Front cover photograph: Detail of Gustav Vigeland's monolith from the Vigeland Sculpture Park, Oslo, Norway.

Published in the United States by FourCats Press
ISBN: 978-1-7320442-0-3
LCCN: 2018935567

Book design by FourCats Press.
First FourCats Press Edition: April 2018
www.FourCatsPress.com
Editor@FourCatsPress.com

The Heterosexual and Homosexual Identities:

The Normalization of Sexual Relationships

John P. DeCecco

and

Michael G. Shively

TABLE OF CONTENTS

Foreword   xv

Preface   xvii

Introduction

Chapter 1 _____ 3
Objectives, Definitions, and General Approach

Sexual identity. Sexual relationships. Normalization. Toxication & detoxication. Medicalization. The scientific discourse. Biological, psychological & sociocultural sexual identity. Heterosexual identity. The structure of sexual relationships. Individualist vs. Collectivist approaches. Psychiatrization & the "implantation of perversions." Biological determinism & biological potentiality.

Chapter 2 _____ 21
Three Cosmological Views of Sexual Relationships

Polytheistic, monotheistic & scientific cosmologies. Greek homosexuality. Pederasty & prostitution. The sexuality of the gods in polytheistic traditions. The monotheistic view of sexual relationships. The scientific philosophy of Descartes, Newton, Locke & others. Scientism.

Chapter 3 _____ 45
From Sodomy to Degeneracy

Changing concepts of sodomy in medieval & modern periods. Sodomy in the Bible. Medieval injunctions. Association with heresy, treason & social disorder. Pederasty. Somaticism vs. Psychologism. Sodomy and degenerative illness. Degeneracy as reversal of evolution.

Part One: The Biological Sexual Identity

Chapter 4 _____ 61
Creation of the Idea of Sexual Identity

The discourse on masturbation & its link to sexual identity. Karl Heinrich Ulrichs & Károly Mária Kertbeny (Karl-Maria Kertbeny). 18th-century medical considerations of masturbation. Onanism. Samuel-Auguste Tissot. Nineteenth-century thought. Claude Francois Lallemand. Benjamin Rush. Sylvester Graham. Ulrichs & the first explicit theory of sexual identity. Benkert/Kertbeny & Prussian law.

Chapter 5 _____ 77

Sexual Identity and Degeneracy Theory

Homosexual conduct as a clinical condition. Paederastia. Tardieu: the medical detection of paederasts. Carl Westphal: "contrary sexual feeling." Julien Chevalier: "inversion of the sexual instinct." Richard von Krafft-Ebing: *Psychopathia Sexualis.* Antipathetic sexual instinct & the taxonomies of perversion. Homosexual conduct as confusion of "natural" sex differences.

Chapter 6 _____ 97

Environmental and Evolutionary Theory

Degeneracy as "imperfect" femininity or masculinity. Benjamin Tarnowsky: "innate perversion of the sexual instinct." Congenital vs. acquired pederasty. Alfred Binet's study of fetishism. Albert von Schrenck-Notzing & the expansion of theories of "environmental causation." Morton Prince's challenge to degeneracy theory. Albert Moll, Uranists, "psychosexual hermaphrodites" & a reformulation of etiological theories of perversion. Libido sexualis. Max Dessoir: stage theory of sexual instinct.

Chapter 7 _____ 119

Detoxication of the Homosexual Identity: Biological Theories

Havelock Ellis & *Sexual Inversion.* The congenital theory. Original bisexuality. Male & female "inverts." Magnus Hirschfeld: *Die Homosexualität.* Pedophiles, ephebophiles, androphiles, gerontophiles, graophiles, pathenophiles, gynecophiles & corophiles. Pseudohomosexuality. Perversion vs. inversion.

Part Two: The Psychological Sexual Identity

Chapter 8 _____ 143

The Creation of the Heterosexual Identity

Sigmund Freud & the "unified theory" of sexual development. The unconscious, preconscious & conscious. The libido. Polymorphous perversity. Oral, anal & genital phases. Sexual objects & sexual aim. Regression & fixation. Kontrarsexuale, Invertierte & die Inversion. The oedipus & castration complexes. The heterosexual imperative.

Chapter 9 _____ 177

From Perversion to Neurosis

Sándor Ferenczi: bisexuality vs. ambisexuality. Helene Deutsch: the preoedipal drama. Karen Horney, primary & secondary penis envy. Hans Sachs. Melanie Klein. The "good penis." Flight from femininity. Wilhelm Stekel: congenital bisexuality. Male homosexuality as disguised sadism toward women. Roy Schafer. Clara Thompson. Frank Caprio: homosexuality as neurotic self love. Sandor Rado: the nonexistence of bisexuality. Genital psychopathology. Harry Stack Sullivan: homosexuality rooted in parental relationships. Lionel Ovesey: homosexuality as retreat from heterosexuality. Preoedipal vs. oedipal homosexuality. Abram Kardiner. Irving Bieber & the fear of heterosexuality. The "close-binding-intimate mother." Robert Stoller. Differentiating homosexual from transsexual development. Reinforcement of heterosexuality as normative sexual identity. Charles Socarides: learned sexual preference. The achievement of normal heterosexual genital primacy. Oedipal & preoedipal homosexuality. Female homosexuality as flight from men.

Chapter 10 _____ 213

Detoxication of the Homosexual Identity: Psychological Theories

Responses to pathologizing of homosexual identity. Thomas Szasz as first "detoxicator." Psychiatry as handmaiden of law & morality. The problem of forcing homosexuals into psychiatric treatment. *The Manufacture of Madness*. Criticisms of Karl Menninger & Irving Bieber. Judd Marmor: prevention of homosexual identity. Marmor's reassessment in *Homosexual Behavior*. Therapeutic efforts to prevent effeminacy & homosexuality in boys. Marcel Saghir & Eli Robins: study of nonclinical homosexuals. Pathologies born in poor parental relationships. Differences between male & female homosexuals. "Incidental" & "situational" homosexual behavior. Marmor & "uncontained" sexuality.

Chapter 11 _____ 239

Pathologizers versus Detoxicators: The Psychiatric Debate

Ideological struggles within the American Psychiatric Association. Revision of the DSM, 1952-1973. Detoxication of homosexual identity. The response of "gay liberationists." Richard Green, Martin Hoffman, Judd Marmor, Lawrence Hatterer, Arno Karlen, Charles Socarides, Richard Stoller , Irving Bieber, Robert Spitzer. Ego-dystonic homosexuality & the DSM-III. The impact of Freud. The psychiatric debate as a reprise of the three cosmological views of sexual relationships.

Part Three: The Sociocultural Sexual Identity

Chapter 12 _____ 265

Cultural Identity: The Anthropological Approach

Sexual identity as a product of biological & cultural forces. Critique of psychological sexual identities. Iwan Bloch: heterosexual relationships as the bedrock of civilization. Adverse effects of masturbation on the vita sexualis. Edward Westermarck & the anthropological view. Bronislaw Malinowski: the sexual customs of the Trobriands. Margaret Mead, sex differences & the role of mothers. Rigid enforcement of masculine & feminine norms as a cause of homosexuality. Ford & Beach. Exclusive heterosexuality or homosexuality as diminution of sexual capacity. Shamans & berdaches. Anthropology's contribution to the normalization of sexual relationships. Sexual relationships in the West limited more by cultural norms than by human biology or psychology. The scientific cosmological view of sexual relationships.

Chapter 13 _____ 289

Behavioral Identity: The Survey Approach

The Kinsey reports. Refutation of psychoanalytic/Freudian theory. Similarities to Freudian approach. Biological determinism. Dissimilarities in male/female "sexual capacity" attributed to "cerebral differences." Sexual identity as a behavioral phenomenon. Homosexuality & neurosis. Impact of sociocultural hostility. Broadening the notion of sexual "normality." Involvement of the Kinsey group in debates over nature/origin of homosexuality. Wainright Churchill & "homosexuality as behavior." Human capacity for "sexual learning." Rejection of psychoanalytic theory. Sex-positive & sex-negative cultures. The "homosexual way of life" as symptom of sex-negative society. The fallacy of romance. Clarence Tripp: *The Homosexual Matrix*. Femininity vs. effeminacy. The origin of heterosexuality & the question of male/female traits. Sexual value systems. Homosexual & heterosexual complementation & resistance. Futility of change therapy. Churchill & Tripp compared.

Chapter 14 _____ 325

Subcultural Identity: The Ethnographic Approach

The "homosexual subculture." Donald Webster Cory: rejection of innate homosexual "nature." Ethnography of gay locales. Maurice Leznoff &William Westley. Secret vs. overt homosexuals. Evelyn Hooker & the total homosexual way of life. Adjustment of homosexual vs. Heterosexual males. Psychoanalytic concepts in Hooker's approach. Gay bars as "markets." Rejection of idea of dichotomized sex roles in homosexual male relationships. Hooker's contribution to detoxication. Albert Reiss: male prostitution & "queers and peers."

Sociocultural vs. Psychological identity. Richard Hauser: homosexual "types" in England. Minority status & stigmatization. Michael Schofield's homosexual types. Social hostility toward homosexuals & promiscuity. Paul Gebhard. David Sonenschein: taxonomy of homosexual relationships. Martin Hoffman: the sexual marketplace & sexual fetishism. Laud Humphreys: *Tearoom Trade*. Sociocultural sexual identity. Variation in ethnologists' portrayals of homosexual relationships reveals assumptions about sexual identity. The embodiment of cosmological concepts in the ethnographic approach.

Chapter 15 _____ 359

The Socially Constructed Identity: Symbolic Interactionism

John Kitsuse: social reactions to deviant behavior. Mary Mcintosh: homosexual identity as social role. John Gagnon & William Simon: distortion of the meaning of sex via biological determinism. Rejection of psychoanalysis. Sexual scripts & "life cycles." Social adjustment of lesbians. Barry Dank: coming out in the homosexual subculture. Shift from heterosexual identity. Kenneth Plummer: symbolic interactionism & meanings attached to sexual activity. Sexuality situationally defined. Western homosexual identity as creation of social intolerance. Stages in the homosexual "career." Erich Goode: the homosexual role. Frederick Whitam: objections to role & deviance theory. Symbolic interactionists' rejection of psychological sexual identity. Minor role assigned to biology. Concepts of sexuality devoid of desire, attraction, pleasure.

Chapter 16 _____ 395

The Demise of Labeling Theory: The Post-Kinsey Sociologists

Labeling theory. Colin Williams & Martin Weinberg. Repercussions of homosexual label on adaptation of male homosexuals. Social intolerance & negative adaptations. Dangers of "the heterosexual world." Subcultural benefits. Contribution to normalization of sexual relationships. Alan Bell: "homosexualities" & social adjustment. Bell & Martin Weinberg's taxonomy of homosexual partnerships: Close-Coupleds, Open-Coupleds, Functionals, Dysfunctionals, Asexuals. Bell, Weinberg & Susan Hammersmith's study of the etiology of sexual identity. Rejection of psychoanalytic & sociological theories. Gender nonconformity & sexual identity. Return to biological etiologies. Summary of studies of homosexuality by post-Kinsey sociologists. Sociocultural homosexual identity as moral discourse on permissible structures of sexual relationships.

Chapter 17 _____ 433

The Collective Homosexual Identity I:
Minority, Community, and Lifestyle

The sociocultural homosexual identity as "minority," "community" & "lifestyle." Laud Humphreys: parallels with racial, ethnic & other minorities. Del Martin & Phyllis Lyon: lesbian identity as minority status. The collective lesbian identity & lifestyle. Applying standards for healthy heterosexual relationships to lesbian relationships. Comparisons of Lyon/Martin approach to work of Donald Webster Cory. Joseph Harry & William Devall: ethnography of gay subculture. Theories of collective identity contribute to claims of homosexual superiority in detoxication efforts. Barry Adam: the gay minority. Gay identity as social construction. Deborah Wolf: lesbian community & lesbian-feminism. The lesbian pair & lesbian mothers. Virginia Brooks: lesbian minority status. Coping with stress. The homosexual "world" transformed into gay & lesbian community. Homosexual identity politicized as gay & lesbian minority membership. Paradoxes in lesbian-feminist ideology.

Chapter 18 _____ 461

The Collective Homosexual Identity II:
Homophobia and the Gay and Lesbian Identity

George Weinberg: homophobia as social prejudice. Criticisms of psychoanalysis & behavioral therapy. The "healthy homosexual." Quantitative techniques for measuring homophobia. A. P. Macdonald: organism deficiency vs. social deficiency. James Millham: Homosexuality Attitude Scale. Eugene Levitt & Albert Klassen: Homosexophobia Scale. James Millham & Christopher San Miguel: studies of aggression toward homosexuals. Stephen Morin & Ellen Garfinkle: latent homosexuality as cause of homophobia. Michael Storms: homophobia as antipathy toward sexual identity or social-sex-role "departure." Rodney Karr: labels & social distance. Heterosexual bias in psychological research. Reverse discourse: homophobes vs. homophiles. Homophobia as relabeling of social intolerance. Joel Hencken & William O'Dowd: three stages of gay identity formation. Carmen de Monteflores & Stephen Schultz: coming out & integration. Vivienne Cass: theoretical model of homosexual identity formation. Eli Coleman: five-stage model. Comparison of "identity formation" approaches & their contribution to normalization of homosexual relationships. Minority status, "community" & resistance to heterosexual oppression.

Part Four: The Recrudescence of the Biological Sexual Identity

Chapter 19 _____ 493

The Hormonal and Genetic Sexual Identity:
Psychomedical and Sociobiological Approaches

Psychomedical & sociobiological approaches. John Money: gender identity, gender role, gender dimorphism & biological imperatives. Facultative vs. obligative homosexuality. Homosexuality as "incongruity" of gender identity. Richard Green: studies of "feminine" boys. Children of homosexual or transsexual parents. Homosexual men/women as "unfinished" or "incomplete" members of their biological sex. Shrinking of the limits of permissible sexual relationships. The search for links between homosexuality & hormone abnormalities. Meyer-Bahlburg. Reviews of hormone studies. "Intersexuals" and "hermaphrodites." Gender-dimorphic behavior in children. Gunter Dörner: prenatal hormonal abnormalities. Genetic origins of homosexuality. Lang & Henry: family studies. Pillard: "familial factor." Kallmann: twin studies. Psychomedical research on sexual identity. Homosexual men & women as contradictions of nature's design. Sociobiology and E. O. Wilson. Natural selection, altruism & kin selection. Michael Ruse. James Weinrich: homosexuals as nonreproductive altruists. Biological sexual identity clothed in trappings of psychological sexual identity. Importance of male-female design. Futuyma & Risch: criticisms of sociobiological approach. Reflections of 19th-century views & earlier psychological & sociocultural formulations in recrudescence of biological sexual identity.

Chapter 20 _____ 543

Identity As Physiology

Masters & Johnson: physiological approach to sexual identity. The phases of sexual activity. Sexual capacities of males & females. Sexual dysfunction & "psychosocial factors." Sexual surrogates. *Homosexuality in Perspective.* Comparisons of physiological & psychosexual behavior in heterosexual vs. Homosexual relationships. Fascination & curiosity regarding "ambisexuals." Sexual inventiveness of homosexuals as response to biologically restricted repertory. "Dissatisfied" homosexuals and conversion/reversion therapy. Tacit belief in biological sexual identity. Contributions to detoxication. Monotheistic constriction of sexual activity within a single relationship. Science & scientism.

Chapter 21 _____ 577

Conclusion: From Sexual Identity to Sexual Relationships—
A Long Look Back and a Short Look Ahead

Works Cited & Bibliography   601

THE HETEROSEXUAL AND HOMOSEXUAL IDENTITIES:

THE NORMALIZATION OF SEXUAL RELATIONSHIPS

John P. DeCecco

and

Michael G. Shively

FOREWORD

In November 1980, Ronald Reagan was elected the fortieth President of the United States. He took office in January 1981 and, by June 1981, the Center for Homosexual, Education, Evaluation, and Research (CHEER) at San Francisco State University had lost all funding. From 1975 to 1981, CHEER had primarily been funded by the National Institute of Mental Health (NIMH—today called the National Institutes of Health). [1]

Initially, the late San Francisco State Psychology Professor John DeCecco[2] and I planned to write a research report on the data CHEER's researchers had gathered regarding individuals whose civil liberties had been abridged in employment or other arenas based on their "departure" (whether actual or perceived) from so-called "norms" of social sex-role (femininity and masculinity) and/or sexual orientation (bisexual and homosexual). The project, known as Civil Liberties and Sexual Orientation or CLIB, had spanned the last half of the decade after Stonewall.

As we began to think about how to organize the CLIB data, however, we realized that no clear historical conception of the notion of sexual orientation (bisexual, heterosexual, or homosexual) existed. In terms of the Civil Liberties and Sexual Orientation research in specific, we began to wonder: When people discriminated against those they identified as "homosexual" or "bisexual," what was the nature of the "identity" to which they believed they were objecting? In cases in which discriminators labeled others as homosexual or bisexual (sometimes erroneously) on the basis of "departure" from social sex-role "norms," what historical and cultural processes had led so-called "masculine" or "feminine" behavior to be seen as proxies for sexual orientation and, thus, to a belief that social sex-role "deviants" were also "deviant" in sexual orientation? Was real or perceived sexual behavior identity at all? Under what theoretical framework did social sex-role constitute an element of sexual identity?

---

[1] Shortly after CHEER lost funding, it was renamed CERES, the Center for Research and Education in Sexuality, principally to broaden the Center's scope of inquiry to include the bisexual and heterosexual identities. CERES' interests later expanded even further, and today it is called the Center for Research and Education in Gender and Sexuality (CRGS).

[2] Dr. DeCecco passed away on November 2, 2017 at the age of 92.

We decided to take a step back and review the conceptualization of sexual identity—that is, how sexual orientation had been conceptually and operationally defined—from its roots. We began by looking at socio-psychological-psychiatric theory and research but ultimately ranged far beyond. In the summer of 1980, our review of the literature on sexual behavior, identity, and orientation began, and, in Fall of the following year, John DeCecco and I began writing *The Heterosexual and Homosexual Identities: The Normalization of Sexual* Relationships as a review and critique of the historical conception of sexual identity.

We worked on the book from the summer of 1980 until the early summer of 1984. When the manuscript was complete, we sent it to a number of prospective publishers and received encouraging feedback. Various academic reviewers asked that particular areas be clarified or expanded, but the response was positive overall. The main obstacle to publication that prospective publishers voiced was the length of the manuscript, and there was discussion about dividing the book into two volumes.

For a variety of personal and professional reasons, however, work on the book came to a halt in the Spring of 1985. Since then, the manuscript has remained untouched, left just as it was when we completed it in the Summer of 1984. In fact, *The Heterosexual and Homosexual Identities: The Normalization of Sexual Relationships* represents a kind of time capsule, reopened at a distance of nearly thirty-four years.

As I read the manuscript now, I am impressed with how well the work has withstood the passage of time. Simultaneously, however, I am amazed by how little progress medicine, psychiatry, and the social sciences have made since the mid-nineteen eighties in conceptualizing sexual identity. These broad and overlapping fields of endeavor continue to conceptually delineate and operationally define sexual identity in ways that keep it confined by and within linguistic and theoretical structures that were born decades and even centuries ago. I have come to believe that *The Heterosexual and Homosexual Identities: The Normalization of Sexual Relationships* remains relevant and useful because it traces a history that may be known in its broadest strokes but which, even today, is rarely considered in detail; and because the terminology and structures of our thinking about sex, sexuality, gender, and relationships have changed so little over a century or more.

Michael G. Shively
Chico, California
February 2018

PREFACE

The idea of the heterosexual and homosexual identities, as adumbrated in medicine, psychiatry, and the social sciences, has had a history of at least one-hundred-thirty years. Its conceptual existence has been chameleonic. Sometimes sexual identity was depicted as a biological entity, at other times a psychological essence, and at still others a personal mirroring of society and culture. Viewed as a whole the discourse on sexual identity can be described as a theoretical labyrinth with strange and fortuitous twists and turns.

This monograph attempts to provide a conceptual map of the largely uncharted terrain occupied by the idea of the heterosexual and homosexual identities. We believe our treatment is comprehensive in that it distinguishes all the major conceptual variations. However, it is not an exhaustive survey of the relevant, available materials; this would require several volumes equal or greater in size. To discern the contours of this immense theoretical forest it has been necessary to step back from a veritable overgrowth of trees.

In two ways our study is broadly historical in tone. First, the presentation of the several conceptualizations of sexual identity roughly follows a chronological order so that later formulations can be seen as the consequences of earlier ones. We departed from a strictly chronological presentation, however, when we were interested in fully developing a particular conceptualization. Second, the roots of each formulation are traced to the historic polytheistic, monotheistic, and scientific cosmologies as central ingredients in western views of sexual relationships.

The treatment is also broadly philosophical. Our basic argument is that the discourse on sexual identity has been a moral disquisition on the permissible boundaries of sexual relationships, dressed up in scientific trappings. This position is elucidated in two general themes. One is that the various ways in which the homosexual identity was pathologized, medicalized, and detoxicated contributed to shoring up the belief in a normative heterosexual identity and in the biological sex of partners as the basic determinant of the structure of sexual relationships. The other is that the several conceptualizations of both the heterosexual and homosexual identities unwittingly served to normalize sexual relationships by containing them within the morally prescribed boundaries of the monotheistic cosmology.

In the present volume we have not attempted to describe the historical contexts within which the idea of sexual identity developed. Social, political, and economic circumstances, to be sure, as well as the apparent accidents of personality and genius, contributed to this development and the favoring of some formulations over others. Drawing an intelligible conceptual map has been complicated enough. An analysis of historical influences, however, would be a significant advance in our knowledge of sexual identity.

The scientific discourse on sexual identity has been rife with political and moral advocacy. To avoid piling another layer of judgment on top of existing layers, we have provided detailed summaries of the contributions made by the major participants in the discourse, frequently quoting their own words. For the most part our commentaries follow the summaries. Occasionally we have placed critical comments in footnotes, particularly when we felt we were dealing with a specific paradox or idiosyncrasy in an author's theoretical approach apart from its general contribution to the discourse on sexual identity. We hope this mode of presentation and analysis will allow readers some independence of judgment.

Besides guiding the reader through the conceptual labyrinth of sexual identity, we hope our book makes other contributions to the field of sexology. We hope that it will alert the student to the need to scrutinize other areas of research on sexual practices and relationships and to discern their tacit moral assumptions and unwitting normative influences. We also hope that it will redirect empirical studies on sexual identity by showing how the failure to examine the theoretical assumptions upon which they are based condemns them to ceaseless duplication of efforts and forestalls any genuine advance in knowledge.

Our major hope is that the book will contribute to a shift in the sexological research in the social sciences from a focus on the individual as an isolated unit to the study of sexual relationships. We believe this shift would constitute a major step in overcoming the biological determinism that has pervaded social science research on human sexuality and would open the way to knowledge about the rich, emerging textures of sexual relationships.

Besides the sexologist and social scientist, we hope the book is illuminating for the general reader who may well be puzzled by popular presentations and discussions of the heterosexual and homosexual identities in the electronic and print media and even bedazzled by the depiction of more exotic sexual identities, such as bisexuality, pedophilia, sadomasochism, transsexuality, and transvestism. After perusing this treatise, the reader can well infer that all sexual identities are names of ideas rather than individuals, and largely scientific homilies on the moral acceptability of particular types of sexual practices and relationships.

In an enterprise of this scope it is hardly possible to recognize all of our theoretical mentors. Most of all we are indebted to F. A. Hayek, the political and economic theorist and philosopher. Hayek drew for us the clear distinction between the study of things, as pursued in the natural sciences, and the study of the relations of individuals, as undertaken in the social sciences and humanities. In Hayek's view, the latter disciplines focus on the growth of the human mind and on individuals as part of a social process to which they spontaneously contribute, which cannot be planned or directed, and which is understood only through retrospective, rational inquiry.

In the introductory chapter we have acknowledged our debt to Freud's notion of unconscious knowledge, to Foucault's idea of the implantation of perversions by nineteenth-century sexology, Jeffrey Weeks' historical locus for the idea of the homosexual identity, and Robert Padgug's and Stephen Jay Gould's demarcation of biology and society. To this we gratefully add the contribution of Richard Hoffman, from whom we borrowed the idea of the polytheistic and monotheistic cosmologies as overarching modes of thought that formed sexual attitudes. Without these seminal ideas this book would have taken a radically different form.

We are also indebted to the National Institute of Mental Health, in particular, Herbert Coburn, Edward Flynne, and Jack Wiener, for furnishing us the support for our empirical studies of sexual identity over a period of six years. In our effort to assess the sexual identity of respondents and to study its impact on their lives we were unwittingly forced to confront the conceptual confusion and ultimately undertake the present survey and analysis.

John P. DeCecco
Michael G. Shively
San Francisco State University
San Francisco, California, 1984

Introduction

1 Objectives, Definitions, and General Approach

The notion that individuals have a sexual identity—bisexual, heterosexual, or homosexual—has a history extending well over a century. Until recently this idea was rarely called sexual identity. It was usually labeled in terms of the sexual variation that absorbed the interest of the writer. The homosexual identity, for example, has been called the third sex, antipathetic sexual instinct, perversion, inversion, homosexuality, homosexual outlet, homosexual orientation (or preference) and, more recently, the gay or lesbian subculture, lifestyle, or community. The bisexual identity, more obliquely, has been labeled sexual perversity (as opposed to sexual perversion), psychical hermaphroditism, acquired (as opposed to congenital) perversion, situational or episodic homosexuality, and, of course, simply bisexuality. The heterosexual identity has rarely been assigned any other name because it has been conceived as the "natural" or "normal" identity—the product of a biological or psychological process of development that squared with moral and institutional prescriptions for sexual relationships.

Popular discourse has readily embraced the general notion that each individual has a palpable sexual identity. Beyond this belief, however, most people would find it difficult to explain exactly what sexual identity consists of. Those explanations proffered would have little in common. Is sexual identity a matter of the flesh, the physical constitution with which the individual is born? Does it reside in fantasy or desire—a "tendency" that may never unfold as sexual conduct? As desire is it reflected by the biological sex of the partners the individual loves rather than lusts after? Or is it a function of sexual behavior, regardless of underlying physical or mental states? Finally, is it a role that society attributes to the individual or that the individual discovers and assigns to the self and others?

The multiplicity of terms denoting sexual identity in medicine and the social sciences is a clue that the confusion in popular usage also prevails there. Sexual identity is treated as a given, an observable characteristic of individuals or the groups to which they belong. Beyond this, however, there is little agreement about what constitutes sexual identity and what force—physical, psychological, or social—determines a specific identity. In some scientific formulations the individual's conformity to or departure from masculine stereotypes for males and feminine stereotypes for females reveals not only sexual identity but also functional biological normality or abnormality. In others, the biological sex of the partners yearned for, consciously or unconsciously, even in the absence of the slightest gesture toward sexual consummation, indelibly marks that person's sexual identity. In more recent conceptualizations sexual identity is treated as if it resides in the social milieu, something institutions impart to individuals or individuals assign to themselves as lifestyle, community membership, or majority or minority status.

Although recent theoretical disquisitions have advocated one formulation over others, none has globally examined the scientific discourse on sexual identity. Such an analysis, at one level, reveals common and disparate conceptual attributes, all parading under the label of sexual identity. These attributes, it can be shown, fall into three general patterns, the biological, psychological, and sociocultural conceptualizations of sexual identity. At another level of analysis, however, it can be shown that the discourse on sexual identity has been a veiled recital of the morally permissible boundaries of sexual relationships.

To present the broad outline of the scientific discourse on sexual identity and to reveal its assumptions about sexual relationships this monograph pursues five objectives. First, it briefly explores the historical genesis of the idea of sexual identity within the moral traditions of western civilization. Second, it examines various conceptualizations within the scientific discourse of the past one-hundred thirty years. Third, it explains how earlier conceptualizations of sexual identity were embodied in those that came later. Fourth, it shows how the discourse was an implicit endorsement of a particular structure of sexual relationships. Finally, it weighs the advantages of shifting the focus of inquiry from sexual identity to sexual relationships.

The key concepts in this analysis are sexual identity and sexual relationships. Sexual identity is conceived as an attribute of an individual that arises from biological, psychological, or sociocultural factors and foreshadows the choice of female or male partners for sexual relationships.

If the partners are of the opposite biological sexes, the individual's identity is called heterosexual. If partners are of the same biological sex, the identity is designated as homosexual. If partners are of either sex, it is bisexual. In our exploration of the emergence of the idea of sexual identity we have used the words heterosexual and homosexual (and their derivative or equivalent forms) as they were employed by the theorists themselves. Following the tradition of scholarship in the field, we have also used these words to refer collectively to several theories of sexual identity. For the most part, our own use has been confined to the original etymological derivation that simply designates whether partners in sexual relationships are of the opposite or same sex.[1]

In this analysis a sexual relationship is defined by its structure. The constituent elements of this structure are the beliefs and attitudes of partners which inform their treatment of each other. Such beliefs can be categorized under headings such as biological sex, complementarity, procreation, permanency, pleasure, choice, and so on. The structure of a sexual relationship consists of the implications of partners holding various beliefs. For example, the structural implications for relationships of individuals who believe that biological sex is the fundamental consideration in the choice of partners and for the success of a relationship would contrast sharply with the relationships of those who believe that considerations of social class of partners far outweigh those of biological sex. As such, the structure is unknown to the partners because it is the invention of the social scientist who notes the implications of partners holding similar or dissimilar beliefs. As stated by F. A. Hayek:

> [I]t is important to observe that … various types of individual beliefs and attitudes are not themselves the object of [social scientists'] explanation, but merely the elements from which

---

[1] The prefix *hetero*-is derived from the Greek *heteros*, which means "the other of two, other, different" (*Shorter Oxford English Dictionary*, 3d Ed., 1944: 895; hereinafter *SOED*). Hetero-is often used in apposition to homo-and sometimes to auto-, homoeo, iso-, ortho-, and syn-. It is used in various combinations in the biological sciences. In zoology, for example, "heterogynous" is applied to species of animals in which the females are of two kinds, perfect or fertile, and imperfect or "neuter," as in bees, ants, etc. (896). The prefix homo-has both Greek and Latin derivation. In Greek, it is derived from *homos*, meaning same (915). In Latin it derives from *homo*, meaning man, or more broadly, human being (915). As a prefix, *homo*-is often used in botany, biology, and zoology in opposition to hetero-. Most uses of the terms heterosexual and homosexual are consistent with the Greek etymological derivation. The suffix -sexual (1859) derives from the Latin *sexualis*, which in turn derived from the Latin *sexus*, meaning sex. The words *heterosexual* and *homosexual*, therefore, in designating whether partners are of the opposite or same sex, derive their meanings from the Greek prefix and the Latin suffix.

we build up the structure of possible relationships between individuals. (68)[2]

Still unanswered is the question of what distinguishes a relationship that is sexual from one that is not sexual. A relationship can be considered sexual from two vantage points: that of a shared moral tradition and that of the individual. Because traditional sexual morality has been chiefly concerned with regulating physical contact between individuals, particularly when it involves the genitalia, a relationship can be viewed as sexual whenever it falls within the purview of strictures placed on such conduct.

> Sexual conduct, however, is not a static reality. Although the Judeo-Christian tradition proscribed forms of sexual conduct such as sodomy and bestiality, it did little to elucidate what particular behavior was forbidden. The institutional fear of fostering the forbidden sexual conduct resulted in only elliptical references to specific behavior. The individual, therefore, was the unwitting heir of the freedom to determine which specific acts were forbidden.

Therefore, a relationship can also be considered sexual because of the individual's understanding of traditional morality and personal beliefs about what constitutes sexual conduct. Moral principles are not ingested or applied by individuals as irreducible substances. They are ideas that are modified by the individual on the basis of conscious and unconscious knowledge and are applied as deemed necessary or appropriate.

It is our contention that the scientific discourse on sexual identity has unwittingly contributed to the normalization of sexual relationships. **NORMALIZATION** refers to the permissible modifications of the structure of sexual relationships.[3] As a process of change, normalization is the unintended result of the reformulation of beliefs about sexual relationships. It is an ideational process and not a social process divorced from individual attitudes and actions. It refers to the implications of what individuals think and do rather than their stated purposes. Normalization was the unforeseen consequence of various theoretical formulations of sexual identity for the structure of sexual relationships.

---

[2] Hayek, F. A. (1979). *The Counter-Revolution of Science: Studies on the Abuse of Reason*. Indianapolis, IN: Liberty Press. (First published in 1952.) References are to the 1979 edition.

[3] Impermissible relationships would be those considered to be illegal, immoral, or pathological.

In tracing the emergence of the notion of sexual identity in scientific literature, it is necessary to deal extensively with the conceptualizations of the homosexual identity with which the discourse was primarily concerned. In identifying the contribution of the various conceptualizations of the homosexual identity to the normalization of sexual relationships, two themes have been pursued. (1) the pathologization of the homosexual identity and (2) its detoxication. The pathologization of the homosexual identity occurred in two ways: it was TOXICATED by forensic psychiatry and later by psychoanalytic theory as a precarious mental condition caused by degeneracy or arrested psychosexual development. It was MEDICALIZED in the psychobiological investigations designed to uncover its genetic, hormonal, or neurophysiological peculiarities.

The major efforts at the detoxication of the homosexual identity, for the most part, have been more recent. Detoxication refers to those theoretical (and sometimes empirical) efforts to demonstrate that the homosexual identity was not associated with mental illness or physical disease. That is, detoxication was the removal from the homosexual identity of its psychiatric and medical penumbra.

The first objective of this monograph is to adumbrate how the discourse on sexual identity emerged from the complex moral tradition of western civilization. In pursuing this objective we have epitomized that tradition as consisting of three cosmologies: the polytheistic, monotheistic, and scientific. Cosmologies are theories of how the universe is organized as a whole and of the general laws that govern it.

In this study the three cosmologies are explored as the basis for the idea of sexual identity and their moral implications for sexual relationships. The polytheistic cosmology, as exemplified in the sexual attitudes and practices of the classical Greeks, condoned individual inventiveness and pleasure and allowed breadth and variety in the structure of sexual relationships. The monotheistic cosmology, as embodied in Judeo-Christian doctrine, made attitudes of genital and procreative sexuality, sexual fidelity to a single partner, and the life-long permanency of monogamous unions pivotal to the structure of sexual relationships. The scientific cosmology, as a product of seventeenth-century natural science and the moral speculations of eighteenth-century philosophers, sponsored the belief that the structure of sexual relationships could be volitional for both men and women. The scientific discourse on sexual identity, we have postulated, consisted of an amalgam of the polytheistic, monotheistic, and scientific cosmologies.

Our second objective is to examine the many conceptualizations of sexual identity. To accomplish this aim we reviewed the scientific discourse on sexual identity, from the middle of the nineteenth century to the present, as it occurred chiefly in European and American psychiatry, medicine, and the social sciences. Because the path we shall traverse is labyrinthine, a map of the conceptual territory lying ahead may be useful.

The scientific discourse led to three major conceptualizations of sexual identity: (1) the biological; (2) the psychological; and (3) the sociocultural. The biological sexual identity consisted of innate physical determinants such as sex drives or instincts, brain centers, hormones, or genes. The psychological sexual identity was conceived as three sets of polarities: physical appearance (female or male sexual characteristics); mental characteristics (feminine or masculine attitudes); and object choice (attractions to female or male sexual partners). The point at which the individual's characteristics fell on each of these continua was a product of natural endowment and the vicissitudes of early developmental experience. The sociocultural sexual identity derived from external forces and circumstances that molded the individual. It assumed a malleable biological sexual capacity that could be shaped by culture.

The first conceptualization of sexual identity was the biological. Karl Heinrich Ulrichs, a lawyer and classical scholar, turned to the nascent science of embryology in proposing that the homosexual identity was a natural variation in the ordinary biological development of the female and male sexes, constituting an admixture of the two and indeed a "third sex." Ulrichs included in his writing both the heterosexual and homosexual identities.

It was the biological homosexual identity that was pathologized by psychiatry. Richard von Krafft-Ebing viewed the homosexual identity as "antipathetic sexual instinct" which stemmed from an inheritable "taint." The afflicted individual slipped from higher to lower stages of human development. Homosexuality, therefore, represented a deterioration of nature rather than an acceptable variation. Although he never wavered from his belief in the congenital origins of homosexuality, Krafft-Ebing later surrendered the degeneracy theory for Albert Moll's evolutionary theory, which attributed "antipathetic sexual instinct" to the failure of the organism to abandon the bisexual for the monosexual stage of development.

The biological line of thought was continued by Havelock Ellis and Magnus Hirschfeld, who both believed that the homosexual identity and, by inference, the heterosexual, were grounded in human biology—either the germ plasm or hormones. Ellis wrote mysteriously about female and male "germs" situated in the fertilized ovum. In normal development the germ plasm of one sex obliterated the other. In the homosexual, however, this process remained incomplete so that remnants of the "conquered" sex persisted. Hirschfeld postulated the existence of female and male sex hormones that controlled sexual desire. A preponderance of female hormones in the male or of male hormones in the female would produce a homosexual identity.

In the recent recrudescence of the biological conceptualization, Hirschfeld's explanation of sexual identity has been revived by those speculating on the influence of maternal hormones on the developing fetal brain. In theory, the to-be-homosexual female is subjected to hormonal excesses that "masculinize" the fetal brain and the to-be-homosexual male suffers a deficiency that "feminizes" the fetal brain. The sociobiologists have subscribed to a biological sexual identity in their postulation of the existence of heterosexual and homosexual genes. Edward O. Wilson could therefore speak of the "fully heterosexual" or "fully homosexual" individual.

It was not until Sigmund Freud that the conception of the psychological sexual identity was clearly delineated. He based his notion of the heterosexual identity on the homosexual. Although both identities in Freud's view represented differentiations of an innate bisexual capacity, they were more psychological than biological achievements. First, the heterosexual identity represented the completion of the individual's psychosexual development: sexual gratification, which had been diffusely concentrated in the oral and anal zones, was surrendered for the higher and more focused gratification possible in the union of female and male genitals. Second, within the framework of his structural theory, Freud thoroughly psychologized the heterosexual identity. Women, obeying their biological destiny, were to be females, feminine and heterosexual. Men were to be males, masculine and heterosexual. What made Freud's conceptualization of the heterosexual identity exceptional was that it was framed within a general theory of sexuality which included both heterosexuality and homosexuality, and within a complex description of psychological development and functioning.

The post-Freudian psychoanalysts continued the psychiatric tradition, begun by Carl Westphal and Krafft-Ebing, of pathologizing the homosexual identity. In the process it was eventually subsumed under the heterosexual identity. In the view of the Irving Bieber group, for example, the heterosexual identity became the "biologic norm." Homosexuality came to be viewed as a twisted form of heterosexuality, a developmental failure of increasingly monstrous proportions.

In the nineteen-seventies the psychiatric discourse on the homosexual identity became a lively and even acrimonious debate. On one side there were those psychoanalysts, such as Bieber and Charles Socarides, who continued to view the homosexual identity as some basic distortion of the fundamental biologic roles of men and women. On the other side there were psychoanalysts, such as Judd Marmor and Robert Stoller, who were willing to grant that individuals could be "healthy homosexuals" while implying that only the heterosexual identity embodied the full promise of happiness and sexual gratification.

The third conceptualization of the idea of sexual identity was the sociocultural. As such it was directly related to the work of Ulrichs, which leaned heavily on the historical analysis of the role of sexuality in the classical age. Two of the earliest historians of sexual identity were Iwan Bloch and Edward Westermarck, whose work argued that there was a fine and perhaps arbitrary line dividing "normal" sexual practices and the so-called sexual perversions.

Some of the earliest anthropological studies of human sexuality were those of Bronislaw Malinowski, Margaret Mead, Clellan Ford, and Frank Beach, who described how different cultures variously defined and encouraged particular forms of sexual expression. The combined impact of the historical and anthropological work challenged the idea of a psychological sexual identity and shifted the responsibility for sexual expression from the individual, where psychiatry had firmly planted it, to the culture. In effect their work was based on the belief in the extraordinary malleability of human sexual expression. Although they showed exceptional understanding and tolerance for homosexuality most of these writers clearly considered heterosexuality to be the happy confluence of biology and culture.

From here the sociocultural line of conceptualization took three forms: the behavioral, social constructionist, and collectivistic approaches. The work of the Kinsey group, Wainwright Churchill, and Clarence Tripp was a steadfast rejection of the Freudian idea of a psychological sexual identity. Sexuality was depicted as the unfolding of a large, undifferentiated mammalian capacity through learned behavior. In the hands of the symbolic interactionists sexual identity was conceived as socially constructed and had only a tenuous connection to human biology. In effect the heterosexual identity was presumably the product of conformity to institutional norms while the homosexual identity represented a deviation from norms.

The individual therefore acquired a sexual identity by interacting with institutions or with those who already subscribed to a particular identity. The theorists of the collective homosexual identity described a sociosexual process which transformed the individual into a true and visible gay person. For those who turned their attention to gay oppression and homophobia, the homosexual social identity was seen as membership in a minority group.

The third objective of this monograph is to show how earlier conceptualizations of sexual identity have been embodied in those that came later. Our analysis of the scientific discourse will reveal that the biological, psychological, and sociocultural conceptualizations of sexual identity were not independent constructions. The biological form was incorporated in the others because all three forms made the biological sex of partners in sexual relationships the crucial distinction between the heterosexual and homosexual identities. It is also possible to show that the psychological form was conceived as a personal identity that combined both biological factors and developmental experiences. The sociocultural form was conceived as an undifferentiated biological sexual capacity molded by cultural determinants.

Tracing the changing contours of the idea of sexual identity will also reveal that conceptualizations of the heterosexual and homosexual identities have been interdependent. Those theorists who entertained the biological notion that the stamp of sexual identity was left on the fetal brain by the vicissitudes of intrauterine development saw the heterosexual identity as the fortunate product of hormonal balance and the homosexual identity the result of hormonal mishaps which feminized boys and masculinized girls. There were also those who held that the heterosexual and homosexual identities were mandated by nature in a strange twist of fate that left homosexuals responsible for the survival and superior fitness of heterosexuals.

Those writers allied with the notion of the psychological sexual identity viewed the heterosexual identity as the expression of mature femaleness or maleness. In the tradition of Freud, the homosexual identity was seen as a stage temporarily occupied by children in their developmental march toward a stable heterosexual identity. Those individuals who never moved beyond the homosexual identity were seen as arrested in their psychosexual development.

Theorists who subscribed to the idea of the sociocultural sexual identity conceived of the heterosexual and homosexual identities as the footprints of culture left on a biology which mandated nothing more than a basic femaleness or maleness. Those who conceived of sexual identity as a product of learning viewed heterosexuality and homosexuality as aggregates of behavioral episodes in which the partners in sexual relationships were of the opposite or same sex. Even in their exclusive forms heterosexuality or homosexuality were not truly identities, because sexual behavior was thought to be labile.

Those who espoused the sociocultural sexual identity treated the two identities as discontinuous and even opposed. Their theories of homosexual identity formation implied that the heterosexual identity was lodged in mainstream society while the homosexual identity was confined to subculture and community. Heterosexual society was seen as the embodiment of the heterosexual identity and, as such, unalterably opposed to the homosexual subculture, attempting either to engulf or crush it. Although a socialization process for heterosexuals was never adumbrated, there was the clear implication that if one were described it would reveal a distinctive heterosexual sociocultural identity.

The fourth objective of this book is to show how the discourse on sexual identity was implicitly a moral discourse on sexual relationships. Although pursued as a scientific enterprise, it is our contention that the discourse on sexual identity normalized the structure of both heterosexual and homosexual relationships by restricting their permissible modifications to fit the Judeo-Christian cosmology. A central ingredient of that cosmology was the belief in the male-female design—that sexual relationships should consist of one male and one female partner. As representatives of the two biological sexes it was believed that males and females provided the necessary physical complementarity. Because that complementarity was essential for procreation, additional restrictions were stability and permanence, which provided the guarantee of a tranquil domestic environment in which to rear offspring and the safeguarding of lineage and property.

The normalized homosexual relationship, although lacking the procreative possibility of the heterosexual relationship, was viewed as essentially duplicating its structure. Both types of relationships were expected to contain as essential ingredients attitudes of complementarity, transcendent purpose, and permanency. In both types human sexuality was viewed as biologically determined a driving force that locked partners together in enduring relationships.

The fifth objective of this monograph is to weigh the advantages of shifting the focus of inquiry in social science research from sexual identity to the structure of sexual relationships. The basic data for our analysis of the discourse on sexual identity are the ideas and opinions of those who contributed to it. In conducting this inquiry it was not our intention to judge the correctness or acceptability of the various theories. Rather our purpose was to elucidate theoretical positions so that recurrent, recognizable, and familiar assumptions about sexual identity and relationships could be discerned. In this sense our task was more one of synthesis than analysis, looking for regularities of opinion and belief beneath the "accidents" of discipline and nomenclature within which these notions were couched.

Such regularities, we believe, represent new entities which were not part of any theoretician's conscious design. Few if any of the writers we examined, for example, consciously intended to contribute to the normalization of sexual relationships by a particular formulation of the heterosexual or homosexual identity. In the case of the normalized homosexual identity, for example, a partner of the same sex could be substituted for a partner of the opposite sex without altering the basic structure of sexual relationships. Perhaps none was aware that by making the biological sex of partners interchangeable they were bringing into serious question the centrality of biological sex and social sex-roles in the structure of sexual relationships.[4]

Our view of the structure of sexual relationships is in the tradition of methodological individualism. In this tradition the social scientist approaches the study of relationships through ascertaining the subjective concepts or ideas that determine individual action.[5]

---

[4] Social sex-roles refer to characteristics that are culturally associated with females or males. These characteristics are perceived as stereotypically feminine or masculine. Social sex-roles refer to the characteristics of appearance, personality, speech, mannerisms, habits, and interests. Based on cultural norms, individuals are expected to behave in ways deemed appropriate to their biological sex. See Shively, M. G. and DeCecco, J. P. (1977). Components of Sexual Identity. *Journal of Homosexuality* 3(1): 41-48; and Shively, M. G., Rudolph, J. R., and DeCecco, J. P. (1978). Identification of the Social Sex-Role Stereotypes. *Journal of Homosexuality* 3(3): 225-234.

[5] Hayek contrasts this approach with that of the natural sciences: "What is true about the relations of men to things is, of course, even more true of the relations between men, which for the purposes of social study cannot be defined in the objective terms of the physical sciences. Even such a seemingly purely biological relationship as that between parent and child is in social study not defined in physical terms and cannot be so defined for their purposes: it makes little difference to people's actions whether the belief that a particular child is their natural offspring is mistaken or not" (1952/1979: 52).

According to Hayek:

> It is only by the systematic and patient following up of the
> implications of many people holding certain views that we can
> understand, and often even only learn to see, the unintended
> and often uncomprehended results of the separate and yet
> interrelated actions of men in society. (1952/1979: 59)

In the individualistic approach it is necessary to distinguish between
the ideas held by individuals which motivate their treatment of each
other and the ideas which they form about their relationships. The
changes in opinion which individuals may entertain about particular
sexual practices and which the social scientist recognizes as causing the
widespread adoption of those practices are in a different class than the
opinions people may have about the causes of those practices. Sexual
practices such as dominance and submission or sadomasochism may be
the result of individuals viewing those practices as the opportunity to
perform roles which ordinarily they believe cannot be enacted in public
life. The participants' explanation of the causes for such practices,
however, may be that they are a reflection of patriarchal society, the
overflow of the association between sex and violence, or the residue of
inhibiting traumas that occurred in the course of their psychosexual
development.

From the vantage point of methodological individualism it is necessary
to question the existence of the social categories popularly used in the
discourse on sexual identity, such as "heterosexuals" and "homosexuals,"
or even the more venerable "female sexuality," "male sexuality,"
"femininity," and "masculinity." In contrast, the collectivist methodology
of the social sciences, in the manner of the natural sciences, assumes that
such categories represent "social phenomena" which are directly
observable. Those who follow the collectivist approach mistake for fact
what Hayek described as "no more than provisional theories, models
constructed by the popular mind to explain the connection between the
individual phenomena which we observe" (1952/1979: 95).[6]

---

[6] Hayek further believed that students of social phenomena ought to learn
never to speak of such entities as "society" or "community" acting, but always to think of individuals acting. He also pointed out the irony inherent in
the collectivist approach. While those who employ it are eager to avoid all
"subjective elements" and confine themselves only to "objective facts," they
end up committing the error they are most anxious to avoid: "namely, that of
treating as facts what are no more than vague popular theories. They have

"Heterosexuals" and "homosexuals," we believe, should be viewed merely as the speculative concepts of popular usage. As Hayek states:

> The naïve realism which uncritically assumes that where there are commonly used concepts there must also be definite "given" things which they describe is so deeply embedded in current thought about social phenomena that it requires a deliberate effort of will to free ourselves from it. (1952/1979: 96)

It is our contention that the discourse on sexual identity was a product of the collectivistic approach to inquiry about sexual relationships. Although that discourse was couched in the language and use the methods of science and was carried on largely under the aegis of medicine, it exemplified the scientific cosmology as transformed into scientism. Scientism is based on the assumptions that (1) there are social forces that direct human affairs in the manner in which physical forces control the material universe and (2) knowledge gained through the social sciences of these forces can be consciously and rationally used to reconstruct social relationships.

Our review of the scientific discourse on sexual identity will reveal that few theorists questioned the scentistic belief in the existence of the heterosexual or homosexual identities. Most treated sexual identity as a given, an observable property of individuals or of the groups to which they belonged. Although there was considerable speculation and debate about the origins, development, meaning, and social status of the heterosexual and homosexual identities, as concepts they were often merely vague and indistinct suggestions of the structure of sexual relationships. Usually they failed to distinguish between the accidental and the significant, the transitory and the permanent.

The shift from a collectivist to an individualist approach would provide important conceptual, methodological, and moral advantages in redirecting the discourse on sexual identity so that the focus is on sexual relationships: (a) attention would be shifted from isolated individuals to their mutual associations; (b) the shift would capitalize on the advantages of the psychoanalytic method (the exploration of personally constructed meanings) and symbolic interactionism (the identification of socially constructed meanings) while avoiding the pitfalls of relying on one of these approaches to the exclusion of the other; and (c) the shift

---

thus become, when they least expect it, the victims of the 'fallacy of conceptual realism' (made familiar by A. N. Whitehead as the 'fallacy of misplaced concreteness')" (1952/1979: 95).

would allow investigators to view sexual relationships from the vantage point of a morality of individual choice and pleasure rather than a traditional morality of externally prescribed obligations.

Our approach to the several objectives of this monograph has been particularly influenced by theories of Sigmund Freud, Michel Foucault, Jeffrey Weeks, Robert Padgug, and Stephen Jay Gould. Following Freud's conceptualization of the Unconscious, we have assumed that attitudes, beliefs, motives, and intentions that compose the structure of sexual relationships may be unknown to the partners. The Unconscious, in Freudian topological theory, consists of "psychic representations" or verbal and nonverbal memory traces of experienced (Freud, 1915/1966).[7]

These forgotten impressions are either inaccessible to consciousness or retrieved with difficulty, often only through psychoanalytic techniques. As the reservoir of the individual's psychic representations of past experience, the Unconscious can exert a significant influence upon the formation of sexual relationships. The attitudes and beliefs that compose the structure of sexual relationships, however, can be ascertained by the social scientist from the actions of partners, although these subjective ingredients may not be consciously known or articulated by the individuals themselves.

Freud's theory of the Unconscious assumes that it is not experience itself that molds the mentality of the individual but the individual's codification of experience. In our inquiry into sexual identity and relationships, we have therefore distinguished between personally constructed meanings that are unique for each individual, and socially constructed meanings, that are shared by individuals residing in particular sociocultural settings at particular points in history. Whereas psychoanalytic theory has emphasized the construction of personal meanings, sociological theory, particularly symbolic interactionism, has stressed the importance of socially constructed meanings in the formation of sexual identity.

Our approach was also influenced by Foucault's conceptualization of the modern history of sexuality.[8] Foucault located the scientific study of

---

[7] Freud, Sigmund (1915/1966). The Unconscious. *Standard Edition* 14: 161-204. Unless otherwise stated, all references in this book to Freud's published works are to the 1966 *Standard Edition* (hereinafter, *SE*).

[8] Foucault, Michel (1976/1978). *The History of Sexuality. Volume I: An Introduction*. New York: Vintage Books. First published in 1976 as *La Volente de savoir* (Paris: Editions Galliamard). References are to the 1978 English translation by Robert Hurley. This volume was a further development of Foucault's general theory that the post-Enlightenment world has been marked

sexuality in the discourse which began obscurely in the sixteenth-century confessional and rapidly gained momentum in the nineteenth and twentieth centuries. Because heterosexual monogamy was the tacit and ubiquitous norm, the discourse focused on perversions:

> [W]hat came under scrutiny was the sexuality of children, mad men and women, and criminals; the sensuality of those who did not like the opposite sex; reveries, obsessions, petty manias, or great transports of rage.... Whence the setting apart of the "unnatural" as a specific dimension in the field of sexuality.... Underneath the libertine, the pervert. (1976/1978: 38-39)[9]

Foucault called the codification of forms of sexuality which were peripheral to heterosexual monogamy the "implantation of perversions" (1976/1978: 48), a responsibility undertaken by medicine in what it touted as the scientific study of sex. This preoccupation of medicine with "aberrations, perversions, exceptional oddities, pathological statements, and morbid aggravations" (1976/1978: 53) composed what Foucault called the "pornography of the morbid" (1976/1978: 54).

According to Foucault the "psychiatrization of perverse pleasure" (1976/1978: 105) was one of the chief means by which medicine established its control over sexuality.[10] This psychiatrization was accomplished by isolating the sexual instinct as a biological or psychical entity, by analyzing the anomalous forms of sexuality with which the instinct could be afflicted, by assigning the instinct a role in normalizing or pathologizing

---

by the "great confinement," the drive to confine and isolate all deviants in society—the mad, the criminal, the poor, and, lastly, the sexually perverted.

[9] In an earlier work (*Madness and Civilization: A History of Insanity in the Age of Reason*. Richard Howard, Trans. New York: Pantheon, 1965), Foucault argued that, beginning in about 1650, a major turn occurred in the treatment of deviants which was based on the belief that madness was shameful and that the best treatment of the mad required their isolation from society and their supervision by medical doctors. For a historical critique of this argument, see Stone, Lawrence (1982, 16 December). Madness. *New York Review of Books* 29(20): 28-36; and Stone's rejoinder to Foucault's reply: (1983, 31 March). *New York Review of Books* 30(5): 42-44. Stone's central criticism of Foucault's position was that it took a pessimistic view of the Enlightenment and the institutions and professions, including psychiatry that grew out of it.

[10] The other three means were the hysterization of women's bodies, pedagogization of children's sexuality, and the socialization of procreative behavior (1976/1978: 104).

all behavior, and by developing a corrective technology to treat the anomalies.[11]

Our inquiry into the scientific discourse on sexual identity has also been inspired by Jeffrey Weeks' conception of the medical model of the homosexual as articulated in the late nineteenth century. The "scientific" theory of the homosexual identity, Weeks has pointed out, was inextricably tangled with old religious notions of sexual immorality and sinfulness. This theory "formed the boundaries within which the homosexuals had to define themselves" (Weeks, 1979: 167).[12]

We have also been guided by Weeks' provocative critique of the basic conservatism of the sexual reform movements, which, for the most part, have been rooted in the belief that there are inherent differences between the female and male sexes, which are genetically or psychologically and socially determined. A more radical view of the attitudinal changes which may lie ahead, in Weeks' prognostication,

> will have to take account of the varieties and diversity of sexual expression, of the arbitrariness of social labels, [and] of the cultural molding of gender and sexual identities: in short, of the historical creation of sexual beliefs and attitudes, and of the radical changes needed to transform them(Weeks, 1977: 7).[13]

Weeks' position implied that "homosexuals" existed as personal and social entities before the medical construction of the homosexual identity. Although homosexual behavior surely predated the scientific discourse on sexual identity, the attitudes individuals had about their homosexual behavior and how these attitudes reflected their sexual relationships remains a subject of historical inquiry.

---

[11] Foucault viewed the psychiatrization of perversion as part of a general strategy to promote a conception of sex that converted it into an instrument of power over social relationship. As a power strategy he believed that sex was essentially alienated from corporeal pleasure. Our own position is that the medical doctors who engaged in the discourse on sex were, as disciples of the Enlightenment, trying to wrest the control of sex from religion and the church by replacing the "theology of sex" with a "science of sex."

[12] Weeks, Jeffrey (1979). Movement and Affirmation: Sexual Meanings and Homosexual Identities. *Radical Historical Review 20:* 164-179

[13] Weeks, Jeffrey (1977). *Coming Out: Homosexual Politics in Britain from the Nineteenth Century to the Present.* London: Quartet Books.

Our approach was based on the distinction between sexuality as biology and sexuality as human behavior, as clarified by Padgug (1979).[14] He observed:

> Biological sexuality is the necessary precondition for human sexuality. But biological sexuality is only a precondition, a set of potentialities, which is never unmediated by human reality, and which becomes transformed in qualitatively new ways in human society. Biology as a set of potentialities and insuperable necessities provides the material of social interpretations and extensions; it does not cause human behavior, but conditions and limits it. Biology is not a narrow set of absolute imperatives. (9)

To try to eliminate biology from human sexuality, however, is misleading according to Padgug because "it denies that sexual behavior takes place within nature and by extension of nature" (1979: 9). In our approach, it is not the biological fact that partners are either female or male but attitudes and beliefs about biological sex which determine the structure of sexual relationships.

Our approach to the question of the centrality of biology in the structure of sexual relationships is also based on the distinction made by Stephen Jay Gould (1983) between **BIOLOGICAL DETERMINISM** and **BIOLOGICAL POTENTIALITY**.[15] In symbolic terms, Gould suggested that whether one was a determinist or a potentialist depended upon one's estimate of the length and tautness of the leash with which biology held onto culture. The determinist believes that the lease is short and holds tightly. The potentialist believes it is loose and unconstraining. This qualitative difference, Gould believed, resulted in qualitatively different conceptions of society. The determinist tended to reduce the complexity of human society to fit the confines of a few known biological universals such as the universality of certain facial expressions and the preference of newborns for sugar over water.

Although biological research in the future will probably extend the list of universals, Gould, as a potentialist, believed that they exerted

---

[14] Padgug, Robert A. (1979). Sexual Matters: On Conceptualizing Sexuality in History. *Radical Historical Review 20*: 3-23. Padgug apparently subscribed to the view that sexual behavior was transmitted through a process of social learning.

[15] Gould, Stephen Jay (1983). Genes on the Brain. *New York Review of Books* 30(11): 5-10. [Gould, who died in 2002, was a paleontologist, historian of science, and evolutionary biologist. —Ed.]

"little constraint upon the incredible richness of detail that so fascinates us and is the subject matter of the social sciences" (1983: 6). It is our contention that the idea of sexual identity reflects an inherent biological determinism in which the partner's biological sex is viewed as a set of constraints on human inventiveness in constructing sexual relationships.

2 Three Cosmological Views of Sexual Relationships

The nineteenth-century notion of sexual identity consisted of an amalgam and transformation of the conceptions of sexual relationships implicit in the dominant cosmologies of western civilization: (1) the polytheistic cosmology, as exemplified in the sexual attitudes and practices of the classical Greeks; (2) the monotheistic cosmology, as embodied in early Judeo-Christian doctrine; and (3) the scientific cosmology, as first expressed in seventeenth-century thinking and later in the Enlightenment. Cosmology has been defined as "the theory of the universe as an ordered whole, and of the general laws which govern it" (*SOED*).

In the polytheistic cosmology, according to Richard Hoffman, the continuity of creation and the sexual nature of the universe worked closely together.[1] Faith in the unbroken chain of creation linked the gods to a primordial realm and human beings directly to the gods. In polytheism, it was believed that the gods emerged from the primordial realm and humans emerged directly from the bodies of the gods or were fashioned by a god out of the bodies of other gods. Although gods and humans were produced through copulation, it was also possible to produce them from bodily substances of the gods such as tears, blood, or urine. Hoffman provided this graphic example from ancient Egypt:

> Here the primordial realm was conceived of as a watery swamp, akin to the Nile during the fertile flood stage. At one

---

[1] Hoffman, Richard J. (1984). Vices, Gods, and Virtues: Cosmology as a Mediating Factor in Attitudes Towards Male Homosexuality. *Journal of Homosexuality* 9(2/3): 27-44. Hoffman also cited Judith Ochshorn's 1981 *The Female Experience and the Nature of the Divine* (Bloomington: Indiana University Press), in which the author explained how the shift from polytheism to monotheism in the ancient Near East resulted in dramatic changes in concepts of femaleness and femininity.

point a mound of clay emerges from the swamp, and from that
mound emerged Ra. Ra masturbated, swallowed his semen,
and then self-fertilized, produced life: he spit to produce the
god Shu; he urinated to produce the goddess Tefnut; he cried
to produce human beings. (1984: 5)

Sexual practices among the gods involved much more than
heterosexual coitus between married partners. It also included bestiality,
adultery, masturbation, homosexuality, and incest. Most important, there
was a blurring of biological sex in the realm of the supernatural. Male
deities could have female organs, particularly breasts and sometimes
uteruses, so that the capacity for bearing offspring was not exclusively
female. Hoffman mentioned examples in Greek, Egyptian, and Hindu
polytheism:

Among the Greeks ... Aphrodite was born of a union between the
male Salt Sea and the genitals of Uranus; Athena and Dionysus
were born of Zeus. Ra reproduced through masturbation and self-
fertilization, Shiva by spilling his semen. (1984: 30)

For the believers in polytheism, deities could have organs of both
sexes or a corresponding deity of the opposite sex. The Hindu Shiva, for
example, was often depicted with female breasts. In Greece, the deities of
war were the male Aries and the female Athena. Hoffman concluded
that few phenomena were thought of as belonging to one biological sex
to the exclusion of the other.

Although the world of mankind was considered to be more circumscribed in sexual behavior than that of the gods, the belief in polytheism,
according to Hoffman, did not make any form of sexual behavior particularly unacceptable and did not rigidly prescribe what was feminine or
masculine. In polytheism as ritualistic practice, for example, a person of
one biological sex could take on the characteristics of a person of the other
sex, a phenomenon Hoffman referred to as ritual role reversal. It was also
possible for individuals to acquire many opposing sexual characteristics.[2]

Hoffman observed: "Although many activities in the Greek social
world were gender-related, sexuality itself was more ambiguous and no
sexual act ... was held to be 'natural' for one specific sex" (1980a: 224).[3]

---

[2] Hoffman provided, as an example, the fact that the Vestal Virgins in Rome
were conceived of as both matrons and virgins, as both men and women
(1984: 32).

[3] Hoffman, Richard J. (1980a). Some Cultural Aspects of Greek Male
Homosexuality. *Journal of Homosexuality* 5(3): 217-226.

Men who were considered paragons of masculinity had homosexual lovers.[4] What was unmanly in the Greek perception was excessive passion, whether it be for females or males.

Their fluid conceptions of biological sex and, correspondingly, of femininity and masculinity, gave the Greeks considerable latitude in structuring sexual relationships. K. J. Dover asserted that, although the Greeks were aware that individuals differed in their relative preference for female or male partners, there were two reasons why they did not believe that such a preference represented a fixed heterosexual or homosexual identity: (1) it was generally assumed that people responded "at different times both to homosexual and to heterosexual stimuli," and (2) that no male who penetrated other males allowed himself to be penetrated at the same period in his life (1978/1980: 1, Note 1).[5]

Dover drew a sharp distinction between later views of homosexual relationships and those of the Greek:

> Greek culture differed from ours in its readiness to recognize the alternation of homosexual and heterosexual preferences in the same individual, its implicit denial that such alternation or coexistence created peculiar problems for the individual or society, its sympathetic response to the open expression of homosexual desire in words and behavior, and its taste for the uninhibited treatment of homosexual subjects in literature and the visual arts. (1)

---

[4] Hercules, for example, had two male lovers with whom he had anal intercourse (Plut. *Moralia* 761D-E), as cited in Hoffman (1980a: 224).

[5] Dover, K. J. (1978/1980). *Greek Homosexuality*. New York: Vintage Books. First published by Harvard University Press in 1978. Page references are to the 1980 Vintage Books edition. Dover frequently cited G. Westwood's 1960 *A Minority Report on the Life of the Male Homosexual in Great Britain*. Westwood was the pseudonym of the sociologist Michael Schofield, who later published studies of homosexuality under his own name. Schofield, as shown later, was one of the early proponents of the idea of the socio-cultural sexual identity. There is some suggestion that Dover's general conceptions of homosexual relationships were influenced by the views of Schofield and did not always represent a reflection of Greek views. The references to "stimuli," for example, are couched in the language of modern behavioristic psychology. The bifurcation of the roles of "penetrator" and "penetratee" may also reflect modern stereotypes of masculine versus feminine homosexual males rather than the sexual attitudes of Greek males.

The centrality of the family in Greece in the Classical Age probably precluded the possibility that the individual could have homosexual relationships to the exclusion of the heterosexual. Hoffman believed that the concept of the autonomous individual did not exist in the Greek world: "Cult, citizenship, material well-being, and survival were all linked to membership in the family unit. Marriage and procreation were foregone conclusions for both men and women" (1978/1980: 218). Those men and women who remained unmarried lived with their closest blood relative. It was not possible for them to establish independent household units. Hoffman continued:

> Nor can I find examples from any period of Greek history prior to Caesar Augustus, of men who had homosexual relations to the exclusion of heterosexual ones. This situation is reflected in the Greek language, where no word was devised to categorize an individual as "a homosexual." To the Greek way of thinking, an act could be described as homosexual or heterosexual, but not an individual. In a world where all men were presumed to marry and have children, the concept of identifying an individual as "a homosexual" was alien. (1978/1980: 218)

Despite the importance of the family, men and women in ancient Greece spent relatively little time together. Hoffman (1980a: 218) described the society as "homosocial": men spent their time with other men, women with other women and children. Husbands and wives did not eat together nor did they sleep together.[6] The only females Greek males had sexual access to were wives, mistresses, and prostitutes.

Outside of marriage it did not appear that males greatly preferred one sex over the other as partners in sexual relationships. The same individual could appreciate beauty in either females or males. Dover noted that KALOS, the Greek word for "beautiful," when applied to a person specifically referred to shape, color, texture, and movement. The Greeks did not make the present distinction between "handsome" males and "beautiful" females. A playwright was quoted by Plutarch as saying: "Is he more inclined toward the female sex or toward the male sex? Where beauty is present, he is ambidextrous."[7]

---

[6] Hoffman (1980a: 219) stated that wives slept behind locked doors with the family heirlooms and the female slaves, which was the way in which the fidelity of the wife was preserved, the family treasure protected, and the breeding of more slaves curtailed.

[7] *Moralia* 767A. The reference is cited by Hoffman (1980a: 219).

The homosexual relationships that occurred in ancient Greece occurred within the context of a profoundly homosocial culture. Hoffman observed that: "Close bonds among men of all ages were the centripetal forces that helped tie society together" (1980a: 219). The Greeks distinguished between two forms of love. One was PHILIA which denoted love or affection for friends, relatives, and family. EROS denoted sexual desire and passionate attachment. Erotic relationships, therefore, generally developed within the context of friendship and civic affiliations.

Dover described how erotic relations between males were conceived and viewed. A distinction was made between the partner who had fallen in love, the ERASTES, and the partner who was the object of love, the EROMENOS. The erastes was viewed as the "active" partner, in the sense that he was older, pursued the other, and was more assertive or dominant in the relationship. The eromenos was the more passive partner, by virtue of receiving from and being subordinate to his erastes.

Dover believed there were a number of rules that governed the actions of the EROMENOS in homosexual relationships: (1) he did not seek or expect physical pleasure from contact with an erastes; (2) he expected the erastes to forego any social contact until the erastes made the requisite concessions; (3) he never permitted penetration of any orifice of his body; and (4) he never assumed the subordinate role of the woman in any physical contact (1978/1980: 103). Dover called these "the rules of legitimate eros" (103). An eromenos who broke any of the rules detached "himself from the ranks of male citizenry and classified himself with women and foreigners" (103). It was even expected that the erastes, as the senior partner in the relationship, would importune the eromenos to bend and even break the rules and for the eromenos steadfastly to refuse. John Ungaretti, however, believed such rules may have expressed public standards but did not necessarily reflect private attitudes and behavior.[8]

Vase paintings showing boys and youths engaged in acts of oral and anal copulation and those of the satyrs which provided a "visual catalog of homosexual acts and creative positions in which to consummate them" (13), suggested to Ungaretti that the eromenos was surely capable of enjoying sexual contact with the erastes.[9] These sexual relationships,

---

[8] Ungaretti, John (1983). De-Moralizing Morality: Where Dover's *Greek Homosexuality* Leaves Us. *Journal of Homosexuality* 8(1): 1-18. Because Greek sexual relationships were noteworthy for their variety and breadth, generalizations about their structure should be treated with skepticism.
[9] Dover also assumed that the relationship with the male eromenos ended with the marriage of the erastes. Ungaretti, however, has presented evidence that

as Ungaretti described them, were pederastic, involving an older man and a male adolescent (Ungaretti, 1978).[10]

The pederastic relationships was "a unique, hierarchical relationship which, in its ideal expression, provided an adult male with the intellectual and sexual company of an attractive youth who, in turn, admired and hoped to learn from his adult lover" (1978: 292-293). The structure of these relationships Ungaretti attributed to several traditions. First, they emulated the sexual relationships the gods had with each other or with mortals. Zeus loved Ganymede. Apollo loved (and accidentally killed) Hyacinthus. Second, on the battlefield, Greek soldiers brought boys along who were too young to fight or captured them in battle. In fact, there was an almost romantic sentiment about the older lover and the younger beloved fighting side by side on the battlefield. Some of the soldiers even took the boys home with them for prolonged relationships. Third, these relationships consisted of notions of masculinity which prompted the older male to assume a superior status and the responsibility for the younger. The typical homosexual relationship, according to Ungaretti, fitted the pattern of "man/wife, man/children, man/parents, and man/slaves" (1978: 295).[11]

Ungaretti concluded:

> [P]ederasty functioned harmoniously with the institution of the family, did not put adult men in direct competition within a sexual relationship, and served a very real social need of the Greek male: It provided the adult male lover with sexual variety, companionship, and a reinforcement of his superior status; it provided the youthful male beloved with a good, responsible model to emulate, as well as someone who could initiate him into the ways of becoming a man. (1978: 299)

Sexual relationships of men with unmarried women or with other men who were not citizens were cast in a different light. A woman who took money from men in return for sexual intercourse was considered a **PORNE**

---

extramarital homosexual relationships were not usually perceived as a threat to the marriage. See Ungaretti, John (1978). Pederasty, Heroism, and the Family in Classical Greece. *Journal of Homosexuality* 3(3): 291-300.

[10] *Pederasty* derives from *pais* (boy) and *erastes*.

[11] For an extended treatment of Greek family life, See Lacey, W. K. (1968). *The Family Life in Classical Greece*. London: Thames & Hudson.

or prostitute.[12] A male prostitute was a **PORNOS**. It was also generally assumed that either a female or male who called a prostitute had sexual intercourse with several different partners and that their clients had no emotional involvement with them. There were also categories of men and women who maintained relatively stable relationships with perhaps only one male client. The dependent man in such a relationship was known as a **HETAIROS**, the woman as a **HETAERA**. Relations with a hetairos or hetaera could involve love and devotion as well as material support.

The Athenian laws against prostitution were aimed at the citizens rather than the prostitutes, who were free to practice their occupation as much and as openly as they wanted. Prostitutes were not citizens. As foreigners, slaves, or freedman they were considered as belonging to the lowest social order. For a citizen to sell his body to a partner was to act as a slave. According to Hoffman:

> Debt bondage and the holding of citizens as slaves had long been abolished, and any reenactment of those conditions for citizens was the occasion for extreme censure. In sum, the law did not care which role was taken in any sex act; it only cared that citizens did not behave in any manner considered appropriate only for slaves. (1980b: 420)[13]

Apparently, therefore, there were no laws which forbade Greek men from patronizing either female or male prostitutes and little or no social opprobrium surrounding these relationships. The breadth and variety of sexual relationships in ancient Greece was made possible by a cosmology which tended to expand rather than constrict individual options. Dover fittingly remarked:

---

[12] Dover points out that *porne* is cognate with *pernanai*, the Greek word for "sell" (1978/1980: 20).

[13] Hoffman, Richard J. (1980b). Review of *Greek Homosexuality* by K. J. Dover. *Journal of Homosexuality* 5(4): 418-421. Dover's view was that in sexual relationships with male prostitutes, the male citizen would perform as the insertor and the prostitute as receiver in acts of oral, anal, or vaginal intercourse. Dover believed that for the Athenian male citizen to allow himself to be penetrated even by a male prostitute would seriously jeopardize his claim to citizenship. This restriction was based on the assumption that the receiver in sexual intercourse was typically female. A male, therefore, who played that role, was behaving as a female and thereby bringing into question the maleness upon which his claim to citizenship rested. Hoffman believed that Dover's interpretation suggested a bifurcation of femininity and masculinity and insertor and insertee roles which was alien to Greek mentality.

The Greeks neither inherited nor developed a belief that divine power had revealed to mankind a code of laws for the regulation of sexual behavior; they had no religious institution possessed of the authority to enforce sexual prohibitions. Confronted by cultures older and richer and more elaborate than theirs ... the Greeks felt free to select, adapt, develop and—above all—innovate. Fragmented as they were into tiny political units, they were constantly aware of the extent to which morals and manners are local. This awareness also disposed them to enjoy the products of their own inventiveness and to attribute a similar enjoyment to their deities and heroes. (1978/1980: 203)

In polytheism the universe was sexually charged and the distinctions between females and males were not rigidly maintained. In effect, the polytheistic view allowed great variation in the structure of sexual relationships. The monotheistic cosmology entertained a theory of creation that differed sharply from that of polytheism. In the Bible, for example, Jehovah, as the sole godhead, did not emerge from a higher realm and therefore did not share his power with other gods. As Hoffman stated, "Thus, not only is Yahweh (Jehovah) unborn, but he does not give birth or father generations" (Hoffman, 1984: 36)."[14]

The belief in monotheism, according to Hoffman, demythologized the universe, which, in turn, had several consequences. It created a clear distinction between the supernatural and natural, the creator and the created. The universe also, in Hoffman's words, became "undeified and desexed" (1984: 36). Nature was also considered to be nonsexual. The believers in monotheism could not imagine that the sea would copulate with some other part of nature to produce offspring. A most important consequence of monotheistic belief was that biological sex was reduced to the observations of genitalia and reproduction. As described by Hoffman:

In nature men and women exist as distinct and obvious forms, and there is no blurring. So too, male and female roles in reproduction are perfectly clear, and are as distinct as Yahweh is from his creation.... What sexuality that does exist, *viz.*, among animals, is unambiguous in its dichotomy of male and female. A blurring of genders is unknown in the natural world of Yahweh. (1984: 36-37)

---

[14] Hoffman described the beliefs of the Israelites in order to exemplify his generalizations about monotheism.

To the monotheists what was sacred in polytheism was considered unholy. The unholy included the ambiguous and anomalous. According to Hoffman, "Everything suggests ambiguity and the breaking down of distinctions is forbidden" (1984: 37). Fields could be sown with only one kind of seed, yokes could be harnessed to only one type of animal, and clothes were to be made of only one kind of thread. The dietary laws were particularly restrictive. Only animals which were pure exemplars of their class were to be eaten: they had to be cloven-hoofed and cud-chewing ungulates. The eating of pork, for example, was forbidden because the pig was cloven-hoofed but did not chew its cud.

In monotheism, the ambiguous categories pertaining to sexual relationships were considered abominations. Transvestism was forbidden for both females and males because human beings were expected to dress in ways appropriate to their biological sex. Humans were not to have intercourse with animals because humans were humans and beasts were beasts. The purpose of intercourse for both humans and animals was reproduction. It was therefore unlawful for one man to give his seed to another for nothing could issue forth from such an act. Hoffman also believed that sexual intercourse between two men was specifically forbidden because it clouded the distinction between the two sexes:

> In monotheism male homosexuality is assumed from the start to be effeminate. Sex with men is an activity appropriate for women only, and those men who are so inclined to act in the same fashion must be like women. Since crossing gender lines is fundamentally wrong and abhorrent, contrary to the nature of the cosmos of Yahweh, male homosexual behavior is equally wrong and abhorrent. (1984: 42)

The only permissible form of sexual relationship was "for the human male to give seed to his wife" (1984: 19). Other relationships were to be punished by death: incest, homosexuality, adultery, a man's fornication with a woman who was not his wife, and bestiality.[15]

In monotheism neither God nor the universe was sexually charged. Sexual expression was controlled for all members of society. The sexual

---

[15] For an alternative interpretation of the prohibitions which appeared in Leviticus 18:22, see Boswell, John (1980). *Christianity, Social Tolerance, and Homosexuality*. Chicago: University of Chicago Press, 120. Hoffman believed that Boswell's interpretation that the prohibitions were against ceremonial uncleanliness rather than homosexual relationships did not reflect the fact that ritual and taboo could not be separated in Biblical monotheism.

attitudes of monotheism were incorporated in the Judeo-Christian and Muslim traditions of sexual morality. This morality implied a belief in the mail-female design. The design assumed basic and complementary differences between the male and female sexes. Although the differences were thought to be essentially biological, by extension the design included a personal and social complementarity to correspond with and augment the biological. The implications of the male-female design for sexual relationships were far-reaching and decisive. One implication was that the individual's genital anatomy prefigured his or her social destiny. This belief resulted in the strict separation of the two sexes which was broadly institutionalized.

The monotheistic cosmology pervaded the writing of the men who became the dominant voices in Christian theology and sexual morality: St. Paul, St. Augustine, St. John Chrysostom, and St. Thomas Aquinas.[16] A major theme in their discussions of sexual morality was what constituted "natural" or "unnatural" practices. The Christian ideal that impermissible sexual relationships were "sins against nature" was expressed by St. Paul in his Epistle to the Romans:

> Wherefore God also gave them (the pagans) up to uncleanness through the lusts of their own hearts, to dishonor their own bodies between themselves: Who changed the truth of God into a lie, and worshipped and served the creature more than the Creator, who is blessed forever. Amen. For this cause God gave them up unto vile affections: for even their women did change the *natural use into that which is against nature.* And likewise also the men, *leaving the natural use* of women, burned in their lust toward one another; men with men working that

---

[16] To treat polytheism or monotheism as cosmologies does not mean that they are the product of monolithic systems of thought and practice. Both Vern Bullough and Boswell have discussed the ascetic and anti-erotic currents in Greek thought, especially Stoicism, neo-Platonism, and even Epicureanism. See Bullough, Vern L. (1976). *Sexual Variance in Society and History.* Chicago: University of Chicago Press, 159-174). Boswell (1980: 163-166) makes the additional point that not all the Church Fathers were intolerant of "love and eroticism" (163). Historians had erred, in his judgment, by focusing on those Fathers whose views ultimately gained acceptance while "disregarding the fact that many equally prominent theologians, some of whom the church regarded as worthy of sainthood, may have held other views" (163).

which is unseemly, and receiving into themselves that recompense of their error which was met. [17]

There has been considerable debate over which sexual acts Paul was condemning. John Boswell argued that Paul was not merely condemning homosexual behavior but all sexual behavior (1980: 108-110). His references to nature were not to universal law or truth but to the ethnic or human character of some particular individual or group.[18]

Bullough believed the appeal to nature was a pedagogical device to convey attitudes about permissible sexual behavior: "It was not really based on observations of what took place in nature because anything contrary to the preconceived notions was ignored" (1982: 57).[19] The only permissible form of sexual behavior was what "nature" intended for production of offspring. Even marriage for Paul was an indulgence in human frailty: celibacy was the highest good.[20]

Paul's view of sexual relationships was largely endorsed by two theologians whose theories were particularly influential in Christian doctrine: St. Augustine and St. John Chrysostom. They were distinguished, among

---

[17] The New Testament, King James Version (Nashville: Regency Publishing, 1975), Romans 1:24-27, 116-117. (Italics added.)

[18] Boswell did believe that Paul "derogate[d] homosexual acts when committed by apparently heterosexual persons" (1980: 109). Boswell's interpretation implied that Paul distinguished between individuals who had heterosexual and those who had homosexual identities or "natures": "It would completely undermine the thrust of the argument if the persons in question were not 'naturally' inclined to the opposite sex in the same way they were 'naturally' inclined to monotheism" (1980: 109).

[19] Bullough, Vern L. (1982). The Sin Against Nature and Homosexuality. In Vern L. Bullough and James Brundage, Eds., Sexual Practices in the Medieval Church. Buffalo, NY: Prometheus Books. For a detailed treatment of the medieval concept of nature, see Noonan, John T. (1966). Contraception: A History of its Treatment by Catholic Theologians and Canonists. Cambridge: Belknap Press of Harvard University.

[20] Celibacy referred to the state of being unmarried. Although loosely associated with celibacy, chastity referred to renouncing all sexual pleasure. In several monastic orders, members took the vow of chastity in addition to remaining celibate. The vow was the expressed intention not to indulge in or derive voluntary pleasure from sexual desire, which included masturbatory fantasies and masturbation. It was possible for married individuals to remain chaste if their sexual intercourse was strictly limited to procreation and avoided pleasurable indulgence. Continence referred to abstaining from sexual intercourse. It was possible that married (and therefore not celibate) individuals could be continent.

several others, as Fathers of the Church.[21] St. Augustine's view reflected the thoughts of leaders in the western church while Chrysostom's reflected eastern thought.

St. Augustine, whose views about sexuality proved to be most influential in Christian doctrine, strongly advocated celibacy, a state he adopted in his own life after his conversion to Christianity in the late fourth century.[22] He equated sexual desire and expression with concupiscence and lust so that all sexual intercourse was tainted with uncontrollable passion, and shame (Bullough, 1976: 193).

Lust, as the excitement of the genitals, was the result of the unlawful intercourse of Adam and Eve (for which Eve was to blame). Therefore, all sexual intercourse was lustful and sinful. Because such an act was necessary to populate to world, Augustine went on to consider the possibility that intercourse could have occurred without lust if Adam and Eve had commanded their genitals to move by will rather than responding to lustful excitement.[23]

Chastity and continence were considered higher states than marriage. Bullough quoted Augustine as concluding: "We ought not to condemn marriage because of the evil of lust, nor must we praise lust because of the good of marriage" (1982: 12).[24] Augustine had no particular rancor against homosexual behavior. He objected to it because, according to Boswell, it was "incongruous" and "contrary to human custom" (1980:

---

[21] In Catholic theology, these were the writers of the first twelve centuries who were considered to have weight and to be worthy of respect. Sometimes the term is reserved for the theologians of the first six centuries. See Attwater, Donald (Ed.). (1941). *A Catholic Dictionary*. New York: Macmillan, 162, 200.

[22] St. Augustine had been a Manichaean, a member of a religious sect that followed the teachings of the prophet named Mani. Mani's teachings embodied Gnostic, Christian, Zoroastrian, and Greek theology. According to his doctrine, there were two eternal first principles: God, the cause of all good; and matter (the Spirit of Evil), the cause of all evil. Evil as a God was equal to the other God. The Elect of the Manicheans, among other things, renounced sexual relationships and worldly goods and embraced celibacy. As a Manichean, St. Augustine never reached the status of the Elect. See Bullough, 1982: 9-10.

[23] St. Augustine's position is described in *The City of God*, Chapters 18-24 (see the 1950 Modern Library edition, Marcus Dods, Trans., 466-472. Peter Gay referred to the speculation of St. Augustine in *The Party of Humanity: Essays in the French Enlightenment* (New York: Alfred A. Knopf, 1964): 157, Note 7.

[24] Bullough was quoting from St. Augustine, *De Nuptiis et Concupiscentia*, I. Chap. 4 (iii).

150) As Bullough observed, Augustine believed every part of the body was created to serve a particular or natural purpose (1976: 355). The external genitals were created only for sexual intercourse and reproduction.

The early Fathers who spoke for the eastern church took a somewhat less conservative view of sexual relationships. This was due to the influence of Judaism which praised marriage and procreation and never held celibacy and chastity to be higher states. Michael Goodich (1979) argued that Christian doctrine represented "the most moralistic and puritanical strain of Judaism" and led "to the suppression of the freer sexual attitudes of the Greeks and Romans" (x). The Jews, however, clearly condemned sodomy.[25]

St. John Chrysostom, one of the Church Fathers most influenced by Judaism, held that it was natural or permissible for the male to have sexual intercourse with his wife even though reproduction were not possible, when, for example, she was sterile, old, or pregnant.[26] Chrysostom also believed that fornication was a sin but at least it was natural: less natural for women, however, than for men.[27]

Although Chrysostom was somewhat easier than Augustine on carnal pleasure when enjoyed by members of the opposite sex, he was harder on homosexual pleasure. He condemned as sodomy both female and male homosexual relationships. Bullough noted that Chrysostom warned parents "not to let their male children's hair grow long because that would make them look effeminate, and such boys were particularly attractive to sodomists" (1982: 18). Chrysostom's intense hostility toward homosexual acts Boswell attributed to "a profound horror of what he considered to be the degradation of one man's passivity to another" (1980: 157). In Bullough's words, Chrysostom considered homosexual relationships "more sinful and destructive than simple fornication because they jeopardized humanity by deflecting the sex organs from their primary ... purpose and sowed disharmony and strife between men and women" (1976: 194).

---

[25] Goodich (1979: 125) cites H. Montgomery Hyde's 1970 *The Love that Dare Not Speak Its Name: A Candid History of Homosexuality in Britain* (Boston: Little Brown), 27-59.

[26] According to Bullough, Chrysostom labored under the notion that it was the word of God and not the act of intercourse itself which led to pregnancy.

[27] Fornication referred to voluntary sexual intercourse between an unmarried man and an unmarried woman. In Scripture its meaning was sometimes extended to include adultery and also to refer to sexual promiscuity.

In the later Middle Ages the grand synthesis of the Christian position on sexual morality was constructed by St. Thomas Aquinas. *The Summa Theologica* was, in Boswell's judgment, less a creative endeavor than a response to conventional beliefs (1980: 321). Aquinas, like Augustine before him, held that sexual behavior, pursued in the interest of pleasure (which he also called "lust") and to the exclusion of procreation, was a sin against nature. He specifically identified four types of unnatural vices (Bullough, 1976: 300), arranged in order from the least to the most grievous: (1) masturbation, which he called obtaining ejaculation and venereal pleasure without copulation; (2) copulation in an unnatural manner, i.e., deviation from the coital frontal position; (3) copulation with an "undue" sex; and (4) copulation with nonhuman creatures. What each of these acts had in common was the misuse of semen, which Aquinas believed was intended by "nature" solely to produce children. Because nature represented the will of God, such practices were therefore sinful.

In order for Aquinas to exclude so many forms of sexual expression he had to stretch his definition of human nature. Boswell pointed out the major inconsistencies (1980: 318-329). Sometimes Aquinas defined human nature as consisting particularly of intellect and reason. At other times human nature referred to that which mankind shared with other beings, the so-called "animal nature." Although in some moral matters Aquinas favored the first definition, in matters of sexual practice he used the second. In Boswell's words:

> Despite his absolute conviction in every other context that humans were morally and intellectually superior to animals and therefore not permitted but obliged to engage in many types of activity unknown or impossible to lower beings, Aquinas resorted again and again to animal behavior as the final arbiter of human sexuality. (1980: 319)

Aquinas' position on human sexuality, as analyzed by Boswell, posed at least two serious paradoxes. It did not explain why human beings, as the superior form of creature, should have to restrict their sexual practices to that of lower species. It also overlooked the fact that most species of animals, with rare exceptions, are not monogamous. Such inherent contradictions suggested to Boswell that Aquinas was propagating under the label of "natural" sexual practices, the popular sexual morality of his time.

In summarizing the attitudes of the most prominent Church Fathers, Bullough had this to say:

The bulk of the Church Fathers tolerated intercourse only in marriage and only for procreation but preferred virginity and celibacy.... Christians were, in spirit, if not always in practice, ascetics, and justifying sexual intercourse only in terms of progeny meant that any kind of sex not leading to reproduction had to be condemned. It also meant that, even when pregnancy resulted, sex was not something to be enjoyed. The Church Fathers regarded sex at best as something to be tolerated, an evil whose only good was in procreation. Western attitudes have been dominated by their concepts ever since. (1976: 196)

In seventeenth-century Europe the scientific cosmology emerged from the development of the natural sciences into a cohesive body of speculation and theory. The new cosmology was to constitute an insuperable challenge to the monotheistic cosmology. The inspiration for the new world view went back to the work of such men as Galileo and Francis Bacon who turned to the empirical investigation of natural phenomena as the royal road to truth. Perhaps the first philosopher to attempt an explicit formulation of the principles of the scientific cosmology was Rene Descartes. This effort was part of his larger plan to weave together into a single fabric truth as handed down by the authority of the church and truth attained through the inductive methods of science.

Although Descartes mostly failed at this task, he unwittingly laid the foundations for the new scientific cosmology. Descartes conceived of God as the divine craftsman who had designed the universe as a well-made machine. The entire earth, organic and inorganic material and animals and mankind, were all machines and parts of the larger machine. In his words:

> I have described this earth, and the whole visible world in general, as if it were a machine in the shape and movements of its parts ... for example, when a clock marks the hours by means of the wheels of which it is made, it is no less natural for it to do so than it is for a tree to produce its fruits.[28]

---

[28] Rene Descartes, *Discours de la Methode*: 1637, Part V, 56. Reprinted by *Libraire Philosophique* (Paris: J. Vrin, 1947). This passage was quoted and translated by R. C. Lewotin in 1983: "The Corpse in the Elevator," *New York Review of Books* 29(1/2): 34-37, 34. Lewotin pointed out that "organism as machine" was intended only as a metaphor by Descartes but has gradually become a form of biological reductionism.

One implication of the Cartesian conception of the universe was that the role of God was relegated to the initial act of creation. God, in effect, created his clock-like universe, wound it up, and let it run its own course.

The task of eliminating the conflict between deductive reasoning and scientific observation fell to Descartes' successor, Isaac Newton, the English mathematician and physicist. In two works, *Principia Mathematica* (1687) and *Opticks* (1704) he was able to make a full statement of the scientific method and to demonstrate how it could be applied in obtaining knowledge which otherwise would be unattainable.[29]

His discovery of the law of gravity showed how a simple mathematical statement could explain seemingly unrelated phenomena such as the fall of an apple, planetary movement, and ocean tides. Gravity was only one example of how the world was governed by natural law. The Newtonian world, in the words of Peter Gay, was one of

> unchanging and unchangeable natural laws, created by God who disdains miracles as paltry admissions of his own inefficiency or impotence; a world of basic constituents like mind or matter whose nature is unknown to us, whose obedience to eternal natural law we can understand and admire. (1954: 22)[30]

Newton was largely unaware of the moral and social implications of his scientific speculations. These were to be explored by John Locke, the English philosopher whose work was to play a dominant role in intellectual currents of the eighteenth century. In his *Essay Concerning Human Understanding* (1690) he claimed that man was born with a *tabula rasa*, a scraped of blank tablet upon which knowledge gained through experience could be written. In establishing sensation and the material world as the basis of knowledge, Locke was challenging the Platonic belief in innate ideas and the Christian advocacy of revealed truth. As J. H. Brunett observed, there was an implicitly democratic tone in Locke's position: "[I]f men were formed by experience alone, they were all originally equal in ability and would, provided their experiences were the same, remain so" (1972: 16). In his later political and religious treatises Locke asserted the existence of a social contract and the right of subjects to overthrow rulers who violated it. In defending religious

---

[29] Brunett, J. H. (1972). *The French Enlightenment*. London: Macmillan Press, 15.
[30] Gay, Peter (1954). *The Party of Humanity: Essays on the Enlightenment*. New York: Alfred A. Knopf.

toleration he urged his readers to retain what was best in religion but to discard superstition and dogma.

The full moral implications of Newton's and Locke's speculations were explored in the intellectual movement of the eighteenth century known as the Enlightenment. The men who led that movement were known as philosophers because they believed that philosophy was the ranking discipline in man's struggle for freedom from error.[31]

Philosophy for them, in Peter Gay's words, was "the mobilization of sound thinking for the sake of right living" (42). Gay characterized the Enlightenment as a series of paradoxes. While the philosophers believed that government should be responsible to its citizens and rule only by law rather than by edict, they also cherished a cultivated elite interested in ideas, the arts, and good conversation. In ethics they believed and even demonstrated stoic courage before death and were dedicated to public service, but they also "enjoyed the dazzle of wit, and play of humor in the face of grim realities" (289).

There were other paradoxes as well. The philosophers were believers in what Gay called "passionate rationalism" (289), defined as a "devotion to the critical spirit that treats all positions as tentative — including their own." That part of their rationalism derived from their scientific view of life. But it was not a frigid view. Gay observed:

> The philosophers at once studied and rehabilitated the passions, tried to integrate the sexual urge into civilized life, and laid the foundation for a philosophy that would attempt to reconcile man's highest thinking with his deepest feeling. In sum, what the philosophers professed was a tragic humanism — humanistic in the sense that they believed in the classics, were active in humanitarian causes, and considered man the center of their moral universe. (289)

In Gay's words "the philosophers were poignantly conscious of the limitations of human efforts, the brevity of human life, the pervasiveness

---

[31] We are following the interpretation of the Enlightenment provided by Peter Gay (1954). Gay's position differs considerably from that of Carl L. Becker in his *The Heavenly City of the Eighteenth-Century Philosophers* (New Haven: Yale University Press, 1932), who believed that, for all their anti-Christian polemics, the philosophers incorporated much of Christian philosophy — in effect demolishing the Heavenly City of St. Augustine only to rebuild it with more modern materials.

of human suffering, man's disappointed hopes, wasted lives, and undeserved misfortunes" (289).

Comparatively little has been written about the philosophers' position on sexual morality although that appeared to have been one of their major concerns.[32] Gay has pointed out the dual nature of their attack on Christianity. It was aimed at both the Christian view of the world (its cosmology) and at the Christian view of man (its morality):

> These two rebellions were equally significant, but they were not equally successful. Christian cosmology found few intellectual defenders—seventeenth-century rationalists had tried in vain to hold the line against scientific empiricism. But Christian morality found two allies: Puritanism and the bourgeoisie. Hence the philosophers' assault on Christian morality was at once more subversive and less effective than their assault on Christian cosmology. (135)

Their attack on Christian morality, in Gay's estimate, stemmed from the view that humans ought to love themselves and their accomplishments. In effect they were trying to free humans from the self-rejection inherent in the belief in original sin. To do this they had to "rehabilitate the emotions." Gay continued:

> Human passions might be blind, unmeasured, but they were not evil. Above all, it was essential to reinstate sexuality in its legitimate place as a joyous, morally acceptable activity. This was a grave and risky enterprise. Catholic social ethics had always found room for the Old Adam—it had tolerated ribald songs, erotic tales, sexual epithets. The very ritual and imagery of the Church freely used sexual symbols. Chivalry celebrated emotions that the Church had condemned as mortal sins. But Catholicism had always looked upon these escapes from the denigration of sexuality as concessions to a fallen humanity. These escapes were tolerated, not happily accepted. They were disguised, reinterpreted, or idealized; divorce was forbidden, but one might divest oneself of one's wife through annulment; chivalry sang of love and pride, but pride was humbled and love rarely successful—sensuality ... was transformed into the craving for self-sacrifice; courtly love was purified by the

---

[32] Again we have relied on Peter Gay, in this case his splendid chapter, "Three Stages in Love's War: Rousseau, Laclos, and Diderot" in *The Party of Humanity* (1954): 133-161.

acceptable motive of loyalty and by the acceptable ending of marriage. These accommodations of Christian virtues to libidinal urges were shrewd concessions, but never more than that. Man was a vessel of wrath, sexuality was lust and concupiscence—the mark of man's folly and disobedience, not of his worthiness. (136-137)

What the philosophers demanded, in Gay's view, was not greater license but a re-evaluation of sexual drives. They wished to break from the constraints of Christian and bourgeois morality because it restricted and demeaned man's nature. In sum, "by exalting man they sought to give a positive value to the strongest and most mysterious of his passions" (137).

To achieve this goal the philosophers had to find a way to reconcile reason and passion. Jean Jacques Rousseau, one of the luminary philosophers, sought this union in the individual's participation in the general social will, an experience, in Gay's words "in which reason and the passions cooperate and ennoble each other" (154).

For Voltaire, passion and reason could be integrated through the gradual process of education, a slow liberation from "perverted and uninformed emotion," and through the channeling of emotions through reason. Voltaire defended pederasty as being natural: Because young boys resembled females and because older males were irresistibly attracted to feminine qualities, it was natural that they would also be attracted to boys.[33]

In his essay on pederasty he posed this question: "How can it be that a vice, one which would destroy the human race if it became general, an infamous assault upon nature, can nevertheless be so natural?" But in the case of homosexual attraction nature was "mistaken":

When the young males of our species brought up together, feel the force which nature begins to unfold in them, and fail to find the natural object of their instinct, they fall back on what resembles it. Often, for two or three years, a young man resembles a beautiful girl, with the freshness of his complexion, the brilliance of his coloring, and the sweetness of his eyes; if he is loved it's because nature makes a mistake; homage is paid to the fair sex by attachment to one who owns its beauties, and

---

[33] Bullough (1976: 494). Bullough was following Voltaire's essay on "Socratic Love" in his *Philosophical Dictionary*.

when the years have made this resemblance disappear, the mistake ends.[34]

Voltaire felt a personal antipathy against homosexual relationships. He disputed the claim that the Theban band of soldiers in ancient Greece was a band of lovers because, as he stated, he preferred not to believe it. Instead, he argued that the soldiers were merely fighting companions. He further implied that homosexual relationships were a threat to the population and that "Greek love" involved friendship but not passion and sexual contact. Although questioning the institution of monogamy, Voltaire adopted the Christian stance on issues pertaining to masturbation and homosexual relationships.

Of all the philosophers, it was perhaps Denis Diderot who best expressed the new sexual morality. Using Tahitian sexual relationships as an example of the natural form, he compared them with the Christian view, which he believed to be the unnatural form.[35] In Diderot's eyes the Tahitians thought of sexuality as an innocent pleasure to which nature, "the sovereign mistress," invited everybody to partake. Fluctuation in sexual impulses was an inherent part of human nature and should be heeded. According to Gay, Diderot's position was that there should be no restrictions on sexual relationships except those that were suggested by nature: "Bigamy, fornication, incest, adultery—these were all imaginary crimes" (161). Diderot's views, in Gay's judgment, "succeeded in breaking the (Christian) antithesis of virtue and gratification, of passion and goodness" (160).[36]

In a later article, published in his famous *Encyclopédie*, Diderot (1751-1772) suggested that the sexuality expressed and enjoyed within a permanent union crowned by children furnished more happiness to the individual than momentary physical gratification.[37]

Gay drew this contrast between the Christian and Enlightenment views of sexual morality:

---

[34] We have quoted the 1962 translation by Peter Gay: Voltaire, *Philosophical Dictionary*, Peter Gay, Trans. and Intro. New York: Basic Books, 76-77.

[35] His *Supplement au Voyage de M. de Bougainville* was written in 1772 as a book review of de Bougainville's report on his world tour, which included Tahiti.

[36] In commenting on Diderot's position Gay stated that Diderot's endorsement of the sexual pleasure of physical union lacked "maturity" because it did not subject love to the "voluntary bonds of affection" (160).

[37] Gay's reference was to Diderot's article, "Jouissance."

Whatever the rationalism of some Christian theologians, fundamental to Christianity was the enmity of passion and salvation: a sense of guilt was to hold back desire—the Fall of Man at once created lust and gave man a weapon against it. In the Enlightenment, the dichotomy of lust versus guilt was softened into the opposition of reason to emotion, and with this softening rose the opportunity of achieving a view of man in which these opposites would be reconciled. (154)

Sodomy was transformed into the medical notion of sexual degeneracy under the aegis of the scientific cosmology. The central faith of this cosmology was the belief that the scientific method would reveal the natural structure and function of physical phenomena. In the nineteenth century, philosophers such as Auguste Comte and Georg Wilhelm Friedrich Hegel argued that social phenomena also possessed a preordained, natural relationship like the physical. They held that social forces determined what people thought and did in the manner in which gravity, for example, determined the descent of falling objects. Like physical phenomena, they believed that once the laws governing social phenomena were discovered, human relationships could be managed.

Their view of social phenomena gave rise to what Hayek called SCIENTISM (1952/1979: 24), which he defined as the slavish imitation of the scientific method by the social sciences. The further belief that the "knowledge" gained through the application of the scientific method could be used to reconstruct society gave rise to what Hayek dubbed the social "engineering type of mind" (1952/1979: 25). He drew this contrast between the Enlightenment and scientistic views of social change:

And while eighteenth-century individualism (of the philosophers), essentially humble in its aspirations, aimed at understanding the possible principles by which individual efforts combined to produce civilization in order to learn what were the conditions most favorable to its further growth, Hegel and Comte became the main source of the hubris of collectivism which aims at the "conscious direction" of all forces of society. (1952/1979: 393)[38]

The discourse on sexual identity that occurred in the nineteenth century was an amalgam of the three cosmologies—the polytheistic,

---

[38] Hayek (1952/1979: 387) noted that both Comte and Hegel disliked Periclean Greece and the Renaissance and shared an admiration for Frederick the Great of Prussia.

monotheistic and the scientific. Each of these cosmologies, as we have explained, implied a different structure for sexual relationships. Each cosmology was resurrected and, in some cases, radically transformed in the normalization of sexual relationships. The discourse, however, was primarily scientific in that it was couched largely in the language of the physical and biological sciences.

Within the polytheistic cosmology sexual relationships could consist of an array of partners who belonged to the opposite or the same sex. Relationships could be contemporaneous so that involvement in one did not preclude the possibility of others. Partners in homosexual relationships could also be involved with other partners in heterosexual relationships. Homosexual partners were not necessarily stereotyped as feminine or masculine. Male partners, for example, could be viewed as masculine even though one or both enacted the role of insertee in anal or oral copulation. Masturbation was not proscribed, and sometimes it was even edified as a practice of the gods. Sexual practices could be diverse and inventive and aimed solely at gratification. Although physical gratification was often linked to love and devotion, it could occur independently of these emotions. Marriage, procreation, and child rearing were considered practical responsibilities rather than the necessary union of love and sexual passion.

The polytheistic cosmology was to survive in the discourse on sexual identity in the nineteenth century—but in a strikingly altered form. The structure of sexual relationships implied by this cosmology was seen as polymorphous sexuality and as perversion. Such relationships were polymorphous because they occurred in various forms rather than the one permissible form, namely monogamy.[39] They were perversions because they turned away from what was considered the true or proper use of the body.

Implicit within the monotheistic cosmology was the belief in the male-female design, that there were basic and complementary differences between the male and female sexes. These differences, as we have stated, were thought to be essentially biological and most visible in genital anatomy. Perceived biological differences, however, prefigured the structure of sexual relationships in the differentiation and complementarity of the two partners. Far from being antagonistic, the biological differences of males and females promised a personal and social

---

[39] "Polymorphous" in biology and medical pathology also has the meaning of various manifestations of eruptive disease (*SOED*: 1540)

compatibility. A permissible sexual relationship consisted of one partner providing the "male" component while the other provided the "female" component.

The monotheistic cosmology was embodied in both the Judaic and Christian conceptions of sexual relationships. To comply with the requirements of Judaic doctrine, sexual relationships were to consist of one male and one female, joined in a life-long marriage, which included devotion to spouse and children. Relationships occurring outside of heterosexual monogamy were viewed as forms of adultery, infidelity, and sodomy. Sexual gratification was permissible as long as procreation was uppermost in the minds of partners. Christian doctrine, however, viewed all sexual pleasure as lustful. Lust opened the gates of passion and ungovernable desire and could consume the soul. Those truly devoted to God's service and salvation, if they were capable, should choose celibacy over marriage and sexual continence over indulgence. Even those females and males who married were expected to guard against lust by limiting coital contact to reproductive requirements.

In the nineteenth-century discourse on sexual identity the monotheistic cosmology was resurrected with only slight modification. Judeo-Christian doctrine had warned against the indulgence in sexual relationships outside prescribed boundaries as seriously jeopardizing one's soul and salvation. Under the aegis of scientism, medicine also warned against the indulgence in impermissible sexual behavior. If the warning was not heeded, the proscribed behavior constituted a serious threat to physical and mental health. Lust, the Church Fathers had severely cautioned, could drive men and women to perdition. Their scientistic successors in the nineteenth century, the fathers of modern medicine and psychiatry, zealously warned individuals that lustful indulgence could drive them to insanity and perversion.

The scientific cosmology, as reflected in the sexual morality of the Enlightenment philosophers, endorsed the polytheistic belief that sexual relationships could exist in various forms. The most important aspect of their sexual morality, however, was the belief that sexual relationships were to be volitional for both partners. By adding the element of choice the philosophers hoped to accomplish two purposes: (1) individuals would be free to exercise their own judgment and thereby form relationships which were harmonious with nature and (2) sexual desire and love would be united in the same relationship.

Within the polytheistic and scientific cosmologies the emphasis was not on prescriptions for sexual relationships but on the broad delineation of freedom for individuals to construct their own relationships. Contrastingly, within the monotheistic cosmology and scientism the emphasis was on prohibitions. Sexual relationships were defined exteriorly, as a set of normative restrictions, rather than as subjective states of individual desire and choice. Choice exercised outside of permissible boundaries was viewed as sinful and harmful for both the individual and the body politic. Consequently, under the monotheistic cosmology and scientism, the history of sexual relationships consisted largely of the description of those that were impermissible.

3 From Sodomy to Degeneracy

The objective of this chapter is to adumbrate the changing conceptions of sodomy that occurred within the monotheistic cosmology, primarily in the medieval and modern periods of western civilization. Sodomy became the emblem for impermissible sexual relationships, although there was no orderly progression of ideas of what sodomy constituted because it ominously represented all the sexual behavior and relationships that lay outside the restrictive boundaries of the permissible.

Sodomy was used to refer to all homosexual relationships (both female and male) and even to all heterosexual relationships outside of marriage. Both within and outside of marriage it described forbidden sexual practices such as oral and anal intercourse or even coital positions in which the male and female were not face-to-face or in which the male was not on top, and it was the name used for all pederastic relationships, particularly if they were homosexual. It included sexual contact between humans and animals, although this was sometimes called by its own name, bestiality. Sodomy was associated with masturbation and even with forms of sexual abstinence such as celibacy. As public knowledge of the inventiveness of individual sexual repertories spread in the eighteenth century, sodomy stood for an interminable list of sexual practices ranging from fetishism to sadomasochism.

Because sodomy referred so generally to whatever sexual innovations individuals may have thought or practiced, it became associated with any type of individual or group nonconformity and dissent or anything perceived as a threat to the social order, such as heresy, sorcery, and treason to the crown.

Finally, under scientism, the idea of sodomy was translated into degeneracy, an amorphous concept that stood precariously at the juncture of evolutionary atavism, moral decay, and physical and mental disease. The idea of sodomy as covering a broad area of impermissible sexual relationships was indigenous to monotheism. As we have shown, within this cosmology the purpose of sexual relationships was limited to reproduction while other forms of sexual behavior were proscribed.

The word sodomy derived from the story in the Old Testament in which Lot, a sojourner in the city of Sodom, received into his lodging two male angels sent by the Lord to investigate the questionable moral status of that community.[1] The male citizens of Sodom gathered around the house in which Lot, his family, and his guests were staying. They demanded that he produce the strangers so that they might "know" them. Lot declined to expose his guests to the men outside, offering instead to send out his two daughters. As stated in the Scriptures:

> And they called unto Lot, and said unto him: "Where are the men that came in to thee this night? Bring them out unto us, that we may know them." And Lot went out unto them to the door, and shut the door after him. And he said: "I pray you, my brethren, do not so wickedly. Behold now, I have two daughters that have not known man; let me, I pray you, bring them out unto you, and do ye to them as is good in your eyes; only unto these men do nothing; forasmuch as they are come under the shadow of my roof.[2]

When the men of Sodom persisted in their demand to meet the angels, whom they called strangers to their city, they were struck blind by the Lord. On the advice of the angels, Lot and his family fled the city the next morning. Sodom along with Gomorrah and other cities were then destroyed by the Lord who caused fire and brimstone to rain upon them.

The possible homosexual implications of this incident hinge on the interpretation of the verb, "know." It is the translation of the Hebrew word YADHA, which, in the Old Testament was occasionally used to mean "engage in (heterosexual) coitus" but usually meant "getting acquainted with." In the old Testament this word was not used to refer to homosexual intercourse. The fierceness of the Sodomites' demand "to know" Lot's visitors, according to Derrick Sherwin Bailey, may have been a response to the violation of a city law by Lot, himself a sojourner

---

[1] The story first appeared in Genesis 19. There were several subsequent biblical references to the incident in Sodom. See Boswell, 1980, 94, Note. 5.

[2] Hertz, J. H. (Ed.) (1972). Genesis. XIX, 3, The Pentateuch and Haftoras: Hebrew Text and English Translation and Commentary, 2nd Ed. London: Soncino Press, 67.

in the city, by receiving and entertaining two possible hostile "foreigners" whose credentials had not been examined by the citizens.[3]

The conduct of the citizens was clearly inhospitable and it was for this transgression, Boswell speculates, that the city was destroyed:

> Lot was violating the custom of Sodom...by entertaining unknown guests within the city walls at night without obtaining permission of the elders of the city. When the men of Sodom gathered around to demand that the strangers be brought to them, "that they might know them," they meant no more than to "know" who they were. (1980: 93-94)

In the Old Testament, Boswell concluded, Sodom became a symbol of wickedness, but the sin of the Sodomites was never specified.[4] It is therefore ironic that the word sodomy was derived from an incident which was possibly not viewed as a sexual encounter by the participants.

The homosexual meaning of sodomy was established by the end of the first century, AD. Bailey quoted from a treatise of the Jewish philosopher, Philo, which appeared at that time. In *De Abrahamo*, Philo wrote of the iniquities, gluttony, and lewdness of the Sodomites. He also made reference to "forbidden forms of intercourse":

> Not only in their mad lust for women did they violate the marriages of their neighbors, but also men mounted males without respect for the sex nature which the active partner shares with the passive; and when they tried to beget children they were discovered to be incapable of any but a sterile seed.... Then as little by little they accustomed those who were by nature men to submit to play the part of women, they saddled them with the formidable curse of a female disease. For not only did they emasculate their bodies by luxury and voluptuousness, but they worked a further degeneration in

---

[3] Bailey, Derrick Sherwin (1955/1975). *Homosexuality and the Western Christian Tradition*. Hamden, CT: Archon Books. (First published in 1955 by Longmans, Green in London.)

[4] Boswell explained that Lot's offering of his daughter was to provide sexual satisfaction as a way to appease the men outside. This proposal was not unusual because female children were considered to be expendable by their fathers.

their souls and, so far as in them lay, were corrupting the whole of mankind. (1955/1975: 22).[5]

According to Bailey, Philo's Sodom did not describe the biblical city but a conception of that city that had gradually established itself among the Jews of Palestine and of the Diaspora during the preceding two centuries.

Over the centuries that followed, the word sodomy had far-reaching connotations ranging, according to Boswell, "from ordinary heterosexual intercourse in an atypical position to oral sexual contact with animals"; sometimes it "referred almost exclusively to male homosexuality and at others almost exclusively to heterosexual excess" (1980: 93, Note 2).[6] In the ninth century, for instance, the theologian Hincmar of Rheims included all non-procreative behavior under the label of Sodomy. He apparently assumed that semen was impure and that its release could be tolerated only under unavoidable circumstances, namely nocturnal emission and procreation (see Boswell, 1980: 264).

A theologian of the twelfth century, Peter Cantor, breaking with theological precedent, used the word sodomy to refer solely to homosexual acts which, incidentally, he equated to murder (see Boswell, 1980: 277).

After reviewing medieval theology and canon law on sodomy, Michael Goodich concluded that "the destruction of Sodom and Gomorrah was considered the just punishment for a sin that violated the natural procreative function of sexuality, was contrary to right reason and the natural order, and denied God's injunction to increase and multiply" (1976: 47).[7]

Arthur Gilbert (1980/1981) pointed out that medieval injunctions against sodomy, as exemplified by Aquinas, assumed that sodomy was a behavioral rather than a relational concept.[8] As behavior, sodomy referred to particular sexual practices irrespective of the biological sex of the partners. As a relational concept, sodomites referred to sexual partners of

---

[5] The original reference is to *OM Abraham*, XXVI: 134-136. The translation is by F. H. Colson, Loeb Classical Library edition of Philo's *Works*, VI: 69-71. London: William Hieneman, 1959-1962.

[6] Boswell inclined toward the view that the variation and ambiguity in the use of the word sodomy reflected its mistaken etymology rather than the different ways of viewing sexual relationships that developed over the centuries.

[7] Goodich, Michael (1976). Sodomy in Ecclesiastical Law and Theory. *Journal of Homosexuality* 1(4): 427-434.

[8] Gilbert, Arthur N. (1980/1981). Conceptions of Homosexuality and Sodomy in Western History. *Journal of Homosexuality* 6(1/2): 57-68.

the same biological sex. Medieval theologians, in Gilbert's judgment, were concerned with sin as behavior, that is, acts against the will of God. Sodomy, therefore, was viewed as a behavioral transgression in both heterosexual and homosexual relationships. He noted that the penitentials, or church rules for prescribing penance for confessed sins, were specific to acts. Anal copulation as a sin was assigned a longer penance than most other forbidden sexual behavior. The fear of sodomy, Gilbert theorized, stemmed from its association with anal copulation which in turn was linked to a general fear of "lower" physical impulses:

> The spiritual strivings in Christian thought clashed with the unassailable fact that life ends in death, that human flesh, like that of all animals, rots and decays. Even more disturbing to the Christian mind was the admission that the living body constantly enacts the drama of death in its physical functions. Excrement was always the clearest and most persistent reminder of the fate of man. Humans usually defecate in secret, and in the Western imagination the anal function became a symbol of evil, darkness, death, and rebellion against the moral order. (1980/1981: 65)

Sodomy, in Gilbert's estimation, aroused the "combined fears of sexuality, animality, and anality"; the venereal pleasures of anal intercourse constituted a "violation of the upwardly striving Christian attempt to find salvation" (66).

It was chiefly during the twelfth and thirteenth centuries that sodomy became associated with heresy through ecclesiastical efforts to tie sexual nonconformity to religious nonconformity. The French Cathers, or Albigensians, for example, were viewed by the church as a heretical sect because they followed the Manichean doctrine which disapproved of sexual relationships which led to procreation. Procreation, they felt, resulted in the entrapment of the spiritual good in the material evil, in the form of a new human being. Because the Cathers explicitly discouraged procreative relationships, it was assumed that they advocated homosexual relationships which, in Boswell's words, were "not only sinless but a desirable means of foiling the devil's efforts to ensnare souls in matter" (1980: 285).[9]

---

[9] Bullough (1976: 390-391) explained how the French *bouggerie* (or "bougre") was the term used to designate the Albigensians (or French Cathers) because it was believed that their doctrine originated in Bulgaria. *Bouggerie* derived from the Latin *Bulgarus* for *Bulgarians*. In the sixteenth century the English word

One Christian writer of the twelfth century was quoted by Bullough as making these charges against the Cathers:

> They condemn marriage and the begetting of offspring through intercourse. And surely, wherever they are scattered throughout the Latin world, you may see men living with women but not under the name husband and wife, and in such a fashion that man does not dwell with woman, male with female, but men are known to lie with men, women with women; for among them it is unlawful for men to approach women. (1976: 392)[10]

The link between heresy and sodomy became sufficiently common-place so that both were applied by French Lawyers to quite orthodox Christians, such as the Knights Templar and members of the clergy, including Pope Boniface VIII (Goodich, 1979).[11]

William Monter noted the association of religious zeal with the punishment of sodomy in the sixteenth century.[12] In studying the records of sodomy trials in sixteenth-century Geneva, Monter showed that the incidence of trials and death sentences increased with the establishment of the moral tribunal known as the Consistory. The Genevan definition of Sodomy included lesbian relationships.[13]

"buggery" became the legal word for sodomy. Bullough believed that the French word was not intended to specify any sexual acts or sins. It appears, therefore, that both the words "sodomy" and "buggery" have had mistaken etymologies. Michael Goodich added that the French *crite* (heretic) was used interchangeably for an Albigensian and a sodomite (1979: 9)

[10] Bullough was quoting Guibert de Nogent, *Histoire de sa Vie* (George Bourgin, Ed. Paris: A. Picard, 1907), as translated in W. Wakefield and A. Evans, *Heresies of the High Middle Ages*, New York: Columbia University Press, 1969, 103.

[11] In some of these cases, the motivation for prosecution was more political than religious. See the description of the case of John Atherton, Bishop of Waterford and Lismore, who was condemned and hanged for sodomy in Dublin in 1640, in Burg, B. R. (1980/1981). Ho Hum, Another Work of the Devil: Buggery and Sodomy in Early Stuart England. *Journal of Homosexuality* 6(1/2): 69-78.

[12] Monter, E. William (1980/1981). Sodomy and Heresy in Early Modern Switzerland. *Journal of Homosexuality* 6(1/2): 41-53.

[13] Even later, in the eighteenth century, a woman was put to death in Prussia for her involvement in a sexual relationship with another woman. See Crompton, Louis (1980/1981). The Myth of Lesbian Impunity: Capital Laws from 1270 to 1791. *Journal of Homosexuality* 6(1/2):11-25; and Erikson, Brigitte (Trans.) (1980/1981). A Lesbian Execution in Germany, 1721: The Trial Records.

One woman was put to death by drowning for the "detestable crime of unnatural fornication" (Monter, 1980/1981: 46). Monter also found that sodomy was defined differently in the city (of Geneva) than in the Swiss countryside. In the city, the term usually referred to sexual relations between men; in the country it meant sex between man and beast. Many more peasants than urban residents were burned for bestiality because, as Monter explained, "peasants have fewer opportunities than towndwellers for homosexual activities but many more opportunities for bestiality" (45). In England during the sixteenth and seventeenth centuries, in addition to heresy, sodomy was associated with treason, sorcery, and even celibacy.[14]

Alan Bray quoted Edward Coke, one of the foremost judicial scholars in the early seventeenth century, as referring to sodomites as part of the infernal trio of "sorcerers, sodomites, and heretics" (1982). Sodomites were treasonous because their sexual behavior was an act against both the Celestial King and the King Terrestrial (i.e., the English monarch). Sodomy was connected with sorcery because witches were believed to have intercourse with the devil. The relationship of witch and devil was considered the antithesis of the relationship of saint and God. Sodomy was tied to celibacy because, in Protestant England, it was believed that the failure of the Catholic clergy to marry led them into the temptation of illicit sex.

All these associations, Bray postulated, were born of the perception that sodomy was a fundamental threat to the social order. The frequent appearance in Renaissance documents of the image of Sodom and Gomorrah destroyed by an angry God revealed the symbolic link between sodomy and social chaos:

> [I]n holding the horrors of homosexuality responsible for the divine wrath a number of needs were satisfied together, for homosexuality...was not part of the created order; rather it was a part of its dissolution. In projecting onto homosexuality the cause of this fundamental malaise and thus placing the cause outside the created order altogether, not only had an explanation for the malaise been found, but one that did not undermine the

---

Journal of Homosexuality 6(1/2): 27-40. The record had been transcribed in 1891 by a Bavarian physician, F. C. Miller, who entitled his notes, "Ein weiterer Fall von konträrer Sexualempfindung."

[14] Bray, Alan (1982). *Homosexuality in Renaissance England*. London: Gay Men's Press. Bray's monograph covers the period of the English Renaissance, roughly from 1550 to about 1700. His treatment, because of the paucity of available documents on female sexuality, is limited to male homosexual relationships.

concept of a single divinely-ordained universal order …it was a disarmingly simple answer operating within a complex system of ideas: It was the fault of the sodomites. (1982: 30)

Bray's thesis that homosexual behavior was associated with social disorder was buttressed by his analysis of the patterns of persecution for sodomy. These persecutions occurred mostly in periods of social upheaval or when individuals had in some way disturbed the public peace through violent behavior. A major theme in Bray's treatment of homosexual conduct in Renaissance England was that there was a yawning gap between enunciated belief and homosexual practice:

This rejection (of homosexuality) was total and unbending; there was no civilization in the world at that time with as violent an antipathy to homosexuality as that of Western Europe. And yet it was faced with the unalterable fact that homosexuality did exist within it on a massive and ineradicable scale. (79)

Compartmentalizing beliefs about homosexuality and the practice of homosexuality made it possible for both to exist side by side. By the eighteenth century, the symbolic association of sodomy with all impermissible modifications in the structure of sexual relationships was firmly entrenched in the discourse on sexuality. It was during the eighteenth and nineteenth centuries that the debate over sodomy gradually took shape. As a contemporary of the French philosophers and a philosopher in his own right, Jeremy Bentham wrote extensively on the subject he called "irregularities of the venereal appetite which are still unnatural" (1785/1978: 389)[15]

Within that circumlocution Bentham included what today are called necrophilia, oral and anal heterosexual copulation, homosexual relationships (which he called "pederasty"), and masturbation, defined as procuring "sensation by one's self without the help of any other sensitive object" (390). It was "pederasty," however, that occupied Bentham's attention over a period of several years.[16] He attempted to refute the

---

[15] The Bentham essay, in its first published form, was edited by Louis Crompton and appeared in two parts in 1978 under the title of "Offenses Against One's Self: Paederasty." *Journal of Homosexuality* 3(4): 383-405 and 4(1): 91-107.
[16] Crompton reported that, during the years between 1774 and 1816, Bentham addressed the subject of pederasty at three different times. Bentham referred to pederasty by such adjectives as "disgusting," "preposterous," and "abominable" even though his essay was a defense of its practice. Crompton believed that these words were employed for political expediency by a man

assertion of Voltaire and others that the practice of pederasty would lead to the under population of the human race. One of his most telling arguments was that males had a sexual capacity that was much greater than was needed only for reproduction:

> [I]f we consider the time of gestation in the female sex we shall find that much less than a hundredth part of the activity a man is capable of exerting in this way is sufficient to produce all the effect that can be produced by ever so much more. Population therefore cannot suffer till the inclination of the male sex for the female be considerably less than a hundredth part as strong as for their own. Is there the least probability that (this) should ever be the case? I must confess I see not anything that should lead us to suppose it. (Bentham, 1785/1978, Part I: 396)

Pederasty, in Bentham's view, was a "natural taste"; it was considered unnatural by others because it was not a procreative necessity: "If the mere circumstance of its not being necessary were sufficient to warrant the terming it unnatural it might well be said that the taste a man has for music is unnatural" (Part I: 402). Nor did he believe that the propensity to be attracted by one sex excluded attraction to the other:

> In all antiquity there is not a single instance of an author nor scarce an explicit account of any other man who was addicted exclusively to this taste. Even in modern times the real womanhaters are to be found not so much among the monks and catholic priests, such of them, be they more or fewer, who think and act in consistency with their profession. (Part 1: 403)

What made pederasty an exclusive practice in modern times was its persecution: "[P]ersecution has and must have...the effect of rendering those persons who are objects of it more attached than they would otherwise be to the practice proscribed" (Part I: 403).

The antipathy to pederasty, Bentham averred, stemmed mainly from moralists and religionists who never allowed the enjoyment of pleasure for its own sake. There had to be some other alleged advantage:

> Eating and drinking by good luck are necessary for the preservation of the individual: therefore eating and drinking are tolerated, and so is the pleasure that attends the course of

---

who sought legal reform. Because, however, the essay was not published, such derogatory modifiers could have also reflected Bentham's own personal taste or ambivalence.

these functions in so far as it is necessary to that end; but if you eat or if you drink for the sake of pleasure, says the philosopher, "It is sinful." The gratification of the venereal appetite is also by good luck necessary to the preservation of the species: therefore it is tolerated in as far as it is necessary to that end, not otherwise. (Part II: 96)

The beliefs of the Marquis de Sade, a contemporary of the philosophers, constituted a radical assault on the traditional restrictions placed on sexual relationships and an endorsement of all sexual practices associated with sodomy. Bullough (1976: 496) observed that, although the philosophers favored the elimination of the old restrictive boundaries, they were fearful of sexual "excess." De Sade was untrammeled by such reservations.[17] He saw fantasy, as the core of language of sexual relationships, as a greater source of pleasure than the actual physical act.

Iwan Bloch quoted de Sade as writing, "Happiness does not lie in actual pleasure, but only in desires, the passionate longings" and that the pleasures "that one impatiently awaits are the best of all" (1934: 275). In de Sade's scheme, power was another key ingredient in sexual relationships because, like fantasy, it aroused strong emotions which intensified sexual experience. Sexual gratification, he believed, could not occur between equals; it capitalized on the differences in the status of the sexual partners. In summing up de Sade's position on sex and power, Bloch declared:

The intensity of erotic sensations is thus relatively proportion-ate to a built-up conception of superiority, the other self in the mind of the enjoying subject. The precondition for highest pleasure is differentiation, and not homogeneity. The analysis of other sensations shows us that there is a kernel of truth in

---

[17] We are following the commentary of Iwan Bloch on de Sade published as Marquis de Sade's Anthropologia Sexualis of 600 Perversions: 120 Days of Sodom or the School for Libertinage and the Sex Life of the French Age of Debauchery, translated and edited by Raymond Sabatier. New York: Falstaff Press, 1934. Bloch discovered de Sade's handwritten manuscript in the private archives of the French government in Marseilles. Unfortunately, Bloch feared that the publication of the original manuscript would be too scandalous and shocking for the reader, so only tantalizing glimpses of what de Sade had written were allowed, generously interspersed with Bloch's explanations of de Sade's views in the language of the nineteenth-century medical sexologist. For example, he called the sexual variations described by de Sade "perversions," a word that in de Sade's lifetime did not have a medical meaning.

the assertion that similar objects do not stand as high in the degree of sensitivity as do dissimilar objects. (1934: 277)

For de Sade the infliction of pain by the powerful partner on the submissive partner was an expression of power, the delineation of their roles, and thereby led to the intensification of passionate and lustful feelings. Such an endorsement of power as the major ingredient in sexual relationships and the substitution of pain and fantasy for physical gratification would have been viewed by the philosophers as blind rebellion against Christian morality rather than the restoration of choice to the individual. Although the philosophers sought to free sexual relationships from the restrictions imposed by Christian and middle class morality, they were not advocates of sexual license.[18]

During the eighteenth century there was a protracted struggle in psychiatry between two schools of thought, SOMATICISM and PSYCHOLOGISM. Somaticism was the belief that mental illness was only a form of physical illness. Psychologism was the belief that mental illness could have environmental as well as physical origins. In the eighteenth century, the somatic position on mental illness was strengthened when many important discoveries about the nervous system were made. According to Ackerknecht there was, however, a question among somaticists about the basis of homosexuality, which at least some regarded as "an illness of the psyche" (15).[19]

It was also during the eighteenth century that psychologism developed in psychiatry. A distinguished leader of this school was Phillippe Pinel.[20] Pinel argued that ordinarily the patient's emotions were disturbed before the onset of mental illnesses. As a disciple of the philosophers, he saw emotional turmoil as interfering with the free exercise of reason. Although he believed that heredity lay at the root of mental illness, the social environment, particularly in the form of faulty education, could be a major factor. Other psychological causes of mental illness, in Pinel's view, were an irregular way of life, spasmodic passions

---

[18] This conclusion contains a note of irony because Bloch's edition of de Sade's *120 Days of Sodom* depicts the eighteenth century as thoroughly libertine and corrupt in sexual practice and some of the philosophers as among the most immoral practitioners.

[19] Ackerknecht, Erwin H. (1968). *A Short History of Psychiatry*. New York: Hafner.

[20] The most comprehensive statement of his views appeared in his *Traite Medico-Philosophique sur l'Alienation Mentale*, published in 1801. Ackernecht called it "a basic text of modern psychiatry" (1968: 41).

such as rage and fright, enervating passions like grief and hate, the change from an active to an inactive life, "gay passions," and a melancholic constitution. Ackerknecht noted that Pinel placed the physical causes of mental illness at the bottom of his list, among which he included "alcoholism, amenorrhea, nonbleeding hemorrhoids, fever, puerperium, and head injury" (Ackernecht, 1968: 42). Pinel rejected the old "theory of possession" which held that the mentally ill were inhabited by the devil and thereby completely insane. Finally, he believed that mental illness was curable.

The somatic school went into decline in the nineteenth century when research on the nervous system, which was intended to uncover the basis for mental illness, failed to achieve its goal. Around the middle of the century, however, the theory of degeneration was proposed, and it revived the hopes of the somaticists. The chief contributor to the degeneration theory was Benedict Augustin Morel.[21] According to Ackerknecht, Morel defined degeneration as "deviations from the normal human type which are transmissible by heredity and which deteriorate progressively toward extinction" (55). The theory was both religious and scientific in concept, with the causes of degeneration linked to both physical and moral injuries.

Insanity was the outstanding example of degenerative illness. It was progressive in form, beginning with eccentrics and instinctive maniacs and ending with idiots and cretins. Degeneration was subject to the "law of progressivity." In Ackerknecht's words, "the first generation of a degenerate family might be merely nervous, the second would tend to be neurotic, and the third psychotic, while the fourth consisted of idiots and died out" (56). Morell believed that degeneracy was becoming more prevalent with the spread of disease and that civilization was approaching extinction. Ackerknecht observed that, by means of the ill-defined concept of "hereditary predisposition," Morel could "attribute the most diverse illnesses in one generation to the occurrence of quite different illnesses in the preceding generations" (56).

It was Valentin Magnan who linked Morel's theory of degeneracy to Darwin's concept of evolutionary regression by discarding the moral elements. Ackerknecht claimed that the "degeneration hypothesis would

---

[21] Morel's theory was set forth in his *Traite des Degenerescences Physiques, Intellectualles et Morales de l'Espece Humaine et ses Causes qui Prodisent ces Varietes Maladives*, which appeared in 1857. Morel had studied theology before taking up medicine and traced degenerative disease to the fall of Adam.

never have acquired the significance it did if it had not coincided with Darwinian Theory, then sweeping all before it" (54).

In the nineteenth century, the biological studies of Charles Darwin were easily absorbed into the scientistic approach to society, including sexual relationships.[22] "Social Darwinism," the application of biological principles to the interpretation of social phenomena, was partly the contribution of Darwin himself.[23] Several tenets of evolutionary theory were applied by Darwin to sexual relationships: (1) that nature was the guiding force in the relationships of the female and male sexes; (2) the two sexes were biologically different in temperament—the female tender, altruistic, passive, and maternal; the male competitive lustful, assertive, and selfish; (3) natural selection favored the "fit" (i.e., the conventional) over the "unfit," (i.e., the unconventional); and (4) conscience and cooperation distinguished civilized man from the primitive savage and were manifested in marriage and fidelity.

Implicit in these Darwinian notions was the idea of the "evolutionary ladder," extending from the simplest organisms all the way up to the subhuman primates and, finally, to humans, who occupied the uppermost rung. Occasionally, however, members of a particular species displayed the characteristics of more primitive forms. The greater resemblance of an organism to its ancestors than to its parent was known as atavism. Atavism in medicine and, later, in psychiatry became the theory of degeneracy which held that defects in one's ancestry could be transmitted through heredity.[24]

Whereas evolution was expected to carry organisms forward to progressively higher levels of development, degeneracy reversed this direction. As applied to individuals, the symptoms of degeneracy were nervous illness, physical weakness, and deviant behavior. Bullough observed:

> Ineluctably, any departure from conventional behavior, whether sexual or social, was regarded as a sign of degeneracy. The popular fear of a "sexual degenerate" was thus based on the idea of an uncontrolled, primitive, animal-like person who

---

[22] Darwin's *On the Origin of the Species by Means of Natural Selection, or the Preservation of Favored Races in the Struggle for Life* was published in 1859.

[23] Darwin's *Descent of Man, and Selection in Relation to Sex* was published in 1871.

[24] The biological use of the word "degeneration" to refer to a change in structure by which an organism assumes the form of a lower type has been dated as occurring in 1884 (*The Shorter Oxford Dictionary of Historical Principles*). Earlier uses referred to a decline in character or qualities.

might do anything. In no way could such a person be regarded as a solid member of the community who happened to be deviant only in some of his sexual inclinations. (1976: 640)

With the evolutionary concepts of natural selection and degeneracy the three cosmologies were brought together to create the stage for the nineteenth-century discourse on sexual identity. The ancestral forms of sexual relationships, once permissible within the polytheistic cosmology, could now be viewed as primitive and their recurrence as atavistic. The sins of concupiscence and sodomy, so graphically described by the theologians of the monotheistic cosmology, now could be seen as the recrudescence of an originally tainted humanity in the form of biological flaws. In the guise of scientism, the forces of the scientific cosmology could be mobilized against all modifications of sexual relationships that were deemed impermissible.

Part One:

THE BIOLOGICAL SEXUAL IDENTITY

4 Creation of the Idea of Sexual Identity

An explicit theory of sexual identity was first set forth in the middle of the nineteenth century. It was preceded by a century of discourse on masturbation, which represented the beginning of the medicalization of sexual conduct. Within this medical discourse the concept of sexual identity was framed in the language of contemporary biology and depicted as a product of nature. The inventors and proponents of the concept were chiefly interested in the homosexual identity. The idea of a heterosexual identity was limited to establishing it as a reference point for their discussions. To show how the discourse on masturbation was linked to the discourse on sexual identity and how the discourse on sexual identity was an intriguing amalgam and transformation of the three cosmological views of sexual relationships, a description and analysis of the idea of sexual identity, as set forth by Karl Heinrich Ulrichs and Károly Mária Kertbeny (Karl-Maria Kertbeny), will be presented.

Medicine began a campaign against masturbation in the eighteenth century. The medical theorist, Hermann Boerhaave, in his 1708 *Institutiones Medicae*, wrote that the "rash expenditure of semen brings on lassitude, a feebleness, a weakening of motion, fits, wasting, dryness, fevers, aching of the cerebral membranes, obscuring of the senses, above all, the eyes, a decay of the spinal cord, a fatuity, and other like evils" (Bullough, 1976: 496).[1]

In 1717, an anonymous text, published under the title *Onania or, the Heinous Sin of Self Pollution and all its Frightful* Consequences, and probably written by a clergyman parading as a medical authority, appeared in

---

[1] Bullough's reference is to S. A. D. Tissot who, in turn, cited Boerhaave's quotation. Bullough speculated that Boerhaave may have based this ominous theory on the observation of the diffuse relaxation of the musculature that occurs in the post-orgasmic period.

England.[2] The author defined "onanism" (or masturbation) as "that unnatural Practice, by which Persons of either Sex may defile their own Bodies, without the assistance of others, whilst yielding to filthy Imaginations" (quoted in Hunter & MacAlpine, 1963: 349). The "licentious masturbators" could be known by their "meagre Jaws, and pale Looks, with feeble Hams, and Legs without calves, their Generative Faculties ... destroy'd..." (quoted in Hunter & MacAlpine, 1963: 349). The author attributed to onanism an impressive roster of physical and moral malfunctions, including several diseases, epilepsy, insanity, lying, and possibly murder.

The medical certification of the dangers of masturbation came with the publication of *A Treatise on Masturbation* in 1758 by the famous Swiss physician, Samuel-Auguste Tissot.[3] For Tissot the single permissible expenditure of semen was in intercourse intended for reproduction, that is, an investment of semen for the purpose of replenishing the supply. Tissot had developed a theory of wastage which held that the human body was constantly faced with depletion through elimination and the loss of blood. Males were further threatened with loss through the emission of semen, therefore, was tantamount to physical emasculation. Tissot spared no detail in cataloging the grave physical consequences of "wasting" semen:

---

[2] Karlen, Arno (1971). *Sexuality and Homosexuality: A New View*. New York: W. W. Norton, 182. Karlen correctly noted that Onan's biblical sin was coitus interruptus, not masturbation. "Onanism" could now join "sodomy" and "buggery" in a trio of mistaken etymologies. By 1730, the fifteenth edition of *Onania* had appeared with a supplement (in its sixth edition). The reputed author was a Dr. Bekkers. See Hunter, Richard and Macalpine, Ida (1963). *Three Hundred Years of Psychiatry, 1535-1800: A History Presented in Selected English Texts*. London: Oxford University Press, 348-349.

[3] Tissot, also known as Simon Andrew Tissot, first published his treatise in Lausanne, Switzerland, in 1758, as part of his "Essay on Bilious Fevers" (*Dissertatio de febribus biliosis, seu, Historia Epidemiæ Biliosæ Lausannensis, An. MDCCLV; accedit Tentamen de Morbis ex Manustupratione*, then later issued separately as *L'Onanisme, Dissertation sur le Maladies Produites par la Masturbation*. The first British translation (by A. Hume, M.D.) appeared in 1766, and American editions followed (the first was apparently the 1832 Collins & Hannay edition [New York], translated by "A Physician," and Otis, Broaders & Co. in Boston published a second edition in 1839, this time with the translation signed by "L. Deslandes, M.D." Tissot used both "onanism" and "masturbation."

(1) cloudiness of ideas and sometimes even madness; (2) a decay of bodily powers, resulting in coughs, fevers, and consumption, (3) acute pains in the head, rheumatic pains, and an aching numbness, (4) pimples of the face, suppurating blisters on the nose, breast, and thighs, and painful itchings; (5) eventual weakness of power of generation, as indicated by impotence, premature ejaculation, gonorrhea, priapism, and tumors in the bladder; and (6) disordering of the intestines, resulting in constipation, hemorrhoids, and so forth. (Bullough, 1976: 498)

Most of these afflictions could occur in females as well as males, but there were more special risks for the females: "hysterical fits, incurable jaundice, violent cramps in the stomach, pains in the nose, ulceration of the matrix and uterine tumors" (Bullough, 1976: 498). Mutual masturbation among women, involving clitoral stimulation, would lead to the deflection of their love from men to other women.

The French contribution to the unfolding medical tale of the horrors of masturbation was made by the surgeon Claude-Francois Lallemand, who, in 1836, invented the diagnosis of spermatorrhea, the involuntary loss of semen.[4] Spermatorrhea was an ailment suffered by adults who, as adolescents, had masturbated in response to reading "lascivious" books and entertaining erotic daydreams. Not only did the ailment presage insanity but it made the masturbator socially apathetic: "He has no other interests; he loves no one; he shows no emotion before the grandeur of nature or the beauties of art ... dead to the call of his family, country, or humanity."[5]

The belief that masturbation led to physical dissolution was extended by later medical authorities to include most forms of sexual indulgence. The author of the first text on medicine published in the United States, Benjamin Rush in 1812, held that excessive sexual indulgence could lead to "seminal weakness, tabes dorsalis, pulmonary consumption, dyspepsia, dimness of sight, vertigo, epilepsy, hypochondriasis, loss of memory, manalgia, fatuity, and death" (Bullough, 1976: 543).[6]

---

[4] Bullough (1976) cited the English translation of Lallemand, Claude-Francois (1836/1839). *Des Pertes Séminales Involontaires: On Involuntary Seminal Discharge.* William Wood, Trans. Philadelphia: A. Waldier.

[5] The translation appears in Karlen (1971: 182). He was presumably quoting from Lallemand's book.

[6] Bullough was quoting from Rush's *Medical Inquiries and Observations* (Philadelphia: Thomas Dobson, 1794-1798, 5 Vols. Vol. 4: 123-129).

Another American physician, Sylvester Graham, believed that even sexual fantasies were a drain upon the nervous system because they could lead to physical arousal.[7] The reproductive system, unlike other bodily systems, was particularly vulnerable to neural assault. All of the organs, according to Graham, were affected by the heat and passion of sexual desire and any excess was serious enough to lead to insanity which, in turn, could further intensify desire. According to Bullough, Graham believed that "the loss of an ounce of semen was equivalent to the loss of several ounces of blood with the result that, every time a man ejaculated, he lowered his life force and thereby exposed his system to diseases and premature death" (1976: 544).[8]

Having transformed masturbation into a clinical condition, the medical profession turned its inventiveness toward prevention, as described by Bullough:

> Some doctors perforated the foreskin of the penis and inserted a ring or cut the foreskin with jagged scissors. Others applied ointments that would make the genitals tender to touch, and others applied hot irons to girls' thighs. In some cases clitoridectomies were performed, and in a few cases actual amputation of the penis was attempted to prevent masturba-

---

[7] Bullough (559) cited Graham, *A Lecture on Epideaic Diseases of the Mind.* Philadelphia: Kimber and Richardson, 1812.

[8] Graham, as the inventor of the Graham cracker, was as austere about eating as he was about coitus, preaching that plain eating led to a diminution of sexual desire. The grave consequences of wasting semen were reiterated in the English and American literature. The English physician, William Acton, wrote that depletion of semen was an assault upon the nervous system. (Bullough, 1976: 544-545.) Bullough (560) cited Acton's 1871 *The Functions and Disorders of the Reproductive Organs in Childhood, Youth, Adult Age, and Advanced Life Considered in Their Physiological, Social, and Moral Relations* (London: J. and A. Churchill, 135-140). For Acton, females were indifferent to sex and provided a fortunate check on the seminal attrition of the male. Only fear of losing husbands to prostitutes and the desire to fill their maternal destiny moved them to coitus. In the United States, Acton's counterpart was the physician John Harvey Kellogg. Bullough (1976: 560) cites J. H. Kellogg's *Plain Facts for Old and Young* (Burlington, Iowa: I. F. Senger, 1882). Kellogg also believed that coitus profoundly jarred the nervous system and that only its guarded and restrained practice would prevent insanity. According to Bullough (1976: 548), females were advised not "to enjoy sex, because women were maternal rather than sexual creatures. Only the diseased female has an 'excessive animal passion.'"

tion. Castration was not unusual. Most popular, however, were mechanical devices that the interested could purchase; ... devices with metal teeth designed to prevent erection in the male, or various kinds of guards to be worn around the pudenda of the female ... devices for patients in mental institutions, including a unique pair of gloves that prevented the patient from touching his or her genitals. There was even a device to prevent bed covers from coming in contact with sensitive areas. By the nineteenth century, according to Hunter and MacAlpine), the sequence of "masturbation—venereal excess—venereal disease—nervous disease—insanity was firmly established not only in the lay but also in the medical mind." Once the pathologization of masturbation was underway, attention was turned to various forms of sexual relationships. (1976: 549)[9]

Within the context of degeneracy theory and the pathologization of masturbation, the German classical scholar and lawyer, Karl Heinrich Ulrichs, formulated the first explicit theory of sexual identity. He was concerned with the plight of individuals whose performance of homosexual acts exposed them to prosecution under the Prussian sodomy statutes. Ulrichs was undoubtedly familiar with the contemporary biological and medical treatises on sexual behavior and development and with the historical research on sexual relationships in ancient Greece and Rome.[10]

---

[9] There was not a consensus of medical opinion on the consequences of masturbation. John Hunter, in his 1786 *A Treatise on Venereal Disease* (London: Privately printed), held that the harm from masturbation came from the idea rather than the practice—that is, from the feelings of guilt, not any direct physical effects (Hunter & MacAlpine, 1963: 491). Another physician, John Gideon Killinger, also doubted that masturbation led to insanity (Hunter and MacAlpine, 1963: 894).

[10] There were both personal and political circumstances that sparked Ulrich's theoretical speculations. He was sexually attracted to males. He was also deeply angered by the arrest and sentencing of his friend, Johann von Schweitzer, for allegedly having sex with a boy in the Mannheim city park. James Steakley (*The Homosexual Emancipation Movement in Germany*. New York: Arno Press, 1975) reported: "In August of that year, two elderly ladies enjoying a quiet stroll through the public park of Mannheim came upon Schweitzer and an unidentified young man in a highly compromising situation" (1-2). Schweitzer was himself a well-known lawyer as well as writer of treatises on socialism. As a lawyer, Ulrichs resented the spread of Prussian law, with its anti-sodomy statutes, to those parts of Germany which had been under the comparatively liberal Napoleonic Code. The spread of Prussian law was the

Between 1864 and 1879, he published twelve short books under the collective title, *Forschungen über das Ratsel der Mannmännlichen Liebe*.[11] As the title implied, Ulrichs presented arguments and case histories to explain the "riddle of love between men." The basis for Ulrichs' explanation of why an individual turned to the opposite or to the same biological sex in forming sexual relationships was the nascent science of embryology.[12] He argued that biological life started from a human embryo which was neither female nor male.[13] The embryo then developed female or male sex organs and feminine or masculine sex drives. As conceived by Ulrichs, the sex drive was apparently a spiritual rather than a physical force. Although he believed it was situated in the sex organs, Ulrichs claimed that the

---

result of the unification of Germany under Bismarck. Even the Kingdom of Hanover, where Ulrichs had long resided and had worked as a public assistant attorney, fell under Prussian hegemony. He was also familiar with the writings of Heinrich Hössli. In 1836 and 1838, Hössli, a Swiss wigmaker, published a two-volume work with a tediously long title which, in part, was *Eros: Die Männerliebe der Griechen (Eros: the Manly Love of the Greeks)* (see Hössli, 1836-1838). H. F. Karsch wrote a biographical sketch of Hössli and a synopsis of his volumes under the title of "Der Putzmacher von Glarus Heinrich Hössli, ein Vorkämpfer der Männerliebe" which was published in the *Jahrbuch fur sexuelle Zwischenstufen*, edited by Magnus Hirschfeld, in 1903 and reprinted under the title *Documents of the Homosexual Rights Movement in Germany, 1836-1927*. New York: Arno Press, 1975: 5-112). The full title of Hössli's treatise suggested that he based his books on the study of Greek history, literature, and philosophy and on "Platonic love." He claimed that the Greeks believed that one man's love for another man was both "natural" and customary. He also implied that some men were born homosexual in character.

[11] The English translation is "Researches on the Riddle of Love between Men." These books or pamphlets of Ulrichs have been reprinted in the Arno Press series entitled *Homosexuality: Lesbian and Gay Men in Society, History and Literature*, General Editor, Jonathan Katz, New York: Arno Press, 1975. Ulrichs wrote the first books of this collection under the pseudonym "Numa Numantius." In the reprinting of the Arno Press series, Ulrichs' own name first appears at the conclusion of the sixth book, *Gladius Furens*.

[12] For the explanation of Ulrichs' theory, we have depended in part on Kennedy, H. C. (1980/1981). The 'Third Sex Theory' of Karl Heinrich Ulrichs. *Journal of Homosexuality* 6(1/2): 103-111; and on the essay by John Addington Symonds, "Ulrichs' Views," in *Sexual Inversion* by Ellis, Havelock and Symonds, John Addington (1897/1936). London: Wilson and MacMillan, Appendix C: 258-272.

[13] Ulrichs, of course, was in error. The original embryo is female in genital structure and remains so unless it is differentiated into the male by the addition of the Y chromosome.

feminine or masculine direction of the drive developed independently of biological sex. Ordinarily individuals with female organs developed a feminine sex drive; those with male organs, a masculine sex drive. Accordingly, such females and males were attracted to members of the opposite sex. Occasionally a biological female developed a sex drive which would propel her toward other females. Similarly, the biological male could develop a feminine sex drive which would attract him to other males. The male with a feminine sex drive, according to Ulrichs, was capable of feeling a woman's love for a man. He summed up his theory (for males) in a Latin couplet:

> *Sunt mihi barba maris, artus, corpusque virile, His inclusa quidem: sed sum maneoque puella.* [Have I a masculine beard and manly limbs and body; Yes, confirmed by these: but I remain a woman]. (Kennedy, 1980/1981: 106)[14]

Later his theory, as applied to males, was summarized in the phrase: *anima muliebris virili corpore inclusa*, "a feminine soul confined by a masculine body."[15] For the basis of his classification system Ulrichs turned to *Phaedra*, one of Plato's symposia. In a speech by Pausanias, a participant in the symposium, Plato distinguished between two sources of love:

> For we all know that Love is inseparable from Aphrodite, and if there were only one Aphrodite there would be only one Love; but as there are two goddesses there must be two Loves. And am I not right in asserting that there are two goddesses? The elder one, having no mother, who is called the heavenly Aphrodite—She is the daughter of Uranus; the younger, who is the daughter of Zeus and Dione—her we call common.... The Love who is the offspring of the common Aphrodite ... is to be of women.... But the offspring of the Heavenly Aphrodite is

---

[14] The couplet appears in the second book of *Forschungen über das Rätsel der Mannmännlichen Liebe*, 4 (cited in Kennedy, 1980/1981: 110).

[15] This phrase first appeared as a subtitle to his seventh book: *Memnon. Die Geschlechtsnatur des mannliebenden Urnings. Eine naturwissenschaftliche Darstelling. Körperlich-seelischer Hermaphroditismus. Anima muliebris virili corpore inclusa.* Wurzburg, 1868. While Ulrichs' theoretical formulations included both biological sexes, his overriding concern was with men and, in particular, male homosexual relationships.

derived from a mother in whose birth the female has no part.... Those who are inspired by this love turn to the male.[16]

By combining his biological explanation of sexual drives with the Platonic distinction between the two sources of love, Ulrichs developed taxonomy of sexual identity. The **URNINGS**, those females and males attracted to partners of their own biological sex, were named after Uranus, the father of the motherless Aphrodite. The **DIONINGS**, those females and males attracted to partners of the opposite sex, were named after Dion, the mother of the common Aphrodite.[17]

Urnings were divided into two broad categories: those attracted exclusively to members of their own sex and those who consorted with either sex. The "exclusive" Urnings were further divided into three groups: (1) the **MANNLINGS**, who preferred adult males who were feminine in appearance, dressed in female clothes, and pursued feminine occupations; (2) the **WEIBLINGS**, who were attracted to males who appeared masculine and powerful; and (3) the **ZWISCHEN-URNINGS**, who sought males in the bloom of adolescence.

There were also three categories of non-exclusive Urnings: (1) the **URANIASTER**, who had sex with men when women were unavailable or, as Symonds stated, "under the influence of special circumstances" (1897: 6); (2) the **URANDIONINGS**, who were attracted to either females or males; and (3) the **VIRILIZED-URNINGS**, who forced themselves to cohabit with and perhaps marry a female.[18] The classification system for female Urnings merely paralleled that for males and, presumably, was not based on extensive knowledge of sexual relationship among women.

Later, in his publication of 1879, Ulrichs placed the various categories of Urnings on a continuum, with the Weiblings at one pole and the

---

[16] Jowett, Benjamin (1937). *Dialogues of Plato*. Two Vols. New York: Random House, 1-309.

[17] Ulrichs' classification scheme is described in *Memnon*. Although Symonds uses *Urning* (after the German), *Uranian* is also a common English translation. As used in English, the term is applied to either females or males. *Uranism* was used for "homosexuality" until the latter term became current. Ulrichs' designations of the sexual states or phenomena he conceptualized varied from *mannmännliche Liebe* ("love between men"), *urnische Liebe* ("Uranian love") to *Urnings-natur* ("the Uranian nature").

[18] Ulrichs also had a class for hermaphrodites, the *Zwitters*. He showed little interest in this group even though, in theory at least, they could claim membership in any of his categories.

Mannlings at the other.[19] This continuum was then placed within a still longer one which located the "normal" female (Dioninge) at one pole and the "normal" male (Dioning) at the other. Ulrichs thereby replaced his original bifurcation of individuals into either Urnings or Dionings with the idea of the Urnings as an "intermediate" or "third" sex. He probably did not view these distinctions as continuous measures on a single scale but rather as discrete points.[20]

Although Ulrichs viewed Urnings as "natural" and even "healthy" forms of females and males, he also saw them as suspended or incomplete phenomena. He believed they were designed to be unhappy not only because of their minority status and persecution but also because they were often attracted to the unattainable object: The Weibling to the powerful male who was most likely an exclusive Dioning and the Zwischen-Urning to the beautiful young man in the full intensity of his sexual attraction to young women. It was perhaps least onerous to be a Mannling because this type could presumably be satisfied with other Urnings, particularly the Weiblings.

Ulrichs' idea of a biological sexual identity was endorsed in a document presented to a Prussian medical commission in 1869 by Károly Mária Kertbeny, a writer who was clearly familiar with Ulrichs' conceptualizations.[21] The document, a series of three open "letters," was addressed to the Prussian Minister of Justice. In the letters Kertbeny outlined his conception of opposite-sex and same-sex relationships.[22] His

---

[19] *Kritische Pfeile: Denkschrift über die Bestrafung der Urningsliebe.* Leipzig: Verlag von Max Spohr, 1898. Reprinted in the Arno Press series, 1975.

[20] In the modern psychology of measurement, Ulrichs was confusing nominal and ordinal scales. In effect, he developed mutually exclusive nominal categories which he then proceeded to arrange along a continuum.

[21] Kertbeny's original name had been Karl Benkert (Kertbeny is an obvious anagram). Although he was born Viennese, the change of his name reflected his love of Hungarian culture. He was hardly a writer of distinction but had established a reputation as a "free-lancer" in France and Germany. The document, which was anonymous, falsely implied that the writer was a physician writing for the illumination of his fellow physicians. Kennedy (1980/1981: 110) noted that Ulrichs referred to K. M. Benkert's 1864 *Erinnerungen aus Charles Sealsfield* (Leipzeig: Ahn) in his fourth book as setting forth some of Ulrichs' ideas. Kertbeny, however, made no reference to Ulrichs in his document and did not use Ulrichs' terminology.

[22] The "letters" are, more accurately, a document of almost seventy printed pages. They were reprinted in 1905 in the *Jahrbuch für Sexuelle Zwischenstufen* (M. Hirschfeld, Ed. Vol. VII: 9-66), under the title § *143 des Preussischen*

chief contribution to the discourse on sexual identity was to coin the term homosexual. In the twentieth century this term was to prevail over all others for describing same-sex relationships.

Kertbeny began by echoing the medical fears of masturbation.[23] He referred to masturbation by such epithets as "lonely self-abuse" and a "truly wicked mania" (10). Masturbation was a particularly pernicious activity because it was stimulated by fantasy rather than another person: "It attacks ... not only the body but at the same time all one's spiritual might, and for that reason is so dangerous to the brain and spinal cord and throat, chest, and lungs" (10) Masturbation easily became a mania because it could destroy the individual's motivation to marry and procreate, turning the practitioner into a "physical eunuch" (11).[24]

The practitioners could also become "mental eunuchs" (11), or "hermaphrodites of the mind," whose feelings would become cold, abstract, harsh, and cynical: "Whenever you meet a cool, remorseless, ironically hard-hearted person, you can be sure that person is a secretive self-abuser" (12). Next, Kertbeny turned to the issue of the unnatural acts of those of "opposite-sexual natures."[25] These activities include cunnilingus, anilingus, fellatio, urination, pedophilia, and masturbation between husbands and wives, all of which went unpunished under Prussian law.[26]

Strafgesetzbuches vom 14. April 1851 und seine Aufrechterhaltung als §152 im Entwurfe eines Strafgesetzbuches für den Norddeutschen Bund (Kertbeny, 1869/1905) [Paragraph 143 of the Prussian Penal Code of 14 April 1851 and its Preservation as Paragraph 152 in the Draft of a Penal Code for the North German Confederation]. The minister was identified as Leonhardt. He, along with the Minister for Religious, Educational, and Medical Affairs, von Mühler, had convened the commission, which consisted of some of the most distinguished physicians and professors of medicine in Germany. The commission was to consider whether there were any medical reasons for not liberalizing the sodomy statutes.

[23] The authors gratefully acknowledge their debt to Michael A. Lombardi, whose unpublished translation of the Kertbeny letters from the German was used in this treatment of Kertbeny's ideas. The page references are to the Lombardi manuscript.

[24] Kertbeny subscribed to the belief that spermatozoa would disappear from the semen of habitual male masturbators.

[25] Kertbeny's word for " opposite-sexual" was *"gegengeschlechtlich"*; he did not use the word heterosexual.

[26] He compared the Prussian statutes with the Code Napoleon, which had been issued in 1806 under the leadership of the French chancellor, J. J. Regis

Same-sex relationships between women also went unpunished. The Prussian penal code, however, did refer to sexual conduct involving two males as evidence of "degeneration and degradation" (12) and as a threat to morality. Kertbeny wryly asked how acts condoned when performed by marital partners or two women could be degraded and degenerate when performed by two men. This contradiction within the Prussian law Kertbeny attributed to the general lack of scientific knowledge of the "homosexual passions."[27] It was here that he set forth Ulrichs' theory of sexual drives, using, however, his own terminology.

> Besides the normal sexual instincts of all mankind and animals, it seems that Nature, in her sovereign judgement, gave the homosexual inclination [der Trieb] to certain male and female individuals at birth and also bestowed upon them a sexual constraint which has physical and mental aspects, which render them, even with the best of will, incapable of achieving a "normal sexual" erection, thus suggesting a specific horror of the opposite sex. This [homosexual inclination] also makes it impossible [for them] to escape the influence which particular individuals of the same sex have on them.[28]

Kertbeny claimed that "homosexuals" had existed throughout history and that, in the time of the Greeks, female homosexuals were known as "tribades," males as "pederasts."[29] For the benefit of his medical

---

Cambaceres. It ignored sexual practices that did not interfere with the rights of others, specifically private, consensual sexual conduct involving adults. The position on sexual conduct was later incorporated in the penal codes of three German states during the period from 1813 to 1840, well before they came under Prussian hegemony. One of these states was Hanover, where Ulrichs had long resided and where Leonhardt, to whom the letters were addressed, had been Minister of Justice. Kertbeny snidely noted that there had been no outbreaks of "immorality" in any of the places governed by the reformed penal codes. The Prussian penal code, however, which became effective in 1851, referred to sexual conduct between males as "unnatural fornication" and made it punishable with up to four years imprisonment.

[27] For "homosexual," Kertbeny used the German "homosexuellen."

[28] This translation has profited from those of both Lombardi and Fred McEnroe. "Der Trieb" was translated as "drive" by Lombardi and as "inclination" by McEnroe.

[29] Kertbeny's word (in the masculine gender) for "homosexuals" was "Homosexualen," which Lombardi translated as "homosexualists." His word for "homosexuality" was "Die Homosexualität."

audience, Kertbeny compared the sexual conduct and relationships of homosexuals with those of "normalsexuals."[30]

Furthermore, Kertbeny thought that the homosexual drive was primarily expressed as attraction to physical beauty and could be maintained in "platonic relationships." The foundation of the homosexual impulse, in Kertbeny's judgment, was masculinity, but this did not mean that homosexuals were indiscriminately attracted to all males. He stated what he believed to be their most prominent characteristic:

> [H]omosexuals almost never give themselves up to solitary self-abuse, no matter how much they are driven to mutual self-abuse, simply because their impulse is not excited by fantasy nor by a superfluous prurigo on their body, but rather by certain personalities which, from mature boyhood to manhood, represent the full features of virility in every detail of its habit, in opposition to the feminine. (26)

Thus there was no reason to fear that homosexuals would seduce young boys. Rather they were attracted to young men such as soldiers, who had achieved full masculinity, and even to men as old as forty. He did acknowledge that homosexuals were attracted to "normalsexual" males, but he did not describe the sexual conduct that occurred between them except to claim that it must be mutually gratifying for that would be the reason for engaging in it. He also believed that copulation occurred only in the case of male prostitutes, who played the role of receiver. He thought both female and male prostitutes were despicable individuals.

The conduct and relationships of the "normalsexuals" sharply contrasted with those of homosexuals. For one thing they cannot resist coitus—"real" or "imitated" (23)—for very long. The "normalsexual" impulse, Kertbeny averred, "cannot maintain itself in the purely platonic state at all and soon finds its way to the touching of the body" (25). For the "normalsexuals," touching led directly to coitus, even when the partners were ugly and unclean, because the basis of the "normalsexual" impulse was sensuality rather than esthetic beauty. "Normalsexuals," he claimed, were therefore much less constrained in their sexual expression than homosexuals:

> For, normalsexuals by nature are totally unrestrained in their ability to become excited; whereas homosexuals, just as mono-

---

[30] In German, "normalsexuals" appeared as *"normalsexualen."*

sexuals, whose secretive self-abuse has become a chronic need, are impotent and, at best, partially constrained. (28)

Consistent with Ulrichs' position, Kertbeny asserted that individuals could not choose to be homosexuals or "normalsexuals" because their governing sexual impulses were congenital. Therefore, there was no "danger" (26) that homosexuals would procreate and that "normalsexuals" would fail to procreate even if the latter occasionally strayed into homosexual relationships. Individuals who had both homosexual and "normalsexual" drives could not be considered "true homosexuals" (33). Rather, they were "normalsexuals" who were "highly blinded by their passions ... [and] their addiction to refinement" (33). True homosexuals were "incapable in the face of women, the majority of them having nothing at all to do with women, but rather always and irrepressively turning towards their own sex from the beginning of puberty" (33).

Kertbeny's letters to the medical commission were evidently convincing because the commission concluded that there was no medical reason for criminal penalties and it unanimously recommended that the sodomy statutes be modified.[31]

The theory of wastage and depletion, formulated by Tissot and embellished by his medical successors, implied that masturbation de-feminized women and de-masculinized men by eroding their basic femaleness or maleness. This erosion endangered and even robbed both sexes of their reproductive capacities. For medicine, reproduction was the reason why nature bequeathed humans a sexual capacity. Masturbation also deflected the love of individuals from the opposite sexes to members of their own sex. It undermined health and exposed individuals to innumerable life-threatening ailments. According to Lallemand, masturbation endangered its practitioners' relationships with family and their social commitments, turning them inward and rendering them apathetic. As the medical discourse on masturbation evolved, there were claims that chronic masturbators were identifiable physical types. A century after Tissot, Kertbeny was able to draw a profile of the chronic male masturbator as an individual who could be quickly identified by his aloof, selfish, and cerebral personality.

---

[31] The statutes, however, were not removed from the criminal code. Von Mühler, as one of the official conveners of the commission and a political figure of great influence in the Prussian parliament, opposed the recommendation because, according to Steakley (1975: 13), he believed that such laws symbolized the "sensibility of the German people."

As the medical discourse on sexual conduct began to replace the religious doctrine of earlier centuries, chronic masturbation as a disease replaced sodomy as the sin against nature. Whereas the unrepentant sodomite was condemned to everlasting punishment, the chronic masturbator was consigned by medicine to insanity. For unrepentant sodomites the church prescribed punishment such as burning at the stake. For the ailing masturbator medicine also invented its own deterrents, which, when all else failed, could include the amputation of the "abused" organs.

In both the ecclesiastical and medical views there was the implicit fear that masturbation would lead to homosexual relationships because the masturbator was absorbed with the organ of his own sex. The link between masturbation and homosexual relationships was made explicit by Kertbeny when he claimed that sex between male partners was usually "constrained" to mutual masturbation. In his judgment this form of shared stimulation provided homosexuals their escape from the lonely practice of self-abuse."

The conception of the homosexual identity by Ulrichs and Kertbeny was an attempt to place it within a biological framework and yet disassociate it from the idea of degeneracy and perversion. They did this by combining ingredients borrowed from sexual relationships as structured in the polytheistic, monotheistic, and scientific cosmologies.

From polytheism they borrowed at least three ideas. One was the idea of androgyny—the belief that femaleness and maleness were transmutable, one into the other, rather than distinct and complementary natural forms. They also incorporated the idea that sexual relationships could be polymorphous, consisting of partners either of the opposite sexes or of the same sex. Finally, they borrowed the Greek notion that while all sexual relationships could include beauty, love, admiration, and adventure, only heterosexual relationships encompassed the practical necessity of begetting and rearing children.

From monotheism they borrowed the idea of the male-female design. This design was based on three implicit beliefs: (1) that females and males were two discrete forms; (2) that these forms were complementary in that one sex provided what the other lacked; and (3) that each form was compelled to seek completeness in the other.

Ulrichs' classificatory scheme for assigning sexual identities was derived from the male-female design. He made the biological sex of partners in sexual relationships the crucial criterion in assigning a sexual identity to the individual. The definitional and normative boundaries of his taxonomy were the pure female and pure male sex, with the intermediate sex situated between them. Because Urnings were not pure representatives of their biological types they looked to partners for completeness, matching their usual femininity or masculinity with the femininity or masculinity of their partners. Finally, Ulrichs conceived the idea of feminine and masculine sex drives to explain the compelling attraction between partners of the same sex or of opposite sexes.

To the monotheistic notion of the male-female design Ulrichs grafted the polytheistic belief in a polymorphous femininity and masculinity. In this way he was able to expand the notion of the "third sex" to include several elaborations in sexual identity, such as Mannlings, Weiblings, and Zwischen-Urnings. In assigning these identities he observed the principle derived from the male-female design that "opposites attract." Homosexual relationships, therefore, in the eyes of Ulrichs and Kertbeny, no matter how the partners' feminine and masculine traits were matched, could never be anything more than dim reflections of heterosexual relationships after which they were modeled.

The homosexual identity, as adumbrated by Ulrichs and Kertbeny, leaned heavily on a medicalized version of the scientific cosmology. They took from Darwin the idea that nature was limitless in producing variations of existing species by claiming that homosexuals represented one such variation of human beings. From medicine they derived the theory that unusual forms of sexual behavior could be innate and degenerate. Ulrichs and Kertbeny retained the idea that homosexual behavior was congenital but they rejected the belief that it was degenerate. For them, homosexual behavior, although presumably muted in expression when compared with "normalsexual" behavior, was equally natural.

Ulrichs and Kertbeny borrowed and transformed the medical idea that forms of sexual practice that habitually excluded heterosexual coitus reflected some basic alteration in human functioning, what was called a condition.[32] Because the idea of "condition" labored under the shadow of disease, by transforming it into an identity, it could remain a central in-

---

[32] Foucault stated that those who were interested in defending behavior which medicine labeled as perverted engaged in a "reverse discourse" (1976/1978: 101), making healthy what medicine called diseased. A detailed examination of the discourse of men like Ulrichs and Kertbeny suggests, however, that some medical ideas were taken over whole-cloth while others were appropriately interpolated to present homosexual behavior in a reputable light.

gredient of the individual, without being associated, however, with pathology.

Sexual relationships, as depicted by the great advocates of the scientific cosmology, the Enlightenment philosophers, were to include free choice of partners and structures as a way of uniting erotic desire with procreative and parental responsibilities. Ulrichs and Kertbeny were defending free choice and desire when they argued that some individuals could love partners of the same sex as most individuals loved partners of the opposite sexes. Rather than basing their argument on the moral principle of individual liberty, however, they chose instead the scientism of medicine. By postulating the existence of independent feminine and masculine "drives," "inclinations," and "impulses," they "biologized" sexual desire. Personal choice was eliminated from sexual relationships by subjecting it to natural forces.

5   Sexual Identity and Degeneracy Theory

B y combining ingredients from the three cosmological views of sexual relationships, Ulrichs and Kertbeny were able to conceptualize
the idea of sexual identity. Their major interest was in the
homosexual identity, which they presented as a distinct yet natural
form of sexual instinct and behavior. Their scientific argument for the
naturalness of the homosexual identity was couched in the language of
evolutionary biological theory. Building on scientized versions of that same
theory, medicine and psychiatry were becoming the moral arbiters of sexual
behavior and relationships. By the time Ulrichs' writings appeared, masturbation had already been pathologized by medicine and associated by
psychiatry with sexual perversion. With Ulrichs' clear assertion of the existence of the homosexual identity, the increasingly influential disciplines of
forensic medicine and psychiatry moved to make it the centerpiece in their
catalogue of sexual perversions.

The idea that homosexual conduct and relationships constituted a
clinical condition appeared in the medical-forensic literature of the mid-
nineteenth century. In 1852, Johann Ludwig Casper, a Prussian medico-
legal expert wrote about homosexual behavior as a form of "disputed
sexual relations" and "disputed natural lewdness."[1] He called it

---

[1] In using the date 1852, we are following the reference of Richard von Krafft-
Ebing (1937). *Psychopathia Sexualis*, 12th Ed. F. J. Rebman, Trans. Brooklyn:
Physicians and Surgeons Book Company, 337). Krafft-Ebing referred to
Casper's "Über Notzucht und Päderastie," *Vierteljahrsschift*, 1852, Vol. 1. He
credited Casper with the "first definite communications concerning this enig-
matical phenomenon of Nature" (337). Casper wrote about the subject of
homosexual behavior in his two major works: Casper, Johann Ludwig (1857-
1858/1864). *A Handbook of the Practice of Forensic Medicine Based Upon Personal
Experience*. G. W. Balfour, Trans. London: New Sydenham Society. Translation
of Casper, Johann Ludwig. First published in 1857-1858 as *Practisches
Handbuchen der gerichtlichen Medicin*. Berlin: A. Hirschwald; and Casper,

"paederastia," although he believed the word was a misnomer because "this method of gratifying sexual appetite between male individuals" (330), far more often involved adults than young people. Paederastia, which, in Casper's view, was a moral vice, criminal act, and metal aberration, could be either congenital or acquired:

> In most of those addicted to it, this vice is hereditary, and appears to be a kind of mental hermaphroditism. These parties have an actual disgust of any sexual connection with women, and their fancy delights in beautiful young men, and in their statues and pictures, with which they delight to surround themselves, and to decorate their apartments. In the case of others, on the contrary, this vice is an acquired one, the result of satiety of the natural sexual pleasures. And it is nothing unusual to find these men, in their gross sensuality, alternating the two sexes! (1857-1858/1864: 330)

Casper associated paederastia with *"imissio penis in anum,"* or anal copulation, but asserted that men who sought sexual gratification from other men, usually limited sexual contact to "reciprocal gratification" (332).[2] Casper also acknowledged that there was "gratification of the sexual appetite between women" (1857-1858/1864: 335), which he called "tribadism," but he asserted that this practice was found in ancient Greece and Rome and in Parisian prisons for women, but surely not in Berlin. Tribadism, according to Casper, was the same aberration as that found to occur between men and, as in the case of the men, consisted

---

Johann Ludwig (1863). *Klinische Sovellen sur gerichtlichen Medicin: Nach eignen Erfahrunger.* Berlin: A Hirschwald. We have cited an English translation of the 1864 third edition of the earlier work: *A Handbook of the Practice of Forensic Medicine Based Upon Personal Experience,* 328-346. Krafft-Ebing also referred to the publication of the biographies of two men "who manifested an enthusiastic love for persons of their own sex" in "Moritz's *Magazin zur Erfahrungsseelenkunde,* Vol. 7, Berlin, 1791" (1886/1935: 337n). One of these men attributed his "aberration" to the following factors: (1) as a child he was caressed only by grown persons and school fellows and (2) his lack of association with women.

[2] By this circumlocution, of course, Casper was referring to mutual masturbation. He quoted one practitioner as stating that "you must not imagine that we practice pederasty [i.e., anal copulation]. I have never done this, and I abominate with many, or most, this inclination" (1857-1858/1864: 332n).

chiefly of "bodily contact and friction for the gratification of the sexual impulse" (335).

For the purposes of forensic medicine, Casper distinguished between those males who took the active (i.e., insertor) or passive (i.e., receiver) role in anal copulation. The latter he variously called "the passive party," "pathicus," or "Cinaedus" (1857-1858/1864: 331). Only the passive partner could be detected through medical examination by (1) "a hollow between the nates [i.e., the buttocks], the sides of which converge towards the anus" or (2) the "smooth condition of the skin around the anus, apparently arising from the frequent stretching and friction of the skin" (333).

The French practitioner of forensic medicine, A. Tardieu, believed that physical abnormalities in both insertors and receivers could lead to their medicinal detection.[3] The penis of the insertor, he reported, grew smaller towards the head and was so twisted that the urinary stream flowed either to the right or left. This unusual shape he attributed to the screw-like movements required to force the penis past the anal sphincter. Tardieu also reported that the oral copulator could be detected by "an awry mouth," short teeth, and thick, turned-in lips. Regarding Tardieu's alleged observations, Casper expressed extreme skepticism: "Such descriptions may cause the hair of non-medical people to stand on end, but medical men know better how to estimate such observations!" (1864: 329n).

In Germany one of the first psychiatrists to turn medical attention to homosexual behavior was Carl Westphal. In 1869, as editor of a new psychiatric journal, he began the publication of case histories of individuals who were possessed with what he called "die konträre Sexualempfindung," or contrary sexual feeling.[4]

---

[3] Tardieu, Ambroise (1857). *Étude Médico-Légale sur les Attentats aux Moeurs*. Paris: J. B. Failliere. Bullough (1976: 670) cited pages 213-255. We have followed Casper's comments on Tardieu. Casper remarked that "Tardieu has written his treatise on this important subject with more ardor and fancy than with the necessary critical caution" (1864: 329n).

[4] Westphal, Carl (1869). Die Konträre Sexualempfindung: Symptom eines Neuropathologischen. (Psychopathischen) Zustandes. *Archiv für Psychiatrie und Nervenkrankheiten* 2: 73-108. Westphal's interests were clinical, anatomical, and physiological. He had distinguished himself in psychiatric research by describing obsessional states (which he called "abortive insanity") and agoraphobia. His work was part of a trend in evaluating neuroses (Schenck, Jerome M. (1960). *A History of Psychiatry*. Springfield, IL: Charles C. Thomas, 123). *Die Konträre Sexualempfindung* was translated for Westphal as "contrary sexual feeling" (Sulloway, Frank J. (1979). *Freud: Biologist of the Mind*. New York: Basic Books, 282). The German *Empfindung* is used to denote *feeling* in

Westphal defined this phenomenon as the "congenital reversal of the sexual feeling with consciousness of the abnormality of the manifestation" (73). One of the first patients to whom Westphal applied the diagnosis of "contrary sexual feeling" was a thirty-five year old woman who, in 1864, was taken by her older sister to the psychiatry department of Charité, a hospital in Berlin. Westphal interviewed both the patient and her sister. The patient was in charge of housekeeping in her sister's boarding school for young ladies. About a week before her visit to Westphal, her sister found the patient grieving and inconsolable. She finally confessed to her sister that she had fallen passionately in love with one of the students. A few days before admission to the hospital she had become violent and begged to see a doctor.

Westphal described the patient's feeling of attraction for other females as a strong pleasure, over which she had no control and against which she heroically struggled. The woman reported that when she was eight she had felt such a tendency toward young girls, whom she would court, kiss, and, if possible, fondle. Between the ages of eighteen and twenty-three, she was sexually active and this, she reported, was also the happiest period of her life. In her sexual fantasies she imagined herself enacting the male role with female partners. She reported that men held no attraction for her, that she had never had sexual contact with them, and that it was possible for her to sleep among men with complete indifference. During most of her adult life her only sexual outlet was masturbation, desire for which reached irresistible urgency shortly before and after her menstrual periods.

Westphal portrayed the woman as average and feminine in appearance. However, her nose turned a little to the left and she had a harelip and severely cleft palate which gave her speech a nasal quality. The patient believed that the harelip was the result of a fetal accident: her pregnant mother had been severely frightened while she was kissing

---

the sense of sensation or *sentiment*, but its meaning can include *instinct* as in: "your remark shows that my *instinct* [feeling] was right" (*The Oxford-Harrap Standard German-English Dictionary*. Oxford: Clarendon Press, 1977, I: 56, under "*empfinden*," II.2: 56). In such usage, *intuition* would probably add some precision over *instinct*. *Instinkt* in German connotes intuition, in the sense: "his instinct told him that." (*Oxford-Harrap*, II: 18). The German, *der Trieb*, which Ulrichs used, meaning "driving force," "impulse," "instinct," and "propensity," was often employed in the nineteenth-century medical discourse in such combinations as *der Geschlechtstrieb* (sex instinct) and *der Naturtrieb* (natural instinct).

someone. Westphal noted that the patient was calm and coherent during the interview.

Westphal's diagnosis was that the patient's contrary sexual feeling was a form of "moral insanity." "Moral insanity" had been defined as a form of madness which consisted of the morbid perversion of "natural" feelings, impulses, love, and moral tendencies. Unlike other forms of insanity, there was no disorder of the intellect, delusions, or hallucinations.[5]

Moral insanity took the form of monomania. In effect, Westphal was classifying the new diagnosis of "contrary sexual feeling" as a form of neurosis, an obsessional state which persisted and occasionally disrupted but did not seriously undermine mental functioning. Although Westphal held fast to the position that the condition was congenital, he wavered on the issue of degeneracy. In the case of his female patient he believed the woman's cleft palate suggested that her condition might have stemmed from an innate predisposition, possibly the result of degeneracy. As editor of a psychiatric journal, he encouraged other psychiatrists to publish additional case histories.

The degeneracy theory became the basis for describing the homosexual identity in the medical discourse, particularly of France and Italy.[6] In 1885,

---

[5] The English psychiatrist and anthropologist, James Cowles Prichard, defined the term in his *A Treatise on Insanity and Other Disorders Affecting the Mind*, which appeared in 1835 (as cited in Schenck, 1960: 117).

[6] Several distinguished psychiatrists published articles and books on sexual perversion before the appearance of Krafft-Ebing's famous *Psychopathia Sexualis* in 1886, most of whom subscribed to degeneracy theory: Lombroso, Cesare (1881). L'Amore nei Pazzi. *Archivio di Psichiatria, Scienze Penali ed Antropologia Criminale* II: 1-33; Charcot, Jean-Martin and Magnan, Valentin (1882). Inversion du Sens Genital. *Archives de Neurologie 3*: 53-60 and *4*: 296-322; and Gley, E. (1884). Les Aberrations de l'Instinct Sexual d'apres des Travaux Recents. *Revue Philosophique 17*: 66-92. Krafft-Ebing (1886/1935: 335n-336n) referred to other contributors (before 1886) of lesser stature: Hoffman, Bernhardi, Tamassia, Coutagne, and Blumer. A comprehensive review of the theoretical speculations on the causes of sexual perversion was provided in Moll, Albert (1897/1933). *Libido Sexualis: Studies in the Psychosexual Laws of Love Verified by Clinical Sexual Case Histories*. David Berger, Trans. New York: American Ethnological Press. (Translation of *Untersuchungen über die Libido Sexualis*. Berlin: Fischer's Medizinische Buchhandlung, H. Kornfeld, 1897: 646-660 and 667-670 (cited in Sulloway, 1979: 228n) and in his 1891 *Die Konträre Sexualempfindung*. Berlin: Fischer's Medicinische Buchhandlung, H. Kornfeld, which appeared in English in 1931 as *Perversion of the Sexual Instinct: A Study of Sexual Inversion Based on Clinical Data and Official Documents*. (Newark, NJ: Julian Press).

Julien Chevalier, a forensic psychiatrist, applied degeneracy theory to what he called *"l'inversion de l'instinct sexuel."* According to Chevalier, there were already a great many terms in French, Italian, and English, in addition to the German *Die Konträre Sexualempfindung*, which referred to the "inversion of the sexual instinct.[7]

The term *l'inversion*, Chevalier claimed, was adopted after the French language was "put through great torture" (1885: 14) in translating Westphal's *die konträre Sexualempfindung*. Despite the variation in terminology, however, he believed that there was substantial conceptual agreement among psychiatrists on the nature of inversion: (1) it was a specific disorder of the sexual instinct; (2) it was congenital and therefore independent of the individual's will; and (3) it was a symptom of a psychopathological or hereditary state, so that the victims could be classified as degenerates.

Chevalier preferred his own definition:

> We will say that inversion is an exclusive and invincible love of
> one individual for an individual of the same sex to which he
> morphologically belongs, with indifference or repulsion for an
> individual of the sex opposite to his own, whatever the cause
> of this state. (1885: 15).

With this definition Chevalier intended to remove the distinction between those individuals who engaged in homosexual behavior for the purpose of "seeking new voluptuousness" and those who pursued members of the same sex because of a "particular anatomical constitution" (14)

In the conclusion to his treatise on sexual inversion, Chevalier clearly endorsed a degeneracy theory of causation. The roots of inversion, he

---

[7] Chevalier, Julien. (1885). De L'Inversion de L'Instinct Sexuel au Point de Vue Medico-Legal. Paris: Octave Doin. In 1893, Chevalier published a second work, *Une Maladie de La Personnalité: L'Inversion Sexuelle; Psycho-Physiologie, Sociologie, Tératologie, Aliénation Mentale, Psychologie Morbide, Anthropologie, Médecine Judiciaire*. Lyon and Paris: A. Storck. Chevalier summarized the synonyms in use by 1885: *"sens genital, instinct sexuel contraire, inverse, perverti, interverti; — attractions, impulsions, sensations sexuelles contraires, inverses, perverties; — attractions des sexes sembables; —sensation croisee de l'individualité sexuelle; — sexualité contraire; —perversion, interversion de l'instinct sexuel; —inversion des attractions sexuelles. Tammassia, le premier, et apres lui Cantarano, se servant du terme inversion, definirent cet etat inversione dell'istinto sessuale; Lombroso l'appela amore invertito; Julien Krueg: perverted sexual instincts; enfin, MM. Charcot et Magnan indiquerent la formule generalement adoptee aujourd'hui: inversion du sens genital"* (1885: 14).

wrote, lay in a congenital malformation or an illness stemming from pathological lesions. It was not a morbid entity or instinctive monomania but rather "an outstanding symptom, a strange episode, a bursting manifestation of a neuropathic or psychopathic hereditary state" (167). To make the diagnosis of inversion, the psychiatrist should look at the genealogical tree of the patient, his medical history, his intellectual faculties, and for the signs of degeneracy. Chevalier averred that the inverted patient was

> not depraved, he is not guilty, he is a lucid madman; to punish him would be a misinterpretation and anachronism.... in spite of its benign appearance, inversion is a manifestation of a serious state. These patients are moral hermaphrodites; they belong to the classification of degenerates. (168)

The psychiatrist who made the most powerful contribution to the pathologization of the homosexual identity was Richard von Krafft-Ebing, the author of *Psychopathia Sexualis*.[8] Krafft-Ebing attributed his interest in "contrary sexual feeling" to the ideas of Ulrichs, which he acknowledged in a letter written to Ulrichs in 1879, before the first publication of *Psychopathia Sexualis*:

> The study of your writing on love between men interested me in the highest degree, ... since you ... for the first time openly spoke about these matters. From that day on, when—I believe it was in 1866—you sent me your writings, I have devoted my full attention to this phenomenon, which at that time was as puzzling to me as it was interesting; it was the knowledge of

---

[8] The first edition was published in 1886 under the title: *Psychopathia Sexualis: Eine Klinisch-Forensische Studie*. Stuttgart: Ferdinand Enke. There were eleven editions published in German before it was translated into English by F. J. Rebman, who translated the twelfth and last German edition. After the first edition, the title was changed to *Psychopathia Sexualis: Mit besonderer Berücksichtigung der konträren Sexualempfindung; Eine Klinischforensische Studie (Psychopathia Sexualis, with Special Reference to Antipathetic Sexual Instinct; A Medico-Forensic Study)*. In later editions of his book, Krafft-Ebing tended to move away from a strict degeneracy theory toward the evolutionary theory of Albert Moll in explaining the origins of contrary sexual instinct. The later editions also show more compassion than the earlier ones, which exhibited great moral consternation.

your writing alone which led to my studies in this highly important field.[9]

Krafft-Ebing's interest in "contrary sexual feeling" was part of his general interest in sexual psychopathology. A large part of *Psychopathia Sexualis* was devoted to cataloging various forms of sexual anomalies such as sadism, masochism, and fetishism. His purpose in pursuing this general study was "to record the various psychopathological manifestations of sexual life in man and to reduce them to their lawful conditions" (1886/1935: vi). He seemed to feel both compelled and repulsed by this work:

> The scientific study of the psychopathology of sexual life necessarily deals with the miseries of man and the dark sides of his existence, the shadow of which contorts the sublime image of deity into horrid caricatures, and leads astray estheticism and morality. It is the sad privilege of medicine, and especially that of psychiatry, to ever witness the weaknesses of human nature and the reverse side of life. (vii)

The catalog of sexual aberrations assembled by Krafft-Ebing was based on his general beliefs about sexual relationships. In his introduction to *Psychopathia Sexualis* he asserted that the propagation of the human race was not left to chance and personal whim but rather was "enforced by a mighty, irresistible impulse" (1). Man, however, should not simply surrender to the gratification of the sexual impulse. To do so was to sink to the level of the beast. Human sexual life could lead to the most sublime virtue or the basest vice: "love unbridled is a volcano that burns down and lays waste all around it; it is an abyss that devours all, honor, substance, and health" (2). Life, he believed, was "a never-ceasing duel between the animal instinct and morality" (5). Will-power and strength of character alone could rescue humans from the shabby side of their nature and teach them "to enjoy the pure pleasures of love and pluck the noble fruits of earthly existence" (1886/1935: 5).

Sexual relationships, Krafft-Ebing thought, were composed of two major ingredients. The chief element was love, "the expectation of unsurpassed pleasure"; the other was the "feeling of dependence" (5). Dependence existed as a stronger element in women than in men, although he believed it could also be found in "men who are of a

---

[9] Kennedy (1980/1981: 108) cited the twelfth volume of Ulrichs' *Forschungen über das Rätsel der Mannmännlichen Liebe*, 108 (Arno Press reprinting).

feminine type" (9). Krafft-Ebing associated dependence with passivity and the receptor role in coitus.

He distinguished among three kinds of love: "sensual," "sentimental," and "true" love. Sensual love was merely fleeting passion and infatuation, which made the body of the partner the sole object of gratification. Sentimental love was a burlesque of true love, nauseating, repulsive, and ludicrous. True love, however,

> is rooted in the recognition of the moral and mental qualities of the beloved person, and is equally ready to share pleasures and sorrows and even to make sacrifices. True love shrinks from no dangers or obstacles in the struggle for the undisputed possession of the beloved. (1886/1935: 12)

True love could only exist between persons of opposite sexes because true sexual desire could occur only when partners were capable of coitus. Heterosexual monogamy, Krafft-Ebing believed, was the foundation of civilization. He did not believe that Platonic love was genuine because those "who love the soul only" (20) despised sexual gratification. True love was "the communion of soul and mind" (20).

The sexual appetites and consciousness of males and females were sharply delineated by Krafft-Ebing. Males, he averred, had the stronger appetite, which made them sensual in their attractions and aggressive in the pursuit of women. "Normal" (14), educated women, on the other hand, had little sexual desire and this made it possible for them to devote themselves to family life. The man wooed the woman for her favor but the woman remained "passive" because "her sexual organization demands it, and the dictates of good breeding come to her aid" (14).

Whereas sexual desire was seen as higher in males, sexual consciousness was supposedly stronger in females. Their need for love was greater, but that love was more spiritual than sensual. As mothers, women divided their love between children and husband, although the first place in their hearts was reserved for offspring. Once the mother's love of children and husband merged, as wife "she accepts marital intercourse not so much as a sensual gratification than as a proof of her husband's affection" (1886/1935: 14).

The distinctive sexual consciousness of females and males, according to Krafft-Ebing, was a product of differentiated visual and olfactory "centers" which lay close to the "psychosexual centers" in the cerebral cortex. The sexual instinct was lodged in the psychosexual centers which served as junctions where visual and olfactory responses to psychic or organic stimuli were routed to the sexual organs. In Krafft-Ebing's words:

The central point of the sexual mechanism is the cerebral cortex. It is justifiable to presume that there is a definite region of the cortex (cerebral center), which gives rise to sexual feelings, ideas, and impulses, and is the place of origin of the psychosomatic processes which we designate as sexual life, sexual instinct, and sexual desire. The center is susceptible to both central and peripheral stimuli. (1886/1935: 29)[10]

The origins of sexual pathology, in Krafft-Ebing's view, could be explained by environmental damage to the sexual organs or by degeneracy, an inherited, diseased condition of the nervous system. All anomalous sexual functions were classified as "sexual neuroses" (49). Some were less serious than others. Those which could be traced to peripheral or spinal nerve damage were of less importance than those attributable to diseased cerebral function. Individuals who suffered from superficial neuroses were free of other mental disease. These superficial neuroses, for the most part, were ailments which today are called "sexual dysfunctions," such as impotence, ejaculatory incompetence, and premature ejaculation.

The four categories of cerebral neurosis were: **PARADOXIA, ANESTHESIA SEXUALIS, HYPERESTHESIA,** and **PARAESTHESIA.** He believed that these sexual neuroses were the symptoms of degeneracy. **PARADOXIA** referred to those sexual neuroses marked by an untimely expression of sexual desire—the premature awakening of sexual desire in childhood or its re-awakening in old age in "a shameless and impulsive manner" (57).[11]

ANESTHESIA SEXUALIS, or absence of sexual feeling, referred to the condition of those individuals who possessed normal genitalia but throughout their lives showed absolutely no interest in the "corresponding emotions of sexual life" (61). **HYPERESTHESIA,** or

---

[10] Krafft-Ebing often referred to "sexual life" as *vita sexualis* and "sexual instinct" as *libido sexualis*. The terminology for sexual instinct he probably obtained from Albert Moll, a contemporary sexologist. Krafft-Ebing believed there was a particularly close association between the olfactory and psychosexual centers in males. He recounted this anecdote: "D., a medical student, was seated on a bench in a public park, reading a book (on pathology). Suddenly a violent erection disturbed him. He looked up and noticed that a lady, redolent with perfume, had taken a seat upon the other end of the bench. D. could attribute his erection to nothing but the unconscious olfactory impression made upon him" (33).

[11] Krafft-Ebing subscribed to the widely held medical belief that childhood was a period of *generis neutrius* (283), during which the child lacked sexual desire.

abnormally increased sexual desire, was defined as "an abnormal presence of sexual sensations and presentations from which necessarily arise frequent and violent impulses for sexual gratification" (69). Krafft-Ebing associated hyperesthesia with imbecility, holding that both defects sprung "from the same degenerative soil" (71). Included in this category were the Don Juans and "apron-hunters" whose "whole existence is an endless chain of sensual enjoyment and whose blunted moral sense does not keep them from seduction, adultery, and even incest" (71).

Most pathological of the cerebral neuroses were those which fell into the category of PARAESTHESIA, which Krafft-Ebing defined as perversion of the sexual instinct.[12] In the individual afflicted by this condition there was a "perverse coloring" (79) of sexual fantasies, which, if disgusting, stimulated sexual arousal and found expression in "passionate, uncontrollable emotion" (79). Behavior sparked by such arousal was regarded as perverse by Krafft-Ebing because it constituted gratification of the sexual instinct in ways that were at odds with nature's purpose for sex, that is, reproduction. In explain paraesthesia, he drew a sharp distinction between "perversion" and "perversity":

> *Perversion* of the sexual instinct is not to be confounded with *perversity* in the sexual act. The concrete perverse act, monstrous as it may be, is clinically not decisive. In order to differentiate between disease (*perversion*) and vice (*perversity*), one must investigate the whole personality of the individual and the original motive leading to the perverse act. (1886/1935: 79-80)

In his taxonomy of paraesthesia, Krafft-Ebing separated those forms that involved sexual activity directed toward the opposite sexes from those directed toward the same sex. In the former category he placed sadism, masochism, and fetishism.[13] Sadism he defined as the "association of active cruelty and violence with lust" (131).[14] Lust and cruelty, he believed, worked in tandem, one impulse feeding the other. Masochism, as he conceived it,

---

[12] In medical pathology, paraesthesia refers to a hallucination of the senses or any disordered sensation (*SOED*: 1427).

[13] Krafft-Ebing coined the terms *sadism* and *masochism*. Sadism he named after the "notorious Marquis de Sade" (80n). Masochism was named after the author and poet Sacher-Masoch (132).

[14] Krafft-Ebing identified many forms of sadism: lust-murder, mutilation of corpses, physical injury to women, defilement of women (e.g., with body wastes), ideal (fantasized) sadism, whipping of boys, and torturing of animals. He believed sadism rarely occurred in women because it was an "intensification of the masculine sexual character" (129).

was the "association of passively endured cruelty and violence with lust" (131).[15]

In masochism, sexual feeling was aroused by the fantasy of being "completely and unconditionally subject to the will of a person of the opposite sex" (131). Masochism, like the other forms of paraesthesia, would be difficult to find in women because both nature and custom were insurmountable obstacles to their [women's] expression of perverse sexual interest" (197). Finally, fetishism he defined as "the association of lust with the idea [fantasy] of certain portions of the female person or with certain articles of female attire" (218).[16]

"Antipathetic sexual instinct" was the name assigned by Krafft-Ebing to the second category of paraesthesia, the perversion which involved individuals of the same sex.[17] He defined it as follows:

> [Antipathetic sexual instinct] is the total absence of sexual feelings toward the opposite sex. It concentrates all sexuality on its own sex. The physical and psychical properties of persons of the same sex alone exercise an aphrodisiac effect and awaken a desire for sexual union. It is purely a psychical anomaly, for the sexual instinct does in no wise correspond to the primary and secondary sexual characteristics. In spite of the fully differentiated sexual type, in spite of the normally developed and active sexual glands, man is drawn sexually to the man, because he has, consciously or otherwise, the instinct of the female toward him, or vice versa. (1886/1935: 54)

Because there was no observable physical malformation, Krafft-Ebing attributed the condition to an "abnormal psychosexual constitution" (285). He referred to those suffering from the condition as "tainted," that is, born with a diseased psychosexual center in the cerebral cortex. In his

---

[15] In Krafft-Ebing's cornucopia of perversions, masochism took may forms: desire for abuse and humiliation (e.g., flagellation), self-humiliation, and latent masochism (e.g., foot and shoe fetishism).

[16] Bestiality was included by Krafft-Ebing in the category of fetishism under his new label, *zoophilia erotica* (281).

[17] In German, he used Westphal's *Die Konträre Sexualempfindung*. Although "empfindung" was translated by Sulloway (1979: 282) as "feeling" for Westphal, he translated it as "instinct" for Krafft-Ebing(282). In translation, the change (in both Sulloway and the Rebman translation of Krafft-Ebing (1886/1935) from "contrary" to "antipathetic" and from "feeling" to "instinct" suggests compulsiveness and a deeper pathologization. It is possible, of course, that Sulloway was merely following the Rebman translation.

words: "[T]his anomaly of psychosexual feeling may be called clinically, a functional sign of degeneracy" (285).

Krafft-Ebing believed that the following functional signs of degeneracy could be found in the victims of antipathetic sexual instinct: (1) their VITA SEXUALIS was abnormal from the start, often accompanied by other forms of sexual perversion; (2) their love was "exaggerated and exalted," expressed with compelling force; (3) in addition to antipathetic sexual instinct, anatomical signs of degeneracy could also be identified; (4) coexisting with the perversion were neuroses such as hysteria and neurasthenia, which were fed by masturbation or enforced abstinence; (5) psychic anomalies, such as brilliance in the arts or imbecility, also coexisted; and (6) in almost all cases the degenerative signs of neuroses or psychoses could be found in blood relatives (1886/1935: 339).

Those males afflicted with antipathetic sexual instinct, according to Krafft-Ebing, had such inherently sensitive nervous systems that a simple embrace or caress, with no genital contact at all, could precipitate immediate ejaculation. Those whose nerves were less easily triggered could have protracted physical contact, usually consisting of masturbation of one partner by the other, mutual masturbation, or interfemoral coitus. Those who could sustain erections and who were "morally perverse" engaged in anal copulation, which Krafft-Ebing called "pederasty" (351).

Whereas perversion, in Krafft-Ebing's formulation, sprouted from the soil of degeneration, perversity was caused by masturbation, sexual excess, or the environmental impossibility for having "natural" coitus.[18]

Among these, masturbation loomed as the major cause of perversity:

> Nothing is so prone to contaminate—under certain circumstances, even to exhaust—the source of noble and ideal sentiments, which arise of themselves from a normally developing sexual instinct, as the practice of masturbation in early years. It despoils the unfolding bud of perfume and beauty, and leaves behind only the coarse, animal desire for sexual satisfaction. If an individual, thus depraved, reaches the age of maturity, there is wanting in him that esthetic, ideal, pure and free impulse which draws the opposite sexes together. The glow of sensual sensibility wanes, and the inclination toward the opposite sex is weakened. This defect influences the mor-

---

[18] In the medical discourse on sexual behavior, homosexual acts committed by sexually aroused men in settings in which there was no access to female partners were said to occur *faute de mieux*.

als, the character, fancy, feeling, and favorable manner, even causing, under certain circumstances, the desire for the opposite sex to sink to nil; so that masturbation is preferred to the natural mode of satisfaction. (286)

Excessive masturbation, Krafft-Ebing believed, could lead the practitioner into a sexual trap. The incapacity to have normal coital gratification because of masturbatory indulgence exacerbated masturbatory desires. When habitual masturbation exhausted the chronic practitioner, he sometimes turned to other male partners with whom he engaged in passive or mutual masturbation. His wild pursuit of masturbatory gratification soon made him mentally indifferent to either sex, so that one blurred into the other. Absorption in solitary masturbation and masturbation with partners, Krafft-Ebing averred, was the highest degree of sexual aberration to be reached by the *"normally* constituted, *untainted,* mentally healthy individual" (288; emphasis added).

Krafft-Ebing's major absorption was with the abnormal congenital manifestations of antipathetic sexual instinct. In tainted individuals the degrees of antipathetic sexual instinct corresponded to the degrees of hereditary predisposition:

> In the milder cases there is a simple hermaphroditism; in more pronounced cases, only homosexual feeling and instinct, but limited to the vita sexualis; in still more complete cases, the whole psychical personality, and even the bodily sensations, are transformed so as to correspond with the sexual inversion; and, in the complete cases, the physical form is correspondingly altered. (1886/1935: 285-286)

The abnormal manifestations paralleled a process of degeneration. The process was divided into four stages: psychosexual hermaphroditism, homosexuality, effemination, and androgyny.

In PSYCHOSEXUAL HERMAPHRODITISM there was a simple reversal of sexual feeling, in which attraction to the same sex replaced attraction to the opposite sexes. The individual remained masculine in character and desired the active role in sexual intercourse with other males. As the term implied there was episodic reoccurrence of the attraction for female partners.

At the HOMOSEXUAL stage there was attraction only to partners of the same sex. Krafft-Ebing referred to the individuals who occupied this stage as Urnings. The love men had for other men corresponded exactly to that which the "normal" man had for women. Urnings were indifferent to and repelled by the beauty and grace of women. Sometimes they made the unfortunate mistake of getting married:

> There are Urnings who are potent for women—men who do not love their wives, but are nevertheless able to perform the marital "duty." In the majority of these cases even lustful pleasure is absent; for it is simply an onanistic act rendered possible by the aid of imagination which substitutes another beloved being. This deception may, indeed, superinduce sexual pleasure, but rudimentary gratification as it is, can only arise from a psychic trick, just as in solitary onanism voluptuous satisfaction is obtained chiefly with the assistance of fancy. As a matter of fact that degree of orgasm which completes the lustful act is entirely dependent upon the intervention of fancy. (1886/1935: 21n)

The EFFEMINATION stage included men who, like those in the homosexual group, were exclusively attracted to males, but, unlike them, felt they were women. When opportunity presented itself, they assumed a female role. "If he can assume the role of a female at a masquerade," Krafft-Ebing stated, "it is his greatest delight" (382). Such men were attracted to masculine men with whom they tried to develop stereotyped female-male relationships.

Men in the ANDROGYNY stage became totally feminine in thought, feeling, and physical appearance. Krafft-Ebing asserted that even the form of the body approached the degree of "abnormal" instinct (336). A male feeling that he was a female was evidence that the individual was "badly tainted" (323). The feminine sensations, at this stage, became imperious and brought about a complete alteration of the VITA SEXUALIS.

For females, Krafft-Ebing had no distinct theory of antipathetic sexual instinct. He believed that the malady probably occurred as frequently in women as in men, but differed from the male form in two respects: (1) it lacked the "predominant character" (397) it had for males and (2) its expression was often inhibited because of women's "chaste" education and because their sexual instinct developed only as they were introduced to male society. However, a "tainted" woman who was "hypersexual" could be led or seduced by other females into masturbation or homosexual acts.

The four degrees of antipathetic sexual instinct in women paralleled those found in men: PSYCHO-HERMAPHRODITISM, HOMOSEXUALITY, VIRAGINITY (equivalent to effeminacy in males), and gynandry (equivalent to androgyny in males). In describing viraginity, Krafft-Ebing's language moved between literacy and the scientific:

The masculine soul, heaving in the female bosom, finds pleasure
in the pursuit of manly sports, and in manifestations of courage
and bravado. There is a strong desire to imitate the male fashion
in dressing the hair and in general attire [and], under favorable
circumstances even to don male attire and impose it. (399)

The diagnosis of antipathetic sexual instinct, according to Krafft-Ebing,
was difficult and problematic. Neither the patient's word nor evidence of
homosexual behavior could be taken as clear indicators. Diagnosis was
easiest when patients came to see the psychiatrist because they were in
trouble with the law, because they were married and impotent, or in order
to avoid suicide. Cases diagnosed as genuine aberration were those in
which the antipathetic sexual instinct exercised an influence over the
individual's "whole psychical being" (1886/1935: 444).

Diagnosis was aided by evidence of hereditary taint, which could be
found by noting the possible existence of other sexual perversions in the
patient or in family members. Those truly afflicted with sexual
degeneracy, Krafft-Ebing reiterated, were abnormal in personality as
well as sexual behavior: "Certain it is that these persons are, as a rule,
also abnormal so far as character is concerned. They are neither man nor
woman, a mixture of both, with secondary psychical and physical
characteristics of the one as well as the other sex" (445).

If diagnosis was difficult, then treatment had even less to offer. For
cases of acquired antipathetic sexual instinct it was usually sufficient,
according to Krafft-Ebing, to prevent masturbation and to relieve sexual
excitability. For congenital cases the only possible way to combat
homosexual impulses was through post-hypnotic suggestion intended
"to remove the impulse to masturbation and homosexual feelings, and to
encourage heterosexual emotions with a sense of virility" (450).

As depicted in German and French medicine and psychiatry, the
pathologized homosexual identity was believed to be biologically
determined. As a somatic identity it was conceptually lodged in the
individual's peripheral or central nervous system. Although conceived as
a biological identity, it was described as particular behavioral
manifestations, sometimes referred to as the functional signs of
degeneracy. These included sexual desire for a partner of the same sex,
feminine behavior in males, or masculine behavior in females. The
behavioral peculiarities were used to account for the absence of any
physical deformities of the genitalia. As a biological entity, the homosexual
identity lay beyond the exercise of moral choice: it was an involuntary
state which fell within the province of medicine rather than religion.

The degree of pathology of the homosexual identity appeared to correspond to the degree of departure from conventional standards for social sex-roles and sexual relationships. Those individuals who sporadically found their way back from homosexual to heterosexual relationships were viewed as less pathological than those who were permanently devoted to homosexual liaisons. Even within homosexual relationships there were degrees of pathology. Those male Urnings who retained their masculine behavior along with the copulatory role of insertor were described as less pathological than those who were feminine and received the penis of their partners. Partners who limited physical genital contact to mutual masturbation were diagnosed as less aberrant than those who engaged in oral or anal copulation. There was even the faint suggestion that oral copulation was less pathological than anal copulation.

The pathologization of the homosexual identity did not include all forms of homosexual behavior. The distinction between hereditary and acquired forms made by Casper was preserved by those theorists of sexual pathology who followed him. It was the hereditary form that became the homosexual identity, in the speculations of Ulrichs, Kertbeny, and forensic medicine. The acquired form was viewed more as a vice than a disease, the hedonism of the voluptuary who occasionally strayed from heterosexual activity in search of ever new forms of erotic gratification.

The provenance of the homosexual identity became more maligned as psychiatric speculations multiplied. Although both Casper and Westphal believed that the homosexual identity was biological, they apparently felt that the afflicted individuals could lead useful lives apart from their ailment. Westphal even held that individuals suffering from contrary sexual feeling could struggle valiantly and successfully against their unfortunate proclivity. In the case of Chevalier and Krafft-Ebing, however, the deep shadow of degeneracy was cast over the homosexual identity. The clue to the presence of degeneracy, Krafft-Ebing believed, was that Urnings fully endorsed and enjoyed their aberration. Within the parameters of degeneracy theory individuals possessed of a homosexual identity were evolutionary throw-backs, psychological hermaphrodites, who could not claim legitimate membership in a human race populated only by true females and true males. Chevalier called the afflicted "lucid madmen" and Krafft-Ebing wrote of the "deep and lasting transformation" of their personalities.

There was an inherent irony in the pathologization of the homosexual identity. The pivotal concept upon which pathologization was based had been articulated by Ulrichs, who had hoped to win some measure of legal and moral toleration of homosexual behavior and relationships. The homosexual identity adumbrated by forensic psychiatrists was the reverse image of the Urning described by Ulrichs. What Ulrichs viewed as a product of inventive evolutionary forces, these theorists depicted as an anomaly or aberration, an evolutionary failure of monstrous proportions. What Ulrichs had conceived of as a third sex, an amalgam of the female and the male, the psychiatrists called "psychical hermaphroditism," a state in which the individual was neither one sex nor the other. The feminine and masculine drives that Ulrichs had formulated to explain the sexual attraction of individuals for others of their own sex, in psychiatric theory became "contrary" and "antipathetic" forces, an "inversion" of nature's intention, an inexplicable twist in the normal course of the VITA SEXUALIS.

Some aspects of Ulrich's vision of the homosexual identity were all but lost in the psychiatric interpolation. Ulrichs and Kertbeny wrote of LIEBE, the love between men, pointing to its spiritual and esthetic qualities. The expression of this love took the form of romantic longing and deep admiration more than it did mundane sensuosity. In the hands of the psychiatrists this affectional aspect of the homosexual identity, as originally conceived, was largely ignored. What Ulrichs called love, Westphal called sexual feeling and Krafft-Ebing a physically embedded sexual instinct. Whereas love and beauty stood at the core of the homosexual identity as conceived by Ulrichs and Kertbeny, for the forensic psychiatrists it was the physical ingredient of lust.

The biological homosexual identity which was pathologized in forensic medicine and psychiatry was an exotic blend of the three cosmological views of sexual relationships. Pederasty, a venerable relationship under the polytheistic cosmology, became the label used by medicine to refer to homosexual behavior until the homosexual identity was delineated by Ulrichs and more "scientific" labels could be invoked. The erotic sensuosity which was a central ingredient of sexual relationships under polytheistic belief was viewed by Krafft-Ebing as an aberration of true love. Pure sensuosity was viewed as transitory and possibly a form of moral perversity. Even Platonic love, which could be sublimely nonsensual, was seen in psychiatry as an unnatural damming up of sexual expression.

The monotheistic cosmology pervaded the psychiatric conception of permissible forms of sexual relationships which had to be heterosexual because that was why nature had created two biological sexes. The female and the male were the major components in a grand design in which males were allocated sexual appetite and pursuit and females the guardianship of love and the family. Heterosexual relationships were to be monogamous and permanent because they were the foundation of the family, and the family was the pillar of civilization.

Homosexual relationships, as conceived in sexual pathology, confused and threatened the biological and psychological differences that identified the two sexes. They were also procreatively barren and thereby mere caricatures of heterosexual relationships. They were aberrations of the LIBIDO SEXUALIS: male homosexual relationships constituted the adding of the lust of one partner to the lust of the other. In heterosexual relationships, however, the lust of the husband could be modulated by a wife who essentially lacked any sexual desire of her own.

The scientific cosmology was also reflected in the view of sexual relationships advanced by the psychiatrists of sexual pathology. The element of individual choice, central to this cosmological view of sexual relationships, was retained, although the options afforded the individual were considerably restricted. As for sexual desire, males had more choice than females. In the psychiatric view it was only the males who really possessed sexual desire so that they rather than females were motivated to pursue partners and therefore had the freedom to choose which to pursue. There were also those profligate persons who indulged in homosexual behavior but had the choice to renounce it for heterosexual monogamy. Indeed, their moral failure to do so could become a serious medical problem because acquired antipathetic sexual instinct, as Krafft-Ebing called it, could in time become an incurable condition.

Then there were those individuals whose sexual perversion was symptomatic of a profound degeneracy. The psychiatrists of sexual pathology believed they should be objects of human pity and understanding rather than targets of moral and legal condemnation. It was indeed one of the great ironies in the scientific discourse on sexual identity that medical compassion replaced ecclesiastical condemnation of homosexual behavior by the pathologization of the biological homosexual identity.

6   Environmental and Evolutionary Theory

D egeneracy theories of sexual identity were based on the belief that the individual's sexual identity was biologically determined. As applied to the homosexual identity, the theories represented the ascendancy of the somatic position in psychiatric speculations about sexual relationships. Impermissible sexual relationships were viewed as pathological forms that theoretically could be traced to some underlying physical abnormality of the sexual instinct.

The symptoms of the homosexual identity were an imperfect femininity in the female and an imperfect masculinity in the male. Although the medical and psychiatric speculations attributed the imperfections to physical causes, the diagnosable symptoms were psychological and social. They consisted of a greater or lesser degree of reversal of the social sex-roles, so that corresponding to the severity of the degeneracy, the individual of one biological sex took on the interests, mannerisms, physical appearance, and personality traits associated with the opposite biological sex.

The idea of a sexual instinct or drive, as we have seen, was the cornerstone of Ulrichs' theory of sexual identity. Within degeneracy theory the sexual instinct became more and more palpable as the catalogue of sexual perversions expanded. The environmental and evolutionary speculations about the origin of the homosexual identity were an attempt to resolve the issue of the relative influence of heredity and social environment as factors that deflected the sexual instinct from its normal procreative path.

Benjamin Tarnowsky, a psychiatrist at the Russian Imperial Academy of Medicine, like his predecessors, distinguished between congenital and acquired disorders of the "genesic" function.[1] Following Krafft-Ebing,

---

[1] Tarnowsky, Benjamin Mikhailovitch [Вениамин Михайлович Тарновский] (1886/1898). *The Sexual Instinct and its Morbid Manifestations from the Double*

Tarnowsky attributed the "innate perversion of the sexual instinct" (14) to the improper constitution and development of the central nervous system. Congenital homosexuality he referred to as "innate pederasty." As a neuropathic condition he grouped it with epilepsy and other sexual perversions, some of which he believed persisted throughout an individual's lifetime while others surfaced only as periodic outbreaks.

The male child who was afflicted with congenital pederasty exhibited several symptoms: (1) he experienced shame in the presence of males but not females; (2) he adored males; (3) he was not sexually excited by the female form; (4) he ejaculated in response to the mere presence of the male love object, without the help of manual stimulation; (5) he took on a feminine appearance and mannerism; (6) he liked feminine activities such as knitting, sewing, and making dolls' clothes; (7) he spent considerable time grooming himself before mirrors; and (8) he became a habitual masturbator if encouraged or left untended by parents. Most notable was his imperviousness to females (11): "Just as any normally constituted and sexually developed man, try as he may, cannot feel any lustful desire for another man, so it is equally impossible for a congenital pederast to accomplish coition with a woman." Although Tarnowsky considered the condition innate, he believed congenital pederasty could be exacerbated if the child were left to the "companionship of similarly morbidly afflicted comrades" (1886/1898: 119).

Tarnowsky's environmental theory of sexual perversion was developed as an explanation for "acquired genesic pederasty" (91). The acquired pederast, unlike his congenital counterpart, was born with a "healthy, well-constituted brain" (5), but had been most likely corrupted by education or example.[2] Boarding schools, Tarnowsky believed, potentially constituted the most contaminating environment:

> When a boy with perverted sexual instinct goes into a large school, particularly if it is a boarding school, comes into contact with a large number of other boys of various ages, among whom it is difficult to watch over and safeguard the regular development of puberty, he generally becomes the source of contamination to a great many of his school-fellows.... the

---

Standpoint of Jurisprudence and Psychiatry. W. C. Costello and A. Allison, Trans. Paris: Charles Carrington. (First published in 1886.)

[2] He also believed that some of them were merely bad characters. Their pederasty sprung from a "willful act of depravity" or as an expression of "vicious propensity" (5).

tendency to embracing, cuddling, sleeping two in a bed,—all these render possible the first attempts at intercourse. To the above may be added the habit and spirit of initiation. (1886/1898: 91)

Once the boy has tasted the lustfulness of pederasty, he may be marked for life by "violent, sometimes morbidly aggravated sexual excitement, which becomes developed as the boy grows up into a youth and remains unsatisfied" (91). Imitation of one boy by others was the chief means of spreading pederastic practice. The "tall, strong, active lad is always the model for the weaker younger ones" (92). Imitation led to the erosion of initial disgust:

Under the influence of example, the wish not to be behindhand, to show their boldness, the unhappy youths conquer their repugnance to the filthy act, heat their imagination with pictures of women, and, at the same time, indulge in pederasty. The more often such abnormal acts are committed, the more the normal, healthy action of sexual instinct gets blunted and modified under the influence of an acquired habit .... The image of woman ... loses its brightness, and the representation of female beauty becomes obscured. More pleasure is found with women who ape the manners of men, with closely cropped hair, breasts but slightly developed, a narrow pelvis. After the vicious habit becomes more and more confirmed, woman finally loses altogether the faculty of exciting sexually. The acquired pederast ... becomes absolutely impotent in the presence of women, or at all events loses the faculty of accomplishing regular consummation. (1886/1898: 92-93)

After a boarding school had become infected with pederasty, the practice was passed along as an institutional tradition:

The vice builds a nest for itself in the establishment, the tradition is transmitted from those who leave [it] to newcomers.... The school has now become the center for a group of pederasts, who continue to draw [in] new victims, and seek only to initiate those into the lowest paths of vice and moral turpitude" (93-94).

Besides boarding schools, Tarnowsky believed that "sailing-vessels on long voyages, prisons, barracks with schools for soldiers' boys, etc., also furnish favorable conditions for the spread and development of acquired pederasty" (1886/1898: 96). Tarnowsky distinguished between the acquired active and passive pederasts. The active pederast, once he got caught up in the vice, lacked the strength of character to abandon it. If his despair did not lead to suicide it drew him to debauchery, "unbroken orgies in the company of similar moral cripple." (95). The passive pederast was even more despicable: "the degraded, lying, and venal Cynede, whose soul is fundamentally depraved, and is physically and mentally ill" (95). Interestingly enough, Tarnowsky thought that a male could become a passive pederast by repeatedly having intercourse with women but without emotional involvement. Such a male eventually lost his desire for women and his sexual powers diminished. By turning to passive pederasty he could again be sexually aroused to erection.

Tarnowsky held that the potential for sexual perversion was probably present "in all times in all people" (143) and that it could spread from one culture to another with the rapid progress of civilization:

> Depravity (degeneracy), which formerly was almost exclusively adduced to account for sexual perversion, now combines with the rapid growth of culture, and for the same reasons, and on account of the rapid progress of intellectual development, unavoidably brings along with it an increase in mental and nervous disease. (144-145)

Although the potential was omnipresent, favorable circumstances were necessary to elicit pederastic behavior. Among these circumstances were the privileged classes and the artisans taking advantage of servants, apprentices, doorkeepers, young porters, and the "droshky drivers." Because of the depraved nature of pederasty and the possibility for contagion, Tarnowsky was firmly opposed to any detoxication. He wrote that pederasty should never be "recognized as normal, regular, and legal. Pederasty, like any other hideous deformity, always and everywhere rouses abhorrence in the mind of a normally developed man, and in that of woman, loathing and contempt" (105).

The French psychologist, Alfred Binet, was one of the first theorists to challenge the degeneracy theory as an adequate explanation for the origin of sexual perversion.[3] Binet held that the theory failed to answer two questions: (1) By what process did individuals afflicted by sexual perversion acquire their perversion? and (2) Why did their perversion take a particular form?

---

[3] Binet, Alfred (1887). Le Fetichisme dans L'Amour. *Revue Philosophique* 24: 143-167. Binet came from a distinguished medical family, but, as a psychologist, achieved fame as the co-author of the first test of general intelligence.

To address these questions Binet turned to the study of FETISHISM, a term he coined, to describe the sexual phenomenon in which parts of a sexual partner's body or articles of clothing became essential ingredients for sexual arousal. Binet thought that almost anyone in love was at least a little fetishistic and that love, itself, as infatuation, was perhaps a form of fetishism. In the fashion of grand and petit hysteria, Binet distinguished between grand and petit fetishism:

> If grand fetishism gives itself away to the outside world by signs so clear that one cannot help but recognize it, it is not the same with petit fetishism; the latter can easily be concealed; it is not apparent, nor noisy; it does not incite the subjects to extravagant acts, such as cutting a woman's hair nor to stealing white aprons; but it exists nevertheless, and it may contain the secret to strange loves and marriages which surprise people. A rich, distinguished and intelligent man marries a woman who has no youth, beauty nor wit, nor anything which would attract the average man. There may be, in these unions, a sympathy of odor or something analogous; this is petit fetishism. (1887: 144-145)

Most cases of grand fetishism described by Binet were heterosexual. He recounts, for example, the description of a male patient whose fetishism centered on white aprons: "At fifteen he sees floating in the sun an apron, which was drying and dazzling in its whiteness; he approaches, seizes it, tightens. the strings around his waist, and goes behind a bush to masturbate" (166-167). Binet also referred to a case involving "SEXUALITÉ CONTRAIRE" (167), published by Charcot and Magnan (1882), in which the patient traced his fetishism for the sight of naked boys and men to an early childhood occurrence: "My sensuality ... was manifested by the age of six, by a strong desire to see boys of my own age, and men, naked. This desire was not difficult to satisfy, for my parents lived near barracks, and it was easy to see soldiers engaging in onanism" (Binet, 1887: 167). In the latter case, Binet granted that some predisposing condition, in addition to the sight of the soldiers, was responsible for the boy's obsession with male nudity.

In contemplating possible causes of sexual perversion, Binet did not believe that heredity alone was a sufficient explanation. For example, heredity could not explain why one individual adored high heels and another a woman's eyes. Even if it were granted that individuals were born with already formed predispositions for attraction to such articles as white aprons or nightcaps, it would still be necessary to explain how ancestors acquired the perversions transmitted to their descendants. In his words: "Heredity does not invent, it does not create anything new; it has no imagination, it has no memory. It has pointedly been called the memory of the species. As such, it does not solve the problem [of explaining perversion]; it only transfers it" (164). To answer the questions about the acquisition and form of perversion, Binet developed a theory of association:

> We have strong reason to suppose that the shape of these perversions is, to a certain point, acquired and fortuitous. Thus … an accident occurred in the history of these sick persons, [usually forgotten by them], which gave their perversion its characteristic shape. (1887: 164)

Binet added that such events took root only because the individual was "degenerate" in the first place: "A healthy man can daily undergo the same analogous influences, without becoming a lover of high heels" (164).[4] In effect Binet had shifted the emphasis in the etiology of sexual perversion from somatic to psychological factors. For this he was criticized by both Chevalier (1893) and Krafft-Ebing(1886/1935).

Binet's theory, according to Chevalier, in its application to sexual inversion, failed to explain why homosexual impulses existed before sexual feelings were associated with sexual fantasy and aversion to the opposite sex, and, in men, with effeminacy. Although Krafft-Ebing granted that some innocuous forms of fetishism might be attributed to accidental associations (222-223, Note 2), he still adhered to the theory that an inherited neuropathic condition was usually the necessary precursor of perversion: "Binet's subtle remark that the lasting presence of such associations is only possible in predisposed (tainted) individuals is worthy of note" (342).

The first recognition of Binet's ideas in psychiatric circles came through Albert von Schrenck-Notzing, a student of Krafft-Ebing and also a psychiatrist.[5] Schrenck-Notzing continued the trend of subordinating

---

[4] We wish to thank Rene La Gloire for the translation of the Binet passages.

[5] Schrenck-Notzing, Albert von. (1892/1956). *The Use of Hypnosis in Psychopathia Sexualis with Special Reference to Contrary Sexual Instinct*. Charles G. Chaddock, Trans. New York: The Julian Press, 1956. (Translation of Die Suggestions-Therapie bei krankhaften Erscheinungen des Geschlechtssinnes, mit besonderer Berücksichtigung der konträren Sexualempfindung. Stuttgart: Ferdinand Enke, 1892.) Page references are to the Chaddock translation. Schrenck-Notzing stated that in all "genuine" cases of "contrary sexual

his mentor's theory of the hereditary origins of sexual perversion to environmental causation. He expanded upon Binet's idea of acquiring perversion through chance conditioning by adding the notion that antipathetic sexual instinct could occur fortuitously in the cultural history of sexual development

> as a result of moral contagion or other external cause, a normal race may come to practice pederasty; this gives birth to contrary sexual instinct, and the latter leads, through transformation of character, to the degeneration of the individual. Therefore, only secondarily can contrary sexual instinct on the basis of hereditary predisposition of the central nervous system, become developed as a symptom of taint. (Schrenck-Notzing, 1892/1956: 144)

According to John Martin, Schrenck-Notzing invented the idea of environmentally induced **MENTAL DISEASE**, one for which there was no necessary biological basis.[6] By making sexual perversion a contagious disease, as opposed to a solely congenital disorder, it became curable. Conveniently enough, psychiatry had a method for treating it: hypnosis. Schrenck-Notzing defended treatment by claiming that "moral health is more important than intellectual qualities for the progress of the individual and the race. Vicious moral instinct led to deterioration and extinction" (1892/1956: 198). Because the basis of mental disease was environmental "contagion," it could be cured through a type of healthy "contagion," the suggestions of the therapist. Schrenck-Notzing, indeed, insisted that to view contrary sexual instinct as incurable was to side with the self-proclaimed Urnings. He further believed that education should be a form of indoctrination for establishing moral habits. If education failed, then the educator and physician should use the power of suggestion (hypnosis) to replace "bad" habits with "good" ones (199).

The American psychiatrist, Morton Prince, delivered a serious challenge to degeneracy theory.[7] Whereas contemporary American psychiatrists adhered to the idea of atavism inherent in degeneracy

---

feeling," the "sexual instinct" was implicated; he believed the instinct was the starting point for the feeling (117).

6. Martin, John R. (1980, April). Sexual Perversion or Vice? A Late 19th Century Debate. Paper presented at the annual convention of the Organization of American Historians, San Francisco.

7 Prince, Morton (1898). Sexual Perversions or Vice? A Pathological and Therapeutic Inquiry. *The Journal of Nervous and Mental Disease* 25: 237-256.

theory, Prince leaned more in the direction of environmental theories, adding, however, a strong moralistic note of his own. [8] In 1898, in an address to physicians and psychiatrists that was published, he defined sexual inversion as:

> the substitution or co-existence of sexual feeling for the same sex in place of, or by the side of, that for the opposite sex. This is also known as *contrary sexual instinct*, or *sexual inversion*. (1898: 237; emphasis added)

His paper raised the following question: How far is sexual perversion the result of nervous disease or "merely indulgences in vice and cultivated habits?" (238). Whereas European psychiatrists in effect "exonerated" perversion because of what they believed was its involuntary, congenital origins, Prince indicated it as moral weakness and culpability. In his article Prince refuted the prevailing etiological theory of sexual perversion as articulated by Krafft-Ebing. First, he dismissed as illogical the idea that a complex psychological phenomenon such as sexual perversion could be explained in terms of "reversion to or inheritance of a nervous system which has never any existence in the lower order of life" (245-246). About the degeneracy theory, he acerbically remarked, "It is only fair to state that credit must be given, if credit is desired, to one of V. Krafft-Ebing's patients, by whom this theory was proposed" (246).

Second, he believed that the idea of "female and male brains" was) a "hazy sort of cerebral localization involving a different cerebral architecture for each sex" (246). He thought that such an argument was analogous to "old-fashioned phrenology."

Prince argued that the evidence for congenital theory rested entirely upon the self-reports of perverts. Such case histories could not be trusted for a number of reasons. It was highly unlikely that any one could recall early sexual feelings. The attributions individuals made to their past experience in recalling their sex histories may be due in fact to sources they have forgotten (e.g., chance associations) or lack of conscious awareness (e.g., unconscious suggestion).

Prince also repudiated the notion that perverts were really a different group of humanity than "normal" individuals. He asserted that there was no clear demarcation between being female and being male but

---

[8] See, for example, Kiernan, James G. (1891). Psychological Aspects of the Sexual Appetite. *The Alienist and Neurologist 12*: 188-219; and Lydston, Frank G. (1889). Sexual Perversion, Satyriasis, and Nymphomania. *Medical and Surgical Reporter 61*: 253-258, 281-285.

rather much overlap in physical characteristics and personalities. Most of the differences in tastes, habits, thoughts, and manners could be accounted for by socialization:

> I think it is extremely probable that if a boy were brought up as a girl and a girl as a boy, and absolutely freed from all counter influences, such as the unconscious influence of public criticism, etc., each would have the non-sexual tastes and manners of the other sex. (1898: 251)

In addition, he believed that, to some degree, all individuals were attracted to persons of their own sex. What distinguished the "perfectly healthy individuals" from the perverts was the ability to suppress this attraction, The truly perverted "does everything in his power to foster and indulge and cultivate the perverse instinct, while in such a soil the feelings themselves acquire monstrous force" (252).

He concluded that all sexual perversion was really moral perversity, that is, vicious habits cultivated to the extreme. Because a lack of volitional control lay at the root of so-called perversion, Prince believed it could be cured by strengthening the will and character and by developing a sense of morality. He concurred with Schrenck-Notzing that direct hypnotic suggestion was the best treatment, with the physician in the role of educator and exemplary model.

The thrust of Prince's argument was to reject biological for environmental explanations. However, much of his reasoning circuitously led him back to innate neurophysiological weakness. He claimed that the ability to resist perverse impulses varied from person to person and, therefore, suggested that perverts had weaker physical constitutions. In addition, he purported that the cultivation of perversity over long periods of time could seriously damage the nervous system, which then became habituated and depraved. Here Prince appeared to be reasserting the degeneracy theory, except now he had shifted the focus from prenatal development to moral irresponsibility.

In his treatise on the homosexual identity, Albert Moll, one of the leading sexual pathologists of the late nineteenth century, embellished the portrait of the male Uranist, as he called them, sketched earlier by Krafft-Ebing and other theorists.[9] Like them, Moll assured his fellow

---

[9] Moll's original theoretical position was stated in his 1891 *Die Konträre Sexualempfindung*, translated by Maurice Popkin in 1931, which is the edition we have used. Before the publication of this book, Moll had established his

medical authorities that Uranists were "perfectly normal physically and anatomically" (1891/1931: 63) and their erections were "normal and vigorous" (64) The one possible physical abnormality was that they could have larger than average mammary glands.

What did distinguish Uranists from "normal" men was their feminine predilections and traits. They often had a passion for the arts, particularly music and acting, and an uncommon talent for sewing. When they chose to disclose their sexual perversion they assumed "an entirely feminine aspect" (65), a process of transformation Moll called "effeminization" (65). Yet their attraction was to "vigorous and normal men" (66).

Moll believed Uranists could be detected by their vocal qualities. They spoke in falsetto, an unusual blend of the female and male voice. It was possible, Moll speculated, that the feminine quality of the Uranist's voice was caused by his vocal cords being shorter than those of the normal male, whose were a third longer than those of females and children. The falsetto voice of the Uranists, according to Moll, could also be due to "moral contagion" (72), that is, their association with other Uranists.

In movement as well as personality Moll believed most Uranists were effeminate. In walking, they balanced themselves on their haunches, taking little steps and raising their knees rather high. They positioned their arms as women, a configuration Moll found difficult to describe: "It consists in applying the forward part of the back of the hand to the cheek and in advancing the forearm from the body, while at the same time, lightly holding the elbow" (73). Like women, in Moll's judgment, Uranists had a tendency to lie, a compulsion fed both by their inherent femininity and the daily necessity for concealing their perversion. They also resembled women in their vanity, jealousy, and envy. Moll cautioned, however, that not all men with feminine traits were Uranists; some were "absolutely normal sexually" (77).

Uranists were sometimes attractive to women because, knowing the ways of women, they were able to ingratiate themselves into their favor. Relationships between Uranists and women, however, were at best platonic and rarely physical. In attempting coitus with women, most Uranists experienced disgust. To become potent with a female, Uranists had to conjure up fantasies of attractive males, an effort that left them fatigued.

The romantic life of the Uranist was one of tumultuous passion: "He thinks day and night of the man he loves, dogs his steps, and floods him

---

position in German psychiatry with the publication of *Der Hypnotismus* (Berlin: Fischer's Medizinische Buchandlung. H. Kornfeld, 1889).

with avowals of his love and demands for a rendezvous" (88). Often Uranists were imprinted for years on the first man they loved. Their attraction was sometimes so extraordinary that it became, what Moll called, erotomania, "a psychic disturbance characterized by an excitation of all the senses having an erotic origin" (93). The impassioned quality of Uranian love distinguished it from the normal man's love for women, which was intense but not consuming. The Uranist's ardor was explained by his typically nervous disposition and also by the fact that his love was unrequited, directed as it was toward normal men who could, of course, never reciprocate. Often Uranists were attracted to military men, especially those in the Calvary. According to Moll, this attraction was so overwhelming for some that they never had intercourse with civilians.

The sexual behavior of Uranists Moll modestly and somewhat ambiguously described in Latin. It consisted of **A PRIMERE MEMBRUM**, pressing the penis against the partner's body; placing the **MEMBRUM** (i.e., penis) **IN ANUM OR RECTUM; IMMISSIO IN ANUM,** taking the penis of the partner into one's anus; placing the **MEMBRUM IN OS** (i.e., the mouth); **IMMISSIO IN OS,** taking the penis and even the testicles into the mouth; and **EJACULATIO SEMINIS IN OS,** ejaculating in the partner's mouth.[10] Contrary to Kertbeny's, Casper's, and Krafft-Ebing's contention, Moll believed that anal and oral copulation were widespread practices among Uranists.

Moll was one of the few sexual pathologists to devote special attention to the occurrence of antipathetic sexual instinct in females. He struggled for a name for this "aberration," finally favoring **TRIBADES** to identify the women and **TRIBADISM** their sexual encounters.[11] However, he believed that even tribadism, as a term, had limited application because several authors used it to describe a specific sexual practice referred to as **CLITORIS IN VAGINAM ALTERIUS** (225). "Lesbian love," he believed, referred only to the act of Sapphism, which he defined as

---

[10] "Immissio" is Latin for "immission" (the antonym of "emission"), which means inserting, introducing, or infusing. Apparently Moll used "placing" when the insertor, and "immissio" when the receiver took the lead in anal or oral copulation.

[11] He also referred to "Lesbian love" (225), a term he claimed memorialized the island of Lesbos where the classical Greek poet, Sappho, had written her love poetry. Despite the explicit references in Sappho's poetry to love between women, Moll did not believe that "Sappho herself practiced love among women" (222). Her poetry was probably depicting the "tenderness of the women of her time."

"women-licking" or cunnilingus. Moll believed that Sapphism was the most prevalent sexual practice among tribades.

The tribades were described by Moll as the female counterparts of the Uranists: "Sexual perversion is similar in all points to that in men" (221). Whereas the Uranists were feminine in appearance and demeanor, the tribades were masculine—clothing themselves as men, keeping their hair short, smoking strong cigars, and playing sports with "Amazonian ardor" (227). They greatly enjoyed dancing with female partners. Their antipathy to men, however, was less pronounced than the Uranists' dread of women.

The individual tribade, in Moll's conceptualization, was attracted to a type of female—either blonde or brunette, short or tall, and so on. Their domestic relationships were emotional, often erupting into fits of jealousy and fighting. In their relationships roles were strictly assigned, one partner enacting the role of "father," the other the role of "mother." In their sexual contacts the "father" licked the genitals of the "mother," and these roles were never exchanged. Occasionally, the "father" introduced her clitoris into the "mother's" vagina, "thus procuring enjoyment for both" (230). Mutual masturbation was also practiced, with partners taking turns in caressing each other's genitals and legs.

In considering the etiology of the homosexual identity Moll originally endorsed the degeneracy theory. He stated his agreement with Morel that a "light" (147) neuropathic condition in parents (hysteria, e.g.) could take on a more serious form in their offspring. The degeneration might lead to sexual inversion rather than epilepsy, for example, because the sexual instinct in those afflicted was the **"LOCUS MINORIS RESISTENTIAE"** (149).

Although Moll held that the precise cerebral site of the antipathetic sexual instinct was unknown, he subscribed to Krafft-Ebing's theory that it was localized in the brain:

> It is in the action of the psyche on the genital senses which the inversion of the genital instinct is not normal. All the mental images that awaken the genital instinct excite the genital organs. The genital senses of man are in a normal state excited by the image of a woman; in the Uranist the excitation is caused by the idea of a man. In him, the influence of ideas on the sexual urge are consequently misdirected. We are thus led to place the seat of sexual inversion in that place where the ideas awaken the sexual instinct. That is to say according to modern notions of psychology in the central nervous system or more particularly in the brain. (1891/1931: 165-166)

Aberrations of the sexual instinct, according to Moll, were on the same order as physical or psychical aberrations in the functions of various body organs. The only reason antipathetic sexual instinct seemed particularly peculiar was because "most individuals who possess the attributes of the masculine sex have a sexual urge for women" (171). Yet, he averred, there was less astonishment about pathological states, for example, in which the stomach functioned normally and yet had no sensations of hunger or abnormal states of the liver in which bile was secreted but did not reach the intestine. Moll tried to explain why the abnormal functioning of the sexual instinct was exceptionally perplexing: "This [surprise] ... is explained by the fact that the sexual instinct is a psychic function which entails the concurrence of another individual and because of this acquires particular social importance" (172).

In addition to this qualified endorsement of degeneracy theory, Moll expressed considerable skepticism about other etiologies advanced to explain the origin of antipathetic sexual instinct. Fortuitous causes arising from childhood experiences, such as a male child's being aroused by having his genitals accidentally touched by a man, could lead to inversion only if there were a latent predisposition in the child. He was very doubtful of the theory that perversion could be spread by moral contagion, for example, by a young Uranist contaminating an entire boarding school for boys, unless there was a voluptuous predisposition in the boys. He wryly remarked: "One can win only those who allow themselves to be won over" (153-154).

Moll was undecided as to whether separation of the male and female sexes led to inversion. He believed, however, that one test of this theory could be made in America where there should presumably be less inversion because there was less segregation of the sexes. He did not believe that masturbation was a cause but rather a result of the early preoccupation of the Uranist with sexual fantasies peopled by males. Nor did he accept the theory that a life of heterosexual debauchery led to Uranism: "It is just as impossible as to see an individual satiated with pastry and cake seized one day with a passion for the dirt and filth that is thrown into the street" (157). As for the etiology of antipathetic sexual instinct in females, Moll inclined toward the view that it was congenital but not necessarily a hereditary neuropathic condition.

In considering the diagnosis and treatment of antipathetic sexual instinct in men, Moll added little to what Krafft-Ebing had already described. The prognosis for psychosexual hermaphrodites was brighter than that for the pure Uranist because the psychosexual hermaphrodites had a prior and more intense heterosexual urge. Prognosis was pessimistic for the Uranist because his psyche was feminine and his sexual fantasies, since childhood, had been populated only with males. If the psychiatrist were to stimulate masculine drives in the Uranist, it would "throw his psychic life out of equilibrium" (188). A cure would not only have to redirect sexual urges away from the homosexual, toward the heterosexual, but also transform "the general psychic state to one of a more masculine nature" (188). The best hope for cure was when the individual was still a child and parents, with psychiatric assistance, could control the child's behavior and environment, directing them toward masculine forms.

Treatment of the adult Uranist would require his being urged to seek the company of women who could charm and captivate him by those qualities quite in accord with his nature. Heterosexual coitus was not to be considered the central goal because failure at intercourse would weaken the Uranist's hope for recovery. Masturbation was to be forbidden because it maintained the old associations between sexual acts and fantasies of males. Deep hypnotic trances sometimes succeeded in dampening homosexual urges and thereby diminished the need to participate in abnormal acts. Through post-hypnotic suggestion it was possible to kindle heterosexual urges. Castration, Moll thought, was a rather drastic treatment.

Before Moll presented his biogenetic theory, several theorists had described an evolutionary process in which the human organism developed from a bisexual to a monosexual stage.[12] By "bisexual," they were referring to the presence in an organism of both female and male sex organs. By "monosexual" they meant that the organs of only one sex were present. They believed that human embryonic and fetal development recapitulated the phylogenic evolution from the bisexual to the monosexual stage. Bisexuality was seen as a primitive form of sexual development. The failure of individuals to develop complete monosexuality was seen as regression. Therefore, the bisexual hypothesis could be encompassed within degeneracy theory.

In what they described as the homosexual resolution of the struggle between female and male elements, traces of the conquered sex remained. As evidence, they pointed to the rudimentary female or male organs possessed by the two sexes. Sexual inversion was the result of one sex not being completely obliterated in progress toward monosexuality.

---

[12] Krafft-Ebing (1886/1935: 344-345) cited Frank G. Lydston, Chevalier, and James G. Kiernan.

Individuals who failed to achieve complete monosexuality would always be neuropathic in their physical and psychological make-up because the struggle between the elements of both sexes continued. In the case of the physical hermaphrodite, the theory had apparent relevance. For the sexually inverted, in whom physical differentiation of the sex organs was complete, the residual sexuality was thought to exist in the central and peripheral nervous system. According to this theory, the degrees of sexual inversion catalogued by Krafft-Ebing corresponded to the amount of the conquered sex which remained in the nervous system.

In 1897 Moll published a treatise that ultimately led to the rejection of degeneracy theory in the twentieth century discourse on sexual identity.[13] In accounting for the origin of the homosexual identity, degeneracy theory assumed that the sexual instinct was a single entity, which could be either normal or perverted in expression. The idea of a unitary sexual instinct was harmonious with the conclusion of degeneracy theory that the homosexual identity represented a hereditary recrudescence of primitive forms of life.

Moll had several reasons for attempting a reformulation of etiological theories of sexual perversion. He had previously expressed skepticism about the persuasiveness of degeneracy theory in explaining those cases of sexual inversion in which the only symptom of degeneracy was the antipathetic sexual instinct itself.[14] He had already questioned theories of accidental associations occurring during childhood, moral contagion, and sexual debauchery, advocated by Binet, Tarnowsky, Schrenck-Notzing,

---

[13] Albert Moll, *Untersuchungen über die Libido sexualis* (Berlin: Fischer's Medicinische Buchhandlung, H. Kornfeld). According to Sulloway (1979: 301 and Appendix D), this work was published in two parts in 1897, the first setting forth a theory of normal sexual development, and the second dealing with clinical and forensic issues. The quotations from Moll are taken from the English translation: Moll, Albert (1933), *Libido Sexualis: Studies in the Psychosexual Laws of Love Verified by Clinical Sexual Case Histories*. David Berger, Trans. New York: American Ethnological Press. Sulloway contended that Moll's theory of sexual development, which Sulloway called "biogenetic," persuaded Freud to abandon the theory of childhood seduction in explaining the origin of sexual perversion. Sulloway (300) also averred that Moll's new theoretical stance led Krafft-Ebing to abandon his advocacy of degeneracy theory in an article published in 1901, a year before his death: "Neue Studien auf dem Gebiete der Homosexualität," *Jahrbuch für sexuelle Zwischenstufen* 3: 1-36.

[14] In documenting this statement, Sulloway (1979: 300) cited Moll (1891/1931: 162, 189-190).

and even Krafft-Ebing. Along with contemporary sexologists, he had discovered that reminiscences of childhood sexual experiences by "perverted" individuals did not substantially differ from those who were "normal." Finally, he became aware of evidence reported by American psychologists that children experienced genital sensations and the emotion of love as early as two or three years of age.[15]

Moll defined the LIBIDO SEXUALIS, or sexual instinct, as (20) "an emotion which strives to express itself in external bodily movement of such a nature that the completion of the movement may bring about the enhancement of pleasure, already present, or the removal of the feeling of unpleasure.[16] Its conscious, subjective purpose was copulation, which was subservient to its unconscious, objective purpose, reproduction.

The libido sexualis consisted of two component drives, both linked to the act of copulation: (1) the "detumescent drive" (DETUMESCENZTRIEB) and (2) the "contrectation drive" (CONTRECTATIONTREIB). The detumescent drive, according to Moll, referred to "an organic impulse to evacuate a secretion just as a full bladder impels to the emptying of the bladder" (1897/1933: 126). In the female this drive was obscurely tied to ovulation while in the male it was clearly associated with ejaculation. The contrectation drive impelled "the male to a physical and psychical approach of a female, and the latter to the approach of the male" (126-127). It was usually gratified by the touching, fondling, and kissing of sexual partners.

Moll believed he had found clinical evidence for the independence of the two drives. As evidence for the detumescent drive, he described case histories of patients who, as children and adults, enjoyed the sensual delights of masturbation without any visual imagery of sexual partners. He further believed that Platonic love and romance, when they did not involve sexual intercourse (or even touching), were evidence of an independent contrectation drive.

For the most part the detumescent and contrectation drives appeared together. Moll wrote: "In the last analysis the sex urge consists in ejaculating semen into the vagina of the female, and on the part of the woman receiving the male's member and absorbing the semen in her vagina followed by detumescence" (29). The two drives, therefore, were conceived as complementary. Detumescence was the lower, more

---

[15] Sulloway (1979: 298, Note 18) referred to the work of Sanford Bell and G. Stanley Hall.

[16] In explicating Moll's theory of *libido sexualis* and its theoretical precursors, we have occasionally relied on Sulloway's excellent discussion and analysis (1979: 298 ff.).

primitive, physical instinct, the raw "desire for sensual pleasure and a dislike for feelings of displeasure" (50). Contrectation was tied to the higher impulses in the form of love: "In that form, devoid of every sensual thought, not only of performing coitus, but also of bodily contact, the spiritual feelings which tying up to the two persons in love, would belong to the higher impulse" (50).

The higher impulse was viewed as corralling the lower in uniting female and male by a spiritual bond. The detumescent drive sprung from the sex glands, but the contrectation drive emanated from the copulatory organs. Contrectation was therefore associated with "social" feelings, while detumescence was associated with purely "sexual" feelings.

Moll was concerned about the line of demarcation between "physical" and "psychical" sexual feelings. He asserted that in humans "the meeting of the sexes is brought about by the sex instinct, and that instinct is consciously perceived" (50). Both components of sexual instinct directed individuals toward the opposite sex. Both females and males, he contended, possessed the innate capacity "to react differently to sense impressions which emanated from woman than to those emanating from man" (166). The psychical feelings came into prominence when humans made "more refined differentiations" (160) in the choice of particular female or male partners:

> I am of the opinion ... that in man the psychical elaboration of the sense impressions received plays an important role, a role which may be observed in everyday occurrences. It is due to such psychical elaborations that sexual excitement will take place in a man and a woman long after a conversation. Every one, according to his own individuality, will elaborate the impressions received in a different manner. This will easily explain the numerous differences in the individualizing direction of the sex impulse which has its highest point in love. The face is the mirror of the soul. (160)

The psychical distinctions made by individuals were essential for the release of the contrectation drive. Some psychical qualities stimulated males while others stimulated females. Moll stated that "the man is often more truly stimulated by a certain reserve and chastity than he is by a woman's forwardness" (254). For her part, "the woman is not only not re-pelled by the man's courage but rather in most cases is excited by it" (254).

Whatever psychical elaborations were made by individuals, however, fell within the constraints imposed by biology. Throughout history and in every culture, Moll averred, "the general bodily formation of the female sex has always been a stimulant to the man and the general masculine bodily formation to the woman" (261). In a more literary vein he wrote: "For the eternal feminine will always remain that which will attract man; and I believe that we must regard the capacity to react to the eternal feminine as inherited in the human sex instinct" (261).

Pivotal to Moll's new theory of sexual instinct were the speculations of his German contemporary, Max Dessoir.[17] Dessoir argued that the sexual instinct developed in two major stages: (1) an "undifferentiated" stage which appeared during puberty and could be either heterosexual or homosexual in expression and (2) a "differentiated" stage in which heterosexual expression became the exclusive instinctual form. Both stages, Dessoir contended, were essential to the normal development of the sexual instinct. Moll applied Dessoir's stage theory to his notion of the two components of the sexual instinct. He postulated a three-stage evolutionary theory: (1) the detumescent drive arose from an ASEXUAL stage in which the human sex organs were undifferentiated; (2) the contrectation drive arose from a BISEXUAL (or hermaphroditic) stage in which humans possessed both female and male sex organs; and (3) a MONOSEXUAL stage developed in which either the female or male genitalia were suppressed.

It was from the monosexual stage that the female and male heterosexual reaction capacity emerged. This capacity was really a complex of reactive capacities that released the sexual impulse toward the opposite sex. Primarily they consisted of visual perceptions but included "various odiferous substances emanating from man and woman, being a stimulus for the opposite sex" (192). In addition, there were the "auditory and tactile senses." Moll believed that almost nothing was known about the release of sexual impulses through the "gustatory senses."

When Moll asserted that heterosexuality was inherited, he referred only to the heterosexual reactive capacities of females and males. He did not believe that the concept of "man" or "woman" was inherited. The innate capacity for discernment of the differences between females and males preceded the development of the sexual instinct in puberty:

> At the time of puberty human beings already know that there
> are two sexes, that man and woman love one another, that the

---

[17] His dual-stage theory of sexual development, Zur Psychologie der Vita Sexualis, was published in 1894 in *Allgemeine Zeitschrift für Psychiatrie*: 941-975 (cited in Sulloway, 1979: 298, 531). Dessoir was a psychologist and philosopher.

genitals of the two sexes are different, etc. But all this does not cause the impulse towards the other sex. It is true that this impulse towards the opposite sex cannot develop without a certain psychical activity. But the latter is not the cause influencing the already developed sex instinct. At most, it is a preliminary condition in order that the sex instinct be developed in a certain direction. (162)

In effect Moll was contending that it was not knowledge itself of the sex differences that set the sexual instinct in motion but the actual perception of the differences in the sexual stimuli emanating from females or males.

Sexual perversion, including the homosexual identity, was explained by Moll as caused by-deficiencies in one or more units of the heterosexual reactive complex, conditions that could be traced to heredity. In the case of the bisexual, Moll suggested the reactive capacity to differentiate between a feminine or masculine body may be absent in the inherited complex: "I only wish to point out that the normal complexes of reactive capacities may be seen to have numerous deviations in many persons" (245). Variations could occur that fell short of "pure homosexuality" (246). They could be placed at intermediate points on a continuum that stretched between "the typical feminine sex instinct directed towards completely mature males, and the typical male sex instinct directed towards completely mature females" (246). For example, there were adult men who were attracted to quite young and almost child-like boys and adult women who were attracted to sexually immature males. Also, Moll reported, that there were men who loved other men who possessed feminine qualities and women who were attracted only to other women possessing masculine qualities. In his summary on sexual perversion Moll wrote:

> Numerous persons exist with incomplete and imperfect complexes of reactive capacities. In some men this complex is not marked exclusively by a receptivity to specific stimuli emanating from woman. This fact explains why some men feel themselves attracted now to males, now to females. Furthermore, that some men will love only such males who possess definite feminine qualities. The reverse is true of women who deviate from the normal. (371-372)

The environmental and evolutionary theorists posed no basic challenge to the belief that the homosexual identity was biological and degenerate. Tarnowsky, in fact, believed degeneracy theory fully accounted for congenital pederasty. Binet could not bring himself totally to disavow the belief that some individuals may be more congenitally vulnerable than others in acquiring perversions. He needed to preserve the notion of congenital predisposition in order to explain why individuals who had similar sexual experiences did not all develop perversion.

The weakness in Binet's argument was not unnoticed by Chevalier and Krafft-Ebing. Chevalier believed that Binet had failed to explain why homosexual impulses existed before sexual feelings were associated with sexual fantasies and why they were accompanied by aversion to the opposite sex and, in men, by effeminacy. Although Krafft-Ebing conceded that some innocuous forms of fetishism might be attributed to accidental associations (222-223, Note 2), he still adhered to the theory that an inherited neuropathic condition was the necessary precursor of perversion: "Binet's subtle remark that the lasting presence of such associations is only possible in predisposed (tainted) individuals is worthy of note" (342).

In the etiological theories of both Schrenck-Notzing and Prince, remnants of degeneracy theory survived. Schrenck-Notzing's theory of moral contagion still preserved hereditary predisposition as at least a secondary cause. The thrust of Prince's argument was to reject biological for environmental explanations. However, much of his reasoning circuitously led him back to innate neurophysiological weakness. He claimed that the ability to resist perverse impulses varied from person to person and, therefore, suggested that perverts had weaker physical constitutions. In addition, he purported that the cultivation of perversity over long periods of time could seriously damage the nervous system, which then became habituated and depraved. Here Prince appeared to be reasserting the degeneracy theory, except now he had shifted the focus from prenatal development to moral irresponsibility.

Moll showed the same reluctance as Binet, Schrenck-Notzing, and Prince, to endorse degeneracy theory as the major explanation for the inversion of the genital instinct. He was also astute enough to observe that no theories of sexual perversions would have been invented if it were not for the fact that the perversions entailed a relationship between two individuals and thereby assumed psychological and social importance. Yet, in the end, he accepted the notion that an innate predisposition determined the individual's sexual identity.

The evolutionary and environmental theories of the homosexual identity introduced new ingredients into etiological speculations. As a mental pathology it could be generated by external circumstances and spread as disease in all-male environments. As a contagion it eroded character and sapped the energy of the normal sexual instinct so that individual practitioners who acquired the vice of perversion were, for all practical purposes, as helplessly caught up in the grip of their homosexual appetite as were the congenitally inverted. Environments were defined with increasing breadth. Although Tarnowsky wrote mostly about the corrupting influence of particular institutional settings, both he and Schrenck-Notzing believed that modern civilization generally strained the intellectual powers and moral strength of the individual and undermined the heterosexual identity.

Also arguing for the environmental position was Binet, with his theory of chance associations, and Prince, with his belief in the socialization process. Binet's theory of acquired sexual perversions tied the homosexual identity to environmental stimuli and reinforcement. Prince believed that the biological line demarcating females and males was faintly drawn and that socialization—the way in which children were reared—determined how typically each child represented her or his own sex. He also implied that sexual indulgence, particularly of an aberrant nature, weakened character and will and that resistance to temptation could ultimately restore character to its original strength.

Each of these theorist provided faint glimmerings of future efforts to detoxicate the homosexual identity. Tarnowsky, who wrote most ominously about congenital and acquired pederasty, was able to distinguish between the wanton decadence of the "infector" and the comparative innocence of the easily beguiled "infected." Binet believed that the biological predisposition toward fetishism was due to sexual precocity, an acceleration rather than arrest in sexual development. Prince held there was no significant gap that separated the normal and the abnormal and that to some extent all individuals were attracted to others of their own biological sex. Moll viewed perversion as a step occupied by all individuals in their evolutionary progress toward the heterosexual reaction complex. Perhaps few individuals, he believed, entirely grew out of the bisexual stage, during which they possessed the sexual characteristics of both females and males, and moved on to an unblemished monosexualism. As a complex of sensory ingredients, Moll thought it was probably unusual that the heterosexual reaction capacity would not be deficient in one component or another: the seeds of perversion were widely scattered throughout humanity.

The new theories of sexual identity, under the influence of medical scientism, tended to blur the boundaries between the physical and the mental. Binet's theory of association was modeled after mechanistic processes described in the physical sciences although it was used to explain psychological states and interpersonal attraction. In Moll's theory the detumescent drive appeared to be the physical dimension of the libido sexualis while contrectation was the psychological and emotional aspect. Moll also held that it was not the mental concept of female or male that aroused the heterosexual reaction complex but the stimuli as actually perceived emanating from each sex. The blurring of the physical and the mental in these theories made it possible to focus on the biological sex of partners as the key determinant of sexual relationships.

7 Detoxication of the Homosexual Identity: Biological Theories

U lrichs had conceived the biological homosexual identity as solidly anchored in nature, although he believed it was rarer and perhaps more fragile than the heterosexual identity. The medical theorists who pathologized the homosexual identity therefore struck at its biological roots, classifying it as a disease of the central nervous system, traceable to a hereditary taint and bearing the stigmata of degeneration. If Ulrichs' original biological vision of the homosexual identity was to be rescued from the jaws of pathology, it had to be rehabilitated by theorists who could claim medical credentials of their own. Although the pathologizers were seldom remiss in noting Ulrichs' pioneering contribution to the discourse on sexual identity, they unfailingly noted that he was a lawyer rather than a physician and, even worse, a practitioner and advocate of Uranism rather than a dispassionate scientist like they believed themselves to be.

In England the physician who assumed the leadership in promoting the idea of a detoxicated biological homosexual identity was Havelock Ellis who, in 1897, published *Sexual Inversion*.[1]

---

[1] The first edition was the work of Ellis and John Addington Symonds. It has been reprinted as: *Sexual Inversion* (New York: Arno Press, 1975). Its preparation was completed by Ellis after Symonds' death. This book was the first in a series of six volumes written and edited by Ellis under the collective title, *Studies in the Psychology of Sex* (1897-1910), to which he added a seventh volume in 1928. Unless otherwise noted, we have cited the American edition: *Studies in the Psychology of Sex*. New York: Random House, 1936, Vol. 1, Part 4: 1-391. Because of English censorship laws, *Sexual Inversion* was first published in Leipzig, Germany under the title *Das Konträre Geschlechts-gefühl* in 1896. The German title suggested the physicality implicit in *Konträre Sexualempfindung*, while the English title appears to be a translation of the French "*L'Inversion Sexuelle.*" The supplement to the *OED* attributes the first English use of

He defined sexual inversion as "sexual instinct turned by inborn constitutional abnormality toward persons of the same sex" (1897/1936: 1). He distinguished it from "homosexuality," which he conceived as including all forms of sexual attraction between individuals of the same sex, especially in circumstances in which members of the opposite sexes were not available. He also distinguished sexual inversion from transvestism, which described the individual who felt like a person of the opposite sex and adopted the tastes, habits, and dress of that sex, while remaining normal (i.e., *heterosexual*) in sexual instinct.[2]

The major focus of Ellis' speculations was on the possible origins of the homosexual identity:

> What is sexual inversion? Is it ... an abominably acquired vice, to be stomped out by the prison? Or is it ... a beneficial variety of human emotion which should be tolerated or even fostered? Is it a diseased condition which qualifies its subject for the lunatic asylum? Or is it a natural monstrosity, a human "sport," the manifestations of which must be regulated when they become antisocial? (1897/1936: 302)

After reviewing contemporary etiologies, Ellis concluded that answers to these questions could be collected under one of two theoretical postures: (1) the view that sexual inversion was acquired or (2) the view that it was congenital.[3] If sexual identity were acquired

---

INVERSION to Symonds, J. A. (1896/1936). *A Problem in Modern Ethics, Being an Enquiry into the Phenomenon of Sexual Inversion.* London: Privately published. (In 1897, it first appeared as an Appendix to Ellis and Symonds' *Sexual Inversion.*) After Ellis, the next use listed is that by R.W. Chambers (1911). *Common Law* I, 29: "This world is full of pale enraptured artists; ... full of unwashed little inverts" (*OED* Supplement).

[2] Ellis did not use the term transvestism, referring instead to "sexo-esthetic inversion" or "Eonism" (2). In a footnote to the original edition of *Sexual Inversion,* Ellis noted: "'Homosexual' is a barbarously hybrid word, and I claim no responsibility for it. It is, however, convenient, and now widely used. 'Homogenic' has been suggested as a substitute" (1897/1936: 1). It was, in fact, suggested by Edward Carpenter in 1895 in a pamphlet entitled, *Homogenic Love and Its Place in a Free Society* (London: Redundancy Press). As Carpenter pointed out, homogenic has two Greek roots: *homos* meaning *same,* and *genos* meaning *sex.* He called homosexual a "bastard word," used in scientific texts (4).

[3] Ellis associated the names of Binet, Schrenck-Notzing, and the Freudians with the "acquired" theories and Krafft-Ebing and Moll with the "congenital" theories.

though the accidents of sexual attraction, Ellis feared for the future of humanity: "We should ... have to admit that the most fundamental human instinct is so constituted as to be equally well adapted for sterility as for that propagation of the race which, as a matter of fact, we find dominant throughout the whole of life" (1897/1936: 303).

Among the theories of acquired sexual inversion, Ellis considered Freud's oedipal construction a particularly tortured explanation of why some male inverts, as children, were close to their mothers. It made more sense to Ellis to view inverted boys as being, from the beginning, vaguely aware of their femininity and therefore prone to share a "community of tastes" (307) with their mothers. Also like their mothers, these boys were "already experiencing the predominant fascination with the male" (307). Ellis clearly favored a congenital theory:

> Sexual inversion ... remains a congenital anomaly, to be classed with other congenital anomalies which have psychic concomitants. At the very least such congenital abnormality exists as a predisposition to inversion. It is probable that many persons go through the world with a congenital predisposition to inversion which always remains latent and unroused; in others the instinct is so strong that it forces its own way in spite of all obstacles; in others, again, the predisposition is weaker, and a powerful exciting cause plays the predominant part. (1897/1936: 322)

His belief in the hereditary basis for inversion stemmed from the view that the sexual instinct was an inborn organic capacity. Childhood and adolescent experience could plant the seed of a heterosexual or homosexual attraction but the seed that would take root depended on the predisposing type of soil.

Ellis endorsed the idea of an original bisexuality. He speculated that the fertilized ovum consisted of half-female and half-male "germs." In normal development either the female or male germs took the upper hand and left behind only a "few aborted germs of the opposite sex" (311). For the invert, however, development steered a different course:

> In the homosexuals ... and in the bisexual, we may imagine that the process has not proceeded normally, on account of some peculiarity in the number or character of either the original male germs or female germs, or both, the result being that we have a person who is organically twisted into a shape that is more fitted for exercise of the inverted than of the normal sexual impulse, or else equally fitted for both. (311)

Germinal peculiarities, Ellis predicted, might eventually be traced to stimulating and inhibiting effects of hormonal secretions. Still the hormones could do no more than shape a basic predisposition for one sexual identity or another.

Although Ellis assumed that "the basis of sexual life is bisexual" (1897/1936: 86), he asserted that its heterosexual or homosexual direction was fixed early and permanently in the individual's life. He distinguished three categories of individuals on the basis of the direction of the sexual impulse:

> [T]hose who, not being exclusively attracted to the opposite sex, are exclusively attracted to the same sex, and those who are attracted to both sexes. The first are the homosexual, whether or not the attraction springs from genuine inversion. The second are the bisexual, or, as they were more often termed, following Krafft-Ebing, psychosexual hermaphrodites. There would thus seem to be a broad and simple grouping of all sexually functioning persons into three comprehensive divisions: the heterosexual, the bisexual, and the homosexual. For Ellis it was untenable to think that the individual who experienced a homosexual impulse could be considered fully heterosexual. (87-88)

For Ellis it was untenable to think that the individual who experienced a homosexual impulse could be considered fully heterosexual. In his estimation, the strength of the heterosexual impulse in bisexuals was questionable: "In the majority of adult bisexual persons it would seem that the homosexual tendency is stronger and more organic than the heterosexual tendency" (88). Therefore, Ellis thought the division of individuals into heterosexual, bisexual, or homosexual was useful but scarcely scientific.

In calling the homosexual identity abnormal, Ellis attempted to draw a distinction between an anomaly and a pathology. At one point he said the homosexual identity could be viewed as a "sport" of nature, "one of those organic aberrations which we see throughout living nature, in plants and animals" (317). He compared inversion to "color-hearing": "Just as the color-hearer instinctively associates colors with sounds … so the invert has his sexual sensations brought into relationships with objects that are normally without sexual appeal" (317-318). The abnormal, Ellis pointed out, was not necessarily diseased: "the study of the abnormal is perfectly distinct from the study of the morbid" (319). Yet he held that sexual abnormality could be traced to some "disturbance" in early embryonic development.

Although Ellis subscribed to a congenital theory of sexual identity, he rejected Ulrichs' idea of a female soul enclosed in a male body (and the converse for female Urnings) and, consequently, the idea of the third sex. In the original edition of *Sexual Inversion*, Ellis wrote:

> We only know soul as manifested through the body; and, although, if we say that a person seems to have the body of a man and the feelings of a woman we are saying what is often true enough; it is quite another matter to assert dogmatically that a female soul, or even a female brain, is expressing itself through a male body. That is simply unintelligible. (1897/1936: 132)

He also rejected the notion that sexual inversion was caused by degeneracy. The invert, he asserted, was "degenerate" only in the sense that the term applied to the color-blind: both had "fallen away from the genus" (1897/1936). Ordinarily the invert showed none of the "stigmata of degeneracy," except perhaps in secondary sexual characteristics that tended to be modified in the direction of the opposite sex.

Portraits of both female and male inverts were provided in Ellis' discussion of sexual inversion.[4] He believed there were two types of female inverts: the feminine or passively inverted and the masculine or actively inverted. The feminine inverts were described as having homely faces but good figures. They were usually neither physically nor emotionally robust and "not well adapted for childbearing" (1897/1936: 222). Because of their general emotional aloofness and relatively tepid attraction to males, they were the type of women whom men often passed by.

Their counterpart was the female invert who possessed "a more or less distinct trace of masculinity" (222), a direct expression of an organic sexual instinct. There was a masculine distribution of hair on her legs and arms,

---

[4] Ellis' treatise was based mostly on his own extensive reading of the medical discourse on sexual identity as well as anthropological and historical studies. He also described thirty-three case histories in the first edition (1897), including the two that appeared in the appendix. This number was later expanded to thirty-nine, which included six cases of inversion in women, one of whom was his wife, Edith Ellis. Edith's case appears as History XXXVI in the later edition and as XXXI in the earlier edition (92-94). Grosskurth, Phillis. (1980). *Havelock Ellis: A Biography*. New York: Alfred Knopf, 186) noted that most of the cases were obtained through Symonds, Edward Carpenter, and J. G. Kiernan, a Chicago psychiatrist. Ellis may have personally known relatively few of the individuals described in the histories. The subjects were preponderantly British but some were Americans. Although thirty-nine case histories appear, Ellis sometimes referred to "my 80 cases" (1897/1936: 264-265).

her muscles were firm and lacked soft connective tissue, her larynx large and voice deep, and genitalia smaller than average in size. She felt more at home in male than female attire, she treated males with directness, sometimes showing comradeship but never sexual attraction: "Usually the inverted woman feels absolute indifference toward men, and not seldom repulsion" (1897/1936: 223). Her demeanor was masculine:

> The brusque, energetic movements, the attitude of the arms, the direct speech, the inflexions of the voice, the masculine straightforwardness and sense of honor, and especially the attitude toward men, free from any suggestion either of shyness or audacity, will often suggest the underlying psychic abnormality to a keen observer. (250)

In the presence of other women, however, her manner could change to one of shyness and embarrassment.

Sexual intercourse between females, according to Ellis, combined affection with sexual gratification. Females enjoyed kissing, sleeping together, close embraces, and resting in the position of "lying spoons." Genital stimulation involved mutual contact and friction and the use of an artificial penis. Clitoral stimulation was rare and CUNNILINGUS was performed by the active type on the passive type of female partner. The sexual relationships of females tended to outlast those of males.

Ellis' portrayal of male inverts was not as clearly delineated as that of females because it tended to emerge from his general conception of sexual inversion. He conceived male inverts as possessing a "more or less feminine temperament" (1897/1936: 201), which impelled them frequently toward suicide but rarely violence toward others. Their faces were child-like, the adult male inverts resembled boys, the adult females, girls.

The feminine tendency of male inverts as well as the masculine proclivities of the female Ellis construed as evidence of arrested development of the normal sexual instinct. This disturbance in development he called a "tendency to infantilism" (291). In the male invert underdevelopment combined with sexual precocity:

> If we are justified in believing that there is tendency for inverted persons to be somewhat arrested in development, approaching the child type, we may connect this fact with the sexual precocity sometimes marked in inverts, for precocity is commonly accompanied by rapid arrest of development. (292)

There were other distinguishing characteristics of male inverts. Many could not whistle. For vocations they favored medicine, literature and the arts, and acting:

[T]he congenitally inverted may, I believe, be looked upon as a class of individuals exhibiting nervous characters which, to some extent, approximate them to persons of artistic genius. The dramatic and artistic aptitudes of inverts are, therefore, partly due to the circumstances of the invert's life, which render him necessarily an actor, — and in some cases lead him into a love of deception comparable with that of a hysterical woman, — and partly, it is probable, to a congenital nervous predisposition allied to the predisposition to dramatic aptitude. (296)

Male inverts had a corresponding tendency to be vain and love applause, perhaps as a compensation for their "consciousness of feminine defect" (298). They also liked to keep their necks uncovered to display feminine grace or, if athletic, masculine brawn. Most of them regarded their appearance and mannerisms as entirely natural.

The sexual practices of male inverts, according to Ellis, ranged from touching and fondling to anal intercourse.[5] Both fellatio and pedicatio, he reported, were infrequent practices, at least in England, where sexual contact between males rarely went beyond masturbation and interfemoral intercourse. He rejected the stereotypic belief that one partner was always active, the other always passive in male sexual relationships.

Most male inverts, he asserted, never had sexual intercourse with females because of their **HORROR FEMINAE**, fear of female genitalia. This aversion stemmed from the male invert's lack of excitable masculine attraction to females. Without sexual excitement, Ellis averred, neither female or male genitalia were especially pleasing: "[T]hey only become emotionally desirable through the parallel excitement of the beholder" (279).

Sexual opposition, in Ellis' view, was a necessary ingredient of both heterosexual and homosexual relationships. He defined it as "the longing for something which the lover himself does not possess" (288), which he later called "heterogamy" (289). Male inverts who were feminine in appearance, for example, could be attracted to "soldiers and other

---

[5] Ellis used the term *pedicatio*, which he defined as "the sodomitical intromission of the penis into the anus" (282n). He believed the term derived from the Greek *pais* for boy and *pedex* or *podex* for anus. Ellis faintly implied that pedicatio was a "grosser" form of sexual practice than fondling and masturbation.

vigorous types" (284). Inverted women, he asserted, were attracted to "more clinging feminine persons" (286). Masculine-looking inverts were attracted to boys or youth because they resembled women. The masculine inverts were more normal than the feminine, in Ellis' eyes, because their attractions required "a less profound organic twist" (286) of the sexual instinct. Although heterogamy was an important basis for sexual relationships, Ellis considered "homogamy" (289), the attraction of likes, to be the more important ingredient because the heterogamous need could be adequately met by superficial differences in physical appearance.

Concerning the treatment of sexual inversion, Ellis was skeptical. Therapy should seek to ameliorate nervous conditions that afflicted most inverts rather than seek to convert homosexual into heterosexual impulse. Physical exercise, keeping mentally occupied, and physical hygiene would relieve the "nervous weakness and irritability, loss of control, and genital hyperesthesia" (332) that constituted the physiological make-up of inverts. Hyperesthesia was the term used by Krafft-Ebing to describe the easy genital excitability of those who suffered from antipathetic sexual instinct. Therapy for inverts would also protect others: "to refine and spiritualize the inverted impulse, so that the invert's natural perversion may not become a cause of acquired perversion in others" (338). It would also protect the invert from himself: "The invert is not only the victim of his own abnormal obsession, he is the victim of social hostility" (338).

Although sexual inversion could not be reversed, according to Ellis, it could be prevented by removing the "exciting causes." One of the chief causes was the school system in which the two sexes were segregated. Here it was possible to arrest heterosexual development through a strong impression of homosexual experience. The remedy, Ellis proposed, was more coeducational activities in the schools. The seduction of a child by an inverted older person was another danger, although Ellis believed that seduction alone could not produce a "taste for homosexuality" (323). Disappointment in a heterosexual relationship could be a precipitating factor. Most vulnerable were those individuals who possessed a latent inverted impulse, because the failure in one heterosexual relationship could turn the person against the possibility of trying others. It was also possible that such disappointment could "poison the normal instinct" (323), so that the individual was rendered incapable of loving either females or males. Marriage, Ellis believed, was certainly no cure for inversion. Marriage for inverts was doomed to failure from the start; it also ran the risk of passing the inversion on to progeny.

Because inversion was incurable, Ellis held that the best that the physician could hope for was to "enable the invert to be healthy, self-restrained, and self-respecting" (338). This was better than trying "to convert him into the mere feeble simulacrum of a normal man" (338). Ellis did not believe sexual abstinence was a solution:

> It is better that a man should be enabled to make the best of his own strong natural instincts, with all their disadvantages, than that he should be unsexed and perverted, crushed into a position which he has no natural aptitude to occupy. (341)

The decision to live according to their sexual impulses was one that the physician should leave to the inverted patient. The social attitude toward inversion should avoid two extremes:

> On the one hand, it [society] cannot be expected to tolerate the invert who flouts his perversion in its face, and assumes that, because he would rather take his pleasure with a soldier or a policeman than with their sisters, he is of finer clay than the vulgar herd. On the other side, it might well refrain from crushing with undiscerning ignorance beneath the burden of shame the subject of an abnormality which, as we have seen, has not been found incapable of fine uses. (355)

The praise of Magnus Hirschfeld was sung by Ellis in the last edition of *Sexual Inversion*. Hirschfeld established a prominent position in the scientific discourse on sexual identity as a German physician specializing in "nervous and psychic illnesses," especially as they pertained to sexual anomalies, as editor of a scholarly journal, as director of an institute for sexual variations, and as a leading advocate for the decriminalization of adult homosexual behavior.[6]

---

[6] Hirschfeld established the quarterly journal, *Jahrbuch für sexuelle Zwischenstufen*, in 1899. (In English, the title is *Yearbook for Sexual Intermediate Stages*.) Between 1899 and 1923, twenty-two volumes were published. In 1919, Hirschfeld founded the *Institut für Sexualwissenschaft* (Institute for Sexology) in Berlin, for research, counseling, and education. The institute collected thousands of case histories from individuals about their sexual relationships and practices. It was destroyed by the Nazis immediately after they came to power in Germany in 1933. See: Haeberle, Erwin J. (1981). Pink Triangle and Yellow Star: The Destruction of Sexology and the Persecution of Homosexuals in Nazi Germany. *Journal of Sex Research* 17(3): 270-287; Steakley, 1975: 30-62; Hoenig, J. (1977). Dramatis Personae: Selected Biographical Sketches of 19th Century Pioneers in Sexology. In John Money & Herman Musaph, Eds.,

Hirschfeld's theory of sexual variations was based on a general conception of sexual desire.[7] He depicted both the strength and direction of sexual desire as shaped by internal and external factors. The internal factors were biological substances and processes, while the external were environmental stimuli such as the attractiveness of the sexual object. The internal factors, he believed, far outweighed the external in shaping sexual desire.

The primary internal or biological factor was the strength of "inner secretions." Hirschfeld was one of the first sexologists to endorse the theory that sexual development and expression were determined by the differential secretion of female and male sex hormones.[8]

Sexual variation, he believed, could be traced to the presence in the individual of one sex of abnormally high amounts of the hormone of the opposite sex. He grafted to Krafft-Ebing's idea of brain centers in which sexual desire was localized, the notion that these centers were fed by massive amounts of sex hormones. This neurochemical interaction ultimately determined the intensity and direction of sexual desire. Hirschfeld believed there was great variation in the strength of sexual desire. Some individuals had practically none but then "there are individuals of both sexes with whom the barely satisfied desire is ever freshly reawakening" (Hirschfeld, 1947: 147). The direction of the desire had nothing to do with the strength of desire. Hirschfeld averred that both

---

Handbook of Sexology I: History and Ideology, 21-43; and Lauritsen, John and Thorstad, David (1974). *The Early Homosexual Rights Movement: 1864-1935*. New York: Times Change Press, 9-10. In 1897 he joined the effort to form the Wissenschaftlich-humanitäres Komitee, which was devoted to winning repeal of the German statutes prohibiting sodomy. In 1921, he organized the first Congress for Sexual Reform. Hirschfeld was the first president of the congress, and Ellis and Auguste Florel the next two presidents.

[7] Hirschfeld, Magnus (1947). *Sexual Pathology: A Study of Derangements of the Sexual Instinct*. Jerome Gibbs, Trans. New York: Emerson Books (originally published in three volumes). In the preface Hirschfeld stated that the first "Psychopathia Sexualis" appeared in Latin in 1844 and was written by Heinrich Kaan, a Ruthenian physician. Then Krafft-Ebing's book appeared in 1886. Hirschfeld viewed his own book on sexual pathology as the third in this series. While the first two books concentrated on individuals, his book intended to concentrate on pathological phenomena. The data for the book, he stated, were obtained in consultation with patients. The book was dedicated to the spirit of Krafft-Ebing.

[8] He was the first to name these hormones: for males it was **ANDRIN**; for females, **GYNEXIN**.

heterosexuals and homosexuals could be "uncommonly passionate, or possess only a weakly developed sexual urge. In the case of bisexual people, the degree to which they are attracted to the one sex or the other is usually widely different" (148).

Hormones influenced sexual development from its embryonic beginnings by determining "the age at which the germ cells and sexual centers start and end their function, which also awakens and enfeebles the other sexual characteristics which, until maturity, are present only in preliminary forms." The rhythm, or periodical rise and fall in sexual desire, was due to the "ebb and flood of sexual hormones" (153). External factors were of lesser importance: "The stronger the effect of the chemical inner stimulus upon the sexual centers, the less of an external nerve stimulus is needed for excitement" (153). When the internal "chemistry" for arousal was lacking, the individual had to lean more heavily on external stimulation. In effect, Hirschfeld formulated one of the first theories of the "chemistry of sex."

In 1913, Hirschfeld published his magnum opus, *Die Homosexualität*, which he intended to be a comprehensive summary of available knowledge of homosexuality.[9] His intersexual theory assumed that there

---

[9] Hirschfeld, Magnus (1913). *Die Homosexualität des Mannes und des Weibes*. In Iwan Bloch, Ed., *Handbuch der gesamten Sexualwissenschaft in Einzeldarstellungen*, III. Berlin: Louis Marcus. The volume is a one-thousand-page summary of all that was known about homosexuality from earliest recorded history. A volume (and the one cited hereafter) that included indices of names, places, and subjects was published a year later, in 1914. *Die Homosexualität* was divided into two sections: (1) Homosexuelle Männer und Frauen als Biologische Erscheinung and (2) Die Homosexualität des Mannes und des Weibes als soziologische Erscheinung. The first section, comprising twenty-three chapters, included several on the diagnosis of homosexuality in men and women based on biological, physical, and psychological evidence. There were also chapters distinguishing homosexuality from same-sex friendships, "pseudo-homosexuality," bisexuality, and homosexual horror of sexual contact with the opposite sex, as well as with hermaphroditism, gender confusion, and transvestism. In Chapter 19, Hirschfeld set forth his "Zwischenstufentheorie" of homosexuality as an intermediate stage of development. In Chapter 20, he considered the question of whether homosexuality was an Enthärtung [degeneracy], disease, or sexual variation. The last three chapters of this section were devoted to prognosis and treatment, one of which described his method of "adaptation therapy." The second section, comprising sixteen chapters, dealt with homosexuality in different regions of the world, including Asia and Eastern Europe. There were several chapters on various sociological and anthropological aspects of homosexuality as an organized or collective phenomenon.

was a continuum of sexual types extending from feminine heterosexual females to masculine heterosexual males, with "sexual anomalies" lying in between.[10]

Sexual types included homosexuals, transvestites, and hermaphrodites. What distinguished homosexuals from transvestites were the types of individuals they "fixated" on: homosexuals on their own sex, transvestites on members of the opposite sex who were atypical in manner and appearance: masculine females and feminine males.[11] This distinction between homosexuals and transvestites, on Hirschfeld's continuum, marked the transition from "heterosexual to homosexual love" (1948: 190). He based his intersexual theory on the hypothesis that bisexuality was a normal part of sexual development:

> [M]en possess feminine and women masculine characteristics not only in the physical and psychological sense, but also as regards the direction of the sexual impulse. In the course of development the characteristics of the opposite sex are outstripped by those of the individual's own sex. If this process does not occur normally, and the development of the sexual impulse is not consistent with the dominant physical and psychological characteristics, the individual so affected may be homosexual. (1948: 232)

---

[10] The following explication of Hirschfeld's theories is largely based on his *Sexual Anomalies: The Origins, Nature and Treatment of Sexual Disorders*. New York: Emerson Books, Inc., 1948. This is a posthumous publication, purportedly a summary of Hirschfeld's works compiled by his students (see title page). It was first published in England. Book 3 is devoted to "anomalies due to a deflection of the sexual impulse ... a deviation from normal direction" (xv). Unfortunately, this is the only summary of Hirschfeld's theories that now appears in the English language.

[11] Currently in human sexuality textbooks, transvestism refers to crossdressing, a person wearing the clothes ordinarily worn by the opposite sex, as a means of obtaining sexual gratification; see, e.g., Diamond, M. and Karlin, A. (1980). *Sexual Decisions*. Boston: Little, Brown, 507. It is generally assumed that most practitioners are heterosexual males. Hirschfeld coined the term *transvestism* and published a monograph on the subject: *Die Transvestiten*. Berlin: Pulvermacher, 1910. Both Haeberle (1981: 272) and Vern L. Bullough (1976: 644) claimed that Hirschfeld was homosexual. Bullough added that he was also transvestite. Haeberle reported that his financial independence provided against his rejection by medical colleagues.

The battle over sexual differentiation was never completely resolved in the lives of homosexuals so that the females were never fully feminine, the males fully masculine. This forestalling of a consolidated identity resulted in the irritability of the "nervous system," a condition Hirschfeld called "hysteroneurasthenia" (204). While he denied that homosexuals were "degenerates," he believed their condition was both congenital and abnormal:

> The relatives of homosexuals very frequently betray an unmistakable neuropathic disposition or characteristics which are known to be unfavorable to the stability of the nervous system in their descendants.... The assumption that Nature makes use of homosexuals to prevent degeneration is borne out by the marriages and descendants of homosexuals. Many of these marriages are childless, but when they are not, the children are mostly of inferior mentality, unless a particularly healthy partner in the marriage brings about a comparative compensation. At all events, from the viewpoint of race hygiene the marriage of a homosexual is a risky undertaking. (235-236)

The intersexual theory of Hirschfeld, like the "third sex" theory of Ulrichs, distinguished "homosexuals" as a unique human form:

> The nature of homosexuality is such that it is most intimately merged with the personality as a whole. Homosexuals of both sexes differ from heterosexuals not only as regards the different directions of the sexual impulse, but also as regards *the peculiar nature of their individualities....* Homosexuality is closely connected with the specific constitution of the personality as a whole, which may be defined as intersexual, since it is neither feminine nor masculine, and intersexuality is always combined with a neuropathic constitution. (1948: 232)

Hirschfeld classified homosexuals according to the characteristics of those to whom they were attracted (1948: 199-200). His major criterion was age. There were four categories of males: PEDOPHILES, those who seek boys below the age of puberty; EPHEBOPHILES, those attracted to youths from puberty to the early twenties; ANDROPHILES, who looked for persons between the early twenties and fifty; and GERONTOPHILES, who loved older, possibly senile men. The corresponding classifications for women were: GRAOPHILES, PATHENOPHILES, GYNECOPHILES, and COROPHILES. Beyond age, Hirschfeld believed that there was an endless variety of "homosexual tastes." He recognized that there were innumerable physical and personal criteria of attraction so that a classification system based on partner choice alone was limited.

He questioned the idea that homosexuals could be divided, on the basis of performance, into "actives" and "passives":

> Strictly speaking, all sexual intercourse is mutual and there is not exclusively active or passive partners; the two partners have intercourse "with each other," though it may be admitted that activity predominates in the one and passivity in the other. This applies with still greater force in the psychological sense. (1948: 194)

He believed that most homosexual intercourse consisted of mutual masturbation or tongue-genital contact. Anal and interfemoral intercourse were much less common. In both homosexual men and women, the anal or vaginal insertor was *never* the insertee. Anal intercourse, moreover, was rare because it is "so like normal intercourse" (198).

Still he assumed a "homosexual mentality" which was the crucial distinction between homosexuals and PSEUDOHOMOSEXUALS: "[T]hese latter are individuals who have physical contact with members of their own sex but lack the homosexual mentality (1948: 191).[12] Correspondingly, there was "pseudoheterosexuality," which marked those occasions when homosexuals had intercourse with the opposite sex: "all such acts are practically equivalent to masturbation" (1948: 192). There were few bisexuals, he believed; they were men and women who loved a type which could be found in either the female or male.

In considering treatment, Hirschfeld believed that "genuine homosexuality" could not be cured either through medical intervention or psychotherapy. It was, however, important that the physician should point out to those seeking treatment:

> that homosexuality is an innate drive, incurred through no fault of the patient, and is not a misfortune in and of itself, but rather becomes so as a result of the unjust evaluation which it comes up against, causing morally fine homosexuals (and we do not include only the abstinent) to suffer more wrong than they commit. (quoted in Katz, 1976: 151)[13]

---

[12] Iwan Block invented the concept and the word PSEUDOHOMOSEXUAL, which, although waning in popularity, is still current in psychiatric parlance.

[13] This quotation, and the following one dealing with treatment, are from an excerpt that appeared in Katz, Jonathan (Ed.) (1976). *Gay American History:*

Hirschfeld recommended various types of treatment. He wanted patients to have contact with homosexuals of "high intellectual callibre" (quoted in Katz, 1976: 152) through reading their books or actually meeting them. He warned, however, that the wish to "meet 'spiritually superior' people [could] be used as a pretext to look for sexual release" (152). Still, he suggested sexual activity as a way for patients to relax. Most important was that the physician provide advice for adjustment:

> [R]egular intensive work, whether manual or intellectual, is the most important condition for [the homosexual's] well-being. There are several reasons for this. First, any useful activity fills the existence of a person, it is an aim it itself; then it makes him forget his problems; further, he can prove his usefulness to himself and his family. And work is an anchor; if anything detrimental should happen, it gives on the inner strength needed, the belief in one's importance. (quoted in Katz, 1976: 153)

The major contribution of Ellis and Hirschfeld to the scientific discourse on sexual identity was to bestow medical authority upon Ulrichs' idea of the homosexual identity as a product of nature. In addition, Ellis' *Sexual Inversion* was the first book to disseminate the idea of a biological sexual identity in the English language. As Grosskurth observed, "Ellis was not the first to proclaim the organic nature of inversion, but he was the first person to write a book in English which treated homosexuality as neither a disease nor a crime" (1980: 185).[14]

There was little that was original in either Ellis' or Hirschfeld's conception of sexual identity. From the contemporary medical discourse they stitched together a conception of sexual identity as biologically determined. Ellis presented it as strictly bifurcated and wholly predetermined by nature. Hirschfeld, following in Ulrichs' footsteps, described various sexual identities, each one a point on a continuum stretching between the pure female and male heterosexual identities.

Lesbians and Gay Men in the U.S.A. New York: Thomas Y. Crowell, 151-153. The excerpt, which is very brief, is translated from Chapter 23, "Adaptations behandeln (Anpassung Therapie) der Homosexualität" in Hirschfeld (1913): 439-461.

[14] Ellis prepared three editions of *Sexual Inversion*. The first appeared in 1897, but only a few copies ever circulated. The second was published in 1901 and the third in 1915. The latter editions were published in the United States. We have treated the final edition, as reprinted in the Modern Library series, as definitive. It does not differ significantly from the earlier ones and has the advantage of considering the theories of Moll, Freud, and Hirschfeld.

To support a dichotomized view of sexual identity Ellis employed the concept of bisexuality for both explanatory and descriptive purposes. He used bisexuality to refer to an amorphous state of femaleness and maleness from which all sexual development originated. In this sense it was an explanation for the presence of both femininity and masculinity in adult females and males. Bisexuality was also used by Ellis as a distinct identity in the array of sexual identities that included the homosexual and heterosexual.

It was circular reasoning for Ellis to use the same concept as biological cause (or process) and a biological product. By collapsing the two meanings of bisexuality into a single conception of sexual identity, however, he was able to preserve the medical normalization of sexual relationships in which femininity was associated with female heterosexuality and masculinity with male heterosexuality. The association of femininity with male homosexuality and masculinity with female homosexuality could then be easily embraced.

The awkwardness of fitting together divergent meanings of bisexuality was evident in Ellis' shifting between qualitative and quantitative distinctions. Qualitatively the two identities were portrayed as entirely distinct and immutable. The bisexual identity, as a categorical distinction, he considered a facade for an essentially homosexual identity. Quantitatively the individual could be a mixture of the two identities, combining various proportions of female or male "germs," when, in the process of prenatal development, one biological sex failed to completely vanquish the other. Thus, it was apparently possible for an individual to "change" identities. For example, the person who was presumably 90% heterosexual, after suffering the pain and anguish of a dismal heterosexual romance, could turn to homosexuality for succorance. The homosexual identity, however, seemed more congealed than the heterosexual, because Ellis hardly suggested that the collapse of a homosexual relationship would send the individual flying off to heterosexuality. Presumably, Ellis believed that it was easier to fall from normality into abnormality than to reverse this process.

The homosexual identity, as depicted by Ellis, was merely an extension of biological endowment. The masculine tendencies of female inverts and feminine tendencies of male inverts could surface in almost any aspect of their lives: in their androgynous physical appearance, mannerisms, and speech; in their labile, nervous, narcissistic temperaments; in their easily triggered sexual precocity; in their heterogamous and homogamous choice of sexual partners and practices; and in their pursuit of vocations and avocations.

Sexual identity, as conceived by Hirschfeld, consisted of sexual instinct formed in an evolutionary process that included a basic bisexuality, localized in specific centers of the brain, and modulated by the sex hormones. As the major component, the sex hormones worked their influence on the other components to produce varied sexual identities, including those of the homosexual and transvestite. By linking his notion of hormonal influences to Moll's evolutionary concept of bisexuality and Krafft-Ebing's concept of localized cerebral sex centers, Hirschfeld was incorporating two etiological theories of the homosexual identity that were central to its pathologization.

In adding the theoretical influence of sex hormones, however, he was able to detoxicate the homosexual identity in two ways. First, as the product of an anomalous imbalance in hormonal secretions, it appeared less pathological than when attributed to biological atavism and tainted brains. Second, Hirschfeld could provide modern scientific trappings for Ulrichs' mystical notion of varied sexual types strung along a continuum stretching from pure femaleness to pure maleness. The individual's position on that continuum was determined by the relative balance in the secretion of female or male sex hormones. Within this scientistic formulation the heterosexual and homosexual identities could be viewed as distinct and continuous. As a natural extension of the heterosexual identity, the homosexual identity could share its aura of normality.

Having reformulated the concept of sexual identity, Hirschfeld could then argue that there were also "mentalities," "sexual practices," and patterns of relationships that corresponded to each identity. He could also speak of individuals who contracted sexual relationships that were antithetical to their basic biological identities as taking a pseudo-identity. In distinguishing between true and false sexual identities, he implied that it was mandatory for the individual to subscribe clearly to one identity or another.

The heterosexual and homosexual identities, as conceived by Ellis and Hirschfeld, lay at the core of the individual's make-up and social relationships. The most that psychotherapy could provide patients, troubled by their sexual desires, experiences, and relationships, was to assist them in searching for and, hopefully, finding their true sexual nature. For those who had taken on a false sexual identity, therapy could possibly help restore their true identity. For true homosexuals therapy could provide practical advice on how to deal with the instability caused by their incomplete feminine or masculine status and possibly with the social prejudice they had to confront. Therapy could also curb the homosexuals' inordinate sexual appetite so that the limits of social tolerance would not be unnecessarily tested and sexual energy could be diverted to creative and social uses.

The plea of Ellis and Hirschfeld for social tolerance of homosexuals was based on their belief that the homosexual identity represented a biological variation. Hirschfeld believed that the unhappiness that sometimes seemed to engulf the lives of homosexuals was due to a profound misunderstanding of their biological nature. Homosexuals did not choose to be abnormal. To conform to institutionalized forms of sexual relationships they would have to sacrifice sexual gratification, but even that could not make them heterosexual. Because the homosexual identity lay at the core of their being, this sacrifice would compromise their integrity as individuals and leave them with only a sham existence.

Although Ellis and Hirschfeld argued, for the toleration of homosexuals, they both invoked social propriety as the structural limit for homosexual relationships, thereby contributing to their normalization, Ellis and Hirschfeld argued, perhaps more eloquently than other contemporary medical writers that if homosexuals could not change themselves, then society should change by allowing them to exist side-by-side with heterosexuals. They never implied that society should foster the homosexual identity but only to recognize it as a fact of nature. By transferring the responsibility for change from the individual to society, Ellis and Hirschfeld were unknowingly laying the foundations for the idea of the social-cultural sexual identity.

The biological concept of sexual identity reflected the three cosmological views of the structure of sexual relationships. The polytheistic cosmology lay concealed in the belief of the biological theorists in the existence of multiple sexual identities, any one of which could determine an individual's relationships. Within the polytheistic cosmology one form of sexual relationships did not exclude the possibility of others; in effect, the individual could have several "sexual identities." In the formulations of the biological theorists, however, the individual was subsumed usually under a single sexual identity. To be a homosexual, for example, excluded the real possibility of being a heterosexual.

The monotheistic cosmology dominated the formulation of the idea of the biological sexual identity in both its heterosexual and homosexual forms. Basic to this cosmology was the rigid delineation of the two biological sexes. The silent, hovering assumption of all the biological theorists was that the basis of sexual relationships was the male-female design. Each sex had its own form and expression as ordained by Nature. The two forms existed as the anatomical male and the anatomical female. The natural expression of the male was his masculinity and of the female her femininity. In this design both form and expression were complementary. Apart from each other neither sex was complete. Nature provided a powerful force, sexual instinct, for uniting males and females. The two sexes, accompanied by their femininity or masculinity, under compelling instinctual influence, united in obedience to the reproductive imperative. The male-female design determined the course of the individuals' relationships; anatomy was destiny.

The depiction by the biological theorists of the homosexual identity lodged it firmly within the male-female design. Their theory of sexual identity, as we observed, accounted for variations within the parameters established by the two biological sexes. It assumed that true heterosexuals were purely feminine women or truly masculine men. Homosexuals were neither truly feminine nor truly masculine. Although they believed that male partners in homosexual relationships usually took both active and passive sexual roles, they implied that the partner who was psychologically more masculine more often took the inserter role. Even the belief in the fragility of the homosexual's general social adjustment seemed to imply that the peculiar amalgam of femininity and masculinity found in their characters was an instable compound that always threatened to dissolve into its basic biological units.

In this light the homosexual identity was more than a PERVERSION: it was an INVERSION. A perversion was a wrong turn, using sex for a defective purpose. Heterosexuals were perverts if they became absorbed in sexual activities that aborted their procreative mission. But homosexuals were INVERTS: they turned the basic male-female design inside out and upside down, substituting the same for the opposite biological sex. Perversion was taking a detour but inversion was driving against traffic. This perceived "reversal" of nature may explain why the homosexual identity became the centerpiece in the discourse on sexual perversion.

Even as inversion, however, the reference point in the definition of the homosexual identity was the heterosexual identity. The inevitable consequence of tying the two identities together was that the future normalization of homosexual relationships would require their reabsorption within the permissible structure of heterosexual relationships. Ulrichs, Kertbeny, Ellis, and Hirschfeld, as apologists for the homosexual identity, all subscribed to the belief that procreative heterosexual relationships were normative. The very idea of "normality" as a moral concept was a product of their age.[15]

In an effort to ground the idea of sexual identity in the scientific cosmology all the theorists assumed the existence of an organic sexual instinct. Under the influence of the somatic school of psychiatry, it was conceived as a powerful, consuming, physical force that determined whether the individual sought either female or male partners for sexual relationships. The theoretical debate over sexual identity never questioned the existence of the scientistic notion of sexual instinct. Rather, it consisted of questions about where and when the instinct originated, where in the body it situated itself, how its direction was influenced and perhaps derailed by endogenous or exogenous factors, and whether it was a unitary or complex phenomenon.

Ulrichs postulated the existence of feminine and masculine instincts that arose independently of the embryo's morphological sex. In the adult the biological instinct manifested itself as mental states that shaped the individual's attraction to either female or male sexual partners of particular physical qualities. Krafft-Ebing called the sexual instinct the VITA SEXUALIS, the sexual life, claiming that it combined both the organic impulse and emotional desire which shaped sexual relationships. So powerful a force needed to be physically housed in an important region of the human anatomy. Krafft-Ebing lodged the sexual instinct in centers located in the cerebral cortex. These centers served as switchboards for routing "psychic" and "organic" stimuli. Cerebral neurosis, his name for damaged psychosexual centers, resulted in the misdirection of sexual response, as in the case of antipathetic sexual instinct.

The environmental and evolutionary theorists also believed in the organic existence of a sexual instinct. What they questioned was its nature and the forces that shaped its expression. Binet, Schrenck-Notzing, and Prince, as environmental theorists, depicted the sexual instinct as malleable by such external factors as fortuitous learning, culture, and socialization. Moll depicted the sexual instinct as consisting of two component instincts, the physical detumescent drive that arose

---

[15] According to the *Oxford English Dictionary*, the word NORMAL derives from the Germanic and Old English and denotes something familiar or standard in measure. In 1840, it was used to refer to something conforming to a common type or standard. In 1849, it referred to positive normality or rightfulness. In 1871, it was applied to the mind in the sense of normal development and reactions. By 1890 it meant "model," as in normal school.

from an asexual stage of human evolutionary development and the psychological contrectation drive that arose from a bisexual stage.

Finally, the detoxicators of the biological homosexual identity, Ellis and Hirschfeld, partly echoing the theoretical stance of Ulrichs, reverted to the belief in an internally directed sexual instinct controlled by female or male germs or hormones. Like Ulrichs they sponsored the belief that the homosexual identity, however anomalous, was as much a creation of nature as was the heterosexual.

By welding together the male-female design of the monotheistic cosmology and the scientistic notion of sexual instinct, the theorists of the biological sexual identity portrayed both heterosexual and homosexual relationships as determined by biological mandate rather than individual choice. The pathologizers of the homosexual identity believed only heterosexuals could have true sexual relationships. The detoxicators believed that homosexuals could also, but only with other homosexuals.

It was the homosexual identity that was first considered problematic in the scientific discourse on sexual identity. The existence of the heterosexual identity was assumed but, with the exception of Moll, never systematically examined. However, as the discourse grew in volume and controversy, it raised questions and exposed assumptions about all forms of sexual relationships, including the heterosexual. An unwitting consequence of the discourse on the homosexual identity was the growing notion that the heterosexual identity was also problematic. The need to address the issue of why individuals entered heterosexual instead of homosexual relationships led to the transformation of the biological sexual identity into the psychological.

Part Two:

THE PSYCHOLOGICAL SEXUAL IDENTITY

8   The Creation of the Heterosexual Identity

In the medical discourse on sexual identity that preceded Freud, the existence of a normal heterosexual identity was taken for granted both by the creators and advocates of the homosexual identity, such as Ulrichs and Kertbeny, and by the psychiatrists who created the homosexual pathology. Freud assumed the leadership of those sexual theorists who considered heterosexuality problematic. He dismissed as untenable theories of sexual identity which provided one explanation for the existence of heterosexuals and another for homosexuals. His intention was to construct a unified theory of normal sexual development that would comprehensively explain sexual variation. In accomplishing this task, he unwittingly created the heterosexual identity and reconstituted the homosexual identity.

Freud's conception of the heterosexual identity was originally framed within a general theory of mental functioning, which has been referred to as the "topological" theory.[1] In the topological theory mental life was organized as three systems: the UNCONSCIOUS, the PRECONSCIOUS, and the CONSCIOUS. The UNCONSCIOUS was the first system to develop in the child. It consisted of elements which were "psychic representations" or verbal and nonverbal memory traces of what the child had experienced during the earliest months and years of life. These forgotten impressions and desires were either inaccessible to adult consciousness or retrieved only with difficulty. The Unconscious derived its energy from sexual instincts,

---

[1] Freud referred to the "topological" idea of mental organization in "The Ego and the Id" (*SE* 14, 1966: 1-66; originally published under the title *Das Ich und das Es* in the *Internationaler Psychoanalytischer* in 1923. In contrasting Freud's earlier topological theory with his later "structural theory," we have relied on the lucid discussion of Arlow, Jacob A. and Brenner, Charles (1964). *Psychoanalytic Concepts and the Structural Theory*. New York: International University Press: 1-113. The chapter also reflects the excellent study of Freud by Frank J. Sulloway (1979).

the goals of which were to satisfy the individual's sexual wishes. The Unconscious was viewed as infantile in nature, seeking instant gratification of its desires. As a reservoir of the psychic representations of past experience, the Unconscious, in silent, circuitous ways, influenced intentions and behavior throughout the individual's lifetime.

The **PRECONSCIOUS** was the system responsible for judging the exigencies of the moment and, accordingly, delaying and modulating gratification of wishes. Freud viewed it as the "adult" part of the mental apparatus. The Preconscious housed those memories which were accessible to consciousness. Before elements in the Unconscious could be retrieved they had to pass through the Preconscious. In this regard, the Preconscious acted as a bridge between the Unconscious and the Conscious systems in the individual's mental life.

The **CONSCIOUS** system embodied perception and included whatever was in the present focus of attention. It was noteworthy in Freud's topological theory, as in the later structural theory, that it was not the raw occurrence of experience that shaped the individual's mental life but what the person perceived as experience. Because the Conscious was the link between the individual and reality, all ingredients of the Unconscious and Preconscious were originally conscious perceptions in the individual's life history.

Within the topological theory Freud postulated the existence of a process of censorship which could either retain memories in the Unconscious or release them into the Preconscious. This censorship acted through repression, a process of withdrawing energy (or cathexis) from a memory trace and thereby keeping it in the Unconscious. For a memory trace to be released into the Preconscious it would have to be associated with some verbal representation. In fact, psychoanalysis, as a therapeutic procedure employing free association by the patient, involves the process of word cathexis, in which energy is invested in memory traces in order to retrieve them from the Unconscious. Even without psychoanalytic intervention, memory traces, in the form of repressed wishes for sexual gratification, could intrude into the Preconscious in the form of neurotic symptoms, often making sexual experience more anxious than gratifying.

In 1905, within the framework of the topological theory, Freud formulated his theory of sexual instinct and development.[2] Freud

---

[2] The original work was published in 1905 under the title, *Drei Abhandlungen zur Sexualtheorie*. It appeared in English in the *Standard Edition* under the title, *Three Essays on a Theory of Sexuality* (Freud, 1905/1966).

accepted Moll's biogenetic theory "that an originally bisexual physical disposition has, in the course of evolution, become modified into a unisexual one, leaving behind only a few traces of the sex that has become atrophied" (1905/1966: 141)[3]

Like Moll, he observed that this theory was supported by the evidence that a certain degree of "hermaphroditism" (141) survived in the normal genitalia of the female and male. However, he rejected the notion that there was an anatomical hermaphroditism that extended beyond the obvious correspondence of the genitalia of the two sexes:

> The theory of bisexuality has been expressed in its crudest form by a spokesman of the male inverts [i.e., Ulrichs]: "a feminine brain in a masculine body." But we are ignorant of what characterizes a feminine brain. There is neither need nor justification for replacing the psychological problem by an anatomical one. Krafft-Ebing's attempted explanation seems to be more exactly framed than that of Ulrichs but does not differ from it in essentials. According to Krafft-Ebing ... every individual's bisexual disposition endows him with masculine and feminine brain centers as well as with somatic organs of sex; these centers develop only at puberty, for the most part under the influence of the sex-gland, which is independent of them in the original disposition. But what has just been said of masculine and feminine brains applies equally to masculine and feminine "centers"; and incidentally we have not even grounds for assuming that certain areas of the brain ("centers") are set aside for the functions of sex, as in this case, for instance, with those of speech. (1905/1966: 142)

The sexual instinct or LIBIDO, in Freud's sexual theory, was a continual flow of internal energy that all individuals possessed as part of their biological endowment. He viewed the libido as an appetite, a sexual "hunger," corresponding to the "hunger" for food. Like Moll, he believed that it consisted of several parts: "It appeared ... that since the original [sexual] disposition is necessarily a complex one, the sexual instinct itself must be something put together from various factors, and that in the perversions it falls apart, as it were, into its components"

---

[3] Freud did not credit Moll with this theory because of the enmity between the two men owing, according to Sulloway (1979: 299), to Moll's published repudiations of psychoanalysis.

(1905/1966: 231). This variegated constitutional disposition Freud described as "polymorphous perverse."

In children the libido could be aroused by many forms of chance contact, such as touching, holding, fondling, and kissing. In the process of sexual development the original diffusion of potential stimulation became organized around three principal centers of arousal, which he called erogenous zones: the oral, the anal, and the genital. This organization occurred in three successive stages, each bearing the name of the dominant zone:

> We found from the study of neurotic disorders that beginnings of an organization of the sexual instinctual components can be detected in the sexual life of children from its very beginning. During a first, very early phase, *oral eroticism* occupies most of the picture. A second of these pregenital organizations is characterized by the predominance of sadism and *anal eroticism*. It is not until a third phase has been reached that the *genital zones* proper contribute their share in determining sexual life, and in children this last phase is developed only so far as to a primacy of the phallus (emphasis added). (1905/1966: 233)[4]

According to Freud's sexual theory, in "normal" development the center of stimulation evolved from the oral to the anal zone and finally to the genital zone, the organizational phase of genital primacy. At this level most oral and anal stimulation was substantially relinquished for the "richer" gratification attainable through the penis or vagina:

> We were then obliged to recognize as one of our most surprising findings, that this early efflorescence of infantile sexual life (between the ages of two and five) already gives rise to the choice of an [love] object, with all the wealth of mental activities which such a process involves. Thus, in spite of the lack of synthesis between the different instinctual components and the uncertainty of the sexual aim, the phase of development

---

[4] The three stages should more properly be called oral, anal, and *phallic* (See Brenner, Charles (1955). *An Elementary Textbook of Psychoanalysis*. New York: International University Press, 20ff.). The third phase Freud later called *phallic* because he assumed, during that stage, that the penis was the center of interest for either the boy or girl and that the girl's chief source of libidinal pleasure was the clitoris, the female analogue of the penis. Brenner explained that the term "genital phase," in a strict sense, applied only to adolescence and adulthood, the periods during which orgasm occurred.

corresponding to that period must be regarded as an important precursor of the subsequent final sexual organization. (1905/1966: 234)

The sexual instinct, within Freud's theory, did not originally serve the purpose of reproduction. Its aim was gratification and its earliest manifestation in infancy was autoerotic, utilizing any erogenous zone of the body. If the child's training were neglected and the autoeroticism not circumvented, the sexual instinct would later be uncontrollable and unserviceable: "In its development the sexual instinct passes from autoeroticism to object-love and from the autonomy of the erotogenic zones to the subordination of these under the primacy of the genitals, which come into the service of procreation" (1908: 26-27).[5]

Freud believed that the boundaries imposed by culture on the expression of sexual instinct had become progressively more restrictive. The historical development paralleled the psychological development of the sexual instinct in the child from the polymorphous perverse to genital primacy. In the first stage the culture allowed the sexual instinct expression which did not lead to procreation. In the second or "civilized" stage the only expression of sexual impulse allowed was that which served procreation. In the third stage, toward which civilization was progressing, procreation only within the institution of monogamy would be allowed. The extravagant price humans paid for the sexual abstinence required by the latter stages could cause much misery:

> Under those conditions the number of strong natures who openly rebel will be immensely increased; and likewise the number of weaker natures who take refuge in neurosis owing to their conflict between the double pressure from the influences of civilization and their own rebellious constitutions. (1908: 30)

Freud posed this dilemma:

> We may thus well raise the question whether our "civilized" sexual morality is worth the sacrifice which it imposes upon us, the more so if we are still so insufficiently purged of hedonism as to include a certain degree of individual happiness among the aims of our cultural development. (1908: 40)

---

[5] Freud, Sigmund (1908/1963). "Civilized" Sexual Morality and Modern Nervous Illness. *SE* 9: 177-204. We have cited the translation in a 1963 collection of Freud's papers entitled *Sexuality and the Psychology of Love*. Philip Rieff, Ed. New York: Collier Books.

The course of normal sexual development was charted by libidinal pitfalls. Therefore, Freud's theory of normal sexual development was based on a theory of perversion. To suggest the myriad paths down which the sexual instinct could travel, Freud introduced two new terms: sexual object and sexual aim: "Let us call the person from whom the sexual attraction precedes the *sexual object* and the act towards which the instinct tends the *sexual aim*" (1905/1966: 135-136). These terms allowed the object to be either female or male and the act to consist of the stimulation of any erogenous zone. The implied flexibility of both object and aim was based on his assumption of the bisexuality or polymorphous perverse capacity with which individuals were congenitally endowed.

In the normal course of sexual development, ending in genital primacy, memory traces of pregenital forms of stimulation were repressed in the Unconscious. In many individuals, however, the mechanism of repression failed and allowed remnants of collateral forms of sexual gratification to re-emerge. When these recollections of infantile gratification penetrated into the Conscious and were repeated by individuals as willful acts of sexual gratification, Freud viewed the practitioners as perverted. When memory traces penetrated only into the Preconscious, and attempts at gratification were inhibited or conflicted, the practitioners were viewed as neurotic. Because the neurotic individual unconsciously wished for the same form of sexual gratification in which the perverted individual actually engaged, Freud concluded that neurosis was the negative or reverse side of perversion:

> We found that in them [i.e., the neurotics] tendencies to every kind of perversion can be shown to exist as unconscious forces and betray their presence as factors leading to the formation of symptoms. It was thus possible to say that neurosis is, as it were, the negative of perversion. (1905/1966: 231)

By interrelating the physical and the psychical, Freud preserved both the congenital and acquired origins of sexual perversion. It was congenital because the libido was part of biological inheritance; it was acquired in the process of psychosexual development. In Freud's own words:

> The conclusion now presents itself to us that there is indeed something innate lying behind the perversions but that it is something innate in everyone, though as a disposition it may vary in its intensity and may be increased by the influences of actual life. (1905/1966: 171)

To account for sexual development that did not stabilize as adult genital primacy, Freud used the concepts of instinctual regression and fixation. **INSTINCTUAL REGRESSION** referred to the process in which the libidinal wishes of childhood remained charged with energy in the Unconscious system. In neurosis these wishes broke into the Preconscious system, causing a change in the equilibrium between the two systems.

FIXATION referred to the stages in sexual development to which the libido regressed. In obsessional neurosis, for example, the libido regressed to the anal stage. Fixation could also refer to the pregenital mode of sexual gratification in which the libido was stuck. In this latter sense, fixation accounted for arrested development. To some degree every individual's sexual development was viewed by Freud as subject to Unconscious instinctual regression. He saw fixation, however, to either infantile sexual wishes or modes of gratification, as implying the presence of perversion or neurosis.[6]

Inversion, in Freud's sexual theory, was one among several possible perversions. He referred to persons for whom the sexual object was their own sex as **KONTRARSEXUALE** (contrarysexuals) but preferred to call them **INVERTIERTE** (inverts) and their relationships "**DIE INVERSION.**" In the inverted object choice, the aim of the libido was to establish sexual relations with an "object" of the same sex. As one piece in the mosaic of sexual perversions, inversion stood closer to normal sexual attraction than other perversions because it involved the love of a partner rather than merely self-love and genital rather than only peripheral sexual stimulation.

According to Freud there were degrees of inversion: (1) the absolutely inverted, those who were attracted exclusively to individuals of their own biological sex; (2) the half-inverted (*"amphigen invertier"*) who were indifferently (*"ebenssowohl"*) attracted to either sex; and (3) the contingently inverted, who were attracted to their own sex only under special circumstances. There were also various temporal patterns in the occurrence of sexual inversion: a consistent pattern lasting a lifetime; an isolated episode occurring in an overall pattern of attraction to individuals of the opposite sex; a pattern than fluctuated between attraction to one sex and the other; or a pattern of reversal in which attraction to the opposite sex was redirected to individuals of the same sex.

Although he maintained that libido was the congenital contribution to human sexuality, Freud rejected the notion that sexual inversion was

---

[6] For a fuller explanation of the processes of libidinal regression and fixation, see Brenner, Charles (1955) and subsequent revisions.

entirely innate. His major objection to congenital theory was that it accounted differently for "absolute inverts" than for the partially inverted: He wrote:

> The very existence of the two other classes, and especially the third [the contingent inverts], is difficult to reconcile with the hypotheses of the innateness of inversion. This explains why those who support this view tend to separate out the group of absolute inverts from all the rest, thus abandoning any attempt at giving an account of inversion which shall have universal application. In the view of these authorities inversion is innate in one group of cases, while in others it may have come about in other ways. (1905/1966: 139)

Freud was, therefore, among the first theorists who did not separate acquired from congenital inversion. He did, however, reject the idea of a congenital "third sex" in favor of the idea of innate bisexuality. Freud held that "without taking bisexuality into account, I think it would scarcely be possible to arrive at an understanding of the sexual manifestations observed in men and women" (1905/1966: 220).

In constructing the psychological etiology of homosexual object choice, he endorsed the idea of the homosexual personal identity. In his treatise on Leonardo da Vinci, Freud referred to male followers of Ulrichs' view as representing a sexual identity:

> Homosexual men, who have in our times taken vigorous action against the restrictions imposed by law on their sexual activity, are fond of representing themselves, through their spokesmen, as being from the outset a distinct sexual species, as an intermediate sexual stage, as a "third sex." They are, they claim, men who are innately compelled by organic determinants to find pleasure in men and have been debarred from obtaining it from women. Much as one would be glad on grounds of humanity to endorse their claims, one must treat their theories with some reserve, for they have been advanced without regard for the psychical genesis of homosexuality. (1910/1964: 98-99)[7]

---

[7] Freud, Sigmund (1910/1955) Leonardo da Vinci and a Memory of His Childhood. *SE* 11: 59-137. (This study was originally published as *Eine Kinderheitserinnerung des Leonardo da Vinci*. Vienna: Deuticke, 1910.)

His conviction that homosexuals and heterosexuals were not distinct forms of humanity was reiterated in the famous footnote he added to *Drei Abhandlungen zur Sexualtheorie* in 1915:

> Psycho-analytic research is most decidedly opposed to any attempt at separating off homosexuals from the rest of mankind as a group of special character. By studying sexual excitations other than those that are manifestly displayed, it has found that all human beings are capable of making a homosexual object-choice and have in fact made one in their unconscious. Indeed, libidinal attachments to persons of the same sex play no less a part as factors in normal mental life, and a greater part as a motive force for illness, than do similar attachments to the opposite sex. On the contrary, psycho-analysis considers that a choice of an object independent of its sex—freedom to range equally over male and female objects—as it is found in childhood, in primitive states of society and early periods of history, is the original basis from which, as a result of restriction in one direction or the other, both the normal and the inverted types develop. Thus from the point of view of psycho-analysis the exclusive sexual interest felt by men for women is also a problem that needs elucidating and is not a self-evident fact based upon an attraction that is ultimately of a chemical nature. A person's final sexual attitude is not decided until after puberty and is the result of a number of factors, not all of which are yet known; some are of a constitutional nature but others are accidental. No doubt a few of these factors may happen to carry so much weight that they influence the result in their sense. But in general the multiplicity of determining factors is reflected in the variety of manifest sexual attitudes in which they find their issue in mankind. (1905/1966: 145n-146n)

In the original formulation of his sexual theory, Freud believed that the component sexual instincts included feelings of love, the drive to propagate, and nongenital forms of sexual pleasure. In 1910 he distinguished between the sexual instincts and the self-preserving or ego instincts, which were manifested by aggression, hatred and destruction.[8]

---

[8] Freud, Sigmund (1910/1957). The Psycho-Analytic View of Psychogenic Disturbance of Vision. *SE* 11: 210-218.

Certain forms of behavior appeared to originate in both ego and sexual instincts. Homosexuality, for example, as an expression of libido provided sexual pleasure, but as ego instinct appeared to be directed toward oneself through the medium of another person of the same sex. In sadism, even more tellingly, sexual pleasure was derived by one partner from inflicting pain on the other. Such behavior, according to Freud, demonstrated that, although both deriving from the libido, sexual and ego instincts could have opposing aims.

To explain such contradictions in his libidinal theory, Freud in 1920 developed the dualistic theory of mental functioning based on the concepts of life instinct ("EROS") and death instinct ("THANATOS").[9]

The mental life of individual was a constant struggle between the forces of life and death. The life instinct now combined the sexual and ego instincts of the older theory. The pleasurable aims of the libido could now be directed toward the self (e.g., as sexual pleasure) or toward others. As life instinct the libido gave rise to new life though the act of reproduction. Love of self and others were united in the life instinct.

The death instinct contained the destructive impulses of mental functioning: to separate and cause conflict between females and males, reduce complex forms of relationships to earlier and simple forms, evade the demands of reality, and dwell on the traumas of the past.

As observed by Sulloway (1979: 403), both forms of instincts were conservative, the life instinct to its beginnings through the reproductive cycle, the death instinct to the primeval conditions out of which mankind developed. Pleasure or "unpleasure" were not the monopoly of either life or death instincts. Sexual instincts, as an example of the life instinct, gave rise to the unpleasurable tension and excitement that preceded gratification. The desire to return to the simplicity of childhood, an example of the death instinct, promised the pleasure of tranquility and protection. Mental life, according to Freud, was struggle between the forces of life and death, each of which doles out quantities of pleasure and pain.

Within this dualistic instinct theory it was possible to take another look at sexual perversion. No longer could it be viewed as the simple derailment of libidinal development because it possibly combined both the life and death instincts. Sadomasochism, for example, joined the destructive impulses of the death instinct to the sexual impulses of life

---

[9] Freud, Sigmund (1920/1966a). Beyond the Pleasure Principle. *SE* 19: 3-64. In his 1914 *On Narcissism: An Introduction* (*SE* 14: 69-102), Freud originally made the distinction between self-love and object-love.

instinct. In a similar vein, the homosexual identity expressed both the ego and object sexual drives of the life instinct but could also represent the destructive thrust of the death instinct if it could be shown that it was a product of disharmony between the two sexes, hate disguised as love, and reenactments of childhood traumas. By making love and hate polar opposites, Freud's new theory had the remarkable advantage of acknowledging the importance of sexual pleasure while pointing to its penumbra of death and destruction.

With this revision of his theory of instincts Freud was able to develop a general theory of mental functioning that was no longer primarily based on conceptions of neurosis and perversion.[10] The new formulation by Freud has been called the structural theory. The topological theory divided mental functioning between conscious and unconscious processes. The conceptualization divided the mental apparatus between three processes dealing with the inner world of instinctual drives and the outer world of realistic demands.[11]

Whereas the focus in the topological theory was the relative equilibrium established between unconscious and conscious functions, in the structural theory the emphasis was on the resolution of conflict among the components of the mental apparatus. Structural theory divided the mental apparatus into three parts: the id, the ego, and the superego. The ID was where the memory traces and fantasies of instinctual gratification resided. It drew upon two sources of energy: libidinal energy derived from the life instinct and aggressive energy derived from the death instinct. Among the memory traces of the id were those associated with sexual gratification with the self (e.g., masturbation) and with another person of the same sex. Because the life and death instincts worked together in a dynamic tension, any act motived by the id contained both erotic and destructive elements.

In the new structure of the mental apparatus the id was at the core of the Unconscious. In itself the id was unaffected by the vicissitudes of experience, although it acted as the repository of both individual and phylogenetic memory. The sole aim of the id was to obtain immediate gratification of instinctual wishes along with their associated fantasies

---

[10] Freud sketched the outlines of the structural theory in *The Ego and The Id*, originally published in 1923. In calling the new theory "structural," we are following the terminology of Arlow and Brenner (1964).
[11] Arlow and Brenner (1964) described the reasons for Freud's theoretical shift more fully than is appropriate here.

and memory traces. By retaining the libido within in the id, Freud was able to incorporate his sexual theory within the structural theory.

Both the EGO and the SUPEREGO, in developmental juxtaposition, evolved from the id. In the beginning of the child's mental life the id constituted the entire mental apparatus. Part of the id, however, consisted of the child's ability to perceive opportunities for instinctual gratification and to manipulate the environment so that those opportunities could be exploited. Arlow and Brenner called these aspects of the id its perceptual and executant functions(1964: 34). From these functions the ego evolved. Freud, borrowing from a philosophical tradition in which the ego stood for the self, defined the ego as that part of the mind which perceived the external world and consciously channeled instinctual energy toward the gratification of its aims.

In the process of development the ego exercised a moderating influence on the id:

> [t]he ego seeks to bring the influence of the external world to bear upon the id and its tendencies, and endeavors to substitute the reality principle for the pleasure principle which reigns unrestrictedly in the id.... The ego represents what may be called reason and common sense, in contrast to the id, which contains the passions. (*SE*, 1923/1966: 25)

Freud compared the ego to the horseback rider and the id to the horse. When the horse knew where it wanted to go, the best rider could do was to guide it in the desired direction: "so in the same way the ego is in the habit of transforming the id's will into action as if it were a part of its own" (Freud *SE, 1923/1966*, 25).[12]

The superego was that component of the mental structure in which the image of the ideal self and moral precepts resided. Freud viewed the superego as evolving from the ego as a result of the "demolition" of the Oedipus complex, a process through which the child identified with one of the parents. Identification chiefly involved the child's taking on moral beliefs, particularly of the parent with whom the identification had occurred.

---

[12] The reality principle, in the topological theory, was the "principle" that regulated the preconscious and conscious systems. The pleasure principle regulated the demands of the unconscious libido. See Freud, Sigmund (1911/1966). Formulations of the Two Principles of Mental Functioning. *SE* 12: 213-226.

The id, ego, and superego could function in harmony or in conflict. The id and ego were harmonious when the ego confined its function to orchestrating the satisfaction of impulses rising from the id. Conflict between the id and the ego broke out when the ego attempted to delay, modify, or frustrate gratification of instinctual impulses. The ego and superego worked in harmony when the ego attempted to delay, modify, or frustrate gratification of instinctual impulses, or when the ego blocked instinctual gratification in accordance with the moral precepts of the superego. They came into conflict when the ego's cooperation with the id allowed the gratification of impulses that were contrary to the moral dicta of the superego. In this latter instance, the superego retaliated against the ego by causing the ego to feel guilt and remorse.

The central psychological event in the genesis of the individual's personal sexual identity was the resolution of the oedipal complex. In 1910, in his psychohistorical analysis of the sexual development of Leonardo da Vinci and before the oedipal complex was fully delineated within the framework of structural theory, Freud asserted that the basis of the male homosexual identity was psychological, arising from a very intense attachment of the male child to his mother. He also averred that "this attachment was evoked or encouraged by too much tenderness on the part of the mother herself, and further reinforced by the small part played by the father during ... (the boy's) childhood" (1910/1964: 99).[13] In Freud's judgment it was the absence of the masculine presence of the father rather than any undue masculinity in the mother that could lead to the boy's acquisition of the homosexual identity.

Freud believed that the boy's passionate love for his mother was repressed in the Unconscious through a process of identification: "he puts himself in her place, identifies with her, and takes his own person as a model in whose likeness he chooses the new objects of his love. In this way he becomes a homosexual" (1910/1964: 100). Thus the process of identification also involved narcissism.[14] The partners pursued by the

---

[13] Freud believed his own psychoanalytic investigations of this mother-child attachment were confirmed by his fellow analysts, Isidor Sadger, Wilhelm Stekel, and Sándor Ferenczi.

[14] At the time he wrote the da Vinci treatise, Freud had not developed the concept of narcissism, but did so in his *On Narcissism* (1914/1966). Later he observed that the break-up of love affairs was often followed by the individual identifying with the former lover and then redirecting the libido to a partner whose sex was the opposite of that of the lover. See Freud, Sigmund

adult male homosexual were really revivals of himself in childhood, "boys whom he loves in the way in which his mother loved him when he was a child" (1910/1964: 100).

By repressing his love for his mother, the 'homosexual remained faithful to her throughout his adulthood. His pursuits of males was really a running away from females who threatened his sexual fidelity to his mother. His homosexual identity was not the result of the absence of heterosexual desire:

> In individual cases direct observation has ... enabled us to show that the man who gives the appearance of being susceptible only to the charms of men is in fact attracted by women in the same way as a normal man; but on each occasion he hastens to transfer the excitation he has received from women on to a male object, and in this manner he repeats over and over again the mechanism by which he acquired his homosexuality. (1910/1964: 100)

In his development of structural theory, particularly in providing a theoretical basis for the origin of the superego, Freud more fully rendered his conceptualization of the Oedipus complex. Focusing first on the male child, he described how the complex emerged:

> At a very early age the little boy develops an object-cathexis [erotic attachment] for his mother, which originally related to the mother's breast ...; the boy deals with his father by identifying himself with him. For a time these two relationships proceed side by side, until the boy's sexual wishes in regard to his mother become more intense and his father is perceived as an obstacle to them; from this the Oedipus complex originates. (1923/1966: 31-32)

The boy's relationship with the father grew hostile and was transformed into a desire to get rid of the father and take the father's place with the mother. From this point the son's relationship with his father was ambivalent: through identification with the father the boy maintained his positive feelings toward him through rivalry with his father to be the mother's lover, the boy had negative feelings toward him. Thus the content of the Oedipus complex in the boy consisted of ambivalence toward the father and love for the mother.

(1920/1966b). Psychogenesis of a Case of Homosexuality in a Woman. *SE* 18: 146-172.

The Oedipus complex, in Freud's formulation, occurred during the phallic period of the child's sexual development. The boy's masturbation during this period was excited by the intensity of his triadic relationship with his parents. In fact, the male's continued practice of masturbation during the adult years Freud attributed to this early oedipal drama.[15]

The Oedipus complex, according to Freud, offered the boy two avenues of sexual satisfaction, both centering on the penis, which during the phallic period was the focus of the most intense erotic sensations. The "active" or masculine option was to put himself in his father's place and engage in intercourse with his mother as his father did. The "passive" or feminine option was to put himself in his mother's place and engage in intercourse with his father.[16]

The exercise of either option could cost the little boy his penis. Freud believed that the boy was motivated to "dissolve" the Oedipus complex by the fear of castration. This fear was elicited by the knowledge that females, including mother and sisters, did not possess a penis. Freud believed that the boy had one of two reactions to the full realization of the fact that females lacked penises: horror of females as mutilated creatures or contempt for them. Either of these reactions, if they became fixed, could contribute to heterosexual or homosexual object choice. The fear of castration led to the conflict "between his narcissistic interest in that part of his body and the libidinal cathexis of his parental objects" (1924/1966: 176).

The heterosexual or homosexual identity was the product of the child's surrendering his libidinal attachment to the mother and thereby saving himself from castration at the hands of his father. By giving up the libidinal cathexis to the mother, Freud held that the boy "destroyed" the Oedipus complex.[17]

The son's surrender of his maternal attachment could occur either by identifying with the mother or intensifying his identification with the father. Freud believed the second was the expected path: "We are accustomed to regard the latter outcome as more normal; it permits the affectionate relation to the mother to be in a measure retained. In this

---

[15] Freud, Sigmund (1924/1966). The Dissolution of the Oedipus Complex. *SE* 19: 172-179.

[16] The implication of the passive option is that the boy surrendered his penis as the precondition of engaging in intercourse with the father.

[17] Freud sometimes preferred "demolished" in *The Ego and The Id* (1923/1966: 32 ff.) and "abolished" or "destroyed" in his later essay on the Oedipus complex (1924/1966).

way the dissolution of the Oedipus complex would consolidate the masculinity in the boy's character" (1923/1966: 32). By "normal" Freud meant that the child took the route to the heterosexual identity. By choosing the first path, that is, destroying the Oedipus complex by identifying with the mother, the boy followed the course leading to the adult homosexual identity.

In Freud's oedipal theory both the vicissitudes of experience and an innate bisexuality conspired to produce either a heterosexual or homosexual dissolution of the Oedipus complex. The vicissitudes of experience consisted of such fateful accidents as having a father who was hostile, distant, unrelated or absent, a mother who emotionally clung to the child, or a mother who was uncommonly masculine. Vicissitudes could also consist of the fateful confluence of events such as the birth of a sibling at the same time the child was caught in the emotional grip of the oedipal drama.

The dissolution of the complex was also preconditioned by the innate bisexuality of the child: "It would appear ... that in both sexes the relative strength of the masculine and feminine sexual disposition is what determines whether the outcome of the oedipal situation shall be an identification with the father or the mother" (1923/1966: 33). The child's congenital bisexuality complicated the oedipal picture by adding both a positive and negative component. The positive component, in Freud's judgment, was the son's love-attachment to the mother and a corresponding ambivalence toward the father-rival. The negative component was his loving attitude toward his father and the corresponding feelings of jealousy and hostility toward the mother-rival.

In the case of the son, a strong feminine component could predispose him to identify with the femininity of the mother and thereby develop a homosexual identity. The little boy, for whom the appropriate parental relationship and biological predisposition fortuitously combined in harmony, would experience a dissolution of the Oedipus complex that ushered him into heterosexual manhood:

> It is only in male children that there occurs the fateful conjunction of love for one parent [the mother] and the hatred of the other [the father] as rival. It is thereupon the discovery of the possibility of castration, as evidenced by the sight of the female genital, which necessitates the transformation of the boy's Oedipus complex, leads to the creation of the superego

and thus initiates all the processes that culminate in enrolling the individual in civilized society. (1932/1961: 284)[18]

Freud initially assumed that there were parallel destructions of the Oedipus complex for both boys and girls.[19] What had been called the Oedipus complex for the boys was called the Electra complex for the girls.[20] When Freud fully addressed the subject of female sexual development, however, he rejected this idea, postulating that the oedipal resolution for girls was much more hazardous than for boys. The girl's task involved two substitutions in her forward march toward the feminine and heterosexual identity. For her, as for the boy, the mother was the first object of love. The little girl had to give up the father for whom she later must substitute another man.

The boy surrendered the mother to save his penis but what motives did the little girl have especially when her biological and cultural destiny was to become a mother herself? To answer this question it was necessary to conceptualize a preoedipal period in the child's psychosexual development.

According to Freud, the preoedipal phase in females was masculine and homosexual in character. The little girl believed that both she and the mother whom she loved had phalluses. It was also a period in which the girl engaged in clitoral masturbation, the clitoris being her obvious claim to a penis.[21] If the girl was to give up the masculinity and infantile homosexuality of the preoedipal period, she had to change the sex of her love-object from female to male, which she did by switching her affections from mother to father.

---

[18] Freud, Sigmund (1932/1961). Female Sexuality. *SE* 21: 223-243. (The article first appeared in the *International Journal of Psycho-Analysis 13:* 281-297.)

[19] See Freud (1923/1966: 32). His new position was adumbrated in two articles: (1) Freud, Sigmund (1925/1966). Some Psychical Consequences of the Anatomical Distinction between the Sexes. *SE* 19: 243-258; and (2) "Female Sexuality" (1932/1961).

[20] Oedipus, in Greek legend, unknowingly fulfilled the prophecy that he would kill his father Laius, King of Thebes, and marry his mother Jocasta. Oedipus, however, did not know at the time that the man he murdered was his father. Electra was much more malevolent. According to legend she had persuaded her brother Orestes to kill their mother, Clytemnestra, and her mother's lover, presumably because of her love for her father, Agamemnon.

[21] One is led to assume that if the girl had the opportunity to see her brother's preoedipal penis, it would be larger than her clitoris but small enough by adult standards to support her phallic fantasies about herself.

To effect this transfer the girl had to acknowledge that she had no penis, that, in effect, she was a castrated individual. She developed an envy for the penis that had several psychological consequences. First it wounded her narcissism; like a scar, the lack of the penis was a mark of inferiority. Later she had to realize that she shared this anatomical defect with all women and that it was not the result of personal punishment. At that point, Freud averred that "the woman begins to share the contempt felt by men for a sex which is lesser in so important a respect, and, at least in holding that opinion, insists on being like a man" (1925/1966: 253). Second, penis-envy was replaced by the character trait of jealousy, which in Freud's judgment, was a more powerful emotion in women than in men. Third, the girl's relationship with the mother as the love object was loosened because the mother was held responsible for sending her daughter into the world ill-equipped. Finally, and perhaps most devastatingly, the little girl had to acknowledge that the clitoris was inferior as an organ to the penis. Freud attributed what he believed to be a greater repugnance to masturbation in women to the discovery of the inferiority of the clitoris.

The little girl's acknowledgement of her castration was the major event in the prehistory of her Oedipus complex. Freud stated: "Whereas in boys the Oedipus complex is destroyed by the castration complex, in girls it is made possible and led up to by the castration complex" (1925/1966: 256). The difference, he asserted, was between a castration threatened (i.e., in the case of the boys) and actually "enacted" (i.e., in the case of the girls). Freud described several motives for the girl to abandon the preoedipal for the oedipal phase of her development: her anger over the perception that her mother never provided her a penis, "the only proper genital organ" (1932/1961: 289); her mother never fed her enough and never returned her love; and her mother even interfered with her clitoral masturbation.[22]

---

[22] See Fenichel, Otto (1930/1953). The Pregenital Antecedents of the Oedipus Complex. In *Collected Papers 1*: 181-204. New York: Norton, 1953. (First published in 1930.) Fenichel listed several aspects of the preoedipal period and their oedipal replacements: (1) prohibitions of masturbation were replaced by the oedipal prohibitions; (2) the loss of the mother's breast and of feces, with the dread of castration; (3) pregenital relations with the father, by the love of the father; (4) mother's breast and feces, by the idea of the penis; (5) the desire for a penis, by a wish for a child; and (6) oral incorporation, by the conception of coitus (184).

Accepting the cruel fact that she had no penis of her own, the girl had to deal with her envy of the male sex, so wondrously equipped. She did this by turning to her father, who, as the love object who replaced the mother, could at least supply (i.e., loan) his own penis. But such an affair with her father was only going to antagonize further her mother whom the little girl already hated and despised and must now learn to fear. It was also hopeless, because her father would not accept her as a replacement for the mother. Realizing that she could not be his wife or the mother of his children, she turned again to the mother whom she now perceived as an identifying figure, a model rather than a lover. She, like her mother, eventually would have a husband and children of her own.

But what about the woman who turned out to be masculine, active, or homosexual? According to Freud, this woman never completely surrendered the preoedipal love of her mother. Such a woman was one who

> clings in obstinate self-assertion to her threatened masculinity; the hope of getting a penis is sometimes cherished to an incredibly late age and becomes the aim of her life, whilst the phantasy of really being a man, in spite of everything, often dominates long periods of her life. The 'masculinity complex' may also result in manifestly homosexual object choice. (1932/1961: 285)

In the analysis of homosexuality in a young woman, Freud pointed out that the dissolution of the Oedipus complex in girls as well as boys involved both biological and psychological factors (1920/1966b). The girl's oedipal love affair with the father was accompanied by the wish to bear him a male child. This wish, of course, was always frustrated. In some girls, however, this frustration was met with great and lasting disappointment, causing them, as adolescents and adults, to repudiate all wishes for a child, the love of men, and even femininity. Freud theorized that greater bitterness was experienced by some little girls than by most because the vicissitudes of the masculine child's developmental history could unwittingly conspire to kindle constitutional tendencies, which, in other girls, growing up in more fortunate circumstances, could remain dormant throughout their lifetimes.

Freud anticipated the opposition to his theory of female sexuality by feminists, female analysts, and their male sympathizers when he coolly remarked:

> It is to be anticipated that male analysts with feminist sympathies, but our women analysts also, will disagree with what I

have said here. They will hardly fail to object that such notions have their origin in man's "masculinity complex," and are meant to justify theoretically their innate propensity to disparage and suppress women.... The opponents [e.g., Freud] of those who reason thus will for their part think it quite comprehensible that members of the female sex should refuse to accept a notion that appears to gain-say their eagerly coveted equality with men. (1932/1961: 285)[23]

The superego, in Freud's structural theory, was the "heir of the Oedipus complex" (1923/1966: 36). By "heir" Freud meant that it was (1) the expression of the powerful libidinal impulses expressed in the incestuous oedipal drama and (2) an edifice constructed by the ego to master the oedipal complex. With the destruction of the Oedipus complex the ego became the representative of the external world and the superego of the psychical world of the id. The superego, which came to represent "the highest in the human mind by our scale of values" (1923/1966: 36) derived "from the lowest part of the mental life" of the individual, i.e., the libidinal impulses of the id. The rise of the superego from the ashes of the demolished Oedipus complex represented, in Freud's words "the victory of the race over the individual" (1925/1966: 257).

As the ideal to which the ego was expected to conform, the superego embodied religion, morality, and sense of social responsibility:

> As a substitute for the longing for the father, it contains the germ from which all religions have evolved. The self-judgment which declares that the ego falls short of its ideal produces the religious sense of humility to which the believer appeals in his longing. As a child grows up, the role of father is carried on by teachers and others in authority; their injunctions and prohibitions remain powerful in the ego ideal and continue, in the form of conscience, to exercise the moral censorship. The tension between the demands of conscience and actual performances of the ego is experienced as a sense of guilt. Social feelings rest on identifications with other people, on the basis of having the same ego ideal. (1923/1966: 37)

---

[23] From "Female Sexuality." Among the women analysts of increasing prominence in the 1920s and 1930s were Freud's daughter, Anna Freud, as well as Helene Deutsch, Jeanne Lampl-de Groot, Karen Horney, and Melanie Klein, later to be joined by Clara Thompson. Among these, Horney expressed the boldest "feminist" beliefs.

The superego, Freud held, was more highly developed in males than females. That was why men had taken the lead in raising the level of civilized morality. This moral superiority of men over women was due to the different ways in which boys and girls abandoned the oedipal situation. For boys, operating under the threat of castration, the surrender of incestuous wishes was immediate and complete. In the case of the girls, however, it was the perception of castration that led them into the oedipal situation; there was no threat of corresponding magnitude to force them to abandon their incestuous wishes. In girls the retreat from the oedipal situation was therefore more gradual and perhaps never completed. This difference in the female and male oedipal denouncement, according to Freud had a permanent impact on the character of women:

> I cannot evade the notion (though I hesitate to give it expression) that for women the level of what is ethically normal is different from what it is in men. Their superego is never so inexorable, so impersonal, so independent of its emotional origins as we require it be in men. Character-traits which critics of every epoch have brought up against women—that they show less sense of justice than men, that they are less ready to submit to the great exigencies of life, that they are more often influenced in their judgments by feelings of affection or hostility—all these would be amply accounted for by the modification in the formation of their superego. (*SE*, 1925/1966: 257-258)

Freud was also willing to admit that most men were far from perfect in the attainment of the masculine ideal. In fact all human beings carried the weight of moral imperfection because of "their bisexual disposition and of cross-inheritance" (*SE*, 1925/1966: 258), which combined "both masculine and feminine characteristics." Pure masculinity and femininity, Freud concluded, were theoretical constructions of "uncertain content" (258)

Homosexuals, particularly the males, were not always wholly imperfect:

> There can be no doubt that a large proportion of male inverts retain the mental quality of masculinity, that they possess relatively few of the secondary characters of the opposite sex and that what they look for in their sexual object are in fact feminine mental traits. If this were not so, how would it be possible to explain the fact that male prostitutes who offer themselves to inverts—today just as they did in ancient

times—Imitate women in all the externals of their clothing and behavior? (*SE*, 1905/1966: 144):

Freud never held out much hope that psychoanalysis, or any other form of psychotherapy, could change a homosexual identity into a heterosexual identity. He believed the homosexual could rarely envision libidinal gratification with a partner of the opposite sex. After all, he observed, it was not any more promising to try to change a heterosexual into a homosexual, although that was never attempted because it was impractical to exchange a normal sexual identity for an abnormal one. The best the therapist could hope for would be to restore the heterosexual option for those patients restricted to the homosexual. This was possible only for patients in whom remnants of the heterosexual object choice survived the homosexual fixation or in whom the libido had stabilized in the interest of living a "normal" life. However, many patients who presented themselves for conversion into heterosexuals harbored a secret plan to fail and thereby resign themselves with easy conscience to their homosexual identity.

A fuller explanation by Freud of the difficulties encountered in psychoanalysis in attempting to persuade a patient to exchange a homosexual for a heterosexual identity centered on his idea of the castration complex.[24] In the female patient this complex took the form of penis envy, the drive to possess the male genital organ. In the male it surfaced as a passive or feminine attitude toward other males. In either case the castration complex resulted in the patient repressing the attraction to the opposite sex. The psychoanalyst, Freud observed, after repeated efforts, often failed to persuade the woman to abandon her futile desire to have a penis or the man that a passive attitude toward other men did not symbolize castration and was, indeed, a necessary element in his relationships with them.

In his frequently quoted letter to the American mother who had inquired about treatment for her homosexual son, Freud voiced more compassion than hope for therapeutic change (Freud, 1960: 423).

Dear Mrs....

I gather from your letter that your son is a homosexual. I am most impressed by the fact that you do not mention this term yourself in your information about him. May I question you why you avoid it? Homosexuality is assuredly no

---

[24] Freud, Sigmund (1937/1966). Analysis Terminal and Interminable. *SE* 23: 211-253.

advantage, but it is nothing to be ashamed of, no vice, no degradation; it cannot be classified as an illness; we consider it to be a variation of the sexual function, produced by a certain arrest of sexual development. Many highly respectable individuals of ancient and modern times have been homosexuals, several of the greatest men among them (Plato, Michelangelo, Leonardo da Vinci, etc.). It is a great injustice to persecute homosexuality as a crime—and a cruelty, too. If you do not believe me read the books of Havelock Ellis.

By asking me if I can help, you mean, I suppose, if I can abolish homosexuality and make normal heterosexuality take its place. The answer is, in a general way we cannot promise to achieve it. In a certain number of cases we succeed in developing the germs of heterosexual tendencies, which are present in every homosexual; in the majority of cases it is no more possible. It is a question of the quality and age of the individual. The result of treatment cannot be predicted.

What analysis can do for your son runs in a different line. If he is unhappy, neurotic, torn by conflicts, inhibited in his social life, analysis may bring him harmony, peace of mind, full efficiency, whether he remains homosexual or gets changed.

If you make up your mind that he should have analysis with me—I don't expect you will—he has to come over to Vienna. I have no intention of leaving here. However, don't neglect to give me your answer. Sincerely yours with kind wishes,

Freud[25]

The letter revealed that Freud was quite firm in his conviction that the homosexual identity should not be viewed as criminal, sinful, or degenerate. Although he also averred that it was not an illness, his references to the normality of the heterosexual identity and to arrested development and prospects for treatment in the case of the homosexual

---

[25] The letter, dated April 9, 1935, was written by Freud. It appears in Freud, Ernest, L. (Ed.) (1960). The Letters of Sigmund Freud. New York: Basic Books, 423-424. It contained the following postscript: "I did not find it difficult to read your handwriting. Hope you will not find my writing and my English a harder task." Three years later, in 1938, Freud was forced to flee Vienna for London in the face of the threat of the German invasion of Austria.

identity, implied that he believed that the homosexual identity was pathological.

Freud's theory of normal sexual development, out of which the heterosexual identity eventually emerged, was constructed in a series of carefully conceptualized steps. The first step was taken within the confines of his topological theory. Sexual instinct, or the libido, was assigned to the Unconscious system, and stimulated through each sensory modality and gratified in zones dispersed over the body surfaces and orifices. This diffuse human sexual capacity, which Freud called polymorphous perverse, was the biological endowment of each infant child.

In the normal course of psychosexual development, as postulated by Freud, the child, in response to parental nurturance and discipline, narrowed the focus of sexual gratification by shifting attention away from the collateral zones of stimulation, particularly the oral and the anal, and centering on the "phallic," i.e., genital zone. By abandoning the sexual pleasure of zones that dominated earlier phases of sexual development for the phallic zone, the child as an adult became heir to both the richest source of sexual pleasure and the grave responsibility to propagate the race.

The second step in developing a theory of normal sexual development was taken when Freud altered his theory of instincts. Originally the sexual instinct reigned supreme in the individual's mental life. He then conceived of the ego instinct as independent of the sexual instinct and both as capable of working toward opposing aims. Because both sexual and ego instincts had individual gratification as their objective, it did not seem logical to conceive of them as working at odds. The formulation of a new theory of instincts was required in which it was possible to assign pleasure and unpleasure to polar opposites, life and death. In this dualistic theory it was possible to show that not all that was pleasurable was constructive and not everything unpleasurable destructive. The dualistic theory was conservative, because it depicted human experience largely in terms of the reproductive cycle (i.e., the life instinct) and regression to the primordial past (i.e., the death instinct). In addition, it made possible the explanation of both the sacrifice and gratification involved in the process of achieving the heterosexual identity.

Freud's last major contribution to a theory of normal sexual development was the idea of the Oedipus complex, as embodied in his structural theory. The incestuous wishes that erupted in the child and fueled the complex had to be demolished as the price the child paid for admission into full adulthood. The destruction of the Oedipus complex gave rise to the superego, the new component that Freud added to the mental apparatus. The superego transformed the energy it derived from the id into sublimated forms of morality embodied in religion, law, and society.

Because the father figure was a more faithful embodiment of moral tradition than the mother, the child's proper alignment with the father was central to the normal resolution of the Oedipus complex. For the boy the achievement of psychosexual normality required identification with the father, renunciation of his sexual attraction to the mother, and her replacement with a wife and children of his own. For the girl it required ending an affair first with the mother, then with the father, and replacing the father with a husband and children of her own.

With the idea of the destruction of the Oedipus complex as the precursor to the emergence of the superego, Freud had woven a comprehensive theory of normal sexual development. Implicit in his theory was the conception of the personal heterosexual identity. It consisted of three sets of physical or psychological polarities: (1) PHYSICAL APPEARANCE, female or male primary and secondary sexual characteristics; (2) MENTAL CHARACTERISTICS, feminine or masculine attitudes; and (3) OBJECT CHOICE, attraction to female or male sexual partners. The original bisexual capacity, therefore, pervaded all aspects of the individual's sexual identity. For each ingredient the individual's biological predisposition and the contingencies of experience combined to determine whether sexual development leaned toward one polarity or the other. Although all possible variations clinically occurred, Freud believed that the normal dissolution of the Oedipus complex involved the consistent alignment of polarities on the masculine side for males and on the feminine side for females. The ideal heterosexual male, therefore, would be solidly male in appearance, wholly masculine in attitude, and choose females exclusively as sexual objects. The ideal heterosexual female would, correspondingly, be wholly female in appearance and purely feminine in attitude and would choose males exclusively as sexual objects.

By the end of the thirties Freud had charted the full course of normal sexual development. The goal for males was to be active and masculine, for females, passive and feminine. By meeting these specifications the heterosexual man or woman provided the proper fit for their differentiated anatomy and mentality. This match allowed for falling in love, marriage, mating, children, and family. By domiciling sexuality securely within the family, Freudian theory set the stage for the pathologizing of a sexual relationship that lay beyond the boundaries of the heterosexual identity.[26]

Freud reconstituted the homosexual identity at each step in the process of creating the heterosexual identity. He began by repudiating theories of the homosexual identity that conceived of it as a natural variation. He therefore dismissed Ulrichs' theory of the "third sex" because he believed it was based on the implausible assumption of an innately "feminine" or "masculine" brain. He also rejected the degeneracy theory by pointing to the exceptional physical, mental, and ethical qualities of homosexuals such as Leonardo da Vinci. He repudiated Krafft-Ebing's theory of localized brain centers, which presumably regulated the VITA SEXUALIS, as lacking scientific verification.

His major break with the medical discourse on sexual identity occurred when he asserted that all homosexual behavior was both congenital and acquired. The homosexual identity, like the heterosexual, was congenital because it emerged from an innate bisexual capacity that consisted of a profusion of component sexual instincts. It was acquired through the vicissitudes of the child-parent relationship.

Freud's first step in restructuring the homosexual identity was to develop the concepts of arrested sexual development and regression. As children, adult homosexuals were described by Freud as having failed to negotiate the process of transferring the focus of sexual gratification from the oral and anal zones to the phallic zone. Development was "arrested," or halted, before the individual reached psychosexual maturity. Regression accounted for those individuals in whom psychosexual development had reached the level of genital primacy but tended to slip back to earlier erogenous stages.

The dualistic theory of instincts also led Freud to recast the homosexual identity. In his original conception, the homosexual identity was classified as a perversion in which the individual was consciously attracted to and

---

[26] Foucault described how psychoanalysis kept sexuality within the nuclear family: "The guarantee that one would find the parents-children relationship at the root of everyone's sexuality made it possible—even when very thing seemed to point in the reverse direction—to keep the deployment of sexuality coupled to the system of alliance.... Parents do not be afraid to bring your children to analysis; it will teach them that in any case it is you whom they love. Children, you shouldn't complain that you are not orphans, that you always rediscover in your innermost selves your Object-Mother or the sovereign sign of your Father; it is through them that you gain access to desire" (1976/1978: 132-133).

pursued sexual partners of the same biological sex. As a perversion the homosexual identity was free of neurotic conflict. It embodied unified, conscious sexual desire. Neurosis allowed the afflicted individual to obtain sexual gratification but not without intrapsychic worry and conflict. Freud's contrast between perversion and neurosis suggested that homo-sexuals could more fully enjoy sexual contact than neurotic heterosexuals.

With the introduction of the dualistic theory, the penumbra of death hung over the erotic pastimes of all individuals. The lubrication, orgasm, and ejaculation that characterized sexual arousal and release, what Freud called the "discharge of sexual substance" (1923/1966: 47), not only provided erotic gratification but also brought the individual face-to-face with death:

> This accounts for the likeness of the condition that follows complete sexual satisfaction to dying, and for the fact that death coincides with the act of copulation in some of the lower animals. These creatures die in reproduction because, after Eros has been eliminated through the process of satisfaction, the death instinct has a free hand for accomplishing its purposes. (1923/1966: 47)

In Freud's etiology of the homosexual identity the life and death instincts were fused. This identity arose, after all, out of the conflict between the two instincts: the erotic desire to possess one parent as the love object (an expression of the life instinct) and the aggressive desire to destroy the other parent as the hated rival (an expression of the death instinct). Regarding the origin of homosexuality, Freud stated: "analytic investigation has only recently taught us to recognize that violent feelings of rivalry are present which lead to aggressive inclinations, and that it is only after these have been surmounted that the formerly hated object becomes the loved one or gives rise to an identification" (1923/1966: 43). In the dualistic conception of the instincts homosexuals were no longer guaranteed unconflicted sexual gratification. The ambivalence engendered by the life and death instincts pervaded and complicated their sexual encounters and relationships, sometimes quixotically transforming passionate love into burning hatred.

The final step in reconstructing the homosexual identity was taken by Freud in conceptualizing the child's alternatives for destroying the Oedipus complex. For those children who would become adult heterosexuals, the complex was destroyed by identifying with the parent of their own biological sex. For those who would become adult homosexuals, identification with the parent of the opposite biological sex occurred. Although Freud had postulated that children developed oedipal attachments to both the father and the mother, he allowed children a single avenue of escape from the Oedipus complex. They had to choose either the father or the mother as the identifying figure or the symbolic love object. It was an inexorable choice, because what was at stake was the biological sex of the future love object and a predominantly feminine or masculine mental attitude.

Freud based his theory of sexual development on the assumption that the heterosexual and homosexual identities were products of a single process. By the time he concluded his developmental speculations, however, sexual identity was as bifurcated in conception as it had been in the theories of his predecessors. In the case of the homosexual identity, object-choice was fixed, usually for life, although physical appearance and mental attitudes could vary from one individual to another. The idea that the child could transform the love of both parents into adult love for both men and women eluded Freud's serious speculations.

An understanding of Freud's use of bisexuality and polymorphous perverse as central concepts in his theory of sexual development illuminates his belief in decisive and exclusive sexual identities. As inherited from Moll and sometimes used by Freud, bisexuality was a biological concept: it pointed to the fact that females and males either share particular physical attributes or that the structure of their genitalia developed from the same embryonic tissue. To this biological concept Freud added the correlates of feminine and masculine attitudes and the choice of a female or male love-object. In this way he psychologized the concept of bisexuality. He then proceeded to use it for explaining variations in sexual development. It was in the course of this theorizing that he unwittingly created the heterosexual identity and reconstituted the homosexual identity.

There was an inherent paradox in Freud's reasoning: he used the concept of bisexuality not only to explain sexual variations but also as evidence that variations existed. The concept, therefore, was utilized for both descriptive and explanatory purposes. Timothy Murphy (1984) suggested that Freud's employment of the idea of bisexuality for both purposes reduced it to little more than a theoretical assertion.[27]

If Freud believed that bisexuality was a basic ingredient of human sexuality, Murphy argued, that it was not necessary for him to explain the

---

[27] Murphy, Timothy (1984). Freud Reconsidered. *Journal of Homosexuality* 9(2/3): 65-77.

presence of either heterosexual or homosexual desire and object choice. The theoretical problem was how an undifferentiated polymorphous perverse sexual capacity, in the process of psychological development, was whittled down to exclusively heterosexual or exclusively homosexual object choice.

The concept of bisexuality was less specious than the idea of polymorphous perverse sexual capacity. Bisexuality implied that the critical dimension of sexual identity was biological sex in its anatomical, psychological, and interpersonal aspects. Polymorphous perverse, as a conception of human sexual capacity, neither located sexual identity in the individual's biological sex nor in genital primacy. Freud's equation of the two ideas was a form of psychological reductionism.

Freud's explanation of sexual relationships was a masterful psychological construction, skillfully bridging between the established disciplines of biology and cultural history. As one support, biology provided the authority of science, which in Freud's time, had already seriously undermined religious doctrine and faith.[28]

History, as the other support, provided the moral authority of tradition and civilization. The biology and history from which Freud borrowed were heavily influenced by evolutionary theory. As applied to social phenomena, the idea of evolution implied that advanced civilized states evolved from primitive societies. In mapping out sexual relationships Freud incorporated large fragments of the polytheistic, monotheistic, and scientific cosmologies.[29]

From the polytheistic cosmology he developed the biological idea of polymorphous perverse sexual instincts. As conceived within that cosmology, sexual relationships could provide gratification through diffuse corporeal stimulation and foster an extensive knowledge of sexual skills, which Foucault described as the "ars erotica of the ancient world. Various avenues of physical arousal allowed sexual contact to

---

[28] Freud's effort to replace religion with science and psychology was best represented in his 1927 *The Future of an Illusion*. *SE* 21: 3-56.
[29] Freud's use of cultural history as support for his psychological theory was illustrated in his *Totem and Taboo* (*SE* 13, 1912-13: 1-161). His excursion into monotheism was notable in his *Moses and Monotheism: Three Essays* (*SE* 23: 3-137, published at the end of his life, in 1939). Although it is not possible to review these works here, they provide persuasive evidence that Freud borrowed heavily from the conceptions of sexual relationships contained in polytheistic and monotheistic cosmologies to support his psychological formulations.

take many forms, 'polymorphous,' and to be independent of or peripheral to the genitals, in Freud's term, 'perverse'" (1976/1978: 57).

In his theory of sexual instinct, Freud psychologized the idea of a diffuse sexual capacity for stimulation, which consisted of several component instincts. The neonate girl or boy was depicted as a hedonic mass, adrift in a libidinal stream. The child's psychological state was comparable to that of polytheistic societies and tribes that imposed few restrictions on sexual relationships and allowed the pursuit of sexual gratification to override procreation as the individual or group priority. Freud used the evidence of primitive societies as proof that an evolutionary historical process paralleled the psychological process of sexual development in the child.

Freud's explanation of sexual relationships leaned heavily on the monotheistic concept of relationships. In that cosmology a sharp distinction was drawn between females and males. By making procreation the sole or primary purpose of sexual relationships, it emphasized the importance of genital contact. The procreative emphasis, in turn, highlighted the single clear anatomical difference between females and males, their genitalia, around which the walls of femininity for females and masculinity for males could be erected.

From the monotheistic cosmology Freud drew the idea of the male-female design. He based upon biology his belief that the anatomical differences of females and males provided the only solid foundation for an authentic sexual relationship. Only within the design could either the male or female find complementarity and completeness.

A full psychoanalytic explication of heterosexual relationships, however, required a clear differentiation of the two sexes beyond anatomy. Unless they were to remain androgynous, the psychosexual theory of heterosexual development had to explain how heterosexuality came to be associated with femininity in females, masculinity in males. There had to be psychological correlates to the biological differences. Implicit in the idea of bisexuality was the belief that humans were innately feminine and masculine. Using the concept of bisexuality, Freud was able to modify the notion of polymorphous perverse capacity to fit the male-female design. Both notions contained the idea of component sexual instincts. However, bisexuality subsumed the classification of the components under the category of biological sex, viewed as physical attributes, mental attitudes, or object choice. By "genderizing" component sexual instincts, Freud in effect reduced them to feminine or masculine instincts.

His adherence to the male-female design was further stated in his portrayal of psychosexual development. Inherent in the idea of a prescribed course was a prescribed outcome: genital intercourse between a female and a male. In following this course Freud's basic implication was that there was the progressive narrowing of stimulation from diffuse involvement of the entire body to a central focus on penis and vagina. A further narrowing of options was implied in the heterosexual resolution of the Oedipal struggle, which required the child to surrender identification with the opposite sex and attraction to the same sex. With the idea of the dissolution of the Oedipus complex, Freud had the means for molding the child to fit the male-female design and achieve the adult heterosexual identity. The homosexual identity represented the failure of the individual to fulfill the design.

Drawing from history, Freud depicted the development of civilization as narrowing the boundaries of sexual relationships so that erotic gratification became permissible only within the institution of monogamy. Although he believed this constriction of sexual relationships often led to rebellion or neurosis, he ultimately accepted it as the sacrifice the individual made for enjoying the advantages of historical progress. Freud believed that civilization teetered on the edge of chaos and irrationality. If the grip of monogamy were broken, society would slip back into primitive stages. His view was a historical and cultural restatement of the degeneracy theory, which he had rejected in its biological and psychological forms. It echoed, however, the belief of his psychiatric predecessors who adhered to the idea that unbridled sexual relationships were a mark of a decaying historical epoch. Freud's etiology of homosexuality broadly suggested that the prevalence of homosexual relationships demonstrated a historical regression that paralleled the psychosexual regression of those individuals who failed to attain the ideal of heterosexual monogamy.

The scientific cosmology, as incorporated in Freud's theory of sexual development, gave his view of sexual relationships the theoretical and methodological authority of science. Freud firmly believed that mental phenomena were like physical phenomena, with lawful relations of their own. He conceived of psychoanalysis as the scientific method for understanding the ingredients and mechanisms of mental life. By treating phenomena as physical he ignored the multifarious options individuals exercised in the formation of sexual relationships.

Freud's view of sexual relationships, therefore, was heavily burdened with the scientism of his age. "Anatomy is destiny," he averred in "The

Dissolution of the Oedipus Complex" (1924/1966: 178), by which he meant that the absence of the penis in the female and its presence in the male shaped the entire course of psychological development for each sex. Sexual instinct as a biological entity, although not an idea original to Freud, was conceived by him as a physical force that drove the individual as it cried out for gratification. Although Freud displayed the proper scientific skepticism about the theory that brain centers regulated the sexual life, he absorbed the idea of sexual instinct without the corresponding doubt about its verifiability. His idea that development occurred in a series of stages in which higher forms of sexual relationships replaced lower forms was a direct application of the biological theory of evolution to social phenomena.

Although Freud presented his topological and structural theories as the science of the mind, they were essentially recapitulations of biology and history. The idea of bisexuality recapitulated contemporary biological theory which held that the biological sex of females and males derived from a sexually undifferentiated embryo. If biology provided Freud the metaphors he needed to describe the apparatus of the mind, history, as the embodiment of institutional morality, supplied the program for developing and operating the mind.

By first combining the topological with the dualistic theory of instincts and then developing his structural theory, Freud was able to make heterosexuality the preeminent goal of mental functioning. In the structural approach the heterosexual imperative was given a permanent home in the superego. Its task was to monitor the ego which, in turn, was charged with the responsibility of managing the id, the repository of libidinal impulses. By moving heterosexuality from the id to the superego, it was possible to explain: (1) why, in the process of development, the ego blocked the expression of some sexual instincts but not others and (2) how the ego held out for the "heterosexual compromise," which, in effect, represented the orchestrated gratification of all the sexual instincts.

Psychoanalysis, as a sophisticated method of gently guided introspection, provided individuals an unparalleled opportunity to plumb the depths of personal belief and attitude which profoundly shaped sexual relationships. To the extent that such introspection restored rationality and freedom of choice, it reflected its Enlightenment heritage. As a program of individual development and a set of criteria by which to judge psychological maturity and adult morality, however, it sacrificed individual choice to social conformity. As a technique for treating unhappy and conflicted individuals, it was often a method of normalizing sexual relationships that did not fit comfortably within prescribed boundaries. Although psychoanalysis had the potential to crystallize options for new forms of sexual relationships, as a scientific enterprise it reduced choice and normalized relationships.

By fortuitously contributing the idea of the heterosexual identity to the scientific discourse on sexual identity, Freud reified both the heterosexual and homosexual identities even though he traced their development to common roots. The unintended creation of the heterosexual identity was a by-product of his using scientism to describe sexual relationships so that they were normalized within the monotheistic cosmology.

Freud's theory of human sexuality has had powerful and lasting impact for two reasons: First, it synthesized all the "known" elements of human sexuality, in forms considered either "normal" or "perverted," into a comprehensive theory. Second, it was exquisitely honed to fit the unspoken tenets of contemporary thought about sexuality, for which it provided a most elegant framework.

9 From Perversion to Neurosis

The heterosexual and homosexual identities, in Freud's theory of psychosexual development, arose from common sources: the child's innate sexual capacity and the vicissitudes of the child's developmental experiences. Either identity, therefore, represented psychological structures erected on an undifferentiated biological potential (polymorphous sexuality) or the biological capacity for both femininity and masculinity (bisexuality). Because of their common origins, Freud believed that neither identity existed in a pure form. Besides there being remnants of feminine attitudes in heterosexual males and masculine attitudes in heterosexual females, all heterosexuals had at least unconsciously made homosexual object choices in the course of their psychosexual development. Correspondingly, the homosexual identity consisted of an admixture of femininity and masculinity and heterosexual and homosexual object choice.

Freud's conceptualization of the heterosexual and homosexual identities restrained his pathologization of the homosexual identity and the normalization of the heterosexual identity. It also embodied his early notion that perversion was the converse of neurosis. The pervert enjoyed sexual gratification even though it was not heterosexual or exclusively genital. The neurotic also obtained sexual gratification but afterwards was tortured by remorse.

Although Freud's theory of psychosexual development had the obvious virtue of encompassing both the heterosexual and homosexual identities within a single theory, in the eyes of many of his followers it appeared that his conception of the heterosexual identity did not give it a solid psychological advantage. In bolstering the position of the heterosexual identity, the post-Freudians reformulated its biological and psychological basis and deepened the pathologization of the homosexual identity.

The problem of reconciling the belief that homosexuality was an acquired neurosis with the idea that it was constitutional bisexuality that had gone awry was addressed by Sándor Ferenczi. In 1911, in a lecture on the classification of homosexuality, he distinguished between ambi-sexuality and bisexuality.[1] **AMBISEXUALITY** referred to that period in the child's development in which erotic feelings were transferred to either sex. **BISEXUALITY**, on the other hand, described prenatal biological development.[2]

He accepted the Freudian notion that all children traversed a stage which had both heterosexual and homosexual components. Normal sexual development, according to Ferenczi, required the repression of the genital aspect of the homosexual component. Too much repression, however, would result in failure to establish emotional relationships with individuals of the same sex.

Ferenczi distinguished two types of inverts, the **SUBJECT HOMOEROTIC** and the **OBJECT HOMOEROTIC**. The "true invert" was the subject homoerotic, a passive creature who represented

> real reversal of normal psychical—and perhaps, also bodily characteristics.... A man who in intercourse with men feels himself to be a woman is inverted in respect to his own ego...; he feels himself to be a woman, and this not only in genital intercourse but in all relations in life. (1914/1963: 5)

He was a "true intermediate sex," in Hirschfeld's terms. He was attracted by "mature powerful men" and had only collegial relations with women. The genuine invert did not need therapy because he was at ease with his passive role and wanted only acceptance for his condition and to be left alone.

---

[1] Ferenczi, Sándor (1914). The Nosology of Male Homosexuality (Homoero-tism). *Internationale zeitschrift für ärztliche Psychoanalyse*. The article is based on his address to the Third Congress of the International Psychoanalytical Association at Weimar in 1911. It is translated and reprinted in Ruitenbeek, H. R. (Ed. and Trans.) (1963). *The Problem of Homosexuality in Modern Society*. New York: E. P. Dutton, 3-16.

[2] Ferenczi attributed the idea of ambisexuality to Freud and bisexuality to Fliess. About a decade later Ferenczi published his own catastrophe theory of psychosexual evolution. Beginning with the development of the sex cells and continuing through ovulation, fertilization, embryonic development, birth, genital primacy and, finally, the latency period, human sexual development recapitulates the catastrophic beginnings and evolution of the formation of life on earth. See Ferenczi, Sandor (1924). *Versuch einer Genitaltheorie*. Leipzig: Internationaler Psychoanalytischer Verlag. Freud's curiosity was piqued, but he later dismissed Ferenczi's theory as he was formulating his structural psychology in the 1920s.

The object homoerotic was not a true invert because:

> he feels himself a man in every respect, is, as a rule, very energetic and active, and there is nothing effeminate to be discovered in his bodily or mental organization. The object of his inclination alone is exchanged, so that one might call him a homoerotic through exchange of the love object. (1914/1963: 5)

Such a homosexual was tortured by doubts and obsessed by the need to conceal and cope with them. He was caught up in a "neurotic flight from women" (12) rather than real attraction to men. His homoerotism was only a substitute for his heteroerotic "sexual hunger." Ferenczi believed that, however difficult, it was possible that object homoerotics who were new to the practice of their aberration could be treated by awakening their "potency" (11) toward women.

Subject homoerotism, Ferenczi held, was congenital, in his words, a "true constitutional anomaly" (1914/1963: 12), but object homoerotism was a "psychoneurotic obsessional state." He believed that the object homoerotics were more numerous and socially important. Unless treated, Ferenczi feared that otherwise valuable men would be excluded from reproduction. By distinguishing two forms of the homosexual identity he was able to preserve the constitutional component of Freud's theory of sexual perversion in viewing one identity as neurotic.

One analyst who agreed with Freud's conception of the preoedipal period in the development of female sexuality was Helene Deutsch.[3] Female homosexuality, according to Deutsch, was a complicated process of retrogression from the oedipal to the preoedipal period. This reversal was evidenced by a "swing to activity" where there should normally have been a "swing to passivity." In normal development, as the little girl entered the oedipal period, she faced a "masochistic peril": she realized that she had no penis and that she could not have a child by her father.

The developmental hazard at this point was that the girls would flee to the preoedipal period where she had felt secure and enjoyed the nurturance and protection of her mother. Because she blamed her mother for not giving her a penis and realizing that her mother did not have one either, she could not turn back. Instead, she harbored sadistic

---

[3] Deutsch, Helene (1933). Homosexuality in Women. *International Journal of Psychoanalysis* 14: 34-69. The article first appeared in the *Internationale Zeitschrift für Psychoanalyse* (1932: 28), and a different English translation of the paper was published in 1932 as "On Female Homosexuality" in *The Psychoanalytic Quarterly*: 484-510.

impulses toward her mother while simultaneously developing a "passive-masochistic attitude" toward her father, resulting in the "swing to passivity" and femininity.

During the oedipal period the little girl had the passive wish to have a child by her father. Because she had not reached genital primacy, she also entertained the fantasy of having and rearing an "anal child." The wish to have a child, Deutsch pointed out, contained elements of both passivity and activity. It was passive with regard to receiving the penis and being impregnated. It was active in the deed of issuing forth and nurturing a child. By taking the symbolic reproductive path the little girl fulfilled her social obligation to become passive, feminine, and heterosexual.

In the oscillation, first toward the mother (i.e., the swing toward activity) and then toward the father (i.e., the swing toward passivity), three outcomes were possible: heterosexuality, neurosis, or homosexuality. In the HETEROSEXUAL outcome the summons consisted of the girl's wish to replace the elusive penis with a child by her father. In NEUROSIS the oscillation was arrested between the mother and the father, blocking sexual expression. In the HOMOSEXUAL outcome, the swing toward the father was obstructed: (52) "The motives which had once induced the little girl to follow the biological summons to her father must be annulled." The homosexual girl, in her retrogressive path from the oedipal to the preoedipal period, took with her the active fantasy of having and rearing an anal child but rejected receiving the father's penis. She turned back, instead, to the relationship she had had with her mother.

In the analysis of female homosexuals Deutsch concluded that their relationships were reenactments of the mother-child situation "in which sometimes the one and sometimes the other played the part of mother" (39). Physical sexual contact, she believed, reenacted the parental relationship:

> In all cases the forms of sexual gratification were the same: sleeping in close mutual embrace, sucking one another's nipples, mutual genital and, above all, anal masturbation and cunnilingus, mainly in the form of sucking, practiced intensively by both parties. Here again the double role of each partner must be specially stressed. (40)

The sexual duality consisted of one woman sanctioning physical initiatives and masturbation in the other and then the partners reversing roles. This scenario reenacted the child's active and passive fantasies about her relationship with her mother in the preoedipal period. Deutsch, therefore concluded that preoedipal more than oedipal factors explained the occurrence of homosexuality in women.

While Deutsch based her view of female sexuality largely on Freud's conception of the preoedipal period, Karen Horney reformulated the theory of the Oedipus complex to avoid presenting women's femininity as little more than defeated masculine aspirations.[4]

Horney questioned the assumptions of Freud and his followers that children in their earliest years were polymorphous in sexuality and androgynous in sex roles. Based on her observation of little girls between the ages of two and five, Horney believed that they were feminine from the start, often behaving "with a certain spontaneous coquetry towards men, or display[ing] characteristic traits of maternal solicitude" (59-60).[5] She also believed that little girls experienced spontaneous sensations in the vagina that preceded clitoral masturbation. "From the very beginning," Horney claimed, "the vagina plays its own proper sexual role."

According to Horney, it was the dominant feminine instinctual component that brought the little girl under the influence of the oedipal attraction to her father. The masculinity and penis envy Horney described in the girl of four or five was the product rather than the trigger of the Oedipus complex and were defenses against attraction to her father. The little girl's desire for a penis sprung from the frustration of knowing that her father belonged to her mother rather than from the desire to be a man. The penis was a part of her father and a substitute for him.[6]

With the resolution of the oedipal conflict the little girl gave up her father as prospective lover and model. Once she surrendered her claim to a penis, her femininity re-asserted itself but now with a residue of post-oedipal masculinity.

Within Horney's theoretical framework the female homosexual identity represented sexual development fixated at the phallic phase of the Oedipus complex. It was the result of the little girl identifying with her father as a way of repressing her love for him and her guilt over these incestuous desires. She envied him and this "leads to a revulsion

---

[4] Horney, Karen (1924). On the Genesis of the Castration Complex in Women. *International Journal of Psychoanalysis 5*: 50-65; and Horney, Karen (1926). The Flight from Womanhood. *International Journal of Psychoanalysis 7*: 324-339.

[5] Horney, Karen (1933). The Denial of the Vagina: A Contribution to the Problem of Genital Anxieties Specific to Women. *International Journal of Psychoanalysis 14*: 57-70.

[6] Horney distinguished between PRIMARY PENIS ENVY, precipitated by the girl's observance of the superior equipment and urinary performance of her brother and SECONDARY PENIS ENVY which was associated with her father in the phallic phase of sexual development.

from the subject's own sexual role.... It is just this identification with the parent of the opposite sex which seems to me to be the point from which in either sex both homosexuality and the castration-complex are evolved" (1924: 64-65). Female homosexuality, then, was a flight from femininity rather than the failure to attain masculinity.[7]

The idea of perversion as representing a double layer of repression was delineated by a follower of Freud and an early leader of psychoanalytic thought in America, Hans Sachs. Although perversion was conscious, it represented, according to Sachs, only the "tip of the iceberg" (1923/1978: 593).[8] Homosexuality in the adult was a substitute gratification for the incestuous heterosexual feelings the person had as a child. In the case of the male child, for example, his sexual fixation on the mother was too strong to overcome and too dangerous to contemplate. The child's substitution of homosexuality for heterosexuality seemed at the time relatively harmless. The infantile experience or fantasy of heterosexual union was preserved "through all storms and stresses of development, especially those of puberty, and remains unconscious" (540). The life of the homosexual was doomed to unhappiness because the repressed portions of infantile heterosexuality broke through in the form of neurotic symptoms. Thus, in Sachs' view, the homosexual was more likely to be neurotic than the heterosexual.

With the portrayal of the battle between the life and death instincts and the ongoing confrontation between the irresponsible id and the realistic ego and moralistic superego, it was possible to entertain more and more macabre and graphic etiologies of sexual identity. Melanie Klein, a child analyst, believed oedipal yearnings occurred in the earliest years of the child's life. She held that incestuous proclivities were released at the time of weaning and made their appearance at the end of the first and the beginning of the second year. These tendencies, she stated "received

---

[7] Horney assumed a corresponding theory for the boy. He started out in the instinctual masculine position but began to show feminine characteristics and entertained fantasies of having breasts and a womb during the phallic phase as a defense against his attraction to his mother. Whereas the phallic girl showed penis envy, the phallic boy showed "womb-envy."

[8] Sachs, Hans (1923/1978). On the Genesis of Perversions. *Internationale Zeitschrift fur Psychoanalyse 19*: 172-182. Reprinted in 1978 in C. W. Socarides, Ed., *Homosexuality*. Hella Freud Bernays, Trans. New York: Jason Aronson, 531-546. In Note 2, Sachs explained that perversion is conscious because gratification can only be conscious. Repression changes gratification (*Lust*) into unpleasure (*Unlust*) (546).

reinforcement through the anal frustrations undergone during training in cleanliness. The next determining influence upon the mental process is that of the anatomical difference between the sexes" (1928/1950: 202).[9]

Klein described the normal resolution of the oedipal conflict:

> The boy, when he finds himself impelled to abandon the oral and anal positions for the genital, passes on to the aim of penetration associated with the possession of the penis. Thus he changes not only his libidinal-position [from oral and anal to genital], but its aim [reception to penetration], and this enables him to retain his original love-object [his mother]. In the girl, on the other hand, the receptive aim is carried over from the oral to the genital position: she changes her libido-position [from oral and anal to genital], but retains its aim [reception], which has already lead to disappointment in relation to her mother. In this way receptivity for the penis is produced in the girl, who then turns to the father as her love-object. (1928/1950: 202)

The oedipal conflict, as Klein described it, was a relentless melodrama occurring over an eighteen-month period, a violent struggle between eros (life) and thanatos (death). It started with the oral-sadistic stage in which "the infant of six to twelve months [is] trying to destroy its mother by every method at the disposal of its sadistic trends—with its teeth, nails, and excreta and with the whole of its body" (130).[10]

But in attempting to destroy the mother, the child was also trying to attract the father who was symbolically represented by one penis or more which the child believed were inhabiting the mother's body. The sadism was fed both by libidinal frustration and by a terrifying sense of punishment and guilt (the early dawning of the superego) which the child experienced from its projected sadistic impulses.

Propelled by the consuming anxieties of the oral period the child, screaming and kicking, entered the anal stage where it faced the added frustration of toilet training. Here the child tried to eject the superego incorporated in the earlier stage. In the latter phase of the anal stage the child began to distinguish a good and bad mother and good and bad penis [father]. Presumably the "good" in the normally developed child was

---

[9] Klein, Melanie (1928/1950). Early Stages of the Oedipus Conflict. *Contributions to Psychoanalysis: 1921-1945*. London: The Hogarth Press.
[10] Klein, Melanie (1932/1975). *The Psychoanalysis of Children*. A. Strachey, Trans. London: The Hogarth Press. (Page references are to the revised edition published in 1975.)

associated with the real parent and the "bad" with the passing fears and fantasies of the pregenital stages of development. In the phallic period the child incorporated the good mother and the good penis: the hate once felt for the parents was now replaced with love which, in turn, was rewarded with love. The boy was then able to turn back to his mother, the girl to her father, in this way, establishing their heterosexual identity.

The derailment within this passionate and murderous oedipal drama that could produce injured femininity in women, injured masculinity in men, and homosexuality in both was less clear for women than for men. For the "normal" boy, according to Klein, the penis "represents his ego and his conscious" (1932/1975: 260).

In the homosexual boy the penis represented his superego and his Unconscious. As ego, the boy claimed ownership and pride in his penis. As superego, the penis was denied, repressed, and hidden. In the male homosexual relationship, by focusing on the partner's penis, the individual had "counterproof of the penis inside of him" and "protection against the punitive superego" (1932/1975: 260). The partner's penis became the good penis, his own internal penis remained the bad and destructive one. The desire to castrate the father also persisted, as Klein described:

> The sexual act between men always serves to satisfy sadistic impulses [of the pregenital period] and to confirm the sense of destructive omnipotence [through male bonding]; and behind the positive libidinal relation to the "good" penis as an external love-object [i.e., the partner] lurk, to a greater or lesser extent, according to the amount of hatred present, not only hatred of the father's penis but also the destructive impulses against the sexual partner and the fear of him that they give rise to. (1932/1975: 262)

In fact, homosexuality was disguised heterosexuality because Klein believed that every homosexual act was motivated by the desire to make the partner impotent for the heterosexual act, to get possession of his penis, and thereby to increase one's own potency with women. Homosexuality also represented the failure of the boy to overcome the oral-sucking stage of development when penis and breast were equated.

As for the development of female sexuality, Klein appeared to agree with Horney that the little girl's flight from femininity represented early oedipal attractions to father rather than, as Freud believed, a failure to achieve masculinity in the preoedipal period. What led the little girl to take on the homosexual identity in adult life was her fear of her mother, which prevented her from forming a strong attachment to her father. Of course, the fear of mother was, as in the case of the boy, merely the projection of the girl's own sadistic impulses.[11]

Klein held that, in the eyes of the little girl, "her father's penis [is endowed] with such enormous powers ... [that make] it the object of her most ardent admiration and desire" (1932/1975: 197). If this penis worship turned to rage for being denied what she most admired and wanted for herself, the little girl permanently took up the masculine and homosexual position. Because she had taken a masculine position in each phase of her oedipal development [identifying with father and his penis], the seeds of female homosexuality were sown throughout the oedipal period. Adherence to the masculine position was a defense against the anxiety of moving on to genitality. It was an act of restitution for pregenital guilt rather than true libidinal development.[12]

Wilhelm Stekel, a disciple of Freud, believed all individuals were congenitally bisexual in disposition; that is, born with both heterosexual and homosexual tendencies which were evident up to the age of puberty.[13]

Men who became heterosexuals repressed their homosexual cravings or sublimated them in social relationships with other males. Those who became

---

[11] It is never clear in the various depictions of the oedipal drama where the child's fantasy ended and knowledge began. For everything to work properly, the assumption was that both parents were present (and brothers and sisters) and that the parents were loving and not indeed sadistic; in effect, that there was an intact, functioning nuclear family.

[12] Otto Fenichel also saw adult homosexuality as the tombstone of oedipal fears. He asserted that fears of castration hung over the homosexual relationships of both females and males. Homosexual men perceived the vagina as capable of biting and tearing off the penis (i.e., the *vagina dentata*). This fearful perception was the repressed form of the original and profound fear of the boy that he would have been castrated by his father for his concupiscent desire for his mother. Homosexual women were also plagued by fears of castration which stemmed from their too intense identification with the mother, whose lack of penis they, as children, had perceived as castration. See Fenichel, O. (1930/1953). The Pregenital Antecedents of the Oedipus Complex. In *Collected Papers 1*. New York: Norton, 181-204; and Fenichel, Otto (1945). *The Psychoanalytic Theory of Neurosis*. New York: Norton.

[13] Stekel, Wilhelm (1922). *The Homosexual Neurosis*. James S. van Teslar, Trans. New York: Emerson Books. This is the second volume of a two-volume work entitled *Onanie und Homosexualität*. We have also referred to Stekel's 1928 *Impotence in the Male: The Psychic Disorders of Sexual Function in the Male*. Oswald H. Boltz, Trans. New York: Boni and Liveright, Vol. 2. Stekel confined his speculations on homosexuality largely to males.

homosexual repressed their heterosexual desires. Repression in homosexuals was accompanied by the painful awareness of being different and led to neurosis because the homosexual's heterosexuality was never completely conquered. Stekel wrote "that, in the case of homosexuals, the heterosexual path is merely blocked, but ... it would be incorrect to hold that the pathway is altogether absent" (1922: 11). Although it was theoretically possible for homosexuals to completely sublimate their homosexuality and thereby appear "normal," this rarely occurred. Stekel believed the homosexual was a neurotic who represented "a type of regression to man's primordial instincts" and that homosexuality was "a sort of compromise healing process in the mental conflict between the abnormal, raw cravings, and the cultural need for their suppression" (1922:290-291).

The male homosexual, Stekel believed, was ruled by fear and hatred of women. This fear was really the fear of his own excessive sexuality and his desire to rape women. Stekel reported that he knew a large number of homosexuals "who have actually confessed to me that they are able to have intercourse with women only when they are in a strong rage" (1922: 19). Stekel asserted: "His is the fear that he may forget himself and strangle one of them" (1922: 20). He also fears that he may assault men: "[T]hat is why he chooses men of strong physique."

It was the emotion of hatred that dominated the life of the homosexual:

> We have seen with what powerful hatred the homosexual encounters his environment. Whether he turns his hatred towards the other sex, his own, or, under certain circumstances, against himself, he remains the inveterate hater, vainly trying to reconcile the feeling of man's aboriginal nature with the ethical requirements of later culture. (1922: 289)

Homosexual relationships excluded love because the "homosexual is incapable of love" (1922: 291). He could love only himself because the hatred of his childhood could never be sublimated.

Stekel, echoing Klein's theory, believed that Freud's conception of the Oedipus complex left out the hate the male child felt for the mother with whom he identified. Stekel was convinced that

> the [male] homosexual parapathy is a flight to the same sex motivated by an attitude of sadism toward the opposite sex. This hatred is a reenactment of the hatred felt for the mother and the jealousy he had felt when she robbed him of his father. (Stekel, 1927: 250)

In Stekel's judgment, the homosexual "clings to his mother because it is all the love he can give to the female sex. The rest is hatred which, with desire, is amalgamated into a sadistic act" (1927: 251).[14] The homosexual, therefore, has good reason to flee from women. It was a matter of preserving his personality. The "inverted sexual attitude" was the homosexual's desperate effort to escape consciousness of his sadistic feelings toward women. The sadism was so deeply repressed, Stekel contended, that homosexual patients could hardly believe that it propelled them away from women.

The purpose of sexuality, in Stekel's estimation, was to overcome the natural hatred that existed between females and males. With the development of civilization the tension between the sexes had increased along with the sexual differentiation between man and woman, particularly in secondary sex characteristics (1922: 294).

Because the homosexual was an amalgam of the two sexes, he represented a retrogression from civilized to primitive forms, a "stage of racial development during which the bisexual character of the organism was more pronounced" (1922: 294). In the heterosexual man and woman love consisted of both love and hatred. In the homosexual these two components were split: love is directed toward the male, hatred toward the female. He was powerless in mediating the natural struggle between the two sexes because of his undervaluing of women and his overvaluing of men. He rejected his own femininity "The hatred of all women corresponds to his scorn of the woman in himself, a reaction due to his personal inability to overcome the woman in his own make-up and become a complete man" (1922: 295).

Stekel attributed the historic struggle against homosexuality to Judaism, with its high valuation on reproduction, the blessings of having children, and the need to curb sexual desire outside of these purposes. Monosexualism, the exclusive forms of femaleness and maleness, he associated with monotheism. Homosexuality, he asserted, was hardly mentioned in the Bible.

Bisexuality, however, he believed was associated with the Greeks. "The Greek," he stated, "was a bisexual being. He was capable of loving his friend and wife and woman slave alongside the boy" (1922: 303). The homosexual was the archaic survival of the Greek male, "carrying with

---

[14] In explaining the type of deed he had in mind, Stekel wrote: "It happens again and again that these mothers' boys suddenly beat up their mothers" (1927, 348n). The translator added the note that this behavior was observed in dementia praecox, also characterized by mother fixation.

him the bisexual instincts of the most archaic developmental stage."
Although Stekel endorsed the steady march of mankind toward
civilization, he also predicted that there would be an increase in the
number of homosexuals as the tension between the sexes increased.
Although the number of individuals who possessed the bisexual
disposition would perhaps remain constant, its eruption into the
homosexual identity would occur more frequently.

In the tradition of Freudian psychoanalysis, Stekel was pessimistic
about changing a homosexual into a heterosexual identity. A long-term
psychoanalysis at least offered the hope of revealing to the homosexual his
deeply ingrained "learnings" and the means for him to "turn his gaze
unrestrictedly over his whole mental horizon" (1922: 309). The
homosexual would have to recognize his preoccupation with males as
being one-sided and that it stemmed from his hatred of women." Stekel
concluded:

> When the homosexual becomes aware of his bisexuality and sees
> the causes of his monosexual learning, we have accomplished
> the requisite educational task. Beyond that point the patient
> must help himself. If he is truly earnest about his desire to get
> well he will accomplish it without being pushed to it. If he lacks
> the inner will the situation is hopeless in spite of the analysis.
> (1922: 312)

In effect he must learn to love in an adult manner. In this way
psychoanalysis could rescue homosexuals:

> Analysis only completes what has long been in preparation in
> the soul of the patient. We see how these individuals ascend
> the steep upward path to the heights of culture. Parapathics are
> miscarried specimens of noble men. (1927: 275)

In this struggle the homosexual recapitulates the progress of the
human race: "The adult fights against the child; the adult race, ripe for
monosexuality, fights against its childhood manifesting itself in bisexuality
and sadism" (1927: 315). The homosexual identity, in Stekel's view, was a
misdirected monosexuality that could be redeemed by recovering the
bisexuality from which it stemmed and through which it could sometimes
be transformed into a heterosexual identity.

In the post-Freudian period, principally under the leadership of Heinz
Hartmann, Ernst Kris, and Rudolph Loewenstein, there was a steady shift
away from the view of the id as the major reservoir of psychical energy to

depiction of the ego as an independent energy source.[15] In its new role the ego had regulatory functions that went beyond screening and managing libidinal impulses. Under the wave of "new environmentalism," as Sulloway called it, the emphasis moved further away from biological constitutionalism to purely psychological processes.[16]

Roy Schafer (1968) summarized five basic theoretical assumptions of the new approach:[17]

(1) The ego developed from a set of primary functions which were aspects of the basic adaptiveness of infants, some of which were perception, memory, motility, and, later, language and reasoning. These functions had energy sources which were independent of the id and "neutral" or available for a variety of practical uses. The neutralized energy was available for discretionary use by the ego and was less imperative than instinctual energy. The development of the primary functions led to the formation of the ego. It was steadier and more predictable than instinctual development as exemplified by the oedipal conflict.

(2) The original sources of ego energy were supplemented by the rewards the child gained through anticipating, guaranteeing, and enhancing the successful use of ego function. By walking and running, for example, without tripping and falling, the child built up a bank of energy it could draw upon when needed.

(3) The ego could use these functions for satisfying libidinal impulses. Perception of the genitals, for example, could turn into generalized curiosity and experimentation. The ego functions continued to develop under the impetus of instinctual energy if they did not become fixated on any one aspect of the

---

[15] See, for example, Hartmann, Heinz, Kris, Ernst, and Lowenstein, Rudolph (1964). *Papers on Psychoanalytic Psychology. Psychological Issues 4.* (Monograph 14). As early as 1939, Hartmann published the German edition of *Ego Psychology and the Problem of Adaptation.* The book appeared in English in 1958 (David Rapaport, Trans. New York: International Universities Press.)

[16] Sulloway contended that Freud believed in the Lamarckian theory of the hereditary transmission of acquired characteristics up to the time of his death (1979: 439-440). According to Sulloway, Freud's followers were embarrassed by their master's steadfast adherence to a discredited biological theory, especially at the time they were attempting to establish psychoanalysis as a mental science free of biological trappings (442).

[17] Schafer, Roy (1968). *Aspects of Internalization.* New York: International Universities Press.

environment. In this way energy could be neutralized and added to the adaptive reservoir.

(4) The reverse, however, could also occur: the reservoir of ego energy could be dissipated as libidinal and aggressive energy, a retrogression that occurred when the child was surrounded by an impoverished or overstimulating environment. When conditions were favorable, according to Schafer, there developed

(5) a predominately positive (pleasurable, reassuring, and optimistic) set of self and object representations [i.e., relationships]; then, the infant's constructiveness, assertiveness, morale, trust, confidence or "will to live" will not be seriously threatened or undermined. (192)

If circumstances were unfavorable (i.e., over- or understimulating), there would be a

preponderance of negative (painful, threatening, and pessimistic) self and object representations; these will be associated with destructiveness, submissiveness, low morale, mistrust, lack of confidence, sense of helplessness and little "will to live." (192)

Unfavorable circumstances would result in the child employing ego functions for protection, revenge, and manipulation, thereby losing the flexibility "to cope with the wide range of adaptive problems that invariably come his way" (192). The basic regulatory aim of the ego was to maintain self-esteem by enhancing positive relationships (or their representations) with self and others. Within the "adaptational" approach, as delineated by these five assumptions, it was possible for the post-Freudian theorists to view sexuality not only as developmental but also as adjustive.

Clara Thompson (1947/1963), agreeing with Freud that all men and women were bisexual, "biologically capable of being sexually aroused by either sex" (42), discussed homosexuality as a symptom which took many forms, and pointed to more basic character problems:

[O]vert homosexuality may express fear of the opposite sex, fear of adult responsibility, a need to defy authority, or attempt to cope with hatred of or competitive attitudes to members of one's own sex; it may represent a flight from reality into absorption in body stimulation very similar to the autoerotic activities of the schizophrenic, or it may be a symptom of destructiveness of oneself or others.[18]

Thompson acknowledged that there were as many different types of homosexual behavior as heterosexual and that homosexual and heterosexual relationships presented the same problems.[19] Thompson argued, however, on the side of heterosexuality: in a culture of no sexual restrictions, "children would eventually develop a preference for the biologically more satisfactory type of sexual gratification and that would prove to be found in the union of male and female genitals" (43).

In keeping with contemporary developments in ego psychology, Thompson looked for the explanation of homosexuality in adaptive failure. In particular, patients displaying the homosexual symptom seemed to be fearful of the unknown and to lack self-esteem. The fear of the unfamiliar led men to be wary of vaginas, women of penises, and both to retreat to comfortable and less demanding relationships with their own sex. Also, in same-sex dyads it was possible for homosexuals to circumvent their fears of intimacy and loneliness, because such relationships were more available as well as less demanding. She was somewhat easier on female than male homosexuals; homosexuality in men usually reflected a character disorder but in women it could be circumstantial because women were forced into each other's company without choice.

Frank Caprio described the female homosexual identity as a "symptom and not a disease entity" (1954: 120).[20] He believed sexual relationships served a dual purpose, procreation and pleasure. Both were linked to survival: procreation to the continuation of the race and pleasure "to make

---

[18] Thompson, Clara (1947/1963). Changing Concepts of Homosexuality in Psychoanalysis. *Psychiatry 10*: 183-189. Reprinted in Hendrick M. Ruitenbeck, Ed. (1963). *The Problem of Homosexuality in Modern Society.* New York: E. P. Dutton, 40-51. (Page references are to the Ruitenbeek reprint.)

[19] Although Thompson claimed that she had not observed a "homosexual love relationship," she was perhaps the first analyst to entertain the theoretical possibility that such a relationship could genuinely exist.

[20] Caprio, Frank S. (1954). *Female Homosexuality: A Psychodynamic Study of Lesbianism.* New York: The Citadel Press. Caprio based his treaties on clinical observation. He also stated that he had "circled the globe with the specific purpose of accumulating scientific information dealing with the prevalence and practices of lesbianism in various parts of the world" (ix). Data, he reported, were "obtained from lesbians themselves via the direct interview method" (ix).

the struggle for existence more endurable and enjoyable" (118). Caprio added: "to live is to love and to love is to live" (120).

In Caprio's view the homosexual identity thwarted both purposes of sexual relationships by turning the individual inward. It was a form of "neurotic self-love" (118), and need for narcissistic gratification that arose from a feeling of insecurity and represented an attempt to over-compensate for thwarting the instinctual need for survival. The narcissism of the female homosexual was evident in her form of sexual contact. Caprio proposed this theory of oral sex:

> Mouth-genital contacts can be explained on the hypothesis that a person wants someone else to do what he is unable to do himself. The desire for fellatio is a projection of an unconscious desire for autofellatio. The desire for cunnilingus in a woman is a projection of an unconscious desire to suck the nipples of her own breasts ("A *retour à l'enfance*"). If we were to accept this concept, then we can conclude that lesbianism is a regression to narcissism. In this respect I would prefer to substitute oral-survival regression for Bergler's term, "oral-masochistic regression." It is my opinion that narcissism and not masochism is the primary drive among sexual inverts. (118-119)

Although the female homosexual identity, as conceived by Caprio, stood in the way of the sexual and self-preservation instincts, it unconsciously led to a neurotic preoccupation with the wish to survive:

> The lesbian unconsciously falls in love with herself. She is in love as it were, inspired by the philosophy that one needs to love in order to survive. Love is feminine in origin. Hence it is logical to conclude that female homosexuality is a regression to mother love, a need for maternal protection and security. (119)

Caprio attributed bisexuality to the child's wish to be loved by both parents. Society, he asserted, prohibited a "bisexual existence" (120). It required the repression of homosexual behavior and the sublimation of homosexual desire. The neurotic, however, either failed to repress homosexual desire or gave vent to homosexual behavior at the price of suffering anxiety and guilt.

Caprio rejected the idea of a biologically determined sexual identity. Every individual, he believed, passed through a homoerotic stage of development. No one emerged from this process as a complete female or male: "There are relative degrees of masculinity and femininity in each person" (303). He believed, however, there were more incomplete females than males and, therefore, more "bisexual lesbians than there were bisexual male homosexuals" (303).

If the lesbian earnestly desired to become a heterosexual Caprio looked to psychoanalysis as the means for a "permanent cure" (307). Treatment would be aimed at changing the whole "personality structure" (307) rather than viewing homosexuality as a separate disease.

The most direct attack on the concept of bisexuality was made by Sandor Rado.[21] Rado argued that Freud had employed the idea of a constitutional bisexuality merely to provide a biological basis for his psychoanalytic speculations and that he always believed that constitutional factors were beyond the reach of psychoanalytic investigation. In Rado's judgment, analysts after Freud unfortunately psychologized the concept of bisexuality and this led to confused notions of biological sex. Since Freud's time, according to Rado, biologists had abandoned the concept of bisexuality. At no point in embryonic development does the gamete contain anything more than the "bipotentiality of differentiation" (181) into the two biological sexes. The whole thrust of embryonic sexual development in humans, Rado asserted, was "differential development, directed toward the construction and perfection of the reproductive system" (180). He concluded:

> Using the term bisexuality in the only sense in which it is biologically legitimate, there is no such thing as bisexuality either in man or in any other of the higher vertebrates. In the final shaping of the normal individual, the double embryological origin of the genital system does not result in any physiological duality of the reproductive function. (182)

In effect, biology only mandated that biological sex was the matter of the reproductive system. In dealing with the reproductive system the province of psychology was the element of genital pleasure. Yet sexual pleasure, in Rado's view, was inextricably tied to the reproductive system: "[W]e see that it is precisely the orgasmic element of the reproductive system that forms the basis of the genital pleasure function. Orgasm is the pivotal point, being also the point of insemination" (1940/1965: 183) Although individuals were capable of deriving sexual excitation by "stimulating sensitive spots" (183) in mind and body other than the genitals, all stimulation, from whatever source it derived and through

---

[21] Rado, Sandor (1940/1965). A Critical Examination of the Concept of Bisexuality. *Psychosomatic Medicine 2*: 459-467. Reprinted in Marmor, Judd (Ed.) (1965). *Sexual Inversion: The Multiple Roots of Homosexuality.* New York: Basic Books, 175-189.

whatever means, acted "upon a single physiological pleasure-effector, the orgasm reflex" (183). This reflex, however, required the differentiation of the female and male sex organs. In the male genital pleasure was necessarily male; in the female it was always female. Rado concluded: "whatever man does or fancies, it is just as impossible for him to get out of the confines of his biological sex as to get out of his skin" (183).

From the vantage point of a revised notion of biological sex, stripped of the concept of bisexuality, Rado looked again at "genital psycho-pathology" (186). The basic problem, he averred, was "to determine the factors that cause the individual to apply aberrant forms of stimulation to his standard genital equipment" (186). He called such sexual behavior a "reparative adjustment" (187) caused by inhibitive processes that ex-tended into early childhood. Reparative sexual behavior could be rigidly confined to one mode of "morbid stimulation" (187) or take several paths. Rado conceded that biological research might someday link pathological sexual behavior to congenital defects of the reproductive system or even to nonsexual factors.

In a final repudiation of the idea of bisexuality, Rado wrote:

> In conclusion, it is imperative to supplant the deceptive concept of bisexuality with a psychological theory based on firmer biological foundations. Reconstructive work of this na-ture is more than an invitation; it is a scientific obligation to the founder of our science, Sigmund Freud, who left us not a creed but an instrument of research. (187-188)

Rado asserted that the male-female design was the fundamental structure of sexual relationships. He claimed it was the most pleasurable as well as the most natural way to have sex. The term "orgastic pleasure" referred to the genital pleasure afforded by the fit of vagina and penis. According to Rado, it was possible to argue that "in man [as distinguished from lower species] we see that coition is dominated by the desire for orgastic pleasure" (98).[22] He went on to state that "orgastic pleasure" was equated to "sexual pleasure" and "orgastic pleasure pair"

---

[22] Rado, Sandor (1949/1963). An Adaptational View of Sexual Behavior. In H. R. Ruitenbeek (Ed.) (1963). *The Problem of Homosexuality in Modern Society*. New York: E. P. Dutton, 94-126. Originally published in P. Hoch and J. Zubin (Eds.) (1949). *Psychosexual Development in Health and Disease*. New York: Grune and Stratton.

to "sexual pair." Fortunately, in humans, although coitus was motivated by pleasure, it was also effective for reproduction.[23]

Rado believed that "homogeneous pairs" [homosexual relationships] were "reparative" caricatures of the male-female design:

> [W]e see at once that the male-female pattern is not only anatomically outlined but, through the marital order, is also culturally ingrained and perpetuated in every individual since early childhood. Those forced to take a mate of their own sex still strive to fulfill the pattern—by approximation. Such is the hold upon the individual of a cultural institution based on biological foundations. (1949/1963: 117)

Rado was assuming that males and females choose same-sex partners for their opposite-sex characteristics. He repudiated Freud's suggestion that there was genuine "homosexual desire" that derived from a basic bisexuality. Had Freud not mistaken, Rado stated, "bisexuality for a proved biologic tenet, he would not have failed to trace the activities of these homogeneous pairs to the original male-female desire and thus recognize its unbroken continuity" (1949/1963: 117). The basis of homosexual relationships was the unconsciously motivated avoidance of the opposite sex: "Male pairs are based on the reassuring presence, female pairs on the reassuring absence, of the male organ" (118).

The masculine homosexual male longed for a female partner with a penis, and ultimately settled for an "effeminate" male. The feminine homosexual male looked for a masculine partner from "he knows how to elicit pleasurable peristalsis of his genital structures through stimulation from the anus, which by variational richness of innervation, may have been anatomically predisposed to this vicarious function" (1949/1963: 118). Rado believed the orgastic nature of these sexual unions only betrayed their imitation of the basic male-female design.

---

[23] Rado developed the "push and pull" principle in the evolutionary differentiation of the female and male sexes. The male germ cell, male copulatory organs, and the male individual sought out, penetrated (as a pressure pump) the females whom they had conquered or seduced. The female egg attracted the sperm, accommodated the penis (as a suction pump), and presented and held onto the males she had attracted. The female's superior capacity for multiple orgasms was due to her biological motivation to collect as much sperm as possible to fertilize her eggs. Simultaneous orgasm was an ecstatic experience because it for shadowed (1949/1963: 101) "the impending union of sperm and egg."

The idea that homosexual behavior could fit into the pattern of normal development was revived by Harry Stack Sullivan. Sullivan, however, believed it was part of adolescent rather than childhood development.[24] Homosexuals were those adults who as children had no chums. Chums had decidedly close relations: "Fantasies, fables, and actual facts about the genitals become common property.... Cooperative or mutual sexual behavior is quite frequently an important part of the gang [peer] life" (169).[25]

Sullivan rejected the Freudian notion that all individuals were bisexual and that heterosexuals had residues of homosexuality in the unconscious. He classified as homosexuals only those individuals in whom both sexual behavior and fantasy were directed toward a person of the same sex. The homosexual identity was the consequence of abnormal attitudes and beliefs that developed out of the child's relationship with parents. It surfaced as the failure of the adolescent to develop solid peer relationships.

Although the homosexual identity was rooted in family pathology, Sullivan believed that physical development and the vicissitudes of experience could erect barriers to the development of the heterosexual identity. For example, a boy who had sexual contacts with an older boy or adult or one who was smaller or slower in physical development than his peers might become a homosexual. Homosexuality might also appear in an otherwise normal boy when no heterosexual expression was allowed. In general, Sullivan considered the homosexual identity as an interpersonal failure to establish intimate, sexual relationships with persons of the opposite sexes.

The general notion that homosexual behavior was a retreat from heterosexuality and the responsibilities of adult relationships was taken up by Lionel Ovesey.[26] Ovesey rejected the Freudian notion that there

---

[24] Although he refers to "adolescents" and "juveniles," Sullivan was apparently considering only males.

[25] Sullivan, Harry Stack (1965). *Personal Psychopathology*. Washington, DC: William Alanson White Psychiatric Foundation. This work is cited extensively in Patrick Mullahy, *The Beginnings of Modern American Psychiatry: The Ideas of Harry Stack Sullivan*. Boston: Houghton Mifflin, 1973.

[26] Ovesey, Lionel (1954/1963). The Homosexual Conflict: An Adaptational Analysis. *Psychiatry* 17: 243-250. Reprinted in Ruitenbeek (1963: 127-140). Ovesey's work is compiled in *Homosexuality and Pseudohomosexuality* (New York: Jason Aronson, 1969). A later statement appears in Ovesey, Lionel and Woods, Sherwyn M. (1980). Pseudohomosexuality and Homosexuality in

were constitutional, instinctive feminine and homosexual components in all male children. Activity and passivity, he believed, were not component sexual instincts but forms of a person's capacity for assertion in varied social contexts. He believed that Freud's constitutional theory of bisexuality was not only too heavily weighted on the side of biology, but also dangerous, because it could lead psychiatrists to view the power and dependency striving of heterosexual patients and expressions of an inherent homosexual identity.

Ovesey distinguished three motivations for homosexual behavior: homosexuality, dependency, and power. Because the homosexual motivation was the only one which the genital gratification was sought, the power and dependency motives could be considered pseudohomosexual: "The dependency and power motivations, as their names suggest, have completely different, nonsexual goals, although the genital organs may be used to achieve them. The patient usually misconstrues these goals as sexual when in reality they are not" (Ovesey and Woods, 1980: 326).

For this reason, the dependency and power motivations are more appropriately designated pseudohomosexual motivations. In overt homosexuality, when the dependency components were primary, the man gave up attempts to be masculine and instead sought masculine partners for purposes of fellatio and anal penetration. When the power motive was ascendant, the man, still too frightened to perform with women, sought as a partner a man who was as much like a woman as possible.

In a later formulation, Ovesey and Woods traced the dependency form of homosexuality to the preoedipal period, when the prehomosexual child incorporated (i.e., introjected) the image of his mother and transferred sexual and dependency needs to his father. Such a child would end up with either a shaky gender identity or with actual gender dysphoria. In adult life "his partner's penis is equated with the mother's breast and incorporated orally or anally as a symbolic substitute. In this way he not only preserves his dependency but [also] gratifies himself sexually" (1980: 332).

While Ovesey called the preoedipal homosexual "obligatory," the oedipal homosexual he called "preferential." The latter did not introject the mother in the preoedipal period but emerged with his male gender identity intact. The childhood obstacle to heterosexual development was excessive parental discipline that inhibited all sexual behavior and

Men: Psychodynamics as a Guide to Treatment. In Judd Marmor, Ed., *Homosexual Behavior: A Modern Reappraisal*, New York: Basic Books, 325-341.

assertiveness. The oedipal period was the time when castration fantasies theoretically occurred, so that the child associated parental discipline with prohibitions against heterosexual behavior, which, in turn, was equated to danger. Unabated sexual needs were then deflected to homosexual behavior as a safe alternative. The ensuing "faulty" resolution of the oedipal conflict "inhibits competition with other men and intensifies regressive longings for dependency (1980: 333).

Fear about being a homosexual, however, could occur in heterosexual males, an emotional state Ovesey called "pseudohomosexual anxiety." It was associated with the man's belief that he lacked the adaptive equipment to survive and be happy:

> Pseudohomosexual anxieties may develop in men at times of self-assertion crisis, precipitated by failures in the masculine role in any area of behavior—sexual, social or vocational. In such circumstances a man may unconsciously represent his weakness through a symbolic equation: I am a failure as a man = I am castrated = I am a woman = I am a homosexual. The ideas in this equation are derived from culturally determined attitudes that favor the male. In our society, masculinity represents strength, dominance, and superiority; femininity represents weakness, submissiveness, inferiority. For the man the former is equated with success, the later with failure. The equation is a caricature of the social demand that every male fulfill certain "masculine" requirements and of the social judgment that "femininity" and homosexuality are failures for which a man must forfeit all respect from his fellows. (1980: 326)[27]

The theme of adaptive failure was also addressed by Abram Kardiner, a psychoanalyst with whom Ovesey collaborated.[28] Both theorists attempted

---

[27] A comparison of the 1980 rendition of this theory with the earlier one (Ovesey, 1954) shows that the latter piece is much more sensitive to what is called "social demand" and "social judgment" and to femininity and masculinity as a social as well as developmental requirements. In 1954, to be self-sufficient, self-reliant, and independent were indicators of mental health; in 1980 they appear as masculine traits and social requirements. The penis-breast equation was originally the mark of dependency and homosexuality whereas, in the later article, it is associated only with pseudohomosexuality.

[28] See the four articles by Kardiner, A. Karush, and Ovesey published in 1959 in the *Journal of Nervous and Mental Disease*, each entitled a "Methodological Study of Freudian Theory." We have relied on a chapter from Kardiner's 1954

to minimize the influence of constitutional and developmental factors and to emphasize the social in the etiology of homosexuality. In abandoning Freud's constitutional theory, Kardiner disclaimed the presence of polymorphous sexuality and androgyny and reiterated that there were fundamental biological differences between the sexes.

He conceptualized five ways in which the male could become homosexual: (1) by being terrorized by a mother who represented the social reality of remasculinization; (2) as a self-preservative device, by prostituting and sacrificing himself for protection by another male; (3) by rejecting the demands of the female which were viewed as depleting rather than complementary; (4) by failing to compete successfully with other males because of his inability or lack of opportunity; and (5) by fleeing to another male with whom he could be alternately passive or active. Homosexuality was both a symptom of distress and a safety valve.

Kardiner believed that there was a sharp rise in homosexual behavior and that it was a symptom of grave social dislocation. The sexual instincts, he contended, could not be relied upon to unite men and women, particularly because human beings can achieve orgastic pleasure outside of procreative roles. This cleavage between procreation and pleasure jeopardized society. The masculine ideal became difficult to achieve in times of war and depression and homosexuality was a protective device against failure.

By the time Irving Bieber and his associates published their psychoanalytic study of homosexuality in 1962, the shift away from the constitutional theory of polymorphous sexuality was complete.[29] In its

---

Sex and Morality, reprinted in Ruitenbeek, H. R. (Ed.). (1963). *The Problem of Homosexuality in Modern Society*. New York: E. P. Dutton, 17-39.

[29] Bieber, I., Dain, H., Dince, P., et al. (1962). *Homosexuality: A Psychoanalytic Study*. New York: Basic Books. The book is based on a study of 106 homosexual males and 100 heterosexual males, all patients in therapy. The research was initiated in 1952, with a questionnaire filled out by psychoanalysts who had homosexual patients. Seventy-seven analysts participated: fifty-nine were designated as "Freudians" (who held that the Oedipus complex was the central event in psychosexual development) and eighteen were "Culturalists" (who viewed the Oedipus complex as occurring only in psychopathological families). Our consideration of the study is limited to its theoretical conclusions as they elucidate the idea of the heterosexual and homosexual identity. It should also be noted that several subsequent surveys have aimed to repudiate in part or in whole the statistical findings of the Bieber group, most notably Bell, Alan P., Weinberg, Martin S., and

place they proposed the theory of constitutional heterosexuality: "We assume that heterosexuality is the biologic norm and that, unless interfered with, all individuals are heterosexual" (319). Following Rado, all homosexuality was viewed as substitute adaptation growing out of fear of heterosexuality: "Homosexuality ... is acquired and discovered [by the child] as a circumventive adaption with fear of heterosexuality" (305).

In the Bieber theory, only male sexuality was described. The initial stages of heterosexual development occurred between the ages of three and six. At this time the little boy began to respond differently to females than to males. He also began to elicit responses from females. Bieber had earlier proposed that little boys could differentiate between the smell of the sexes: "Olfaction ... plays an important part in the organization of the capacity for heterosexual responsivity and differentiation" (312).[30]

Because his initial attraction was to the mother, the little boy developed competitive feelings towards the father and males in general: "The sexual response to the mother and rivalrous feelings to the father constitute the fundamentals of the Oedipus complex" (312) if the parents loved each other, the mother was not seductive toward her son, and the father was not threatened by the boy's competitiveness. The parent-child configuration fostered and supported the heterosexual development of the boy and the ability "to sustain a gratifying love relationship" as an adult. (Bieber, et al., 1962: 312-313.)

Homosexual identity, on the other hand, was traced to an unhappy and unfulfilling relationship between the mother and father: "Where the marital relationship is unsatisfactory, the parents may make attempts to fulfill frustrated romantic wishes through the child" (313). The mother of the prehomosexual boy was described as sexually seductive, "close-binding-intimate," and openly preferring her son to her husband, whom she also dominated. In reaction to the mother, the father was distant, hostile, and

---

Hammersmith, Sue Kiefer (1981), *Sexual Preference: Its Development in Men and Women*, Bloomington, IN: Indiana University Press.

[30] Experimentation in rhinology has demonstrated that infrahuman organisms respond sexually to olfactory stimuli. It is unclear which research on humans Bieber had in mind in making this particular claim, or whether he was reviving a notion of Krafft-Ebing (1886/1935: 27ff). The name *pheromone* was given to the odor to which sexual responses were made; see Parkes, A. S. and Bruce, H. M (1961). Olfactory Stimuli in Mammalian Reproduction Odor Excites Neurohumoral Responses Affecting Oestrus, Pseudopregnancy, and Pregnancy in the Mouse. *Science 134*: 1049-1054. The Parkes and Bruce article is a review of experiments on the pheromone.

openly competitive with the son. The result of this mother-son-father triangle was the impaired development of the son's heterosexuality.[31]

To support this theory of the male homosexual identity, the Bieber group depicted adult homosexual relationships as efforts to restore lost heterosexuality: "A reparative mechanism ... included the selection of homosexual lovers who were quite masculine—the 'large penis' type.... Not infrequently the homosexual lover is perceived as a potent rival or the most likely threat to heterosexual goals" (314). Like Melanie Klein, they believed that the goal of the homosexual male was to keep his partner away from women. Homosexual relationships were doomed to failure:

> Such twosomes are usually based on unrealistic expectations.... These liaisons are characterized by initial excitement which may include exaltation and confidence in the discovery of a great love which soon alternates with anxiety, rage, and depression as magical expectations are inevitably frustrated.... These relationships are generally disrupted after a period of several months to a year or so; they are generally sought anew with another partner and the cycle starts again. (317)

Because homosexuality, in their view, was psychopathological, the worst thing that adult homosexual males could do was to participate in the homosexual subculture: "Life within this society tends to reinforce, fixate, and add new disturbing elements to the entrenched psychopathology of its members" (317).

The Bieber group believed that homosexuality was a distinct clinical diagnosis, easily detected because of its behavior patterns. They rejected the notions of Thompson and Ovesey that it was symptomatic of underlying character disorders. Inhibited masculinity, as demonstrated in the fear of the unknown, lack of self-esteem, lack of self-assertion, and yearnings for dependency were the "*consequences* of psychologic injury and not the *causes* of it" (309). The homosexual identity in the Bieber

---

[31] In the perspective of the Bieber group (as in the theory of Melanie Klein before them), the mother replaced the father as the central parental figure in the oedipal drama. The mother of the prehomosexual boy was described as follows: "the CBI [close-binding-intimate] H-mother exerted a binding influence on her son through preferential treatment and seductiveness on the one hand, and inhibiting, over-controlling attitudes on the other. In many instances, the son was the most significant individual in her life and her husband was usually replaced by the son as her love object" (27). Fathers were depicted as "detached" or "not-detached" and, in their negative relationships with sons, as hostile, indifferent, minimizing, dominating, exploitative, and ambivalent.

view was fully psychiatrized, given its own clinical morphology and etiology, and, by implication, its course of treatment.[32]

Robert Stoller, in the tradition of the Bieber group, looked to the early relationship between the child and mother for the origin of adult homosexuality.[33] Stoller's view of the homosexual identity derived chiefly from his study of male-to-female transsexuals and his theory about the development of masculinity. As he wrote, "the sense of maleness and the later development, masculinity, are a bit less firmly established in males than the sense of femaleness and femininity in females" (1975/1976: 296). The transsexual was the individual whose identity as a child merged into the femaleness of the mother: "[N]either the mother nor infant will want to separate from each other — and the *principal effect is extreme femininity in the little boy*" (293).

Stoller took issue with Freud over the latter's belief in the biological origin of the homosexual identity. In Stoller's eyes, this identity was the response to a "non-biological threat to one's sense of core identity, of existence, of being" (1975/1976: 296). He did not believe, as did Freud, that maleness was biologically firmer than femaleness and that males were off to a better start toward the heterosexual identity than females. Boys were indeed off to a worse start because they had to avoid primitive merging with the mother at a time when they possessed little ego structure. The vulnerable position of the little boy would "leave him [a] less fixed and dependable identity, put him in great jeopardy in oedipal development, and, as a result, make him more prone to the development of perversion" (296). Homosexuality, Stoller argued, was a particular threat to males because "the pull toward merging again into

---

[32] Although the Bieber group did not consider female sexuality in this study, Irving Bieber himself, as late as 1966, quoted the following description of female sexuality by Krafft-Ebing [cited in Bieber, Irving (1966). Sadism and Masochism. *American Handbook of Psychiatry* 3]: "In women voluntary subjection to the opposite sex is a physiological phenomenon. Owing to her passive role in procreation and long existent social conditions, ideas of subjection are, in women, normally connected with the idea of social relations. They form, so to speak, the harmonics which determine the tone quality of feminine feeling" (257-258).

[33] Stoller, Robert (1975/1976). *Sex and Gender. Volume II: The Transsexual Experiment*. New York: Jason Aronson. This work was first published in 1975 in England by the Hogarth Press. His views on homosexuality were less clearly stated in two subsequent books: *Perversion: The Erotic Form of Hatred* (New York: Pantheon, 1975) and *Sexual Excitement: Dynamics of Erotic Life* (New York: Pantheon, 1979).

the mother's femaleness terrifies and enthralls men; it is the Siren's Song" (296).

In normal male development, as Stoller conceived it, the boy first established his identity as a biological male, then a masculine identity, and finally a heterosexual identity. But none of this was inevitable:

> One ought not to define heterosexuality and homosexuality anatomically but rather according to identity. Anatomy is not really destiny; destiny comes from what people make of anatomy. For the little boy is only anatomically, not psychologically, heterosexual in the first period of his life; that heterosexuality comes only after a massive piece of work, performed with some difficulty and pain. We know of that struggle—separation and individuation. (293)

The developmental course that separated transsexuals from homosexuals was the oedipal relationship. Because the pretranssexual boy had no heterosexual relationship with his mother, there was no chance of oedipal conflict: "Had this only occurred, the less profound pathology—homosexuality—might have resulted" (165). In a subsequent treatise on perversions, Stoller relegated homosexuality to a subsidiary theme because it was a subject "on which many social issues are fought" (1975: 196).[34]

One apparent motive for the book was Stoller's intention to defend heterosexuality as the normal sexual identity against the inroads being made by contemporary sexological research in biology and the social sciences as well as to dispel the growing misgivings of psychiatrists who were reading that research. Like other post-Freudian analysts, Stoller believed perversions, including homosexuality, were efforts to restore a damaged heterosexuality. He gave full endorsement to the idea of heterosexuality as the normative sexual identity:

> However restrictive the myth of heterosexuality may be, however sex militants hate it, and however bitter people are at how far its reality has fallen below perfection, heterosexuality with love—affection, respect, honesty, decreased selfishness, fidelity, joy in children, and creation of a unit larger and more original than the two people making it up [i.e., the family]—Is the criterion. This is so not because it is ordained by heaven, biology, or economic theory but because almost all members of

---

[34] It is safe to assume that the book on perversions followed that of sex and gender because the later was listed in the bibliography of *Perversion*.

society accept it somewhere within themselves as the ideal that haunts them. (1975: 204)

The book on perversion was also an effort to distinguish clearly between perverse and normal sexuality and to explain why even individuals who were essentially heterosexual in identity occasionally engaged in errant sexual behavior, including homosexuality. To identify sexual perversions, one had to look to the motives of individuals rather than their behavior alone. In Stoller's view, the perverse act was motivated by hostility, the desire to harm the partner. The hostility stemmed from fantasies of revenge born in childhood traumas. The traumas to which Stoller referred were those experienced by the child in the course of establishing its heterosexual identity, including the appropriate femininity for the little girl and masculinity for the little boy. The traumas were converted into triumphant, risk-taking erotic ventures (often confined to fantasy in adulthood). The risk-taking stemmed from the need to introduce novel elements into what would otherwise be a monotonous reenactment of the encrusted childhood trauma and its associated residual anxiety. The individual took a big enough risk to attain sexual potency but small enough to avoid a heightening of the anxiety.

Stoller, like the forensic psychiatrists of the nineteenth century, recognized and opposed the social and legal oppression of homosexuals. He warned against the use of psychiatry and the diagnosis of mental pathology to bolster that oppression. He also believed that perversions were not necessarily crippling: "I do not believe these dynamics [childhood psychosexual traumas] cripple most of their owners any more than does the conflict solving [of the oedipal situation] that produces normative [heterosexual] behavior" (43). Some oppression of homosexuals, however, he thought was provoked by the homosexuals themselves:

> For multiple, complicated reasons, many homosexuals are committed to clowning, mimicry, caricature, whenever an audience—heterosexual or homosexual—Is present. An ingredient of these performances is sarcasm—hostility in which there is a joke: "When I seem to be making fun of myself, I am actually making fun of the straight world—with the additional bonus that they are too dumb even to know what I am doing to them. (200-201)

Stoller explained such behavior, which he attributed more to homosexual males than females, in psychoanalytic terms: the transfer by homosexuals of hatred they originally felt toward parents to authority figures in the society and their persistence in inducing self-punishment because of the self-hatred they felt as children. An additional explanation of how homosexuals provoked retaliation from heterosexuals was by undermining their heterosexuality: "Homosexuals can threaten the heterosexual stance of the militant straight, bullying him with insight into his own homosexual or effeminate potentials. To prove himself, the heterosexual may retaliate" (202).

After the Bieber group, the psychoanalytic argument that the homosexual identity represented a pathology, with distinct clinical forms, was taken up by Charles W. Socarides.[35] Socarides stated several assumptions about normal sexuality in the process of weaving his theory of homosexuality. First, there was no innate connection between sexual instinct and choice of sexual object: sexual preference was acquired through learning rather than dictated by genes or hormones. Echoing Rado, however, he believed biology did make its own contribution:

> [T]he male-female design is taught to the child form birth and is culturally ingrained through the marital order. This design is anatomically determined, as it derives from cells which evolved phylogenetically into organ systems and finally into two classes of individuals reciprocally adapted to each other. This is the evolutionary development of human beings. The male-female design is perpetually maintained, and only overwhelming fear can disturb or divert it. (1978: 5)

In essence, Socarides distinguished sharply between the "inside" and "outside" of human sexuality. The outside, female and male anatomy, was fixed by nature and served as the mold for the expression of sexuality. The "inside" was the unformed, malleable substance derived from childhood sexual fantasy and experience. The biological exterior and the psychical interior were harmoniously combined only in the heterosexual identity.

---

[35] Socarides' major work on the subject is *Homosexuality* (New York: Jason Aronson, 1978). His earliest paper on male homosexuality was "Theoretical and Clinical Aspects of Overt Male Homosexuality," *Journal of the American Psychoanalytic Association* 8, 1960, 552-556; on female homosexuality, "Theoretical and Clinical Aspects of Overt Female Homosexuality," *Journal of American Psychoanalytic Association* 10, 1962, 579-592. Both of the journal articles were reports of panel discussions. Socarides is interested in the whole spectrum of sexual "perversions," including fetishism and transsexualism.

This idea of harmony and completeness only in the achievement of the heterosexual identity was the basis for his discussion of femininity and masculinity. At birth there was a feminine and masculine tension in females and males. In heterosexual development the female directly discharged the feminine tension and sought vicarious satisfaction of the masculine tension in a male partner. Similarly, in the male, while the masculine tensions were personally and directly discharged,

> the feminine needs become object-invested, that is, the ego feels the need for a feminine sexual partner whose feminine urges it cares to satisfy…. The more an ego "egotizes" the urges of its own sex and externalizes to a proper object representation the urges of the opposite sex, the more such an ego feels complete. (1978: 113)

Socarides also held that heterosexual genital primacy was an achievement rather than an assured course of development, one that could easily be blocked by psychical events occurring in the first five or six years of the child's life. Unless blocked, psychosexual development of the child normally proceeded to the orgastic pleasure of penis-vagina intercourse. Any sexual perversion, including homosexuality, represented an exaggerated emphasis on the gratification of a partial sexual instinct at the expense of the orchestrated instinctual possibilities: "[T]he true homosexual has only one way of gaining pleasure and his energies are concentrated on one particular partial instinct" (106). Socarides believed that homosexual orgastic pleasure was not as intense as the heterosexual because the latter resulted from the unification of all the component sexual instincts (1978: 108).[36]

With the criteria for adult sexual normality stated, Socarides embarked on his theory of homosexuality. Although he distinguished

---

[36] In modern psychoanalytic discussions, there has been at least the implicit distinction between sexual stimulation and gratification. Only gratification is associated reliably with pleasure. Although there may be pleasure associated with non-genital stimulation, it is considered to be of an inferior quality to that resulting from penile-vaginal orgasm. Non-genital stimulation has been equated to the partial sexual instincts. In homosexual intercourse, because there is the absence of either penis or vagina, there is the assumption of more stimulation than gratification. The presumably compulsive nature of homosexuality can thereby be explained as superabundant stimulation with relatively little gratification.

several types of homosexuality, his theoretical interest centered on the preoedipal and oedipal forms.[37]

In the oedipal form the individual's sense of self was unimpaired and the homosexual tendencies were felt as foreign to the ego. Socarides felt that the prognosis for changing an oedipal homosexual identity into a true heterosexual identity was very good.

The preoedipal homosexual represented a developmental fixation occurring in the first three years of life. Socarides distinguished two forms of preoedipal homosexuality. Individuals of either type showed signs of narcissism, anxiety, and impulsiveness. Preoedipal Type I, which he considered less pathological, was characterized by a more realistic sense of self, less self-absorption, greater ability to relate to others, less sexual compulsivity, and the tendency to deal with anxiety by engaging in sexual acts. Preoedipal Type II, in which development had been arrested in the earliest years, was characterized by the individual being wrapped up in some grandiose version of the self, the instantaneous and gross acting out of sexual impulses, and extreme anxiety and feelings of emptiness and remorse. The preoedipal form of the homosexual identity caught the afflicted individual up in futile and obsessive efforts to achieve true emotional intimacy and sexual gratification with a member of the same sex.

Socarides described a process of "resonance identification":

> The aim of the homosexual act is ego survival and a reconstitution of a sense of sexual identity in accordance with anatomy. The male achieves "masculinity" through identification with the male sexual partner; this lessens castration fear. The female achieves 'resonance' identification with the woman partner; this lessens castration fear. She also creates the good mother-child relationship. (93-94)

---

[37]Besides the preoedipal and oedipal forms of homosexuality, Socarides (1978: 91-98) distinguished three non-obligatory forms: (1) *situational*, which arose when partners of the opposite sex were "inaccessible"; (2) *variational*, which resulted from desire for new sexual excitement or sexual disappointments suffered with the opposite sex; and (3) *latent*, in which there was no overt sexuality but in which existed the same psychic structures as in the oedipal and preoedipal homosexual. He stated that situational and variational homosexuality were non-obligatory because heterosexual functioning was possible and preferred(475). He also stated that these forms of homosexuality were consciously motivated.

Only preoedipal homosexuality represented true perversion in Socarides' view. He wrote: "the homosexual has been unable to pass successfully through the later stages of the separation-individuation phases of early childhood.... Homosexuality serves the repression of a pivotal fixation in which there is a desire for, and dread of, merging with mother in order to reinstate the primitive mother-child unity" (86).

Socarides diagnosed male homosexual behavior as follows:

> At a conscious level the patient attempts to compensate for his primary nuclear conflict by certain activities designed to enclose, ward off, and encyst the isolated affective state of the mother-child unity. He does not, therefore, approach any other woman, especially sexually; this will activate his fear of her [his mother]. He does not attempt to leave mother because he fears provoking engulfing, incorporative tendencies on her part and on his own. Any attempt to separate produces an exacerbation of his unconscious ties. He instead attempts to keep the safest closeness to her, all the while remaining asexual regarding other females. All sexual satisfactions are carried out through substitution, displacement and other defense mechanisms. Having already made a feminine identification (a result of the continuance of the original feminine identification), he restores strength and reaffirms a sense of self through transitory male identification with his male partner. The homosexual is unconsciously enjoying sexual closeness to both mother and father simultaneously by substituting a man for sexual intercourse. (86)

About the female homosexual identity, he had this to say:

> The homosexual woman is in a flight from men. The source of this flight is her childhood feelings of rage, hate, and guilt toward her mother and a fear of merging with her. Accompanying this primary conflict are deep anxieties and aggression secondary to disappointments and rejections, both real and imagined, at the hands of the male (father). Any expectations of her father's fulfilling her infantile sexual wishes poses further masochistic danger. On the other hand, her conscious and unconscious conviction that her father would refuse her love, acceptance, and comfort produces a state of impending narcissistic injury and mortification. The result of this conflict is to turn to the earliest love object, the mother, with increasing ardor. (133-134)

Freud's early notion of innate polymorphous sexuality, shaped through the vicissitudes of experience was steadily eroded in the speculations of the psychoanalytic theorists of sexual identity who followed him. With the trend toward biological determinism in Freud's structural theory, the sexual instincts lost some of their autonomy to the superego. With the addition of the adaptational approach, they were to lose more to the ego, which was promoted from a managerial to an executive position. Under the ego, a sexuality that, in Freud's early psychosexual theory, had been imperative and hedonistic, was corralled, scrutinized, and cautiously orchestrated according to a plan that was to guarantee the individual both sexual pleasure and adaptive harmony .

Adaptation implied willful constraint so that it was necessary for the post-Freudians to explain how the harnessing of sexual desire could still provide enough pleasure to make the sacrifice worthwhile. Nature, they claimed, had guaranteed gratification in the "natural fit" of penis and vagina. In the very act of coitus, the male "push" was exquisitely coordinated with the female "pull," a performance that was nothing less than the reenactment of the union of sperm and ovum. Simultaneous orgasm was the highest gratification because it joined sexuality as a pleasure to sexuality as reproduction.

In the strict dichotomization of sexual identity into the heterosexual and homosexual, Freud's contemporaries, as well as the post-Freudians, attacked the concept of bisexuality. Ignoring Freud's attempt to bring all forms of sexual identity within the framework of a single theory, Ferenczi reverted to the notion that there were two distinct homosexual identities, the subject and the object homoerotics. The subject homoerotic, the "true inverts," in Ferenczi's view, were described as having a congenital biological sexual identity. In avoiding the notion of a biological bisexual identity, Ferenczi classified the object homoerotics as psychoneurotics having a purely psychological homosexual identity. Stekel conceived of bisexuality as both a primitive embryological state and an archaic historical condition that civilized people had abandoned in the steady march toward monosexuality and, by implication, the heterosexual identity. Homosexuals, decent enough people in Stekel's eyes, were unfortunately caught between the bisexuality of ancient times and the monosexuality of inexorable historical progress.

Although Deutsch, Horney, and Klein did not directly attack the notion of bisexuality, their preoedipal theories implied that the femininity of little girls and the masculinity of little boys were inborn qualities or acquired in the earliest months of infancy. The idea of an innate feminine or masculine identity, like the heterosexual or homosexual identity, was based on the belief that the biological options that children were born with were strictly dichotomized and determined their psychological destiny. Although Stoller considered femininity in females and masculinity in males as psychological achievements rather than natural endowments, he never questioned the normative belief in the need for the rigid delineation of the biological sexes.

The frontal attack on the notion of bisexuality was launched by Rado who claimed that it was based on Freud's misconception of embryological development. Apart from the incipient bipotentiality that existed in the fertilized ovum, Rado asserted that the biological differentiation of the female and the male reproductive equipment created two distinct sexes. Along with this, nature provided the design for fitting this equipment together in an ideal union that combined reproductive practicality with sexual gratification. The cultural institution of marriage and family fleshed out the anatomical outline that nature had sketched. Rado's assault on the concept of bisexuality was joined by Sullivan, Ovesey, Woods, Kardiner, the Bieber group, and Socarides and congealed the belief that the heterosexual identity constituted the biological norm.

With the normalization of the heterosexual identity the pathologization of the homosexual identity was deepened in several ways. As a psychological etiology it was pushed back farther and farther in time, from the oedipal to the preoedipal period, as in the theories of Deutsch and Horney, and then to the earliest relationship of mother and child, as described by Klein. In this way the homosexual identity became an increasingly indelible quality of the individual. In being transformed from a perversion, as Freud had originally conceived it, into a neurosis, as Sachs and Stekel portrayed it, the homosexual identity could still provide the sexual gratification of perversion, but now at the price of the consuming anxiety and gnawing guilt of neurosis. For Thompson, Caprio, Sullivan, Ovesey, Woods, and Kardiner, the homosexual identity signaled a character structure that was narcissistic, underdeveloped, and essentially unable to cope with reality. As a clinical entity, it was described by the Bieber group and Socarides as being so deeply rooted in early experience and personality that only the laborious process of psychoanalysis could possibly restore the heterosexual identity.

The homosexual identity represented failure in past relationships and futile attempts to repair the ensuing psychological damage. There was the homosexual's initial failure in relationships with parents, for which the parents were to blame. For Stekel, the sexual attraction of homosexual males did not reflect their love of men so much as the reeling away from their hatred of women. For Sullivan, homosexuals suffered from the adolescent failure to establish solid relationships with same-sex peers. For Ovesey, Woods, and Kardiner, men who failed to stand their ground in competition with other men retreated to homosexual relationships for protection and security. For Klein, the Bieber group, and Socarides, homosexual relationships were attempts by men to reclaim the penis they symbolically lost as children and for women to regain access to the mother's breast.

Whether classified as its own pathology or symptomatic of massive disruptions in character and adjustment, the homosexual identity was associated with weakness, powerlessness, inadequacy, shame, and failure. When the homosexual woman was considered at all, she was seen as empty and lonely, castrating and vindictive, narcissistic, and wracked by penis envy. Her only solace was retreating with another woman to a preoedipal mother-child symbiosis. For males, the homosexual identity was the ultimate failure. Arising from a denial of the penis, it was a symbolic attempt to be and act like a female.

Within the post-Freudian discourse on sexual identity the polytheistic view of sexual relationships was pitted against the monotheistic. The diffuse sexual identities and practices condoned under the polytheistic cosmology, when embodied in contemporary sexual relationships, were seen as the individual's failure to keep stride with the progress of civilization. The lack of differentiation between the two biological sexes, which Stekel conceived as both biological and psychological and a mark of polytheistic cultures, was seen in contemporary life as primitive and anachronistic. Homosexuals, as Stekel asserted, were incomplete specimens of their respective biological sexes living amidst those individuals whom civilization had sharply delineated as one or the other biological sex.

The element of sexual pleasure, central to the *ars erotica* of the polytheistic culture, was absorbed within the male-female design as the only structure of sexual relationships permitted under the monotheistic cosmology. Within the monotheistic cosmology, the post-Freudians viewed the heterosexual relationship as both a biological imperative and a psychological achievement. In the words of Rado, the male-female pattern was "anatomically outlined"; for the Bieber group it was the "biologic norm": and for Socarides it was "anatomically determined" and "culturally ingrained." Because they believed it was fundamental to human nature and society, they could declare that attempts to fulfill the design by overriding or ignoring differences in biological sex or social sex-role were evidence of staggering pathology.

The scientific cosmology, in the scientistic guise of biological determinism, was used in the post-Freudian discourse on sexual identity to bolster the belief in a monotheistic conception of sexual relationships. With the abandonment of the concept of bisexuality the post-Freudians moved away from the position of the biological potentialists to that of the biological determinists. Their rigid delineation of the two biological sexes made explicit their allegiance to the belief in the male-female design. The post-Freudian theorists of sexual identity, by the mid-twentieth century, made no secret of their advocacy of the design as the inviolable pattern of human biology and culture. It became a credo, a banner in the forward march of destiny, resisted by the individual at the price of self-mutilation, personal opprobrium, and social upheaval. If not exactly destiny, anatomy at least prefigured the consonance of the two sexes which normal development should achieve in adulthood. There was the added note of irony that the new scientistic, biological orthodoxy of the post-Freudians arose during a period in the history of psychiatry, and in psychoanalysis in particular, when its connection to the biological sciences, including medicine, was more tenuous than ever.

10

Detoxication of the Homosexual Identity: Psychological Theories

Within the formulations of the post-Freudian adaptational and reparative theorists, the homosexual identity was thoroughly
pathologized. The pathologizers, however, retained the distinction between homosexual identity and homosexual behavior: individuals
who engaged in the behavior but lacked the identity were considered less
pathological than those who both possessed the identity and engaged in the
behavior.

The pathologizers' blanket proscription of the homosexual identity led
to a reaction within the psychiatric profession.[1] Those psychiatrists who
wished to distinguish between pathological and nonpathological forms of
the homosexual identity were unable to do so within a theoretical framework that rejected the Freudian notion of bisexuality and viewed
homosexual relationships as entirely reparative. In developing the notion
of pathological and nonpathological forms of the homosexual identity the
detoxicators were able to draw a distinction between permissible and impermissible structures of homosexual relationships. Failure in permissible
relationships was attributed to social intolerance while failure in the
impermissible was traced to homosexuals themselves, those who still bore
the taint of pathology.

In 1965, the effort to detoxicate the homosexual identity was launched
by Thomas Szasz, a professor of psychiatry as well as a psychoanalyst.[2]

---

[1] Identification of the historical circumstances leading to the detoxication of the
homosexual identity is beyond the scope of this treatise, which focuses on the
ideas comprising scientific discourse on sexual identity.
[2] The discussion here is limited to two of Szasz's earliest defenses of the
homosexual identity: Szasz, Thomas (1965). Legal and Moral Aspects of
Homosexuality. In Judd Marmor, Ed., *Sexual Inversion: The Multiple Roots of
Homosexuality.* New York: Basic Books: 124-139; and Szasz, Thomas (1970). *The
Manufacture of Madness.* New York: Delta Books, Chapters 10 (160-179) and 13
(242-259).

For over a decade Szasz had been arguing that psychiatry was in the business of promoting majoritarian morality by diagnosing as mentally ill those individuals whose lives expressed divergent or dissenting values. Psychiatry, in his view, was merely the handmaiden of law and morality. Individuals whose lives conformed to conventional morality were deemed mentally healthy; the nonconformists were the mentally ill.[3]

Szasz thought the very notion of mental illness was based on shaky ground. In aping the medical concept of organic illness, the idea of mental illness provided biological trappings for disguised moral judgment. The psychiatric judgment of mental health, as in the case of heterosexuality, was an unmitigated expression of moral preference: "The main reason for adopting this standard is the value of heterosexuality for procreation and therefore for the survival of the species" (1965: 132). Such a standard appeared to be a biological requirement until one recalled that survival of the human race was threatened by too much rather than too little reproduction.

The dread of homosexuality, rooted in society and embodied by psychiatry, Szasz proposed, stemmed from the social perception of the homosexual as a subversive who undermined heterosexuality:

> Because he rejects heterosexuality, the homosexual undermines its value. So, of course, does the priest. The homosexual, however, respects one type of sexual conduct in favor of another, whereas the priest eschews the pleasures of the flesh to emphasize the value of the spirit. The homosexual thus threatens the heterosexual on his own grounds. He makes the heterosexual fear not only that he too may be homosexual but also that heterosexuality itself is not as much "fun" as it has been made out to be. Many people behave as if sexual satisfaction were one of their main interests in life. If the value of their favorite game is undermined, they may lose interest in it, and then what will they do? (1965: 135)

The social abhorrence of homosexuality also reflected "strongly anti-sexual" attitudes (1965: 131). Statutes that prohibited homosexual conduct also frequently limited heterosexual intercourse to genital insertion. Cultural sexual antipathy informed the laws against contra-ception, abortion, and the heterosexual "perversions," as well as those opposed to homosexuality.

---

[3] One of Szasz's earliest volleys against psychiatry was *The Myth of Mental Illness*. New York: Hoeber-Harper, 1961.

The major issue confronting psychiatry, according to Szasz, was whether or not "homosexuals should be forced to submit to psychiatric treatment against their wills" (1965: 132). He suggested two ways in which psychiatrists could become complicit with enforced treatment. One was by diagnosing individuals as homosexual in public institutional settings such as government service, the military, and prisons. The other, in the context of psychoanalysis, was for the analyst to go beyond his purely analytic responsibility of helping the patient learn about himself and try to convert homosexuality into heterosexuality. In the eyes of Szasz, the analyst was confused if he equated the biological value of heterosexuality with its social value: "The jump from biological value to social value is the crux of human morality" (1965: 136).

Apparently Szasz himself had serious reservations about sexual expression in general and about homosexuality in particular. He inclined toward the position that homosexuality was a disease in the sense that "it is an expression of psychosexual immaturity, probably caused by certain kinds of personal and social circumstances early in life" (1965: 124). He also viewed the homosexual male as "preoccupied with and intent on homosexual cravings and gratifications" and "the mirror image of the ever-lustful, ever-frustrated heterosexual" (135). There were insinuations that heterosexuals, in an effort to escape their puritanical backgrounds, could and did become obsessed with sex. In his estimation, both Christian ethics and psychoanalysis made too much of sex: "It is implicit in their orientation (i.e., approaches to human conduct) that sexuality is one of the most important and most interesting facets of life. But is it?" (135).

Five years later, in *The Manufacture of Madness*, Szasz intensified his attack on the psychiatric conception of mental illness. In this work he traced the history of homosexuality as heresy in the eyes of the Catholic Church to show how it was converted to mental illness under the dominion of medicine and psychiatry. The equation of homosexuality and heresy Szasz attributed to biblical sources which he believed sponsored anti-homosexual attitudes which were perpetuated in the medieval period.[4]

Homosexuality, in Szasz's view, was condemned because it was "unnatural," associated with carnal lust and sexual pleasure rather than

---

[4] John Boswell (1980) provided an interpretation of Scriptural passages which was at considerable variance with that of Szasz. In general, Boswell's position was that the Scriptures were "moot" on attitudes toward homosexuality (117). Szasz, following past scriptural scholarship, assumed that passages such as those describing Sodom and Gomorrah were references to homosexuality.

reproduction. During the medieval witch hunts, homosexuality as sexual deviance was directly associated with homosexuality as religious deviance or heresy. This connection between homosexuality and heresy persisted even into the twentieth century when Senator Joseph McCarthy equated the "social sin of Communism with the sexual sin of homosexuality" (1970: 166).

The dilemma of homosexuals exactly paralleled that of the witches in the medieval period. According to Szasz, witches felt neither sinful nor considered themselves to be witches. In a similar vein, homosexuals did not consider themselves sick or see themselves as patients requiring treatment. In Szasz's view there was a sharp distinction between physical and mental illness: "It is necessary to keep in mind ... that most people diagnosed as physically ill feel sick and consider themselves sick; whereas most people diagnosed as mentally ill do not feel sick and do not consider themselves sick" (1970: 176). Homosexuals did not feel ill or think of themselves as being ill and, therefore, did not seek psychiatric help. But help was forced on them because the government gave to psychiatrists the power the Church once gave to the Inquisitor:

> My contention [is] that the psychiatric perspective on homosex-
> uality is but a thinly disguised replica of the religious
> perspective which it displaced, and that efforts to "treat" this
> kind of conduct medically are but thinly disguised methods for
> suppressing it. (1970: 170-171)

In viewing homosexuality as a disease, psychiatry was medically stigmatizing homosexuals and participating in their social persecution: "The noise generated by their [the homosexuals'] persecution and their anguished cries of protest are drowned out by the rhetoric of therapy" (1970: 168).

Szasz leveled specific criticisms against fellow psychiatrists who had written authoritatively on the subject of homosexuality. For example, Judd Marmor, he thought, was pretending that conventionality was Nature when he wrote that homosexuality was an illness that could be "corrected" (1970: 167). Karl Menninger, another psychoanalyst, obviously betrayed a religious frame of mind when he referred to homosexuality and prostitution as ranking high in the "kingdom of evils" (1970: 172). Nor could Szasz restrain a footnote in which he quoted Irving Bieber as referring to bachelorhood as "symptomatic of psychopathology" (1970: 175). By promoting such beliefs, psychological ideology threatened individual liberty as religious ideology had once done.

Szasz's essay on the legal and moral aspects of the homosexual identity was published in a volume edited by Judd Marmor, a prestigious psychoanalyst who later became president of the American Psychiatric Association.[5] Marmor's intention was to present the multiple roots of homosexuality by publishing articles based on biological, historical, and social science research as well as clinical observations and practice. His own position, expressed in a lengthy introduction, reflected contemporary post-Freudian psychoanalytic thought on homosexuality. Unlike Szasz, Marmor considered the homosexual identity to be psychopathological and both treatable and reversible. He believed that with greater knowledge of its complex origins, the homosexual identity would eventually be preventable.

Marmor defined "the clinical homosexual" as "one who is motivated, in adult life, by a definite preferential erotic attraction to members of the same sex and who usually (but not necessarily) engages in overt sexual relations with them" (1965: 4). By emphasizing a "strong and spontaneous capacity to be aroused" by (4) a member of the same sex, Marmor intended to include those individuals with intense homosexual fantasies and to exclude adolescents, sailors, and prisoners who are "driven to transitory homosexual patterns of behavior as a consequence of intense heterosexual frustration" (4).

In speculating on the causes of the homosexual identity, Marmor was skeptical of the biological evidence as found, for example, in studies of monozygotic homosexual twins. He sided with the post-Freudian psychoanalysts in rejecting Freud's theory of an innate bisexuality and of homosexuality as a normal phase of psychosexual development. He endorsed the reparative view which held that the homosexual identity would not develop, particularity in hostile social environments, unless there were monumental fears of the opposite sex which blocked the path

---

[5] Marmor, Judd (Ed.). (1965). *Sexual Inversion: The Multiple Roots of Homosexuality*. New York: Basic Books. The biological articles were by R. H. Denniston (ambisexuality in animals), W. H. Perloff (hormones), and C. M. B. Pare (on genetic determinants). The social-cultural research was by E. Hooker (male homosexual society), M. K. Opler (anthropological aspects), T. Szasz and G. R. Taylor (historical and mythological aspects), and S. H. Fisher (homosexuality in Ancient Greece). The clinical contributions were by S. Rado (on bisexuality), R. Stoller (on gender identity), L. Ovesey (pseudo-homosexuality), L. Salzman (latent homosexuality), I. Bieber (male homosexuality), C. Weber (female homosexuality), M. E. Romm (female homosexuality), and P. Mayerson and H. I. Lief (a follow-up study of psychotherapy). Marmor's introduction constitutes Chapter 1: 1-24.

to heterosexuality: "For our time and culture, therefore, the psychoanalytic assumption that preferential homosexual behavior is always associated with unconscious fears of heterosexual relationships appears valid" (1965: 12). He believed these fears in men were associated with the difficult demands placed on them in Western society, which intensified the desire to flee the masculine role.

Thus far his position reflected the pathologization of the homosexual identity found in contemporary psychoanalytic thought. There were, however, several indications that his future position might change in the direction of detoxication. He reminded his fellow analysts that their concepts of homosexuality derived from their homosexual patients. If individuals were shaped as homosexuals by life experiences, then they could not be inherently "unnatural ... except insofar as this preference represents a socially condemned form of behavior in our culture and consequently carries with it certain sanctions and handicaps" (Marmor, 1965: 16).

Marmor distinguished between the "pure scientist's" and clinician's approach to homosexuality. For the scientist, homosexuality and heterosexuality were merely areas of behavior in the broad spectrum of sexual conduct. The clinician, however, reflected the cultural beliefs of what was optimal personality development and adaptation. He implied that clinicians had to be ready to change their standards as society changed.

Marmor agreed with Szasz that a heterosexual adaptation should not be forced on reluctant clients. The authoritative intervention of psychiatry was warranted only in the case of youngsters:

> [W]e could argue with justification that psychiatric intervention is prophylactically indicated for children or adolescents who seem to be failing to make appropriate gender-role identifications. As long as we live in a society that regards homosexuality as an undesirable behavior deviation, the ultimate adaptations of such children to their inner and outer worlds will be potentially better ones if they can be prevented from developing homoerotic patterns. (1965: 18)

Marmor rejected the idea of the "homosexual personality" which he believed in the future would "appear as archaic as the old description of the 'typical' tuberculous or epileptic personalities now appear" (26). What he was implying was that the belief that homosexuals were less able to control their sexual impulses or were less dependable than heterosexuals was little more than social prejudice. He did think, however, that homosexuals generally tended to be more neurotic than heterosexuals simply because social intolerance made life more difficult for them:

> [T]here is, nevertheless, as wide a personality variation among homosexuals as among heterosexuals; from introverts to loud and raucous extroverts; from hysterics to compulsives; from sexually inhibited and timid types to sexually promiscuous and self-flaunting ones; from irresponsible sociopaths to highly responsible and law-abiding citizens. Their psychiatric diagnoses, apart from the homosexual symptom, run the entire gamut of modern nosology. Their physical appearances are equally varied, of course, and cover a wide spectrum from extreme "femininity" of physique and manner to extreme "masculinity." (1965: 19)

Fifteen years after the publication of *Sexual Inversion*, Marmor edited a second volume entitled *Homosexual Behavior: A Modern Reappraisal.*[6] The

---

[6] *Homosexual Behavior: A Modern Reappraisal.* New York: Basic Books, 1980. The biological articles were by H. R. Denniston, "Ambisexuality in Animals"; G. Tourney, "Hormones and Homosexuality"; and J. Money, "Genetic and Chromosomal Aspects of Homosexual Etiology." The social-cultural articles where by A. Karlen, "Homosexuality in History"; J. M. Carrier, "Homosexual Behavior in Cross-Cultural Perspective"; C. Warren, "Homosexuality and Stigma"; L. Humphreys and B. Miller, "Identities in the Emerging Gay Culture"; B. Ponse, "Lesbians and Their Worlds"; J. Kelly, "Homosexuality and Aging"; R. Slovenko, "Homosexuality and the Law: From Condemnation to Celebration"; S. Hiltner, "Homosexuality and the Churches"; and B. Voeller, "Society and the Gay Movement." The clinical articles were by R. Green, "Patterns of Sexual Identity in Childhood: Relationship to Subsequent Sexual Partner Preference"; Marmor, "Clinical Aspects of Male Homosexuality"; M. T. Saghir and E. Robins, "Clinical Aspects of Female Homosexuality"; B. Reiss, "Psychological Tests in Homosexuality"; L. Salzman, "Latent Homosexuality"; L. Ovesey and S. M. Woods, "Pseudohomosexuality and Homosexuality in Men: Psychodynamics as a Guide to Treatment"; D. S. Sanders, "A Psychotherapeutic Approach to Homosexual Men"; M. Kirkpatrick and C. Morgan, "Psychodynamic Psychotherapy of Female Homosexuality"; and L. Birk, "The Myth of Classical Homosexuality: Views of a Behavioral Psychotherapist." There was a final piece by Marmor: "Epilogue: Homosexuality and the Issue of Mental Illness." Only two authors were retained from the first volume: Denniston and Salzman. The social science section was greatly expanded and was largely sociological and political in character. Some of the authors were leaders in the Gay Liberation Movement, such as Bruce Voeller. In the clinical section, authors who had been strongly associated with the position of homosexuality as psychopathology, such as Rado, Stoller, Bieber, Mayerson,

change in title from *Sexual Inversion*, with its connotation of psychopathology, to *Homosexual Behavior*, with its broad social implications, hinted at Marmor's new approach. In the introductory essay Marmor gave greater credence to the "biological roots" and "sociological roots" of homosexuality and shifted away from heavy dependence on the psychological sexual identity.

The most notable change was in his discussion of social intolerance and discrimination under the rubric of **HOMOPHOBIA**. In its most flagrant forms, Marmor held, homophobia "represents a pathological fear of homosexuality, usually based on one or more of the following factors: (1) deep-seated insecurity concerning one's own sexuality and gender identity; (2) strong religious indoctrination; or (3) simple ignorance about homosexuals" (1980: 19). Homophobia, in Marmor's view, was an affliction of heterosexual men and women who were ignorant of the etiology of homosexuality, believing that it was chosen or contagious:

> Many people still tend to think of homosexuality either as a pattern that is freely chosen by a conscious act of will, or as something that is 'caught' from others, either as a result of seduction or by an 'infectious' imitation or modeling of oneself after homosexuals to who one has been exposed. (19)

Assertions that children who have homosexual teachers would become homosexual he labeled as "ignorant or malicious" and having "not an iota of evidence" (19). The die of sexual orientation, he believed, was cast before the age of six. The presence of the homosexual teacher could be beneficial to heterosexual children by creating "more tolerance and understanding toward homosexuals as people, and to dispel the widespread prejudicial myths about them, thus reducing homophobia" (20). Their presence could also benefit "that small percentage of children who for prior developmental reasons are already struggling with homosexual feelings, with all the guilt and self-hatred attendant upon such feelings in our culture" (20).

Finally, Marmor made his plea for statutory protection and for compassion:

---

and Lief, were replaced by authors who took a much more benign position, such as Green, Riess, Sanders, Kirkpatrick, Morgan, and Marmor himself. The volume moved distinctly in the direction of Szasz's indictment of the pathologization of homosexuality (see pp. 275-276), although Szasz's article was not retained.

[T]he legalization of homosexual behavior between consenting adults and the outlawing of discriminatory practices against homosexuals is a first and necessary step in making it possible for millions of men and women whose early life experiences, through no fault of their own, have rendered them erotically responsive to their own sex, to live lives of dignity and self-respect. This is a mental health issue of the first magnitude, one with important and widespread implications for homosexuals and heterosexuals alike. (20-21)

In his discussion of the "clinical aspects of homosexuality," Marmor distinguished between two groups of homosexuals: those who maintained extended relationships and those who were promiscuous in sexual behavior. Homosexuals who searched for a "meaningful human relationship" were "more emotionally mature" (269). Promiscuous homosexuals were less psychologically and sociologically stable. Psychologically they feared "interpersonal commitment, intimacy, or responsibility that may play a part not only in the avoidance of heterosexual involvement but may also operate in regard to homosexual relationships" (269-270). Sociologically, the promiscuous homosexual was doing what a heterosexual man would do in the same situation—taking advantage of easily available sex. But Marmor appeared to favor the psychological explanation:

[H]omosexuals who cruise in public parks, streets, and public restrooms are often individuals who are seeking relatively impersonal sex and who have strong neurotic components to their homosexual behavior. The drive for impersonal sex sometimes has an enormously compulsive quality. Some of these individuals may be involved in a dozen or more transactions in the course of a single day or evening. Most homosexuals who seek passing relationships but are less neurotically driven look for them in homosexual baths and gay bars where there is a higher degree of safety. (270)

In contrast with the promiscuous, the coupled homosexuals had relationships that "involved the same kind of emotional exchange and commitment that heterosexuals experience in love relationships" (270).

As in 1965, Marmor endorsed the "prevention of homosexual development" (274) in children: It was "obviously" (274) what all heterosexual parents wanted. Even most homosexual parents wanted to spare their children "the difficulties that a homosexual way of life entails in our culture" (274). Finally, effeminacy in boys should be treated to prevent their homosexual development and to spare them "merciless teasing and hazing from their peers" (274). Therapeutic efforts at prevention should involve the whole family.

Marmor echoed Szasz's sentiments as expressed in 1965 that no adult homosexual should be forced into treatment: "Homosexual behavior that violates standards of decent behavior in public, or that involves the seduction of minors, should be handled by legal sanctions just as analogous behavior by heterosexuals should be" (275). Most adult homosexuals who sought therapy did so for the same reasons as heterosexuals: "loneliness, dissatisfaction with their partners, breakups of meaningful love relationships, problems in self-realization, or a wide variety of neurotic or depressive reactions" (275). Those who sought treatment after having been arrested for public homosexual behavior should be treated in a manner that would deepen their "understanding of the unconscious significance of their need for impersonal sex and their (usual) inability to establish a meaningful dyadic relationship" (276). Homosexuals who were most likely to succeed in switching to the heterosexual identity were those under thirty-five, who had more heterosexual than homosexual experience, and who were masculine-looking men or feminine-looking women.[7]

In the epilogue to *Homosexual Behavior*, Marmor attempted to refute the psychoanalytic arguments upon which the case for the homosexual identity as a pathology rested. The first was "that homosexual behavior is a disorder of sexual development resulting from disturbed family relationships" (395). Marmor viewed this as merely the assertion that individuals who did not turn out to be heterosexual were mentally ill. It was in the same league as diagnosing political dissent as mental illness or labeling masturbation (as in the nineteenth century) as serious mental disturbance.

The second argument was that homosexuality "represents an obvious deviation from the biologic norm" (395). Here Marmor took the position that mammalian inheritance was essentially bisexual and that only through its conversion to heterosexuality or homosexuality did one sex become an exclusive source of sexual arousal. Marmor questioned conceptions of "natural" behavior:

---

[7] In a footnote (279), Marmor criticized Masters and Johnson for not making the distinction among homosexuals in their treatment program. He also took issue with their claim that heterosexual performance was blocked by anxiety. He believed their program did not change "the underlying homosexual eroticism or fantasy life" of the patients.

The argument that homosexuality is biologically unnatural becomes even more specious when one considers that all civilized human behavior from the cooking of food to the wearing of clothes is a departure from the strictly "natural." We do not label vegetarianism or sexual celibacy as automatic evidences of psychopathology, even though these behavioral patterns do not follow "natural" biological expectations. Actually, one of the most distinctive characteristics of human beings is their extraordinary capacity to modify and transform their "natural" biological drives into widely diverse patterns of behavior, whether this be in terms of sexuality, eating, devising shelters, worshiping gods, or developing the mathematical precision that enables them to land a man on the moon.(395)

The third argument was that "when homosexuals are studied psychodynamically they are found to be emotionally disturbed and unhappy people" (395). In psychoanalytic theory a number of emotional disturbances were identified in the homosexual male: (1) entrenched castration anxiety which led to the fear of women and reparative efforts to regain the penis through intercourse with males; (2) narcissism; (3) fear and hatred of women (evidenced by fantasies of the dentate vagina); and (4) effeminacy traceable to identification with the mother as the more loving or stronger parent. Marmor believed that the first assertion did not explain bisexuals, who had intercourse with both sexes. The second and third assertions applied equally well to heterosexual males who were most of the diagnosed narcissists and who also had dreams and fantasies of dentate vaginas. The fourth assertion did not explain "non-feminine" homosexual males.

Under psychoanalytic scrutiny Marmor believed that all individuals would appear at least a little unhealthy: "It must be recognized that there are very few individuals indeed, heterosexual or homosexual, in whom deep psychoanalytic probing would not elicit some evidences of deviance from ideal normality. No one is perfectly healthy, psychologically, in an absolute sense" (399-400).

In 1973 two psychiatrists, Marcel Saghir and Eli Robins, published a study of non-clinical samples of homosexual females and males.[8] Their

_____

[8] Saghir, Marcel T. and Robins, Eli (1973). *Male and Female Homosexuality: A Comprehensive Investigation.* Baltimore: Williams and Wilkins. A sample of eighty-nine homosexual males was recruited primarily from homophile organizations: in Chicago, from Mattachine Midwest and One, Inc., and, in San Francisco, from the Society for Individual Rights. A sample of fifty-seven

intention was to present the results of a study of female and male homosexuality which described homosexual development, adolescent and adult sexual practices, psychopathology, family relationships, and the sociological concomitants of being homosexual.[9]

The study was presented as exploratory and objective. The authors stated that they began with no hypotheses, avoided definitive stands, and "felt emotionally neutral" (4) toward their subject matter.[10]

---

homosexual females were obtained primarily through the Daughters of Bilitis. Respondents who qualified as homosexuals identified themselves as having had "a history of repetitive overt homosexual activity continuing beyond the age of 18" (6). A control group of thirty-five unmarried males and forty-four unmarried females were selected from an apartment complex in St. Louis County. To qualify as heterosexuals, respondents had to be exclusive in "sexual psychologic preference and behavior after the age of 18" (7). It was not clear why the authors used age 18 as the cut-off point in defining sexual orientation given that adolescence was defined by them as occurring between ages 14 and 19 and adulthood as beginning at age 20. A fifty-page interview schedule, which took between three to four hours to complete, was used to collect data on demographic background, occurrences of psychopathology, the development of sexual orientation, sexual practices, family relationships, interpersonal relationships, and relationship to social environment. Although most of the questions on the interview schedule were answered with a "yes," a "no," or a number, all the affirmative answers and some of the other responses were probed. The authors distinguished between CASUAL RELATIONSHIPS (lasting less than four months), LIAISONS (lasting between four and twelve months), and AFFAIRS (lasting over one year). Because the heterosexuals showed considerably less interest in being interviewed than the homosexuals, the heterosexuals were paid $15 for their time. The authors believed that the homosexuals in their samples were "hard core confirmed homosexuals" (16) who were adjusted to their homosexuality and their world and, therefore, could not be considered "sick."

[9] George Winokur, also a psychiatrist, stated in the preface to the book that the authors were following the tradition in psychiatry of fully describing the "clinical syndrome" (viii) as the first step in formulating an etiology and treatment. He referred to homosexuality as a "condition." For example, he praised the authors for having "written the classic psychiatric work on the homosexual condition" (viii). He also commended them for using a control group of "single" persons because they "are more likely to show psycho-pathology than married individuals" (viii). Such statements implied that Winokur felt that the authors had studied homosexuality as psychopathology.

[10] A few sentences later they appeared more divided than neutral when they stated that they tried to strike a balance between excessive feelings of prejudice

The authors' first conclusions were about homosexual males. As boys these males displayed a "well circumscribed picture of polysymptomatic effeminacy or sissiness" (28). The "symptoms" were the boys' preferring the companionship of girls to that of other boys, playing with dolls, staying around the house, and shunning sports and rough games. There was also the constant desire of the boys to become girls and several solitary occasions when they dressed up as females.

The "sexual psychologic responses" of the homosexual respondents were reported as basically homosexual. These included their romantic attachments, fantasies and imagery, and sexual arousal. It did not include sexual behavior, which the authors acknowledged was not always congruent with psychologic responsiveness. Homosexual males were depicted as masturbating more than heterosexual males "at every period throughout their [the homosexuals'] sexual histories" (62). Single heterosexual males gave up masturbation usually by the age of thirty. The greater frequency and continuance of masturbation by homosexual males was explained by the observation that they started their sexual practices earlier than the heterosexuals. This running start provided the opportunity for sexual activity to reach a crescendo by the time the homosexual males became adults:

> During adolescence and in adult life his homosexual practices become more intense. There is usually a multiplicity of partners with 'one-night' stands and short-lasting relationships. His sexual pursuits are often impersonal and serve an immediate need for orgasmic discharge. (63)

Partners exchanged sexual roles so that both acted as insertees as well as insertors in fellatio and anal intercourse: "There are no strict 'masculine' or 'feminine' roles although a minority tends to subscribe to such a behavior" (63).

Although homosexual men experienced unabated sexual ardor, they sought and were often able to maintain intimate relationships. Although most of these "affairs" lasted less than four years, some lasted for decades. For the most part partners in these relationships did not require sexual fidelity.

The psychologic preference for homosexuality, the authors reported, did not exclude heterosexual behavior "[d]uring a specific period in their lives most homosexual males date, about one-half of them engage in

---

and compassion. They felt "some prejudice and some compassion" (4). Neither of attitudes suggested an untroubled acceptance of homosexuality.

intercourse, and over one-half establish a relationship with a woman lasting for a year or longer" (103).[11] This high level of involvement in heterosexual relationships was explained chiefly as the capitulation of these men to social pressure in their vain effort to become "one" with heterosexual society. Some heterosexual behavior was due to "genuine responsiveness, curiosity, and self-reassurance through a process of experimentation and testing" (101). When heterosexual activity lead to marriage it was to satisfy the need of the homosexual male "for social acceptance and the longing for children and the domestic life" (104). Those men who did marry chose wives who were "strong-willed, demanding, and pushy" (104). The marriages rarely lasted because the males soon discovered that their homosexual desires did not vanish.[12]

In dealing with the issue of psychopathology, the authors avoided the question of whether or not homosexuality itself was pathological, clearly expressing a desire not to involve themselves in the "sickness-health controversy" (130) and not to take "fixed positions concerning the pathologic nature of homosexuality or its normalcy.[13] Instead, they tried to determine if "the rates of definable psychopathology" (130) were higher among homosexuals than a comparable group of heterosexuals. In searching for psychopathology in their respondents the authors focused on the "degree of symptomatic dysfunction" rather than "an ideal state of mental health" (8). Specifically, they looked for anxiety neurosis, antisocial personality, alcoholism, affective disorders, phobias, paranoid tendencies,

---

[11] These last two proportions are confusing because one would assume that all the men who established relationships were also having sexual intercourse.

[12] Saghir and Robins reported that only 19% of the homosexual males had nocturnal emissions, as compared with 94% of the heterosexual males (102). They recognized that this notable difference could be explained by the higher frequency of masturbation of homosexual males, but they then added the curious speculation that the higher incidence of masturbation was "possibly also a result of the inadequate or arrested heterosexual responsiveness among them [the homosexual males]" (102). It was not clear why heterosexual responsiveness would lead to a dampening of masturbatory interest. The explanation also attributed what could be considered the superior performance of the homosexual males to an incapacity rather than to an entirely acceptable cultivation of interest and taste.

[13] Saghir and Robins, however, noted the intensity of the conflict between the "Gay Liberation Front," and psychiatrists who took negative positions on homosexuality in the professional literature "that are far from supported by objective scientific evidence" (136).

and psychosomatic disorders. Finally, they made a general assessment of intrapersonal and interpersonal functional disability.

The authors identified some differences in the psychopathology of the homosexual and heterosexual men. In the homosexual group they found more feminine identification and personality traits, less competitiveness, more visits to physicians when depressed, more dropping out of college, and a greater number of different jobs. There were also greater trends toward alcoholism, heavy drug usage, more suicide attempts, more affective disorders, and greater likelihood of being fired. There were no indications of differences in the ways of handling anger, concern for the opinions of others, prevalence of psychiatric disorders, depression, psychosomatic illnesses, psychotic or paranoid patterns, educational and occupational achievement, and overall personal and functional disability. The authors concluded:

[I]t is apparent from our findings that homosexual men are strikingly similar to single heterosexual men in most areas of psychopathology. Despite the finding that a majority of the male homosexuals had had a symptomatic disorder at one time or another in their lives, such disorders were often situational rather than an ongoing neuroses or addictions. (136)

Despite findings regarding the mental health of their homosexual respondents, the authors held the opinion that most homosexuals could benefit from psychotherapy that was limited to problems of adjustment:

Promoting adjustment and defusing conflict are primary goals. A small proportion of homosexuals will come to psychiatrists demanding a change in orientation. These individuals, where feasible, should be offered the help they are seeking. However, the majority of male homosexuals who go to a psychiatrist do so not to be "changed" but to be helped to adjust and tolerate. For these individuals such goals should be adequate and practical. (136)

Saghir and Robins intended to shed light on the etiology of male homosexuality by investigating the parental home and family relationships of their respondents. In turning to the family, they noted they were following psychiatric tradition in tracing the origins of mental illness: "It seems reasonable to say that what cannot be explained now by anatomy, physiology, and chemistry or by genes and chromosomes be-comes automatically a disorder with a 'functional' component, with roots in early life events often involving the parents and the early environment at home" (149).

Their reported findings tended to confirm many of the conclusions of the Bieber group about poor parental relationships and homosexuality. The parental homes were marked by "intense discord and fighting" (152). Fathers were almost always described by homosexual males as "indifferent and uninvolved at home" (152), particularly with the prehomosexual son. Mothers were seen as the dominant parent who made decisions, carried out discipline, and showed more drive and involvement. However, some of the homosexual males had closer relationships with fathers than mothers while some of the heterosexual males had closer relationships with mothers. The Bieber group had concluded that a breakdown of the parent-son relationship was the cause of homosexuality. Saghir and Robins, in a more cautious vein, concluded that poor parental relations accompanied but did not necessarily cause male homosexuality.

The report on the "sociologic considerations" of homosexuality followed the style of ethnographic description. The authors noted the increased militancy of the "Gay Liberation Front" since 1969 and its strong advocacy of the individual's public disclosure of homosexuality. They saw the older homophile organizations as more suitable for the individual: "the homosexual does not need a greater emphasis on his homosexuality but rather on himself as an individual, not dissimilar in his goals, aspirations and accomplishments from his heterosexual counterpart" (180). One of the advantages of homosexual organizations was that they provided opportunities for "homosexuals to meet other homosexuals for the purpose of sexual liaisons" (181).

Discrimination against homosexuals by organized religion and the military, the authors believed, should be actively opposed by homosexuals. "Cruising," they thought, led to problems caused by homosexuals themselves:

> While he labors under a variety of discriminatory practices against him, the homosexual does not help matters very much by certain patterns of his sexual behavior. In his search for sexual partners the homosexual male spends a good deal of his time "cruising" bars, streets, parks and numerous other places. As a result he is often arrested by the police through direct intervention or entrapment. It is surprising to find that close to one-half of the homosexual men [who were respondents] were arrested, assaulted, robbed or threatened, usually in the context of their homosexual behavior. (185)

The final portrait of the male homosexual rendered by Saghir and Robins was that of the man who carried on as a socially useful and productive worker while remaining stoically resigned to the difficulties of personal and social relationships:

> Ultimately and at some point in his life he reconciles himself to his problems and despite the early conflict and emotional turmoil, manages to remain without disability or handicap. In doing this, he runs into a great deal of difficulty, specifically in his social and personal relationships. His close friendships are most often limited to other homosexuals and his parental connections are often severed because of his homosexuality. (187)

As the homosexual male grew older, his life became still lonelier: "the homosexual man grows older without a family and without children and most often without a stable relationship" (188). His only heterosexual friends were usually fellow workers. He came to view his homosexuality as more and more the source of his unhappiness.

The second set of conclusions presented in the report by Saghir and Robins pertained to female homosexuality. As a childhood phenomenon, homosexuality in girls could be observed as tomboyishness, a "syndrome" which included "persistent aversion to girls' activities and to girls as playmates" and "a definite preference for the company of boys and for boys' activities" (192). Tomboys had little identification with the mother and recurring wishes to be boys. But boy-like behavior in girls was more prevalent than girl-like behavior in boys. Tomboyishness, the authors concluded, was much less a predictor of future homosexuality than sissiness in boys.[14]

Homosexual women masturbated more than heterosexual women and began the practice earlier. Manual-genital stimulation was the most common practice among homosexual women. Cunnilingus was added later and was an almost "universal" practice (220). Almost all the homosexual women were both insertors and insertees in performing cunnilingus. A relatively small proportion used dildos as part of sexual intercourse. Many had affairs lasting more than a year, a far larger proportion than for the males. The female relationships were characterized by sexual fidelity. The primary reason for the breakup of these affairs was that one of the female partners was "not basically

---

[14] The authors revealed an uneasiness with tomboyishness and homosexuality when they stated that tomboyishness was "not altogether an innocuous behavior" (201) when it led to homosexuality.

homosexual" (227). Homosexual women were reported as more promiscuous than heterosexual women but far less than men of either orientation. The majority of homosexual women stated that they had no feeling of fear or guilt about their homosexual activity. The homosexual women seemed to have been more involved in heterosexual activity than the homosexual men. More of the women engaged in intercourse and more got married. They were not disgusted by the sight of male genitals, did not mind talking about them, and had not turned to homosexuality as a result of a traumatic heterosexual experience.

As for psychopathology the homosexual women fared worse than the heterosexual women in three areas: they drank alcohol excessively over a number of years; they viewed themselves as more masculine and less feminine than the average woman; and they dropped out of college at a higher rate than heterosexual women. It can be inferred from Saghir and Robins' discussion that the reason for excessive drinking by homosexual women was linked to their denial or rejection of traditional female roles:

> Equality and opportunity for women do not preclude or elimi-
> nate some of their essential and basic roles as women, wives,
> and mothers. Thus, while the traditional roles of women are be-
> ing redefined and reoriented, they are not and cannot be
> eliminated. Contrastingly, for a large proportion of homosexual
> women such roles are denied and thus are absent in their tradi-
> tional and even redefined models. (291)

The higher rate of college dropouts was explained by the assertion that homosexual women came to grips with their homosexuality most intensely during their early college years.

Aside from these differences the authors concluded that the patterns of psychopathology in homosexual and heterosexual women were strikingly similar. Both types of women were reported as suffering from "neurotic and psychophysiologic disorders and premenstrual depressions and menstrual irregularity and disability are also not much different between the groups" (293-294). As in the case of the homosexual men, the homosexual women ultimately became resigned to their homosexuality: "At least on a conscious level they arrive at a point in their daily lives when homosexuality becomes well tolerated and accepted as an unalterable and an integral part of the personality" (294).

The early family relationships of the homosexual female respondents tended to show a pattern of conflict similar to that of the male respondents. The females reported much domestic conflict in their childhood homes, often leading to the divorce of parents. They had remote or hostile relations with mothers. They had few siblings, usually more brothers than sisters.[15]

Because the homosexuals reported that their awareness of cross-gender behavior stretched back to early childhood, Saghir and Robins suggested that the discord that characterized their family relationships was the result of the parents' failure to realize that they were dealing with a "different" and possibly prehomosexual child:

> The possibility remains that due to the behavioral and temperamental peculiarities of the prehomosexual child, the parents respond to cues based on those peculiarities that become already established at a very early age. Thus, the father of the sissy boy dissociates himself emotionally from such a child and the mother of the tomboyish girl finds little in common with her disinterested girl. Consequently, a situation is created whereby the behavior of the prehomosexual child instigates rejection from the same-sexed parent and the acceptance and involvement from the opposite-sexed parent. As this situation is perpetuated, it creates strain and conflict between the parents that eventually might lead up to divorce in certain instances. (301)

The authors reported a number of comparisons between the "sexual psychologic responses" of homosexual females and homosexual males. In females the overt homosexual activity and romantic attachments occurred later, toward the end of adolescence. Their first conscious homosexual arousal stemmed from a romantic relationship which was nongenital, while for the males it was the result of genital contact with another male. Female like male homosexuals had both heterosexual and homosexual fantasies and dreams, but the homosexual predominated and the heterosexual were not usually indications of "true heterosexual responsiveness" (213). The reason that homosexuals did not continue heterosexual activity was that it lacked emotional gratification. This deficiency Saghir and Robins attributed to the basically homosexual content of the homosexuals' dreams and fantasies, which represented "ideational rehearsals in wakefulness and sleep" (213).

---

[15] Saghir and Robins proposed that a shortage of sisters might promote a feminine identity in boys while an excess of brothers might foster tomboyishness in girls (304). It is possible that they were tacitly assuming that femininity was less attractive to boys than masculinity to girls.

The authors explored the reasons for the heterosexual marriages of female and male homosexuals. They did not believe that the females married more frequently than the males because they were more bisexual or heterosexual. It was more likely because the females did not have to produce erections and could limit their role in heterosexual intercourse to passive reception. It was the fear of erectile failure that kept homosexual males away from heterosexual intercourse. Most of the heterosexual marriages involving a homosexual partner were not durable. Those that did last were maintained on an affectionate basis without sexual intercourse or based on the agreement that the homosexual spouse would continue to have sexual relations with the marital partner while also engaging in homosexual intercourse outside the marital bed.[16] The authors believed that it was more likely that the homosexual spouse kept the heterosexual partner ignorant of her or his homosexual involvements.

Because the homosexual women were depicted by the authors as more aggressive than the average woman and the homosexual men as less demanding and more passive than the average man, they were naturally curious as to why homosexual men and women did not marry each other. Their conclusions rested on the assumption that such liaisons could only be marriages of convenience in which no sexual intercourse occurred. They predicted that the contrast in personalities, which in heterosexual relationships could serve as a stimulus for sexual arousal, in homosexual liaisons would become potential sources of friction: "opposing personality traits might only lead to conflict and disharmony despite the temporary arrangement of the marriage between opposite-sex homosexuals" (265).

The differences between female and male homosexuality were attributed to the biological and cultural differences between men and women. The promiscuity, violence, and unstable relationships that the authors believed epitomized the life of the homosexual male was attributed to the fact that: "the male is more prone to aggressive, sexually and socially unstable behavior because he is more likely to be punished for it" (305). Because aggression was denied to women the homosexual female was not involved in arrests and violence. Their lives were private. Sex for them was wedded to love:

---

[16] The authors were following the conclusions reached in a study by Ross, H. L. (1971). Models of Adjustment of Married Homosexuals. *Social Problems 18*: 385-393.

> Unlike the homosexual male, incidental homosexual activity is rarely practiced by the homosexual female. One-night stands occur but are the exception rather than the rule. In her search for sex, the homosexual woman looks first for a relationship and usually establishes a relationship prior to any sexual activity. (313)

The women were not engulfed by their homosexuality as were the men; they had more close heterosexual friends than the men; few felt that their homosexuality set limits to their ambitions, and they were also much less anxious about growing old.

Saghir and Robins believed that both psychological responsiveness and overt behavior were essential considerations in classifying individuals as heterosexual or homosexual. As psychiatrists, however, they tended to discount behavior in favor of psychological or mental states: "Being a homosexual, like being a heterosexual, is primarily a psychologic preference and responsiveness" (101). They drew a distinction between the homosexual behavior of homosexuals and what they called "the incidental homosexual behavior" (177) of heterosexuals:

> Homosexual behavior as an incidental practice represents a common behavior among non-homosexuals. Preadolescence and adolescence are periods of development in which homosexual practices occur frequently among heterosexual preadults. Such a behavior is often a result of curiosity, and of sexual strivings made intense by hormonal changes during adolescence. Often, homosexual behavior at this time is more accessible than heterosexual behavior and has a great deal less guilt and anxiety attached to it. (177)

The authors then went on to claim that homosexual practices were dropped by heterosexuals during the adult years, except in cases of psychotic individuals, thrill-seekers, and prisoners. To explain behavior that appeared to be bisexual, the authors came up with the ideas of "situational" and "limited" homosexuality and heterosexuality. Both concepts were based on the assumption that the individual was basically homosexual or heterosexual in responsiveness.

SITUATIONAL sexuality was not the result of basic responsiveness but of special factors such as group pressure or lack of availability of partners of the preferred sex. For example, "situational heterosexuality" was practiced by homosexuals "not out of basic responsiveness, but due to the 'primacy' of heterosexuality in society and consequently to the social, family, and personal pressure that the individual homosexual finds himself subjected to during adolescence and young adulthood" (262). "Situational homosexuality" of heterosexuals was the result of the absence of partners of the opposite sex.

The idea of a LIMITED homosexual or heterosexual identity explained why individuals who were basically homosexual or heterosexual could still possess the responsiveness associated with the opposite identity . The limited heterosexuality of homosexuals, the authors believed, "could reflect a genuine degree of psychological responsiveness." The limited homosexuality of heterosexuals, the authors thought, could have been due to "an adaptational response to avoidance fear of heterosexuality" (263).

As an example of this reasoning, in a later essay on female homosexuality, Saghir and Robins reported that there was an increasing tendency for some heterosexual women to form homosexual relationships.[17] Such behavior, they conjectured, partially reflected the increased emphasis of women on independence and assertiveness. Despite these homosexual involvements, the authors still considered the women to be heterosexual: "The most crucial aspect that defines homosexuality is the lifelong psychological tendencies to homosexual preferences, rather than the behavior itself.... They form a separate group of women associated with homosexuality but not truly homosexual" (294).

The efforts of Szasz, Marmor, Saghir, and Robins to detoxicate homosexual relationships were based on the belief in the psychological homosexual identity. For Szasz this identity was transhistorical, existing at least from the Middle Ages to the twentieth century. It was also psychological because it represented a form of "psychosexual immaturity." For Marmor it was a "definite preferential attraction to members of the same sex, "a strong and spontaneous" homosexual capacity, and "intense homosexual fantasies." The homosexual identity for Saghir and Robins consisted of "lifelong psychological tendencies to homosexual preferences." Most of these men rejected the notion that engaging in homosexual behavior was proof of the homosexual identity. Homosexual behavior in individuals who lacked the homosexual identity was described as "situational," "limited" or "incidental." When it was situational for males it was attributed to the unavailability of female partners.

---

[17] Saghir, Marcel T. and Robins, Eli (1980). Clinical Aspects of Female Homosexuality. In J. Marmor, Ed., *Homosexual Behavior: A Modern Reappraisal.* New York: Basic Books, 280-295.

Marmor, Saghir, and Robins were cautious about the forms of homosexual practices and relationships they detoxicated. At the time Marmor endorsed Rado's theory of an innate heterosexual identity, he accepted the reparative view of homosexual relationships. In his later thinking, when he returned to Freud's theory of an innate bisexuality and the belief in a diffuse mammalian sexual capacity, he abandoned reparative theory as the necessary etiology of all homosexuals, reserving its application to those who did not form "stable" sexual relationships and who were seemingly caught in the grip of promiscuity.

Saghir and Robbins, instead of looking for traces of pathology in all forms of homosexuality, tried to assess the extent of pathology in homosexuals who had never sought psychiatric treatment. The psychopathology they claimed to have found was that which they did not detoxicate: femininity in men, masculinity in women, depression and despair, wavering commitments to education and job, heavy drinking and drug usage, and "cruising." They did detoxicate homosexuals who became "reconciled" to their homosexual identity as an unalterable part of their personalities. By implication the pathologized homosexuals were those trapped in the futile struggle to escape their sexual identity.

The psychiatric effort to detoxicate the homosexual identity reflected the three cosmological views of sexual relationships. The polytheistic view was still proscribed by the detoxicators as it had been by the post-Freudian reparative theorists. Transitory sexual relationships with unfamiliar partners found in public meeting places were seen by the detoxicators as motivated by the inner torment of homosexuals who were running away from their sexual identity. Such self-denial presumably closed the door to intimacy and love. These were the homosexuals who had been severely traumatized as children and for whom sexual promiscuity was merely a reparative mechanism. The polytheistic belief in sexual relationships that promised only excitement and pleasure was essentially rejected by the psychiatric detoxicators.

Marmor, for example, implied that "uncontained sexuality" was disruptive for the individual and society; the less contained, the more neurotic. It was the form of sexuality practiced in public settings and outside paired relationships. Marmor had several objections to such practices. As sex in restrooms, parks, and on sidewalks, it was a potential source of shock to the general public. It was also dangerous for practitioners because it could lead to arrest. As a "driven" sexuality it could lead to licentiousness (e.g., a dozen partners in one evening). There were two ways Marmor suggested for containing rampant homosexuality.

To protect themselves from danger, those homosexuals who were sexually very active should limit their sexual contacts to those individuals they found in gay bars and baths. Marmor did not add that this institutionalization of homosexuality also kept it from public view. It was possible that the driven homosexuals could find in psychotherapy ways of containing their sexuality within coupledom. Stable relationships were the ultimate containment because they enveloped sexuality within the folds of emotion and intimacy.[18]

The monotheistic conception of the structure of sexual relationships, therefore, was endorsed by the detoxicators as it had been by the pathologizers before them. This endorsement was obscured by the bold attacks the detoxicators made on the institutional proscription of homosexuality. Szasz and Marmor both attacked psychiatry. Szasz compared psychiatry, in its treatment of homosexuals, to the Inquisition, the ecclesiastical tribunal erected by the medieval papacy for the purpose of discovering, punishing, and preventing heresy. Under the guise of medicine and mental health, psychiatry was bent on uprooting the "error" of homosexuality. Marmor condemned the social intolerance and discrimination he called "homophobia." He implied that the fulminations of fellow psychiatrists such as Socarides were evidence of homophobia within the profession. Saghir and Robbins, attempting to maintain the posture of scientific neutrality, did not point the finger of blame at psychiatry but lamented the discrimination against homosexuals by the military and organized religion. The plea of the detoxicators for tolerance and compassion was the corollary of their belief in the psychological homosexual identity. If homosexuals could not change their sexual identity, then it was incumbent upon society to change its attitudes toward homosexuals from one of moral condemnation to tolerance and fair treatment.

Despite their ringing political defense of homosexuals, the detoxicators expected that homosexual relationships fit within the view of the monotheistic cosmology. Marmor expected normalized homosexuals to join together as partners in relationships modeled after heterosexual monogamy. He left the impression, however, that the major function of homosexual monogamy was to contain the rampant sexuality that lay at the roots of the homosexual identity. For homosexuals, as for heterosexuals, "marriage" was the mark of personal stability and maturity.

---

[18] Marmor betrayed a little reservation about homosexual coupledom. The homosexual liaisons were described as "significant emotional exchange" while the heterosexual liaisons were described as "love relationships" (1980: 270).

Although Saghir and Robbins did not directly address the issue of homosexual pairings, their comparison of homosexual respondents with unmarried heterosexual respondents implied that married individuals were usually mentally healthier than single individuals of either sexual identity.

The monotheistic cosmology was also reflected in the detoxicators' view of biological sex. The normalized homosexual was to be true to her or his own biological sex, behaving in a feminine manner if female or in a masculine manner if male. For Saghir and Robbins, the adjustment of the adult homosexual was a constant struggle against childhood sissiness or tomboyishness.

In all the detoxicators there was the hint of the discomfort and distaste they felt for homosexuals who departed in appearance and personality from the established sex-role stereotypes. The greater the departure, they appeared to believe, the greater the homosexual's pathology. As part of sex-role conformity the detoxicated homosexual was to acquire the other credentials of adulthood: complete a college education, obtain and hold a job, and be productive and dependable. Because all this had to be done under the shadow of stigma and oppression, the detoxicated homosexual was supposed to face life with grit and stoicism.

None of these writers appeared to question the popular belief that males were more sexual than females. Females had to turn to love and nest building even if they lacked the children for whom nests were built. Males found satisfaction in sexual pursuit and conquest. Their accounts of the cruising of male homosexuals were redolent with sexual intensity, the result of uniting the sexual capacities of two or more males. Within the scientific discourse on sexual identity, it was always more difficult to bring male than female homosexual relationships within the ambit of the monotheistic view because of an almost primordial fear of the presumably ungovernable sexual capacity of males.

The psychiatric detoxicators of the homosexual identity clothed their conceptions of the homosexual identity within the scientific cosmological view. The elements of love, intimacy, and passion were included in their depiction of sexual relationships, with the clear implication that the ideal was more easily achieved by heterosexuals than homosexuals. The detoxicators also retreated to scientism in order to support their moral views with the authority of science. Marmor claimed the authority of clinical evidence. Saghir and Robbins laid claim to the authority of the scientific method.

11 Pathologizers versus Detoxicators: The Psychiatric Debate

The outcome of a quarter-century of pathologization and the later detoxication of the homosexual identity resulted in an ideological struggle within the American Psychiatric Association during the period 1972 to 1981.[1]

The ensuing debate revealed not only the divergence of opinion among psychiatric leaders but also the lingering reluctance on the part of almost all psychiatrists to detoxicate completely the homosexual identity so that it occupied a status equal to that of the heterosexual identity.

In the first edition of the *Diagnostic and Statistical Manual of Mental Disorders (DSM-I)*, published in 1952, homosexuality was listed under the heading "sexual deviation." Sexual deviation was defined as follows:

> This diagnosis is reserved for deviant sexuality which is not symptomatic of more extensive syndromes, such as schizophrenia and obsessional reactions. The term includes most of the cases classed as "psychopathic personality with pathologic sexuality." The diagnosis will specify the type of the pathologic behavior, such as homosexuality, transvestism, pedophilia, fetishism, and sexual sadism (including rape, sexual assault, mutilation). (*DSM-I:* 38-39)

"Sexual deviation" appeared under the general heading, "sociopathic personality disturbance," which included "antisocial reaction" and "dyssocial reaction" as diagnostic categories. "Antisocial reaction" referred to:

---

[1] For a journalistic overview of this struggle see Bayer, Ronald (1981). *Homosexuality and American Psychiatry: The Politics of Diagnosis.* New York: Basic Books. Bayer described the role of Gay Liberation leaders in bringing pressure upon the APA. For an analysis of problems involved in defining sexual disorders and mental illness, see Suppe, Frederick (1984). Classifying Sexual Disorders: The Diagnostic and Statistical Manual of the American Psychiatric Association. *Journal of Homosexuality* 9(4): 9-28.

[c]hronically antisocial individuals who are always in trouble, profiting neither from experience nor punishment, and maintaining no real loyalties to any person, group, or code. They are frequently callous and hedonistic, showing marked emotional immaturity, with lack of sense of responsibility, lack of judgment, and an ability to rationalize their behavior so that it appears warranted, reasonable, and justified. The term includes cases previously classified as "constitutional psychopathic state" and "psychopathic personality." (*DSM-I:* 38)

"Dyssocial reaction" was applied to

[i]ndividuals who manifest disregard for the usual social codes, and often come in conflict with them, as the result of having all their lives in abnormal moral environments. They may be capable of strong loyalties. These individuals typically do not show significant personality deviations other than those implied by adherence to the values or code of their own predatory, criminal, or other social group. The term includes such diagnoses as "pseudosocial personality" and "psychopathic personality with asocial and amoral trends." (*DSM-I:* 38)

The classification "sexual deviation" was followed by the section on alcoholism and drug addiction.

In the second edition of the *Manual (DSM-II)*, published in 1968, the diagnosis of sexual deviations appeared under the general category of personality disorders, including "inadequate" and "immature" personality. The deviations were described with much more specificity than they had been in the first edition:

This category is for individuals whose sexual interests are directed primarily toward objects other than people of the opposite sex, toward sexual acts not usually associated with coitus, or toward coitus performed under bizarre circumstances as in necrophilia, pedophilia, sexual sadisms, and fetishism. Even though many find their practices distasteful, they remain unable to substitute normal sexual behavior for them. This diagnosis is not appropriate for individuals who perform deviant sexual acts because normal sexual objects are not available to them. (*DSM-II:* 44)

The explanation of the category, "sexual deviation," was followed by a list which included homosexuality, fetishism, pedophilia, transvestism, exhibitionism, sadism, masochism, and other "unspecified sexual deviations." Apart from its listing under this category, nothing more was said about homosexuality, although it was the deviation that headed the list. The section on deviation was preceded by a category called "inadequate personality" and still followed by the categories of "alcoholism" and "drug dependence."

Detoxication of the homosexual identity at the organizational level began in 1972 when the Northern New England District Branch of the American Psychiatric Association enacted a resolution which called for the deletion of homosexuality per se from *DSM-II* and its replacement with the diagnostic category of "sexual dysfunction." Along with frigidity and impotence, homosexuality was to be included when the therapist believed it was a "problem" for the patient. The resolution, setting the ideological tone for others to follow, called for an end to discrimination against homosexuals, repeal of legislation against adult consensual homosexual intercourse, and the inclusion of homosexuality as a topic in sex education courses for young people.[2]

On the national level, the controversy within psychiatry was aired in two leading professional journals, the *International Journal of Psychiatry* and the *American Journal of Psychiatry*.[3] The earlier symposium was led by Richard Green, who presented a paper that raised a number of questions about the biological, psychological, and sociological bases of homosexuality.[4]

The questions, Green believed, were those his fellow psychiatrists should consider in responding to the request of the Gay Liberation movement to remove homosexuality from *DSM-II* as a category of mental disorder. Green distinguished between facultative (i.e., situational) and obligatory homosexuality, declaring that his essay dealt only with the

---

[2] According to Bayer (1981: 122), two psychiatrists who led this effort were Lawrence Hartmann and Richard Pillard. Hartmann was the son of a leading psychoanalytic theorist, Heinz Hartmann. Richard Pillard was also known as a gay activist. The action of the Northern District, later in 1973, was endorsed by the New England District and Area Council of the national organization.

[3] The first symposium appeared in the *International Journal of Psychiatry* 10(1), 1972: 72-128. It included contributions from Richard Green, Alan Bell, Lawrence Hatterer, Martin Hoffman, Arno Karlen (a journalist and author), Judd Marmor, and Charles Socarides. The assistant editor of this journal was Robert Spitzer.

[4] Green, Richard (1972). Homosexuality as a Mental Illness. *International Journal of Psychiatry* 10(1): 77-98, 126-128. He identified himself as a "heterosexual psychiatrist" (94). The paper was not exactly a statement of his position because, as Bell (1972: 99) observed, it contained eighty questions.

latter type. Apart from this distinction, "obligatory" homosexuality was treated as a unitary phenomenon and as a sexual identity.

The thrust of Green's argument was that psychiatry had adopted the idea of homosexuality as a form of mental illness without the supporting scientific theory and evidence. The theories that psychiatry did subscribe to were uncritically received as dogma. He also stated that psychiatry took heterosexuality as a form of mental health for granted although the same etiological questions could be raised about it as about homosexuality. He recalled zoological research which showed that neither exclusive hetero- sexuality nor homosexuality was known in subhuman animals. He be- lieved that there was sufficient evidence to indicate that there was a biological substrate for both orientations and that the exclusive forms were probably the result of experience. As for psychological explanations of the origins of homosexuality, Green believed that psychoanalytic theories were no more convincing than social learning theory. In his view both lacked scientific support. Nor could homosexuality be considered a form of social deviance, for it occurred with great frequency in North American culture and was considered normal in many other cultures.

Heterosexuality, Green asserted, was undoubtedly accorded prefer- ential treatment by psychiatry. For example, the promiscuity and instability in intimate relationships that were attributed to homosexuals went largely unremarked in heterosexuals. Yet exclusive heterosexuality could be considered a rigid form of sexuality:

> Some predominantly homosexual or ambisexual persons argue that exclusive reliance on heterosexual orgasms is restrictive of a wider breadth of genital and interpersonal experience in the same manner that psychiatry argues the converse. Is ambisexuality evidence of a fuller range of interpersonal experience? Furthermore, is the anatomic configuration of the sexual object the only or even the critical variable? Or is it more in the quality of the relationship? One might argue that exclusive sexuality in either direction is by definition restrictive. What should be the psychiatrist's responsibility if consulted by a *heterosexual* who wants to overcome some of his *homosexual* inhibitions? Consider that such a person's reasons were to increase his means of sexual satisfaction and promote a more extensive manner of relating with men—motivation of reasonable merit, when comparably advanced by the homosexual who wishes to overcome heterosexual inhibitions.

Would many (any) psychiatrists be willing to work with the patient toward such a goal? (90-91)

Green could not believe that heterosexual relationships were more fulfilling for heterosexuals than homosexual relationships for homosexuals:

I question the given state of 'knowledge' that orgasms between males and females are by definition better than between females and females or males and males, that the components comprising the major factor, "love," are by definition superior between males and females to between males and males or females and females." (95)[5]

In the responses that followed Green's paper, the writers either agreed or disagreed with his proposition that homosexuality per se was not a mental illness. Bell, a psychologist from the Kinsey Institute, found the essay "refreshing" because it avoided siding with Gay Liberationists who preached that their being gay "makes them experts on the meaning and nature of their own and others' homosexuality" (Bell, 1972: 99).

Green also avoided the doctrinaire attitudes of clinicians whose views on homosexuality were restricted to patient contacts. Bell agreed that the choice of females or males as sexual objects revealed little about the individual's sexual experience. Sex was not equally important to all people and, in an erotophobic society, all people had trouble with it: "homosexuals and heterosexuals alike have difficulty integrating the affectional and sexual aspects of their personhood" (102).

Martin Hoffman, a psychiatrist who had published on the subject of homosexuality, echoed Green's contention that homosexuality and heterosexuality were not mutually exclusive.[6] Hoffman believed that holding on to the notion that homosexuality was a mental illness alienated "many potential, and needy, patients" (106). Through the *DSM* "psychiatry has quite unreflectively carried over … the moral values of the culture from which it arose" (106).

---

[5] Green enlisted the support of Freud, quoting the letter Freud had written in 1935 to an American mother who had inquired about treatment for her homosexual son.

6 Hoffman, Martin (1972). Philosophical, Empirical, and Ecologic Remarks. *International Journal of Psychiatry* 10(1), 105-107.

Judd Marmor also believed that the issue of homosexuality as mental illness was moral rather than medical.[7] By calling it a mental illness, psychiatry justified society's invasion of individual lives. In a democratic society the sexual preference of individuals should be respected as were their religious preferences: "I submit that the entire assumption that homosexual behavior per se is 'unnatural' or 'unhealthy' is a moral judgment and has no basis in fact" (115).

The fact that a significant number of homosexuals suffered from "emotional conflicts" and "impaired self-images" (116) was attributed by Marmor to social intolerance. He believed that neither heterosexuality nor homosexuality were ordained by "nature":

> I wish to reemphasize the fact that both obligatory homosexuality and obligatory heterosexuality are uniquely human conditions. Neither pattern is truly "natural," and there is no more justification for calling one an illness than the other. As an obligatory heterosexual, I would strongly object to any social pressure to alter my sexual preference. I can fully empathize, therefore, with the obligatory homosexual's similar resentment. (117)

Three of the participants in the symposium took issue with Green. Lawrence Hatterer, a psychoanalyst, believed that Green failed to appreciate the "multideterminant" and "multidimensional" nature of homosexuality and complexities involved in its treatment.[8] Homosexuality, he contended, had varied forms with respect to etiology, subculture and lifestyle. He implied that some of these forms were more normal than others. Green had failed to make the necessary distinctions: "He has lumped every kind of homosexuality with every other kind and unfortunately leaves us with another straw man beyond 'society'—the psychiatrist" (104).

Arno Karlen, a medical journalist, argued that Green's search for the cause of homosexuality in genes or hormones was "simplistic" (1972: 109).[9] He also contended that homosexual behavior as penetration of penis did not exist in the animal kingdom; mounting was not the same as

---

[7] Marmor, Judd (1972). Homosexuality: Mental Illness or Moral Dilemma? *International Journal of Psychiatry* 10(1): 114-117.

[8] Hatterer, Lawrence J. (1972). A Critique. *International Journal of Psychiatry* 10(1): 103-104.

[9] Karlen, Arno (1972). A Discussion of Homosexuality as a Mental Illness. *International Journal of Psychiatry* 10(1): 108-113.

insertion. Yet he did believe that heterosexuality was found throughout nature. It was "biologically efficient behavior" (110). Although Karlen recognized man's capacity for learning, he also believed that there was a "biosocial nature": "Man is not only a sexual animal, but a pair-bonding, group-bonding, and child-rearing animal. His sexual behavior cannot be unrelated to his broader sociosexual nature" (111). He chided Green for referring to marriage as merely "virtuous." Homosexuality in humans showed how their superior capacity for learning made them "vulnerable to maladaptive learning" (110). Finally, he accused Green of taking on the "Gay Lib's" hostility toward heterosexuality, marriage, and the family" (113).

The final adversary was Charles Socarides,[10] who bitterly attacked Green's paper for "its total lack of scientific veracity" (1972: 118). Socarides stated his belief that homosexuality was not biologically determined by "genetic or hormonal propensity" (118) but rather that heterosexuality was an emergent biological endowment:

> Heterosexual object choice is determined by two-and-a-half billion years of human evolution—a product of sexual differentiation, at first solely based on reproduction but later widened to include sexual gratification; for example, from one-celled nonsexual fission to the development of two-celled sexual reproduction, to organ differentiation, and finally to the development of two separate individuals reciprocally adapted to each other anatomically, endocrinologically, psychologically, and in many other ways ... [heterosexuality] is supported by universal concepts of mating and the tradition of the family unit and the complementariness and contrast between the two sexes. (1972: 120)

Homosexuality, Socarides thought, was caused by "massive childhood fears" (120) which "damaged and disrupted the standard male-female design." It was "a round-about method of achieving orgastic release" through "instituting male-male or female-female patterns" (120). Homosexuality could be traced to the childhood failure to undergo "the separation-individuation phase" (118) of development. Homosexuals, therefore, were "unable to form a healthy sexual identity in accordance with their anatomical and biological capacities" (119).

---

[10] Socarides, Charles W. (1972). Homosexuality: Basic Concepts and Psychodynamics. *International Journal of Psychiatry* 10(1): 118-125.

As an adult "solution," homosexual relationships were "doomed to failure" (1972: 119) because of their underlying "destruction, mutual defeat, exploitation of partner and self, oral-sadistic incorporation, aggressive onslaughts, and attempts to alleviate anxiety" (119). Homosexual male seduction consisted of disguised attempts to vanquish other males. The vanquished partner could obtain gratification through identifying with the victor: "Grasping the penis through the aperture in a toilet stall door without face-to-face contact is an enactment of the fundamental nature of their object relationships, relating to part, not whole, objects" (119). Homosexual males were afraid of women and hostile towards men. Homosexuality was reparative, a "compromise adaptation" (122) in which one male chose another for "sexual gratification in order to save the self from the intolerable anxiety that could ensue were he to approach the female" (122). In their genital contact, homosexuals hoped "to achieve a 'shot' of masculinity in the homosexual act through the mechanisms of identification with their male partner, his body, and his penis" (122).

He believed that those homosexuals who sought treatment were the healthier, "far less masochistic and self-destructive than their partners or associates, who will not even attempt any realistic effort to relieve their anguish" (1972: 122). He lashed out against psychiatrists who through misguided compassion would declare homosexuality natural and normal:

> Few physicians and other specialists devoted to the principles
> of scientific rigor and professional integrity will yield to such
> propaganda. It is the homosexual who will be victimized by
> these false "friends." True, it is difficult to know that one is ill,
> but it is far worse to keep experiencing symptoms and yet be
> told by supposedly qualified people that: "You're all right.
> There is nothing the matter with you. Relax and enjoy it. It's all
> society's fault. (1972: 123)

Green's reply was aimed mostly at Socarides. He satirically pointed to the absence of "scientific rigor" in an article by a man who attacked another for a lack of scientific veracity. Green also remarked that if the homosexual could be challenged for excluding half of mankind from meaningful relationships so could the heterosexual. The emotional plights described as occurring in the relationships of homosexuals, Green believed, were also found in heterosexual relationships.

The second symposium was a debate among psychiatrists over whether or not homosexuality should be retained as a diagnosis in the *DSM*.[11] Richard Stoller, Marmor, and Green argued for its removal. Stoller urged this action because homosexuality could not be "succinctly and accurately" (1973: 1208) described so as to make it a useful diagnostic category: "There *is* homosexual behavior; it is varied. There is no such *thing* as homosexuality. In that sense it should be removed from the nomenclature" (1207).[12] However, he wanted homosexuals to know that, by listing their sexual orientation as a diagnosis, psychiatry had at least "signified that the homosexual is part of the natural realm and not a member of the species of damned sinners" (1207).

Stoller went on the express what was to become his theory of perversions. In his opinion the ideal sexual relationship lay "buried in most of us" (1208). It was "a male preferring a female and vice versa, in which both wholeheartedly enjoy the sexual and loving aspects of their relationship" (1973: 1208). The sexual styles of most individuals failed to manifest this ideal. Yet the fact that children grew up in families kept the ideal alive: "[E]ven in childhood we know we are the result of an intimate, highly charged, astonishing, mysterious, unquestionably heterosexual act" (1208).

Perversions bridged the gap between ideal and actual behavior: "So I see [sexual] perversion (but not all sexual deviations and not all homosexual behaviors) as modifications one must invent in order to preserve some of one's heterosexuality" (1208). He also held that homosexual relations, among other perversions, were "heterosexual distortions, compromises nonetheless filled with excitement that allow one to give up certain desires if only others can be salvaged" (1208).

---

[11] The abstracts of the papers presented at this symposium were published in 1973 under the title, "A Symposium: Should Homosexuality Be in the APA Nomenclature?" *American Journal of Psychiatry 130*, 1207-1216. The contributors were Robert Stoller, Judd Marmor, Irving Bieber, Ronald Gold (of the Gay Activist Alliance in New York City), Charles Socarides, Richard Green, and Robert Spitzer. The published contributions for this symposium were abstracts of papers delivered at a session of the annual meeting of the APA in Honolulu, Hawaii, on May 9, 1973, devoted to the question "Should Homosexuality Be in APA Nomenclature?" That symposium followed the near-confrontation in New York City between the Gay Activist Alliance and the Nomenclature Committee in February 1973. See Bayer, 1981: 115-121.

[12] Stoller, Robert (1973). Criteria for Psychiatric Diagnosis. *American Journal of Psychiatry 130*(11): 1207-1208.

Marmor apparently viewed homosexuality as a "personality idiosyncrasy" that resulted from unusual parent-child relationships, most of which were disturbed.[13] Although such a background resulted in deviant behavior, people did not "have the right to label behavior that is deviant from that currently favored by the majority as evidence per se of psychopathology" (1208). To engage in such labeling, he held, tended

> to define normality in terms of behavioral adjustment to cultural conventions rather than in terms of ego strengths and ego-adaptive capacities, and it puts psychiatry clearly in the role as an agent of cultural control rather than a branch of the healing arts. (1209)

In Marmor's estimation, it was the task of "psychiatrists to be healers of the distressed, not watchdogs of our social mores" (1209).

Green argued for classifications of sexual behavior and distress that were free of cultural bias and untested psychoanalytic theory and that was "patient-activated" (1973: 1214).[14] As in the earlier symposium, Green focused on forms of heterosexual behavior as eligible for classification in the *DSM*—what he specifically referred to as "ego-dystonic neurotic uses of heterosexuality" (1214). A common heterosexual problem was

> instability in maintaining a love relationship and neurotic uses of sexuality—in which sexuality is used to control others, as a substitute for other feelings of self-worth, or as a defense against anxiety and depression. (1213-1214)

Such uses of heterosexuality were not listed in the *DSM* although they were recognized as characteristics of homosexuality. Green felt that in "gross psychologic social functioning" (1214) the homosexual was identical to the heterosexual. Green proposed a compromise taxonomy in which both heterosexual and homosexual behavior would be classified merely as sexual dysfunction. The new schema would distinguish between dysfunctions that were basically physiological (e.g., erectile failure, anorgasmia) and those basically psychogenic (e.g., anxiety, depression, and inability to maintain stable object relations).

Bieber and Socarides, of course, argued against the removal of the word "homosexuality" from the *DSM*. Bieber stoutly maintained that

---

[13] Marmor, Judd (1973). Homosexuality and Cultural Value Systems. *American Journal of Psychiatry 130*: 1208-1209.
[14] Green, Richard (1973). Should Heterosexuality Be in the APA Nomenclature? *American Journal of Psychiatry 130*(11): 1213-1214.

"human beings born with normal gonads and genitals are biologically programmed for heterosexual development (1973: 1210).[15] Olfaction played a major role in steering the infant's sexual development in the direction of the opposite sex. Homosexuality represented an interruption in heterosexual development. It was caused by a pathological relationship of parents and child which denied the boy the needed masculine figure for identification. Homosexuality was a "substitutive adaptation" in which "attempts are made to acquire missing sexual and romantic gratification" (1210).

Bieber suggested that homosexuality could be reclassified as a "sexual inadequacy" because its present classification as a sexual deviation was ambiguous and not useful. By describing it as sexual inadequacy, the particular disabilities exclusively homosexual males had in functioning with females could be specified. He rejected the notion that the appearance of homosexuality in the *DSM* was responsible for discrimination against homosexuals. However, to remove the classification would be a scientific error. It would interfere with efforts for preventing homosexuality in prehomosexual boys and discourage treatment of young men in conflict over their sexual orientation.

In arguing for the retention of the homosexual diagnosis, Socarides adumbrated his preoedipal theory of causation.[16] Adult obligatory homosexuals, as three-year-old children, had been unable "to make the progression from the mother-child unity of earliest infancy to individuation" (1973: 1212). This, according to Socarides, was caused by the parents: "a domineering, psychologically crushing mother who will not allow the child to attain autonomy from her and an absent, weak, or a rejecting father who is unable to aid the son to overcome the block in maturation" (1973: 1212). The emotional life of homosexuals was therefore fixated in the preoedipal period. In adult males this psychological failure to separate was exhibited as a "deficit in masculinity" (1212) and the "continuation of a primary feminine identification with the mother." These males also suffered from "primitive fears of injury by women" (1212). Socarides believed that adult homosexuality was a diagnosable entity:

---

[15] Bieber, Irving (1973). Homosexuality: An Adaptive Consequence of Disorder in Psychosexual Development. *American Journal of Psychiatry 130*: 1209-1211; and Socarides, Charles (1973). Homosexuality: Findings Derived from 15 years of Clinical Research. *American Journal of Psychiatry 130*: 1212-1213.

[16] Socarides, Charles (1973). Homosexuality: Findings Derived from 15 years of Clinical Research. *American Journal of Psychiatry 130*(11): 1212-1213.

"There are symptoms and there is a course of development and there is a treatment—often very effective treatment" (1213).

Socarides was adamantly opposed to the reclassification of homosexuality from a sexual deviation to a sexual dysfunction. Dysfunctions, he stated, occurred within the "standard pattern" of "sexual release" (1212). He was referring, of course, to penis-vagina intercourse. Dysfunctions could be easily remedied by couples varying their sexual techniques, for example, of foreplay. The implication was that the actual orgasm occurred only during the time the genitalia were connected. It was the failure to achieve "sexual release" during coitus that turned people to "modified patterns of orgastic relief" (1213), which Socarides called sexual deviations. He believed that there was an "immutable distinction" between sexual dysfunctions and deviations, which, if blurred would lead to "formidable scientific chaos" (1213).

It was left to Robert Spitzer to search for a compromise between those psychiatrists who viewed homosexuality as a mental disorder and those who called it a normal sexual variant. Spitzer was faced with the problem of formulating an acceptable proposal for revising *DSM-II*.[17]

The first question Spitzer addressed was the definition of mental disorder. For a mental condition to qualify as a disorder it had to meet one of two criteria: "[I]t must either regularly cause subjective distress or regularly be associated with some generalized impairment in social effectiveness of functioning" (1215). Spitzer held that neither criterion applied to homosexuality: "Clearly homosexuality per se does not meet the requirements for a psychiatric disorder since ... many homosexuals are quite satisfied with their sexual orientation and demonstrate no generalized impairment in social effectiveness or functioning" (1215).

The failure to function heterosexually, Spitzer argued, should not be used as a standard of mental disorder. He preferred to think of homosexuality as an "irregular form of sexual behavior" (1215), less optimal than heterosexuality for functioning in our society. If the *DSM* were to list all the "less than optimal" forms of psychological functioning, along with homosexuality, it would have to include, for example, celibacy,

---

[17] Spitzer, Robert L. (1973). A Proposal About Homosexuality and the APA Nomenclature: Homosexuality as an Irregular Form of Sexual Behavior and Sexual Orientation Disturbance as a Psychiatric Disorder. *American Journal of Psychiatry 130*, 1207-1216. Spitzer's paper was written after the Honolulu meeting of the APA. He was a member of the APA Nomenclature Committee, whose titular head was Henry Brill. Spitzer took the lead in resolving the dispute over the reclassification of homosexuality in *DSM-II*.

revolutionary behavior, religious fanaticism, vegetarianism, and male chauvinism.

Spitzer attempted to carve out areas of professional consensus on homosexuality. He asserted that psychiatrists would agree: (1) that homosexuality was "interest in sexual relations or contact with members of the same sex"; (2) a "significant number" of homosexuals were satisfied with their homosexuality and functioned effectively; and (3) a "significant number" were "quite bewildered by, in conflict with, or wish to change their sexual orientation" (1215). Because there were homosexuals who felt "subjective distress" with regard to their homosexual behavior and feelings, Spitzer proposed a new category, "sexual orientation disturbance," to replace the "undefined category of homosexuality" (1215) in *DSM-II*. If this revision of the *DSM* were made, psychiatrists could "continue to help homosexuals who suffer from what we can now refer to as 'sexual orientation disturbance,' helping the patient accept or live with his current sexual orientation, or, if he desires, helping him to change it" (1216).

Spitzer was emphatic in the declaration that the revision was not a capitulation to "homosexual activist groups," who, he predicted, would claim that the change made "homosexuality ... as 'normal' as heterosexuality."[18] That claim, he averred, would be wrong. The proposed revision would not align psychiatry "with any particular viewpoint regarding the etiology or desirability of homosexual behavior" (1216). The removal of homosexuality from the nomenclature would, however, have a beneficial political effect. When the civil rights of homosexuals were threatened or abridged on the grounds that they were mentally ill, the burden of proof would be on their accusers.[19]

---

[18] Immediately after the APA Board of Trustees adopted Spitzer's proposal, the APA President, Alfred Freedman, stated to the press that the decision did not mean that his organization believed that homosexuality was "normal" or as "desirable" as heterosexuality. (See Bayer, 1981: 139.)

[19] Ronald Gold, a leader of the Gay Activist Alliance in New York City, also presented a paper with the satirical title, "Stop It, You're Making Me Sick!" (*American Journal of Psychiatry* 130(11): 1211-1212). Gold recounted his own unhappy experiences at the hands of psychiatrists who tried to change his homosexual identity to heterosexual. Gold believed that homosexuals could be accomplices of their own oppression in turning to psychiatry with the hope of becoming heterosexual. Psychiatry, he held, had helped to create "the irrational fear and hatred of homosexuality" (1211). He believed that psychiatrists should no longer accede to request of homosexual patients to change to a heterosexual identity. Instead, they should help patients to realize

The APA Board of Trustees adopted Spitzer's proposal at its December meeting in 1973. This resolution provided a definition of the category "homosexuality," which was listed but left undefined in the first version of *DSM-II*. The following classification appeared in a revision of *DSM-II*:

> Sexual orientation disturbance [Homosexuality] This is for individuals whose sexual interests are directed primarily toward people of the same sex and who are disturbed by, in conflict with, or wish to change their sexual orientation. This diagnostic category is distinguished from homosexuality, which by itself does not constitute a psychiatric disorder. Homosexuality per se is one form of sexual behavior, and with other forms of sexual behavior which are not themselves psychiatric disorders, is not listed in this nomenclature. (44)[20]

The description of sexual deviation was not changed with the exception of the addition of a footnote indicating that the Board believed its definition was now inconsistent with the addition of the category of "sexual orientation disturbance." The list of "deviations" that followed the definition remained unchanged.

Because the decision of the APA Board of Trustees was seen as a defeat by the psychiatrists who had taken the position that

---

how many homosexuals were professional people who were successful and well-adjusted. He enjoined psychiatrists: "Take the damning label of sickness away from us. Take us out of your nomenclature. Work for repeal of sodomy laws, for civil rights protection for gay people.... You've got to tell the world what you believe—that Gay is Good" (1212).

[20] This revision appeared in the reprinting of *DSM-II*. At the same meeting the Board of Trustees (14-15 December 1973) passed the following anti-discrimination resolution, which appeared in 1974 the *American Journal of Psychiatry* 130(11): "Whereas homosexuality in and of itself implies no impairment in judgment, stability, reliability, or vocational capabilities, therefore, be it resolved, that the American Psychiatric Association deplores all public and private discrimination against homosexuals in such areas as employment, housing public accommodation, and licensing, and declares that no burden or proof of such judgment, capacity, or reliability shall be placed upon homosexuals greater than that imposed on any other persons. Further, the APA supports and urges the enactment of civil rights legislation at local, state, and federal levels that would insure homosexual citizens the same protection now guaranteed to others. Further, the APA supports and urges the repeal of all legislation making criminal offenses of sexual acts performed by consenting adults in private" 497).

homosexuality was pathological, they immediately organized their forces and challenged the decision in an organizational referendum.[21]

The pathologizers argued that the criteria for mental disorders, proposed by Spitzer, would wreak havoc in psychiatric diagnosis. The absence of "subjective distress" was often symptomatic of most serious psychopathologies and adequate social functioning as a standard would further exempt a whole spectrum of sexual perversions. They added that the decision was politically motivated, a capitulation to ideological and political pressure and manipulation by gay groups.

Much of the debate centered on the issue of which group was being less scientific or more political. The Board was scandalized that the opposition politicized what it believed was a scientific issue, by forcing a referendum for the general membership. The opposition believed the Board had confused the issue of discrimination against homosexuals with the issue of pathology. In the referendum held during the spring of 1974, the general APA membership upheld the Board's decision.[22]

The dispute, however, was far from resolved even with the failure of the referendum. It erupted in the APA Task Force on Nomenclature and Statistics, which was established in 1974 and which Spitzer headed. Over the next few years the Task Force was to undertake a major revision of *DSM-II*. Spitzer had to contend with three factions in resolving the continuing conflict over homosexuality. One group of detoxicators considered homosexuality as a normal sexual variant; they wanted no classification at all.[23] Another group of detoxicators wanted to keep the revised classification, sexual orientation disturbance. The third group, the pathologizers, who had led the drive for the referendum, still wanted homosexuality included as a mental disorder.

In developing the drafts of the proposed revision of *DSM-II*, various terms and categories were suggested and discarded as substitutes for "homosexuality" and "sexual orientation disturbance": homodysphilia, dyshomophilia, and amorous relationship disorder.[24]

---

[21] This effort was led by Bieber, Socarides, Kardiner, Robert McDevitt, and Harold Voth, a psychoanalyst from the Menninger Clinic. Voth bitterly attacked the decision as a capitulation to the Gay Liberation Movement.

[22] The results of the referendum indicated that 58% favored the Board's action, 37.8% opposed it, and 3.6% abstained. (See: Marmor, 1980: 292.)

[23] This group was led by Richard Green and Richard Pillard, with support from Marmor, Saghir, and Stoller.

[24] Spitzer, R. L. and Endicott J. (1978). Medical and Mental Disorder: Proposed Definition and Criteria. In R. L. Spitzer and D. F. Klein, Eds., *Critical Issues in*

Spitzer proposed dyshomophilia to refer specifically to an individual's subjective distress over homosexuality. As dyshomophilia, homosexuality was to be listed with the classical sexual disorders such as fetishism, pedophilia, bestiality, exhibitionism, voyeurism, sadism and masochism. The etiology of dyshomophilia, which was also to appear in *DSM*, was to be that which the Bieber group had formulated for male homosexuality over a decade earlier. In defending his proposal, Spitzer presented it as scientifically sound:

> The concept of dyshomophilia takes a middle position regarding the pathological status of homosexuality, even though the text clearly states that homosexuality per se is not to be regarded in *DSM-III* as a mental disorder. I believe that in our current state of ignorance this is a scientifically defensible position. I believe that if we remove dyshomophilia ... we could be justifiably accused of responding to political pressure. (Bayer, 1981: 174)[25]

Spitzer's attempt to include the post-Freudian etiology of homosexuality in the new edition of *DSM* was vigorously opposed by the group of detoxicators led by Green and Pillard. Finally, after a laborious effort at compromise, Spitzer won the support of several psychiatrists from each faction with a new proposal.[26]

The final resolution was to list EGO-DYSTONIC HOMOSEXUALITY under "psychosexual disorders" in the new edition, *DSM-III*. The new category was described as follows:

> The essential features are a desire to acquire or increase heterosexual arousal, so that heterosexual relationships can be initiated or maintained, and a sustained pattern of overt homosexual arousal that the individual explicitly states has been

---

Psychiatric Diagnosis. New York: Raven Press, 15-39. Selected documents of the work of the Nomenclature Committee appear in Bayer, Ronald and Spitzer, Robert L. (1982). Edited Correspondence on the Status of Homosexuality in *DSM-III. Journal of the History of the Behavioral Sciences* 18(1): 32-52.
[25] Bayer was quoting a memorandum from Spitzer to the committee of the task force charged with considering proposals on psychosexual disorders (5 October 1977). Serious consideration was never given to the category "amorous relationship disorder."
[26] Green and Pillard remained adamant in their opposition to any listing of homosexuality per se. Bayer (1981: 174-178) described what he called Spitzer's heroic, precarious, and not entirely successful effort to win a compromise.

unwanted or a persistent source of distress. This category ... should be avoided in cases where the desire to change sexual orientations may be a brief, temporary manifestation of an individual's difficulty in adjusting to a new awareness of his or her homosexual impulses. Individuals with this disorder may have either no or very weak heterosexual arousal. Typically there is a history of unsuccessful attempts at initiating or sustaining heterosexual relationships because of the expectation of lack of sexual responsiveness. In other cases the individual has been able to have short-lived heterosexual relationships, but complains that the heterosexual impulses are too weak to sustain such relationships. When the disorder is present in an adult, usually there is a strong desire to be able to have children and family life. Generally individuals with this disorder have had homosexual relationships, but often the physical satisfaction is accompanied by emotional upset because of strong negative feelings regarding homosexuality. In some cases the negative feelings are so strong that the homosexual arousal has been confined to fantasy. (281)

This description of ego-dystonic homosexuality was then followed by a list of associated features: loneliness, guilt, shame, anxiety, and depression (281). The most common "age of onset" was early adolescence "when the individual becomes aware that he or she is homosexually aroused and has already internalized negative feelings about homosexuality" (281).

Instead of an etiology, *DSM-III* described a "course" in which the homosexual identity could be consolidated in individuals suffering from ego-dystonic homosexuality:

There is some evidence that in time many individuals with this disorder give up the yearning to become heterosexual and accept themselves as homosexuals. This process is apparently facilitated by the presence of a supportive homosexual subculture. It is not known how often the disorder, without treatment, is self-limited. However, there is general consensus that spontaneous development of a satisfactory heterosexual adjustment in individuals who previously have a sustained pattern of exclusively homosexual arousal is rare. The extent to which therapy is able to decrease homosexual arousal, increase heterosexual arousal, or help homosexuals become satisfied with their sexuality is disputed. (281-282)

No etiology was provided because "homosexuality that is ego-dystonic is not classified as a mental disorder" (282). Its cause was attributed to "negative societal attitudes toward homosexuality that have been internalized" as well as to the desire for having children and a "socially sanctioned family life" (282). Particular complaints about being homosexual were excluded from the classification: distress over homosexuality that stemmed only from the conflict between the homosexual and society; individuals with generally inhibited sexual desire; and homosexuals who developed a major depression. The section was concluded with the statement of the two diagnostic criteria for ego-dystonic homosexuality:

> A. The individual complains that heterosexual arousal is persistently absent or weak and significantly interferes with initiating or maintaining wanted heterosexual relationships.
> B. There is a sustained pattern of homosexual arousal that the individual explicitly states has been unwanted and a persistent source of distress. (282)

The section on psychosexual disorders ended with a "residual category" for those not covered by any of the specific categories in the diagnostic class of Psychosexual Disorders. Examples of unlisted clinical disturbances included feelings of inadequacy about one's masculinity or femininity, size and shape of genitals, or sexual performance. Also included were impaired enjoyment of orgasm, distress about (283) "a pattern of repeated sexual conquests with a succession of individuals who exist only as things to be used (Don Juanism and nymphomania)," and "confusion about preferred sexual orientation."

Spitzer was astutely aware that the specific issue of listing homosexuality in *DSM* raised the broader issue of defining mental disorder. In the debate over homosexuality terms such as *disease, illness, disorder, sickness, pathology, dysfunction, deviation,* and *disturbance* were used interchangeably.[27]

Even Bieber and Socarides did not always call homosexuality the same thing. Socarides used a variety of terms while Bieber insisted that homosexuality was a sexual deviation and a psychopathology but not a

---

[27] Frederick Suppe (1984) discussed the conceptual confusion and entertained the possibility that the confusion could be reduced if the psychiatrists had turned to the philosophical literature on the concepts of *disease* and *illness* as distinct but related ideas.

serious disturbance or a mental illness. The latter two terms, he held, connoted psychosis and therefore were not applicable to homosexuality.[28]

In his attempts to build a consensus in the Task Force, Spitzer pressed for his earlier definition of mental disorder as involving either subjective distress or impaired social effectiveness and functioning.[29] Spitzer was therefore arguing that the consequences of a mental condition and not its etiology determined whether or not it should be considered a mental disorder. The criteria for classifying a condition as a mental disorder were included in the introduction to *DSM-III*:

> In *DSM-III* each of the mental disorders is conceptualized as a clinically significant behavioral or psychological syndrome or pattern that occurs in an individual and that is typically associated with either a painful symptom (distress) or impairment in one or more important areas of functioning (disability). In addition, there is an inference that there is a behavioral, psychological, or biological dysfunction, and that the disturbance is not only in the relationship between the individual and society. (When the disturbance is *limited* to a conflict between an individual and society, this may represent social deviance, which may or may not be commendable, but is not by itself a mental disorder.) (6)

Homosexuality was exempted from the classification of mental disorders, Spitzer contended, because it was not a source of distress to homosexuals and because any disability in social functioning was the result of discrimination against homosexuals and the normative expectation that all individuals be heterosexuals. In this context Spitzer defined the homosexual identity as a "persistent pattern of homosexual arousal" and a "persistent pattern of absent or weak heterosexual arousal" (212). He fully acknowledged that using the heterosexual identity as the norm for sexual relationships was "a value judgment and not a factual matter" (212). If homosexuality were a disadvantage, it was "because of our society's interference with the pursuit by homosexuals of basic needs." It was not a disadvantage in other cultures and in the homosexual subculture. In responding to the question of why *DSM-III* did not list ego-dystonic heterosexuality, Spitzer averred: "[T]here is not

---

[28] Suppe was following Bieber, Irving (1980). On Arriving at the APA Decision. Unpublished working paper, Hasting Center Closure Project: 11-22.

[29] Spitzer, Robert J. (1981). The Diagnostic Status of Homosexuality in DSM-III: A Reformation of Issues. *American Journal of Psychiatry 138*(2): 210-215.

a single case in the scientific literature that describes an individual with a sustained pattern of heterosexual arousal who was distressed by being heterosexually aroused and wished to acquire homosexual arousal in order to initiate or maintain homosexual relationships" (213). He went on to assert that the inability of heterosexuals to function as homosexuals "puts them at no disadvantage except in extraordinary situations, such as confinement in jail" (212).

There was little willingness on Spitzer's part to detoxicate the "paraphilias" listed in *DSM-III*, such as pedophilia, fetishism, voyeurism, and masochism. He defended their inclusion as mental disorders on the basis that "unusual or bizarre imagery or acts are necessary for sexual excitement" (212). The paraphilias qualified as mental conditions even though the practitioners did not claim subjective distress or face social hostility. However, "the necessity of the unusual or bizarre imagery or acts for sexual arousal" (212), Spitzer argued, constituted impairment in an important area of sexual functioning and therefore "justified the inference of a behavioral or psychological dysfunction."

Building on the idea of the biological sexual identity as conceived in the nineteenth century, Freud delineated the notion of the psychological sexual identity. He did this by creating the psychological heterosexual identity and restructuring the psychological homosexual identity. Both identities had common biological and psychological roots: The innate bisexuality of all humans and the unitary process of psychosexual development. From Freud's perspective, the development of the individual embraced both the heterosexual and homosexual identities. That which prevailed was attributed to biological propensity and the vicissitudes of developmental experience.

In the ensuing discourse on the homosexual identity, Freud's conception of the heterosexual identity was never questioned. Both the pathologizers and detoxicators of the psychological homosexual identity accepted the Freudian notion that normal females were feminine in appearance and attitude and heterosexual in choice of partners; normal males were masculine in appearance and attitude and chose females as partners in sexual relationships.

What was challenged was Freud's conception of the homosexual identity. The pathologizers retained Freud's reparative view of the psychical origin of the homosexual identity. They were, however, critical of the Freudian idea that the heterosexual and homosexual identities derived from a common biological and psychical source because this conceptualization could lead to the belief that both identities were equally healthy and acceptable. For Freud's biological notion of innate bisexuality they substituted the idea of innate heterosexuality. In doing this they purged the heterosexual identity of any homosexual taint.

Having sharply distinguished between the heterosexual and homosexual identities, the pathologizers went on to make the homosexual identity completely inferior to the heterosexual. The homosexual identity was associated with the biological failure to reproduce the species, the psychological failure to establish a lasting relationship with a member of the opposite sex, the social failure to shoulder the responsibilities of adult men and women, and the cultural failure to participate in civilization's steady progress toward monosexuality. The homosexual identity came to represent a pathology of monstrous proportions that hovered between obsessional neurosis and schizophrenia.

The detoxicators attempted to revive the original Freudian notion of sexual identity by viewing the heterosexual and homosexual identities as products of common biological and psychical processes. Richard Green perhaps most articulately defined this position when he asserted that there was a biological substrate for both identities and that an exclusively heterosexual or homosexual identity was probably the result of experience. He even entertained the notion that heterosexuals might be aided through therapy to overcome their homosexual inhibitions.

The detoxicators, however, showed a lingering reluctance to give the homosexual identity a clean bill of health. Green mused over the possibility that medical science would someday discover the genetic abnormalities or prenatal hormonal imbalances of homosexuals and thereby reveal the biological etiology of homosexuality. Pillard, who vigorously and successfully worked for the APA anti-discrimination statement, in his own research, looked for evidence of the genetic basis of homosexuality. Stoller viewed the heterosexual identity as a Platonic ideal lodged in the human anatomy and cultural tradition; even in its more propitious aspects, the homosexual identity was only a dim reflection of the heterosexual identity. Marmor saw the homosexual identity as a personality idiosyncrasy produced by some early twisting of the parent-child relationship.

Although Green, Stoller, and Marmor were among the stalwart advocates of detoxication there was the strong inference in their arguments that they basically agreed with Spitzer that homosexuality was an "irregular form of behavior," hardly equal to heterosexuality in untainted origin, the quality of sexual fulfillment, romantic pairing, or social contribution. All these men believed that sexual identity was congealed in the individual as "obligatory" heterosexuality or homosexuality. Most of them made clear their belief that they were obligatory heterosexuals. Their efforts at detoxication of the homosexual identity owed more to medical compassion for individuals who could not be changed than it did to an untroubled acceptance of the homosexual identity as psychologically equal to the heterosexual.

When the theoretical positions of the pathologizers and detoxicators are compared, the debate appears to take on the disputatiousness of medieval theologians arguing over the possible number of angels who could stand on the head of a pin. Clearly both groups believed the homosexual identity required some special explanation that would distinguish it from the heterosexual identity. Both looked for the beginnings of sexual identity in the earliest months and years of experience — prenatal if not postnatal. They probably all believed that "prehomosexual children" formed relationships with parents that were disturbed either because they were born "different" or became "different." They all believed that homosexual relationships were reparative although they disagreed on exactly what had to be repaired: An innate biological defect or an innate heterosexual capacity that had been short-circuited by parental mismanagement. All believed that life was not very easy for homosexuals not only because of social intolerance but also because of an inherent fragility that left them ill-equipped to fulfill feminine or masculine destinies in a society organized on the basis of biological sex.

Neither pathologizers nor detoxicators used the debate over *DSM* as an opportunity to explore alternative structures of sexual relationships, although this issue was approached in the Nomenclature Committee. The pathologizers, resisting any modification in the structure of sexual relationships, desperately defended the institution of heterosexual monogamy. The detoxicators, while recognizing that traditional psychiatric attitudes toward the homosexual identity were raw incorporations of sexual mores, failed to see that the diagnostic view of other sexual variations or identities, was no different.

The psychiatric debate over the homosexual identity embodied the three cosmological views of sexual relationships. Both the pathologizers and the detoxicators were distinctly uncomfortable with the polytheistic view which embraced variation in sexual relationships and practices and did not view them as mutually exclusive or entrenched in biology or personality. In the first two editions of *DSM* sexual relationships and practices that lay outside the purview of heterosexual monogamy were proscribed as sexual deviations. They were symptoms of unbridled psychological appetite, to be grouped with excessive drinking and drug addiction. *DSM-III*, although detoxicating "obligatory" homosexuality, held open the door for the diagnosis and treatment of all forms of homosexual identity in which the possibility of change was present. The possibility that individuals who were limited to heterosexual relationships would wish to enjoy sexual relationships with partners of the same sex, or with both sexes, was dismissed as clinically unknown. Obligatory homosexuality, as viewed by the detoxicators, could lay claim to the mantel of health only if it were contained within an established homosexual union.

The monotheistic view of sexual relationships was endorsed by both pathologizers and detoxicators. The pathologizers viewed heterosexual monogamy as mandatory: It was the conforming of sexual relationships to the male-female design as ordained by nature. For the detoxicators, heterosexual monogamy was the ideal sexual relationship, seldom attained in its purest form by heterosexuals, although it remained the model that both heterosexuals and homosexuals should emulate. Deviations from the ideal sexual relationship, the detoxicators assumed, required medical and psychiatric explanation.

The debate also embodied its version of the scientific cosmology. For both pathologizers and detoxicators, however, the element of choice that characterized the Enlightenment view of sexual relationships was eliminated. Sexual identity for both groups was tied to embedded impulses and fantasies that were hardly eradicable and which drastically narrowed individual options for the structuring of sexual relationships.

The psychiatrists of the twentieth century, no less than their predecessors in the nineteenth century, disingenuously used appeals to science and medicine to advocate transparently moralistic views of sexual relationships. Both sides used science as the ultimate source of truth and authority. Scientific knowledge, however, could never resolve this debate because it was not motivated by scientific curiosity in the first place. The motivation was moral but the argument was scientific. The pathologizers, under the guise of psychoanalysis, argued the issue as agents and enforcers of the monotheistic morality. The detoxicators, although more open to viewing the homosexual identity as a political and moral issue, also couched their arguments in the language of science.

In airing their own views and criticizing those of others, both sides inadvertently contributed to the normalization of sexual relationships. The pathologizers advocated the transmutation of the homosexual identity into the heterosexual to accommodate the male-female design. The detoxicators viewed the homosexual identity as a natural variation, although they believed that homosexuals could be reconciled to their identity only if they institutionalized their relationships so that they resembled those of heterosexuals.

Part Three:

THE SOCIOCULTURAL SEXUAL IDENTITY

12 Cultural Identity: The Anthropological Approach

The environmental and evolutionary theories of sexual perversion that were constructed in the nineteenth-century discourse on sexual identity gave rise to the belief that sexual identity was a product of both biological and cultural forces. During the twentieth century, the study of the formative influence of culture on sexual practices and relationships was to become the major focus of the discourse on sexual identity. In the process the biological and psychological sexual identities were gradually absorbed into the idea of the sociocultural sexual identity.

This sociocultural conception was based on the belief that individuals were both biologically and psychologically malleable. Theoretically, individuality was shaped by social forces and conferred through membership in groups. In the case of the individual's sexual identity, social forces were conceived as institutionalized constraints that prescribed sexual practices and relationships. Membership in groups could be the product of either conformity to or deviation from these institutionalized norms.

The sociocultural sexual identity was constructed within various disciplinary and methodological traditions. Its original form was provided by the historical and anecdotal surveys of sexual practices and relationships in both western and non-western cultures and in civilized and tribal societies. It was embellished in the anthropological investigations of the cultural roles assigned respectively to the female and male sexes and the permissible structure of sexual relationships. Next it was quantified as a wide variety of sexual practices, many of which had been viewed as pathological in the medical discourse on sexual identity. Chiefly in the hands of the sociologists and psychologists, the sociocultural identity was conceived as sub-cultures existing within the mainstream culture, sexual meanings individuals derived from interaction with established norms for sexual relationships, and, finally, as a collective or group identity.

The sociocultural identity stood as a critique of the biological and psychological sexual identities. Within this conceptualization these latter identities were viewed as highly restrictive of sexual practices and the structure of sexual relationships.

The first contribution to the idea of a sociocultural sexual identity was provided by Iwan Bloch who, in 1902, published his *Beiträge zur Aetiologie der Psychopathia Sexualis.*[1] As a medical historian, Bloch believed that the history of religion was the history of perverse sexual practices, including ordinary debauchery, prostitution, fetishism, and contrary sexual instinct, as well as the somewhat rarer sadism, masochism, and exhibitionism. Further, he thought that any sensory organ, including the nose, could serve as the locus of sexual excitement and that there were adult individuals who possessed abnormal physiological sensitivity. He subscribed to Binet's idea that external stimuli could be conditioned to sexual responses. Bloch's view of sexual relationships grew out of his studies of sexual practices in primitive and modern civilizations.[2]

His major criticism of the biological theories of sexual perversions was that they focused exclusively on the "sick man" (Bloch, 1910: 455) while ignoring the broader anthropological and historical picture of primitive and civilized man. In particular, he believed that Krafft-Ebing's doctrine of degeneracy had to be "amplified and rectified by anthropological evidence" (1910: 456).[3] This information, Bloch believed, would prove that sexual aberrations always existed everywhere in history and they were nothing less than the rudiments from which normal sexual behavior had evolved: the tendency for sexual aberrations was intrinsically human. After surveying many civilizations, Bloch concluded:

> Degeneration cannot be employed as von Krafft-Ebing has em-
> ployed it in his Psychopathia Sexualis, as a heuristic principle
> in the investigation, recognition, and judgment of sexual
> aberrations and perversions. At the most, degeneration is no
> more than a favoring factor of the diffusion of sexual abnor-

---

[1] The title translates as *Contributions to the Etiology of Sexual Perversion.* Bloch was a dermatologist who had considerable familiarity with the treatment of sexually transmitted diseases. He has also been credited with naming the field of sexology, in German, *Sexualwissenschaft* (Hoenig, 1977: 40).

[2] Bloch, Iwan. (1910). *The Sexual Life of Our Times in Its Relation to Modern Civilization.* M. Eden Paul, Trans. New York: Allied Book Company. This translation is of the sixth edition. The original volume was published as *Das Sexualleben unserer Zeit in seinen Beziehugen zur modern Kultur* (Berlin: Louis Marcus, 1907). Chapter 17, "The Anthropological Aspect of Psychopathia Sexualis," 454-477, was based upon Bloch's earlier work (Bloch, 1902).

[3] Information was not collected in the field by Bloch; it was obtained through primary and secondary accounts of others.

malities, an influence which increases the frequency of their appearance. On the contrary, the ultimate cause of all sexual perversions, aberrations, abnormalities, and irrationalities, is the need for variety in sexual relationships peculiar to the genus homo, which is to be regarded as a physiological phenomenon, and the increase of which to the degree of sexual irritable hunger is competent to produce the most severe sexual perversions. (1910: 463)

Bloch held to the belief, however, that heterosexual relationships represented the culmination of human sexual development and the bedrock of civilization: "There are two sexes only on which the true advance in civilization depends—the genuine man and the genuine woman. All other varieties are ultimately no more than phantoms, monstrosities, vestiges of primitive social conditions" (1910: 13).[4] Further, he asserted that in the "love between a normal man and a normal woman ... it is possible to find an unimpeachable sanction. Only this love, continually more differentiated and more individualized, will play a part in the future course of civilization" (1910: 14).

Bloch's conception of heterosexual relationships contained elements of choice, pleasure, and passion that went well beyond an exclusive focus on genital primacy and procreation. He acknowledged the tactile diffuseness of sexual stimulation, conceiving it as associated with intense tickling.[5] He believed that biting, cursing, and crying out were a part of normal intercourse. He rejected the notion that men had a greater erotic intensity than women. Sex was of course necessary for procreation but, more important, it was essential to the psychological growth and happiness of the individual.

Bloch was an ardent champion of "free love" and foe of the "coercive marriage" arranged by families with disregard for the desires and personalities of their children. The obligatory marriage was "the sole cause of the increasing diffusion of *prostitution*, of *wild sexual promiscuity*,

---

[4] The anomalies included hermaphrodites and other types represented by Hirschfeld's theory of intermediate stages. Any individual in whom the sex differences were blurred or mixed were seen by Bloch as instances of retrograde development.

[5] "[T]he voluptuous sensation is merely a special case of general cutaneous sensibility; it is closely allied with the cutaneous sensation of tickling; properly speaking, it is no more than excessively powerful tickling" (Bloch, 1910: 43). Bloch's specialization in dermatology may have led him to favor tactile explanations for various sexual practices.

and of *venereal diseases*" (1910: 237). It drove husbands and wives to seek love and sexual passion outside of marriage. "Free love" allowed a man and a woman, as two independent personalities, to construct a marriage in which they had equal rights and responsibilities. Their love should precede sexual contact; sexual continence was to be practiced by women who had not reached twenty and men who were not twenty-five. "Free love" was not "wild love," what today would be called casual sex, which Bloch condemned as "a continued succession of superficial sensual pleasures, as preparatory stimuli for an equally fugitive and debased sexual act" (1910: 282).

Within prescribed limits, Bloch viewed masturbation as normal: the precursor of sexual development, the occasion for releasing sexual tensions, as a way to induce relaxation and sleep, and as a distraction from pain. One had to be cautious about masturbation, however, because it could be symptomatic of disease:

> Frequently local morbid changes in or near the genital organs lead to the practice of masturbation, such as skin troubles, intestinal worms, phimosis, inflammatory states of the penis or near the entrance of the vagina, prurigo and other itching infections of the penis, constipation, urinary anomalies, etc. Further, mental disorders, epilepsy, and degenerative nerve troubles, are frequent causes of masturbation. (1910: 417)

Masturbation could have adverse effects on the VITA SEXUALIS, dulling the desire for normal intercourse or even entirely usurping its place.[6]

Bloch viewed perversions as basic to human sexuality. Sexual arousal was possible with many forms of stimulation. The frequent repetition of sexual acts could make them habitual. Seduction and imitation could rapidly cause particular practices to spread. If the sexual perversions arose in childhood they were due to chance conditioning; those in adulthood could be traced to the need for heightened stimulation. The activity of men and the passivity of women were also fertile soil for such practices as masochism and sadism. Perversions, he believed, could be implanted in the early childhood experiences of otherwise "healthy individuals":

---

[6] Bloch supplied the following examples: the "homosexual persons [who] are only able to have intercourse with their wives after preliminary caresses by their male friends" (1910, 455) or the masochist who had to be whipped before his penis became erect.

From all these facts may be deduced the *untenability* of a purely *clinical and pathological* conception of sexual aberrations and perversion. We must now accept the point of view that although numerous morbid degenerate and psychopathic individuals exhibit sexual anomalies, yet these *identical* anomalies and aberrations are extraordinarily common in *healthy* individuals. (1910: 466)

In 1908, Edward Westermarck, as a historian, moral philosopher, and sociologist, joined the discourse on sexual identity in his commentary on "homosexual love."[7] Westermarck defined "homosexual love" as "intercourse between individuals of the same sex" (456). He considered it a form of gratification of the sexual instinct that fell "outside the pale of nature" (456). It was widespread throughout the animal kingdom and the human race: "It is frequently met with among the lower animals. It probably occurs, at least sporadically, among every race of mankind, and among some people it has assumed such proportion as to form a true national habit" (456).

In his chapter on homosexual love Westermarck described various "homosexual customs" and the places in which they had been reported, such as the native tribes of America, the peoples of the Bering Sea, in the Malay Archipelago, the natives of the Kimberley District of West Australia, and Madagascar. These customs frequently included the relinquishing of the masculine sex role by the male boy or adolescent for the feminine role. As transvestites these males played the roles of sorcerers, entertainers of men, boy-wives, prostitutes, and priests. Westermarck observed that homosexual practices were also reported to have occurred among women in such places as Brazil and Zanzibar. In Brazil some tribal women imitated men in such activities as making war and hunting. They also married other women. Westermarck remarked:

From Greek antiquity we hear of "Lesbian" love. The fact that homosexuality has been much more frequently noticed in men than in women does not imply that the latter are less addicted to it. For various reasons the sexual abnormalities of women

---

[7] Westermarck, Eward (1908). *The Origin and Development of the Moral Ideas*. 2 Vols. London: Macmillan. We have cited the 1926 reprinting of the second edition (1917), which left the text of the first edition unchanged. Westermarck's interest in sexual relationships was reflected in his earlier studies of the history of marriage and marriage ceremonies in Morocco. His book on moral ideas consisted largely of the amassing of published materials.

have attracted less attention, and moral opinion has generally taken little notice of them. (446-465)

Homosexual love, in Westermarck's view, had both its biological and cultural side.[8] In his words "homosexual practices are due sometimes to instinctive preference, sometimes to external conditions unfavorable to normal intercourse" (456). Most observers of homosexual practices, he held, found it impossible to decide whether particular cases were congenital or acquired. Westermarck was mostly interested in the external circumstance that favored homosexual love. He believed that medical authorities such as Krafft-Ebing, Moll, and Ellis underestimated the influence that culturally ingrained habits could have on the "accidental turning of the sexual instinct into abnormal channel" (467). He continued:

> I take the case to be, that homosexual practices in early youth have a lasting effect on the sexual instinct, which at its first appearance, being somewhat indefinite, is easily turned into a homosexual direction ... Of course, influences of this kind "require a favorable organic disposition to act on"; but this predisposition is probably no abnormality at all, only a feature of the ordinary sexual constitution of man. (468-469)[9]

Among the external conditions that supported homosexual practices, according to Westermarck, were the absence or unobtainability of the opposite sex, methods of training youth that placed them under the tutelage of lovers of the same sex (as in ancient Sparta), and the great gulf that mentally separated males and females, as in ancient Greece and in Muslim countries.

Besides summarizing reports on homosexual practices in various regions of the world and historical periods, Westermarck considered the question of its "moral valuation" (471). That valuation, he believed, varied greatly. Sometimes the existence of homosexual love was ignored, as in tribal societies. In some cultures it was recognized but not condoned. In others it was despised but not legally punished. In Chinese culture little distinction was made between heterosexual and homosexual offenses: age and consent were the legal issues in either

---

[8] Westermarck referred to "congenital sexual inversion" (456) as a "psychological" phenomenon even though he was referring to an inherited physical state.

[9] The quoted material within this passage is drawn from Ellis' *Sexual Inversion*.

case. In some cultures, most notably ancient Greece, homosexual love was given a higher status than the heterosexual:

And this attachment [between a man and a youth] was not only regarded as permissible, but was praised as the highest and purest form of love, as the offspring of the heavenly Aphrodite, as a path leading to virtue, as a weapon against tyranny, as a safeguard of civic liberty, as a source of national greatness and glory. (478)

The strongest abhorrence of homosexual love Westermarck attributed to the Judeo-Christian tradition. The Hebrew rejection of homosexual love (which was called sodomy) Westermarck believed was due to the hatred of foreign cults, the sin of people not under Yahweh, particularly the lustful Canaanites. This rejection was shared by Christianity, which waged a "veritable crusade" (481) against homosexuality after it became the religion of the Roman Empire.

Westermarck's own attitude toward homosexual love apparently combined both personal antipathy and moral tolerance. In explaining the censure to which homosexual practices were subject he wrote: "This censure is no doubt, in the first place, due to that feeling of aversion or disgust which the idea of homosexual intercourse tends to call forth in normally constituted adult individuals whose sexual instincts have developed under normal conditions" (483). While endorsing the Code Napoleon, however, Westermarck questioned "whether morality has anything to do with a sexual act, committed by the mutual consent of two adult individuals, which is productive of no offspring, and which on the whole concerns the welfare of nobody but the parties themselves" (483).

Bloch's and Westermarck's historical and second-hand excursions into the realm of human sexuality sparked the interests of anthropologists in obtaining first-hand evidence of sexual customs by visiting primitive societies. One of the first to do so was Bronislaw Malinowski, who led an expedition to New Guinea between 1914 and 1918.[10]

---

[10] Malinowski, Bronislaw (1929). The Sexual Life of Savages in North-Western Melanesia: An Ethnographic Account of Courtship, Marriage and Family Life Among The Natives of the Trobriand Islands, British New Guinea. New York: Eugenics Publishing Co. The subtitle indicates that the book was an anthropological account of courtship, marriage, and family life among natives of the Trobriand Island in what was then British New Guinea. Malinowski used the term "savage" in the sense of Rousseau's "noble savage" rather than with derogatory connotation. Our selection of anthropologists has focused on

Like Bloch, Malinowski made clear that he associated sex with love rather than prurient interest. He thought there were close links between sexual practices in civilized and primitive societies: "Sex is not a mere physiological transaction to the primitive South Sea Islander any more than it is to us; it implies love and love-making; ... *Sex* ... is rather a sociological and cultural force than a merely bodily reaction of two individuals" (xxiii). The anthropological interest in the study of sex, in his view, addressed the societal consequences of blending physical sexuality with romance. In this union the mystery of love resided.

In his observations of the sexual customs of the Trobriands, Malinowski reported that, because of living arrangements, children saw and heard the sexual intercourse of their parents, what he called the "sexual enjoyment of parents" (54). Children also learned about sex from companions, their own age and older. They were allowed by adults to indulge their curiosity about the genitalia, and to manipulate these organs by hand or mouth. The only "regulation" of children's interest in sex was "their [own] degree of curiosity, of ripeness, and of 'temperament' or sensuality" (56).

The sexual life of adolescents was more serious, manifesting itself as a series of affairs. As the adolescents grew older their affairs lasted longer until it occurred to the male partner to make one of these liaisons permanent. Every marriage was preceded by an extended period of premarital coitus, usually in the privacy of the bachelor's house in which the single males resided. Sexual practices included sadism and masochism: "the cruel forms of caress—scratching, biting, spiting—to which a man has to submit to a greater extent even than the woman—show that as elements in eroticism, they are not absent from native love-making" (475). Fellatio was practiced in the "intimacy of lovemaking" (475).[11] Although individuals indulged in masturbation, it was generally regarded as undignified and demeaning. There was general contempt and disgust for exhibiting the genitals.

The boundaries of sexual expression were established by two sets of taboos: The general and the sociological. The general taboos branded

---

those scholars whose contributions have been theoretical and seminal as well as empirical in shaping later thought and scholarly inquiry in sexology. For a review of empirical, anthropological studies of homosexuality see Carrier, J. M. (1980). Homosexual Behavior in Cross-Cultural Perspective. In Judd Marmor, Ed., *Homosexual Behavior: A Modern Reappraisal.* New York: Basic Books, 101-121.
[11] Malinowski noted that the men would only admit that women fellated the male genitals(475). He believed, however, that the men practiced cunnilingus.

some forms of sexuality as "objectionable, indecent or contemptible" (453). The sexual taboos limited the options for selecting sexual partners. "Homosexuality, bestiality, exhibitionism, masturbation, fetishism, and anal eroticism" were some of the sexual behaviors that fell under the general taboos. Such practices were discouraged by ridicule rather than punished under law:

> The natives regarded such practices ... as but poor substitutes for the natural act, and therefore as bad and only worthy of fools. Such practices are a subject for derision, tolerant or scathing according to the mood, for ribald jokes and for funny stories. Transgressions are rather whipped [i.e., punished] by public contempt than controlled by definite legal sanctions ... Nor would a native ever use the word taboo (*bomala*) when speaking of them, for it would be an insult to assume that any sane person would like to commit them. (46)

Malinowski did not believe that homosexuality as genital contact existed. As close friendship it did exist:

> It is allowed by custom, and is, indeed, usual for boyfriends to embrace one another, to sleep together on the same couch, to walk enlaced or arm-in-arm.... Sometimes such a friendship is just a passing whim, but it may survive and mature into a permanent relationship of mutual affection and assistance. (471)

He appeared to be troubled by these strong emotional ties between males particularly because the natives made no linguistic distinction between close alliances between men and those between men and women.[12] Malinowski criticized imprecise uses of the word homosexual:

> Difficult as it is exactly to draw the line between pure "friendship" and "homosexual relation" in any society—both because of laxity in definition and because of the difficulty of as-certaining the facts—it becomes almost impossible in a community such as the Trobriands. Personally, I find it mis-leading to use the term "homosexuality" in the vague and almost all-embracing sense that is now fashionable under the in-fluence of psychoanalysis and the apostles of "*Urning*" love. If inversion be defined as a relationship in which detumescence is regularly achieved by contact with a body of the same sex, the

---

[12] The word for both relationships was *lubaygu*. Malinowski assured the reader that identical meanings did not signify identical emotional content.

male friendships in the Trobriands are not homosexual, nor is inversion extensively practiced in the islands. For, as we know, the practice is really felt to be bad and unclean because it is associated with excreta, for which the natives feel a genuine disgust. And while the ordinary caresses of affection are approved as between members of the same sex, any erotic caresses, scratching, nibbling at the eyelashes, or labial contact would be regarded as revolting. (472)

Other general taboos discouraged particular forms of heterosexuality; sexual intercourse in public, sexual greed in pursuing many partners, and sex with those who were generally believed to be repugnant in appearance or behavior. Periods of sexual abstinence had to be observed: for males when they were engaged in war, sailing, hunting, and farming and for females when they were pregnant. The sociological taboos restricted those to whom individuals had sexual access. They barred sex with another man's wife, particularly the wife of the chief, and with those considered social inferiors.

Using anthropological methodology, Margaret Mead examined prevalent cultural attitudes about sex-roles and human sexuality.[13] She claimed that male sexual functioning worked best "when it is most automatic, when the response is to a simple set of signals that have been defined as exciting, whether those signals be bodily exposure, a special perfume, a woman's reputation for compliancy, or simply a woman alone—on a bush path or in an empty apartment" (1949/1955: 158).

Female sexuality, in Mead's view, was less urgent and more rhythmical and responsive. The man was required to be potent and active but the woman's

---

[13] Mead, Margaret (1935). *Sex and Temperament in Three Primitive Societies.* London: Routledge and Kegan Paul; *Male and Female: A Study of the Sexes in a Changing World.* New York: William Morrow, 1949. (In citing *Male and Female,* we have used the Mentor Book edition, published in New York by the New American Library in 1955.) Beginning in 1925, Mead studied several societies of Oceania, including Samoa, the Manus (in the Admiralty Islands), and the Arapesh, the Mundugumor, Iatmul, and the Tchambuli of New Guinea and Bali. Her material on the United States was less formally gathered through teaching, public lectures, seminars, and serving on commissions, councils, and committees dealing with problems of child-rearing and adolescence. *Sex and Temperament* and *Male and Female* were two of her more comprehensive and influential books.

receptivity requires so much less of her—merely a softening and relaxing of her whole body, and none of the specific readiness and sustained desire that is required of the male—she can learn to fit a simple compliancy together with a thousand other considerations of winning and keeping a lover or a husband, balancing the mood of the moment against the mood of tomorrow, and fitting her receptivity into the whole pattern of her body. (1949/1955: 161)

Mead assumed that the basic potency of males and receptivity of females was the substrate of differences between the sexes in all societies. Because these sex differences were clearly geared to reproductive functions, they guaranteed the continuation of the human race. In Mead's view, attitudes toward these capacities varied from individual to individual and culture to culture, ranging from an eager willingness to an adamant resistance to the fulfillment of the reproductive mandate. In particular, male sexuality could easily be deflected from its procreative mission because it was geared to immediate gratification. The male's spontaneous sexuality was threatened by a civilization that bridled it with considerations of morality, love, and creativity: "Put very succinctly, the more he thinks, the less may he copulate" (1949/1955: 159). It was the responsibility of men to resist curbs on their sexual impulses:

The male can maintain, in all honesty, that a culture which does not protect his spontaneous sexuality will in the end perish, because there will be no children to carry it on. He can demand, and demand most vehemently and with full social responsibility that social forms which hamper and over-define his impulses must be altered. The need for cultural forms in which spontaneous sexual impulse can be happily expressed serves as a testing-point in every human society. This is perhaps one reason why men are so often regarded as the progressive element in human history. (1949/1955: 160)

Mead believed, however, there was a conflict, on the one hand, between men's sexual impulsiveness and the impregnating of women and, on the other the social responsibility of parenting children within the family "It is society that provides the male with a desire for children, patterned interpersonal relationships, that order, control and elaborate his original impulses" (1949/1955: 17). For women there was an easier coalescing of biology and society in their desire for children because they actually bore and reared them. Society could take away the desire for children: "Girls can be placed in learning contexts in which being a woman and bearing a child is a synonym of having one's body invaded, distorted, and destroyed" (1949/1955: 176).

Boys and girls learned their respective roles in the process of growing up. It was the mother's task to reinforce maleness in the little boy and femaleness in the little girl. Nursing provided both boys and girls their first lesson in membership in their respective sexes.[14] The female infant received "a picture of muted complementary behavior within its own sex" (1949/1955: 116). The male infant also formed a complementary relationship; his, however, was with a person of the opposite sex.

The next two lessons involved the child's relationship to the mother's breast. For the male child, demanding and active sucking was to be reinforced; for the female it was to be discouraged. The experience of weaning had fatefully contrasting meanings for boys and girls. For the girls it signified leaving behind the relationship with her mother with the reassuring knowledge that someday she would reenact it with a child of her own. The boy, however, had to abandon the maternal relationship forever because he could never bear a child.[15]

The final childhood lesson in sex membership was learned in training for elimination. Mead believed that there was too much concern and secrecy surrounding the child's toilet training. She espoused a casual attitude so that the anatomical differences between boys and girls would be conspicuous and viewed as different rather than superior or inferior. Penis envy of little girls was not inevitable; it resulted from encouraging exhibitionism in boys and engendering despair in little girls.

The psychological process that accompanied the acculturation of the child was the resolution of the Oedipus complex in which the child "must accept the own-sex parent as in some way a model for his or her own behavior" (1949/1955: 88). This process also involved the recognition by the child that the parents belonged to each other. The oedipal resolution, Mead held, was most successful when the maleness or femaleness of the child was developed as counterpoint and contrast to the parent of the

---

[14] By nursing, Mead meant breast feeding and lactation. She feared that modern technology obscured the relationship between mother and child and endangered sex differentiation by replacing the breast with the bottle and the mother's milk with formula.

[15] Mead believed that women preferred over all other relationships those they had with their suckling son (1949/1955: 118). The son knew the high valuation his mother placed on their relationship. As a husband the son had to be willing to step aside when his wife preferred nursing his son to having sexual intercourse.

opposite sex rather than as rivalry with the parent of the same sex. The resolutions for boys and for girls were viewed as very different. The boy "has to face the need to grow, to learn, to master a great variety of skills and strengths, before he can compete with grown males" (1949/1955: 122). His path was less certain than the girl's; it constituted a struggle and required traversing a long distance before he could possess a woman of his own and become a father. The girl's future, however, was prefigured in her mother's life and was thereby more certain from the start. Whereas the boy had to forge ahead toward manhood the girl had to be restrained: "Implicit in the abundant rules that are laid upon her, the prohibitions against the freedom, the exhibitionism, the roaming and marauding, permitted in her brother, is the message 'It might happen too soon. Wait.'" (1949/1955: 123). Mead summarized the oedipal odyssey:

> So the life of the female starts and ends with sureness, first with the simple identification with her mother, last with the sureness that that identification is true, and that she has made another human being. The period of doubt, of envy of her brother, is brief, and comes early; followed by the long years of sureness. For the male, however, the gradient is reversed.... Instead he must turn out from himself, enter and explore and produce in the outside world, find his expression through the bodies of others. This imposed uncertainty, this period of striving and effort, never really ends ... he may marry, and his wife may have a child, but the child his wife bears is probably never the absolute assurance to him that it is to her.... So while in the end the female in societies in which every woman marries is practically certain of resolving all her doubts about her sex membership, ... the male needs to reassert, reattempt, to redefine his maleness. (1949/1955: 124-125)

Although she believed in basic sex differences as mandated by reproductive roles, Mead argued vigorously against the idea that definitions of femininity and masculinity were rooted in biology. On the basis of anthropological studies, she claimed that societies had different beliefs about what men and women were "naturally" like and different standards for determining deviation. Building on an idea of Ruth Benedict, Mead distinguished between sex differences, as physical and biological characteristics, and temperament or personality traits.[16]

---

[16] Benedict, Ruth (1934). *Patterns of Culture.* New York: Penguin Books.

Children were born with a wide variety of temperaments but it was society that selected from the potpourri of traits those believed to be desirable. The selected traits were inculcated by every means possible, in childrearing, recreation, politics, religion, and the arts. The assignment of particular traits to men or women was not dictated by biology:

> [M]any, if not all, of the personality traits which we have called masculine or feminine are as lightly linked to sex as are the clothing, the manners, and the form of head-dress that a society at a given period assigns to either sex.... We are forced to conclude that human nature is almost unbelievably malleable, responding accurately and contrastingly to contrasting cultural conditions. The differences between individuals within a culture are almost entirely to be laid to differences in conditioning, especially during early childhood, and the form of this conditioning is culturally determined. (1935: 280)

Every society had prescribed personality forms for females and males to which children were molded. Each varied in the strictness with which they assigned traits to one sex to the exclusion of the other. Societies without rigid sex-dichotomies merely pointed out to the child who deviated that he or she was not fulfilling expectations for achieving status in that society without challenging the child's membership in its own sex. In cultures like the United States, however, the enforcement of sex-role norms took a different form. The deviant boy was reproached for not behaving like a male and confronted with the dismal prospect of becoming a sissy instead of a man like his father. The little girl was scorned for not behaving like a female and warned of the possibility that she would grow up to be a tomboy:

> Every time sex is invoked as the reason why it [the child] should prefer trousers to petticoats, baseball bats to dolls, fisticuffs to tears, there is planted in the child's mind a fear that indeed, in spite of anatomical evidence to the contrary, it may not really belong to its own sex at all. (1935: 297)

The etiology of homosexuality was located by Mead in the imposition of rigid feminine and masculine norms upon the behavior of boys and girls:

> In addition to, or aside from, the pain of being born into a culture whose acknowledged end he can never make his own, many a man has now the added misery of being disturbed in his psychosexual life. He not only has the wrong feelings but,

far worse and more confusing, he has the feelings of a woman.... In extreme cases in which a man's temperament conforms very closely to the approved feminine personality, and if there is an existence a social form behind which he can shelter himself, a man may turn to avowed inversion and transvesticism. (1935: 293-294)[17]

In viewing homosexuality as inversion, Mead distinguished between congenital inversion, which she presumed had physiological origins, and homosexual practice which she traced to temperamental variation.[18] She believed that "the most careful research has failed to tie up endocrine balance with actual homosexual behavior" (1935: 104). The "practicing homosexuals" were "those individuals whose adjustment to life is conditioned by their temperamental affinity for a type of behavior that is regarded as unnatural for their own sex and natural for the opposite sex" (1935: 295). Such maladjustment was the cultural result of assigning and limiting personality types to one of the two sexes. Psychiatry, she held, should look for the explanation of passivity in men not only in the boy's identification with his mother but also in the culturally dichotomized assignment of temperamental traits.[19]

Rigid definitions of sex roles, according to Mead, caused confusion in those individuals when they met those who did not conform as, for example, the submissive woman who established a relationship with a dominant woman:

Trained from childhood to yield to the authority of a dominant voice, to bend all of her energies to please the more vulnerable egotism of dominant persons, she may often encounter the

---

[17] Mead, in both volumes, devoted more of her attention to male than female homosexuality, an emphasis that may have stemmed from her belief that the responsibility for the progress of civilization lay more heavily on the shoulders of men than women.

[18] In *Sex and Temperament*, Mead described an American Indian youth she had observed as "in all probability a congenital invert" (294-295). It is not surprising that Mead used the term "inversion" because she viewed homosexuality as the abdication of one's membership in one's own sex for membership in the other sex.

[19] She repudiated the notion that individuals of one sex who showed traits that were culturally linked to the opposite sex where "latent homosexuals." The issue of "latent homosexuality" was reflected in Ovesey's conceptualization of pseudohomosexuality. Presumably any lapses in the masculine behavior of males kindled the suspicion of homosexuality.

same authoritative note in a feminine voice and thus she, who is by temperament the ideal woman in her society, may find women so engrossing that marriage adjustments never enter the picture. Her involvement in devotion to members of her own sex may in turn set up in her doubts and questions as to her essential femininity. (1935: 306)

The cross-cultural comparison of sexual behavior was provided in a treatise published by Clellan Ford and Frank Beach,[20] a survey of vast bodies of information gathered over many years by anthropologists, zoologists, and physiologists.[21]

Ford and Beach described their perspective as being threefold. To determine the full range of human sexuality, they compared several cultures or societies, including the United States, for differences and similarities in sexual behavior. They also compared human sexual behavior with that of animals, particularly the other primates, to determine the "basic mammalian pattern" (251) of sexuality. After identifying this pattern they believed they would be able to assess which aspects of human sexuality could be attributed to biological development or social influence. Finally, they examined evidence of sexual behavior and physiology, to explain differences between humans and animals. The investigation into physiology rested on the assumption that "sexual relations are in part an expression of deep-rooted urges and needs, and the behavior through which these find expression is organized by the physical machinery of the body" (251).

Ford and Beach asserted that human mammalian heritage included sex play in childhood, masturbation, and foreplay preceding coitus. Sexual activity among children and adolescents was found in every society

---

[20] Ford, Clellan S. and Beach, Frank A. (1951). *Patterns of Sexual Behavior*. New York: Harper and Row.

[21] Although the two authors worked in close collaboration, Ford handled the anthropological evidence, most of which was drawn from the Human Relations Area Files at Yale University, which, at that time, contained information gathered by anthropologists and lay people from about 200 different societies. One-hundred-ninety of these were utilized in this study. They were scattered over Oceania, Eurasia, Africa, North America, and South America. Beach had collected information on the sexual behavior of animals over a period of fifteen years. He had also conducted several experimental studies on the physiological effects of hormone administration on the sexual behavior of animals such as rats and dogs. See Beach, F. A. (1948). *Hormones and Behavior*. New York: Paul Hoeber.

that permitted it and appeared, although less frequently, in restrictive societies, It was implied that sexual experimentation in childhood could lead to more satisfying coitus in adulthood. Masturbation was universal among humans and animals: "the basic mammalian tendencies toward self-stimulation seem sufficiently strong and widespread to justify classifying human masturbation as a normal and natural form of sexual expression" (166). They found great variability in types and duration of foreplay but it existed in almost every society. While some forms of foreplay were found among infrahuman species, kissing and breast stimulation were almost exclusively human practices, Bestiality was also brought within the purview of normal sexuality as evidence "that man is biologically equipped to respond sexually to a great range of stimuli and potential partners" (152).

Ford and Beach believed that both exclusively heterosexual or homosexual relationships represented a cultural diminution of sexual capacity:

> Men and women who are totally lacking in any conscious homosexual leanings are as much a product of cultural conditioning as are the exclusive homosexuals who find heterosexual relations distasteful and unsatisfying. Both extremes represent movement away from the original, intermediate condition which includes the capacity for both forms of sexual expression. In a restrictive society such as our own[,] a large proportion of the population learns not to respond to or even to recognize homosexual stimuli and may eventually become in fact unable to do so. At the same time a certain minority group, also through the process of learning, becomes highly if not exclusively sensitive to the erotic attractions of alike-sexed partners. Physical or physiological peculiarities that hamper the formation of heterosexual habits may incline certain individuals to a homosexual existence. But human homosexuality is not basically a product of hormonal imbalance or "perverted" heredity. It is the product of the fundamental mammalian heritage of general responsiveness as modified under the impact of experience. (258-259)

Although homosexuality in adulthood was never the dominant cultural form, it could be found even in the most sexually restrictive societies, such as the United States. In those societies in which homosexuality was institutionalized, it was usually allowed only for males. The most prevalent institutionalized form was the **BERDACHE** or male who "dresses like a woman, performs a woman's tasks, and adopts some aspects of the feminine role in sexual behavior with male partners" (130).

In some societies these feminized men could be figures of status and power known as SHAMAN because of the belief that their masculine to feminine transformation was the result of supernatural intervention. Some shaman entered into marriages with other males in which they played the role of receiver in anal copulation. Some also had female mistresses by whom they had children. Even the shaman's husband usually had a second wife, a female with whom he could have heterosexual coitus.[22]

For the most part, in those societies which did not incorporate homosexuality into some form of marital relationship, it was institutionalized as an ancillary or transitional sexuality. Anal or oral copulation between adult and adolescent males, with the adult in the role of insertor, was sometimes viewed as the means for ushering young males into manhood, a process anthropologists euphemistically called "puberty rites." In at least one society, the bachelors, who had been insertees as adolescents, spent their premarital years as insertors of young males, taking on, as it were, the responsibility for their masculinization.[23]

---

[22] Although Ford and Beach explained the acquisition of a second wife by a shaman's husband in terms of sexual desire, it seems equally probable that these men would have wanted to have children of their own.

[23] This society was the Keraki of New Guinea, in which the adult men, before their marriages, inseminated the younger males (see Ford and Beach, 1951: 132). A 1981 study by Gilbert Herdt (*Guardians of the Flutes: Idioms of Masculinity*. New York: McGraw-Hill) provided a detailed description of institutionalized homosexuality of a warrior society located in Papua New Guinea and pseudonymously identified as the Sambia, which he observed from 1974 to 1976. From the ages of seven to ten the boys were "taken from their mothers when first initiated into the male cult, and thereafter experience the most powerful and seductive homosexual fellatio activities" (2). For about five years the pubescent boys engaged in the sexual practice of sucking the penises of older boys who ejaculated into the younger males' mouths. According to Herdt the practice of fellatio was highly ritualized, allowing little interpersonal variation: "Younger initiates may act only as fellators, ... older males cannot suck younger boys, and they evince no interest in doing so" (3n). These homosexual practices excluded anal intercourse and transvestism. Through the ingestion and storage of semen the younger boys were supposed to be masculinized and purged of any residual femininity left over from long association with their mothers. After serving as fellators for several years the young males became the individuals who were fellated. At the height of these sexual relationships there was strict avoidance of women who were feared as possible pollutants. There was, however, a transition period from sixteen to

Those societies in which the majority of males engaged in homosexual activity, according to Ford and Beach, furnished clear evidence that any exclusively physiological explanation for homosexuality (e.g., abnormal glandular balance) was contradicted by the cross-cultural evidence. Within the ambit of normal behavior the authors described what they called assaultive behavior:

> It is our conclusion that for most people high levels of erotic arousal tend to generate moderately assaultive tendencies. And, furthermore, that for the majority of human beings painful stimulation which is not too intense is likely to increase rather than decreased the level of sexual excitement. The inherited capacity to derive satisfaction from this kind of stimulation is greatly modified by learning and experience. Our cross-cultural evidence suggests that societies which incorporate painful stimulation in the approved forms of foreplay also provide ample opportunity for the developing individual to learn the facilitative effects of the resulting sensations. (67)

Assaultive behavior consisted of scratching, biting, and pulling hair. In human sexual expression, each partner assaulted the other: "[I]f the man bites the woman, she is permitted and expected to bite in return. If the girl scratches her lover, he retaliates. This is not true of lower animals. In their case it is almost always the male who wounds the female, very rarely the reverse" (67).

The implication of the emerging formulation of the sociocultural sexual identity by Bloch and Westermarck was that if that identity were a product of culture then it could be tolerated in both its heterosexual and homosexual forms. Within his general view of sexual perversions, Bloch can be credited with furthering the detoxication of the homosexual identity by directing attention to anthropological and historical evidence. In his mind homosexuality remained a perversion because it was not reproductive and therefore did not transmit to future generations any valuable uniqueness. Yet homosexuality was nothing more than a

---

twenty-five years of age during which the young men, known as bachelors, would take up sexual activity with women while still being fellated by the boys. With the arrival of marriage and, certainly, of fatherhood, heterosexuality was expected to be exclusive. Herdt was careful to point out that Sambian boys did not entertain (and, one may add, probably were ignorant of) the idea of a homosexual identity (3n-4n). They showed excitement over women's appearance even during the period when their sexual contact was exclusively homosexual.

human aberration. According to Bloch aberrations were ubiquitous and the raw material out of which civilized sex was created. When they did not overtake the individual's vita sexualis, homosexuality and other perversions could even be viewed as "healthy," occasional dalliances of the adventurous heterosexual.

Westermarck's emphasis on moral values as determinants of sexual relationships and practices continued the trend of attributing the formation of sexual identity to external rather than internal factors. This shift in emphasis by Westermarck, as in the case of Bloch, was proposed within a general endorsement of heterosexual monogamy. Westermarck, the sociologist of marriage, implied that moral progress was contingent upon the achievement of the male-female design as the model sexual relationship. Malinowski assumed that monogamous heterosexual relationships were the ideal held in tribal society. He was uncomfortable with the use of the word homosexuality to describe the emotionally close relationships of tribal men.

Mead's view of child development was clearly modeled after Freud's conception of the psychological sexual identity although, like the post-Freudians, she moved the central focus of the oedipal drama from the father and penis to the mother and breast. She also claimed that exhibitionism in boys and penis envy in girls was not the inevitable consequence of psychosexual development but the detritus of cultural stereotypes of men and women, which emphasized rivalry within and between the sexes rather than "complementarity." Even with an amelioration of conflict, she believed the successful oedipal resolution yielded passive, feminine girls and active, masculine boys, solidly heterosexual in object choice.

As an educator she shouldered the responsibility of enlightening the public about innate sex difference, individual temperament, and cultural conditioning. She saw herself as the guardian of the sexual development of adolescents. In this role she decried the wide dissemination of the first Kinsey report:

> I believe one should put oneself in those readers' place, and not force them either to accept or to reject interpretations the implications of which they would not have chosen to hear had they been fully aware of them.... This is one of the most serious criticisms that can be leveled at the way in which the Kinsey report was permitted to become a best-seller. The sudden removal of a previously guaranteed reticence has left many young people singularly defenseless in just those areas where

their desire to conform was protected by lack of knowledge of the extent of non-conformity. (1949/1955: 329, 329n)

There is little question that Mead considered the homosexual identity to be pathological, in her words, serious confusion and maladjustment, that blocked the afflicted from fulfilling their reproductive and parental roles. But the finger of pathological blame that was formerly pointed at the individual for alleged developmental or moral deficiencies, now was aimed at a culture that forced men and women of unusual temperaments to achieve self-expression at the price of renouncing membership in their respective biological sexes.

Her contribution to the redefinition of heterosexuality was, perhaps, more noteworthy. She made the heterosexual identity roomier than Freud allowed by showing how femininity and masculinity were relational concepts that depended almost entirely on cultural perspectives. Although acknowledging the great malleability of men and women, she held steadfast to the belief that there was an essential femaleness and maleness, nature's endowment of potency to men and receptivity to women. The basic sex differences were cast in terms of reproduction and childrearing which, in her formulation, inextricably tied sexuality to procreation.

The contribution of Ford and Beach's work to the normalization of sexual relationships was considerable. In some ways it was only an endorsement of prevalent sexual attitudes and practices. Their conclusion that the fact that stable heterosexual "mateships" existed in all societies favored the acceptance of marriage as the natural form of sexual relationship. While these unions were described as monogamous, the authors acknowledged that males in some cultures had sexual relationships with more than one woman. The frontal position in human coitus was explained by the location of the clitoris and vagina which in human females is further forward than in other mammals. The general practice of coitus in private surroundings was attributed to "the widespread human desires for concealment" (83). By viewing assaultive behavior as mutual it was easier for Ford and Beach to normalize a sexual relationship sometimes classified as sadomasochistic.

There were explicit beliefs and assumptions upon which Ford and Beach grounded their survey. One was that human sexual behavior was the product of evolutionary development and social conditioning. In their view it was difficult to separate social from biological influences. In any case they believed that social conditioning had more influence and better explained the cross-cultural variations.

There were other assumptions that were only implied. They assumed in several ways that males were more sexual than females. They believed that females engaged in less masturbation, were less often homosexual, and were less attracted by physical appearance. Because they bolstered these beliefs with zoological evidence, the implication was that the attenuated sexuality of females was a product of biology.[24]

The authors were convinced that human sexual expression was not limited to reproduction and that it could be flexible in form. Occasional references to homosexuality as inversion, combined with their view of female sexuality, however, at least implied a belief in the male-female design as the bedrock of social organization.

One final assumption was that high frequency of behavior defined normality. Much of the authors' acceptance of conventional practices, such as marriage, frontal coitus, foreplay, and children's sexual activity, was predicated on the evidence of their frequent occurrence in many cultures. Normalization of the less conventional, such as masturbation, homosexuality, bestiality, and assaultive behavior, also resulted from showing their reoccurrence in many cultures.

The theoretical perspective of Ford and Beach generally supported the belief in the sociocultural sexual identity. In attributing variability in human sexual behavior largely to conditioning, in recognizing the lability in sexual practice, and in equating frequency and normality, the authors were emphasizing the importance of external factors in shaping sexual identity.

Their sociocultural conception of sexual identity, however, included both psychological and biological elements. The psychological ingredients included their acknowledgment of childhood sexuality, the minimization of female sexuality, and their belief in sexual "urges." The biological ingredients were contained in their references to the mammalian basis of human sexual behavior and physiological factors undergirding sexual urges. The authors rejected the concept of sexual identity as basically biological, however. The greater encephalization of humans, they held, rendered a strictly biological account of human sexual behavior simplistic:

> Review of the changes which have taken place in the structure
> of the brain during mammalian evolution showed that this
> structure has become increasingly complex and important as
> the primates and finally our own species developed. In

---

[24] Although the report documents the cultural occurrence of polygamy, it had almost nothing to say about polyandry.

particular, the cerebral cortex has assumed a greater and greater degree of direction over all behavior, including that of sexual nature. It appears that the growing importance of cerebral influences accounts for the progressive relaxation of hormonal control over sexual responses. At the same time, increasing dominance of the cortex in affecting sexual manifestations has resulted in greater lability and modifiability of erotic practices. Human sexual behavior is more variable and more easily affected by learning and social conditioning than is that of any other species, and this is precisely because in our own species, this type of behavior depends heavily upon the most recently evolved parts of the brain. (1951: 249)

In essence, Ford and Beach conceptualized sexual behavior as responses and stimuli that were physical, psychological or cultural: "Human learning ... customarily occurs in a social context. For this reason the impact of learning upon human sexuality is best understood within the frame of reference provided by the society of which the individual is a member" (1951: 262-263).

The anthropological contribution to the discourse on sexual identity included polytheistic, monotheistic, and scientific views of the permissible boundaries of sexual relationships. In their study of polytheistic societies the anthropologists became acquainted with a wide range of sexual practices, including masturbation, oral copulation, nibbling and cursing during coitus. They also learned more about sexual relationships among children and individuals of the same biological sex. This knowledge led them to ponder the possibility that the structure of sexual relationships found in western civilization was limited more by cultural norms than by human biological or psychological capacity.

The monotheistic view of sexual relationships prevailed, however, in the anthropological contribution to the discourse on sexual identity. Bloch asserted that the future course of civilization depended on the male-female design, the union of the "normal" man with the "normal" woman. Malinowski drew a firm line between "friendship" among individuals of the same biological sex and "homosexual love." Although arguing against the imposition of sex-role stereotypes, Mead subscribed to the belief in an essential femaleness and maleness as biological guarantees of reproduction, the rearing of children, and the future of civilization. The biological difference in the sexuality of females and males, Ford and Beach implied, provided the basis for their "natural" mateship.

The anthropologists incorporated the scientific cosmological view of sexual relationships in their belief that human sexual capacity was far greater than the forms it took in a single culture. They tried to show how basically impressionable and malleable this capacity was to the touch of societal attitudes and regulation. This potentialist view of sexual capacity admitted the element of choice, although choice appeared to pertain more to partners than to the structure of their relationships. There was also the inevitable scientism in the contribution of the anthropologists. With the exception of Westermarck, who acknowledged the moral tone of his discussion of sexual relationships, the anthropological contribution to the discourse on sexual identity was dressed in the scientific garb of ethnography.

13 Behavioral Identity: The Survey Approach

The sociocultural sexual identity, as conceived by the anthropologists, was largely a product of eternal forces, which they described as cultural imperatives and injunctions. In the discourse on sexual identity that followed the idea of the cultural identity was transformed into the behavioral sexual identity. In this formulation culture, or "environment," was conceived as an array of stimuli and the individual as a repository of learned physical and psychical responses.

The formulation of the behavioral sexual identity was launched by Alfred Kinsey and his associates at Indiana University in their survey of sexual practices in the United States.[1] The individual's sexual behavior was described as a "total sexual outlet" or the sum of the orgasms derived from various sources: masturbation, nocturnal emissions (in the male), heterosexual petting, heterosexual intercourse, homosexual intercourse, and intercourse with animals.[2]

---

[1] The main body of their work is contained in two volumes: Kinsey, Alfred C., Pomeroy, Wardell B., and Martin, Clyde E. (1948). *Sexual Behavior in the Human Male*. Philadelphia: W. B. Saunders; and Kinsey, Alfred C., Pomeroy, Wardell B., Martin, Clyde E., and Gebhard, Paul H. (1953). *Sexual Behavior in the Human Female*. Philadelphia: W. B. Saunders. The volumes are dedicated to their respondents, 12,000 males and 8,000 females. In summarizing the contribution to an expanded conception of human sexuality we have relied on the excellent 1976 summary by Paul Robinson: *The Modernization of Sex: Havelock Ellis, Alfred Kinsey, William Masters and Virginia Johnson*. New York: Harper & Row. Our assessment of the Kinsey contribution differs from Robinson's, especially over the issue of sexual identity.

[2] The Kinsey studies did not include practices that absorbed the attention of psychiatrists such as fetishism, transvestism, and sadomasochism. There is recent evidence that Kinsey himself was very interested in sadomasochism and the sexual motives involved in obtaining tattoos. See Steward, Samuel (1981). *Chapters from an Autobiography*. San Francisco: Grey Fox Press, Chapter VI, "Doctor Prometheus," 95-106. Kinsey even persuaded Steward to play the

The Kinsey group assessed the psychological identity in developing their idea of the behavioral sexual identity by taking issue with various aspects of Freud's theory of psychosexual development. They believed that children rarely ascribed sexual meaning to what were little more than games: "[E]ven when the small boy lies on top of the small girl and makes what may resemble copulatory movements, there is often no realization what genital contacts might be made or that there might be an erotic reward in such activity" (Kinsey et al., 1953: 108). They did not deny, however, that such contacts could become sexual with greater knowledge on the part of the child:

> Freud and the psychoanalysts contend that all tactile stimulation and response are basically sexual, and there seems considerable justification for this thesis, in view of the tactile origin of so much of mammalian stimulation. This, however, involves a considerable extension of both the everyday and scientific meanings of the term sexual, and we are not now concerned with recording every occasion on which a babe brings two parts of his body into juxtaposition, every time it scratches its ear or its genitalia, nor every occasion on which it sucks its thumb. If all such acts are to be interpreted as masturbatory, it is, of course, a simple matter to conclude that masturbation and early sexual activity are universal phenomena; but it is still to be shown that these elemental tactile experiences have anything to do with the development of the sexual behavior of the adult. (Kinsey, Pomeroy & Martin, 1948: 163)

They also argued against the idea that there was a linear progression in development which shifted the child's sexual interest from the self (the narcissism of masturbation) to homosexual and ultimately to heterosexual relations. On the contrary, they thought that the child's attention fluctuated among all of these interests. Finally, they disputed the idea of discontinuities in sexual interests as held in the theory of preadolescent latency. Interruptions in sexual interest, they contended, could be traced to cultural restraints placed on the behavior of children as they approached puberty.

Psychoanalytic theory, especially the adaptational approach, entertained the possibility that the individual could channel sexual energy

---

role of the masochist in an encounter filmed by him. Steward also recounts Kinsey's allergic reaction to the word normal: "Just what do you mean? ... Usual? Usual for whom—you, me, the rest of the world?" (99).

into cognitive pursuits. Much of artistic expression, for example, was attributed to this process, known as sublimation. This theory, the Kinsey group believed, assumed uniformity in sexual capacity. For them sublimation was merely the modern form of an ancient asceticism. They believed that, in males, "sublimation is so subtle, or so rare, as to constitute an academic possibility rather than a demonstrated actuality" (Kinsey, Pomeroy & Martin, 1948: 213). In contrast they attributed differences in capacity to individual sexual endowment; what was believed to be "sublimation" owed more to sexual apathy than to sexual restraint and denial: "No one who knows how remarkably different individuals may be in morphology, in physiologic reactions, and in other psychologic capacities, could conceive of erotic capacities (of all things) that were basically uniform throughout a population" (209).

Apart from these refutations of psychoanalytic theory, there were some striking similarities between the two approaches. Although psychoanalytic thought wavered in its commitment to being a pure psychology, it never abandoned the notion that mental functioning had a biological basis. In a similar vein, the Kinsey group took the position that the distinctions among anatomy, physiology, and psychology were nebulous:

> Whatever we may learn of the anatomy and physiology and of the basic chemistry of an animal's responses, must contribute to our understanding of the totality which we call behavior. Those aspects of behavior which we identify as psychologic can be nothing but certain aspects of that same basic anatomy and physiology. (Kinsey et al., 1953: 643)

Both psychoanalytic theory and the Kinsey approach used biology to explain human sexuality. The former, however, tied biology to interior states of mental functioning, while the Kinsey approach linked it to descriptions of sexual conduct.

Freudian theory was profoundly influenced by evolutionary concepts, as exemplified by adherence to the doctrine that complex forms of sexuality evolved from simple forms. Although the Kinsey group was wary of explaining human behavior in terms of animal behavior, their belief in evolution was demonstrated by their many analogies between the two. The response to touch, for example, presented as basic to sexual stimulation in humans, they believed was characteristic of all mammalian forms.[3]

---

[3] The Kinsey authors wrote: "In the higher mammals, including the human, tactile stimulation is the chief mechanical source of arousal" (1948: 157).

A less obvious but more important similarity between the two approaches was the unquestioned belief in irreducible differences in female and male sexuality. In the psychological sexual identity, this belief was expressed as the superordinate male-female design, indelibly stamped upon human anatomy, physiology, and culture, the prescribed mold for human erotic experience. The Kinsey group also believed that human sexuality was ultimately shaped by innate differences between the sexes.

This biological determinism was considerably less apparent in the Kinsey reports because of their ringing endorsement of female sexuality. An initial reading of their position suggests that they were minimizing and even eliminating the notion that male sexuality was unique and superior. The obvious differences in female and male genitalia notwithstanding, they insisted that the physiological bases of sexual response were identical in the two sexes: increase in pulse rate, blood pressure, and respiration, tumescence, loss of sensory perception, and the development of pelvic thrusts. There was equally rapid intense response to tactile stimulation and orgasms could be equally satisfying. The single significant physiological difference was that males ejaculated.[4]

The Kinsey group also defended the clitoris as equal to the penis (Kinsey et al., 1953: 591): "The penis, in spite of its greater size, is not known to be better equipped with sensory nerves than the much smaller clitoris. Both structures are of considerable significance in sexual arousal." In the psychoanalytic perspective the vagina was the seat of maximum, mature sexual satisfaction for the woman. The Kinsey group entertained serious doubts about the existence of the vaginal orgasm as an isolated sexual response and berated the efforts of countless clinicians

---

Robinson believed that Kinsey evaluated all forms of human sexual experience in terms of the sexuality of lower species. "Nothing," Robinson stated, "was more characteristic of Kinsey than his reliance on the argument *de animalibus*" (1976: 56). Robinson's position may be somewhat overstated because the Kinsey group did believe that "psychologic stimulation" was unique to humans and that, in the adult, it gradually replaced physical stimulation (see, for example, Kinsey, Pomeroy & Martin, 1948: 157-158).

[4] The second volume of the Kinsey Report claimed that "there is no such phenomenon [as ejaculation] in the female" (1953: 641). This claim has now been questioned with the discovery of the Grafenberg spot, located on the anterior wall of the vagina. It swells when sexually stimulated and, in some women, causes an expulsion of fluid from the urethra. See Calderone, Martha (1981). Orgasmic Expulsion of Fluid in the Sexually Stimulated Female. *SIECUS Report (10)*2: 23.

to transfer clitoral to vaginal reaction—attempts that were a "biological impossibility" (584). The male authors of these reports showed some feminist sympathies when they suggested that the vagina received undue attention because it contributed more to the sexual arousal of the male than the female:

> In brief ... we conclude that the anatomic structures which are most essential to sexual response and orgasm are nearly identical in the human female and male. The differences are relatively few.... If the females and males differ sexually in any basic way, those differences must originate in some other aspect of the biology or psychology of the two sexes.... They do not originate in any of the anatomic structures which have been considered here. (Kinsey et al., 1953: 593)

After this moving declaration of anatomical equality, the Kinsey group went to depict differences in female and male sexuality that were as basic and immutable as those of psychoanalytic theory. The locus of sex differences was transferred from genital to psychic response. Using the language of learning theory and conditioning, the Kinsey report stated the following:

> In general, males are more often conditioned by their sexual experience, and by a greater variety of associated factors, than females. While there is great individual variation in this respect among both females and males, there is considerable evidence that the sexual responses and behavior of the average male are, on the whole, more often determined by the male's previous experience, by his association with objects that were connected with his previous sexual experiences, by his vicarious sharing of another individual's sexual experience, and by his sympathetic reactions to the sexual responses of other individuals. The average female is less often affected by such psychologic factors. (1953: 649-650)

When one considers the multiplicity of factors classified as "psychologic," it is clear that the differences in responsiveness between the sexes was considerable indeed: portrayals of nude figures, erotic art, live or filmed sexual activity, burlesque and floor shows, animal coitus, peeping and voyeurism, preferences for light or dark during the primal act, fantasies, nocturnal sex dreams, literary materials, responses to painful erotic stimuli, fetishism, transvestism, and promiscuity. In only three items, films, romantic fiction, and being erotically bitten, were females

equal to males in sexual responsiveness. The authors believed that observations of sexual behavior in infrahuman mammalian species confirmed
their conclusions about the differences in the sexual capacities of men and
women.[5]

To what did the Kinsey group attribute this sharp difference in
capacity? Their answers appear to hark back to the evolutionary theory
of the nineteenth century, recalling notions of Krafft-Ebing and Moll:
"We are inclined to believe that differences between female and male responses to psychologic stimuli may depend on cerebral differences"
(Kinsey, et al., 1953: 712). Although confessing ignorance of the nature of
these differences, they ventured the idea that there were sex centers in
the cerebrum that acted as a "master switch-board which controls all the
individual elements but brings them together as a unit during the sexual
response" (712).

The Kinsey group, despite its emphasis on sensory hedonism, viewed
the family and home as the basic unit of society: "Society is interested in
maintaining the family as a way for men and women to live together in
partnerships that may make for more effective functioning than solitary
living may allow" (Kinsey, Pomeroy & Martin, 1948: 563). The family
performed several functions: it provided for the care of children who were
the products of coitus, a dependable sexual outlet for adults, and the
means to curb promiscuity. Although more tolerant of premarital coitus
than the Freudians, the justification for this sexual activity rested upon the
belief that men and women who were sexually active before marriage had
more successful unions than those who were inactive. Premarital sex, they
believed, preserved some of the adult's original uninhibited capacity to
enjoy physical contact and even enlarged their ability to respond
emotionally to people outside the family.[6]

---

[5] The later report (Kinsey et al., 1953: 650) referred to the 1951 Ford and Beach
study as stating that, in infrahuman mammals, males were more capable of
sexual learning and conditioning than females. The Kinsey reports tended to
treat psychological and physical stimuli as unidimensional in their capacity to
elicit responses, as if governed by the same physical laws of learning. The
Kinsey studies were carried on during the heyday of American behavioristic
psychology, which took an early and especially firm hold on American
Midwestern universities.

[6] Kinsey's own academic interest in human sexuality grew out of his
participation in a pioneering marriage course introduced in 1938 for seniors at
Indiana University. The course required individual conferences with students

The idea of sexual identity was addressed by the Kinsey group in their reporting of the frequency of homosexual behavior among their respondents:

> [W]e ourselves were totally unprepared to find such incidence data.... Over a period of several years we were repeatedly assailed with doubts as to whether ... a selection of cases was biasing the results. It has been our experience, however, that each new group into which we have gone has provided substantially the same data. (1948: 625).

In viewing sexual identity as a behavioral phenomenon, the Kinsey group challenged the belief, inherent in the notions of the biological and psychological identities, that the individual's sexual identity was equivalent to personality. In their view, masturbation, homosexuality and heterosexuality were only names of sources of sexual stimulation:

> The mammalian record thus confirms our statement that any animal which is not too strongly conditioned by some special sort of experience is capable of responding to any adequate stimulus. This is what we find in the more uninhibited segments of our own human species, and that is what we find among young children who are not too rigorously restrained in their early sex play. Exclusive preferences and patterns of behavior, heterosexual or homosexual, come only with experience, or as a result of social pressures which tend to force an individual into an exclusive pattern of one or the other sort. (1953: 450)

The sources of stimulation, however, in common parlance, became designations of the individual: the masturbator, the homosexual, or the heterosexual.[7] The Kinsey remedy was quite direct:

---

and, in effect, marked the beginning of the Kinsey interviews. See Christenson, Cornelia V. (1971). *Kinsey: A Biography*. Bloomington: Indiana University Press.
[7] The 1948 report contains two philological errors: (1) It claimed that the word "homosexual" was patterned after the word "heterosexual" (612), whereas in the Kertbeny letter, the idea (not the word) of the heterosexual identity was conceived in the image of homosexuality; (2) It defined sexual perversion as males playing female roles and females playing male roles (614), whereas, as explained by Chevalier and employed by Freud, the term had broader meaning. The report was, however, historically accurate in claiming that such terms as sexual inversion, intersexuality, the third-sex, and psychosexual hermaphroditism imply that those who are homosexual are ambiguously female and male (612). The authors also pointed out that the term bisexual

It would clarify our thinking if the terms could be dropped completely out of our vocabulary, for then socio-sexual behavior could be described as activity between a female and a male, or between two females, or between two males, and this would constitute a more objective record of the fact. For the present, however, we shall have to use the term homosexual in something of its standard meaning, except that we shall use it primarily to describe sexual relationships, and shall prefer not to use it to describe the individuals who were involved in those relationships. (Kinsey et al., 1953: 447)

In explaining their theory of the etiology of the homosexual identity, the Kinsey group rejected genetic and hormonal explanations, as well as theories of pathological psychosexual development and moral degeneracy.[8] Their explanation rested squarely on social conditioning: accidents that lead the child to have its first sexual experience with a person of the same sex and the powerful effect of people's opinions and social codes in promoting acceptance or rejection of the experience.

The Kinsey group believed that if homosexuality were less socially toxic then those who engaged in sexual experience with individuals of their own sex would be less inclined to deny or minimize their involvement as being "not really homosexual":

It is amazing to observe how many psychologists and psychiatrists have accepted this sort of propaganda, and have come to believe that homosexual males and females are discretely different from persons who merely have homosexual experience.... Sometimes such an interpretation allows for only two kinds of males and two kinds of females, namely those who are heterosexual and those who are homosexual. (Kinsey, Pomeroy & Martin, 1948: 616)

---

confused matters further because its biological meaning had nothing to do with sexual outlet and its usual behavioral definition required that the individual's sexual activity concurrently involve both females and males. At one point in the report, the biogenetic theory which held that the individual anatomically possessed both female and male structures and physiologic capacities (one version of the theory of bisexuality) was clearly rejected as lacking supporting evidence (Kinsey, Pomeroy & Martin, 1948: 657).

[8] The reports called "unacceptable" theories that viewed homosexuality as biological and unmodifiable. Such explanations were not even possible until the rival theories of homosexuality as shaped by learning and cultural mores were thoroughly considered and disproved.

The report declared that there was no homosexual personality and nothing in the physical, psychological or spiritual make-up of the homosexual female or male that made them distinct from the heterosexual:

> It is commonly believed, for instance, that homosexual males are rarely robust physically, are uncoordinated or delicate in their movements, or perhaps graceful enough but not strong and vigorous in their physical expression. Fine skins, high-pitched voices, obvious hand movements, a feminine carriage of the hips, and peculiarities of walking gaits are supposed accompaniments of a preference for a male as a sexual partner. It is commonly believed that the homosexual male is artistically sensitive, emotionally unbalanced, temperamental to the point of being unpredictable, difficult to get along with, and undependable in meeting specific obligations. In physical characteristics there have been attempts to show that the homosexual male has a considerable crop of hair and less often becomes bald, has teeth which are more like those of the female, a broader pelvis, larger genitalia, and a tendency toward being fat, and that he lacks a linea alba. The homosexual male is supposed to be less interested in athletics, and more often interested in music and the arts, more often engaged in such occupations as bookkeeping, dress design, window display, hairdressing, acting, radio work, nursing, religious service and social work. The converse to all of these is supposed to represent the typical heterosexual male. (Kinsey, Pomeroy & Martin, 1948: 637)[9]

Behaviors such as these were observed in cities. Homosexual relationships among ranchmen, cattle men, prospectors, lumbermen, and farmers were virile and active: "such a background breeds the attitude that sex is sex, irrespective of the nature of the partner with whom the relation is had" (Kinsey, Pomeroy & Martin, 1948: 457). In rural areas homosexual relationships were merely an extension of the masculine pursuits of the male inhabitants: "Such a group of hard-riding, hard-hitting, assertive males would not tolerate the affectations of some city groups" (459).[10]

---

[9] The report on female sexuality contained no corresponding description of the stereotypes for the homosexual woman.

[10] The country later invaded the city so that cowboy hats, jeans, colored handkerchiefs, boots, and leather accouterments became de rigueur in the gay male scene of the nineteen seventies. See Peter Fisher (1972), *The Gay Mystique: The Myth and Reality of Male Homosexuality*. New York: Stein & Day: 81-94.)

To replace the concepts of the biological and psychological sexual identities, the Kinsey group proposed the notion of a heterosexual-homosexual balance. It consisted of the continuity of gradations between exclusively heterosexual and exclusively homosexual experience. Based on this notion they developed the heterosexual-homosexual rating scale which could be used to evaluate the physical contacts and psychic reactions the individual had to either sex. To maintain the idea of "balance," a rating of 0 (exclusively heterosexual) was at the opposite end of the scale from a rating of 6 (exclusively homosexual), a rating of 3 represented the midpoint of the scale and an exact balance of heterosexual and homosexual response.

The idea of the heterosexual-homosexual balance constituted a behavioral or experiential version of the sociocultural sexual identity, as suggested in this passage:

> The histories which have been available in the present study make it apparent that heterosexuality or homosexuality of many individuals is not an all-or-none proposition. It is true that there are persons in the population whose histories are exclusively heterosexual, both in regard to their overt experience and in regard to their psychic reactions. And there are individuals in the population whose histories are exclusively homosexual.... But the record also shows there is a considerable portion of the population whose members have combined, with in their individual histories, both homosexual and heterosexual experience and/or psychic responses. There are some whose heterosexual experiences predominate, there are some whose homosexual experiences predominate, and there are some who have had quite equal amounts of both types of experience. (Kinsey, Pomeroy & Martin, 1948: 638-639)

Where homosexuality and neurosis were associated, the Kinsey group maintained that was often the result of society's hostile reaction to the individual's homosexual behavior. American culture was particularly intolerant. Except for England, the report contended, no European culture had become as disturbed over homosexuality. Religion bred fear and hatred because both Jewish and Christian doctrine viewed all forms of non-procreative sexual activity as perversion. The law made its own contribution to oppression. In every state of the Union there were forms of homosexual activity and desire which were punishable under such labels as sodomy, buggery, perverse or unnatural acts, crimes against nature, public or private indecency, and unnatural, lewd or lascivious behavior (Kinsey et al., 1953: 483). Nor were legal attitudes toward homosexual conduct consistent since they were more punitive toward males than females.

In sexual relationships the Kinsey authors believed that social mandates should be replaced with personal choice:

> It must not be forgotten that the basic phenomenon to be explained is an individual's preference for a partner of one sex, or for a partner of the other sex, or his acceptance of a partner of either sex. This problem is, after all, part of the broader problem of choices in general: the choice of the road one takes, of the clothes one wears, of the food one eats, of the place in which one sleeps, and of the endless other things one is constantly choosing. A choice of a partner in a sexual relation becomes more significant only because society demands that there be a particular choice in this matter, and does not so often dictate one's choice of food or clothing. (Kinsey, Pomeroy & Martin, 1948: 661)

The Kinsey group's conception of sexual identity followed in the footsteps of the historians and anthropologists who preceded them. Sexual identity, in its sociocultural aspect, was viewed as a product of forces external to the individual. In the Kinsey conception "stimuli" and "responses" could range from tactile contact and visual imagery to institutional prescriptions for sexual relationships and social intolerance. "Culture," "society," "conditioning," and "learning" were various designations of the external forces which shaped the individual's sexual identity.

Although the Kinsey group repudiated the traditional notions of the biological and psychological sexual identities, elements of these concepts survived in their behavioral version of the sociocultural sexual identity. The idea of the biological sexual identity was preserved in their distinction between female and male sexuality and their tacit assumption of physical complementarity. Moreover, the heterosexual-homosexual rating scale was conceived in terms of the biological sex of partners, even though it assumed a greater fluidity of choice than did the conceptions of the biological sexual identity. The psychological sexual identity was retained in the distinction between "behavioral" and "psychic" response, as embodied in the heterosexual-homosexual rating scale. "Psychic" response occurred in the individual's mind even in the absence of any overt behavior. Although cast in the language of behavioral theory, "psychic" response implied mental processes that were akin to the mental activity that constituted the psychological sexual identity.

We have reviewed some important ways in which the Kinsey reports broadened the notion of what was sexually normal. Tactile stimulation, which in an older view of sexuality focused on the genitals, was extended to the oral and anal orifices and entire body surface. Stimulation was not limited to the physical; there were rich deposits of psychologic stimuli to be mined, erotica that stirred eye, ear, and nose and kindled nascent sexual fantasies. Finally, normal sexuality included women whose sexual capacity and performance was depicted as the anatomical and physiological equivalent of men's. Be it experienced by female or male, an orgasm was an orgasm was an orgasm.

Theories about the biological or psychological origins of sexual identity were repudiated for the belief that sexual taste and conduct were products of learning through conditioning.[11] Learning theory and the Kinsey view of sexuality were both essentially hedonic. In the Kinsey view the human body and environment provided infinitely fertile soil for the association of stimuli and responses to occur and, correspondingly, the capacity for gratification was enormous. In matters sexual, however, society in the form of religious injunction, custom and taboo, and psychiatry and the law intruded into this simple mechanism by declaring which forms of gratification were permissible.

The reports showed that many individuals ignored these societal intrusions and, by avoiding clashes with institutions and customs, enjoyed their erotic penchants with impunity. Institutionalized restrictions of free-ranging sexual relationships were unwittingly perpetuated by those individuals whose sexual anxieties and indiscretions involved them with clinicians, clergy, and the courts. What the Kinsey reports emphatically proclaimed was that there was precious little that was unusual or peculiar in sexual practice. Sex in itself was not the difficulty. Declared the report:

> The real clinical problem is the discovery and treatment of the
> personality defects, the mental difficulties, the compulsions and

---

[11] In learning theory, there were two basic forms of conditioning. Classical conditioning (as in the Pavlov experiments with dogs) trained the organism to make the same response to the substitute (conditioned) stimulus that it originally made to the unconditioned stimulus (e.g., to salivate at the sound of the bell which became associated with the sight and smell of food). In operant conditioning (also known as behavior modification), responses ordinarily emitted by the organism (e.g., pecking in the pigeon) are shaped to some predetermined criterion (e.g., pecking a white disk) by reinforcing successive approximations of the targeted performance. The differences between the two forms of conditioning are probably more procedural than substantive.

the schizophrenic conflicts which lead particular individuals to crack up whenever they depart from averages or socially acceptable custom. (Kinsey, Pomeroy & Martin, 1948: 201-202)

Institutions were slow to change, according to the Kinsey group, because there was little or no contact with the millions who were moved by the same desires and engaged in the same behavior and who were free of personal distress.[12]

The legal and moral dicta that pathologized variant forms of sexuality under the banner of science were hardly empirical truth: "[T]here is no scientific reason for considering particular types of sexual activity as intrinsically in their biologic origins, normal or abnormal" (Kinsey, Pomeroy & Martin, 1948: 202). What had passed for the science of sexuality was a disguised form of theology: "Either the ancient philosophers were remarkably well trained psychologists, or modern psychologists have contributed little in defining abnormal behavior" (203). Their advice to the mental health professions was to forget about those who departed from sexual custom and instead to try to understand why so many individuals conformed to customs which were highly restrictive of sexual experience and pleasure.

The position of the Kinsey group on the issue of sexual identity involved them in the historic debate over the nature and origin of homosexuality. Their position, ironically enough, placed them at odds with those who believed in homosexuality as a natural biological identity, such as Ulrichs, Ellis, and Hirschfeld. While the Kinsey group agreed with these men that the homosexual identity was as "natural" and free of pathology as the heterosexual, they did not believe it was innate or that, as individual behavior, it signified a unique character or mentality.

The Kinsey group could find no biological or psychological reason why homosexuality should not be included in the broad spectrum of normal sexual relationships. In their view homosexual relationships had no special etiology. Like all sexual relationships they were learned, the result of the chance pairing of stimuli and responses. In a less sexually repressive culture, the reports suggested, individuals would be able to respond to partners of either sex. Exclusive homosexuality was the product of the same restrictive attitudes that promoted exclusive heterosexuality. The harsh, punitive attitude toward homosexual

---

[12] Robinson (1976: 75) correctly noted that the Kinsey reports retained the notion of sexual maladjustment but attributed it mainly to sociogenic rather than the usual psychogenic causes.

relationships, as embodied in religion, medicine, and the law, were seen in the reports as unshakeable evidence of the rigid social control of human sexual expression.

Wainright Churchill, writing as a psychotherapist and student of sexology, in 1967 published a book which took a sweeping view of male homosexual behavior.[13] Following the lead of the Kinsey group and Ford and Beach, Churchill was clear that his interest was in "homosexual behavior" rather than homosexuality" or "homosexuals." "In this book the word 'homosexual' is used in its historic and literal context to refer to any sexual phenomena that involve like-sexed partners, and all such phenomena are regarded as worthy of consideration" (10). The phenomena could be "overt or psychic" (35). He considered the responses as homosexual regardless of the contexts in which they occurred or the motivations of the individual responding. Distinctions between individuals who were "truly homosexual" and those "not really homosexual," he believed, were spurious and bred in the belief that homosexuality was unnatural and pathological.

If homosexuality were viewed simply as behavior, Churchill did not think it was uncommon or remote from everyday life. Relying on the Kinsey reports he held that millions of people have had homosexual experiences. Historically homosexual experience was "as old as the race itself" (33). Practitioners shared no common characteristic except perhaps "a sense of guilt" (42). The very lack of common features gave rise to myths, superstitions, and stereotypes about so-called homosexuals: "[I]t is easy ... to find whatever one is looking for in the homosexual population simply because the population is not homogeneous" (43).

---

[13] Churchill, Wainright (1967/1971). *Homosexual Behavior Among Males: A Cross-Cultural and Cross-Species Investigation.* New York: Prentice Hall. (Citations are to the paperback edition published by Prentice-Hall in 1971.) Churchill dedicated the book to Kinsey and relied heavily on the two volumes of the Kinsey group. Churchill did not include female homosexuality for two reasons: (1) he agreed with the Kinsey group that there were important psychosexual differences between the sexes and (2) he felt that the social repercussions of female homosexuality were very different than those of male homosexuality (10). The author did not make clear his professional affiliation although, as the holder of the copyright, he was identified as "Dr. Wainwright Churchill." Within the text he referred to himself as a psychotherapist and clinician. He claimed to have known about 1,500 homosexual males over a period of twenty years "within the clinical setting and outside of it" (269). The book was based on his personal and professional knowledge and on published anthropological and historical studies. The preface was written in Rome.

With the exception of western culture, Churchill believed that exclusive heterosexuality was rare and not observed in mammals other than humans. The conventional belief was that heterosexuality was innate and that the sex drive was instinctually directed toward the opposite sex. Objects that became attached to the sex drive, in his opinion, did so as a result of experience: "Heterosexuality, therefore, no less than homosexuality, is learned in the context of one's experience, and neither has anything to do with 'instinct'" (98). The capacity for heterosexual or homosexual response was innate but the tendency to be heterosexual or homosexual was acquired. Specifically, the homosexual capacity was part of the mammalian inheritance of human beings: "It has been more widely recognized by scientists that the capacity to respond to stimuli originating in an individual of the same sex is potential in all human beings; with the wider recognition of this fact has come the tendency on the part of many scientists to reinterpret the meaning of homosexual behavior" (172).

Sexual learning, as conceived by Churchill, was the result of pairing sexual stimuli and responses. Those responses that proved to be gratifying were preserved in the individual's sexual repertory; those that turned out to be painful or distasteful were avoided in future encounters. Learning was not an intention or conscious process: "emotional response and even attitudinal postures are also learned, more often than not without the knowledge or cooperation of the learner" (105). The essential fluidity of the learning process kept open possibilities of acquiring new sexual tastes: "There are instances in which persons who have been exclusively heterosexual for many years have developed homosexual interests, and other instances in which persons who have been exclusively homosexual for many years have developed heterosexual interests" (106).

The capacity for sexual learning was less impaired in young people than adults. In fact young people responded to any type of erotic situation unless they had learned to avoid it by an "unsympathetic or obnoxious person" (107). Sexually precocious adolescents quickly expanded their sexual repertories:

> The fact that homosexual activities occur much more frequently in this group suggests that it is males with the strongest sex drive who respond most vigorously to a variety of sexual stimuli and who more often find it necessary to breach convention in order to satisfy the imperious demand this drive makes upon them. (56)

Within the formulation of an innately undifferentiated sex drive and sexuality as learned responses, Churchill viewed the psychiatric concept of sexual perversion as moralistic and arbitrary:

> In reality ... the sex drive has no inherent aims or objects other than the release of tension. Before this drive becomes conditioned through learning the individual may respond sexually to any sufficient stimulus. Thus many young children may respond sexually in many situations that appear "perverse" in the context of our moral belief, simply because they have not learned to avoid certain taboo" sexual stimuli. The so-called pervert is an individual who ... has never learned to avoid certain taboo sexual stimuli. Or he may be an individual who has never learned to respond positively and exclusively to certain approved stimuli. Often various conflicts during childhood are responsible for the type of sexual learning that produces what clinicians call "perversion"; but childhood conflict is, by no means, the only factor that may facilitate the learning of socially unapproved sexual tendencies. (244)

Churchill rejected the psychoanalytic theory that homosexuality was caused by fear of heterosexuality because he did not believe that attraction to one sex precluded attraction to the other: "we are compelled to assume that homosexual stimuli may, as a result of learning, come to have an attractiveness of their own quite apart from the individual's positive orientation (or lack of it) to heterosexual stimuli" (272).

The cultural context within which learning occurred, Churchill believed, circumscribed what was learned. Each society had a SEXUAL MYSTIQUE (16) which consisted of sexual dogmas and taboos for regulating the sex drive in the social interest: "Because human beings have always been fearful of the range and intensity of their sexual desires and because human sexuality seems particularly apt to play some role in almost every kind of social and interpersonal relationship, men have everywhere and at all times attempted to regulate this drive" (15). Some societies allowed more "human libidinousness" (17) than others. SEX-POSITIVE cultures were those which encouraged sexual expression. SEX-NEGATIVE cultures regarded "sex as a kind of necessary evil, inherently dangerous, and to be hedged about on all sides by restraints and avoided except in very particular and very scrupulously defined circumstances" (17).

Within sex-negative cultures there existed EROTOPHOBIC psychologies in which "sex is regarded not merely as somehow inherently evil, but also inherently dangerous" (19). The Judeo-Christian attitude toward sex was the stellar example of erotophobia. A culture could also be specifically **HOMOEROTOPHOBIC**, rejecting homosexual behavior as acceptable for any member of the community. It could also be **HOMOEROTOPHILIC** allowing homosexuality at least for some members of the community. Churchill believed that Western culture, including the United States, was for the most part sex-negative and erotophobic.

Psychiatric diagnosis, motivated by erotophobia, lay behind the characterization of all those who departed from sexual conventions as psychopaths: "[T]he wayward husband, the promiscuous female, the prostitute, and, above all, the 'homosexual' and other so-called 'deviates'" (28). In sex-negative cultures, sexual freedom was greatly curtailed by implanting fears of sexually transmitted diseases and unwanted pregnancies. In the minds of the sexually conservative, little effort was made to distinguish between "true pathology," as in the case of these diseases, and the putative pathology of homosexuality.

Where there was erotophobia, Churchill believed, one would also find homoerotophobia. The North American culture, as far as Churchill was concerned, was strongly homoerotophobic. There was little warmth or affection expressed in the social relationships of males with other males because of their fear that such demonstrations might result in their being seen as homosexuals. It also affected the relationships between fathers and sons:

> These relationships are so often lacking in tangible affection as to lend credence to the idea that many males adopt a compulsive pattern of overt homosexuality in later life in an effort to compensate for the emotional indifference they felt on the part of their fathers. (160)

It was important for a son to have trust in his father: "A boy in particular must feel that he is accepted and loved by his father to whom he looks for the kind of guidance that can only be provided by another more experienced male" (161). Homoerotophobia, paradoxically, did more to deny males emotional closeness than to prevent homosexual contact. The toughness and touchiness of American youth and the ease with which they resorted to violence Churchill partly traced to homoerotophobia. It was even possible that some of the most active homosexual men were the most homoerotophobic: "This is, of course, an exceptionally ironic turn of events and helps to explain how it is that excessively homoerotophobic cultures tend to give rise to the development of exclusive homosexuality more often than less homoerotophobic cultures" (165).[14]

The emotional distance produced by homoerotophobia generally impoverished the sexual relationships of men with women. It denied men a woman's appreciation of the nuances and joys in mental and emotional life. It made the men poor lovers of women:

> For any man—or woman—to become complete, and thus to become capable of sexual communication with a partner of the opposite sex, he must possess in some measure, through cultivation or intuition, certain of the qualities of the partner. He must be capable of empathizing with his mate.... The chief complaint that women make about their husbands or lovers is that they are insensitive, self-centered, and rough. These are among the most prominent traits that American males associate with masculinity, and their opposites—sensitivity, consideration and tenderness—are thought by many of these males to be feminine characteristics. (164)

In fact, Churchill speculated, some males may turn to homosexuality because they know far better how to please another man sexually than to please a woman.

What later authors called the "gay lifestyle," Churchill described as the "homosexual way of life" (174), considering its existence to be a "morbid symptom of our sex-negative society" (193). The homosexual way of life consisted of the adjustments made by those males who came to regard themselves privately or publicly as "homosexuals." Although Churchill believed there was no such thing as a "homosexual," he recognized that there existed within society the stereotype: "The 'homosexual' in our society is pictured as a perverted, dissolute, unscrupulous, and emotionally warped individual who is unworthy of trust or confidence" (176). The homosexual possessed the less admirable qualities associated with femininity (e.g., vanity, emotional instability). Part of the stereotype was that homosexuals were organized as an international conspiracy and that they infiltrated and dominated certain professions.

---

[14] Churchill had described the differences in attitudes toward homosexuality of the Mediterranean world as compared with trans-Alpine Europe. Exclusive homosexuality was rarer, he believed, in the Mediterranean world which was less erotophobic to begin with and allowed the male personality some of the emotionality that in Northern Europe was associated with femininity in males. See, for example, 167 ff.

The homosexual stereotype, Churchill believed, hardly reflected reality:

> Acceptance of the stereotype represents a type of adjustment rather than an appreciation of reality. In reality no one is a "homosexual" any more than anyone is a "heterosexual"—or any other reification of sexual life. Belief in the contrary only leads to homosexual chauvinism or heterosexual chauvinism. It is better and more accurate to regard oneself as a human being first and last, and to accept that one is in possession of various unrealized and unexplored potentialities. (184)

Nor did the "gay" life, in his estimation, fare any better. He saw it as superficial although he recognized that it fulfilled needs for "companionship, understanding, and acceptance" (181). It offered to those who pursued it an escape from isolation and loneliness. In the "gay" world the individual found "the refutation of perhaps the first and most horrible thought he had to face when he discovered himself a 'homosexual'—the thought that he was the only person of his kind on earth" (193). The adhesive holding together the homosexual world was persecution. As an oppressed minority it had "all the vainglorious pride, all the contempt for itself, all of the chauvinism, and all the sense of alienation coupled with the desire for conformity that are characteristic of any other persecuted minority" (187). In particular, it attempted to emulate majoritarian attitudes toward love:

> In almost every detail they [homosexuals] ape and in the end caricature heterosexual values and usages. "Homosexuals" are condemned by "heterosexuals," and condemn themselves for not regularly maintaining monogamous marriages of a sort designed for child-rearing, which are only truly meaningful in the context of domesticity. We hear also of "homosexuals" bemoaning the lack of offspring and pleading for the right to adopt children. Many homosexual couples have even sought to have their unions recognized by official religious ritual. (187)

The "homosexual" showed the mark of oppression in both his public and "gay" life. In public, he was subdued and remote, but he was no better off in the gay setting:

> Often in "gay" society this person is so busy "letting his hair down" that he has no opportunity to reflect upon the real nature of his deepest feelings. When many people who are ordinarily subdued and distant come together in permissive

surroundings for the purpose of relaxing and "being themselves," the ensuing atmosphere is usually one of forced hilarity in which no one really reveals his true identity. This is often the atmosphere of "gay society," and there can be little doubt that this is why the word "gay" has become associated with homosexuality. (191)

Most men who engaged in homosexual behavior rejected the homosexual way of life because they wanted to maintain their connection to heterosexual society and also to continue having sex with women. Although these men represented "the vast majority of all males in whom homosexual responsiveness is manifest" (191), most books on the subject were about males who were exclusively homosexual. If there were greater social tolerance of homosexuality, many more males would have both heterosexual and homosexual relationships: "It is as if our society is willing to tolerate a large number of exclusively homosexual males—if current attitudes and practices can be called at all tolerant—in order to prevent the occurrence of an even larger number of actively bisexual males" (192).

Churchill viewed psychiatry as acting more in the interest of social conformity than the welfare of patients. By urging patients toward "socially acceptable" sexual values and practices or toward "good adjustments," psychiatry was defining mental health as mere social convention:

> [U]ntil orthodox psychiatry, psychoanalysis, and clinical psychology can establish more objective criteria of mental health and mental disease, and until these disciplines can achieve at least as much detachment from conventional value judgments as is ordinarily achieved in the other social and behavioral sciences—all of which leave much to be desired—it does not seem necessary for anyone to feel called upon to accept psychiatric pronouncements as final or infallibly authoritative. (257)

The treatment of individuals who considered themselves "homosexuals," Churchill believed, should involve a general exploration of both their heterosexuality and homosexuality. Based on his own clinical experience, Churchill averred that all "homosexuals" who sought therapy had the "secret or avowed motive of escaping from their homosexual urges" (252). Those most upset about their homosexuality were the exclusively homosexual in behavior. Treatment had to confront their pervasive erotophobia:

> The treatment of the homosexual patient or any other patient, if it is to be worthwhile, must bring about a confrontation on the part of the individual with his attitudes toward sex and toward himself as a sexual being. All the near and sometimes outright insanity about sex that the patient has accumulated in the erotophobic atmosphere of our culture must, as is said in clinical jargon, be "worked through" if the patient is to reach a rational sex adjustment. The object of therapy should not be that the patient accept heterosexuality, homosexuality, or autoeroticism, but simply that he accept sexuality. Having done so, it is entirely within his own province—and indeed his own responsibility—to discovery for himself what particular modalities of the sexual drive fulfill his needs as an individual. It is very likely that a patient who received the benefits of such therapy will be alive to a number of different sexual possibilities, but those that may constitute the greater part of his sexual pattern should be a matter of complete indifference to the therapist; certainly the therapist should never exploit his authority in order to propagandize on behalf of his own particular sexual preferences. (253-254)

In effect Churchill was arguing that the homosexual patient had to achieve two objectives in the acceptance of his sexuality: (a) The resolution of guilt and conflict over his homosexuality and (b) resolution of his conflicts over heterosexuality. This dual acceptance of both heterosexuality and homosexuality was necessary for both patient and therapist:

> We do not believe that any patient—or therapist—can take a nonjudgmental attitude toward homosexuality if he fears and despises heterosexuality. Nor, for that matter, do we believe that any patient, therapist, or any other person can unequivocally accept heterosexuality if he fears and despises homosexuality. (282)

Churchill did not believe that homosexuality itself was pathological. Although he was critical of the general claims of the Bieber group about the etiology of homosexuality, he did agree that there were homosexual men who were severely disturbed. What the Bieber group missed was the connection between pathological homosexuality and pathological heterosexuality as it occurred in the families of their patients: "it is perhaps even more correct to say that pathological homosexuality can only develop in an erotophobic environment such as that engendered by the sexual mystique of our Judeo-Christian culture" (290).

As embodied in Judeo-Christian doctrine, heterosexuality was based on a false assumption about the human sexual drive. That assumption was the hopeful belief that the average individual was monogamous by nature or could be made monogamous by a devoted mate. This assumption gave rise to the romantic search for the ideal marital partner who could fulfill all present and future needs:

> Each must be a devoted friend, a stimulating social companion, an aggressive breadwinner (or expert homemaker), an alluring sexual partner whose charms (no matter how often enjoyed) never stale, a wise parent, and in general the source of all things joyful, estimable, and rare. (301)

Because there seldom was an individual who could be all these things to another, husbands and wives spent enormous efforts in artful deception and flattery. But the mutual demands placed on the partners often lead to unspeakable boredom "with the monotony that may often result from the necessity of having to find satisfaction for all of one's most intimate needs in a single individual" (302). In reality many individuals were not suited for marriage or parenthood.

The individual caught up in a romance, in Churchill's perception, was seriously incapacitated in reason and judgment. Romance distracted people from their work and responsibilities. Their total absorption was in one person to the exclusion of friends and associates. When the fantasy shattered, as was inevitable, it led to bitterness and disappointment. If the relationship continued beyond this point it became entrenched in conflict.

If romance lacked solid foundations, the family that it often led to also had its serious flaws. The seamy side of the family often went undescribed. Where the family had a firm grip on the lives of its members their outside relationships were seriously deficient:

> The superficiality of the relationships between individuals who are not related by family ties is quite incredible. Alliances are narrow; friendships are brittle, perfunctory, and seldom get beyond the formality appropriate to mere acquaintanceship. It is only relatives with whom one has real and meaningful social contact, There is little feeling for society at large and hardly any sense of social responsibility. (304)

The family gave rise to greed (justified by concern for its welfare), the boredom of everyday life, petty gossip, the creation of litanies of ideas and beliefs, blind acceptance of the conventional as "normal," and the association of evil with dissent. It was indeed the seedbed of much mental illness. Churchill did not question the value of love, intimacy, and sustained relationships. He believed, however, that individuals should decide the forms their sexual relationships should take. This placed the moral responsibility for sexual relationships in the hands of individuals. Morality, to be anything more than hypocrisy, required individual conviction and decision: "a conventional morality that is neither felt nor believed in is no morality at all" (317).

In 1975, Clarence Tripp, a clinical psychologist, published an essay which discussed homosexuality within the social and cultural "matrix" of heterosexuality.[15] Tripp started with the statement that human beings were born with a polymorphous sexual capacity that was neither heterosexual nor homosexual. This undifferentiated sexuality was given direction by learning which he described as "a host of experiential events" (17). Not everyone had the same innate sexual capacity, however. Some had greater cortical ability to organize their sexual experience. Some were more impressionable or susceptible to conditioning than others. Once sexual experience became organized by the brain, the individual's sexuality "eventually becomes keyed to specific cues" (18). Personalized patterns of sexual responses were gradually built up which included selection of partners and situations and the development of areas of exquisite physical sensitivity (i.e., "hot spots"). These sexual patterns were described as "batteries of responses" which could be triggered at any

---

[15] Tripp, C. E. (1975). *The Homosexual Matrix*. New York: McGraw-Hill. The book leaned heavily on previously published material as it pertained to male sexuality, particularly the sociological research of the Kinsey group, the cultural and biological surveys of Ford and Beach, and the psychomedical research and speculations of John Money. In the preface the author stated that he was "associated" with the "Kinsey Research Staff" (viii) over a period of nine years, presumably from 1948 to 1957, although (as he also stated) he was not part of the staff. The author occasionally called his book a "study" (e.g., ix), but it was not clear to which data he referred because the book is in the form of an essay rather than a research report. He implied, however, that he studied a group of fifty-two non-homosexual transsexuals, eight of whom he came "to know and like very much in close, friendly surroundings" (viii). He also got to know twelve persons who had been connected with the federal government and who supplied information on the "politics of homosexuality."

moment. The polymorphous sexuality of childhood was progressively channeled into specific responses to specific cues:

> With the coming of puberty and an increased sex drive, this diversity of response quickly begins to narrow down, first to general sexual situations, then to people and finally to particular kinds of people. Under the spotlight of attention and affection, this narrowing-down proceeds to ever smaller and smaller segments of time and detail—moments of intense arousal fixing their focus on a particular person, on particular traits that epitomize that person, then on to one trait, a particular detail that stands for that trait, and so on. (20)

Tripp speculated that the increasingly refined focus of sexual development was "probably neurologic at bottom" (121).

The development of exclusive heterosexuality or homosexuality was one instance in the narrowing down of choice. As the individual followed one of these paths, the other was left behind. Original choice dissolved into psychological imperatives that drove the individual still further along a single path.

Besides an innately diffuse sexual potential, there was also the mammalian capacity for inversion. Whereas Freud used inversion to refer to homosexuality, Tripp defined it as "a reversal of the commonly expected gender-role of the individual, whether animal or human" (23). A female dog who mounted males or other females or "even the leg of her owner" (22) was displaying inverted behavior. When the human female assumed the role of the initiator or "top" in coitus, both she and her male partner were engaging in inverted behavior. The major forms of human inversion identified by Tripp were male transvestism, transsexualism, and effeminacy. Transsexualism was the most spectacular form because the male renounced both "gender-role" and "gender-identity" (30). In their inverted roles, however, he believed that transvestites and transsexuals were less interested in sex than in the drama of enacting the feminine sex-role. Transvestism was momentary while transsexualism and effeminacy were continuous inversions.

Tripp distinguished between "femininity" and "effeminacy." Femininity apparently described the behavior of biological females. Effeminacy defined the feminine-like behavior of the biological male, but was not the male's caricature of femininity. Tripp asserted that the "effeminate male is naturally so and is quite unaware exactly what is effeminate in his own behavior" (177), yet when Tripp distinguished four types of effeminacy, he utilized descriptions of feminine styles of behavior. **NELLIE** referred to the "quite purely feminine" (177) manner-isms of effeminate males. **SWISH** described masculine exaggerations of feminine movements. **BLASÉ** referred to the "classical postures of hetero-sexual females" (182). **CAMP** was an exaggerated swish: "Remember that in swish there was high animation coupled with masculine forcefulness; camp extends this contrast much further" (185). Camp was also charac-terized by **DUPLICITY** or "polarity between opposite gestures, movement, or intents" (185) and by **STACKING** or piling up of emphasis in speech, mannerism, or appearance.

Tripp was apparently implying that males were incapable of authentic feminine behavior. Although he provided no corresponding analysis of "masculine" female behavior, one could assume that he would not have viewed it as genuinely masculine. Tripp asserted that most male transvestites and transsexuals were heterosexual but implied that most effeminate men were homosexual. He also implied that homosexual men, particularly those who were effeminate, lacked the masculine confidence to risk engaging in inverted behavior. Heterosexual men, in his view, would more willingly risk inversion because they were more confident of their gender-identity and gender-role "[I]t is the sure-footed, squarely aggressive males who most readily invert their expected roles, both in heterosexual and homosexual relations" (34).

The key tenets of Tripp's approach to sexuality were set forth in his discussion of the "origin" of heterosexuality. Heterosexuality, in his formulation, sprang from the biological differences between females and males. The males were depicted as more urgent in their sex-drive, more aggressive in their sexual behavior, and more sexually active: "The promiscuity of most uninhibited males rest partly on biological traditions—a high sex-drive, an easily triggered responsiveness, and perhaps a species-history of the sexual chase" (153). These biological differences were fueled by still others, the male capacity to be visually oriented and "to imagine sexual possibilities" (153).[16]

Males, "as [they] go about their daily interactions ... are, in effect, immersed in a pool of arousing sexual stimuli made up of actual and suggestive cues—cues which are assembled into active fantasies" (153). In comparison, females were portrayed as sexually phlegmatic: "Their

---

[16] Tripp believed that the richness of the individual's sexual experience depended on that person's cortical ability to organize sexual experience, Because sexual fantasy is essentially a cortical phenomenon, it is possible to infer from Tripp's assertion that he thought males were inherently more intelligent than females.

[the males'] situation is in sharp contrast to that of most women, who are neither so 'driven' nor so visual, and who usually require a certain psychological preparation (later even tactile stimulation) before attaining an equivalent arousal" (153). He dismissed as "fashionable" the notion that there was no essential difference between female and male sexuality by citing studies that concluded that many women had little or no sexual responsiveness and that many others responded more slowly and with less intensity than men. Such biological deficiencies made women slower in developing sexual attraction, impoverished their sexual fantasies, and kept them from becoming promiscuous. The differences in female and male sexuality prevailed over sexual identity. The "simplicity and plainness" (107) of the lesbian approach to sexuality stemmed from the more definite, more focused, and more genital techniques of males."

Tripp's view of the biological differences between the sexes was the foundation for his speculations on the psychological basis of heterosexuality. He saw the heterosexual relationship as emanating from a state of tension which arose from the different sexual endowments of the two sexes. This tension was alternately reduced and increased to keep sexual interest alive and satisfied. The process of tension-reduction was called complementation. It involved females and males "exporting" the feminine and masculine traits associated with their respective sexes and "importing" those of the opposite sex:

> To round himself out and thus correct his cultivated masculine eccentricity—that is, to regain much of what he has systematically eliminated from his personality and to savor softness in a hundred-ways—he needs the company of women. Conversely, a woman's cultivation of less robust qualities tends to leave her short on the kinds of stability and symbols of security which are the specialties of men, and that are obtainable from them. (55)

This transaction was described as quite profitable for the male by way of import. The male recovered from his female partner the vulnerability, emotionality, and domesticity he sacrificed in the development of his masculinity. Even in the act of export the male gained the import of the female's admiration and validation. What females might gain in the process of complementation was never made clear by Tripp.

The successful complementation of feminine and masculine attributes in heterosexual relationships, however, was achieved at the "price of dwindling erotic tensions—a descent that can threaten the whole erotic enterprise" (59). The most erotic relationships were those in which the level of compatibility did not rule out the possibility or actuality of conflict. To keep sexual relationships exiting it was necessary for the partners to increase tension through a process of distancing and resistance: "Something within the sexual psychology of man requires a higher level of stress between the sexes than biology alone supplies" (48). To keep relationships tense, "people are ready to pay whatever price they must in order to keep a certain disparity, a 'resistance,' or distance between the sexes" (48).

In Tripp's psychology of the sexes the comforts of intimacy were at odds with sexual attraction. Without an "alienating resistance between the sexes, sexual attraction would dissolve" (60). Sexual resistance, he thought, explained the culturally-sanctioned forms of abuse such as pinching and biting during coitus and the tribal practice of exogamy, obtaining wives only from other tribes. Even the derogation of females by males was an effort of both to "sharpen the breach between the sexes, increase tension [resistance] between them, and add spice to their relations" (61). In a favorite metaphor Tripp declared that friction set "the gap for the spark of sex to jump" (40). Relationships, Tripp concluded, could be destroyed by either too much disparity or too much closeness.

Tripp viewed females as the primary architects of intimacy. He therefore believed that the chief responsibility for distancing and resistance in heterosexual relationships fell to males. To arm men for this challenge there was the male bond—the tendency of men "to cluster and affiliate with each other into tight-knit cliques, and into larger groups" (49). Male groups were devoted more to "seeking a personal intimacy than a group of solidarity" (51). Although affectionate relationships among men could be seen as homosexual, Tripp believed that the male bond really enhanced male heterosexuality: "[The male bond's] homosexual component is ordinarily much too far from anything erotic to offer sexual competition to heterosexuality" (58).

In heterosexual relations, women's engulfing femininity constituted a threat to the masculinity of men. The male bond was the means for men to restore the masculinity which was drained by their contact with women:

> By supplying relief—in a sense, putting gas back in the tank—it satiates male needs and refreshes a man's appetite for a forceful return to heterosexual contacts. Many women intuitively understand this refueling operation, and although they may miss their men who are "off with the boys," they use the time themselves to recuperate, correctly sensing that they are the ultimate benefactors of men's diversion from them. Their hunch

is right, as is the hunch of other women who feel a pensive disquietude with men who have no close male ties. (58)

The sexual psychology of Tripp was further explicated in his ruminations on the origins of male homosexuality. He repudiated the theory that homosexuality sprang up when women were not available because there were few cultural and historical circumstances in which they were in short supply. He rejected the theory that homosexuality was a damaged heterosexuality because it excluded the possibility that those who engaged in homosexuality could do so for positive motivations.[17] He also rejected the theory that homosexuality originated in the person's life with "a single impressive [homosexual] experience" (80). Instead, Tripp held that there was a psychological predisposition in people which made some sexual experiences more impressive than others.

In outlining an etiology of homosexuality Tripp formulated the notion of SEXUAL VALUE SYSTEMS, the ingredients of which appeared to be more cognitive than experiential. In claiming, for example, that "eroticization always tends to raise the value of the items it touches" (84), there was the suggestion that some mental predisposition led the individual to sexualize some stimuli but not others. The idealization of a particular male or of masculinity by homosexual males, he thought, revealed a "quite definite sexual value system" (90). These systems seemed to be superordinate: "[V]alues more often lead to experience than vice versa" (90). The sexual identity of the individual depended on the development of a particular sexual value system:

> The final existence of any sexual orientation depends upon the extent to which its various parts have reinforced each other in producing a structure, a system of values, a pattern of responses. The directionality of the whole system and much of its force depend upon the effectiveness with which it purifies its aims and wards off competing alternatives. (92)

Although Tripp used his concept of sexual value systems to explain development of various sexual identities, he also equated these systems

---

[17] Tripp failed to distinguish between Freudian and post-Freudian etiological theories of homosexuality, referring to both as reparative. In Freudian oedipal theory, heterosexuality represented an achievement rather than a biological given. It resulted from the positive resolution of the Oedipus complex. In the later formulations of Rado and the Bieber group, heterosexuality was a biological given rather than an achievement. For them, homosexuality represented a failure to develop an innate heterosexual capacity.

with those identities. For example he referred to the "homosexual value system" (84) and to the "double value system" (95) of bisexuals. In males, sexual value systems appeared to be anchored to their biological sex. In theorizing about the origin of homosexuality Tripp proposed two ideas. A boy's intense admiration for the "seemingly wondrous attainments of a usually older male model" (81) may become eroticized when focused on a particular man. Or boys who were precocious masturbators developed an intense interest in their own genitalia that could become associated with finding sexual excitement in the contemplation of the genitalia of other males.[18]

The progressive refinement of a sexual value system both dictated and stabilized selection of the sex of partners: "Once started, an organized preference quickly begins to extend itself throughout a whole inventory of gender-related items" (93). It also ruled out the possibility of attraction to characteristics associated with the other sex: "As soon as a person starts to develop a sexual interest in the qualities and traits of one sex, he usually begins to view the analogous features of the opposite [i.e., other] sex not only as different but as dissonant" (93). Thus the full development of a sexual value system reduced the scope of sexual interest and tasted.[19]

The particular characteristics which individuals sought in partners were those which they had never developed in themselves. These attributes were eroticized by the individual who then developed a (98) "near-insatiable" appetite for them. Because such differences existed between partners of the same-sex as well as those of the opposite sexes, the process of homosexual and heterosexual complementation were identical (100): "the symbolic possession of those attributes of a partner which, when added to one's own, fill out the illusion of completeness."

---

[18] Tripp's comment that the Kinsey group's study of male sexuality showed that homosexual males started masturbation at an earlier age than heterosexual males was misleading because that study distinguished only between homosexual and heterosexual response rather than identity. That report (1948: 507), however, did state that males with the highest frequencies of masturbation were those who reached adolescence at earlier ages.

[19] For reasons not entirely clear, bisexuals were exempt from this constriction of choice. They developed a "double value system" which allowed them to enjoy what they liked in females or males "without allowing the unwanted aspects of either to get in his way" (960). Tripp stated that bisexuality need not result from the individual actually having had experiences with both females and males, thereby suggesting that there was some type of mental predisposition toward bisexuality.

The themes of complementation and resistance were pursued by Tripp in his portrayal of homosexual and heterosexual relationships.[20] It was his belief that homosexual relationships duplicated the heterosexual. Because the homosexual had no notion of what form a relationship should take (72) "he is almost forced to squeeze it into fitting the stand-ard male-female format he knows, and thus heterosexualize it." Tripp did identify what he claimed were distinguishing characteristics of homosexual relationships. Because the partners were of the same sex they could not rely on traditional sex-roles in which men occupied the position of dominance and leadership and women the position of sub-mission and service. The assignment of roles had to be negotiated rather than taken for granted. Tripp held that because homosexual partners were of the same sex, there was a high degree of rapport which facilitated the process of complementation.

The "high rapport of same-sex partners" (163), however, had some disadvantages. When conflict did arise, one partner could aim at the chink in the psychological armor of the other: "[A]n angry male partner knows exactly where a man's ego rests and how to zero in on it—just as an angry lesbian can be far more cutting to a woman's pride than a man can" (163). But most of the time homosexual partners avoided conflict: "[H]omosexuals are relatively intolerant of clash and ... they are not particularly good at contending with it or reducing it" (163).

High rapport also resulted in short-lived and sharply declining sexual interest between partners. The dwindling of sexual interest was "ex-traordinarily fast and deep" (164) in lesbian couples because of the "relatively low libido of many women" (164). In fact lesbians' interest in nest building stemmed from the need to) "extract more nonsexual re-wards from a close relationship than men can" (164). Homosexual males sometimes revived sexual interest in their relationships by bringing in third parties or openly or tacitly agreeing to sexual "infidelity."

In comparison, according to Tripp, heterosexual relationships, depended on the differences between partners:

> The heterosexual blend tends to be rich in stimulating contrasts and short on rapport—so much so that popular marriage-counseling literature incessantly hammers home the advice that couples should develop common interests and dissolve their

---

[20] He distinguished between "ongoing relationships," which could last from a few months to several years, and "durable relationships" which partners expected to last a lifetime.

conflicts by increasing their "communication." By comparison, homosexual relationships are over-close, fatigue-prone, and are often adjusted to such narrow, trigger-sensitive tolerances that a mere whisper of disrapport can jolt the partners into making repairs, or into conflict. (167)

It was possible, therefore, for heterosexual relationships to be immersed in conflict because of "major collision between the whole outlook and style of two people" (169). But sex differences could also strengthen heterosexual relationships. To the extent that male and female partners thought of these differences as embodied in traditional sex-roles, the "leadership" role automatically fell to the males and the role of providing "labor" to the females. The male-female contrast often kept sexual interest alive: "It is not unusual for a man and wife to retain a workable if not very intense sexual interest in each other for twenty years or longer, but such time-spans are rare in male relationships and exceedingly rare among lesbians" (164).

In addition to ongoing homosexual relationships Tripp described ephemeral relationships, which he called as "brief encounters" (150). The many forms these relationships took demonstrated "certain fundamental differences between the sexes" (151). Males were more promiscuous than females because of their sexual biology. But there were social and psychological motivations as well: to win status and attract the envy of less sexually active and successful friends; to search for a suitable partner; to avoid ongoing relationships; and to vainly enjoy being attractive to several partners. Ephemeral relationships flourished among males for both biological and circumstantial reasons: "[M]ales have an abounding capacity to quickly respond to new partners, a readiness which is activated primarily by their ability to read value-connotations into such fragmentary cues as the bodily features of the particular kinds of partners they have previously eroticized" (159).

Not all ephemeral relationships were without affection. It was often expressed when one man viewed the other as the ideal partner. Affection could also flow from sexual contact which was intended to be only friendship without sex or ongoing relationships in which sex and affection were combined. Sometimes transitional relationships were "a kind of life affair in microcosm" (158), what Tripp also described as "a telescoped version of an entire meeting-to-mating sequence" (158).

Tripp considered psychotherapy for the purpose of transforming male homosexuals into heterosexuals to be a futile undertaking. It was doomed because "the adult human being's sexual response rests at bottom on a massive, cortically organized, sexual value system which is impervious to the trivial intrusions launched against it by what amount to social concerns" (258). Change therapy was a badly informed effort of clinicians who were largely ignorant of research on homosexuality and whose knowledge was limited to patients who were tormented by their homosexuality. Finally, such treatment involved the therapist using every opportunity presented by patients for undermining their homosexual attachments. Therapists pointed out the patients' hate for their partners, the lack of durability in homosexual relationships, and the patients' repeated attempts to end earlier relationships. In effect, the therapists used "whatever the patient says of his doubts, hesitations, or guilt feelings to wipe out whatever hope he may still harbor of finding a satisfactory homosexual life" (256). Patients were often complicit in this effort to undermine their homosexuality because they had internalized most of the psychiatric theories of its etiology.

Instead of attempting to change the homosexual's orientation, Tripp advised therapists to focus on problems that truly troubled homosexuals, "problems having to do with the management of aggression and, in some instances, a higher than average vulnerability to hysteria" (260) particularly at times of crisis and high stress. Therapists were to concentrate on assisting the homosexual patient in building up his psychological defenses. To protect himself against the resurgence of primitive guilt over his homosexuality at times of crisis, the patient was to develop "devotion, a commitment, or some other target of interest" (262). If an interest became "obsessional," then it might provide his life a "gyroscopic directionality, no matter how rough the seas" (262). A focal interest also enabled the individual to "compartmentalize" his problems so that he could carry on in non-troubled areas of his life. Above all, the homosexual had to learn to meet crisis by "simply standing pat" (265), what Tripp also called "a kind of attentive nonparticipation in untoward events" (266). In effect, the homosexual patient had to learn "how to keep from being stampeded into joining the forces one finds lined up against him" (265).

Writing within the context of anthropological and sociological surveys of sexual behavior, both Churchill and Tripp endorsed the idea of the sociocultural sexual identity. For both men, sexual identity was the consequence of the process of shaping an undifferentiated sexual capacity through learning. Learning, in turn, was conceived as an essentially mechanical process of wedding stimuli to responses through reinforcement. Churchill believed that the learning of sexual behavior occurred under the sway of cultural attitudes, which, in western civilization, were "sex-negative," "erotophobic," and "homoerotophobic." Tripp viewed learning as an accumulative process in which cue-response patterns gradually became entrenched in the cortex as sexual value systems.

Both men accepted the belief that there were basic biological differences in female and male sexuality that accounted for contrasting roles in sexual relationships. Largely subscribing to the views of the Kinsey group, both saw female sexuality as receptive and modulated and male sexuality as aggressive and impulsive. As clinicians, both writers believed that troubled homosexuals could benefit from psychotherapy, although they sought different therapeutic goals. Churchill hoped to expand their sexual options by including at least the possibility of having both female and male sexual partners. Tripp sought to adjust homosexuals to their emotional instability, a characteristic he apparently believed to be an intrinsic personal vulnerability.

There were striking areas of disagreement. Churchill, a biological potentialist, took an expansive view of human mammalian sexual capacity, conceiving it as embracing the possibilities for both heterosexual and homosexual relationships. Exclusive heterosexuality or homosexuality was diagnosable and treatable ailments. As a biological determinist, Tripp believed there were several prior constraints on the learning of sexual behavior. Biology ordained that females be more concerned with establishing the proper fit and stability for sexual relationships. It also ordained that males be more concerned with providing the spice of excitement and tension. Also, individuals differed in their cortical capacities, some more capable than others in organizing the products of learning. Furthermore, in Tripp's view, earlier learning precluded what could be learned later as cue-response patterns and sexual value systems became embedded in the cortex.

Tripp's view of sexual relationships was more conventional than Churchill's. Tripp essentially provided a treatise on why heterosexual relationships worked and why homosexual relationships were inevitably modeled after them. The processes of complementarity, distancing, and resistance were common to both types, even though they needed to be introduced by more artifice in homosexual than in heterosexual relationships. In contrast, Churchill believed that the traditions of romantic love, monogamy, and the family were basically at odds with the biology of sexual impulse. In most individuals, Churchill implied sexual impulse could be satisfied in various relationships with different partners.

At least by implication, Churchill and Tripp entertained different conceptions of a homosexual male subculture. Calling it "the homosexual way of life," Churchill depicted it as superficial and escapist, a product of western erotophobia. In a sardonic and bemused vein, Tripp presented it as a culture of effeminacy that took many subtle forms and emphases.

The Kinsey group, Churchill, and Tripp, confronted the issue of sexual identity. Although the Kinsey group stated their objections to identifying individuals as "heterosexuals" or "homosexuals," they subscribed to the notion that all sexual behavior was the product of environmental conditioning and that exceptional forms of behavior, both social and sexual, branded individuals with an identity other than the heterosexual. Churchill also viewed sexual identity in behavioral terms, proposing the idea that exclusively heterosexual or homosexual relationships were products of erotophobic cultures. Finally, Tripp endorsed the belief in sexual identity as derived from external sources. He described sexual identity as a learned acquisition, embellishing it with cerebral components.

As conceived by these writers, the behavioral sexual identity did not stand in opposition to the biological and psychological sexual identities but rather was an incorporation of them. It absorbed several aspects of the biological identity. It was anchored, of course, to the biological sex of partners in sexual relationships in its varied bisexual, heterosexual, and homosexual forms. While insisting that the physiological differences between female and male responses were insignificant, the Kinsey group believed there were definitive "psychologic" differences associated with each sex. Churchill who, among these writers was perhaps the least biologically deterministic, vigorously sponsored the belief that individuals innately possessed the biological capacity of sexual responding to both sexes. Tripp made the cortical ability to organize sexual experience and a neurologically-based sexual value system pivotal ingredients of his conception of sexual identity.

Although conceived partly in reaction to the idea of the psychological identity, the behavioral sexual identity incorporated several of its elements. Psychological along with physiological response was important in rating individuals on the heterosexual-homosexual rating scale of the Kinsey group. Churchill wrote of the emotional distance among North American men and the toughness of American youth. Tripp's processes of inversion, complementation, distancing, and resistance were rendered in essentially psychological language.

The behavioral version of the sociocultural sexual identity included elements of the polytheistic, monotheistic, and scientific cosmological views of sexual relationships. The discovery of a rich variety of sexual belief and practice led to these writers conceiving human sexuality as a polymorphous potentiality hardly tapped by the institutionalized sexual relationships with which they were familiar. By viewing sexual relationships as consisting of discrete behaviors and behavioral patterns they incorporated polytheistic elements into the discourse on sexual identity.

With few exceptions, however, none of these contributors to the discourse on sexual identity strayed very far from the monotheistic conception of sexual relationships. Although lamenting the lack of western tolerance for homosexual relationships, the Kinsey group looked to marriage and the family for the containment of sexual "outlet" and as the mainstay of society. Tripp applied the male-female design to homosexual relationships by claiming that they were based on a psychological complementarity that duplicated the physical complementarity of heterosexual relationships. Churchill alone challenged the male-female design by pointing to the mendacity and selfishness inherent in the western institutions of romance, marriage, and the family.

Elements of the scientific cosmology were present in the discourse on the behavioral sexual identity. By viewing sexual identity as a repertory of sexual behaviors, the element of choice was restored to partners in sexual relationships. Sexual behavior was presented as a menu of erotic choices which could be variously blended in the unceasing search by individuals for novel gratification.

The couching of essentially moralistic views of sexual relationships in the language of science continued, however, with the formulation of the behavioral sexual identity. The raw empiricism of the Kinsey group was intended to be a scientific tour de force. Churchill and Tripp anchored their conceptions of sexual relationships in behavioral psychology, which they accepted as the science of human behavior. Tripp spiced his behavioral speculations with contemporary research on hormones and brain physiology.

14 Subcultural Identity: The Ethnographic Approach

T aking their cue from the anthropological studies, the sociologists during the decades of the fifties and sixties joined the discourse on sexual identity. They conducted a series of ethnographic studies that were based on the assumption that individuals with either a heterosexual or homosexual identity lived in distinct cultures.[1]

These ethnographic researchers portrayed what they perceived to be the homosexual subculture, describing the social manifestations of homosexuality in western, urban settings the way anthropologists had depicted the sexual practices and institutions of primitive societies. In advancing the urban ethnography of sexual identity, the sociologists developed a version of the sociocultural sexual identity that was essentially divorced from the biological but retained remnants of the psychological sexual identity. An unwitting consequence of their efforts was to hypostasize a heterosexual culture that possessed its own sexual traditions and could be subjected to its own ethnographic scrutiny.

One of the first ethnographies was provided by Daniel Wester Cory.[2] Although writing as a homosexual and advocate of homosexuality rather

---

[1] Ethnography is a branch of anthropology that deals descriptively with specific cultures.

[2] Cory, Daniel Webster (1951). *The Homosexual in America: A Subjective Approach*. New York: Greenberg. It is now known that "Cory" was the pseudonym used by Edward Sagarin, a well-known American sociologist. The introduction was written by Albert Ellis, a psychoanalyst and sexologist, who openly disagreed with the author on the natural origin of "homosexual drive," the impossibility of changing homosexuality to heterosexuality, and the individual and social advantages of homosexuality. The book contains a number of useful appendices, particularly Appendix D, a list of novels and dramas in which homosexuality was a basic theme.

than scholar, Cory had a wide knowledge of relevant historical, legal, psychiatric, and literary materials.[3]

Cory rejected the biological conception of sexual identity in favor of the psychological. Although he considered "the homosexual drive" compelling, he did not believe the homosexual identity was innate. The view that it was inborn, he contended, was sponsored by those who thereby hoped to win acceptance and be exonerated of all guilt. The psychological basis of sexual identity, however, did not allow the possibility of change:

> [B]eing homosexual ... is as involuntary as if it were inborn, despite the fact it is not inborn.... The fact of retaining homosexual desires, whether one indulges or suppresses them, and whether or not a bisexual adjustment is made, is virtually as ineradicable as if it involved the color of one's skin or the shape of one's eyes. (4-5)

The author's version of the etiology of male homosexuality was largely psychoanalytic and oedipal.[4] Among the major causes of the homosexual identity, which could operate singly or in concert, were: the boy's intense love and physical desire for his mother, from which he could not free himself; his identification with his mother and desire to emulate her; his attempt to become his mother's lover to replace an absent or inadequate father; his effort to become his father's lover to replace a lost or loveless mother. The boy's idealization of women as immaculate, his predisposition to femininity, and chance homosexual experiences occurring in his adolescence could also be contributing factors.

What made Cory's conception of the homosexual identity sociocultural was the emphasis he placed on external formative influence, what he referred to as the "hidden sources" (15) of hostility:

> [T]he superiority feeling engendered in the insecure heterosexual; the use of condemnation as a means of suppressing that portion of libidinous urge directed towards one's own sex; the assignment of deviltry and witchcraft toward the unknown;

---

[3] Although the author wrote as a homosexual, he stated that he was husband and father as well as the lover of another man. Sagarin later changed his identity to heterosexual.

[4] The book dealt with male homosexuality because the author believed that little was known about lesbians and because he was writing as a male homosexual, often about his own experience. In 1964, he published *The Lesbian in America* (New York: Citadel Press).

the difficulties of a searching study to understand; the social advantage gained from joining the chorus of condemnation; the ease of stereotype thinking by the dominant group; the challenge of homosexuality to the [male] sexual ego; and the use of condemnation as a means of suppressing the envy for the attainment of a certain degree of sexual freedom in the homosexual way of life. (27)

The minority status of individuals who possessed the homosexual identity also made it sociocultural. As a minority status it was less cohesive and visible than other minorities because it lacked a biological means for identifying those who belonged. There was also the reluctance of its members to acknowledge that they were homosexuals. It was a large, unrecognized minority:

> As a minority, we homosexuals are therefore caught in a particularly vicious circle. On the one hand, the shame of belonging and social punishment of acknowledgment are so great that the pretense is almost universal; on the other hand, only a leadership that would acknowledge its membership would be able to break down the barriers of shame and resultant discrimination. Until the world is able to accept us on an equal basis as human beings entitled to the full rights of life, we are unlikely to have any great numbers willing to become martyrs by carrying the burden of the cross. But until we are willing to speak out openly and frankly in defense of our activities, and to identify ourselves with the millions pursuing these activities, we are unlikely to find the attitudes of the world undergoing any significant change. (14)

Much of the discrimination against homosexuality, he believed, stemmed from a basically "anti-sexual world" (232). The future acceptance of homosexuality would be part of the acceptance of all sexuality. Cory also contributed to the sociocultural homosexual identity by charting the territory of the "homosexual subculture" for future ethnographic exploration. In this field he introduced the terminology of GAY and STRAIGHT and the argot of the homosexual sub-culture.[5]

---

[5] The word *gay* appeared in the sociological literature of the fifties, although its use predated that time. John Boswell (1980, 43n) documents the use of the French *gai* from the thirteenth century and its associations with courtly love, the "art of poesy," and still later, sexual looseness and prostitution. He stated, "One can easily imagine transference of the idea of the sexual looseness of

He described gay locales such as streets and bars, where sexual contact was made, festivities such as drag balls, and the emotional qualities of intimate relationships between men. His advice on how homosexuals could make a satisfactory adjustment contributed to the normalization of sexual relationships. Marriage was the adjustment he most strongly recommended: the heterosexual marriage, with the homosexual lover on the side; the "front" marriage between a homosexual female and male; or the "homosexual marriage." His advice to parents of homosexual sons was to be patient and understanding.

In 1956, Maurice Leznoff and William Westley published an ethnographic study of the male "homosexual community" and "homosexual groups" in Montreal.[6] The sociocultural homosexuality of respondents, locales, and groups was treated as a given. The members of these groups, according to the authors, looked to their fellows for the acceptance they could not find in any other social context. Presumably, the "other social context" (163) referred to a sexual community. The authors described the members' deep attachment to the group:

> Since the homosexual group provides the only social context in which homosexuality is normal, deviant practices [are] moral, and homosexual responses [are] rewarded, the homosexual develops a deep emotional involvement with his group, tending toward a ready acceptance of its norms and dictates, and subjection to its behavior patterns. (163)

Besides emotional support, the group provided occasions for gossiping about sexual exploits, adopting exaggerated feminine behavior and

---

prostitution or the immorality attributed to homosexual persons in hostile environments" (43). Boswell believed that the use of gay was common in the English homosexual subculture in the early twentieth century. Outside of pornographic fiction, its first public use in the United States was in the 1939 movie *Bringing up Baby*. Cory (1951: 107-108) stated that the word was used in pornographic literature soon after 1918. Psychoanalysts told him that their patients were using the word in the nineteen twenties. He believed it had wide currency in the nineteen forties in the print and broadcast media. Cory was less enlightening about the word *straight*, although he implied that its use was more current on the East than the West Coast of the United States in the forties and early fifties. *Gay*, according to Cory, was obviously preferred by homosexuals because it avoided the odious connotations of *queer, fairy*, and *faggot*.

[6] Leznoff, Maurice and Westley, William (1956). The Homosexual Community. *Social Problems* 3: 257-263. The article was reprinted in Ruitenbeek (1963: 162-174). Page references are to the Ruitenbeek reprint.

speech, and occasionally cross-dressing. Sexual relationships within the group were prohibited "in a manner suggestive of the incest taboo" (163).

The study identified two subgroups of homosexuals, the secret and the overt, distinguishable by the ways in which they avoided legal and social sanctions against homosexuality. The secret homosexuals tried to conceal their homosexuality from coworkers and heterosexual friends. They held jobs with relatively high social status and regularly mixed with heterosexuals in occupational and social activities. Their involvement (170) "in the homosexual world" was largely limited to the search for sex partners. The overt homosexuals were the separatists. They worked and played in surroundings where they could be open in the espousal and practice of their sexuality. This social confinement meant that they worked in low status occupations and formed social relationships only with other open homosexuals.

There was reciprocal hostility between the secret and overt groups even though they were linked by "sexual interdependency" (172). According to Leznoff and Westley, "it is the casual and promiscuous sexual contacts ... which weld the city's homosexuals into a community" (172). The sociocultural conception of sexual identity attracted the attention of clinical psychologists and psychiatrists.[7]

As early as 1956 Evelyn Hooker advocated a sociocultural approach to the study of homosexual men.[8] Her attention focused on men who had identified themselves as homosexuals since their adolescence or early adulthood. Hooker believed that once the individual recognized his ho-

---

[7] See, for example, Opler, Marvin K. (1965). Anthropological and Cross-Cultural Aspects of Homosexuality. In Judd Marmor, Ed., *Sexual Inversion: The Multiple Roots of Homosexuality*. New York: Basic Books, 108-123. Opler was a psychiatrist interested in both anthropology and sociology. In this article he maintained that cultures defined norms of sexual conduct as they defined standards for other relationships. In his view, the sexual was linked to the social and personal: "There are, in all cultures, *social* definitions of conduct linked with *sexual* definitions and with notions of proper *personal* behavior" (115). He believed that Freud placed too much emphasis on the restrictive and prohibiting aspects of culture and too little on its prescriptive and facilitative influence. He also believed it was impossible to separate the psychic aspects of sexual development from social and personal aspects. Psychological identification had to be expanded, in Opler's view, to induce social identification.

[8] Hooker, E. (1956). A Preliminary Analysis of Group Behavior of Homosexuals. *The Journal of Psychology* 42: 217-225. This article was based on a paper she presented at the American Psychological Association meeting in San Francisco in 1955.

mosexuality, he sought other homosexuals not only for sexual gratification but also for the rewards and support of "the total homosexual way of life" (1956: 221). Research on homosexuality, she contended, should be concerned "with ways in which the patterns of attitudes and behavior of the homosexual majority are shaped, both by homosexual groups and by attitudes of the dominant majority toward him as a member of a socially outcast minority" (1956: 218). She believed that personality characteristics stereotypically attributed to homosexual males, such as "obsessive concern," "withdrawal and passivity," and "protective clowning," could be explained as defenses used by minority group members to ward off victimization.[9]

Hooker described the characteristics and activities of several types of homosexual groups. There were the public groups found in gay bars and on the streets and the private, informal, social groups. Whereas finding sex partners was the major preoccupation of the public groups, conversation was the consuming activity of the private groups. The major topics of discussion were art, music, theater, and literature and the gossip was about the latest conflicts in the relationships of homosexual couples. Hooker also drew a distinction between healthy and pathological groups. Pathological groups were those that became absorbed in sexual excitement, rigidly enforced group norms, and excluded those, particularly women, who could possibly modify in-group prejudices. In developing her social psychological approach, Hooker removed the onus of mental illness from the shoulders of the individual homosexual male and placed it at the doorstep of public homosexual groups.

One of the first efforts to marshal clinical evidence to dispel the belief that male homosexuality was a "symptom of pathology" was made by Hooker in an article published in 1957.[10] While this article was based on an

---

[9] Hooker was choosing from a much longer list of "traits due to victimization," developed by the social psychologist Gordon W. Allport in *The Nature of Prejudice* (1954). In addition to those traits mentioned above, Allport, in Chapter 9, listed denial of group membership, strengthening of in-group ties, slyness and cunning, identification with the dominant group (self-hate), aggression against own group, prejudice against out-groups, sympathy for other minorities, fighting back (militancy), enhanced striving, symbolic status striving (expressed in pomp and circumstance), neuroticism (split-living), and self-fulfilling prophecy (leading to a benign or vicious circle).

[10] Hooker, E. (1957). The Adjustment of the Male Overt Homosexual. *Journal of Projective Techniques* 21: 18-31. A footnote by the editor of the journal indicated that this report was "preliminary." An earlier version of this article (the text of a

experimentally designed study, it was part of a larger effort to gather data on the life histories of a group of homosexual men and their cultural milieu. Psychiatric conceptions of homosexuality had been based almost entirely on men and women who were in therapy or institutionalized. Hooker selected for her study men who were not referred by a clinical agency, not seeking psychotherapy, not unemployed, and who lacked (1957: 20) "evidence of considerable disturbance." She found many of them through the Mattachine Society located in Los Angeles.[11]

In attempting "to secure homosexuals who would be pure for homosexuality, that is, without heterosexual experience" (20), Hooker had to include three subjects who "had not had more than three heterosexual experiences" but "identified themselves as homosexual in their patterns of desire and behavior" (20). She also looked for "thorough-going" (20) heterosexual men who were well adjusted. The description of the recruitment procedure suggested that Hooker had some difficulty finding bona fide heterosexuals and that, despite her screening precautions, some "who have strong latent or concealed overt homosexuality" (20) may have slipped through.

The purpose of the study was three-fold: (1) to compare heterosexual and homosexual males for possible differences in personality structure; (2) to compare overall adjustment; and (3) to find out if experienced

---

paper read at the American Psychological Association convention in Chicago in 1956) was published in Ruitenbeek (1963: 141-161). Hooker published two subsequent articles based on this research in the *Journal of Projective Techniques*: (1958). Male Homosexuality in the Rorschach. *Journal of Projective Techniques 22:* 33-54 and (1959). What is a Criterion? *Journal of Projective Techniques 23:* 273-281.
[11] Hooker described the purpose of the Mattachine Society as "the development of a homosexual ethic in order to better integrate the homosexual into society" (1957: 19). She revealed more about her initial contact with respondents in a later publication: Hooker, E. (1967). The Homosexual Community. In J. Gagnon and W. Simon, Eds., *Sexual Deviance*. New York: Harper and Row, 167-184. In response to an entreaty by a former student, "a highly successful businessman," to study homosexual males who "did not seek psychiatric help, and who led relatively stable, occupationally successful lives," she accepted the opportunity to study homosexuals. This student and his friends provided entree to social circles and public gathering places. It was later that Hooker made "independent contacts with official homosexual organizations" which "led to other social strata in the community" (1967: 170).

clinicians could distinguish men of one orientation from those of the other, on the basis of their test records.[12]

In the reported findings most of the men, either heterosexual or homosexual, were judged to have average or better adjustment, which led Hooker to conclude that (1957: 23) "clearly there is no inherent connection between pathology and homosexuality," Presumably no differences in the personality structures of the heterosexual as compared with the homosexual men were found. As for distinguishing sexual orientation, the raters misjudged it in about half the cases. When they were correct it was often because there was self-disclosure of homosexuality (and one can assume, heterosexuality) in the records.

There were several indications that Hooker and her collaborators approached this study from a psychoanalytic point of view. The list of "cues" that Hooker believed could be used in reviewing the test records to detect the homosexual were:

> anality, open or disguised; avoidance of areas usually designated as vaginal areas; articles of feminine clothing, especially under-clothing, and/or arts objects elaborated with unusual detail; responses giving evidence of considerable sexual confusion, with castration anxiety, and/or hostile or fearful attitudes toward women; evidence of feminine cultural identification, and/or emotional involvement between males. (1957: 23)

These indicators appeared to have been imbued with psychoanalytic concepts of homosexuality: the fear of women, particularly female genitalia; dread of castration; the replacement of the masculine for the feminine identification; and the exclusive substitution of males for

---

[12] The instruments used to assess personality and adjustment were well-known projective tests: the Rorschach, in which individuals described the configurations that appeared to them as they perused a series of inkblots; the Thematic Apperception Test (TAT) in which individuals were asked to compose a story of nineteen ambiguous scenes presented on cards; and the Make-A-Picture-Story test (MAPS) in which individuals selected a cardboard figure and setting for which they composed a story. In a subsequent article, the purposes of this study were stated more broadly: "[T]he primary objectives were to study the developmental sequences in the life history of the individual leading to the adult identification as a male homosexual and to determine the correlates in personality structure and adjustment of such identification." See Hooker, E. (1965). "An Empirical Study of Some Relationships between Sexual Patterns and Gender Identity in Male Homosexuals." In John Money, Ed., *Sex Research: New Developments*. New York: Holt, Rinehart & Winston, 24-52: 28.

females in emotional relationships. In describing men who received very low adjustment ratings, references were made to emotional relationships that lacked depth and warmth (1957: 29), a high level of narcissism, and homosexuality as a defense against psychosis.

The assessment of "good" adjustment, however, appeared to rest on how closely the homosexual man approached conventionality. One man's attitudes toward sexuality were seen as "fairly moral" (1957: 27). About the same man Hooker wrote: "Although in his early life he passed through the 'cruising' stage, he now has highly stable personal relationships, including a 'homosexual marriage'" (26). Another subject with high ratings was described as involved in "'homosexual marriage' of some six years' duration. He tried very hard to change his sexual pattern but was unsuccessful and has now accepted the homosexual 'life'" (28). About another she wrote: "He is thoroughly immersed in the homosexual way of life but apart from this I see no particular evidence of disturbance" (27).

Possibly because the study was based on unexamined psychoanalytic assumptions about sexual identity, Hooker never speculated on what the homosexual identity consisted of. The title of the article, the search for "pure homosexuals" as respondents, and the effort to discern a unique personality structure all suggest that Hooker never questions the existence of a psychological homosexual identity. Yet she was emphatic in concluding that "efforts thus far to establish clear-cut differences between the two groups as a whole have been relatively fruitless" (1957: 24).

Along with the test records Hooker had gathered information on the "life histories" of her respondents. She suggested that scrutiny of these records would show "with some certainty" that there would be a difference between heterosexual and homosexual men "Comparisons between number and duration of love relationships, cruising patterns, and degree of satisfaction with sexual patterns and the love partner will certainly show clear-cut differences" (1957: 30). These were the areas in which homosexual relationships were viewed by Hooker as departing from conventional heterosexual relationships. She implied that the psychological homosexual male identity could be described in terms of these departures and that the heterosexual identity would prove to be superior. Consequently, homosexuality as pathology was not completely exonerated. Perhaps, she speculated, what would be found to be truly pathological was the "erotic situation"; pathology would be "limited to the sexual sector alone" (31).

In a subsequent article, Hooker (1959) claimed there were no unique clues that the clinician could use in detecting homosexuality in responses given to projective tests. By 1959 her position was "that homosexuality is not an entity but is, rather, a multi-manifested phenomenon. We need to get beyond the fact that the individual is homosexual, to the kind of homosexual he is" (279). In later publications Hooker's conception of sexual identity was predominantly sociocultural. Her studies focused on what she called the homosexual "subculture" or the homosexual "worlds."[13]

The outline she sketched in 1956 for describing the homosexual community was followed in portraying "gay life" and the "gay scene" (1967: 172) in Los Angeles.[14] Hooker pictured gay bars as markets for social concourse, training, and sexual contact. In their social functions the bars were places where friends gathered to gossip and look over new faces. They also served as induction centers for young men entering the homosexual community. As "a sexual market," the bar was a "place where agreements are made for the potential exchange of sexual services, for sex without obligation or commitment—the one night-stand" (1967: 175). In Hooker's view, the "promiscuity of the homosexual" was determined less by the homosexual's "psychodynamic structure" (1967: 176) than by the structure of the gay world:

> The relative absence of women in the homosexual world, the negative sanctions of society against homosexual relationships, the pressures toward secrecy and the risks of revealing one's own personal identity as a homosexual, and the market character of the bar setting in which meetings occur, combine to produce the kind of sexual exchange which we have described as a stable feature of the "gay" world. (1967: 177)

The public aspect of the homosexual community was only the tip of an iceberg. Most homosexual males inhabited a private world of social cliques, groups, and networks. There were also the relationships called

---

[13] Hooker described the male "homosexual community" in at least two articles: (1) Hooker, E. (1962). The Homosexual Community. *Proceedings of the 14th International Congress of Applied Psychology, Personality Research.* Copenhagen: Munksgaard, 40-49. (A revised version of this paper was reprinted in *Perspectives in Psychopathology.* New York: Oxford University Press, 1965, and later, in Gagnon, J. and Simon, W., Eds., *Sexual Deviance.* New York: Harper and Row, 1967: 167-184.); and (2) "Male Homosexuals and Their 'Worlds'" in In J. Marmor, Ed., *Sexual Inversion: The Multiple Roots of Homosexuality.* New York: Basic Books, 83-107. This latter article, which appeared in 1965, is substantially the same as the former.

[14] Our page references are to the reprinting of "The Homosexual Community" in Gagnon and Simon (1967).

marriages. In Hooker's eyes "the hope of many who engage in the 'one night-stand' round of activities is that a particular encounter may lead to a more permanent relationship" (1967: 182).

As early as 1962 Hooker challenged the conventional belief that the sexual relationships of male pairs were based on the rigid assignment of an exclusively masculine role to one partner and an exclusively feminine role to the other. In a paper presented in 1963 she reported evidence she had gathered to disprove that such dichotomization or roles existed in homosexual male relationships.[15]

She questioned the contention of Ferenczi that there two distinct kinds of homosexual males, the passive feminine and the active masculine. The implicit corollary belief was that the passives were the insertees in sexual intercourse and the actives the insertors. While she found that Ferenczi's typology fitted a small number of the men she studied, most were neither rigidly feminine nor masculine and most acted as both insertors and insertees. She attributed variations in sexual practice and expressed femininity and masculinity to the particular segment of the homosexual subculture to which the men belonged. Some segments were strict in enforcing normative standards of masculinity or femininity, while others had no discernible requirements and therefore were without influence in shaping behavior. Her parting advice was that psychological research on male homosexuals should include variations in subculture and the social interaction of partners in sexual relationships.

The idea of a fixed homosexual identity was an important feature of the homosexual sub-culture as described by Hooker:

> The majority believed either that they were born as homosexuals or that familial factors operating very early in their lives determined the outcome. In any case, homosexuality is believed to be a fate over which they have no control and in which they have no choice. It follows that the possibility of changing to a heterosexual pattern is thought to be extremely limited. Current pessimism in psychiatric circles about the results of psychotherapy for homosexuals has been assimilated. To fight against homosexuality is to fight against their own "nature" in its essential form as they experience it. They be-

---

[15] Hooker (1965). This article was based on a paper presented at the annual meeting of the New England Psychological Association in Boston in 1963.

lieve that homosexuality is as "natural" for them as heterosexuality is for others.[16]

Hooker's major contribution to detoxication was to show that there was no inevitable connection between psychopathology and homosexuality; but hers was a guarded acceptance. As demonstrated here normalization would be accomplished by the absorption of homosexual relationships, as far as possible, into patterns of conventional heterosexual relationships, and by the possible exclusion of those behaviors that were seen as uniquely homosexual, such as numerous liaisons with different partners and the fluidity of emotional relationships.

One aspect of research on the homosexual subculture was the investigation of male prostitution. This research fitted the theoretical predilection of sociologists interested in "deviant" and criminal behavior. Homosexual prostitution combined the social deviance of delinquent boys who were the prostitutes with the sexual deviance of their clients.[17]

Albert Reiss, as a sociologist, looked at the practice of homosexual prostitution as a form of social and sexual deviance.[18] He focused on the sexual relationship between "delinquent peers" and "adult queers" (249). The exchanges between them were described through the perceptions of the "peers," who were teenage boys. They viewed themselves as neither hustlers nor homosexuals; their interest in clients was portrayed as entirely monetary and part of an extensive pattern of delinquent activities. The "queers" were described as men who sought sexual gratification outside of adult homosexual groups, thereby hoping to protect their anonymity.[19]

---

[16] Hooker, E. (1968) Homosexuality. *International Encyclopedia of the Social Sciences*, Vol 14. New York: Crowell, Collier & MacMillan, 222-223. In this article Hooker still believed that "it may be possible to differentiate personality patterns among homosexuals" (227).

[17] See, for example, Butts, William (1946-1947). Boy Prostitutes of the Metropolis. *Journal of Clinical Psychopathology* 8: 673-681; Ross, H. Laurence (1959). 'The Hustler' in Chicago. *The Journal of Student Research 1*: 13-19; and Jersild, Jens (1956). *Boy Prostitution.* Copenhagen: C. E. Grad.

[18] Reiss, Jr., Albert J. (1961). The Social Integration of Queers and Peers. *Social Problems* 9(2): 102-120. Our page references are to the Ruitenbeek reprinting (1963: 249-278).

[19] Reiss apologized for the use of the word "queer" and stated that "getting a queer" was the phraseology used by the boys to describe their contractual relationship with their clients (249). In explaining the motivation of the "queers," Reiss did not explore the possibility that these men were attracted to adolescent boys.

The queer-peer relationship, according to Reiss, was regulated by a set of norms, apparently conceived and enforced by the boys: (1) sexual gratification had to be clearly subordinated to the purpose of making money; (2) sexual contact had to be confined to oral copulation of the boy by the man; (3) neither partner was allowed to show emotion; and (4) violence was to be used by the boy only if the rules were broken by the adult. As explained by Reiss, infractions were met with violence because they threatened the boys' view of themselves as heterosexual and masculine and endangered membership in their gangs:

> The prescriptions that the goal is money, the sexual gratification is not to be sought as an end in the relationship, that the affective neutrality be maintained toward the fellator, and that only mouth-genital fellation is permitted, all tend to insulate the boy from a homosexual self-definition. So long as he conforms to these expectations, his "significant others" will not define him as homosexual; and this is perhaps the most crucial factor in his own self-definition. The peers define one as homosexual not on the basis of homosexual behavior as such, but on the basis of participation in the homosexual role, the "queer" role. The reactions of the larger society in defining the behavior as homosexual is unimportant in their own self-definition. What is important to them is the reactions of their peers to violation of peer-group norms which define roles in the peer-queer transaction. (274-275)[20]

Reiss's subscription to the idea of the sociocultural sexual identity is evident in his belief that sexual identity depended essentially on a social contract with clients, and the boys' reputation with peers. Because he never questioned whether money was the only or major motivation for the boys entering homosexual relationships with their clients, Reiss clearly separated the boys' sociocultural from their psychological sexual identity.

A composite view of the homosexual subculture in England based on the idea of the sociocultural sexual identity was provided by Richard Hauser in 1962.[21] He showed its many facets by describing different

---

[20] Reiss's depiction of the boys exemplified the psychiatric belief that to be homosexual one must be homosexual in mentality as well as behavior.

[21] Hauser, Richard (1962). *The Homosexual Society*. London: The Bodley Head. The report was commissioned by the British Home Office and followed by about four years the *Report of the Departmental Committee on Homosexual Offenses and Prostitution*, the famous "Wolfenden Report."

forms of homosexual behavior and relationships, developing taxonomy
of homosexual "types," suggesting the differences in homosexual
"subcultures," and revealing what he believed were typical homosexual
attitudes. Because he did not believe that homosexuality was a unitary
psychological identity, his taxonomy included classes of men who could
be considered more heterosexual than homosexual.[22]

Hauser distinguished among three levels of homosexual behavior: (1)
the man who behaved and thought like a woman; (2) the man who was
thoroughly masculine and "would never for a moment consider acting a
woman's role" (120-121); and (3) the individual "who wishes to be
neither a woman nor a man, but thinks himself to be a part of third sex
(believing himself to be a true invert or homosexual). He may live as a
homosexual but is neither male nor female in outlook" (121). Hauser
believed that men in the last two categories were probably bisexual
although they might deny this if asked.

For each level of behavior there were several types of homosexuals. As
a subculture there was little homogeneity: "All homosexuals have only
one thing in common: they have sexual feelings for their own sex. It cannot
be implied that they all practice in the same way and even less that they do
so with the same attitudes" (19). Of all the types the one which had
Hauser's greatest admiration was the "fully sublimated homosexual or
bisexual"; such an individual "has made his peace with his handicap often
after an exceedingly tough struggle. He knows that if he ever gives way
the whole defense mechanism inside of himself would collapse" (43).

Like many of the sociological studies which were to follow, Hauser
viewed homosexuals as a minority who shared with other minorities a
sense of grievance over stigmatization and who resisted majority
pressures. The minority attitudes included a mythology about superior endowment, use of a secret language, preference for homosexual companionship, a sense of alliance, and the ability for mutual recognition. The
formation of the homosexual ghetto he believed was for the purpose of
withstanding majority pressure.

Hauser devoted a portion of his book to "the reconsideration of the
normal cultural relationship between man and woman to see whether all
is well there (we think it is not)" (25). For this purpose he developed a
stage theory of relationships which, presumably, could be applied to
both heterosexual and homosexual relationships:

---

[22] For example, the "bisexual," the "married man," the "demoralized married
man," the "young bisexual."

Stage 1: Sex only and physical courtship. In this stage the "sex organs are used to penetrate the other person's body—only for sex purposes and for no other major relationship or satisfaction" (123).

Stage 2. Passionate love and emotional courting. Here the courting focused on emotion and sought possession. It did not necessarily include the full sex act.

Stage 3. The pair created a nest. They lived together with the warmth and security of a real family.

Stage 4. Social relationship. A sense of comradeship, sharing of hopes and worries strong links of friendship and interests.

Stage 5. Lasting relationship. Here the pair was united in an unselfish love in which there was complete trust and full confidence in the permanence of the relationship. (123-127)

The idea that some homosexual males could rate higher marks than others in psychological health and social adjustment was expanded by Michael Schofield in his study of homosexual men in England.[23] Three types of men were included: those convicted of homosexual offenses, patients in therapy, and men who had not sought therapy or had not been arrested or convicted. Schofield compared these three groups with three others: convicted pedophiliacs, heterosexuals in psychotherapy, and a nonpatient, nonprisoner heterosexual group.[24]

Schofield's assumptions about the possible ingredients of a detoxicated homosexual sociocultural identity are clearest in his discussion of homosexual males who had not run into trouble with the law and had no need for therapy. Except for the choice of male sex partners, their adjustment profile showed more similarity to that of their heterosexual counterparts than to the profiles of the troubled homosexuals. In Schofield's view sexual practices of this group were not sordid, often consisting of "genital

---

[23] Schofield, Michael (1965). *Sociological Aspects of Homosexuality: A Comparative Study of Three Types of Homosexuals.* Boston: Little, Brown. Schofield was the research director of the Central Council for Health In London. His previous research had dealt with the sexual behavior of young people. Schofield had written earlier works on homosexuality under the pseudonym "G. Westwood."

[24] The total number of men interviewed was 300, fifty for each of the six groups.

apposition."[25] They sought only authentic homosexuals as partners, and were attracted to masculine men and not male transvestites or "effeminate poufs."[26]

Schofield tried to expose as groundless the public fear that homosexuals "actively proselytized" (112) heterosexuals. Few were interested in non-homosexuals because they sought affection and companionship in a permanent homosexual relationship:

> There is no doubt that a homosexual can experience a very strong emotional attachment to another man. This intense feeling has many of the same observable features as one found in the love of a man for a woman. Many people are surprised to learn that most homosexuals seek companionship and community of interest as well as sexual satisfaction. Some homosexuals do develop relationships as loyal and as closely knit as the best kind of marriages. (112)

Men who had successful homosexual relationships did not come into conflict with the law and did not require psychotherapy because "they find enough satisfaction and contentment in a secure home life" (116). Schofield believed homosexual relationships were difficult to preserve because of "some masculine personality feature" (115) but not because of some flaw in the homosexual personality.

The men with the longest relationships were also the most solidly homosexual. Few had ever felt attraction to women, engaged in heterosexual intercourse, or believed that they would ever develop interest in having sexual intercourse with women. Most inhabited all-male social groups. Schofield concluded that the homosexual men he viewed as best adjusted were those who would be least likely to become heterosexual through psychotherapy. Those men who composed the homosexual patient group, Schofield believed, were more homosexual than those in the prisoner group. In viewing the prospects for changing sexual orientation, Schofield rather wryly remarked that psychiatrists "stood a better chance with the men in prison ... than with their own patients" (121).

---

[25] Schofield (1965: 111) described genital apposition as a preference for a situation where orgasm is produced, not by manual stimulation of the genitalia, but by the close proximity of the whole body."
[26] A *pouf* (see Schofield, 1965: 112) is literally a puff, like a soft roll of hair or a powderpuff, but was used in England to refer to males who displayed stereotypic feminine behavior.

Schofield compared the well-adjusted group of homosexual males with the other groups. The homosexual prisoners came from more disturbed homes, had stronger heterosexual than homosexual impulses, were mostly insertors, could not establish stable relationships with either men or women, and had sex more often, with more partners, and in public places. The men in the homosexual patient group, in Schofield's estimation, were less accepting of their homosexuality than those in the adjusted group. They tended to be less sexually active, preferred "less sophisticated homosexual techniques," but were more likely to visit public places to make sexual contacts.[27]

The pedophiliacs, men who had been convicted of having sexual encounters with boys, were more heterosexual than any of the other homosexual groups. They were often married men who had given in to a momentary impulse during times of stress or weakness or after losing interest in heterosexuality. In attempting to rid the homosexual identity of the taint of pedophilia, Schofield claimed: "The results of this research indicate that pedophiliacs are more likely to be heterosexually oriented than homosexually oriented" (59). It was clear in his mind that pedophilia was not the same as homosexuality. Indeed, he found that the homosexuals who sought adults for sex shared the public intolerance for sexually molesting children.

Apparently, Schofield subscribed to the idea of the sociocultural sexual identity. A homosexual, he believed, was a person who was willing to say to the interviewer that he regarded himself as a homosexual. The heterosexual only had to make the same declaration of his heterosexuality. To Schofield, whether homosexuals were born or made was an issue of small consequence:

> There seems to be an earnest desire to believe that homosexuals are born not made. Perhaps this is because people wish to show that a man cannot be held responsible for his homosexual desires. But this would be equally true if the homosexual condition was formed in early childhood, as the Freudians believe. As far as responsibility is concerned, the difference between an inborn

---

[27] Schofield (1965: 83) presumably considered "genital apposition" less sophisticated than anal intercourse. Presumably, "less sophisticated" sexual practices to Schofield were more acceptable. There was that faint implication that Schofield felt that "rubbing" was less sophisticated than "inserting." The report did not deal with fellation, but did distinguish between "active" and "passive" anal entry.

condition and a condition acquired before the age of five is purely academic. (164)

Schofield was also unhappy with the idea that homosexuality was caused by early conditioning because that belief played into the hands of politicians and moralists who viewed it as an infectious disease. A predetermined sexual identity could not be spread. There are indications however, that he favored the idea of the psychological identity over that of the biological identity. He believed that the etiology could be traced to the early environment, particularly to "disturbed homes" and to the flawed performance of the father in his parental role. Schofield did not abandon the belief that homosexual impulses stemmed from pathogenic sources and that treatment consisted of uncovering unconscious origins and breaking down and reorganizing the personality structure.[28]

Although the individual could not be blamed for being homosexual, society could be held responsible for its intolerance:

> Homosexuality is a condition which in itself has only minor effects upon the development of the personality. But the attitudes, not of the homosexual, but of other people towards this condition, create a stress situation which can have a profound effect upon personality development and can lead to character deterioration of a kind which prohibits effective integration with the community. A proportion of homosexuals are unable to withstand the pressures from outside and become social casualties. These are the homosexuals most often found in prisons and clinics. Their difficulties may take a form not directly associated with the homosexual condition, although originally caused by social hostility shown toward homosexuality. On the other hand, the homosexuals who have learned to contend with these social pressures can become adjusted to their condition and integrated with the community. These men are hardly ever found in prisons and clinics. (203)

This social hostility led to forms of sexual practice that Schofield believed were damaging to both the homosexual and society. Promiscuity resulted when the homosexual decided to enjoy his status as outcast and to make his own rules of sexual conduct. Promiscuity,

---

[28] Schofield (1965: 162-168). Unless the patient was bisexual, young, and affluent enough to afford a long course of therapy, however, he considered efforts to switch patients to heterosexuality to be useless.

however, was a heterosexual as well as a homosexual problem and, in Schofield's conception, unacceptable for either sexual identity:

> The objection to promiscuity is, or ought to be, not so much unbridled pleasure of intemperance, as the consequences such as disease, evasions, lies, thoughtlessness, self-centeredness, and lack of responsibility. The fact is that even the most ardent practitioner very rarely gets much satisfaction from his promiscuity, and the feckless use of another person's body to gratify the sexual urge is a very limited and unrewarding exercise. (175)

Schofield believed there were dangers to the larger society from the existence of the homosexual subculture, what he called "introverted groups" (180). Such groups, which are a direct response to their outcast status, tenuously subscribe to moral norms and may turn to alcohol, promiscuity, and techniques of sexual gratification "forbidden by normal society" (185). There was also the risk of associating with criminal elements such as drug addicts, prostitutes, and other criminals. These subgroups could breed anti-social attitudes.

Tolerance of homosexuals, Schofield argued, could promote social progress. Because homosexuals were unencumbered by families they could devote their whole lives to their jobs and thus were an important economic asset. The homosexual identity could be valued for its nonconformity: "In some people a homosexual disposition brings out a tough intellectualism that rejects many things accepted without question by the majority" (179).

In 1965, Paul Gebhard led a group of investigators in the study of heterosexual sex offenders.[29] The seven classes of sex offenders that the Gebhard group described revealed the ways in which they though adult male heterosexuality could go awry. The ASSAULTIVE MALE had to include violence in his sex acts with women in order to achieve full gratification. The AMORAL DELINQUENTS were the adult hedonists who viewed women as sex objects and always expected females to submit to their sexual impulses. The DRUNK's behavior ranged from pawing and grappling with the woman and went on to assault and battery if she resisted. The EXPLOSIVE MALE could be the model husband or student with an unblemished sexual past who suddenly and inexplicably became

---

[29] Gebhard, Paul H., Gagnon, John H., Pomeroy, Wardell B., and Christenson, Cornelia V. (1965). *Sex Offenders: An Analysis of Types*. New York: Harper-Hoeber.

sexually assaultive, There were the men who were called the **DOUBLE-STANDARD VARIETY**. They divided females into "good" and "bad," feeling free to importune "the bad girls," even with a little threat and force, in order to have sex with them. There were the **INCEST OFFENDERS**, fathers who had sex with their adolescent daughters or stepdaughters. Finally, there were the comparatively harmless **PEEPERS** who obtained sexual gratification by spying through windows of bedrooms and dormitories in the hope of seeing nude females. The taxonomy of the Gebhard group suggested three of the ways in which the heterosexual identity went awry: (1) by aberrant and criminal behavior; (2) by assaultive or coercive sex; and (3) by the perverse use of violence to achieve sexual potency.

As part of the description of the homosexual subculture, some ethnographic studies focused directly on homosexual relationships as reflections of a sociocultural **SEXUAL IDENTITY**. In 1968, David Sonenschein published a description of the variety of male homosexual relationships he had observed in a city in the southwestern United States.[30] Sonenschein asserted that the work of Hooker, Leznoff, Westley and Reiss formed the basis for his description of the homosexual community. Psychology, he acknowledged, had heretofore furnished much of the available information on homosexuality, a corpus that mostly contained bizarre case histories involving sexual pathology. According to Sonenschein, it was left to anthropology and sociology to provide a systematic picture of the homosexual relationship:

> Basically, the kinds of answers one seeks then now centers around the question: "Given a homosexual individual, what does he do about it, what does he do with it, and what happens to him as a result? This writer feels that this is a much more immediately important and crucial approach—to the homosexual and heterosexual alike—rather than what seems to be at this time, the unanswerable question of etiology. (141)[31]

[30] Sonenschein, David (1968). The Ethnography of Male Homosexual Relationships. *The Journal of Sex Research 4*(2): 69-83.
[31] Sonenschein, David (1966). Homosexuality as a Subject of Anthropological Inquiry. *Anthropological Quarterly 68*: 188-193. Reprinted in Weinberg, Martin S. (Ed.) (1976). *Sex Research: Studies from the Kinsey Institute*. New York: Oxford University Press, 140-155; page references are to the 1976 reprinting. Sonenschein identified himself as a "heterosexual friend" (141) of the homosexual community, over a period of eighteen months.

Sonenschein developed a fairly elaborate taxonomy of homosexual relationships, distinguishing between permanent or non-permanent relationships and among those that were both sexual and social (sociosexual), only social, or only sexual. Permanent SOCIOSEXUAL relationships were modeled after the heterosexual marriage: (1) a ritual which copied heterosexual matrimony; (2) an exchange and wearing of wedding rings; (3) a romantic conception of unending love; and (4) the dichotomizing of feminine and masculine roles. As Sonenschein pointed out, these were the marriages that the psychiatrists described as parodies of heterosexual relationships. The most common type of "marriage," however, was what Sonenschein called cohabitation:

> It too was based on a conception of love but the relationship was
> less predominately sexual as was the previous variety; there was
> a more conscious attempt by the individuals involved to aim at
> congruence of values and interest. (152)

The cohabitation relationship was more stable than the marriage. In fact "the [marriage] ritual, rather than being an attempt to cement the relationship, was more of an excuse for the ever-present and ever-needed party" (152). Sonenschein also believed that when individuals entered sociosexual relationships they wanted to last, they decreased their participation in the homosexual community. He held that non-permanent sociosexual relationships between individuals who were just friends or acquaintances were very rare because of the tendency to separate sexual and social partners.

The permanent SOCIAL relationships consisted of individuals alike in interests, intellect, occupations, social status and attitudes. These individuals supported each other socially and psychologically. In the non-permanent social relationship there was less consonance of attitudes and expectations. Sonenschein believed that the social relationship consisted either of individuals who had never had sex with each other or who were once sex partners but had moved on to a nonsexual relationship.

Sonenschein contributed to the detoxication of the homosexual identity by dispelling the belief that homosexual male relationships invariably involved sex. By describing the variations of social and sexual relationships, he shattered the notion that all homosexual relationships were one-night stands. Homosexual relationships were normalized by Sonenschein when he implied that the values and considerations upon which they were based were similar to those for heterosexual relationships.

Writing as a social psychiatrist, Martin Hoffman presented an ethnography of the homosexual subculture that combined a sociological analysis of its organization and practices with a psychological portrait of its inhabitants.[32] He also showed how the subculture was the defensive response to the social intolerance of homosexuality. Whereas earlier ethnographers of the gay world had described it with the curiosity and neutrality of the anthropologists, Hoffman viewed it with compassion and pessimism. For him it was essentially a sexual marketplace: the search for suitable sex partners was the driving force behind personal interaction, particularly in the bars and baths, Everywhere the accent was on youth, beauty, and romance, Everyone lived with the hope that a young prince would walk through the door of the bar, and sweep him off his feet and into the prince's bedchamber. Rejection by prospective partners added insult to injury: the insult consisted of being rejected for not being beautiful enough in a world in which beauty counted for more than anything else. The injury was the reopening of the wound to self-esteem, one incurred by the individual knowing he was a homosexual. It was true that homosexuals also went to bars to socialize, but the thought that they might find the ideal sexual partner was always at the back of their minds.

The gay world, as Hoffman described it, was shot through with "sexual fetishism," which he defined as the devotion of "an inordinate amount of time to sexual matters" (1968: 78). The obsession with sex, he believed, was the inevitable product of the oppression of homosexuals for their homosexuality. In his view, there would be less emphasis on sex if social intolerance did not make it necessary for homosexuals to meet in anonymous places:

> [I]f homosexuals could meet as *homosexuals* in the kind of social settings in which heterosexuals can (e.g., at school, at work) where the emphasis on finding sexual partners is not the controlling force behind all social interaction which transpires, a great deal of anonymous promiscuity which now characterizes homosexual encounters would be replaced by a 'normal' kind of meeting between two persons. (50)

---

[32] Hoffman, Martin (1968). *The Gay World: Male Homosexuality and the Social Creation of Evil*. New York: Basic Books. Hoffman conceived of the social psychiatrist as the investigator interested in examining how social arrangements create personal misery and how this misery could be eliminated. He stated that his study was based on interviews with 157 homosexual men and many hours spent in private homes and gay bars (9). The bulk of the data was collected in the San Francisco Bay Area.

Following the psychoanalytic tradition that viewed homosexual practice as reparative, Hoffman explained what he believed were some of the psychosexual forces that led to homosexuality. The "compulsive fellator" (1968: 142) was the man who attempted to feed on the masculinity of virile men to compensate for his own male inadequacy. The attraction of the older homosexual to younger partners was a narcissistic object choice in which the older partner treated the younger the way he wanted his mother to treat him. Hoffman also accepted the theory that overly intimate and binding mothers could explain the development of some types of homosexuals.[33]

He felt that such etiological conceptions explained some homosexuals, especially those who sought treatment, but not others. Although all of his illustrations of psychodynamic theories explained pathological development, Hoffman held open the possibility that nonpathological ways of becoming homosexual could also be discovered.

The chief symptom of an ailing homosexual world was the apparent inability of homosexual males to establish stable relationships with other males. Hoffman attributed this "failure" to the psychodynamic "roots" (1968: 141) of homosexuality. However, the adverse vicissitudes of psychosexual development only partly explained why intimate relationships were difficult to maintain. Hoffman placed the major blame on social attitudes which forbade sexual intimacy between males: "the same social forces which act to prevent most males from becoming homosexual reach into the lives of those that do become homosexual and prevent them from developing closeness in a sexual relationship with another man" (177). It is at this juncture in his portrayal of the gay world that Hoffman most boldly questioned the concept of homosexuality as pathology:

> What is fundamentally wrong with the conventional disease concept of homosexuality is not that there is no connection between homosexuality and pathology, for there is, in fact, such a link. What is incorrect is that all the phenomena of gay life are analyzed in terms of individual pathology, as if there were no social forces acting upon the homosexual. The problem of paired intimacy, which in my judgment is the central problem of the gay world, is a problem which cannot meaningfully be

---

[33] Although Hoffman criticized the research of the Bieber group's being methodologically unsound, he endorsed their theory about the close-binding-intimate (CBI) mothers of homosexual sons.

understood without considering the social context in which it occurs. It is this failure to consider the social milieu in which the gay world is situated, namely, the hostile character of the surrounding non-homosexual world, that accounts for the simplistic explanations of so much current analysis of the problem. (1968: 178)

Hoffman contributed to the efforts of his contemporary ethnographers by asserting that there were many different kinds of homosexuals and that those seen as patients were not typical. He also held that the question of why a man was homosexual implied as little pathology as the question of why a man was heterosexual. He accepted the doctrine of the Kinsey group that sexual arousal was triggered more easily in males than females. Hoffman thought all sexuality was learned through parents and was based on the human capacity to respond to either female or male stimuli. Unless one believed that the purpose of sexual behavior was procreation, homosexuality, along with nonreproductive heterosexuality, was natural. The stereotype of homosexual males as the "effeminate, limp-wristed, obvious fairy" (1968: 23) described only a small number. Underneath their licentious behavior, homosexual men were romantics, seeking passionate, stable relationships. The condemnation of homosexuality rested on the evidence, as Hoffman conceived it, of the widespread instability in homosexual relationships. That instability was itself the very product of social condemnation.

What Hoffman contributed to the normalization of sexual relationships was more by implication than assertion. Heterosexual relationships, he held, were not more natural than the homosexual but appeared to be so because from birth the boy was encouraged to prefer girls and was denied the alternative possibility of preferring boys.[34]

Some of the hostility heterosexual males showed toward homosexuals could be explained by postulating that they were projecting the guilt they felt about their own homosexual feelings. Along with Hooker and Schofield, for example, Hoffman saw the stable homosexual relationship as the *sine qua non* of the healthy homosexual. He viewed the gay world as a passing phenomenon, ultimately to be absorbed by the general social order as tolerance for homosexual relationships became widespread. At

---

[34] Hoffman did not discuss the possibility of a second alternative, the encouragement of the boy to like both boys and girls. He did, however, refer to parents who pass on to children the covert message that heterosexual behavior is less desirable than homosexual behavior (134-135).

this point heterosexual and homosexual relationships would presumably enjoy equal status and success.

The ethnographic approach to the sociocultural sexual identity was used by Laud Humphreys in a study originally intended as a broad sociological survey of homosexual behavior.[35] In selecting research clientele for launching his project, he turned to men who met for chance sexual contact in public restrooms in the parks of a Midwestern metropolitan area.[36] Utilizing a model of social interaction and observation developed by Erving Goffman, Humphreys portrayed these men as players in a game of chance.[37] He developed a catalog of roles to cover all the players, even those individuals who unwittingly used the restrooms for their customary purposes. The central actors in this situational drama were insertors and the insertees (the "cock-suckers").[38]

The supporting roles were provided by three types of lookouts or "watch-queens": the WAITERS who were poised for involvement in sexual activity already underway or who were looking for a particular person or sexual type; the MASTURBATORS, who might also be biding time as

---

[35] Humphreys, Laud (1970). *Tearoom Trade: Impersonal Sex in Public Places.* Chicago: Aldine. Humphreys stated that the etymology of TEAROOM was unknown but suggested that it may be associated with the British slang use of "tea" to denote "urine" (2). The British also used "tea" as a verb meaning "to engage" or "to encounter." The research occurred in two phases between 1965 and 1968: (l) "participant-observation" and (2) interviewing. In the first phase, "under the guise of being another gay guy" (24)and acting as a "voyeur-lookout" (27-28), Humphreys observed twenty restrooms in five different parks (9n). He systematically" observed 173 participants (102) in fifty sexual encounters and fifty-three acts of fellation (12n: 34). In the second phase he interviewed about fifty of the participants, twelve, the "intensive dozen," at greater length than the others. Fellatio was almost the only form of sexual practice Humphreys reported, although he twice saw couples engaged in anal intercourse and others in sexual contacts limited to mutual masturbation. In carrying out his research project, Humphreys was once arrested "in the line of duty" and briefly incarcerated (94-96).

[36] The basis for selection of public restrooms as the research site was described by Lee Rainwater in the foreword to Humphreys' book (vii-xv). The restrooms were chosen for two reasons: (1) there were no earlier studies of restrooms as there were of gay bars and (2) it was easier to observe sexual activity in restrooms than to locate and interview bar patrons or teenage hustlers.

[37] Goffman, Erving (1961). *Encounters.* Indianapolis: Bobbs-Merrill; Goffman, Erving (1967). *Interactional Ritual.* Chicago: Aldine.

[38] Humphreys noted that, contrary to the associated feminine stereotype, the insertees were often the initiators of the sexual encounter(1970: 52).

waiters; and the VOYEURS, who simply enjoyed watching others performing fellatio.

There were also special categories of participants. The teenagers or "chicken" could be watchqueens, hustlers, or toughs. The hustlers played the role of insertors, and the toughs would harass and sometimes attack other participants. There were the agents of social control such as police or park attendants. Finally, there were the naive visitors to the restrooms whom Humphreys classified as the "straights."

Humphreys believed there was a slippage by participants from one role to another:

> By "instability" of a role, I mean its observed tendency to melt, slip, fuse, or drift into another of the standard roles. This tendency is manifested regardless of who may take up the role in the course of an encounter. The role of "straight" is transient. In a deviant encounter, this label is not adhesive; it does not stick to a person for an extended period of time. (55)

The "straights" who came back repeatedly ceased to operate as straights, and this even applied to members of the vice squad. Humphreys believed he had found evidence in his research for the aphorism, "today's trade is tomorrow's competition."[39]

---

[39] There is considerable conceptual confusion in Humphreys' use of the term "straight" at different points in his treatise. At times it appears to refer to men who did not participate in restroom sex because they were ignorant of its occurrence or because they were "too heterosexual" or "too inhibited" (1970: 49). It appears, however, that those who did participate could also be straight, as in the cases of those men classified as "trade." In providing examples of men who fitted the "trade" category, Humphreys implied that most of their sexual contact may have been homosexual even though they did not "seek homosexual contact as such" (115). It appears that Humphreys, despite his antipathy to psychoanalytic theory, apparently accepted the psychoanalytic doctrine that men who are, for whatever reason denied heterosexual outlets, can engage in homosexual intercourse as insertors and still retain their psychological heterosexual identity. Humphreys even carried this doctrine one step further by implying that a biological or psychological heterosexual identity could be retained even when men played the role of insertee (113, Table 6.1). Although Humphreys was careful to note that his study was not about "homosexuals but of participants of homosexual acts" (18), his treatment of the men classified as "straight" or "gay" suggests that he believed that his participants had heterosexual or homosexual identities, established prior to and independently of their restroom behavior.

Much of Humphrey's analysis of restroom behavior consisted of a description of moves and countermoves of the sexual participants. There were patterns of approaching, signaling, maneuvering, contact, foreplay, payoff, and clearing the field. All of these were performed with minimal disclosure of personal identity:

> From one viewpoint, tearoom encounters may be analyzed as structured interaction that evolves from the need for information control: signals and strategies are developed to exclude the potentially threatening and uninitiated intruder, while informing potential partners of one's willingness to engage in sex; silence serves to protect participants from biographical disclosure; and locales were chosen for an ease of access that keeps wives, employers, and others from discovering the deviant activity. (131)

Participants in restroom sex were also assigned to sociological categories. Men classified as TRADE, most of whom were married, presumably did not identify themselves as homosexual, although several were insertees in restroom sex. Many were truck drivers whom Humphreys portrayed as unhappy in lower-class marriages that provided minimal sexual gratification. They turned to the restrooms for a sexual outlet that was quick, inexpensive, and impersonal. The AMBISEXUALS, who shared Humphreys' admiration, thought of themselves as bisexual. Although often maintaining model marriages and families, they could turn for personal support to networks of homosexual friends. The GAY participants, also admired by Humphreys, were the proud and open bearers of the sociocultural homosexual identity. The restrooms were not the primary setting for their sexual activity because they had free access to and movement within the homosexual subculture. The restrooms provided the anonymous opportunity for sex without their lovers finding out. The CLOSET QUEENS, although "painfully aware of their homosexual orientations" (129), turned to the restrooms because they feared exposure, arrest, or stigmatization for open participation in the gay subculture. Humphreys also suspected that they preferred teenage boys as sex partners.

Sociocultural sexual identity, as conceived by Humphreys, comprised two elements: (1) the individual's role as a participant in restroom sex and (2) his social network outside the restrooms. This conception was based on the implicit assumption that the individual walked into the restroom already stamped with a biological or psychological sexual identity. While he might exchange one role for another, it was still possible for him to retain his original identity. Humphrey's conception of sexual identity precluded any meaningful exploration of the individual's motives for engaging in restroom sex. In fact, Rainwater noted this shortcoming in his foreword to Humphreys' book:

> This study does not seek to analyze in any detail the personal significance of the participants or their homosexual behavior. It says little about why they engage, what role it plays in their inner psychic life or in the maintenance of ego identity. This aspect of the social psychology of homosexuality represents an important area for future research. (xiv)

In place of the exploration of personal motives, Humphreys substituted moral judgment in assessing restroom behavior. He decried the hypocrisy of the "covert deviant" who hid behind a "refulgent respectability" and a "breastplate of righteousness" (134-135). Humphreys sermonized:

> In donning the breastplate of righteousness, the covert deviant assumes a protective shield of super propriety. His armor has a particularly shiny quality, a refulgence, which tends to blind the audience to certain of his practices. To others in his everyday world, he is not only normal but righteous—an exemplar of good behavior and right thinking. However much the covert participant may be reacting to guilt in erecting this defensive barrier, he is also engaging in a performance that is part and parcel of his being. (135)

Humphreys conjectured about the domestic situations of married men which prompted them to engage in restroom sex. Sometimes he viewed their behavior as remarkable, exciting sexual exploits while, at other times, he portrayed their lives as barren and duplicitous. Restroom sex, he believed, was more exciting than masturbation because it was a personal encounter, a game, a risky adventure. It also combined detached excitement with convenience:

> What the covert deviant needs is a sexual machine—collapsible to hip-pocket size, silent in operation—plus the excitement of a risk-taking encounter. In tearoom sex he has the closest thing to such a device. This encounter functions, for the sex market, as does the automat for the culinary, providing a low-cost, impersonal, democratic means of commodity distribution. (1970: 154)

All of these encounters were also viewed by Humphreys as avoiding the integration of sex and commitment. Yet he recognized that sex without love met with special condemnation in Western society which required that "a respectable level of romantic intent has been reached" (60) as a necessary prelude to sexual involvement.

Humphreys' ethnography of restroom sex made several contributions to the detoxication of the homosexual identity. The elaborate rituals of encounter he believed provided considerable assurance that the uninterested or unwary restroom visitor would not be recruited into homosexual relationships or surprised or shocked by accidental observation of homosexual acts. The participants were presented as much more likely to be menaced by teenagers, particularly the toughs or blackmailers, than the teenagers were to be seduced or molested. The major risk for participants was that of arrest. According to Humphreys there was little chance of the participants being infected by sexually transmitted diseases.

By implying that marital sex had limitations, Humphreys unintentionally contributed to the toxication of the heterosexual identity. With the exception of the married ambisexuals, Humphreys believed marriages fell short of providing sexual gratification for many husbands. Severely limited by "religious teachings" (115), their sexual contact with wives was infrequent. If the old bordellos had survived, Humphreys believed that many married men would have turned to them for cheap, quick, and anonymous sex. These men "did not seek homosexual conduct as such; rather, they want a form of orgasm-producing action that is less lonely than masturbation and less involving than a love relationship" (115). Even the homosexual "marriages" were viewed by Humphreys with some cynicism: the restroom participants he classified as "gay" were often men who used the anonymity of the restrooms to conceal their sexual infidelity from partners.

By the mid-twentieth century, the ideas of the biological and psychological sexual identities were recast as a sociocultural sexual identity. This transition was made possible by the earlier anthropological research which had asserted that wide variations in human sexual expression were attributable to what particular cultures or societies fostered and allowed. The Kinsey group also played a major role in this transition by reporting that sexual variations, which anthropologists believed existed in most primitive societies, were ubiquitous at all social levels in the United States.

Within the ethnographic research the homosexual sociocultural identity was defined in a two-pronged effort. First, on the psychological level, the link between homosexuality and psychopathology was weakened when, for example, Hooker and Schofield identified groups of well-adjusted homosexual males. Second, on the sociological level, ethnographers described and classified homosexuals by observing where they lived and how they socialized. The change in methodology, from the analytical couch to field observation, reflected a considerable metamorphosis in the conception of the homosexual identity. The psychological methodology was based on the belief that one could know about homosexual relationships by listening to homosexual patients describe their subjective states and conflicts. The premise of the new methodology was that one could only understand homosexual relationships by observing homosexuals in their own social milieu. Once the link between the homosexual identity and psychopathology was weakened, the discourse on sexual identity moved away from the investigation of the mental life of individual homosexuals and devoted full attention to the study of their existence as a sociocultural group.

Remnants of the biological psychological identities were retained in the construction of the sociocultural sexual identity so that it represented more a merging than a replacement. It remained a biological identity, a label for individuals who had sexual relationships with members of their own sex. It retained its biological origins as a basic mammalian and human capacity. Although mostly viewed as acquired rather than inherited, the sociocultural sexual identity was still a fixed psychological identity.

The absorption of the biological and psychological into the sociocultural identity made it possible for the social theorists to view sexual identity as a given and heterosexuals and homosexuals as social units. How the units fitted into the social fabric became the focal point of inquiry. It also freed the investigator from the necessity of pondering the origins of homosexuality or, for that matter, heterosexuality.

The sociocultural sexual identity, as conceived in the ethnographic studies, retained some elements of the psychological sexual identity. This can be seen most clearly in the postulations of Cory, Hoffman, and Hooker, and, to some extent, Hauser and Schofield. To varying degrees these writers subscribed to the etiological theories of sexual identity propounded in contemporary psychoanalytic theory. Because they believed that external, societal factors were preponderant in shaping the observable manifestations of sexual identity, however, their conceptions were more sociocultural than psychological.

Their idea of a "psycho-social" sexual identity served as a transition to the more refined sociocultural versions that were to emerge in the scientific discourse. The foundations for a sociocultural sexual identity, free of both a biological and psychological past, were laid in the work of the other ethnographers, Leznoff and Westley, Reiss, Sonenschein, and Humphreys.

The relative importance the ethnologists attributed to the psychological aspects of sexual identity shaped their views of sexual relationships. This can be seen in the contrasting portrayals of homosexual relationships offered by Hoffman and Sonenschein, both published in the same year. Hoffman conceived homosexual relationships as pervaded by sexual motivation and fantasy, while Sonenschein saw some relationships as more sexual than others and some as entirely nonsexual. Hoffman believed that homosexual relationships were doomed to failure because both psychosexual development and social hostility undermined them. Sonenschein viewed some types of relationships as more lasting and, presumably, more successful than others and believed that purely sexual relationships could evolve into socio-sexual or purely social liaisons.

The wide divergence in their conclusions can be attributed to differences in their governing assumptions about sexual identity. Sonenschein treated homosexuality as a purely sociocultural identity, an acquisition requiring no etiological explanation. He was able, therefore, to note the different types of social and sexual relationships that individuals who took on this identity were able to construct. For Sonenschein the homosexual was an actor who could play in many different interpersonal scenarios, some of which were more enduring than others. Hoffman, however, viewed homosexuality as both a psychological and sociocultural identity, created out of the individual's psychosexual past and deeply flawed by the intrusion of socially hostile attitudes. For him the homosexual was the victim of psychological and social forces over which he had no control, a man condemned to play his role in a bitter drama to its tragic conclusion. For Hoffman it was a question of fixing the blame for a social problem. Sometimes he blamed the homosexual's family, particularly his mother; sometimes he pointed an accusing finger at the homosexual himself, berating his cosmetic existence, his sexual monomania, and his flight from intimacy; mostly he blamed society for its fear and hatred of homosexuality and the insuperable barriers it erected against the possibility of two men finding emotional solace and contentment in a relationship with each other.

To understand homosexuals as sociocultural units it was necessary to examine their relationships with each other. This exploration was based on the assumption that homosexuals, ay and large, were capable of accurate recognition of each other: it took one to know another. The public knew only those homosexual males given to feminine extravagance. The

assumption of an interlocking awareness within the homosexual subculture presumably provided homosexuals the prescience for selecting
those individuals who would be likely partners. Much of the
ethnography of the period, as in Sonenschein's study, focused on
homosexual relationships as friendship networks and permanent or
impermanent pairs.

The ethnographers eventually arrived at some common judgments
about homosexuality as a social and cultural amalgam. The basic adhesive
that tied and kept homosexuals together was their sexual interest and
involvement with members of their own sex. The ancient stereotype that
all that homosexuals could do together was have sex was dispelled by the
description of relationships that were entirely nonsexual. Sex, however, if
only in the form of romantic fantasy and the steady outpouring of gossip,
was still viewed as the adhesive of homosexual society.

Taking their cue from the anthropologists, ethnographers of
homosexuality described the subculture as they would have some
primitive, exotic society. They portrayed the shadowy ambience of bars,
baths, streets, and restrooms, the mannerisms of speech, posture,
gesture, and movement, the dress and general physical appearance, the
cruising for sex partners and the search for lovers, hoping to extract from
this mélange what was uniquely "gay."[40]

As the social terrain of the homosexual identity was charted in
greater and greater detail, its biological and psychological character
seemed to recede further and further into the background. Apart from
noting that sexual partners can be alternately insertors and insertees,
itself part of the larger effort to defend homosexual males against the
stereotype of effeminacy and passivity, little was revealed about the
sexual treatment of partners afforded each other in their relationships.
To the extent that the sexual was associated with the psychological and

---

[40] There were more ethnographies than those we have reviewed, for example:
Achilles, Nancy (1967). The Development of the Homosexual Bar As An
Institution. In J. H. Gagnon and W. Simon, Eds. *Sexual Deviance*. New York:
Harper and Row, 228-244; and Giallombardo, Rose (1966). *Society of Women: A
Study of Women's Prisons*. New York: Wiley. In 1974, Richard Troiden
published Homosexual Encounters in a Highway Rest Stop. In E. Goode and
R. Troiden, Eds., *Sexual Deviance and Sexual Deviants*. New York: William
Morrow, 211-228; and Carol B. Warren's *Identity and Community in the Gay
World* (New York: John Wiley) also appeared. More have been published since
then. For example, Kenneth E. Read's 1980 *Other Voices: The Style of a Male
Homosexual Tavern*. Novato, CA: Chandler and Sharp.

the psychological with the pathological, sexual conduct was largely jettisoned in the construction of the homosexual sociocultural identity.

The ethnographers seemed to have mixed reactions to what they uncovered in their examination of the homosexual subculture. At one level they appeared fascinated with the extravagances of an all-male society. As social outcasts the inhabitants of the homosexual demimonde were unfettered in their relationships by the normative restriction of conventional society. The ethnographers believed that the subculture was created by homosexuals to express their deviancy in settings that avoided the social sanctions against homosexuality. Still, they did not always agree that immersion in the subculture was in the best interest of the individual. At times it appeared that those individuals who were more solidly homosexual in identity were the better adjusted. Hooker, for example, looked for well-adjusted respondents in a political group dedicated to winning social tolerance for homosexuality. Schofield asserted that those men who were most thoroughly homosexual in identity were least likely to have problems of adjustment. Like the post-Freudians, however, most ethnographers viewed immersion in the homosexual subculture with skepticism. They believed that it was ruled by sexual preoccupations, excluded women, and isolated individuals from the culturally richer heterosexual society.

The creation of the homosexual sociocultural identity hardly left the heterosexual identity completely intact because they were both products of the same discourse. It too became sociocultural, a "straight" as opposed to a "gay" identity. The ideal form of heterosexual relationship, however, seemed harder and harder to find. In the study by the Gebhard group, some forms of heterosexual relationships were described as abusive, coercive, and intrusive. As Cory, Hauser, Humphreys, and Schofield revealed, a heterosexual marriage was no guarantee of the partners' sexual identity being solidly heterosexual. Schofield believed that the pedophiliacs were more heterosexual than homosexual. Hooker had some difficulty locating "thoroughgoing" heterosexual males as research subjects. The heterosexual "peers" in Reiss's study earned significant portions of their income from indisputably homosexual activity. Promiscuity, as scornfully viewed by Schofield, was both a heterosexual and homosexual problem. Hauser believed that heterosexuals as well as homosexuals needed instruction on the qualitative differences between lustful and loving sexual relationships. One can well conclude that the detoxication of the homosexual identity was not achieved without adding a noticeable tarnish to the heterosexual identity.

The ethnographic approach to the discourse on sexual identity embodied ingredients of the three cosmological conceptions of sexual relationships. The polytheistic conception survived in the descriptions of the homosexual subculture, which sometimes betrayed envy and relish for its racy and adventurous sexual peccadillos and unembarrassed devotion to youth and beauty. Most ethnographic descriptions of the homosexual subculture assumed that sexual encounters, anonymous, transient, and numerous, were the glue that held it together. The metaphor of "sexual marketplace" implied that it trafficked in sexual goods that were exchanged among strangers with no prior or future relationships. Cruising, one-night stands, prostitution, and tearoom sex were polytheistic strands woven into the fabric of the homosexual subculture.

These remnants of polytheism, however, combined with a basic adherence to the monotheistic view of sexual relationships in the ethnographic reports. Whether the individual was heterosexual or homosexual, being paired and, more importantly, staying paired, was viewed as a happier and healthier state than being and staying single. Pairing implied the integration of love and sex and love implied a lasting relationship. Sex without love, they assumed, led to promiscuity, the *bête noire* of an all-male society, which could and did degenerate into rampant lustfulness. The implied preference of the ethnographers for stable coupledom was a clear endorsement of the monotheistic structuring of sexual relationships as a means of containing an otherwise ungovernable and socially disruptive libido sexualis.

The ethnographers of sexual identity presented themselves as investigators of sexual relationships, impartial observers implacably in search of truth. Their work in both theory and methodology, was conceived within the scientific cosmology. Hooker, for example, used a quasi-experimental design to obtain evidence that would rescue the homosexual identity from inevitable pathology. Hauser and Schofield gathered demographic data from which they constructed their sexual typologies. Humphreys played the role of the fascinated spectator watching a game of sexual sport. Yet they, along with the other ethnographers, under the aegis of science were conducting a moral discourse on the permissible structure of sexual relationships.

15 The Socially Constructed Identity: Symbolic Interactionism

The biological and psychological sexual identities concentrated on the individual as an isolated unit. The sociocultural sexual identity, as adumbrated in the anthropological, survey, and ethnographic studies, characterized the individual essentially as a reflection of a cultural or subcultural milieu. In the contributions of the sociological theory that were to follow, the sociocultural sexual identity was partially reconstructed by adding a subjective dimension to external, cultural factors. This reformulation came to be known as the socially constructed sexual identity. Although it contained remnants of the biological and psychological identities, it chiefly consisted of ingredients drawn from symbolic interactionist theory, including concepts of societal reaction to sexual deviance and stigma, the homosexual role, sexual scripts, "coming out" in the homosexual subculture, and sexual meaning as the shaper of sexual roles and sexual career.

One of the first contributions to this reformulation of the sociocultural sexual identity was a study by John Kitsuse of the reactions of college students to individuals whom they identified as homosexuals.[1] Kitsuse believed that the idea of social deviance had been used by earlier sociologists to classify and analyze deviant behavior but rarely had been applied to the study of societal reactions to deviance. Societal reactions, in his formulation, referred to a tripartite process in which (1) particular behavior was interpreted as deviant; (2) persons who so behaved were defined as a type of deviant, (e.g., criminals, drug addicts, or psychotics); and (3) the labeled persons were treated as deviants.

---

[1] Kitsuse, John I. (1962). Societal Reactions to Deviant Behavior: Problems of Theory and Method. *Social Problems 9*: 247-256. The report is based on seventy-five interviews with college men and women who described experiences in discovering that someone was homosexual. Subjects were asked about the first signs revealing that the other person was a homosexual, the situation, what in particular they noticed, and how they reacted to the discovery.

Each aspect of this process of societal reaction to homosexual behavior was studied by Kitsuse. Interpretations of behavior as homosexual were based on indirect evidence such as rumor, general reputation, or the reports of others. They were also based on direct observations such as noting a behavior "which everyone knows" (251) is a sign of homosexuality (e.g., bringing up the topic in casual conversation), the homosexual departing from "behavior-held-in-common" (251) (e.g., not dating someone of the opposite sex), or the homosexual making an overt sexual proposition. Defining the individual in question as a homosexual was "documented by retrospective interpretations" (253), in which the respondents reviewed past interactions with the suspect individual "searching for subtle cues and nuance of behavior" (253) as evidence.

Most interesting was how the individuals making the discoveries treated the homosexuals. Kitsuse grouped their reactions into four categories: (1) explicit disapproval and immediate withdrawal (e.g., in response to a clear proposition); (2) explicit disapproval and subsequent withdrawal (e.g., the individual accepts a ride with a person who identifies himself as a homosexual but later resists sexual contact); (3) implicit disapproval and partial withdrawal (e.g., "we can remain roommates but you go elsewhere to have sex with your partners"); and (4) no disapproval, with maintenance of the relationship (e.g., the "live and let live" attitude).

Kitsuse seemed surprised that none of the reactions involved violence, name-calling, or the filing of criminal charges. Their mildness was attributed to the high educational level of respondents. He believed the findings brought into question the supposition of societal reaction theory that there were "a set of specific behavioral prescriptions which will in fact be normatively supported, uniformly practiced, and socially enforced by more than a segment of the total population" (256). In modern society, he concluded, societal reactions were contingent on a variety of factors—situation, place, social and personal biography, and the activities of control agencies.

This study was based on the assumption that individuals had sociocultural sexual identities, either heterosexual or homosexual. Kitsuse assumed that the college students who acted as respondents were bona fide heterosexuals and that the encounters they described were with bona fide homosexuals. In focusing on the clues for detecting homosexuals, the study showed how sociological research perhaps unwittingly began to crystallize the norms for sexual relationships. The investigatory results also represented one of the early disappointments in the application of social deviance theory to the study of the homosexual identity in the discovery that the societal reactions against homosexuals were considerably more varied than theoretically expected.

A major theoretical effort to shift consideration of the homosexual identity from psychiatry, where it was conceived of as a psychological condition, to sociology, where it could be viewed as a social role, was made by Mary McIntosh.[2] McIntosh believed that viewing the homosexual identity as a psychological condition failed to explain why individuals who were not homosexual engaged in homosexual behavior, why those who were homosexuals sometimes engaged in heterosexual behavior, or why some homosexuals did not engage in homosexual behavior. The introduction by psychiatry of the notions of bisexuality, latent homosexuality, or pseudo-homosexuality, she believed, were not explanatory because they were usually defined as transition points between the only two possible identities—the heterosexual or the homosexual.

The idea of homosexuality as a psychological condition also acted as a process of social control for both heterosexuals and homosexuals. For the heterosexuals, "it helps to provide a clear-cut, publicized and recognizable threshold between permissible and impermissible behavior" (32). For the homosexual, the idea "appears to foreclose on the possibility of drifting back into normality and thus removes the element of anxious choice.... The deviancy can be seen as legitimate for him and he can continue in it without rejecting the norms of society" (Mcintosh, 1968/1981: 32-33).

As an alternative theory, McIntosh proposed the concept of the homosexual role, which was defined by the expectations of both heterosexuals and homosexuals. She implied that the expectations of the heterosexuals for homosexual males would probably be negative:

> He will be [seen as] effeminate in manner, personality, or preferred sexual activity, the expectation that sexuality will play a part of some kind in all his relations with other men, and the

---

[2] McIntosh, Mary (1968/1981). The Homosexual Role. *Social Problems* 15(2): 182-192. This article was reprinted in Plummer, K. (Ed.) (1981). *The Making of the Modern Homosexual*. Totowa, N J: Barnes & Noble, 30-44, with a postscript on a discussion involving Plummer, Weeks, and the author (44-49). The page references for quoted materials are to the reprinting. Although McIntosh was an English sociologist, the article appeared in *Social Problems*, a sociology journal published by the American-based Society for the Study of Social Problems, which was receptive to articles on homosexuality. McIntosh stated that "*Social Problems* was the main forum for labeling theory" (45).

expectation that he will be attracted to boys and very young men
and probably be willing to seduce them. (33)

Both homosexuals and heterosexuals would expect that "a
homosexual will be exclusively or predominantly homosexual in his
feelings and behavior" (33). Reviewing published anthropological and
historical evidence, McIntosh showed how the homosexual role was
conceived differently in various tribal societies and historical periods.
The development of the modern homosexual role she traced to early
eighteenth-century England.[3]

According to McIntosh's theory, the homosexual and, by implication,
the heterosexual roles, should shape sexual behavior so that homosexuals
as they age would engage in less heterosexual behavior and heterosexuals
as they age in less homosexual behavior. Utilizing data from the Kinsey
studies she noted that "proportionately more 'homosexuals' dabble in heterosexual activity than 'heterosexuals' dabble in homosexual activity"
(Mcintosh, 1968/1981: 40). The "dabbling" appeared to drop off as men in
both groups grew older. She also found that men more than women were
concentrated in an exclusively homosexual role. Because the male homosexual role was more thoroughly delineated than the female homosexual
role, McIntosh believed the greater exclusivity of male homosexuals was
confirming evidence that the existence of the role influenced behavior.

Her conceptualization of the homosexual role illustrated how sociologists, on the one hand, argued against the idea of the psychological
homosexual identity as a pathological condition while, on the other
hand, advancing the belief in a socially constructed sexual identity. Her
discussion of sexual "dabbling," however, although free of the judgment
of mental illness, strongly suggested that either a biological or psychological identity or, for that matter, the heterosexual identity pre-existed
in the early years of a man's sexual experience. In this formulation homosexual behavior and, by implication, heterosexual roles gradually
took control of sexual behavior so that it was brought in line with the
pre-existing sexual identity of the individual. Even her anthropological
and historical treatment of homosexuality strongly suggested that there

---

[3] This line of research was continued by Trumbach, Randolph (1977). London's
Sodomites: Homosexual Behavior and Western Culture in the Eighteenth
Century. *Journal of Social History* 11(1): 1-33; and by Bray (1982: 81-114).

was an underlying homosexual identity which all owed particular forms of expression in different societies.[4]

In short, she proposed the exchange of the psychological homosexual identity for the socially constructed sexual identity. Although this transfer allowed the detoxication of the homosexual identity, it left individuals who bore the sociocultural homosexual identity encapsulated by social expectations as they once had been by medical diagnosis.

The effort to reintroduce the individual into a reformulated concept of the sociocultural sexual identity was represented in the work of John Gagnon and William Simon.[5] The sociocultural perspective of Gagnon and Simon was developed in contradistinction to the psychosexual stance of the psychoanalysts and the behavioral approach of the Kinsey group. These earlier views of sexuality, they believed, were rooted in biological determinism. Both were based on the belief in a sex drive and in drive reduction as the primary motivation for sexual behavior:

---

[4] Jeffrey Weeks, in the postscript to the reprinted 1981 article suggested that her approach was "latent essentialism" (47).

[5] Our discussion of their views is based primarily on the following: W. Simon, W. and Gagnon, J. H. (1967). Homosexuality: The Formulation of a Sociological Perspective. *Journal of Health and Social Behavior 8*: 177-185; Gagnon and Simon (1973). *Sexual Conduct: The Social Sources of Human Sexuality.* Chicago: Aldine; Gagnon (1973). Scripts and the Coordination of Sexual Conduct. In J. K. Cole and R. Dienstbier, Eds., *Current Theory and Research and Research on Motivation: Nebraska Symposium on Motivation* 21: 27-59. Lincoln: University of Nebraska Press; Simon (1973). The Social, the Erotic, the Sensual: The Complexities of Sexual Scripts. In J. K. Cole and R. Dienstbier, Eds., *Current Theory and Research and Research on Motivation: Nebraska Symposium on Motivation* 21: 61-83. Lincoln: University of Nebraska Press; and Gagnon (1977). *Human Sexualities*. Glenview, Illinois: Scott, Foresman. Other major and collateral works are: Gagnon and Simon, Eds. (1967). *Sexual Deviance*. New York: Harper & Row and Gagnon and Simon (1970). *The Sexual Scene*. Chicago: Aldine. Both men received their graduate training at the University of Chicago, in the school of sociological thought known as symbolic interactionism. Both had been influenced by the work of Kenneth Burke: *A Rhetoric of Motives*. (Berkeley: University of California Press, 1969); and *Language as Symbolic Action* (Berkeley: University of California Press, 1966). They also had been research collaborators at the Alfred C. Kinsey Institute before the publication of *Sexual Conduct*. They collaborated on the pilot research in Chicago that led to the full-scale study by the Institute of Homosexual Men and Women in San Francisco. We have freely moved to and fro among these contributions, spread over a decade (1967-1977), because there was relatively little shift in their conceptualization of sexual identity.

> The Freudian and Kinseyian traditions share the prevailing
> image of the sexual drive as a basic biological mandate that
> presses against and must be controlled by the cultural and
> social matrix.... It presses for expression, and in the absence of
> controls, which exist either in laws and mores or in appropriate
> internalized repressions learned in early socialization, there
> will be outbreaks of "abnormal sexual activity. (1973: 11)

Gagnon and Simon believed that this view of human sexuality distorted the meaning of sex in two ways. It gave rise to a dramatic image of man as the noble savage who struggled against the restraints of civilization in order to achieve sexual gratification. It also attributed to sexuality a power and significance that promised more fulfillment than could ever be delivered. A sociocultural approach to sex, they believed, would demythologize sexuality and present it as a "simple and pleasant capacity." They wrote: "perhaps the last act of resistance to Big Brother and 1984 is properly an act of copulation—it can be allowed because it is of no danger to anyone" (Gagnon and Simon, 1973: 108).[6]

They aimed specific criticisms at the psychoanalytic depiction of sex and of homosexuality.[7] First of all they questioned its evidential basis. Psychoanalytic theory depended on adult memories of childhood which, in the post-Freudian era, were inevitably influenced by the "rhetoric of psychoanalysis" that "permeated the culture" (Simon & Gagnon, 1967: 178). For most people "the rehearsed past and real past become so intermixed that there is only the present" (178). Psychoanalysis used the language of adults to describe childhood sexuality from the point of view of the child. Children could not have viewed the acts and feelings of childhood in the adult sense.[8]

In the view of Gagnon and Simon, the child probably experienced apparently sexual behavior less dramatically and fearfully than adults because the child did not have access to adult language in which

---

[6] The community created by George Orwell in his novel *1984* was ruled by Big Brother who enforced, among many other prohibitions, an edict against sexual activity.

[7] The authors made no distinctions between earlier and later ruminations of Freud or between Freud and the post-Freudians, thus treating psychoanalysis as a monolithic doctrine.

[8] Although Jean Piaget's cognitive theories of development were not explicitly cited by Gagnon and Simon, criticisms of psychoanalytic theory and their own depiction of the stages of sexual development suggest that they were influenced by Piaget's work. See, for example, Gagnon and Simon, 1973, 100-102.

"overenriched" conceptions of sexual behavior resided (Gagnon and Simon, 1973: 16). In the psychoanalytic view, sex was the lurking motive behind all behavior and there was little appreciation of the possibility that the sexual could be used to express nonsexual intentions.[9]

There was even the suggestion that adults should recapture the sexual equanimity of childhood:

> Most of the time, sex is really a relatively docile beast, and it is only the rare individual who through the processes of self-invention or alienation from the normal course of socialization is prepared to risk occupation, present comfort, spouse and children, or the future for the chancy joys of sexual pleasure. (Gagnon and Simon, 1973: 104)

Finally, psychoanalysis tended to disembody human sexuality, linking it to ideas and psychic structures and divorcing it from people engaged in the acts and the social context of their performance.

These criticisms were also applied to the psychoanalytic theories of homosexuality. Because of its preoccupation with the sexual, psychoanalysis viewed homosexuality as a dominant trait of character, one which was acquired in childhood and shaped the individual's entire life. The various forms of homosexuality were explained by altering the childhood scenario. It was the fusion of sexual identity and personal identity that Gagnon challenged: "Just because people call themselves homosexual or queen or dyke does not mean that everything they have been, are, or will be is affected by that label" (1977: 237).

Gagnon and Simon also found wanting the Kinsey groups conceptualization of sexuality. If Freud had decorporealized sexuality so that it could be located only in the mental functions of the individual, the Kinsey group took the opposite thrust:

> Here we have sexual man in the decorticated state; the bodies arrange themselves, orgasm occurs, one counts it seeking a continuum of rates where normalcy is a function of location on a distribution scale. Once again our search for the natural sources of behavior, the meanings that actors attribute to their own behavior and that the society collectively organizes are left out. (Gagnon and Simon, 1973: 6)

---

[9] The authors occasionally endorsed the theories of Lionel Ovesey (1954) which repudiated the notion of "latent homosexuality" of men who were heterosexual and who substituted the idea of pseudo-homosexuality. They did this without indicating that Ovesey was a psychoanalyst.

They believed it was this strictly behavioral view of human sexuality that led the Kinsey group to construct the heterosexual-homosexual rating scale and to reject the idea of sexual identity. According to Gagnon, individuals do not view their sexuality as a point on a scale:

> [W]e do not experience ourselves or the world around us as a continuum, but rather as a series of discrete categories. People do label their behavior and themselves; they do not count up acts, but call themselves gay, straight, or bisexual, and the world around them offers them opportunities for sex depending on the label they present and on the scripts associated with it. People who think of themselves as gay may approach a specific sex act in one way; those who think of themselves as bisexual may approach the same act in another; male prostitutes may approach it in a third; and people at an orgy may approach it in still a fourth way. These differences in scripting for the same act will determine the meaning of the act in the personal history of the individual.[10] (1977: 262)

Gagnon and Simon proposed an alternative conceptualization of human sexuality which steered a course between the individualism of psychoanalysis and the behaviorism of the Kinsey group. The pivotal concept in their approach was the idea of sexual scripts. In their early work (Gagnon and Simon, 1973: 20-23, 292) these scripts were described as INTERPERSONAL, or shared beliefs of partners in sexual relationships, and INTRAPSYCHIC, or motivations that led to arousal and engagement in sexual activity. The scripts acted as gatekeepers, who released biological states, allowing them to be expressed in sexual activity. Without this mediational role of scripts, Gagnon and Simon believed that neither the biological states nor the situations alone would lead to sexual conduct.[11]

---

[10] One could argue that many people, besides not experiencing their lives as a continuum, also lack the passion of American social scientists for categorizing behavior, particularly sexual behavior.

[11] Gagnon and Simon preferred to use "conduct" instead of "behavior," apparently to avoid identification with the behaviorism of the Kinsey group. CONDUCT is more sociological in connotation while BEHAVIOR is more biological and psychological. Simon and Gagnon (1967: 183), following the definitional path laid down by Ernest Burgess, identified CONDUCT as behavior that was prescribed or assessed by the group while BEHAVIOR was simply observable performance. Sexual outlets fell or were assigned to a category of conduct because they occurred within socially prescriptive and judgmental contexts. (See Burgess, Ernest W. (1949). The Sociological Theory of Psychosexual

Sexual scripts, according to Gagnon (1973) were mental plans or schema individuals had for coordinating their conduct in particular sexual encounters. These scripts "name the actors, describe their qualities, indicate the motives for the behavior of the participants, and set the sequence of appropriate activities, both verbal and nonverbal, that should take place to conclude behavior successfully and allow transitions into new activities" (29). Gagnon identified additional characteristics of sexual scripts: (1) they were incomplete specifications for behavior in concrete situations, thus allowing for adaptability; (2) they provided guidance to actors without the actor's awareness that they were following the scripts; (3) they included sexual fantasy which could be invoked in situations lacking particular concrete elements; and (4) they contained the practical explanations that people made about the motives for their sexual behavior. Sexual scripts, in Gagnon's formulation, were learned in various "sociocultural and historical contexts" (38) and applied in others. Scripts, Gagnon emphasized, were not exact matches for concrete situations:

> The elements in the scripts do not exist in any one-to-one relation to elements in the concrete activities, and in this sense they are not a direct map of the concrete situation. It is this loose relationship between scripts and concrete behavior that make inferences about the meaning of concrete behavior so problematic and invalidates much of the cross-cultural and historical psychologizing. (39)

Although practical motives were variable ingredients of scripts, Gagnon held that "once the subsidiary skills are learned it is possible for the person to perform a concrete sexual repertoire with all the thoughtless grace of dancing a minuet" (58).

In his later work, Gagnon listed the characteristics of scripts. They were: (1) blueprints people carried in their heads for guiding, understanding, and remembering their sexual activity; (2) specifications of the whos, whats, whens, wheres, and whys of sexual activity; (3) more important than concrete sexual acts; (4) products of culture and history; (5) learned and applied in the process of growing up; and (6) rarely

---

Behavior. In Paul H. Hoch and Joseph Zubin, Eds., *Psychosexual Development in Health and Disease*. New York: Grune and Stratton, 227-243). The idea of sexual script was first addressed in Simon and Gagnon (1969). On Psychological Development. In D. A. Goslin, Ed., *Handbook of Socialization Theory and Research*. Chicago: Rand McNally, 733-752.

modified in any significant way by the individuals who followed them (1977: 6-19). Gagnon stated: "very few people have the desire, energy or persistence to create highly innovative or novel scripts" (1977: 6). It is clear that Gagnon and Simon assumed that the culture was the "author" of the scripts and the individual was the "actor." Although they recognized that some actors were more innovative than others, they believed that few became authors.

Individual awareness was another characteristic of scripts. The individual was sometimes presented as acting with full conscious awareness and rational purpose: "as we act, we think about what we are doing, the people we are doing it with.... We use scripts to choose courses of action, to check our behavior against our plans: (Gagnon, 1977: 6). At other times the individual was depicted as befuddled and vulnerable:

> [I]in any given society, at any given moment in its history, people become sexual in the same way they become everything else. Without much reflection, they pick up directions from their social environment.... Their critical choices are often made by going along and drifting. (2).[12]

Their description of sexual development contrasted sharply with that of psychoanalytic theory. Development was a social rather than organic process, in which individuals pieced together their sexuality out of socially defined and available outlets, objects, and attitudes. After infancy, there was not biological fixity in development. At every age the individual "assembled" or "reassembled" a sexual posture:

> The word assembly is used quite deliberately. It was selected to indicate the collage-like, constructed, put-together, indeed artificial character of human development and to oppose an imagery of the natural flowering of an organic process. (Gagnon and Simon, 1973: 100)

In their view the adolescent period (ages 11-18) was paramount for two reasons. Adolescents had to assemble the appropriate feminine or masculine roles and attitudes about physical sex as well as to integrate these attitudes with beliefs about love and marriage. By describing

---

[12] Because symbolic interactionists did not subscribe to the Freudian notion of the Unconscious, they could only present individuals as already possessing full "meaning" of their acts or as fortuitously being urged along the path toward full meaning.

learning in terms of *what* was learned and the order in which it was acquired, they circumvented the question of *how* learning occurred.

The approach of Gagnon and Simon to sexual identity predisposed them to search out which of the available societal and sexual norms apparently shaped the individual's sexual and nonsexual experience:

> The aims, then, of a sociological approach to homosexuality are to begin to define the factors—both individual and situational—that predispose a homosexual to follow one path against others; to spell out the contingencies that will shape the career that has been embarked upon; and to trace out the patterns of living both in their pedestrian and their seemingly exotic aspects. Only then will we begin to understand the homosexual. (1967: 185)

There were, they believed, as many ways of being homosexual as being heterosexual because both types of individuals encountered the same basic choices and crises in their lives. They contended that if one could look past the homosexual label and the sexual content of the homosexual life one would find that "homosexuals.... vary profoundly in the degree to which their homosexual commitment and its facilitation becomes the organizing principle of their lives" (Simon & Gagnon, 1967: 179).

By "homosexual commitment" Simon and Gagnon were apparently referring to individual ratings on the heterosexual-homosexual rating scale of males in the Kinsey study who had "extensive histories of homosexuality" (Simon & Gagnon, 1967: 180). They distinguished between those who were "exclusively homosexual" and the "mixed heterosexual and homosexual." They concluded that the more highly educated respondents within the mixed heterosexual-homosexual group had less trouble with the police and their families and in their occupations. Large proportions of homosexuals, regardless of commitment and educational attainment, engaged in casual sex with strangers, often "picked up" in public places. Simon and Gagnon believed that: "These data, then, suggest a depersonalized character, a driven or compulsive quality of sexual activity of many homosexuals, which cannot be reckoned as anything but extremely costly to them" (1967: 181). There was the faint suggestion that if homosexuals stayed in their own community, away from public restrooms and parks, that their sexual ardor would be appropriately dampened:

> "[T]he homosexual community] allows for the dilution of sexual desire by providing social gratification in ways that are not directly sexual. Consequently, the homosexual with access

to the community is more protected from impulsive sexual 'acting out'" (1967: 182).[13]

Their advice to social scientists was to spend less time worrying about sex and pay attention to the general problems of living faced by homosexuals and, for that matter, heterosexuals: earning a living and maintaining a residence and relations with family.

Gagnon and Simon compared the "life cycles" of heterosexuals and homosexuals. The cycles were punctuated by crises. The "coming out" of the homosexual male, a time when he recognized his identity as a homosexual, was parallel to the heterosexual "coming out," a time when coitus was pursued with great vigor. For the homosexual, it was also the period in which he "acted out" his femininity in a public manner, a "pseudo-feminine commitment" (Simon & Gagnon, 1967: 182) few retained. There was also the crisis of aging, difficult for both the heterosexual and homosexual in a "youth-oriented society" (182) but more troublesome for the homosexual who lacked the support of wife and children and who inhabited a community in which physical attractiveness was paramount.

There was the implication that departures from the social sex-role stereotypes in both childhood and adolescence could start the individual down the path of what was retrospectively recognized as homosexuality (Gagnon & Simon, 1973: 192-193; Gagnon, 1977: 242-244). Nonconforming adolescents noticed that they were different from their peers. They felt uncomfortable conforming to the sex-role stereotypes, the "heterosociality" and "heterosexuality" of the adolescent social life (Gagnon, 1977: 243). When they identified their homosexuality "the experience of being different, of being invisible or too visible, is profoundly demoralizing for many young people" (Gagnon, 1977: 241).

Gagnon and Simon believed that lesbians closely identified with feminine patterns in their sexual relationships. Lesbians, in their conception, were women first and lesbians second: "Almost all the women we interviewed saw themselves as women who wanted to become emotionally and sexually attached to another woman who would, in turn, respond to them as a woman" (Gagnon and Simon, 1973: 199). As a woman the lesbian did not view her body as an instrument for sexual

---

[13] The term "acting out" derives from psychoanalytic theory and designates the individual's expression in behavior of infantile impulses and fantasies which are stirred up in the process of therapy. It is often misapplied, as in this case, in describing general behavior viewed as impulsive or extravagant.

gratification. Her intimate relationships started on an emotional plane and only later became sexual. The lesbian, in their eyes, was not immune to the rhetoric of romantic love:

> Romantic love as a mass experience is an invention of the modern world. As such, it plays a peculiarly important role in stabilizing social life. This is particularly true for that form of love that embodies, and is partially expressed through, sexuality. Few people grow up in our society without an understanding of the desirability of love. Even fewer doubt that its absence represents a crucial personal impoverishment, and extremely few fail to respond to the rhetoric that emerges from it. The lesbian is no exception to this. (Gagnon and Simon, 1973: 208)

The social adjustment for the lesbian was more problematic than for her heterosexual counterpart. She had to earn her own living because there was no husband to support her. Her homosexual commitment could endanger or compete with her job. She had to find self-acceptance in a society that gave approval to women as wives and mothers. Finally, in the view of Gagnon and Simon, she had a greater need for a love relationship and this intensity of yearning could lead to greater frustration.

They argued that homosexuality was no more or less "unnatural" than heterosexuality because the basic source of all human sexuality was social rather than biological. The law was a source of suffering for homosexuals in their estimation: "The law is at the center of a good many of the male homosexual's dilemmas, because it converts an unchosen condition into a legal disability" (1973: 161). They dismissed the psychoanalytic doctrine that adult homosexuality could be traced to pathological relationships between children and parents as at least unverifiable and at most improbable.

Gagnon and Simon offered predictions for the sexual future. Males would have to surrender some of their assertiveness and absorption in their penises to gain emotional closeness with women and reprieve from the stoic demands of a flawless masculine image. Females, partly through marriage and divorce, would gain increased awareness of themselves as sexual beings. Individuals of both sexes would come to an earlier recognition of their sexual identities but this would be expressed only as erotic feeling until the ideology of "'sex is fun' or 'sex is good in itself' became more widespread" (Gagnon and Simon, 1973: 291). Although they stated that marriage was in trouble, in their vision the young would still search for romantic love and intense dyadic attachments, but sexuality, in itself, would become a less powerful force in people's lives:

> Sex will be experienced like eating—as important and indeed
> luxurious experience in some circumstances, but not the
> emotional center of experience. It cannot stand for fidelity and
> infidelity, probably its most common social connection today,
> nor can a woman's surrender of virginity be a major gift any
> longer. (Gagnon and Simon, 1973: 305)

Finally, the ideology of sex as private choice will be exercised by individuals chiefly to enhance their own happiness.

One of the earliest endorsements of the idea of a socially constructed sexual identity was provided in a study by Barry Dank on "coming out" in the homosexual subculture.[14] "Coming out," as defined by Dank, meant "identifying oneself as being homosexual" (181). This self-appraisal could occur without ever having engaged in an overtly homosexual act. Dank drew a distinction between sexual acts and sexual fantasies, suggesting that it was fantasy rather than the act that revealed sexual identity: "a male actor may have a sexual contact with a female, but fantasize the female as being another male or himself as being a female; in such a case he might view the act as being homosexual" (181n).[15]

Presumably, fantasy revealed sexual desire and, in his study of coming out, Dank emphasized desire because "it is quite possible for one to have

---

[14] Dank, Barry M. (1971). Coming out in the Gay World. *Psychiatry* 34: 180-197. The study was based on interviews with fifty-five "self-admitted homosexuals" (180), observations and conversations with many others, and a one-page questionnaire administered to 300 self-admitted homosexuals at a meeting of a homosexual organization. Interviewees, all of whom were males, were asked the age at which they first were aware of any desire or sexual feeling they had for persons of their own sex, the interval between the first desire and the decision that one was homosexual, and, most particularly, the social context in which the individual came out—through meeting self-admitted homosexuals, by meeting knowledgeable heterosexuals, or by reading about homosexuality. Presumably the questionnaire dealt with the same areas of interest as did the interview. Dank indicated that he presented himself "correctly as being a heterosexual who was interested in doing a study of homosexuals" (181).

[15] This illustration was followed by Stoller's name within parentheses, suggesting that the example or idea was Stoller's. The author had been a member of the colloquium on gender identity led by Stoller at the University of California, Los Angeles.

homosexual desires, fight against those desires, and have no homosexual contacts of any type for an extensive period of time" (182n).[16]

Some people, either unaware of their desires or resisting the necessity to decide they are homosexuals, marry and beget children. In Dank's view such individuals were homosexuals who inadvertently or deceptively had become parents. Such crossing over from one sexual identity to another, according to Dank, was not uncommon.

What Dank intended to study was the social circumstances under which males, who presumably once viewed themselves as heterosexual in identity, began to view themselves as homosexual.[17] This change in sexual identity could occur without engaging in homosexual behavior, in a variety of social contexts, and with frequent exposure, which allowed the concentration of knowledge of homosexuals and homosexuality. The usual contexts, as identified by Dank, involved having an affair with another man, attending gay parties, and frequenting parks, restrooms, and gay bars. None of these contexts "forced" his respondents to come out, as would have been the case had they been "publicly labeled" by being arrested or dismissed from employment.

The change from a heterosexual to a homosexual identity, according to Dank, was a two-step cognitive process. First, the individual learned of the existence of the social category "homosexual." Then he fitted himself into the category after he had cleansed it of the "negative stereotype of the homosexual held by most heterosexuals" (189). The heterosexual stereotype, in Dank's words, depicted homosexual males as "dirty old men, perverts, Communists, and so on" (197).

This change was not without its paradox. On the one hand, the homosexual male had to resign himself to a deviant status and adjust to societal reactions to those occupying that status while, on the other hand, denying that being a homosexual made him a deviant. Dank believed that

---

[16] As the findings were reported (182n), more individuals engaged in homosexual acts before than after "desire," which leaves the reader ignorant or confused regarding the motivation for the acts.

[17] This probably overstates Dank's position. In the excerpts of the interview protocols published in the article, it is not clear whether respondents once believed they were heterosexuals or simply did *not* believe they were homosexuals. Whereas Dank treated "admitting to oneself" as the decisive change in identity, the excerpted protocols suggest that the self-admission (as self-recognition) of homosexuality came early in the lives of his male respondents and the decisive change occurred when they decided to convert their awareness of their homosexuality into an exclusive homosexual identity.

coming out resolved the dilemma for the homosexual by giving him access to the positive gay image supplied by the homosexual community.

Dank addressed the question of why some homosexuals came out while others did not. He believed the crucial factor was access to knowledge about homosexuals that challenged and disproved the negative stereotype. This knowledge, supplied by gay organizations and disseminated through the gay press and the public media, presented "homosexuality-as-a-way-of-life" (195). Although Dank did not describe the ingredients of the homosexual lifestyle, he assumed that it would not lead to "the creation of a gay community in which one's sex life ... became less fragmented from the rest of one's social life" (195). Those homosexuals who did not come out, men he called "closet queens" (190-192), were those who viewed "homosexuality-as-mental-illness" (195). As depicted by Dank the closet queens were the proverbial unhappy homosexuals:

> In a sense the closet queen represents society's ideal homosexual, for the closet queen accepts the societal stereotype of the homosexual and feels guilt because he does the same sort of things that homosexuals do, yet believes he is really different from homosexuals in some significant way. This inability of the closet queen to see himself in other homosexuals prevents him from placing himself in the cognitive category of homosexual, and he will not come out until some new information is given to him about homosexuals which permits him to say, "there are homosexuals like myself" or "I am very much like them." (193)

Dank claimed that he had contact only with "ex-closet queens" (193), who always reported that they were happier after they had come out, only regretting that they had not done so earlier.

Although contributing to the notion of a socially constructed sexual identity, Dank appeared to believe that there was a pre-existing psychological sexual identity. He used intrapsychic concepts such as sexual fantasy and desire as a test of the individual's sexual identity. Behavior in itself was not a criterion for establishing sexual identity because the individual could engage in heterosexual acts and still be homosexual in identity. To cast an identity in terms of "fantasy" and "desire" also suggested a psychological identity because these are mental and emotional states. The theoretical basis of the notions of sexual fantasy and desire was not identified so that they appear as pieces of dismembered psychoanalytic theory.

His description of "closet queens" also revealed his assumption that there was a psychological homosexual identity which was being denied.

They were presented as tortured by guilt for behaving like but not identifying themselves as homosexuals. Denial appears to have been borrowed directly from the arsenal of psychoanalytic defense mechanisms.

The social contexts that he believed precipitated coming out provided homosexuals their sociocultural sexual identity. Coming out, in Dank's conception, was apparently motivated by the need for a supportive social context in which to express and define a homosexual identity. Because no homosexual would refuse a supportive environment if one were available, the concept of coming out resolved a dilemma only for the sociologists who theoretically required the homosexual to be viewed as a social deviant and who viewed the locus of change as being outside the individual. Coming out was not so much a psychological process of becoming a homosexual but the sociological process of being identified as a homosexual.

The theoretical underpinnings of the symbolic interactionism employed by Gagnon and Simon to develop a general conception of human sexuality were explicitly stated and amplified by Kenneth Plummer, an English sociologist.[18] In the interactionist approach to sexuality, as articulated by

---

[18] Plummer, Kenneth (1975). *Sexual Stigma: An Interactionist Account*. London: Routledge and Kegan Paul. The foundation of symbolic interactionism, according to Plummer, was laid by George Herbert Mead (e.g., *Mind, Self, and Society: From the Standpoint of a Social Behaviorist*. Chicago: Chicago University Press, 1934) and Herbert Blumer (*Symbolic Interactionism: Perspective and Method*. Englewood Cliffs, NJ: Prentice-Hall, 1969). There were two basic concepts in symbolic interactionism: SELF and ROLE. Regarding the SELF, there were some basic tenets: (1) The individual was capable of becoming an object to itself. The self emerged out of social encounters particularly during childhood; (2) The self had two components, the "I" and the "Me." As the more active of the two parts, the "I" formulated intentions and initiated actions. The "Me," as the more passive part, anticipated the reactions of others to the behavior of the "I"; (3) The basic meaning of social life was to be found in the part played by others in influencing and shaping an individual's actions. ROLE was the other important concept, an idea sociologists borrowed from dramaturgy. Plummer explained the interactionist view of role by comparing it with the view of structural sociology. The structural school described roles as a predetermined set of expectations for the behavior of the individual occupying a certain social position, such as professor or physician. It depicted social life as a classical drama in which actors were fully versed in their parts. Plummer believed the structural conception of roles had two weaknesses: (1) It assumed there was a pre-existing consensus of expectations where none could be found; and (2) It made the idea of role "a mechanical, overdetermined, overscripted, static conception" (18). He concluded, "No 'role structures' pre-

Plummer, sexual acts and partners were conceived as social objects whose meanings were derived from the group to which the individual belonged. In this view, while physiology made sexual activity possible, sexual intentions and roles were shaped by sexual meaning. These meanings were bestowed on sexual biology through social encounters and language: "Nothing is sexual but naming it makes it so. Sexuality is a social construction learnt in interactions with others" (Plummer, 1975: 30).

A range of meanings became attached to sexual activity: There was the UTILITARIAN meaning of procreation. EROTIC meanings emerged when the idea of pleasure was attached to tactile and visual sensations. ROMANTIC meanings, either publicly or secretly held, were based on the idea of loving one other person. GENDER meanings were connected to beliefs about being female or male. SYMBOLIC meanings linked sexuality to religion, worship, and lurking Freudian motives.

Sexual meanings emerged from two types of realities: the objective and the intersubjective. OBJECTIVE realities were the product of centuries of encounters. They provided both constraints and cues for sexual activity. The sources of objective realities could be discovered through historical analysis. INTERSUBJECTIVE realities consisted of the meanings created in everyday encounters. The two types of realities were interactive: the meanings that emerged from objective realities provided constraints and cues for the intersubjective realities, which, in turn, furnished modified meanings for objective realities:

> The contemporary sexual reality, for example, contains divergent strands from the Judeo-Christian tradition, evangelical religions, jurisprudence, laws, power struggles over economic and status factors, philosophical debates, organizational dilemmas, public-opinion polls, moral crusades, medical theories, and psychiatric theories, not to mention large chunks of everyday interaction over hundreds of years. It would be nice to posit in such strands a unity, a logic, a system, but it is at least as reasonable to see the

---

exist that men simply 'fit into' like some huge waxwork effigy" (18). In symbolic interactionism, roles were conceived as dramatic improvisations: "The focus of the interactionist perspective on roles starts out from the notion of men in everyday life busily constructing images of how they expect others to act in given positions (role-taking), evolving notions of how they themselves expect to act in a given position (role-making), and also imaginatively viewing themselves as they like to think of themselves being and acting in a given position (role identity)" (18).

contemporary sexual reality that partially constrains its members as not having any underlying order. (Plummer, 1975: 53)

In Plummer's theory, the individual was not born but was made sexual:

> Man is born with a varying biological capacity for "sexual experience," including the physiological capacity to respond to sufficient stimulus.... While there may be biological constraints, he is essentially characterized by plasticity and "world-openness...." Man is born into an historically created "objective reality," which contains a socially constructed series of "sexual" meanings. The process of becoming sexual is ... a learning process [occurring through identification, conditioning, or imprinting]. It is not simply the unfolding of biological tendencies, though these may act as constraints. [Whatever the mode of learning] ... an interactional account is required to show how such [sexual] experiences are interpreted as sexual. (1975: 56)

There were two basic tenets of interactionist theory as Plummer applied it to sexual identity. In the first place, the individual was viewed as inherently asexual; sexuality was a mental construction of the individual and society. In addition, personality was viewed as a process of becoming rather than as a stabilized entity. In Plummer's terminology, it was more precise to refer to "personality drift" (131), a striving for structure that never arrived. The major thrust of Plummer's application of symbolic interactionism was to the study of sexual deviancy and stigma, in his words "becoming sexually different" (56).[19]

---

[19] As in the case of the idea of role, Plummer drew a distinction between the structural and interactionist concept of deviancy. In structural sociology, deviancy was a classification of particular acts that led to negative reactions on the part of control agencies. The deviants, so to speak, were those judged as malefactors. The symbolic interactionists took the opposite route (e.g., Becker, Howard S. (1963). *Outsiders: Studies in the Sociology of Deviancy*. New York: MacMillan; and Lemert, E. M. (1967). *Human Deviance, Social Problems and Social Control*. Englewood Cliffs, NJ: Prentice-Hall). They believed that "societal reactions" created deviancy by applying rules and sanctions to an "offender." Important in this process of creating deviancy was the individual's "self-reaction" and "self-labeling" (Plummer, 1975: 22). In this way individuals could come to think of themselves as deviant even in the absence of official designation: "[in] sexual labeling it is not official labeling that matters but rather the self-labeling that takes its cues from an externalized, reified stigma

Sexual deviance referred to forms of sexual activity that violated norms and which both society and the individual viewed as stigmatized. Within this conceptualization, homosexuality was a form of sexual deviance. From the individual perspective, sexual deviance originated as a sense of sexual "differentness" (a primary deviation) and later became the core around which the individual organized his life (secondary deviance). From the social angle "the more things are defined in a society as deviant the more deviance that society will have, and when a given experience is defined as deviant, it develops the consequences of deviancy" (Plummer, 1975: 74).

Applying the interactionist principle that sexuality is situationally defined, Plummer developed a new typology of the homosexual identity. His categories were based on whether the identity stemmed from primary or secondary deviance and on the degree of importance it had for the individual's life (1975: 98-100). CASUAL HOMOSEXUALITY referred to fleeting encounters occurring in fact or fantasy which had little significance for the actors (e.g., school-boys' mutual masturbation). PERSONALIZED HOMOSEXUALITY became a central concern for the individual who, however, was isolated from other homosexuals (e.g., the patient in psychotherapy). HOMOSEXUALITY AS SITUATIONAL ACTIVITY included those experiences in which individuals engaged in homosexual activity but did not make it pivotal to their lives (e.g., participants in restroom sex). Finally, there was HOMOSEXUALITY AS A WAY OF LIFE, a sociocultural identity for the individual who accordingly participated in

---

label" (23). Plummer also distinguished between "situational deviance," conduct that "emerges as deviant in interpersonal encounters" (26) and "societal deviance ... the conduct described as deviant in the public, abstract and reified value systems which all societies must have" (26). There were publicly held norms that remained absolute, but they too were the product of social process rather than givens. In becoming a deviant the individual had to move from *primary deviation*, which had its source in biology, psychology, and culture, to *secondary deviation*, which was a product of the responses people made to problems created by societal reaction to their primary deviance. Sociologists of the period described strategies they believed individuals used in coping with the problems created by deviance, most notably Erving Goffman's 1963 *Stigmas: Notes on the Management of Spoiled Identity*. (Englewood Cliffs, NJ: Prentice-Hall), in which he wrote about "defensive cowering," "hostile bravado," and "passing." Goffman also distinguished "discredited" and "discreditable" identities. In the former the deviancy was immediately apparent while in the latter it was possible for the individual to manage "information about his failing" (42).

both the formal institutions, such as bars and baths, and the friendship cliques of the homosexual subculture.

Plummer believed that the homosexual identity in western culture was created by social intolerance: "the perceived hostility of the societal reactions that surround it" (1975: 6). To study societal reactions it was necessary to conduct research "which depicts the ways in which members actually perceive, respond to and reflect upon homosexuality in face-to-face encounters" (113). Most survey studies of attitudes toward homosexuality, he believed, had "an oversimplified notion of attitude [and] most of them fail to take into account the discrepancy that is likely to arise between words, deeds, and feelings" (113). The studies tapped what people said but reflected imperfectly what they did and felt. As the results of these surveys were fed back to society and homosexuals they conveyed a monolithic picture of hostility:

> Indeed, homosexuals may come to see what was originally an uncrystallized, contradictory, ambiguous, ever-changing, weakly focused and highly variable individual reaction towards homosexuality as a unanimous, stable, well-defined, consistent and powerfully strong form of hostility. They may even come to perceive hostility where none exists. (113)

There were three levels of reaction to the homosexual identity, as conceived by Plummer: the SOCIETAL, the INDIVIDUAL, and the HOMO-SEXUAL SUBCULTURAL. At the societal level, hostility to homosexuality was expressed in a two-step process. First, the homosexual identity was perceived as a threat to the established order, in particular, to sex-role stereotypes, family, and reproductive sexuality. Second, the existence of the homosexual identity was explained in ways that could assimilate it to conventional society. This could be done by denying its existence or dismissing it as a rare peculiarity.

At the individual level, the reaction to homosexuality was embodied in "the homosexual career" (Plummer, 1975: 122). The concept of "career" derived from the interactionist conception of development, which was seen as "a life-long activity involving the interaction of self with others, while personalities and conditions are transformed into 'roles' strung together by the slender thread of memory and entailing various degrees of commitment" (122). In Plummer's formulation, any individual could become homosexual because all that was required was the construction of the necessary sexual meanings through interaction with others. The crucial element was the attitudes of significant others such as parents, siblings, peers, and teachers.

The homosexual career, as outlined by Plummer, consisted of four "stages or sequences of socialization" (134). It was a process whereby the individual moved from seeing himself as "asexual" to believing he was homosexual.[20] Throughout the process, the homosexual identity acquired at one stage was carried over to the next stage. Each stage required its own efforts at problem-solving. However, the stages were not clearly delineated in the mind of individuals evolving a homosexual identity. Rather, the stages appeared as "turning points" at which the homosexual acted in a "semi-slumbering mood" (174).

The first stage Plummer called SENSITIZATION, during which the individual came to perceive himself as potentially homosexual. Sensitization could result from: (1) some fortuitous sexual or emotional involvement with another male, an experience culturally defined as homosexual; (2) "gender confusion" which became defined by the individual as "sexual differentness"; or (3) sexual labeling (e.g., "sissy") by adults or peers, especially during adolescence. SIGNIFICATION AND DISORIENTATION was the second stage. During this period the homosexual experiences acquired meaning through their association with guilt, secrecy, and solitariness. Thus, individual reactions were constructed out of societal reactions.

COMING OUT was the third stage, a time when the homosexual explored the homosexual subculture.[21] At this point in a sexual career the individual surrendered the secrecy of the earlier stages and exposed himself to the homosexual role-models and belief systems that legitimated his homosexual identity. The culminating stage was the stabilization of homosexuality. At this point the individual experienced the advantages of his sexual identity: "Unwillingness to leave the homosexual role arises not least because of the intrinsic delights of being homosexual: the acts of falling, making, and being 'in love' with a member of the same sex can be both pleasurable and satisfying" (151-152). The individual who embarked on a homosexual career may also reach a point of no return. He was

---

[20] Plummer described the socialization of the male only, without references to a similar process for the female.

[21] Plummer stated (147) that he was following the definition of Simon and Gagnon (1967: 181) rather than that of Barry M. Dank (1971). Simon and Gagnon in fact stated two criteria for coming out: self-recognition of one's homosexual identity and involvement in the homosexual community. Dank believed that these were separable events because self-identification (181) "may or may not occur in a social context in which other gay people are present."

blocked from heterosexual experience as his homosexual experience became more engulfing. His access to willing females became difficult, and contemplation of heterosexual coitus disturbing.

Plummer's third level of reaction to the homosexual identity was the collective response of the homosexual subculture. To describe this level he used the ethnological literature of the preceding period, adding "my own direct observations of homosexual life in London between 1968 and 1970" (154). He distinguished between a "pull" theory and a "push" theory for explaining the emergence of the homosexual subculture. The pull theory held that it emerged because it provided solutions to problems uniquely faced by homosexuals, for example, finding friends and sex partners. The push theory emphasized hostile societal reactions as crystallizing a subculture and splitting it off from mainstream society. While the pull theory explained segregation, the push theory focused on societal rejection. Plummer recognized the plausibility of a third theory: the subculture was a product of homosexuality per se.[22]

Plummer believed this latter explanation was untenable because the homosexual subculture focused on problems of sexual identity, legitimacy, and guilt. If social intolerance were totally eliminated,

> it is plausible that subcultures would not even be necessary for the purpose of joining with mutual enthusiasts. For it is part of [my] argument ... that in a non-repressive society, homosexuality would most probably not take the exclusive form that it currently does—there may well be no 'homosexual condition,' only homosexual experiences available to everyone. (170-171)

Plummer did believe that the sexual future might be different from the past. As sexual mores changed, the process of becoming homosexual would be less salient and significant: "This may result in a decrease of polarization so that individuals come to see themselves as simultaneously occupying homosexual and heterosexual roles, with an accompanying decrease in rigid, exclusive norms of sexuality" (153).

The divisions in the sociological conceptions of sexual identity were revealed in a debate published in 1981 over the "homosexual role"

---

[22] In current parlance, this is the theory of the gay esthetic, the gay sensibility, or the gay personality. Dennis Altman referred to the "gay culture" (156), which he believed was a lifestyle and the esthetic products that it gave rise to. See Altman's 1982 *The Homosexualization of America and the Americanization of the Homosexual*. New York: St. Martin's Press.

among sociologists.[23] The homosexual role, as conceived by Erich Goode, was a set of social and behavioral expectations for those individuals who assumed the role. It was not created by the homosexual but by the society which viewed homosexuality as a form of deviancy, as it did prostitution and drug usage. The homosexual subculture was the product of the effort of homosexuals to "normalize" their behavior and generate a community of "like-minded practitioners." Goode's view, in the tradition of symbolic interactionism, assumed that there was an underlying lability in sexual identity which, of course, diminished as the individual met more and more of the expectations which comprised either the heterosexual or homosexual identity.

Becoming a homosexual, therefore, was a "socially influenced variable" (81) rather than a constant. It did not always occur at the same age or at an early age. Referring to his (and Troiden's) study on acquiring the "gay" identity," Goode stated:

> We were interested in the age at which our respondents suspected that they might be homosexual, identified their feelings as homosexual, defined themselves as homosexual, began associating with other homosexuals, and entered their first love relationship with another man. All of these dimensions were acquired or experienced at significantly different ages by members of different categories or social groups in our sample. For instance, the younger the respondent the earlier in his life he acquired or experienced all these dimensions. Heterosexually experienced gay men in our sample "became" homosexual (along these five dimensions) at a later age than our respondents without heterosexual experience. Highly educated respondents were later in "becoming" homosexual than less well-educated respondents. (1981b: 81)

He acknowledged that the men he studied reported that they "felt different" (1981b: 81) from their peers as young children but did not have a label to apply to this feeling: "it is not unreasonable to assume that a wide range of 'non-sexual behavior' which entails an 'outside'

---

[23] Goode, Erich (1981a). Comments on the Homosexual Role. *Journal of Sex Research* 17(1): 54-65; Whitam, Frederick L. (1981). A Reply to Goode on the Homosexual Role. *Journal of Sex Research* 17(1): 66-72; Omark, Richard C. (1981). Further Comment on the Homosexual Role: A Reply to Goode. *Journal of Sex Research* 17(1): 73-75; and Goode, Erich (1981b). The Homosexual Role: Rejoinder to Omark and Whitam. *Journal of Sex Research* 17(1): 76-83.

status would be particularly attractive to individuals who feel like 'outsiders' to begin with" (1981b: 81-82).

In defense of the concept of role, Goode compared female and male homosexuals. He noted that lesbian sexuality was expressed within relationships while male homosexuality was manifested as cruising and public sex. Also, lesbians became aware of their homosexuality later than males. These differences in homosexual females and males, he believed, reflected the content of male and female roles in our society: "homosexuals are males, or females, first and homosexual second — and that much of what they do in and out of bed is a function of the gender ideas they learn" (1981b: 82). Such differences, he concluded, illustrated the powerful influence of roles.

Frederick Whitam had several objections to the application of the idea of role and of deviance theory in general to the study of homosexuality. He held that homosexuality should be viewed as a sexual orientation rather than a role. It was certainly an orientation for persons classified as "fives" and "sixes" on the Kinsey heterosexual-homosexual rating scale:

> These persons do not choose their sexual orientation. While sexual orientation is not completely fixed ... it remains relatively so, as countless homosexuals who have spent years in therapy will attest. A small group — perhaps 5% — of such persons called homosexuals appear in all societies and so far as we know have always appeared. (67)

Although he identified the males he was discussing in terms of the Kinsey rating scale he held: "Homosexuality as a sexual orientation does not appear to be—as a conceptualized by Kinsey—merely a point on a sexual continuum, but appears to be related to nonsexual behaviors" (67). Whitam had in mind such behaviors as "the tendency [of homosexuals] toward entertainment and the arts" (68), including musical comedy. The homosexual subculture, therefore, was considerably more than "the superficial creation of the heterosexual world" (69). It was the product of the homosexual identity and its accompanying "complex cross-gender" (68) behavior.

Whitam believed there was evidence that "elements of homosexuality emerged at a very early age when it is unlikely that role and labeling are efficacious" (68). He summarized his position as follows:

> My view ... is that a small percentage of persons of homosexual orientation appear in all societies and all historical epochs, that sexual orientation, appearing very early, has important

biological components, that all societies produce homosexual subcultures which tend to have many of the same behavioral elements, and that these behavioral elements result in activities that are socially useful for the larger society. (71)

Whitam commented on the political implications of the belief in a fixed sexual "orientation" and gender identity. The opposing view "that homosexuality as an orientation is a superficial, learned, flexible aspect of one's personality feeds the primordial fears of the Anglo-Saxons that homosexuals are dangerous people and that homosexual orientations can be taught to others" (70). The belief in the homosexual orientation as an "immutable characteristic," he predicted, could win judicial rulings as favorable as those for other groups identified by fixed biological characteristics, such as blacks, other ethnic groups, women, and the handicapped.[24]

Richard Omark contended that Goode's view of the homosexual role did not include the fact that some males "clearly had a preference for sexual relationships with other males but ... did not have knowledge or contact with a gay community" (73). He also argued that Whitam failed to distinguish between homosexual object preference and gay identity when Whitam asserted that the gay identity could emerge without a gay community:

> Without contact with a gay community and the normative constraints involved in the performance of the homosexual role, one would predict that sexual preference and homosexual behavior would be extremely labile. With such contact with the gay community, the consequence for behavior is likely to be nearly exclusive same-sex contacts and decreased interest and opportunities for heterosexual contact. When an individual is congruent in terms of homosexual preference, gay identity, and homosexual behavior, there is little incentive to continue to question existentially if one "is" a homosexual. (74)

The symbolic interactionists were particularly adamant in their rejection of the idea of the psychological sexual identity. They were severely critical, for example, of the psychoanalytic account of sexual

---

[24] In his rejoinder Goode (1981b) expressed the opinion that for "anti-gays," "[s]aying some activity has congenital roots designates it as *even worse and even more worthy of punishment* than if it were freely chosen. Anti-gays would remove homosexuals from teaching positions *even if the condition' were congenital* .... Congeniality is simply an *affirmation of the depth of depravity* of the 'deviant'" (67).

development. Studious theoretical efforts were made to replace what they believed to be the static concepts of psychoanalysis with the "open-ended concepts of "encounter," "process," "role," and "career." Despite these efforts, there were striking similarities between the psychoanalytic and symbolic interactionist accounts of sexual development and identity.

In psychoanalytic perspectives the male child, for example, who did not meet all the requirements of the heterosexual identity would be a misfit, with varying degrees of conscious or unconscious awareness of his condition. The full meaning and consequences of his developmental failure would not be known by him until adolescence and adulthood. According to Plummer, the male launched his homosexual career in the stage called "primary deviation." The individual's awareness or sensitization to his "differentness" arose out of the misty confluence of biology, psyche, and culture, first described by psychoanalysis. Although symbolic interactionism temporarily relocated the time this deviation occurred, moving it from early childhood to adolescence, the resemblance to psychoanalysis is clear. Indeed, the chief area of sensitization identified by both psychoanalysis and symbolic interactionism, was the area of social sex-roles, the failure of the male child to adopt masculine, to the exclusion of feminine, traits (or roles).

In psychoanalytic theory the channeling of libido down the path of same-sex object choice was not easily reversible in adults because of the summative aspects of psychosexual development and the difficulty of decathecting eroticized objects. In symbolic interactionism, the move from primary to secondary deviancy was also not an easily reversible process so that the homosexual male (and, by implication, the heterosexual) was stuck with his adult sociocultural sexual identity. Reversal was difficult for many reasons: what was acquired at earlier stages of the sexual career was utilized in consolidating sexual identity at later stages; meanings and roles tended to solidify and exclude possibilities of acquiring new sexual identities; and the social context within which the identity was formed became constrictive and isolating. The possibility of exchanging a homosexual for a heterosexual identity was entertained chiefly by the post-Freudians who viewed the homosexual identity only as the twisted shadow of the heterosexual and removed the control of sexual relationships from the id and libido to the cognitive functions of the ego.[25]

---

[25] It may be useful to point out that, in their attacks on psychoanalysis, symbolic interactionists tended to treat it as a monolithic system of thought,

In post-Freudian psychoanalysis the psychological homosexual identity had two requirements: engagement (through fantasy or deed) in sexual activity with an individual of the same sex and gratification of basic emotional and sexual needs through this activity. In a similar vein, the symbolic interactionists distinguished between those individuals whose "commitment" to the homosexual identity was a central theme in their lives and those for whom it was an opportunistic or fortuitous experience. By adding this subjective element to an essentially experiential and situational analysis of the homosexual identity, the symbolic interactionists allied themselves with the idea of the psychological homosexual identity. In both theoretical frameworks the "meaning" the homosexual experience had for the individual was at least as essential as the experience itself.

The fact that symbolic interactionists preserved the notion of the psychological sexual identity was also revealed in Plummer's typology of homosexual experience. Those individuals who experienced "personalized homosexuality" or "homosexuality as a way of life" apparently were the "congenital" homosexuals of Krafft-Ebing or the "subject homoerotics" of Ferenczi. Those who engaged in homosexuality on a casual basis or as a "situated activity" resembled the lapsed heterosexuals, Ferenczi's "object homoerotics."[26]

Although symbolic interactionism hoped to render an account of sexual relationships that was less tempestuous and engulfing than that of psychoanalysis, it still resorted to the language of dramaturgy. Individuals became "actors" who had sexual "roles" or "careers" or followed sexual "scripts." Sexual development was marked by "turning points" or "crises," the type of disjunctures in the development of character and plot that are familiar in the theatre. There was more than a little Greek (if not oedipal) tragedy in symbolic interactionism: those who embarked on deviant sexual careers faced an inescapable fate—enmeshment in personal guilt, societal intolerance, and cultural isolation.

The heterosexual identity in symbolic interactionism was as solidified and immutable as the homosexual identity. This can be most clearly seen

---

ignoring the changes introduced by Freud in his own lifetime and the more radical departures of post-Freudian psychoanalysts, particularly those trained in the United States. In fact, there are striking parallels between the ideas of the symbolic interactionists and those of the post-Freudian analysts.

[26] All homosexuality in symbolic interactionism was situational so that the more "stable" forms had to be partly distinguished by the types of situations in which they were expressed.

in the description of male prostitution and of homosexuality in schools, military forces, and prisons. Gagnon's belief that once a heterosexual, always a heterosexual is reflected in his portrayal of male hustlers: "At no point before, during, or after the sexual act do these young men define themselves as homosexuals or as experiencing or performing a homosexual act" (Gagnon, 1977: 264). Nor did Gagnon believe in the adage "this year's trade is next year's competition" (265). The "heterosexual script" of the hustler rarely broke down to the point where he continued his occupation for sexual pleasure. The impression that hustlers became homosexuals, Gagnon believed, was left by those male prostitutes who were homosexual to begin with but concealed their sexual identity from customers who sought "real" heterosexual masculine males.

The customers apparently were as confirmed in their homosexual identity as the hustlers in their heterosexual identity. Gagnon and Simon's description of the customer's motives is redolent with Kleinian drama:

> Contact with men who are symbolically more powerful gives the sexual act a greater sense of tension through increased risk. At the same time, a desire for power over the heterosexual is evoked. By the act of arousing the prostitute and "making" him ejaculate, the homosexual male acts out a drama in which he is in power over the heterosexual male. He also reduces his own deviance by confirming his belief that there is an element of homosexuality in all men. (Gagnon and Simon, 1973: 168)

There was still the problem of accounting for heterosexual men who had sex with other men when no pecuniary gain was involved. Gagnon used the idea of "substitutive homosexual scripts" that were enacted and later discarded. The substitutions occurred when "groups of healthy and active people of one sex" (Gagnon, 1977: 266) were isolated from the opposite sex. In the army, schools, and prisons the homosexual script was substituted by heterosexual males to relieve boredom or, particularly in prisons, to validate their masculinity and positions of dominance."[27]

---

[27] In an earlier explanation of homosexuality in prisons Gagnon and Simon (1973: 258-259) added the motive of affection to that of preserving masculinity. Whatever needs homosexuality gratified, however, homosexual contacts remained facsimiles of heterosexuality: "The inmates are acting out their needs for self-expression, control over their own behavior, affection and stability of human relationships. The homosexual relationship provides one of the few powerful ways of expressing and gratifying these needs. Unless these needs are met in some other way, there is little opportunity for adequate control of homosexual activity in the prison environment" (259).

Gagnon held that men who thought of themselves as heterosexual sometimes turned to homosexual relationships out of disenchantment with the demands of heterosexual relationships.[28] Those men and women who viewed themselves as bisexual, Gagnon obliquely implied, had an underlying heterosexual or homosexual identity: "[They] rarely simply do (or feel) the same things with both women and men. Using the same script and revising it only by substituting one gender for the other is rarely done" (1977: 259).

More striking were the contrasts between psychoanalytic and symbolic interactionists thought. In psychoanalysis the individual was conceived as a psychological entity, possessing a unique mental apparatus that operated and expressed a unique personality. The foundations for the structure of personality were laid down in early childhood and the sturdiness and internal harmony of the design and its execution made mature development possible. Individuals knew little about what went into their formation or even the motives that propelled them into daily action. They had, however, the ultimate responsibility for their decisions and actions because the primary site of conflict was the mental apparatus of each individual. Because the individual alone represented all the parties to a conflict, the full contemplation and resolution of conflict was possible. Psychoanalytic theory provided for creativity, allowing the individual to invent new actions and relationships and to create new solutions for old conflicts.

In the view of symbolic interactionists, psychoanalysis was seen as preoccupied with early childhood experience and as downgrading the importance of adolescent and adult development. Symbolic interactionists not only disputed the lurking pervasiveness of sexual motives in human activities and relationships but also claimed that much that appeared as sexual in psychoanalysis was really symbolic of the mundane world in which one earned a living and maintained a home. Psychoanalysis, in their view, conceived of the individual as socially isolated, walled off in a small, private world.

Symbolic interactionism saw the individual as embedded in society. No longer containers of an autonomous inner life, individuals were seen as membranes that were permeable on all sides. Membranes are suspended passively in space, acted upon by the fluids and substance that flow over or against them. Similarly, in symbolic interactionism

---

[28] Here Gagnon is following the view of Lionel Ovesey (1954) who distinguished between pseudo-homosexuality (fear of masculine responsibility) and the genuine article.

individuals were portrayed as suspended in social space, creatures of the encounters and contingencies to which they were fortuitously exposed.

The sociological self as actor, with accompanying roles and scripts, was constructed from ingredients essentially outside the individual. For a particular person the assemblage of social ingredients may show some degree of individuality (or peculiarity) but such uniqueness could be explained by a fine-grain analysis of the objective or intersubjective realities to which the individual had been exposed. Because the individual was believed to be formed from the outside the basic responsibility for actions was shifted from the individual to society. The important point was that nothing really original was ordinarily contributed by the individual because there were no mechanisms within the self for creativity.

Within this formulation individuals were given a mentality but not a mind, in the psychoanalytic sense of mental apparatus. Mentality was invested with imported consciousness, rationality, and foresight. At times symbolic interactionists softened their view of individuals who were fully conscious beings, reflecting on encounters, with references to "drifting" and "semi-slumbering" states. Individuals who were products of their interactive destinies, however, had to remain fully conscious of social reactions, one's own and those of others, because one's fate in either mainstream or deviant society depended on the discrete management of roles. Indeed, for actors to perform well they must be uncommonly conscious of the nuances of their own words and deeds and finely tuned to the varied impact of their behavior on the audience.

In a conception of the individual where there is little uniqueness, responsibility, or creativity, there can be no underlying motives. To explain the basis for human actions, symbolic interactionists imbued social encounters with meanings and conscious interaction. In the course of living the individual was seen as assimilating these meanings, which then became the basis for future actions. Because the meanings were understood by individuals and were the sole reasons for acting, everything that was done had a strictly rational basis. Meanings were also the basis for weighing options in particular encounters. Individuals, therefore, were seen as possessing foresight because they were always busy reviewing and selecting options in their myriad social encounters. As Martin Dannecker observed:

> The interaction theory, then, if it does not completely overlook the active contribution people make to their own destiny, at least reduces this to so minimal a role as to produce an image

that degrades the human being to an unresisting object of social norms. (81-82)[29]

In the very ways in which symbolic interactionism contrasted with Freudian psychoanalysis, it strikingly paralleled post-Freudian analytic thought, particularly psychoanalytic adaptational theory. In that formulation of the mental apparatus the ego took the control of human behavior which, in the topological conception of Freud, was under the influence of the impulses of the id and libido. The lustful impulses of the libido, under the supervisory eye of the ego, were monitored and managed so as to avoid their undermining the individual's social adjustment. Adaptational psychoanalysis, as a managerial psychology, turned the individual's attention away from the raging conflict between sexual impulses and moral imperatives of the superego and toward the interaction of the ego with the world outside.

In a parallel development, symbolic interactionism replaced instinct, impulse, and motive with "meanings" that became the foundation for the performance of roles and scripts. Like the cognition of the adaptational ego, these meanings were conscious, intellectual, and willful, essentially occupying their own sphere and presiding over individual experience. The meanings, however, derived from societal reactions and norms. Both adaptational theory and symbolic interactionism stressed adjustment—the fitting of societal expectations or roles. In both theories society deeply invaded the individual's identity, in one case by the ego taking on the responsibility of enforcing social norms on recalcitrant impulses and in the other by making the individual's identity a product of societal reactions.

In the light of this introjection of social norms, it comes as no surprise that, in conceptualizing the homosexual identity a major concern of both the post-Freudian and symbolic interactionist approaches was the individual's departure from normative feminine or masculine roles. For Thompson, overt homosexuality in the male could be a symptom of his fear of shouldering adult responsibility or of competing with other males. The pseudo-homosexuality of heterosexual males, as conceived by Ovesey, was precipitated by failures in the performance of the masculine role. Kardiner believed that males sometimes fled to homosexual relationships to win the protection of another male. In the etiological speculations of the Bieber group, the greatest damage the

---

[29] Dannecker, Martin (1981). *Theories of Homosexuality*. London: Gay Men's Press. Originally published in Frankfurt am Main (West Germany) by Syndikat *Autoren-und Verlagsgesellschaft* in 1978.

seductive, possessive mother wreaked on her prehomosexual son was to inhibit the development of his masculinity, autonomy, and assertiveness. The early infant son-mother symbiosis, in Stoller's formulation, was an incipient threat to the development of the son's masculinity. Symbolic interactionism, in a similar vein, identified as the earliest sense of "differentness" experienced by prehomosexual children their noncon-formity to "gender roles."

The "delibidinization" of sexual activity that Freud unwittingly commenced in his structural theory of the mental apparatus was carried to extreme lengths in the adaptational psychology of the post-Freudian period. In these latter approaches the ego was given a larger and larger independent source of energy and could neutralize and divert more and more sexual energy of the Id for its own intellectual and managerial purposes. This de-erotization of the individual was carried even further by symbolic interactionism in its claim that individuals began life with an innocence and *tabula rasa* that became sexual only with experience interpreted by society and understood by the individual to be sexual. In this view "sexuality" was a social construction rather than a biological or psychological capacity for gratification.

The sociology of the groups studied by the ethnologists, operating within the theoretical framework of symbolic interactionism, including homosexuals, prisoners, and prostitutes, was devoid of detailed discussions of sexual practice and of sexuality as pleasure. Because, as a system of thought, symbolic interactionism was rooted in "experience" or "situated activity," it is surprising to find so little was written about the sexual experiences of the people the ethnologists observed. Researchers were even urged by Simon and Gagnon (1967) to pay less attention to the sexual aspects of the homosexual's life than to the practical problems of jobs, home, and relatives. Some ethnological studies did make references to acts of fellatio and insertion but with little or no allusion to the sexual gratification these activities may have had for the individuals who engaged in them.

Symbolic interactionism also shared ideas with the Kinsey group in its approach to sexuality. References of Plummer, Gagnon, and Simon to social "contingencies" or "situated activities" had the same import as the Kinsey group's references to stimuli or conditions. Indeed, as the inquiry of the Kinsey group extended to the cultural context of sexual behavior, the words "stimuli" and "responses" lost their Pavlovian precision and were broadly used to refer to social conditions, attitudes, and constraints.[30]

The relatively minor role that symbolic interactionism assigned to biology in the conceptualization of sexual identity is the major point of contrast with the position of both the Kinsey and Freudian groups. In the latter view, human sexuality was grounded in biology and in the general mammalian sexual capacity. It held that more of this capacity would be expressed if society did not impose restrictions on man's sexual nature. While not denying that there were biological constraints on human "sexual plasticity," the sociological view held that they were clearly subordinate to the individual's socially constructed sexual meanings. In rejecting the notion of sexual instincts, Plummer had this to say about the relative influence of biology and sexual meanings:

> Now the history of the social sciences can, in one sense, be seen as an ongoing struggle to rescue man from such explanations which constantly stress his instincts as the basis for his action. At one time, every form of human behavior could be interpreted by evoking the notion of an instinct, but today this status is reserved for a very limited range of man's social activities, with sex to the fore. Now the central point about man's social life—as contrasted with sub-human species—is that it is a symbolic life. This means that man's sexual feelings constantly have to be placed in the context of his symbolic interpretation of them; he does not have to act on the basis of biological forces pushing him from within to behave in certain ways; rather he constantly sets about interpreting inner feelings, and making sense of the world around him. To talk of man as having a sexual instinct is a crude reification of a complex symbolic system; rather he has a biological capacity ..., which is capable of great variation as he moves and manipulates his symbolic environment. The notion of a drive or instinct builds into the whole idea of sexuality a strength to control human life that I suspect it simply cannot have. (1975: 37)

Given this perspective on sexuality as principally *symbolic*, it is difficult to determine where the symbolic interactionists locate physical desire, attraction, sensation, and pleasure. Is it possible that individuals

---

[30] This conceptual similarity should come as no surprise because both symbolic interactionism and behavioral psychology had their theoretical origins in the experiential, pragmatic philosophy of John Dewey.

can discover new sources of arousal and sensations that exist outside any of their definitions of pleasure? Does thought shape physical pleasure without pleasure shaping thought? A portrayal of sexual relationships in terms of the constraints of biology and society which does not include the unfolding of sensation and gratification within sexual experience and for which the participants may have no pre-codified meanings appears as an ascetic, prosaic, and encapsulated version of sexual relationships. If, as the symbolic interactionists claim, the Kinsey group decorticated sex, have they not decorporealized sex? One recalls Michel Foucault's definition of the *ars erotica* of ancient polytheistic cultures:

> In the erotic art, truth is drawn from pleasure itself, understood as a practice of accumulated experience; pleasure is not considered in relation to an absolute law of the permitted and forbidden, nor by reference to a criterion of utility, but first and foremost in relation to itself; it is experience as pleasure, evaluated in terms of its intensity, its specific quality, its duration, its reverberations in the body and soul. Moreover, this knowledge must be deflected back into the sexual practice itself, in order to shape it as though from within and amplify its effects. (57)

16 The Demise of Labeling Theory: The Post-Kinsey Sociologists

In the decade of the 1970s, a series of sociological studies of the homosexual identity were published by investigators at the Alfred C. Kinsey Institute for Research on Sex, Gender, and Reproduction.[1] These studies were empirical applications of a theoretical perspective derived from symbolic interactionism and known as labeling theory.

Colin Williams and Martin Weinberg applied labeling theory to the study of the effects on men of receiving a less-than-honorable discharge from the military for reasons pertaining to homosexuality.[2] Labeling

---

[1] It had been originally named the Institute for Sex Research and renamed in honor of its founder in 1981. The social psychologists and sociologists who conducted these studies will be referred to as the post-Kinsey sociologists.

[2] Williams, Colin J. and Weinberg, Martin S. (1971). *Homosexuals and the Military: A Study of Less than Honorable Discharge.* New York: Harper & Row. Their study involved sixty-three World War II veterans, thirty-two of whom had received honorable and thirty-one less than honorable discharges. Respondents were recruited through two homophile organizations, the Mattachine Society in New York City and the Society for Individual Rights in San Francisco. They were given an initial questionnaire, interviewed, and then given a second questionnaire. The first questionnaire was used to select the sample. It contained questions on the respondent's background, early homosexual experiences, service experiences and discharge, involvement with homosexuals at the time of induction, and involvement with the police or therapists. The interview was divided into two parts, the first containing questions about how the respondent perceived himself and believed he was perceived by others and the second containing questions dealing with his military service, including his sexual experiences while in the military. Those respondents who received less than honorable discharges were asked how they came to the attention of the authorities, how their cases were processed, and how the discharges affected their lives. The second questionnaire repeated some of the items in the first one, but they were reworded "at the present time" rather than "at time of induction." There were also questions on

theory, they believed, tended to view the deviant as victim, subject to the arbitrary procedures of control. As a departure from earlier applications of the theory, they gave attention to the deviants as well as the labelers. They were interested in exploring the contribution made by the deviants to their discovery as homosexuals, that is, the extent to which they played an active role in the process.[3] In their study the deviant label, as applied by the military, was the less-than-honorable discharge. Because this was the type of discharge given to those who were reputedly homosexual, the authors considered the less-than-honorable discharge tantamount to being officially labeled homosexual.[4]

In comparing these individuals with male homosexuals who received honorable discharges, the authors hoped to determine the effects of

occupational history, friends, public identity as a homosexual, heterosexual experiences, religious and political behavior, and psychological adjustment. The data were collected in 1968.

[3] There appears to be a continuing debate over the conceptualization of labeling as a theory or perspective. Williams and Weinberg (1971: 2) believed it was more a perspective than a theory, although they used "theory" in their applications. By calling it a perspective they signified that labeling was more a collection of assumptions than a series of testable propositions. In her foreword to their book (vii-viii), Hooker commended the authors for their critique of labeling theory "for its failure to take into account the role of those who engage in deviant acts." Kenneth Plummer, in his 1981 "Building a Sociology of Homosexuality" claimed that the authors applied labeling theory but not the labeling perspective (19-20). Plummer made these distinctions. Labeling theory was based on two principles: (1) deviant labels are applied without regard to the behavior of those labeled; and (2) this labeling produces the deviant and deviant behavior. The labeling perspective raised questions rather than tested propositions. It addressed the following issues: (1) the nature of deviant labels; (2) how they arose; (3) the situations in which they were attached to behavior; and (4) the individual and social consequences of labeling.

[4] There was some practical difficulty with this equation because the less-than-honorable discharge was also given for reasons unassociated with homosexuality. Additionally, on the discharge document, only the type of discharge but *not* the reasons for discharge appeared. Kenneth Plummer had a theoretical objection to the claim that the study was a real test of labeling theory. The discharge label "is in no way comparable to the all-pervasive, powerful, denigrating label of homosexuality that exists … in American society generally…. In other words, it is abstract societal symbolic labeling that is more important than the specific formal labeling of the military. To show that specific, direct labeling has little impact misses the point; it is the whole weight of cultural hostility that counts" (1981: 22).

being labeled homosexual. The first question addressed was: Why did one group but not the other get labeled as homosexuals? There were three reasons given by the authors. First, some men were relatively inexperienced in making sexual contact with other men. Although their contacts were infrequent, they were unfortunately indiscreet, primarily involving other servicemen. Others "voluntarily admitted" (178) their homosexuality. Finally, there were those who had frequent sexual contacts and consequently had run the greater risk of discovery. These reasons, the authors asserted, demonstrated how the deviant contributed to his own victimization:

> We hope to have thus shown that discovery exhibits certain patterns and does not necessarily involve arbitrary selection procedures by the military. Members of our sample did not appear to have suffered from a "bumrap" in that, regardless of the propriety of these rules, they had engaged in a type of behavior which, as members of a certain social system, was expressly proscribed. (179)

Because, in theory, the individual labeled homosexual was expected to suffer adverse social consequences, the authors studied how the post-military lives of the men who received less-than-honorable discharges were affected. Compared with those men who had received honorable discharges, the effects were minimal and short-term. Those who received less-than-honorable discharges in the long-run were not barred from employment nor were they left with a paralyzing sense of injustice. This conclusion, of course, did not empirically support labeling theory, and therefore raised doubts about its validity in the authors' minds.

The first doubt was over methodology. In the research applications of labeling theory either the role of the deviant or that of the labeler was stressed while less attention was paid to the interaction between the two roles:

> Labeling theory draws its main strength from symbolic interactionist theory in sociology. This school of sociology has suffered from a relative lack of empirical work, the main reason being the difficulty researchers have faced in translating the theory into empirical terms. We feel that for labeling theory in particular, more work should be done on specifying the nature and types of interaction that characterize labelers and deviants and in developing a methodology that comes to grips with the unfolding, emergent, and dynamic nature of such processes. (183-184)

Their second doubt pertained to the possibility that labeling theory may have been "an oversimplified conception" (185). It reified both society and the individual by assuming that society invariably took steps to exclude the labeled individuals and that the individuals, resigned to their fate, became socialized as deviants:

> Labeling theory often has been reduced to a theory of stigma determinism, of people locked into deviant careers, never to escape. If the labeling approach is to continue to excite sociologists, the intricacies of social reality must be faced—its social psychological aspect must increase in sophistication, and its sociological aspect must be extended to fulfill its most important promise. (185)

Three years later the authors published a second sociological study based on labeling theory, which, in this work, was called "societal reaction theory."[5] This study, they believed, was in the tradition of the

---

[5] Weinberg, Martin S. and Williams, Colin J. (1974). *Male Homosexuals: Their Problems and Adaptations*. New York: Oxford University Press. The authors did not explain the change in terminology. They studied four cities: New York, San Francisco, Copenhagen, and Amsterdam. For each city, there was a general description of the legal situation (statutory offenses pertaining to homosexual conduct), law enforcement, homophile organizations, and the geographical distribution of homosexual bars. In addition, 2,497 presumably homosexual respondents in the four cities completed a questionnaire of 145 items. They were contacted through homosexual organizations, social clubs, and bars. The questionnaire for homosexual respondents was divided into three parts. The section on "relating to the heterosexual world" contained items about their public identity as a homosexual, putative prejudice or discrimination, passing, official labeling as homosexual, social involvement with heterosexuals, and identification with traditional values. The section on "relating to the homosexual world" contained items about social involvement with homosexuals, sexual practices and partners, homosexual social situations (friends, bars, and lovers), and conceptions of homosexuality (normality and choice). The final section dealt with "psychological problems." These included self-acceptance, stability of self-concept, depression, psychosomatic symptoms, anxiety regarding homosexuality, nervous breakdown, interpersonal awkwardness, faith in others, loneliness, and psychiatric experience. The responses of the research subjects from the United States were compared on the psychological items in the questionnaire with the responses of a sample of 3,101 American males selected "from the general population" (9) for a study published ten years earlier (Kohn, Melvin L. (1969). *Class and Conformity: A Study in Values*. Homewood Illinois: Dorsey Press). For a similar comparison

original Kinsey group.[6] The choice of societal reaction theory was itself a reaction against the psychoanalytic conception of the homosexual identity as a psychological condition, pathological in origin and possibly amenable to treatment and cure.[7]

With the intention of redirecting the research on homosexuality, Weinberg and Williams concentrated on the sociocultural conception of the homosexual identity and the possible repercussions of the homosexual label on the adaptations of male homosexuals. As a role or status, the homosexual was shaped as much by the values and social structures surrounding him after he became aware of sexual identity as by the events of early childhood. The focus of research, they believed, should shift from psychological causation to the investigation of how the homosexual was affected by the social situation he had to confront:

> Taking into account the social context in which the homosexual lives leads to a fundamental change in the conception of re-search. Instead of talking about homosexuality as condition ... and seeking the causes of the condition, primary attention is directed to the ways in which the homosexual is affected by his social situation, for example, how the connotations and expecta-tions surrounding homosexuality affect the homosexual's behavior and self-concept. (Weinberg & Williams, 1974: 7)[8]

---

random samples of presumably heterosexual males were selected from the telephone books in Amsterdam and Copenhagen.

[6] They referred to the investigations of the Kinsey group as the first large scale sociological study of homosexuality even though it was done by a zoologist, Alfred C. Kinsey (5).

[7] Weinberg had collaborated with Alan P. Bell in the publication of over 1,200 abstracts of investigations of homosexuality (Bell, Alan P. and Weinberg, Martin S. (1972). *Homosexuality: An Annotated Bibliography.* New York: Harper and Row). Based on this compilation, Weinberg and Williams (1974: 3-4) concluded: (1) most of the research focused on the etiology of homosexuality; (2) the basis of the research was (4) "Freudian," concentrating on (4) "child-parent" experiences; (3) the samples of respondents were small and largely comprised of patients in therapy; (4) the studies failed to compare homosexual adjustment with heterosexual adjustment; and (5) most studies were (4) "culture-bound," limited, that is, only to the United States. Weinberg and Williams also noted the general lack of sociological research on homosexuality.

[8] This passage echoes the position of Simon and Gagnon (1967) who recommended the refocusing of research on homosexuality, from viewing it as a condition to examining it in its social context.

From the vantage point of societal reaction theory, homosexuality as deviance was not a characteristic of a sexual act but a sociological phenomenon:

> [W]hat makes homosexuality "deviant," according to reaction theory, is not anything about the behavior per se but rather the fact that people differentiate, stigmatize, and penalize alleged homosexuals. (7-8)

Within their sociological framework, homosexuality was "a variant of sexual expression" (6), a manifestation of human sexual capacity, originally undifferentiated "that becomes attached to certain objects and situations through a complex learning process" (6). Whatever the mysteries of etiology, they believed the homosexual male was more than his origins.

In this second test of labeling theory, Weinberg and Williams studied the adaptations of male homosexuals in three cultures they believed showed contrasting degrees of sexual tolerance. They reasoned that homosexuals who faced more intolerance, as in the United States, should show more "negative adaptations" than those who faced less, as in the European cities they studied. The assumption that there was greater tolerance in Europe than in the United States rested chiefly on the fact that homosexual acts between consenting adults were not illegal in the European locales they studied although they were classified as criminal offenses in the United States.

The social reality to which the male homosexual had to adapt was conceptualized as two dichotomous "worlds," the heterosexual and the homosexual, both of which could be a source of "psychological problems." The most direct threat posed by the heterosexual world was discovery and exposure of the individual's homosexual identity:

> Being known about ... can propel a person whose homosexuality is of little salience for him into a homosexual role. Being publicly identified as homosexual means that others may relate to him in terms of this status rather than his other statuses and attributes.... Thus, fear of exposure and concern with secrecy may determine in important ways the manner in which the person's homosexuality is managed and may affect his psychological well-being. (Weinberg & Williams, 1974: 9)

The heterosexual world had a less direct impact on the adaptation of the homosexual: as the embodiment of traditional values and morality it stood in conflict with his sexuality:

Such is the power of heterosexual society that the homosexual may take over the beliefs that it propounds, creating problems of self-acceptance for himself. He may feel forced to hide his sexual orientation, often beset with fears and anxieties about its exposure. (12)

Whereas they described the homosexual as inescapably ensnarled by the heterosexual world, his relationship to the homosexual world afforded him more choice, a "range of ways of being homosexual" (11). The individual could preserve his anonymity and limit his involvement to a series of sexual encounters with strangers or he could assume a known homosexual identity within the homosexual world and thereby expand his involvement to social and political activities.

The psychological dangers posed by the heterosexual world could be partially allayed by the social support and freedom provided by the homosexual world. Because the homosexual world was shaped by the condemnation of the heterosexual world, however, it could also be a source of psychological problems: homosexuals, fearing exposure, could be consumed in anonymous sexual encounters, eschewing opportunities to establish "intimate, lasting relationships" (Weinberg & Williams, 1974: 12).

As in the case of their first study, the empirical results did not support theoretical predictions. They had expected that European homosexuals would be psychologically better adjusted than American homosexuals because there was greater tolerance for homosexuality in Europe. What they found was that there were no significant differences in the psychological well-being of European and American homosexuals. Within the framework of societal reaction theory they tried to account for the unpredicted results. First they questioned the assumption that the legal status of homosexual acts was a reliable index of social tolerance. There were differences, they asserted, between formal laws against homosexual behavior and their actual enforcement, particularly in cities like New York and San Francisco. The impact of the sexual laws in any case was indirect—the laws symbolized more than enforced society's rejection of homosexuality. Finally, morality, they believed, was "situated" (268). How heterosexuals actually treated homosexuals depended on the social context of their interactions, their relationships, their purposes and interest, what was relevant, and their perceptions of the situations:

What we can say for now is that the [societal reaction] model is not specific and detailed enough to avoid reifications and overgeneralizations. For example, the key variable may not be the societal reaction so much as how the person adapts to it.

> Thus, the negative effects of societal reaction may be neutralized by living with another homosexual and being involved in the homosexual subculture.... Thus, some theoretical clarification is needed regarding the extent to which the impact of societal reaction is limited by the person's adaptations. (Weinberg & Williams, 1974: 269)

What their theory correctly predicted, they asserted, was that open associations among homosexuals within the confines of the homosexual subculture promoted a "sense of well-being" (Weinberg & Williams, 1974: 271). The subculture, they suggested, should not only be viewed passively as a place where deviants were concerned "primarily with bandaging wounds their members receive from a hostile conventional world" (271), but also as a political launching pad from which homosexuals could create a "new style of 'being different'" (271) and voice their political demands.

Another theoretical expectation that was not verified was that homosexuals would experience stress in moving between the heterosexual and homosexual worlds. They believed this expectation went unsupported because homosexuals were socialized to meet heterosexual norms and that they did not think of themselves as having "two highly distinct lives" (Weinberg & Williams, 1974: 272). Whatever stress was experienced the authors attributed to worry and concern about exposure rather than any difficulties homosexuals faced in moving between two worlds. This interpretation was bolstered by the finding that there was as little psychological stress due to fear of exposure for bisexuals and non-exclusive heterosexuals.

Williams and Weinberg (1971) contributed to the detoxication of the homosexual identity by showing the apparent injustice done by the military in discharging men who were identified as homosexuals regardless of how meritorious their service was. Their contribution to the normalization of homosexual relationships was contained in recommendations to homosexuals on how to improve their adaptation. Homosexuals were advised to become involved in their subculture and in this way learn that homosexuality was equatable to heterosexuality: "[A] homosexual identity may not have all the negative consequences they feared" (1971: 276). The authors suggested that homosexuals could obtain guidance and support in the homosexual world for adapting to the heterosexual world. In this way the authors used heterosexual values as the standard for integrating the homosexual and heterosexual identities. They also contributed to normalization by implying that those homosexuals who received the less desirable discharge were the victims of their own improprieties by having sex with fellow servicemen or in being sexually very active. They urged homosexuals not to abandon religion but rather to appreciate that its stand on sexuality was a product of history rather than contemporary thinking. They counseled homosexuals not to make the homosexual subculture the basis for their lives:

> The homosexual shares far more in common with many heterosexuals than he may realize. While he should enjoy the homosexual aspect of his life and while identification with other homosexuals is functional, he need not make his sexual orientation the central part of his identity. (Williams & Weinberg, 1971: 278)

Their recommendations for change in societal attitudes were an explicit contribution to the normalization of sexual relationships. They urged repeal of laws against consenting adult homosexual conduct. Because these laws prohibited sexual acts regardless of the biological sex of partners, it was implied that their repeal would broaden the scope of permissible heterosexual behavior to include oral and anal intercourse. They inadvertently endorsed this expanded notion of sexual practice when they supported bisexuals continuing the enjoyment of sex with both females and males (Williams & Weinberg, 1971: 278). They castigated the use of entrapment to obtain evidence against homosexuals in the enforcement of laws against solicitation as a violation of civil liberties. In effect their argument questioned the justification of all governmental regulation of sexuality, as for example the use of entrapment against female prostitutes.

They strongly urged the end of employment discrimination against homosexuals in both public and private institutions. The claim of the federal government that homosexuals were security risks because they could be blackmailed "overlooked that the same logic applies to others, such as married heterosexuals having extramarital affairs" (Williams & Weinberg, 1971: 282), an argument that was perhaps an unintentional condoning of nonmarital sex. Finally, they suggested that sex education should not be restricted to heterosexual behavior and reproduction but include accurate information on homosexuality even though some people might fear that this would "encourage experimentation with homosexuality" (284n). In the authors' opinion, "even if people did experiment with homosexual behavior we have no evidence that in a tolerant and nonmoralistic atmosphere this would be harmful" (284n).

The question of homosexuality as a sexual identity was recurrent in the early sociological publications of the Kinsey Institute. The idea that there was a range of "homosexualities" which varied in character was discussed at length by a social psychologist at the Institute, Alan Bell.[9] Bell criticized earlier investigators for obtaining sexual orientation ratings for their respondents on the heterosexual-homosexual rating scale only to collapse them to form dichotomous groups of heterosexuals and homosexuals. Bell believed that two rating scales were necessary for assessing sexual orientation, one for sexual behavior, the other for sexual feelings.[10]

It was theoretically possible, he stated, for a person to be both exclusively heterosexual in behavior and exclusively homosexual in feeling. He implied that feeling more than behavior ratings revealed sexual identity because the individual had less control over feelings. It was also implied that sexual feelings were more diffuse than sexual behavior, which would explain why behaviors were frequently rated at the ends of the heterosexual-homosexual rating scale. Bell also held that the labels of "heterosexual" or "homosexual," even as self-applied, were not reliable indications of the individual's sexual feelings and behavior. The diversity of sexual behavior, he observed, led many people to reject labels: "The bisexual's experience certainly belies the notion that homosexuality and heterosexuality are mutually exclusive.... In summary, how one defines one's sexual orientation and the basis on which the definition is made differs from one individual to the next" (Bell, 1975b: 204).

Bell postulated that the real differences between heterosexual or homosexual groups could only be determined when more attention was paid to the "differences" that existed within each group. By "differences" he alluded to the sources from which respondents were recruited and the character of their sexual practices. He believed that future research should emulate his sampling procedure by obtaining respondents from as many sources as possible: "through public advertising, in public and private

---

[9] Bell, Alan P. (1973). Homosexualities: Their Range and Character. In James K. Cole and Richard Dienstbier, Eds., *Current Theory and Research on Motivation: Nebraska Symposium on Motivation 21*. Lincoln: University of Nebraska Press, 1-26. The research to which Bell referred was the Kinsey Institute study of homosexuals in the San Francisco Bay Area, which he led from 1969-1970. Bell was trained as an Episcopalian priest and clinical psychologist but functioned in the role of a research social psychologist at the Kinsey Institute.

[10] Bell, Alan P. (1975b). The Homosexual Patient. In Richard Green, Ed., *Human Sexuality: A Health Practitioner's Text*. Baltimore: Williams and Wilkins, 52-72. Reprinted and abridged in Weinberg, Martin S. (Ed.)(1976). *Sex Research: Studies of the Kinsey Institute*. New York: Oxford University Press, 202-212. Page references are to the reprinting.

bars, steam baths, and other public places, through personal contacts, and by means of various mailing lists" (Bell, 1973: 5). Heterosexuals, he believed, should be recruited by block sampling of cities, utilizing stratified random samples.

To determine the character of respondents' sexual identity it was necessary to obtain more than a rating on the heterosexual-homosexual rating scale because that revealed little about "where one is sexual" (1973: 8). For more complete information on heterosexual and homosexual research subjects, Bell proposed a list of "sexual parameters":

> [The] level of sexual interest (how important is sex vis-a-vis other areas of a person's life); the conditions under which we become aroused sexually and the secondary feelings associated with that arousal; the extensiveness of sexual experience (how often does sexual activity occur and what is the range of one's sexual repertoire); the number and type of sexual problems (does guilt or inferiority predominate); the number of sexual partners; and the nature of our temporal and emotional involvement with them. (1973: 8)

There were additional areas of inquiry that were particular to homosexuals: "the amount and kind of cruising they do, their feelings about and attitudes toward homosexuality in themselves and others, and the extent to which they are covert" (8-9). Only by attending to these dimensions of sexuality, Bell asserted, would research uncover "the exact size or nature" (9) of the differences between heterosexuals and homosexuals. This approach to homosexuality, Bell proffered, would lead to a typology of homosexuality that would include far more than the classifications of insertor and insertee and a greater range of emotions than Ovesey's homosexuality, dependency, and power. He suggested other possible motivations:

> [F]or some homosexuals the prominent feature of their homo-sexuality is their attempt to deal with the guilt which they experience over their behaviors; for others it may be the management of the tension they experience between the gay and straight worlds; for others it might become experienced primarily as social protest, as the search for long-lasting rela-tionships, or as an attempt to overcome sexual inhibitions. (24)

The psychological dimensions of adjustment, in Bell's formulation, included feeling states such as loneliness, depression, or happiness, thinking of suicide, and seeking psychotherapy. In these aspects of adjustment Bell believed that homosexuals differed more from each other than they did from heterosexuals. Social adjustment included occupation, church affiliation, voting, and involvement with homosexual or heterosexual friends:

> Some [homosexuals] leave the field entirely, becoming ghetto-ized occupationally, residentially, and emotionally. Such persons may live in one of the "lavender" ghettos which can be found in any large urban center, seeking employment in vari-ous enterprises where most of their fellow workers are known to be homosexual, frequent gay-owned establishments, and limit their social contacts to those provided by various gay set-tings. At the other end of the continuum are those who are relatively uninvolved in, if not rejecting of, the gay subculture. (1973: 19)

There were also social consequences of being homosexual. For some these were "but one of the many masochistic features in their personality" (19)—being robbed, arrested, and fired. For others the homosexual minority status enabled them to "develop in themselves very useful and important capacities for social criticism, enhanced their creative abilities, or made them more sensitive to the needs of others" (19).

Bell believed that variations in psychological and social adjustment could be traced to variations in patterns of child development, with par-ticular regard to relationships with parents and with peers. Some patterns, he believed, would conform to the psychoanalytic model by appearing disturbed while others would appear normal. Bell therefore assumed that there were "multiple routes" (1973: 22) to the homosexual identity.

Although he described a range of homosexual etiologies, motives, and adjustments, Bell evidently held to the belief that heterosexual and homosexual were two distinct identities which remained untouched by experience and time: "I prefer to view homosexuality (like heterosexuality) as all of one piece, in which temporal distinctions are acknowledged as arbitrary, artificial and not always useful" (20).

The first comprehensive report of Bell's research on homosexuality appeared in 1978.[11] Bell generally followed the outline for research on

---

[11] Bell, Alan P. and Weinberg, Martin S. (1978). *Homosexualities: A Study of Diversity Among Men and Women*. New York: Simon and Schuster. The study reported in this volume grew out of a pilot study of 458 male homosexuals in Chicago in 1967. That project was led by Paul H. Gebhard as Director of the Kinsey Institute and by John Gagnon and Paul Simon (the data reported in the

homosexuality he had proposed in his articles.[12] Unlike the earlier studies of Weinberg and Williams, which were inspired by labeling perspective, Bell and Weinberg, in this study, professed no particular theoretical position. Proceeding in an apparently purely empirical manner, the authors cast a broad net in an attempt to assess and compare sexual

---

article by Simon and Gagnon, 1967, appear to be those gathered in the pilot study). Data for the Bell and Weinberg investigation were gathered in 1970 in the six counties of the San Francisco Bay Area. Homosexual subjects were recruited from June to October in 1969 from a wide variety of sources. The final homosexual sample consisted of 979 respondents, 293 females and 686 males. Four hundred seventy-seven heterosexual respondents, preponderantly male, were obtained through a random block-sampling procedure. Respondents were interviewed, using a schedule 175 pages in length and containing 528 questions. The questions fell into three broad areas: sexual experience, social adjustment, and psychological adjustment. Under sexual experience the following were included: ratings on two heterosexual-homosexual rating scales, one for behavior, the other for feeling; overtness (public disclosure or knowledge of homosexuality); incidence, locales, and time spent cruising; sexual partners, including number, affairs or relatively stable relationships, and duration of relationships; sexual appeal to others of the same sex; sexual techniques such as masturbation, tribadism, fellatio, and anal intercourse; level of sexual interest; sexual problems such as orgasmic dysfunctions, erectile difficulties, finding partners, maintaining affection for partners, and sexually transmitted diseases; acceptance of homosexuality (e.g., regret, negative feelings, and attempts to discontinue). Under social adjustment there were questions dealing with occupational history, church affiliation, political affiliation, marriage, friendships with men and women, social activities (alone, others, at home, bars, baths, and homophile organizations) and, finally, social difficulties with the law, assailants, and blackmailers. Under psychological adjustment there were questions on general health, psychosomatic symptoms, happiness, exuberance, self-acceptance, loneliness, worry, depression, tension, paranoia, suicidal feelings and impulses, and psychotherapy. In his preface to the book, Paul Gebhard stated that Alfred Kinsey had intended to publish a study of homosexuality as a third volume to follow the two volumes on male and female sexuality. After Kinsey's death, the Institute turned to other projects. Attention was refocused on homosexuality because of the efforts of Stanley Yolles, who, as director of the National Institute of Mental Health, established a Task Force on Homosexuality, which held its first meeting in 1967, and was first chaired by Evelyn Hooker. Both the Chicago and San Francisco studies were funded by the National Institute of Mental Health.

[12] In addition to the two articles already cited, Bell reiterated his position in Bell, Alan P. (1975a). Research on Homosexuality: Back to the Drawing Board. *Archives of Sexual Behavior* 4(4): 421-426.

experience and social and psychological adjustment. By first identifying the different types of homosexuals, they believed they could discover the basic difference between the heterosexual and homosexual identities.

Consistent with Bell's notion of the existence of pluralistic forms of homosexuality, they developed a typology that contained five classes of homosexuals: CLOSE-COUPLEDS, OPEN-COUPLEDS, FUNCTIONALS, DYSFUNCTIONALS, and ASEXUALS. The Close-Coupleds were sexually and emotionally "close": "First, the partners in this kind of relationship are closely bound together. Second, the partnership is closed in that the Close-Coupleds tend to look to each other rather than to outsiders for sexual and interpersonal satisfactions" (219). Bell and Weinberg stated that they

> resisted the temptation to call this group 'happily married,' although some of its members described themselves that way, because we did not want to imply that heterosexual relationships and marriage in particular are standards by which to judge people's adjustment. (219)

The Open-Coupleds lived with a special sexual partner but "tended (despite spending a fair amount of time at home) to seek satisfactions with people outside their partnership" (Bell & Weinberg, 1978: 221). The Functionals were compared with the heterosexual "swinging singles" (223). They were the homosexual men and women who "were not particularly interested in finding a special partner to settle down with, engaged in a wide variety of sexual activities, considered their sex appeal very high, and had few if any sexual problems" (223). They were also extensively involved in the "gay world" (223).

The last two types of homosexuals were described in terms of the deficiencies in their lives. The Dysfunctionals were depicted as closest to "the stereotype of the tormented homosexual" (Bell & Weinberg, 1978: 225). They were uncoupled individuals "whose lives offered little gratification" (225). They searched for and had many sexual encounters that proved to be largely unsatisfying. The Asexuals, finally, lacked both stable partnerships and sexual activity and gratification. The authors thought their "withdrawn lives … [were] the inevitable product of an underlying apathy toward the panoply of human experience" (228).

According to Bell and Weinberg this typology was based on five particular aspects of sexual experience included in their interview questionnaire.[13] First was sexual partnerships, often referred to as "affairs." The nature of the first "relatively stable relationship" was examined with respect to

> the partners' ages, its duration, whether they lived together, whether respondents were in love with their partners, the partners' relative social positions, what each got out of the relationship, how it differed from any later affairs, its impact on the respondent, the reasons for its termination, and the respondents' reaction to the breakup. (Bell & Weinberg, 1978: 84)

A second aspect was the level of sexual activity or "the number of times our respondents reported having had sex with partners of the same sex during the year just prior to the interview" (Bell & Weinberg, 1978: 69-70). The third was cruising or "the purposive search for sexual partners" (73). In addition to frequency and locations, respondents were asked about whether they or their partners made the first approach, where they would go to have sex, how much time they spent with each partner, how much they worried about cruising, how satisfactory the sex was, how they felt about being rejected by a prospective partner, difficulties in conversing, the adequacy of their performance, inadvertently cruising heterosexuals, and experiencing violence, blackmail or arrest. Sexual problems was the fourth aspect. It included

> orgasmic difficulties ..., ejaculatory control and erectile problems ..., insufficient frequency, difficulties in finding a suitable partner, their own or their partner's failure to respond to whatever sexual requests were made of them, concerns about their ability to perform sexually, difficulties in maintaining affection for their partners, and whether they had ever contracted a venereal disease from homosexual contact. (Bell & Weinberg, 1978: 117)

The last aspect was acceptance of homosexuality, which included

> the amount of regret the respondents had over their homosexuality, whether they ever considered discontinuing their homosexual activity, whether they wished they had been given a magic pill at birth which would have guaranteed their

---

[13] Other aspects of sexual experience, asked about in the questionnaire but not used as criteria in developing the typology, were ratings on the heterosexual-homosexual rating scale, familial and extrafamilial disclosure of homosexuality, level of sexual interest, and sexual techniques.

becoming heterosexual, and whether they would take such a pill today if one were offered to them. (122)

They were asked about their views of the possible immorality or pathology of homosexuality and how upset they would be if they were to have a homosexual child.

The investigation of each of these aspects, as postulated by the authors, constituted a valid test on the "heterosexual majority's negative view of homosexuality" (Bell & Weinberg, 1978: 121). By studying partnerships the authors felt they could evaluate the stereotype of the homosexual man as being "highly 'promiscuous,' unable to integrate his emotional and sexual needs, incapable of maintaining a longstanding sexual partnership, and doomed to an eternally hopeless quest for the ideal relationship" (81). By determining the level of sexual activity, the authors could challenge "the old stereotype of homosexuals as constantly engaged in all sorts of sexual activity, except during occasional breaks to eat or sleep" (69). By investigating cruising, the authors were testing "the stereotypic notion of the homosexual person (especially the male) … constantly on the lookout for sex, no matter where, no matter when" (73). By looking into possible sexual problems or dysfunctions the authors intended to fill a deficiency in knowledge that grew out of the common assumption that homosexuality itself was a sexual problem and the fear of clinicians that to treat the sexual dysfunctions of homosexual patients was to reinforce "behaviors which they consider unfortunate if not pathological" (116). Finally, by exploring the homosexuals acceptance of their homosexuality, the authors could question the sociological assumption that homosexuals "assimilate the heterosexual's negative view of homosexuality, thus becoming alienated from their deepest sexual needs and interests" (121).[14]

Before comparing the levels of social and psychological adjustment for each type of homosexual, the authors made some general comparisons between heterosexuals and homosexuals for social adjustment. Homosexuals showed about the same degree of job stability. Few were discriminated against to the point where their homosexuality forced them to leave a job. Homosexuals were more alienated from religion than the heterosexuals either because of guilt over their homosexuality or disagreement with church doctrine. There were no differences in voting

----

[14] This putative heterosexual view was also referred to by the authors as "lacking others' endorsement of their [the homosexuals'] private identity" (Bell & Weinberg, 1978: 121).

patterns, a conclusion the authors attributed to the fact that their data were gathered before the effects of gay liberation were felt by the population they surveyed. There were some differences between the strictly heterosexual marriages and those heterosexual marriages in which one partner was homosexual. The authors stated that these "mixed" marriages were of shorter duration than their strictly heterosexual counterparts because of the lack of sexual gratification for either the heterosexual or homosexual partner.

They also drew some general conclusions about homosexual and heterosexual friendships. The homosexual males, not surprisingly, had more good, close friends who were male than did the heterosexual males. The homosexual males believed that males had "better personalities" (Bell & Weinberg, 1978: 175) than women. Both the heterosexual and homosexual men "tended to think that other males were more enjoyable to socialize with" (175). The homosexual women preferred other women because they viewed women as superior psychologically. The homosexuals had more friends than the heterosexuals because, in the authors' view, the homosexuals were free of family constraints. They also concluded that homosexuals had more heterosexual friends than heterosexuals had homosexual friends, something they attributed to the relative abundance of heterosexuals.

As for general psychological adjustment, the heterosexual men in some respects outstripped the homosexual:

> The homosexual men tended to feel less self-accepting and more lonely, depressed, and tense than did the heterosexual men. They also tended to worry more and to display more paranoia and psychosomatic symptoms. On the other hand, the homosexual men tended to be more exuberant than their heterosexual counterparts. They were much more likely to have considered suicide, although, according to the respondents, this was not necessarily connected to their homosexuality. Far more of the homosexual than the heterosexual men had ever sought professional help for an emotional problem. (Bell & Weinberg, 1978: 207)

The authors declared that if they had made only gross comparisons of heterosexual and homosexual psychological adjustment, without delineating homosexual types, they would "have been forced to conclude that homosexual adults in general tend to be less well-adjusted psychologically than heterosexual men and women" (215-216).

After comparing heterosexuals and homosexuals, Bell and Weinberg turned to the question of the relative adjustment of their five different types of homosexuals. Those men and women classified as Close-Coupleds were portrayed as being the best adjusted:

> They were the least likely to seek partners outside their special relationship, had the smallest amount of sexual problems, and were unlikely to regret being homosexual. They tended to spend more evenings at home and less leisure time by themselves, and the men in this group seldom went to such popular cruising spots as bars or baths. (Bell & Weinberg, 1978: 219)

Although their sexual techniques were limited, their sexual activity was evidently gratifying. In some ways their adjustment was superior to that of married heterosexuals. The Open-Coupleds, compared with the Close-Coupleds, were "less happy, self-accepting, and relaxed" (221). Although they were more sexually active, they were also more worried about cruising and the possibility of being arrested and exposed as homosexuals. Their sexual activity tended to be anxious and ungratifying.

The Functionals were remarkable in being able to combine a high level of sexual activity with good adjustment:

> They reported more sexual activity with a greater number of partners than did any of the other groups.... [They] were least likely to regret being homosexual, cruised frequently, and generally displayed a great deal of involvement in the gay world.... They were particularly unlikely to complain about not getting enough sex or difficulties in their sexual performance. Of all the groups, they were the most interested in sex, the most exuberant, and the most involved with their many friends. (Bell & Weinberg, 1978: 223)

The only flaw appeared to be that they were the homosexuals most likely to be arrested, which the authors attributed to "their high attendance at gay bars, and, perhaps as well, their relative lack of worry or suspicion of others—or even a certain degree of recklessness" (224). The generally successful adjustment of the Functionals the authors attributed to their personalities: "They are energetic and self-reliant, cheerful and opportunistic, and comfortable with their highly emphasized sexuality" (224). The encomiums, however, were reserved by Bell and Weinberg for the Close-Coupleds: "One should not conclude, however, that Functionals are an ideal type as regards coping with a homosexual orientation. It is rather the

Close-Coupled men and women who have made the best adjustment" (224).

As their name unambiguously implied, the Dysfunctionals were the least well adjusted. Their active sex lives gave them little satisfaction. They regretted their homosexuality, suffered from an array of sexual dysfunctions, seemed unable to find suitable sex partners, and had difficulties with the law and employment. One dysfunctional male was described as interested in young males:

> He seems to have an adolescent religious hang-up. I see his admission to being a "chicken-queen" as a way for him to re-live or act out his lost youth. He drives to the Tenderloin "meat rack," picks up young hustlers, drives them to Redwood City, and then pays them for sex. (Bell & Weinberg, 1978: 225).

The authors' description of the Asexuals implied a reticence on the part of men and women in this category to accept their homosexuality: "They were the least likely of all groups to describe themselves as exclusively homosexual, and, among the males, they were the less overt [i.e., disclosed] about their homosexuality and had fewer same-sex friends" (Bell & Weinberg, 1978: 227). Their lifestyle was described as solitary: "Despite their complaints of loneliness, Asexuals are not very interested in establishing a relationship with a special partner or in any of the rewards a gay world may offer" (228).

The development of their taxonomy of homosexuals enabled Bell and Weinberg to detoxicate the homosexual identity by drawing distinctions between its pathological and nonpathological forms. Following in the footsteps of the psychiatrists and earlier sociologists, they claimed that, while homosexuality itself was not pathological, some types of homosexuals showed attitudes and behaviors that revealed mental illness:

> Perhaps the least ambiguous of our findings is that homosexuality is not necessarily related to pathology. Thus, decisions about homosexual men and women, whether they have to do with employment or child custody or counseling, should never be made on the basis of sexual orientation alone. (Bell & Weinberg, 1978: 231)

The two types of homosexuals whose normality they did question recalled earlier psychiatric views of homosexuality as perversion and neurosis. The Dysfunctionals resemble psychiatric descriptions of the perverts whose monomaniacal absorption in the quest for sexual gratification aborted any possibility of sustained relationships and even led to mounting sexual frustration. The Asexuals recalled Freud's early description of neurotics as individuals whose sexual energy lay trapped between perverted and normal expression.

The efforts of Bell and Weinberg at detoxication extended beyond banishing the specter of mental illness. It included a defense of homosexuals against charges of criminal, sexual behavior and public indecency:

> Homosexuals' sexual activity ... begins with highly cautious pursuits in places not normally frequented by heterosexuals or in more public surroundings where heterosexuals are not aware of what is taking place. Most often it is consummated with full consent of the persons involved in the privacy of one of the partners' homes. Even this description, however, disregards the numerous instances in which homosexual contact occurs solely between persons whose commitment to each other includes sharing a household. (230)

In keeping with the practice to detoxicate the homosexual identity at the price of pathologizing the heterosexual identity, the authors reminded readers of such heterosexual criminal offenses, all by males, as seducing adolescent female students, preying on pre-pubescent girls, and the rape of women of all ages. Such behaviors the authors sharply contrasted with that of some types of homosexuals whom they described as "models of social comportment and psychological maturity" (230).

The contribution of Bell and Weinberg to the normalization of homosexual relationships rested mostly on their portrayal of the homosexual men and women they described as Close-Coupleds and Functionals.[15] The Close-Coupleds were distinguished by their stable relationships, sexual fidelity, and domesticity. Although there were occasional dis-

---

[15] We are assuming that the typology adopted by Bell and Weinberg was reflective of their beliefs about the relationship of heterosexuality to homosexuality. Although the typology was based on a statistical technique known as cluster analysis and purportedly objective, Frederick Suppe (1981) explained that it had subjective components. For example, the researcher who uses cluster analysis must decide which taxonomies, among the several "candidate taxonomies" generated, are more natural (i.e., reflecting real divisions in nature) than others. In addition, the grouping of individuals is highly influenced by variance patterns in the sample and is usually not replicable for other samples drawn from the same population. It should also be noted that a large number of respondents could not be classified, using their typology.

claimers by the authors that they were employing a marital standard in describing this group, it is quite clear that they believed that the best homosexual adjustment was that which imitated heterosexual monogamy.[16]

Although the Functionals were not monogamous, as a group, they were almost as happy as the Close-Coupleds. Of all the homosexual groups, it was the Functionals who moved most freely and comfortably within the homosexual subculture. The implication was that the *normal* homosexual, therefore, was as solidly homosexual as a *normal* heterosexual was consummately heterosexual.

The Functional group was also comparable to the heterosexual swingers. The contribution of Bell and Weinberg to the normalization of sexual relationships was the implied message that the individual could be sexually "promiscuous" and still socially and psychologically well adjusted. In fact their description of the members of the Functional groups as physically attractive, personally appealing, energetic, cheerful, and opportunistic made them indistinguishable from the uncoupled heterosexual female or male who had the physical appeal, economic means, and social connections to enjoy the good single life.

By concluding that there was a diversity of heterosexualities and homosexualities, it appeared as if Bell and Weinberg were repudiating the notion of sexual identity:

> It should be clear by now that we do not do justice to people's sexual orientation when we refer to it by a singular noun. There are "homosexualities" and there are "heterosexualities," each involving a variety of interrelated dimensions. Before one can say very much about a person on the basis of his or her sexual orientation, one must make a comprehensive appraisal of the relationship among a host of features pertaining to a person's life and decide very little about him or her until a more complete and highly developed picture appears. (Bell & Weinberg, 1978: 329)

Indeed, the quantitative differences they found in the sexual behavior of homosexuals most certainly could have been found among heterosexuals. There were homosexuals who equaled and even surpassed heterosexuals in good adjustment. If there were dysfunctional and asexual

---

[16] The authors never considered the importance of parenting children to the institution of marriage or the absence of children, for the most part, in the homosexual partnerships.

homosexuals, surely their counterparts could be found among the heterosexuals.

The reader, therefore, was left to ponder the question of what was
quintessentially heterosexual or homosexual within this pluralistic framework. The typology described the different configurations of homosexual
relationships without questioning the assumption of an underlying homosexual identity. Acceptance of this identity by the homosexual was, in fact,
a major criterion for good adjustment. If the authors intended to question
the idea of the homosexual identity, they could have investigated the
widespread heterosexuality found in the "behavior" and "feelings" of
their homosexual respondents.[17]

In the absence of any explicit distinction between heterosexuals and
homosexuals, the reader was left to conclude that the only real difference
was the obvious one: heterosexuals usually have sex with members of
the opposite sex while homosexuals usually have sex with others of the
same sex. All that remained for Bell and Weinberg was to search for
some prior conditions in the lives of heterosexuals and homosexuals that
dictated their respective identities.

In 1981, Bell, Weinberg, and Hammersmith published their study of
the etiology of sexual identity.[18] The study had interlocking goals: to explain both the heterosexual and homosexual identities; to review the
many scientific explanations of the causes of sexual identity; and to determine if heterosexual and homosexual respondents could be
distinguished by their developmental histories.

---

[17] Twenty-six percent of their respondents were not exclusively homosexual in
behavior and forty-four percent not exclusively homosexual in feelings.
Seventy-one percent had engaged in heterosexual coitus sometime in the past.
See DeCecco, John. (1981). Definition and Meaning of Sexual Orientation.
Journal of Homosexuality 6(4): 51-67.

[18] Bell, Alan P., Weinberg, Martin S., and Hammersmith, Sue Kiefer (1981).
Sexual Preference: Its Development in Men and Women. Bloomington, IN: Indiana
University Press. This book was based on data collected from the same
respondents used in the previous study by Bell and Weinberg (1978). The data
carne from a separate set of 200 questions on childhood and adolescence in the
175-page interview schedule. In the "Introduction" Bell was identified as a
"psychologist and therapist" and "relatively supportive of psychodynamic
theory" (8). Weinberg and Hammersmith were described as sociologists "with
quite a different theoretical perspective" than that of Bell. We have used
"sexual identity" in place of the authors' use of "sexual orientation."

To reach these goals the data were subjected to a path analysis.[19] This statistical technique required the authors to arrange the independent variables in sequences that they believed reflected the developmental stages during which those variables contributed to the formation of sexual identity. For this sequencing the authors used two guidelines. One was simple chronology so that data on the grade-school years, for example, were placed before those on the high-school years. The other was the application of theoretical models, such as one holding that parental personalities preceded and influenced the development of the child's social sex-role. When there were conflicting theoretical stances, the sequence was determined by "the broadest consensus among the various theories we were attempting to test" (29). Based on these guidelines, they arranged their data into the following sequence:

Stage 1. Parental Traits. These data included adjectives used in describing parents as individuals and descriptions of parents' sexual attitudes.

Stage 2. Parental Relationships. This included general perceptions of which parent dominated the other, possible friction, and parents' mutual affection.

Stage 3. Parent-Child Relationships. This included reports of closeness, acceptance, protectiveness, the favoring of one child, and parental seductiveness.

Stage 4. Parental Identification. This stage was based on reports of how respondents resembled or wanted to resemble a particular parent and parental encouragement of identification with the parent of the same sex.

---

[19] Path analysis is a statistical technique developed for use in the biological sciences for relating a large number of independent variables, arranged in sequential stages, to a dependent variable. The hypothesized sequences are based on theory and on an assumed sequential occurrence of various events. In this study path analysis was used to determine differences in the childhood and adolescent experiences of heterosexual and homosexual respondents and to examine differences among subgroups of homosexuals such as the exclusively homosexual and the bisexuals, black and white homosexuals, and those who fitted, as compared with those who departed from, the sex-role stereotypes. The term "path" indicated that some variables, particularly those early in the sequences, could be related to sexual preference through intermediate variables.

Stage 5. Sibling Relationships. Respondents indicated the degree of closeness they felt toward brothers and sisters.

Stage 6. Sibling Identification. Respondents described identification with either female or male siblings.

Stage 7. Gender Conformity. Respondents assessed their relative conformance to feminine or masculine stereotypes while growing up, their relative enjoyment of boy or girl activities, and their personality traits as children.

Stage 8. Grade-School Years. Here respondents referred to peer relationships in grades 1 through 8, numbers of friends and general popularity, feelings of being left out, close girlfriends and boyfriends, and sexual experiences (both homosexual and heterosexual), including arousal, physical contact, or being called a derogatory sexual epithet.

Stage 9. High-School Years. In addition to questions like those in the preceding stage, respondents were asked about dating, sexual intercourse (both heterosexual and homosexual), masturbation, feeling sexually different, and being called a name suggesting a difference.

Apparently stages 1 through 7 were formulated as tests chiefly of psychoanalytic theory of sexual identity. The major focus was on the theory set forth by the Bieber group, which viewed the psychological homosexual identity as the dismal product of the child's intrafamilial failure to resolve the Oedipus complex and to achieve the appropriate heterosexual identity. The healthy oedipal resolution, it may be recalled, not only enjoined the child to develop a heterosexual object choice but also required the female child to become feminine in attitude, the male child masculine.[20]

The last two stages (8 and 9) flowed mostly from sociological theory (including labeling theory) which focused on the pre-adolescent and adolescent years of sexual development during which children were presumably socialized into peer groups.

In the analysis of data for this study, the stages were viewed as groups of independent variables that theoretically contributed to the development

---

[20] Although the work of Socarides and of Stoller was listed in the bibliography of this book, the stage model did not test more recent theories of the psychological homosexual identity, based on concepts of merging, individuation, and separation. Nor was there evidence that the research attempted to distinguish systematically between psychoanalytic theories of the female and male homosexual identities.

of either the heterosexual or homosexual "preference." In the context of their research, adult sexual preference specifically referred to the ratings on the heterosexual-homosexual rating scales, which respondents assigned to themselves presumably on the basis of their adult sexual adjustment at the time they were interviewed in 1969 or 1970.[21]

By the last page of the major text of their book, however, the authors acknowledged the limitations of their title:

> Although we have entitled our present work *Sexual Preference,* we do not mean to imply that a given sexual orientation is the result of conscious decision or is as changeable as the many moment-by-moment decisions we make in our lives. Neither homosexuals nor heterosexuals are what they are by design. (Bell, Weinberg & Hammersmith, 1981: 222)

The authors also acknowledged that they were not interested in explaining degrees of homosexuality or heterosexuality in respondents whose personal histories involved both identities: "the placement of respondents into two boldly defined groups—homosexual versus heterosexual—represents a natural division between respondents as well as the distinction most theoretically important for our study" (32).[22]

Although Bell, Weinberg, and Hammersmith eventually concluded that psychoanalytic etiological theories of the homosexual identity were unconfirmed by their findings, there seemed to be at least some support. They reported that homosexual more than heterosexual males, for example, described their mothers as strong individuals and the dominant parent and their fathers as distant and hostile figures with whom they

---

[21] The sexual preference rating for each respondent was the average of two ratings, one for "sexual behavior," the other for "sexual feelings." Although most homosexual respondents averaged either 5 or 6, anyone with an average rating of 2 or higher was classified homosexual. Respondents with ratings of 0 or 1 were classified as heterosexual. The authors stated (200) that only 55% of the white homosexual male respondents and (207) 45% of the white homosexual female respondents rated themselves as exclusively homosexual. This procedure for assessing sexual orientation departed from that of the Kinsey group in three ways: (1) in obtaining separate ratings for behavior and feelings; (2) by having respondents rate themselves rather than the researchers rating respondents on the basis of their sexual histories; and (3) by obtaining only a single assessment of adult sexual orientation rather than rating respondents for successive periods of their adult sex histories.

[22] It is not clear whether "natural" was used in the sense of "biological" or "popular."

had little identification. The greatest consonance with psychoanalytic theory was the finding that "childhood gender non-conformity" was a strong predictor of the homosexual identity in the prehomosexual boy. Gender nonconformity was revealed by the boys' dislike of conventional male choices of play activities (e.g., baseball or football) and the enjoyment of typical girls' activities. It was also revealed by the respondents' retrospective assessments of their femininity and masculinity at the time they were growing up. Although few homosexual men described themselves as feminine in their early lives, most did not see themselves as stereotypically masculine. They did not describe themselves as having been very strong, active, or dominant; these adjectives occurred more frequently when the heterosexual men described themselves as children.

Gender nonconformity was also related to factors occurring earlier and later in the path analysis. It was related to closeness to mothers, mothers as strong and dominant parents, and distant, negative relations with fathers. It was also related to later stages in which homosexual arousal and behavior occurred.

As for peer socialization, the authors summarized their findings in this way:

> Compared with their heterosexual counterparts, the homosexual males reported less social involvement with peers during childhood and adolescence, a greater sense of feeling different from other boys (especially for reasons related to gender role), and a higher incidence of feeling sexually different and being labeled as such. They also reported more negative feelings about dating, less happiness, and more negative self-images. (Bell, Weinberg & Hammersmith, 1981: 95)

In itself, however, a lack of peer socialization was not a predictor of a future homosexual identity. The factor which best predicted whether the future sexual identity would be heterosexual or homosexual was the direction of sexual arousal:

> What differs markedly between the homosexual and heterosexual respondents, and what appears to be more important in signaling eventual sexual preference, is in the way respondents felt sexually, not what they did sexually. A homosexual predisposition became evident, for the majority of our homosexual respondents, through their feelings of homosexual arousal or feeling sexually different, which in most cases occurred years before any advanced homosexual activities took place. (113)

Although they reported that many heterosexual males had homosexual experiences, often preceding their sexual experiences with females, and that many homosexual males also had sexual intercourse with females, the authors tended to view the sexual contacts of the homosexuals as "superficial" and "not especially gratifying" (Bell, Weinberg & Hammersmith, 1981: 113). Because sexual experience did not determine sexual identity, the authors concluded "that sexual preference is likely to be established quite early in life and that childhood and adolescent sexual expression by and large reflect rather than determine a person's underlying sexual preference" (113).

Their developmental findings for homosexual females also lent partial and indirect support to psychoanalytic theories, although, as in the case of the males, they were not predictive of a future homosexual identity. Homosexual females, when compared with heterosexual females as children, identified less with mothers, had more negative relationships with mothers, and described fathers as colder and weaker. As in the case of the homosexual males, the greatest consonance with psychoanalytic theory was the authors' conclusions on childhood gender nonconformity in prehomosexual girls. These girls, they believed, displayed gender nonconformity in play activities and personality traits: "Among the females, as among the males in the study, Childhood Gender Nonconformity appears to have been much involved in the process by which respondents came to be homosexual" (Bell, Weinberg & Hammersmith, 1981: 151).

The authors denied, however, that this conclusion corroborated psychoanalytic theory because the nonconformity of the prehomosexual girls did not appear to be a product of family constellations. During the elementary and secondary school years the peer relationships of the prehomosexual girls were as troubled as those of the prehomosexual boys: "the lesbian respondents more often described themselves as lonely, unhappy, and alienated while growing up" (163). This isolation, the authors asserted, could not be traced to being labeled as different. Their sense of difference came from their gender nonconformity and growing awareness of their attraction to other females.

The extensive and not unpleasant heterosexual experiences of female homosexuals, the authors believed, furnished evidence that the girls' homosexuality could not be attributed to insufficient or coercive heterosexual encounters. In the authors' judgment the key to future sexual identity was the same for women as for men: arousal and gratification. Heterosexual women were aroused and gratified by heterosexual experience while homosexual women were gratified by homosexual experience. Sexual *feelings*, the authors reiterated were the key to sexual identity:

> [A]mong females it appears to be one's covert sexual feelings that play a role in the development of a homosexual orientation. Sexual feelings, however they may be engendered, are less subject to the individual's conscious control and less modifiable by social circumstances. When a girl's feelings take a homosexual turn (e.g., in feeling sexual attracted to other females) there seems to be an increased probability that eventually she may express an adult homosexual orientation. (Bell, Weinberg & Hammersmith, 1981: 180)

The conclusions of Bell, Weinberg, and Hammersmith on the etiology of the homosexual identity freed it from pathological, familial and socially deviant origins. This detoxication was first accomplished by the disavowal of psychoanalytic theories which explained the homosexual identity as a form of mental illness resulting from pathological child-parent relationships. Regarding these relationships the authors concluded: "We find the role of parents in the development of their son's sexual orientation to be grossly exaggerated" although "relationships between girls and their parents seems a bit more influential" (184).

Nor could the homosexual identity be traced to the child's identification with the parent of the opposite-sex, a key ingredient of oedipal theory. The authors claimed, in fact, that "the homosexual men did not identify more with their mothers, and the homosexual women identified less with their fathers, than did the heterosexuals with whom they were compared" (189).[23]

Although they held that cold and detached fathers predisposed their children toward homosexuality, this influence was "considerably overstated in psychoanalytic literature" (184). Contrary to the theories of the Bieber group, Socarides, and Stoller, the father replaced the mother as the chief villain in the etiology of homosexuality: "For both the [homosexual] men and women in our study, poor relationships with

---

[23] Later in their book, the authors stated that it was the effeminate male homosexuals (44% of their sample) who lacked identification with fathers (198-199). The authors confessed that they were at a loss to determine whether the boys were born effeminate and therefore could not identify with fathers or whether the initial failure to identify with fathers led to their effeminacy.

fathers seemed more important than whatever relationships they may have had with their mothers" (Bell, Weinberg & Hammersmith, 1981: 189).

There were homosexuals, the authors reported, who were alienated from their fathers and peers. These were the men and women who possessed family backgrounds and showed developmental patterns that fitted the clinical portrayal of the homosexual identity. They were the homosexuals who the authors believed were most likely to enter psychotherapy.[24] For the men that meant detached-hostile fathers, negative relationships with fathers, and images of fathers as cold. For the women it meant gender nonconformity and a sense of peer alienation in childhood and adolescence.

Sociological theory did not fare better than the psychoanalytical as an explanation for the causes of the homosexual identity. Its origins could not be explained by theories that "attributed homosexuality to poor peer relationships" (Bell, Weinberg & Hammersmith, 1981: 184). Although the authors believed it was true that homosexual children were more isolated than heterosexual children from their peers, this alienation could be better explained as a product of their gender nonconformity than by peer name-calling or rejection. Thus the labeling of the child or adolescent as homosexual, the authors held, was not a causative factor in the development of homosexuality. Nor could the cause be found in the lack of heterosexual experience: "The homosexual men and women in our study were not particularly lacking in heterosexual experiences during her childhood and adolescent years. They are distinguished from their heterosexual counterparts, however, in finding such experiences ungratifying" (188).

After detoxicating the origins of the homosexual identity the authors turned to the normalization of homosexual relationships. Their task here was to retain the exceptionality of homosexuality as a distinct and comparatively rare sexual identity while fitting it into a normal process of psychological and social development. In detoxicating the homosexual identity, however, they had almost entirely ruled out family and peer socialization, in either its negative or positive aspects. It was therefore necessary to find a concept that could be applied to a psychological and social process of development. They turned to the concept of gender conformity which in the case of the homosexual they called gender

---

[24] The authors reported that more than half (58%) of the white males and two-thirds of the white females classified as homosexuals had had some counseling or psychotherapy (204, 210).

nonconformity. The term GENDER established a link to biology while NONCONFORMITY was a link to development. For the authors gender nonconformity in children and adolescents was the key indicator of an ensuing homosexual identity: "One of the major conclusions of this study is that boys and girls who do not conform to stereotypical notions of what it means to be a male or a female are more likely to become homosexual" (221).

The lack of gender conformity was closely associated with the presence of homosexual feelings. Sexual feelings were viewed by the authors as deeper than behavior and ultimately revealing of sexual identity. Homosexual feelings, they claimed, preceded homosexual activity for their respondents by three years or so and "it was these feelings, more than homosexual activities, that appear to have been crucial in the development of adult homosexuality" (187).

By lodging sexual identity in feelings, the authors could discuss the homosexual identity as deeply ingrained:

> In other words, our data show that childhood and adolescent homosexuality, especially pronounced homosexual feelings, cannot be regarded as just a passing fancy that every child goes through at one time or another. Rather, in most cases this inclination seems to be relatively enduring and so deeply rooted that it is likely to continue as a lasting homosexual orientation in adult life. (Bell, Weinberg & Hammersmith, 1981: 186)

The heterosexual identity was as deeply embedded as the homosexual: "Our findings could be interpreted as simply reflecting the emergence of a deep-seated propensity toward either homosexuality or heterosexuality, which begins to emerge while a person is growing up and then continues into adulthood" (187). It was clear that the authors believed that sexual identity was an essence that unfolded in the process of development. It was not a characteristic parents could change: "You may supply your sons with footballs and your daughters with dolls, but no one can guarantee that they will enjoy them" (191).

The question remained as to the source of these profound sexual feelings. Because they could not be traced to psychological or sociological circumstances the authors turned to biology: "Indeed, homosexuality may arise from a biological precursor (as do left-handedness and allergies, for example)" (Bell, Weinberg & Hammersmith, 1981: 192). Acknowledging that their study did not include biological data, the authors claimed that their findings "are not inconsistent with what one would expect to find if, indeed, there was a biological basis for sexual preference" (216). They suggested that a biological theory would: (1) explain why homosexuality operated more powerfully for those who were exclusively homosexual than for bisexuals; (2) probably account for gender nonconformity; and (3) explain familial factors as the result of the son or daughter being different from birth.

The most powerful statement revealing how the authors employed a biological explanation to the detoxication of the homosexual identity follows:

> Those who argue that homosexuality is "unnatural" will be forced to reconsider their belief, because something that is biologically innate must certainly be natural for a particular person, regardless of how unusual it may be. People might ultimately come to the conclusion that everyone is unique, biologically and socially, and that natural physiological factors will make it inevitable that a certain percentage of people in a society will be fundamentally homosexual regardless of whether they are momentarily (or even continuously) engaged in heterosexual behaviors. (Bell, Weinberg & Hammersmith, 1981: 218-219)

These conclusions led to some theoretical difficulties for the authors. For example, the future sexual identity of black homosexual males was signaled by homosexual activities occurring in childhood and adolescents rather than homosexual feelings. This relatively early occurrence of sexual activity for black as compared with white males, the authors explained, possibly reflected "the freer sexual attitudes of the black community" (191). Bisexuality also posed a problem. The bisexuals were those men and women who rated themselves in the middle range of the heterosexual-homosexual rating scale. As in the case of the black males, their homosexual relationships were not traceable to homosexual feelings occurring in childhood and adolescence. The authors felt that bisexuals learned their homosexuality after the age of nineteen, thereby implying that the bisexuals were born heterosexual in identity: "exclusive homosexuality tends to emerge from a deep-seated predisposition, while bisexuality is more subject to influence by social and sexual learning" (201). The authors were also implying that the acquired homosexual behavior of bisexuals was less deeply entrenched than an innate homosexual identity and therefore more amenable to therapeutic change.

There was one final difficulty that also appeared to be a theoretical embarrassment. The authors discovered that they could find no "notable" relationships (Bell, Weinberg & Hammersmith, 1981: 204, 210) between their typology of homosexuals (e.g., Close-Coupleds, Functionals) as described in the previous volume and differences in childhood or adolescent development. Without these connections the two books on homosexuality (the first on adjustment, the second on etiology) stand as isolated works even though they were based on the same interviews with the same respondents. The reader was left with no integrative or coherent statement of the author's theory of sexual identity.

The first two sociological studies of homosexuality by the post-Kinsey sociologists were designed as empirical tests of the socially constructed sexual identity. Weinberg and Williams intended to determine the extent of the social and psychological victimization homosexuals encountered and how such mistreatment affected their general adjustment. Both studies, as we have seen, failed to provide the empirical support that the authors had anticipated. In the study of military discharges, for example, they concluded that those homosexuals who had less-than-honorable discharges did not make significantly different adjustments in their post-military lives than those who had received honorable discharges. They believed those men who were expressly labeled and expelled as homosexuals were able to return to a civilian status and often to lead productive and satisfying lives. In their study of homosexuality in particular cities in the United States and Europe, they found that the prejudice against homosexuality, as represented in laws prohibiting homosexual conduct, was not always accompanied by actual enforcement of the law. Thus the legal status of adult homosexual conduct was not a reliable indicator of the tolerance shown towards homosexuals.

The two initial attempts of the post-Kinsey sociologists to provide empirical support for labeling theory and to document the treatment of homosexuals as deviants had therefore failed. With these failures, the post-Kinsey sociologists quietly abandoned the labeling perspective and, with it, symbolic interactionism.[25] What they did not abandon was the belief in the sociocultural sexual identity. They never questioned the fact that soldiers discharged for homosexual tendencies or conduct or denizens of gay bars and social clubs were homosexuals. Whatever sexual involvement their male respondents had with women were treated as an insignificant eddy in the main homosexual current of their sexual relationships.

---

[25] Labeling theory was casually mentioned in the etiological study in connection with the sexual labeling of homosexual children by peers.

The attention of the post-Kinsey sociologists increasingly focused on those homosexuals who had never been arrested or fired for homosexual conduct and never sought counseling or psychotherapy. Their portrait of the psychologically healthy homosexual was essentially ethnographic. It described a man who fitted comfortably into the homosexual world, finding in it emotional support, friendship, love, and sex as well as advice on how to cope with the heterosexual world. The ethnologists and the symbolic interactionists had expressed their fears of the homosexual subculture as a sexual marketplace and ghetto. The post-Kinsey sociologists viewed it as both a refuge and a launching pad for re-entering and even perhaps changing the attitudes of the heterosexual world about homosexuality.

The next two studies by the post-Kinsey sociologists, those on homosexual adjustment and etiology, were offered mainly as comprehensive assessments of psychiatric and social stereotypes. No explicit theoretical formulations for this research were proposed to replace labeling theory. The implication was that the authors had no beliefs and attitudes of their own about sexual identity. That they indeed did have notions was implicit in the manner in which they approached the general topic of sexual relationships, their conceptualization of social and psychological adjustment, and in the way they distinguished between adult sexual preferences.

First, their approach to sexual relationships was in the sociological tradition which provided an abstract description of sexual behavior without revealing much of its substance, Bell's list of "sexual parameters," such as time spent cruising, number of sexual partners and affairs, level of sexual interest, and number of sexual dysfunctions provided a disembodied and purely externalized view of sexual relationships. Although information was obtained from respondents on sexual techniques, it was not utilized in classifying homosexuals into types. In fact, their approach to sexual relationships was almost entirely quantitative. It has been argued that an external, quantitative approach to sexual relationships is tied to the ideology of sexuality as performance, production, and reproduction rather than to sexuality as eros, art, and enjoyment.[26]

The absorption by the post-Kinsey sociologists of the idea of a psychological sexual identity was implicit in their treatment of sexual

---

[26] Marcuse, Herbert (1955). *Eros and Civilization A Philosophical Inquiry Into Freud*. Boston: Beacon Press. Marcuse referred to the transformation of the Freudian pleasure principle into the post-Freudian performance principle.

orientation. Although the authors acknowledged that many of their presumably homosexual respondents had been involved in sexual activity with members of the opposite sex, in some cases extending over several years, there was no systematic effort to compare these homosexual and heterosexual experiences to determine if there were any consistent qualitative differences. When respondents reported that experiences with the same sex were more gratifying than those with the other sex, the reader was left to conclude that *every* experience with an individual of the same sex was more gratifying than *every* experience with an individual of the other sex.

Within the general framework of the sociocultural sexual identity the post-Kinsey sociologists endorsed the idea of a basic biological identity. Their theoretical posture was best illustrated in the use of the notion of gender conformity and nonconformity. The psychoanalytic explanation, in which the child identified with the parent of the opposite sex because of inadequacies in the relationship with the parent of the same sex, was rejected on empirical grounds. As a substitute for the psychological etiology of gender conformity or nonconformity they speculatively substituted a biological explanation—the belief that the child was born with the propensity for conformity or nonconformity, and, correlatively, for a heterosexual or homosexual identity.

The concept of gender conformity or nonconformity, divorced from its Freudian psychological context and used to explain the result of an investigation in the social sciences, formed the link between the ideas of the biological and sociocultural sexual identities. Gender conformity was the key to the heterosexual sociocultural identity, while nonconformity was the link to the homosexual. The term "conformity" implied the existence of standards for social conduct phrased in terms of feminine appearance and behavior for females and masculine appearance and behavior for males. It was gender nonconformity in young children that heralded their future homosexual identity and would later stand in the way of their constructing sexual relationships with partners of the opposite sex.

The use of the word "gender," which connotes a biological characteristic, obscured the fact that the post-Kinsey sociologists were referring to social sex-roles, a sociological concept.[27] It was easy for these

---

[27] In the discourse on sexual identity of the last decade, "gender" has increasingly replaced "sex" in references to the individual's biological sex. As most dictionaries indicate, however, this use of gender is colloquial because

authors to link gender non-conformity to a homosexual sociocultural identity, transmuted by homosexuals into the "gay subculture," which, in turn, could be generously viewed as the celebration of their biological uniqueness. Membership in the gay subculture, however, clearly represented a sociocultural rather than a biological sexual identity. The endorsement of the biological sexual identity brought the post-Kinsey sociological studies full circle with Ulrichs' conception of 120 years earlier, also rooted in the prenatal biology of the developing organism.[28]

The sociocultural sexual identity of the post-Kinsey sociologists, as an overlay of the biological and psychological, was used to detoxicate the homosexual identity. If the homosexual identity derived from natural and social forces external to the individual, treating homosexuals as criminal, immoral, or pathological was clearly inhuman. Homosexuals therefore could be viewed as objects of liberal compassion. To exercise their full rights as citizens, homosexuals needed the special attention of the law and courts to protect them from incarceration and discriminatory practices. As children homosexuals needed the special compassion of parents and teachers who would understand but not try to change them into heterosexuals. As patients homosexuals needed therapists who would not question their sexual identity or implant guilt or hope for change. All such considerations, however, rested on the assumption that homosexuals were unlike heterosexual in their abilities to assume responsibility for their own lives.

The sociocultural homosexual identity, as conceived by the post-Kinsey sociologists, established the boundaries for the socially and psychologically well-adjusted homosexual. Within these boundaries, the image of the "truly homosexual" individual developed. The "truly homosexual" were those who most fully assimilated the "gay subculture" in the choice of partners, friends, political allegiances, and sometimes work. The subculturally assimilated homosexual was considered by the post-Kinsey sociologists to be the adjusted homosexual. This implicit endorsement of the gay subculture served two purposes. It tied the popular belief in the

---

the word is essentially a grammatical term. In languages in which nouns have gender, it is interesting to note that those referring to natural phenomena (e.g., rivers, mountains) can be feminine or masculine as well as those referring to people. This linguistic blurring of gender suggests the polytheistic origins of several languages.

[28] Ulrichs, of course, also made the visible evidence of homosexuality the femininity of the males and the masculinity of the females, a notion that was taken over whole cloth by psychiatry and psychoanalysis.

existence of this subculture to their concept of the homosexual sociocultural identity and gave this identity at least the appearance of social palpability. It also enabled them to view the gay culture as a staging ground for the re-entry of homosexuals into mainstream society. Endorsement, however, carried the implicit expectation to meet requirements, in this case the necessity for the homosexual subculture to shape up to the standards for sex roles and sexual relationships as institutionalized in mainstream society.

The sociocultural homosexual identity, as conceived by the post-Kinsey sociologists, contained ingredients borrowed from the three cosmological views of sexual relationships. The polytheistic view prevailed in their descriptions of some aspects of the gay subculture. The homosexuals described as "functionals" energetically formed sexual relationships with many partners, enjoying the status of the sexual elite. There were, however, the "dysfunctionals" who were similarly occupied with sexual pursuits but appeared to be plagued by guilt and self-rejection. They formed the sexual underbelly of the gay subculture, the remnants of an unbridled sexual paganism. The key distinction between the functionals and dysfunctionals presumably was that the functionals engaged in homosexual relationships under the aegis of the homosexual sociocultural identity. The dysfunctionals engaged in relationships that were furtive and transitory because they rejected their sexual identity. One could imagine, in the context of the studies by the post-Kinsey sociologists, that it was the dysfunctionals who were dishonorably discharged from military service, remained secretive about their "gay identity," and maintained a sexual, to the exclusion of a social and political, involvement in the gay subculture.

The "purely sexual" remained suspect because the socially constructed sexual identity was conceived primarily within the monotheistic view of sexual relationships. The clear endorsement of the belief in the biological origin of sexual identity by the post-Kinsey sociologists merely revealed that the notion of the male-female design was implicit in the idea of sexual identity. For homosexuals to be happy they had to approximate that design as closely as possible, as in the "close-coupled" relationship. Their depiction of the "open-coupled" relationship as troubled reflected their uneasiness with partners who toyed with that design by combining polytheistic and monotheistic ingredients in the same relationship.

If the post-Kinsey sociologists' notion of close-coupled homosexual relationships is grafted on to their idea of homosexual gender nonconformity, there is the clear implication that they assumed that two imperfect females or males could form stable relationships when their feminine or masculine biological deficiencies were mutually compensatory. Homosexual relationships would then be flawed but substantial reflections of the putative biological complementarity of heterosexual relationships. This structuring of homosexual relationships on the basis of a biological principle presumably governing heterosexual relationships represented the chief contribution of the post-Kinsey sociologists to the normalization of homosexual relationships.

Their research restricted the use of choice that characterized the scientific cosmological view of sexual relationships. Individuals, of course, could not choose a biological sexual identity because that was predetermined. Choice was drastically restricted to the one available option. Individuals could choose the appropriate sociocultural sexual identity by willing self-endorsement or they could reject or circumvent it. The tacit assumption of the proponents of the sociocultural sexual identity was that the heterosexual and homosexual were to occupy their assigned sociocultural niches. For one to try to occupy the position of the other would wreak havoc on the sexual order and on personal and social adjustment.

What constituted a moral discourse on permissible structures of sexual relationships was couched in the scientistic language of empirical research. The statistical manipulations of data became more and more convoluted so that the conclusions drawn from them by the researchers were less and less accessible to general scrutiny. The authority of science, thereby, was summoned by the post-Kinsey sociologists, just as their predecessors, the biological and psychological identity theorists, had used medicine and psychiatry to advance their particular conceptions of permissible sexual relationships.

17

The Collective Homosexual Identity:
I. Minority, Community, and Lifestyle

In the scientific discourse that was to follow, the sociocultural homosexual identity was presented as a collective social phenomenon. As the collective homosexual identity it was conceived as a "minority" or as a "community" and "lifestyle," with the implication that the heterosexual identity constituted a majoritarian community and lifestyle of its own. As a "minority" status the collective homosexual identity was framed as the product of heterosexual oppression. This was called "homophobia," a form of social intolerance that paralleled the racism and sexism to which other minorities were subjected. As a "community" and "lifestyle" it was depicted as an affirmative gay and lesbian identity that had tradition, integrity, and uniqueness of its own as well as being embodied in a process of social development that transcended the individual and set the mold for sexual relationships. The collective homosexual identity remained a sociocultural identity because its formation and maintenance depended largely on external factors: the unmasking of and resistance to oppression and the enhancement and celebration of gay community and lifestyle.

One of the first sociological description of the homosexual collective identity as a minority status was provided by Laud Humphreys.[1] One of Humphreys' intentions was to explain the social movement to which the oppression of homosexuals had given rise. The movement was fueled, in his view, by the hope of liberation, that which had been sparked by the report of the Kinsey group on male sexuality. Humphreys conceptualized various forms of oppression and the social and political efforts of homosexuals to evade or battle it. In Humphreys' formulation, the way the homosexual viewed himself was merely the image of himself that others

---

[1] Humphreys, Laud (1972). *Out of the Closet: The Sociology of Homosexual Liberation*. Englewood Cliffs, NJ: Prentice-Hall.

projected. Society projected the image of hatred that the homosexual absorbed as self-hatred:

> Proof that homosexuals constitute an oppressed minority in our society is to be found in the existence of the gay world with its own argot, institutions, social structure, and norms. Even stronger evidence may be seen in the lives of millions of men and women who reject that world in fear and horror, choosing rather to pass as something they are not—heterosexual. (Humphreys, 1972: 41)

Humphreys believed there was more self-hatred in the covert than overt homosexual. In depicting the oppression of homosexuals, Humphreys drew parallels with racial and ethnic minorities and the physically disabled. The temptation of most minorities was to evade rather than confront stigmatization. Evasion included succumbing to shame, attempting to repair the affliction in oneself, passing, mimicking majority customs, and associating only with "fellow sufferers." The aping of the heterosexual marriage by homosexuals was an evasive tactic Humphreys called "covering" (139), which was used "to ease the burdens of oppression by stressing acceptable modes of behavior and diverting attention from traits straight society finds intolerable" (139-140).

Homosexual oppression was not without advantages because it developed novel social skills. Humphreys called these "STREET SKILLS" (66). They consisted of the abilities to "con" others and to use words and wit to outmaneuver the opponent and, of knowledge of a "community's under-life" (66). These skills and this knowledge made it possible for gays (and blacks) to make quick and strategic assessments of other's motives, intentions, and meanings. The homosexual was a "scanner of possibilities" (74), like an actor who experimented with different roles and developed a repertory of identities. The homosexual became an adept cue taker and developed an uncanny sense of when the time was ripe for the portrayal of a particular role. In Humphreys' view, the oppression of homosexuals was not entirely stultifying.

Homosexuals could also "confront" their stigma in two ways. They could "convert" the stigma by exchanging social for political marginality. This conversion was possible by making open declarations of their homosexuality. The other way was to convert the stigma into a new, proud identity: the closet queen became a liberation leader. Besides conversion, which was the "sociopolitical method" (148) of removing stigma, there was a "moral-religious mode" which he called STIGMA REDEMPTION:

Stigmatized persons redeem their own discredit by demanding reparation for suffering endured. They confront condemnation with their own moral indignation, cashing in a lifetime of stigma borne for the right to make moral demands on their accusers. (Humphreys, 1972: 149)

The idea of the homosexual identity as minority status and a lifestyle was propounded in a personal and exhortatory account of the lesbian by Del Martin and Phyllis Lyon.[2] Their book was based on knowledge growing out of their own experience as lesbians and their involvement in the American homophile and women's movements. They noted the lack of research on the lesbian for which they gave several reasons: (1) lesbians were not easily studied because they hid for their own protection; (2) most researchers were men and chiefly concerned with male homosexuality; (3) lesbians resisted being studied by male researchers; and (4) female researchers, who would have met with less reluctance, would not investigate lesbianism for fear of becoming suspect in the eyes of colleagues.

In delineating the lesbian identity as a minority status, Martin and Lyon identified sources of oppression that had been previously described for male homosexuals: intolerance embodied in institutions like the church, law, and psychiatry and prejudice that took the form of attitudes about sex roles and sexuality. Martin and Lyon examined each of these forms of oppression.

Religion came in for particular battering: "To us, the church is a monolithic monster that preys upon people's fear of death" (Martin & Lyon, 1972: 39). As reflected in the mirror held up by the church, the image of the lesbian was distorted: "less than human, sinner, celibate, unnatural, perverse, immoral, graceless, shameful, unstable, unworthy, evil-minded, accursed, wicked, impure" (31). Although church liberals condescendingly offered tolerance for the inescapably lesbian woman, they resisted the idea "that the homosexual can partake of the good life within the homosexual experience" (35).

---

[2] Martin, Del and Lyon, Phyllis (1972). *Lesbian/Woman.* San Francisco: Glide Publications. The authors were founders of the Daughters of Bilitis in 1955, the organization which was to play the leading role in the national women's homophile movement. The organization's newsletter, *The Ladder*, which first appeared in 1956, was edited by Lyon (under the pseudonym, "Ann Ferguson"). In 1958 she was succeeded by Barbara Gittings. Since 1968, Martin and Lyon have played major roles in the women's movement, particularly in the National Organization for Women.

While granting that the laws against homosexual behavior were al-most exclusively enforced against males, they noted that the sexual acts proscribed were as illegal for women as for men. Lesbians, however, felt the brunt of legal intolerance in employment. The chief offender was none less than the federal government, in the form of the Civil Service Commission and the armed services. Both the civilian and military branches of government conducted *sub rosa* investigations to identify and purge from its ranks women who allegedly engaged in homosexual behavior or had homosexual "tendencies."

Martin and Lyon saw psychiatry as making its gloomy contribution to social intolerance, The "pseudo-science of psychoanalysis" (Martin & Lyon, 1972: 46) was blamed for the shift over the years from viewing homosexuality as "sin" or "crime" to viewing it as "mental illness." The most ordinary fears and feelings of women were singled out by psychiatry as possible "causes" of lesbianism:

> fear of the opposite sex, fear of injury or of being emotionally hurt by a man, fear of pregnancy, fear of venereal disease, fear of submission, fear of penetration, fear of rejection, fear of the un-familiar (as contrasted with the familiar), fear of inadequacy, fear of rivalry, fear of growing up and assuming the adult re-sponsibilities of motherhood. These fears are accompanied by other feelings, according to the malady-mongers, of love and/or hate for mom and/or dad, sibling jealousy and rivalry, loneli-ness, rejection, neurotic dependency, strong masochistic impulses, orality and sadism, lack of self-restraint, self-pity, nar-cissism, insecurity, inferiority, hurt pride, defiance, lack of self-confidence, loss of self-esteem, and the excessive wish to survive (to which we might add, "What for?"). (Martin & Lyon, 1972: 47)

There were some bright spots in this thick overcast of oppression. A few Protestant churches formed and supported councils and committees on homosexuality and one church ordained a seminarian who had de-clared that he was a homosexual.[3] As Martin and Lyon pointed out, these

---

[3] The churches involved were the Methodist, Episcopalian, and the United Church of Christ in the period from 1965 to 1972. As a minister in the Methodist Church, Ted McIlvenna led the formation of the Council on Religion and the Homosexual in San Francisco in 1965. Since the publication of the book by Martin and Lyon, a number of homosexual men and women have been ordained by various Protestant denominations after disclosing their sexual identity.

changes within the "'namebrand' Protestant denominations" (264) did not deter a fundamentalist preacher from Alabama, Troy Perry, from starting the Metropolitan Community Church for gay men and women. They lamented the fact, however, that women in that church were relegated to the usual role of "Ladies Auxiliary" (264).

On the legal front they noted the passage of ordinances for protecting homosexuals against employment discrimination and the litigation by homosexuals against employers who had fired them for their sexual orientation. They also observed that research undertaken by psychiatrists and psychologists had eroded the link between homosexuality and mental illness.[4]

Lesbians faced other forms of social prejudice. One stemmed from rigid beliefs in sex-role stereotypes as norms for female or male behavior. As interpolated and applied to lesbians, this took the form of the stereotyped "butch-femme" relationships between women. Martin and Lyon believed they had seen the steady decline of such relationships:

> The minority of lesbians who still cling to the traditional male-female or husband-wife pattern in their partnerships are more than 'likely oldtimers, gay bar habitués or working-class women. (Martin & Lyon, 1972: 80)

Such relationships, they believed, floundered on the rocks of jealousy which itself stemmed from viewing one's partner as property.

Beliefs about lesbian sexuality were not an insignificant source of prejudice:

> Once aware of the lesbian's existence, most people tend to view her solely as a sexual being. She is seen as a sad caricature of a male, trying to dress and act in the manner she deems "masculine," and generally aping some of men's worst characteristics. Or she is conceived of as a hard, sophisticated female who indiscriminately seduces innocent girls or women into the mysteries of some "perversion" they know little or nothing about. On the other hand, she is seen as an unfortunate, pitiable spinster, who, unable to catch a man, has settled for a less desirable substitute in another woman as her lover—whom, of course, she will immediately abandon when and if she meets "him." Some men fantasize the lesbian as a voluptuous, sensuous mistress who is unscrupulous in her sexual tastes, insatiable in her sexual appe-

---

[4] They referred to the research of, among others, Saghir and Robins (1973) and Freedman (1971).

tite and therefore indiscriminate in her choice of sexual partner. (Martin & Lyon, 1972: 9)

When all sources of social oppression were considered, the lives of lesbians were fraught with danger and impediments. Each form of prejudice was a stumbling block which made her life a "never-ending obstacle course" (28). To negotiate around the barriers and ultimately to survive, the lesbian had to develop her inner resources:

> The facts the public has been led to believe are based on mythology, fantasy, rationalization, theory, conjecture, personal bias and hysterical hyperbole. Because of this, the lesbian must go it alone. She must find her own destiny out of her own guts. How she manages her difference, how she feels about herself on learning of her homosexuality, how she confronts those societal attitudes that proclaim her less than human because of a state of being; these are part of every lesbian's story. Some lesbians succumb to society's disregard for people and wind up in purgatory or jail or in an asylum. But hopefully most learn, after years of bitter warfare, that they are people—people of worth and dignity—and that what is important really is not how others view them, but how they view themselves. (Martin & Lyon, 1972: 61)

The conceptualization by Martin and Lyon of the lesbian identity was a major contribution to the literature on homosexuality because the issue had been heretofore generally neglected.[5] The first sentence of their book contained this definition: "A lesbian is a woman whose primary erotic, psychological, emotional, and social interest is in a member of her own sex, even though that interest may not be overtly expressed" (1). Although this definition could be appropriately modified and applied to male homosexuals, the authors believed "that the lesbian differs greatly from the male homosexual in attitudes, problems, and lifestyles" (1). If anything bound homosexual men and women together it was their "many common

---

[5] The authors explained terms that were current in social scientific, journalistic, and political literature on homosexuality. The term HOMOPHILE (as in "homophile movement"), they stated, was used by the Mattachine Society in the 1950s to contrast with HOMOSEXUAL: "Homosexual ... means sex with same, while homophile means love of same" (3). The word GAY, they claimed, was originally used as an "in-group password: to deceive heterosexual society: "It was a word you could use to let someone else know you were homosexual without fear that anyone overhearing it would understand" (5).

concerns" (1). Perhaps the key element of their definition was the apparently innocuous word, "interest." "Interest" in their extended delineation of the lesbian identity spanned biology, psychology, and sociology.

Central to their concept of the lesbian was biological identity:

> Neither our [lesbian] bodies nor the way they function is different from those of other females.... For most lesbians are not women who are pretending to be men, but rather women who cannot express their normal sexual drive in relationships to men, but must direct it toward other females instead. Even in the sexual sphere, the lesbian remains essentially feminine, with the natural desires and reactions of a woman. (13-15)

Because the sex drive of lesbians was natural, they claimed that the lesbian identity was "merely a variation in the total spectrum of human sexuality" (58). Lesbians were not biological anomalies: "For lesbians are *women* who are attracted to *women*" (17).

The lesbian identity, as conceived by Martin and Lyon, was also psychological. Indeed, they repudiated the idea of a purely biological identity: "sex is not just biology and reproduction: it is emotion, sensations, pleasure and pain" (Martin & Lyon, 1972: 184). They defined lesbians' psychological sexual identity more as inner, subjective states than as behavior, "which is only the outward expression of a much deeper, emotional and psychic life" (23). The inner life of the lesbian was variously described. It consisted of sexual fantasies peopled by women. It included dawning proclivities that preceded overt behavior: "Lesbians ... become aware of their homosexual tendencies gradually during their growing-up process" (200). It was, above all, an emotional identity: "female homosexuality could not be defined simply in terms of the sex act itself, but had to do with emotional involvement between women" (19). The emotional qualities of the lesbian identity were seen as diffuse, "encompassing the structure of her whole personality, one facet of which is, of course, her sexuality. For her it is the expression of a way of feeling, of loving, of responding to other people" (10). This psychological identity, had pervasive significance for the lesbian:

> Behind that simple statement—"I am a Lesbian"—are implications so vast that the individual who would survive with any measure of sanity must examine all that she has ever been taught, all that she has ever experienced, all that she has ever hoped or dreamed. Some never make it through this long and lonely journey. (27)

There was a positive aspect of the collective lesbian identity, described by Martin and Lyon as the lesbian lifestyle.[6] It was characterized by one-to-one relationships between women who often successfully pooled their monetary resources. In the suburbs the lesbian lifestyle took the form of "inbred lesbian cliques" (117) composed of professional and middle-class women who cautiously limited their choice of friends and partners. In general, the lifestyle was quiet and unassuming, and included sexual fidelity between partners. For some lesbians, presumably those in cities, the lifestyle was described as increasingly political, as earlier hopes for "tolerance" gave way to demands for acceptance, liberation, and equality:

> It is indeed time that society redefines and reevaluates homosexuality as a preference, an orientation and a propensity for a certain lifestyle which is equal to and on a par with heterosexuality—with all that entails.... The homophile community of fifteen years ago (mid-fifties) might have settled for "tolerance." But not today: no halfway measures will do. In our several identities (as citizens, as women, and as lesbians) we want equal rights and full citizenship—whether in relation to marriage, joint income tax returns, inheritance, property, adoption of children, job opportunity, education or security clearances. (Martin & Lyon, 1972: 309-310)

As for the social behavior of the lesbian, "the only thing that distinguishes her as a lesbian is her choice of another woman as her sex, love, or life partner" (24). They rejected as fallacious the notion that "it takes one to know one" (14) and stated that the lesbian was not distinguishable by her departure from conventional femininity:

> Like other women we come in all sizes and shapes. Some of us are tall and lanky; some of us are short and fat. We are young and old, beautiful and homely, blonde and brunette, short-haired and long-haired, fair-skinned and dark-skinned—

---

[6] Lifestyle is a term that lies at the intersection of personality and culture. Its wide usage first occurred in the nineteen-sixties to describe the unconventional tastes and practices of such groups as the beatniks, flower children, and the hippies. It is currently employed euphemistically to refer to unconventional sexual practices and liaisons, including homosexual relationships. It is sometimes used interchangeably with "subculture" or "community" as in the "gay lifestyle." Martin and Lyon used "lifestyle" in both its personal and collectivistic senses.

whatever the combination or variation.... The lesbian looks, dresses, acts and is like any other woman. (13-14)

Because the lesbian identity was at first a private, personal one, it was the responsibility or choice of the individual lesbian to convert it into a public, social identity. The authors distinguished between the early and current meanings of the term, "coming out." They noted that it once referred to the first sexual experience one woman had with another (which presumably led to an unending series of such experiences). It now described the event of publicly disclosing one's homosexuality, as it were, "coming out of the closet" (126).

Their conceptualization of the lesbian as a collective identity that included logical and psychological ingredients was consistent with their postulations on how the identity was acquired. At one point they surprisingly endorsed psychoanalytic versions of etiology: "the preponderance of psychoanalytic theory suggests that homosexuality is either a learned pattern of behavior or an expression of one facet of the ambisexual nature of human beings" (159). However, they did not subscribe to the Freudian theory of sexual instinct. Unlike animals lower on the evolutionary scale, they believed that humans learned sexual behavior.[7]

Lesbianism could also be a socially-induced identity. Referring to two adolescent girls of uncertain sexual orientation, the authors predicted that "they will probably be lesbian because they were pushed, marked, and stereotyped as lesbians by those adults who most feared such a result" (Martin & Lyon, 1972: 186). As a label, "lesbian" was socially imposed by men as a "psychic weapon" (292) against those women who functioned

---

[7] In their discussion of bisexuality (85-90), Martin and Lyon suggested that all women have the natural capacity for pleasurable sexual relations with both men and women, which unfortunately had been "obscured by biological and biblical scripting" (86). Although they believed lesbians could have pleasurable sexual intercourse with males, they thought it lacked the emotional involvement present in relations with women. Yet they postulated a human ambisexuality: If the idea of sex could be cleansed and the guilt we have felt about it could be purged from our minds, we would be rid of our sexual frustrations and hang-ups. We could expand our consciousness beyond our present preoccupation with the who-what-why-where-and-how of the mechanics of genital contact and fascination with the measurements of physical attributes.... Allowed the freedom to be human, we might find that a new sexuality would emerge, encompassing not only the sensual, but also the trans-physical qualities of love, empathy and concern for one another's personhood, regardless of gender" (89-90).

autonomously outside the "feminine role" as defined by men. It was possible for heterosexual women to take on the lesbian identity as a step toward liberation from male sexual exploitation. Rather than sacrificing all sexual gratification, such women turned to other women as a "stopgap" (297), waiting for the time when men would treat them with equality:

> The point is that as women become women-identified rather than male-defined, they are opening themselves up to the discovery of the many options available to them. No longer are they constrained to the limitations of the nuclear family and husband or the alternative of "going it alone." Some are experimenting with communal living—either same sex or mixed groups. Others are what we have called "instant" lesbians, making a conscious choice for relationships with other women rather than the unconscious choice typical of the lesbians.... These women, no longer trapped in the Freudian hoax of vaginal versus the clitoral orgasm, know that they can find sexual satisfaction, emotional and spiritual fulfillment, and human understanding with a woman; and they know that at this time in history they cannot find these things with a man. (Martin & Lyon, 1972: 298)

Martin and Lyon's contribution to the normalization of homosexual relationship was contained in their depiction of intimate relationships. They believed that standards for healthy heterosexual relationships could be validly applied to lesbian relationships: "The established criteria for heterosexual marriage (love, commitment, concern, and responsibility) can be, and often are, found in homosexual relationships" (34). It was their belief that most lesbians formed intimate pairs, some of which, like heterosexual relationships, could endure:

> [W]hether or not these pairings last, as in heterosexual marriages, depends upon the degree of their maturity, their level of sexual adjustment, how well their personalities mesh, how much they have in common, and how well they manage their outside commitments. (103)

Even lesbian sexuality met heterosexual standards: "What do lesbians do sexually? Very much the same thing a man and a woman (or a man and a man) can, with the exception there is no penis" (64). While lesbian relationships were sexual, their key element was emotional involvement: "What keeps us together is feelings—of love, commitment, and mutual respect" (109).

Because the requirements for heterosexual relationships closely corresponded with those of lesbian relationships, Martin and Lyon argued for the legalization of homosexual marriages. This endorsement, they believed, would provide homosexuals a sense of well-being. When lesbian relationships became troubled, the individuals involved needed the same kind of counseling available to heterosexuals especially because most lesbians could not turn to families for support. They often did not seek professional help because they feared exposure of their homosexuality and therapists who might focus on their sexual orientation rather than attend to the problems in their relationships.

Many lesbians, the authors believed, had been married to men. Some married because they had minimized or had been unaware of their homosexual feelings. Others were put off by the "seamier" (128) side of gay life and, in the quest for security and stability, retreated into marriages. Married lesbians frequently became mothers. If their homosexuality was discovered and precipitated divorce, the question of their fitness as mothers arose: "The ability to reproduce has nothing whatever to do with child-rearing. What is involved is the love, concern, responsibility and maturity of the parent, not whether that parent is heterosexual or homosexual" (176).

These ideas contributed to the normalization of sexual relationships. The proposal to include homosexual pairings in the institution of marriage expanded the notion of heterosexual monogamy. By distinguishing between reproductive and parenting roles, they expanded the notion of parenthood by including the single mother. Finally, by reminding parents of their familial responsibilities to their homosexual children, they presented the possibility that children could develop and express either a heterosexual or homosexual identity.

The subjective account of the lesbian experience by Martin and Lyon was remarkably similar in concept and tone to the portrayal, twenty years earlier, of the homosexual male and subculture by Cory. Both books were pioneering efforts to detoxicate the public view of the homosexual identity by showing the crippling consequences of moral intolerance and legal oppression on the lives of harmless individuals. Both subscribed to the psychoanalytic theory of homosexual etiology, a sexual identity forged in early childhood and difficult if not impossible to reverse; both favored marriage as the normalized form of homosexual relationships as well as the most desirable and healthy form; and both counseled parents on the compassionate acceptance of their homosexual children. Their narratives struck different notes, however, because they were describing a set of conditions they believed were contingent on differences in biological sex. Cory, in what was to become the ethnographic fashion of the next two decades, exotically described the "male homosexual subculture." Martin and Lyon dwelt on the "lesbian lifestyle," anchored in the lesbian couple and merged with the political determination of women to win equality.

The concept of the lesbian lifestyle, as developed by Martin and Lyon, had two components: one was the autonomous individual and the other was the relationship between individuals. Their concept of the individual as lesbian had three elements. The lesbian was a female, held feminine values, and was emotionally or physically attracted to women. This concept was both biological and social in construction. It was biological because the lesbian was identified as a female and as potentially having sexual relationships with women. It was social in the feminine values held by her.

In the relationship between individuals the characteristics of the lesbian were combined and expressed. These relationships embodied a solidarity with women at interpersonal, societal, and political levels. While the lesbian lifestyle was predicated on the biological concept that all lesbians were women and described in terms of their relationships with women, these relationships were not necessarily sexual. They were based on a set of values traditionally associated with stable relationships: love, commitment, concern, and responsibility.

What Martin and Lyon provided was a juxtaposition rather than a merging of the sexual and social elements of the lesbian lifestyle. The social element appeared more likely to stumble over the sexual; lesbians and heterosexual women who sought to express the solidarity of feminine values in an intimate relationship had to confront the problem posed by antipathetic sexual desires. Because the social element took precedence, the "comprise" possible for such pairs was to sacrifice the sexual for the social relationship at least until that time when men could be found who shared the values of heterosexual women.[8]

It was also possible for the sexual to stumble over the social, although this possibility was less well delineated by the authors. The wife and mother, for example, who became sexually involved with women

---

[8] In such a compromise it would appear, at first blush, that the heterosexual woman would be making the greater sacrifice because the lesbian was attracted to women in the first place. To keep the costs and benefits equal, it would be necessary to cast those relationships along the order of "love without sex."

jeopardized her love, commitment, concern, and responsibility for her family and faced the possibility of losing custody of her children. With the minimization of the sexual, the author's conception of the lesbian lifestyle was clearly sociocultural.

There were sociological treatises, contemporary with those of the post-Kinsey sociologists. Before the publication of the last volume of the post-Kinsey sociologists, Joseph Harry and William DeVall presented a description of the gay subculture that attempted to correct the image of "cultural impoverishment" (Harry & DeVall, 1978: 151) presented by the ethnologists of the sixties.[9] The authors commenced their work with an attack on theories of the psychological homosexual identity. According to the authors, one theory held that homosexual males identified themselves as females. Although they entertained this as a possibility wherever cultural settings restricted the choice of "gender identity" to female or male, the authors believed that this theory may have had no basis other than the assertion of both gay men and psychiatrists that "a homoerotic choice implies a female gender identity" (3).

The authors referred to a second theory that held that the origins of homosexuality lay in the dominance-power motivations of homosexual men which, in turn, derived from their resolution of the oedipal conflict. It was based on evidence that homosexual males preferred masculine partners. Harry and DeVall argued that a simpler explanation for this preference was that homosexual men had "internalized their culture's conception of what is desirable in men" (Harry & DeVall, 1978: 4). A third

---

[9] Harry, Joseph, and DeVall, William B. (1978). *The Social Organization of Gay Males*. New York: Praeger. The authors presented their work as a serious "structural and analytical treatment of important questions for both social theorists and for those who make public policy" (x) regarding male homosexuality. The book was primarily based on questionnaires filled out by 243 respondents in the Detroit metropolitan area in 1975. Respondents were contacted through gay bars, private and professional social circles, and homophile organizations. Questions focused on negative attitudes toward gays, interest in emotional intimacy with other gays, bar cruising, self-esteem, enduring sexual liaisons, homosexual marital relationships, homosexual marital status (i.e., married, single, or divorced), and teenage heterosexual and homosexual interests. Most responses were indicated on Likert scales. Although those who responded to the questionnaire apparently were not interviewed, the authors did interview men in different parts of the United States and Canada, particularly in San Francisco and New York. They read gay publications and historical materials as well as observed gay street life and the lesbian-gay freedom day parades in San Francisco.

theory, that homosexuality was caused by pathological childhood fear and trauma, they thought was less convincing than the psychological theory that "a homosexual orientation was acquired during childhood through positive motivations and rewarding erotic experiences with same-sex persons" (3)[10]

If this was how the homosexual identity was acquired, they thought its social prohibition would be indeed perplexing for the child:

> Once a child has had such rewarding erotic experience with same-sex persons, those experiences prove to him that a person of the same sex can be a source of sexual pleasure. Having eroticized same-sex persons, it then becomes extremely difficult to later learn that such persons cannot be sources of sexual pleasure. In contrast, heterosexuals have learned to define same-sex persons as not being sources of physical pleasure. Hence the homosexual remains puzzling to them and is seen as something that must be motivated by perverse feelings rather than by erotic ones. (6)[11]

The speculations of Harry and DeVall on labeling theory reflected the increasing skepticism and caution of sociologists in applying it to the study of sexual identity. The authors argued that informal labeling was a more potent force than formal labeling by social control agencies. Informal labeling consisted of heterosexuals keeping homosexuals at arm's length: "Heterosexuals prefer to keep homosexuals at a distance because the latter often provoke anxiety in the former" (14). Homosexuals also had more varied reactions to labeling than formal labeling theorists had originally imagined. Labeling theory was "nullified" in those cases when gay men successfully concealed their homosexuality. Even when their sexual orientation was fortuitously discovered, serious punishment or ostracization rarely resulted. In addition, when gay men publicly "came out" the consequences of labeling were circumvented.

The point of view generally adopted by Harry and DeVall was that of gay men as collectivity, facing the challenges of overcoming the cultural push toward heterosexuality, constructing personal relationships among

---

[10] The authors attributed this theory to C. E. Tripp (1975.).

[11] The authors noted Tripp's theory and their extensions of it did not explain bisexuality or sexual abstinence. The exclusivity of choice they suggested may be due to the fact that "society defines sex roles, and particularly sexual roles, as mutually exclusive.... Thus the homosexual child may assume that one is allowed to eroticize only one sex" (6).

themselves, and confronting social and political discrimination. They saw adolescent gays as facing the problem of surmounting the "intense and omnipresent expectations" (78) to adopt a heterosexual script even though they know that it was at odds with their male identification and homosexual orientation. Repeated attempts by homosexual adolescents to adopt the heterosexual script were defeated. Their resistance to adopting the homosexual script could have deleterious psychological effects: "[A] teenager's guilt about his homosexuality seems to give rise to a delayed coming out and a later stage of identification of self as gay. Late entry into the gay world is also associated with a lessened interest in emotional intimacy with other gay males and with lessened self-esteem" (79). When the gay adolescent exercised his freedom as an adult he "rejects heterosexual expectations, comes out, and devises a lifestyle more in keeping with his delayed sexual identity" (79).[12]

The expectations of gay males for their sexual relationships was a key area of attention of Harry and DeVall. They addressed the question of whether or not there were a set of expectations that were generally shared so that it would be possible to speak of the "social organization" of gay marriage. On the surface it appeared that gay marriage as an institution was in a state of "disorganization" because these marriages lacked longevity and sexual fidelity. The authors, however, held that the EMOTIONAL fidelity of male partners, more than the SEXUAL fidelity, was the key ingredient of gay marriage. To the extent that the men insisted on sexual fidelity they "have borrowed their marital model from the heterosexual culture" (94). It was such insistence on sexual fidelity, not infidelity itself, that disrupted gay marriage. Yet the authors recognized that "sustained emotional intimacy" was the goal of the gay marriage and that this aspiration was at odds with "the sexual market mentality" (94) of the gay subculture.

The issue of dominance, the authors believed, was not a disruptive influence on gay marriage: "Since gay males seem to model their marriages after the egalitarian model of best friends, matters of dominance are substantially irrelevant to their relationships" (100). Nor did they believe that dominance intruded upon sexual roles: "the most common set

---

[12] The author's treatment of adolescent homosexuality was based on their assumption that sexual identity "is established during the first years of life and that subsequent efforts to change it, either by the individual or psychotherapeutic agents, are likely to be ineffective" (78). The gay male adolescent was therefore faced with the problem of expressing rather than identifying his homosexuality.

of preferences among gay men is for all roles—both oral and anal and active and passive" (109).The use of both orifices and the taking of both roles was fostered by membership in the gay subculture: Perhaps we can infer ... that participation in gay sexual and social activities encourages sexual flexibility rather than the sexual role speculation that popular or psychoanalytic thought alleges" (109). This inference, the authors claimed, rested on the evidence that gay "bar frequenters" were more flexible in role taking than "nonfrequenters" (110). The issue of dominance emerged only in the relationships of those gay males they identified as "nonegalitarians" (113). Egalitarians, contrary to psychoanalytic theory, "seem to pattern their activity more on a model of equality and reciprocity" (118). The authors asserted that middle and upper-class gay men preferred egalitarian to nonegalitarian relationships.

The confronting of discrimination by gay men was another major focus of their book. The authors based their conclusions on the development of gay communities, personal adaptations to discrimination, and the gay liberation movement. Variation in gay communities was discussed in terms of "institutional completeness," the degree to which a particular community was capable of providing services required by its members. The first step in this direction was the establishment of urban gay bars; the second, the development of neighborhoods in which gay residents were concentrated. The highest degree of completeness was achieved in the "gay ghettoes" (143) of cities like Boston, Chicago, New York, Los Angeles, and San Francisco.[13] As each of these communities became diverse the authors thought they overcame the "cultural impoverishment" feared by the ethnologists of the sixties.

Under "getting ahead gay" (159), the authors described how gay men dealt with the problem of employment in the face of either direct discrimination, as exemplified by being fired or passed over for promotion, or indirect discrimination, where gay males avoided certain positions in anticipation of ill treatment. In spite of discrimination the authors claimed that gay males often enjoyed more occupational success than heterosexual males because of their superior education, greater geographical mobility, and, in particular, deeper devotion to jobs:

---

[13] The requirements for urban locales to qualify as gay ghettoes were stipulated in Levine, Martin P. (1979). Gay Ghetto. *Journal of Homosexuality* 4(4): 363-375. The authors did not explain why they excluded Detroit from their list even though it was the place where their questionnaire data had been collected.

They are freed from the tensions of balancing work demands against the demands of spouses and children.... While the higher-status jobs call forth more effort from employees, it is likely that gays have more to give to their jobs due to their freedom from familial obligations.... These [factors] have enabled some male homosexuals to partially offset discrimination against them. Gays in higher white-collar occupations often have better records of job performance than heterosexuals. (Harry & DeVall, 1978: 164-165)

The Gay Liberation movement was viewed by the authors as the effort to develop a "collective identity" which "embodied explicit criticisms of the status quo and provided a justification and rationale for homosexual lifestyles" (173). While recognizing the amelioration of public intolerance in recent years, they expressed great concern over the "antigay crusades and neo-conservatism" (116) of the late seventies.

Their recommendations for changes in public policy included liberalization of laws pertaining to consenting adult sexual conduct: "A more rational approach by legal authorities to homosexuals' behavior would be to decriminalize homosexual acts in private and to allow, even encourage, the development of explicitly gay settings, such as bars and baths" (190). They also believed that sex between adults and minors should not be based on the presumption of force by the adult: "[W]e note that the presumption of coercion is an assumption and need not be a necessary part of adult-minor [sexual] transactions" (194). Public sex among gay men should become a police concern only when "the volume of sexual transactions is sufficiently large that it is likely that visitors to the locale might become unwilling observers to such transactions" (198). The legalization of gay marriages "could be a measure of symbolic support for enduring relationships within the gay community" (201). Their alternative recommendation was the "delegalization" (201) of heterosexual unions. Based on this policy "sexual unions of all kinds—other than coercive ones—would be matters of private concern, which would not be within the state's domain of interest" (201-202). They also recommended the passage of laws that prohibited discrimination on the basis of "affectional or sexual preference" (202). In support of such laws the authors proclaimed: "Since the vast majority of gay persons hold down jobs and perform them satisfactorily, it has become clear to many informed persons that job discrimination based on sexual orientation is palpably unjust" (208).

The assertions by Harry and DeVall of the superiority of individuals who were homosexual to those heterosexual struck the increasingly militant note which was to characterize the detoxication of the homosexual identity by the theorists of the collective identity. What had once been entreaties for tolerance became at least implied critiques of heterosexual relationships as a set of inflexible, non-egalitarian, sexual practices held together more by legal than affectional ties. As an acquired sexual identity, homosexuality was given developmental beginnings which were at least as respectable as those of heterosexuality and free of any serious threat to the individual's membership in his own biological sex. The gay marriage continued to be the chief means whereby homosexual relationships was normalized. It was also the standard whereby one could judge the individual's self-acceptance of his homosexual identity and the real depth of his immersion in the homosexual community.

In 1978, Barry Adam published a volume in which he compared what he called the "gay minority" with the black and Jewish minorities.[14] His intention was to show the commonality of "coping strategies" used by the three groups in overcoming their "inferiorization" by the dominant social order. Within Adam's formulation the dominated were viewed as contributing to their own domination:

> Evidence from such disparate groups as Jews, blacks, and gay people allows us to understand how inferiorized people cope with living oppressed on a day-to-day basis. The story of how people survive domination through resistance, accommodation, and compliance tells us much about how domination survives and an inequitable social order is reproduced. (Adam, 1978: x)

By "domination" Adam referred to the "social structuring of life limitations, by which one group (the dominators) successfully maximize its life chances by minimizing those of another (the dominated)" (8). The systematic restriction of "life chances" (18) resulted in the everyday "inferiorization" of the dominated group: "The struggle to survive, resist, and overcome the processes of inferiorization marks the history of dominated groups" (1).

The major focus of his treatise was to describe "the coping strategies employed in the *everyday life* to meet the exigencies of inferiorization" (1).

---

[14] Adam, Barry D. (1978). *The Survival of Domination: Inferiorization of Everyday Life*. New York: Elsevier. The volume appeared to combine elements of symbolic interactionism, existential philosophy, and Marxist political theory with the social psychology of Theodor Adorno and the social philosophy of Friedrich Nietzsche.

There were several methods of coping: ESCAPE FROM IDENTITY as, for example, the desire or even the pretense of the homosexual to be a heterosexual; SOCIAL WITHDRAWAL from the larger society into the minority community; PSYCHOLOGICAL WITHDRAWAL, as exemplified by the constriction of behavioral and emotional expression; guilt-expiation rituals such as the self-mutilation of the transsexual; construction of MAGICAL IDEOLOGIES as a sham explanation of the goals and process of domination; and IN-GROUP HOSTILITY in which one segment of an interiorized group shows intolerance toward a still more degraded segment.

In-group hostility, in Adam's view, had particular application to the gay minority. Such hostility was shown by gay people as contempt for others who embodied the gay identity. This contempt was a profound self-hatred that could take several forms: disdain for effeminate men, the inability to have an intimate relationship with another gay man, the genitalization of sex (in the fashion of heterosexuality), engaging in sex while repressing emotional involvement, and attachment to heterosexuals: "Gay men living with other gay men … showed more self-acceptance and less guilt" (Adam, 1978: 11).

The coping strategies described by Adam were presented as methods of compliance and accommodation by minorities to the dominant social order. With the development of their own communities the minorities were able to shift to strategies of resistance and thereby take the first steps in overcoming their inferiorization. The strategies for casting off domination were learned within the community at the price of limiting one's life aspirations to those provided by the community. Within the minority community the art of resistance flourished for the purpose of undermining the dominant order through such means as social parody and satire.

In the tradition of symbolic interactionism Adam conceived the "gay identity" as a social construction: "Black or Jewish or gay identity arises from no intrinsic or biologic quality in itself. Intrinsically they are nothing. Only the image of the self reflected by *others able to influence or control one's life or survival*, necessarily organizes the self's priorities and orientations" (11). What gave the gay minority its identity were the social meanings which accrued to the homosexual erotic preference.

In the year following the appearance of Adam's book, Deborah Wolf published an ethnographic study of the lesbian community.[15] Wolf

---

[15] Wolf, Deborah Goleman (1979/1980). *The Lesbian Community*. Berkeley: University of California Press. Page references are to the paperback reprinting

described the development of the community as occurring in three stages. The first stage, "the old gay life" (Wolf, 1979/1980: 23), was characterized by dichotomized butch-femme sex-roles, the bar as the central social setting, and a generally "depressed lifestyle" (24) accepted by lesbians as their just lot in life. "Homophile organizations" marked the next historical stage. These organizations, which developed in the fifties within the context of social norms, hoped to educate the public about lesbians and to serve as an alternative setting for them to meet. The third stage was characterized by "militant lesbian-feminism" (24). Lesbians were viewed "as the vanguard of the feminist future" and they demanded "a basic reconstruction of both self and society" (24).

Because Wolf studied the lesbian community during its third stage, much Of her attention was devoted to lesbian-feminist ideology and politics. According to Wolf the leading proponents of lesbian-feminism believed that "lesbian" was a label invented by men for any women who dare to be their equal and applied by men to any relationship of real solidarity among women. The goal of lesbian-feminism was to exchange the women's male-given identity for "the woman-identified-as-woman" identity. This new perspective represented for lesbian-feminists the creation of a new consciousness and revolutionary force.

In her ethnographic description of lesbians in San Francisco, Wolf explained the concept of "community":

> The terms "community," "lesbian community," and "women's community" are commonly used by women themselves to refer to the continuing social networks of lesbians who are committed to the lesbian-feminist lifestyle, who participate in various community activities and projects, and who congregate socially. The concept "socio-psychological unity" is to them an important part of their sense of what a community is and who belongs to it. (Wolf, 1979/1980: 73)

Wolf pointed to the "support of one's sisters" (77) as the basic value of lesbian-feminism. In the expression of this value the local community in San Francisco was linked to other lesbian communities across the nation in a vast social network.

(1980). Wolf described herself as a "heterosexual anthropologist" (6). She intended that her book serve as a description of the "development of the San Francisco lesbian feminist community during the years 1972-1975" (ix). The work, she stated, was inspired by the earlier publication of Martin and Lyon which had urged research on lesbians.

Wolf described the structure of the lesbian community as consisting of overlapping social networks without any official leaders, although some networks are dominated by women with strong personalities. Individual women were characterized in a number of ways: "within the community, women are identified by their special interest or skills, by their friendship networks, and by their present and former lovers" (81).

The lesbian pair, Wolf held, was the "building block of the community, the ideal to which the community aspires" (81). This relationship she described as romantic, sexually egalitarian, and mutually nurturant. The benign quality of lesbian sexuality pervaded the entire relationship: "The fact that lesbians can be tender with each other in bed and that the nature of lesbian lovemaking can be inherently egalitarian means that, for many women, the trust and good feelings established during lovemaking carry over and help reinforce the emotional relationship" (91). Although coupledom was the ideal, the most enduring relationships were those between close friends who, in some cases, may have been former lovers.

As a community the women, according to Wolf, stressed "anti-materialism" (101), choosing "not to compete for high-salaried, pro-fessional jobs, which they equate with middle-class capitalistic values." Leisure time was spent with friends, usually at home, but also in the women's coffeehouses, bars, and bookstores.[16]

The issue of the sociocultural identity clearly emerged in Wolf's discussion of the marginal position of lesbian mothers: "To members of the lesbian community she is in an ambiguous position: because of her association with the father of her children, they are not certain she is a 'real' lesbian" (136). Wolf depicted lesbian mothers as struggling with their lesbian identity. Some women had been aware of their homosexual identity before marriage but entered marriage with the hope that it would "cure" them. Others became aware after marriage, particularly when they fell in love with another woman. Some left their marriages behind, a decision which Wolf believed required difficult social and financial adjustments. In the interest of their children, other women maintained their marriages but had an affair on the side:

---

[16] Wolf devoted a chapter to the description of two projects that were undertaken by two classes of women in the lesbian community. One group she referred to as "middle-class cultural feminists, the other as "working-class women with a strong class analysis" (108). The two groups were presented as representing an ideological split within the lesbian community.

Such women hesitate to identify themselves as lesbians; rather they are inclined to feel, as do some newly emerging lesbians who are unmarried, that the affair in which they find themselves is a special one between two people who love each other, but that it will not be repeated. Such "special" relationships can last for years, and the heterosexual marriage is maintained as well. In recent years, however, with the spread of feminist politics and the emergence of lesbian-feminist self-help organizations, many such women, who traditionally would have stayed married, do leave their husbands and move with their children and a partner into the lesbian community. (Wolf, 1979/1980: 137-138)[17]

Wolf believed there were implicit assumptions that community members made about self, others, and society, which she collectively called their "world view" (169). The female self was a reservoir of life-affirming and unfulfilled potential dammed up by a male-dominated society. The world was divided into males and females and the females subdivided into lesbians and nonlesbians. Lesbians were seen as strong:

Lesbians are viewed as epitomizing the strength, the creativity, and the tenderness in all women but is stifled in heterosexual women because they are trained to be dependent on and deferential to men. Lesbians are also seen as latter-day Amazons, fearless warriors, yet caring and loving friends. (Wolf, 1979/1980: 171)

Relations with men exposed women to the risk of contamination:

[I]t is felt that the more contact one has with men, the more one's inner strength and resourcefulness are sapped, since men, even inadvertently, try to dominate any situation and to cannibalize the strength of women. (171)

Women were seen as the élan vital:

Women are viewed as nurturing, intuitive survivors, who by their nature are more likely to be in harmony with the life force. If our present society had been structured in terms of women's characteristics rather than men's, some community members believed that all people would have the opportunity to develop according to their potential, and cooperative, caring lives would

---

[17] Wolf also described the "unmarried lesbian mothers," women who acquired children by adoption or artificial insemination through anonymous donors (Wolf, 1979/1980: 138-139).

be led by all. The political system of the realm of women might be called something like a "socialist matriarchy." (170)

As part of this world view, the patriarchal god was to be replaced by a "Mother Goddess" (173) who was the fountainhead of healing, intuition, and the unity of the human race.

A study of the homosexual identity as a lesbian minority status was conducted by Virginia Brooks.[18] The focus of her research was the exploration of how the lesbian minority status was related to stress, which she defined as situations or agents that required the individual to make readjustments. In a vein similar to that of Adam, Brooks conceived of a minority in terms of the restrictions imposed on the lives of its members:

> (1) A minority group may be defined as any group of people who, on the basis of one characteristic, are categorically ascribed inferior status, denied equal access to legitimate socio-economic opportunities, and denied equal participation and fair repre- sentation in major societal institutions. (2) This condition as defined here has persisted over time, is systematically embed- ded in the culture, and requires institutional change as opposed to individual change for alleviation and prevention. (Brooks, 1981: 56)

Because lesbians occupied two minority statuses, as women and as homosexuals, Brooks believed that they would be exposed to stress on both counts.

The lesbian identity, in Brooks' conception, consisted of elements of power, social scripts, and social learning. She believed that "the power model argued that lesbianism is not only a sexual preference but also a political stance against (male) domination" (30). Negative social meanings accruing to the heterosexual script reduced the attractiveness for women

---

[18] Brooks, Virginia R. (1981). *Minority Stress and Lesbian Women*. Lexington, MA: D.C. Health. The study was based on the questionnaire responses of 675 women recruited from women's meeting places in three major metropolitan areas of California: Los Angeles, San Diego, and San Francisco. In addition to the customary demographic items, there were questions on sexual orientation, social sex-roles, self-disclosure, childhood activities, psychotherapy, use of drugs, friendships, political views, and life goals. Brooks defended her use of the term LESBIAN WOMAN against the charge of redundancy. She stated that "cognitively it is important to shift the classification of the individual to *woman* and the descriptive modifier to *lesbian*" (8). Her subjects were not called homosexual women because she claimed that the word homosexual was traditionally associated with men.

of relationships with men. She thought these negative meanings were the result of the "power differential" that greatly favored men. Concomitantly, through social learning women found that relationships with other women were more reinforcing.

According to Brooks, the term sexual orientation was misleading because lesbian women were expressing a cultural as well as a sexual preference for a feminine social environment over a masculine one. The central issue in women's relationships with either men or women appeared to be sex-roles rather than sex. In the hope of balancing the cultural and sexual implications, she employed the term sociosexual orientation.

Lesbians were portrayed as freer from the constraints of the feminine sex-role than heterosexual women. This conclusion suggested to her that "lesbian women … have been more resistant to the male reward systems that reinforce sex-typed behaviors" (47). In the sense that lesbians were described as androgynous, Brooks implied that they were freer to develop both their femininity and masculinity. Through her study Brooks hoped to discover if this psychological autonomy of lesbians led to greater social stress.

Brooks apparently concluded that the stress experienced by lesbians was not solely the consequence of their minority statuses. Lesbians of lower-class status, for example, experienced more stress than those of middle-class status. Being a woman resulted in more stress than being a lesbian. Being disclosed as a lesbian was more stressful than being undisclosed. Exposure to the feminist ideology and viewing lesbians and women as reference groups, she believed, were associated with reduced stress in her respondents.

Brooks provided a diagrammatic conception of the process through which lesbian women as a minority could learn to cope with stress. Her emphasis was on increasing the individual's behavioral repertory so that she could operate capably in novel and critical circumstances. The first step in the management of stress involved the lesbian woman's redefinition and acceptance of self. At this step she had to cast off the stereotypes and adhere to her own personal beliefs about herself. At the next step she had to develop "a broader empathy with other minorities" (Brooks, 1981: 125), a step made difficult because each group stereotyped the others. The third step occurred when the lesbian woman joined efforts with other lesbian women, a task requiring the alteration of any stereotyped beliefs about others like herself. The final step was taken when she understood the importance of supporting equal rights for other minorities as well as her own. Because progression through these steps increased tension, it was important for her to believe in the beginning that temporary increases in stress were necessary in order to attain an ultimate reduction.[19]

The homosexual "subculture" or "world" as conceived in earlier versions of the sociocultural identity was transformed into the gay and lesbian "minority," "community" and "lifestyle" in the analyses of Humphreys, Harry, DeVall, Adam, Wolf, and Brooks. The collectivization of the homosexual identity as conceived by these writers, was largely attributed to the majoritarian society, variously described as the dominant order, capitalism, the middle class, male-dominated society, or, most simply, men. The ruling groups were portrayed as acting solely in their own interests, maximizing their own opportunities for material and political gain by minimizing those of the minorities, such as gay men and lesbian women.

While the monolithic oppression of the rulers created the gay and lesbian minorities, it was the collective efforts of individual minority members which created the gay and lesbian communities and lifestyle. This consolidation of effort was made possible by the members' recognition of the commonality of their oppression and the ways they coped with it. These new communities were treated with much more tender care by the collective identity theorists than that which had been given to the male homosexual subculture by the ethnographies of preceding decades. The sociologists of the fifties and sixties were ambivalent about the "homosexual world," on the one hand representing it as a safe and necessary refuge for sexual outcasts while, on the other hand, expressing

---

[19] We have selected the books by Brooks, Lyon and Martin, and Wolf as representative of social-scientific efforts to depict the three facets of the lesbian identity discussed in this chapter, as minority, community, or lifestyle. Several journalistic and literary depictions of the lesbian identity appeared in the seventies and early eighties: Abbot, Sidney and Love, Barbara (1972). *Sappho Was a Right-On Woman.* New York: Stein and Day, 1972; Califia, Pat (1980). *The Book of Lesbian Sexuality.* Tallahassee, FL: Naiad Press; Faderman, Lillian (1981). *Surpassing the Love of Men: Romantic Friendship and Love Between Women from the Renaissance to the Present.* New York: William Morrow; Johnston, Jill (1973). *Lesbian Nation: Feminist Solution.* New York: Simon and Schuster; Lewis, Sasha Gregory (1979). *Sunday's Women: A Report on Lesbian Life Today.* Boston: Beacon Press; Millet, Kate (1977). *Sita.* New York: Farrar, Strauss, and Giroux; Vida, Ginny (1978). *Our Right to Love: A Lesbian Resource Book.* Englewood Cliffs, NJ: Prentice-Hall; and Wolf, Charlotte (1971). *Love Between Women.* New York: Harper, Colophon.

disdain for its rampant sexuality and "cultural impoverishment." The gay and lesbian communities, as collectivities, were endorsed without qualification and assigned a station alongside the historic ethnic and racial minorities.

The transmutation of the homosexual subculture into gay and lesbian communities signaled an increasingly strident, political note in the scientific discourse on sexual identity. Harry and DeVall condemned what they saw as the palpable injustice of job discrimination against gay men. Adam described how the coping strategies of compliance, with the backing of the communities, were jettisoned and replaced by strategies of resistance. The lesbian-feminist programs described by Wolf, with their emphasis on political correctness, could be viewed as organized political indoctrination. Brooks outlined a process of political development for the lesbian woman which began with political awareness of her social position and ended with her joining the struggle of all minorities to revolutionize the social order.

As the descriptions and analyses of the sociocultural identity became more collectivistic, the description of sexual relationships became less and less polytheistic. The delibidinization of the homosexual relationship was evident in the authors' treatment of sexual identity. Adam and Brooks divorced it from biology. By conceiving it as entirely a social invention, they were able to separate sexual identity from purely personal gratification. The homosexual identity was politicized by making it into a gay and lesbian identity symbolizing minority or community membership.

As a political entity, sexual identity revealed little about the individual's sexual proclivities and practices. The gay marriage, as portrayed by Harry and DeVall, was more an affectional than sexual bonding, one threatened by the promiscuity of the gay subculture. Wolf and Brooks explained that it was possible for a heterosexual woman to be a political lesbian as an expression of solidarity with other women. The implication was that there were pure lesbians and political-only lesbians. It was never clear if and when solidarity between members of the two groups was expressed as physical congress. Brooks, for example, believed that the concept of sexual orientation should be renamed "sociosexual orientation" because what bound lesbian women together was not so much the rejection of heterosexuality but their preference for feminine over masculine social environments. For this reason one could not be sure that pure lesbians did not enjoy heterosexual intercourse.

With the purging of the polytheistic conception of sexual relationships, the monotheistic was fully endorsed. The ability of either a gay man or lesbian woman to enter and maintain a "paired relationship" with a person of his or her own sex was of paramount importance in the establishment of the collective homosexual identity. For Harry and DeVall the ability of one man to establish emotional intimacy with another was the key test for full membership in the gay community. For Adam and Brooks such relationships were the visible signs that individuals had accepted their homosexual identity and aspired to membership in their communities. Wolf described paired relationships as the foundation of the lesbian community, the nuclei of the social networks that held it together. For Brooks the individual's conscious recognition and acceptance of her lesbian identity was almost reflexively followed by her desire for a stable sexual relationship with another woman. Apparently, in the perception of these writers, the paired relationship symbolized the community at the personal level.

The collective homosexual identity had the appearance of choice as embodied in the scientific cosmological view of sexual relationships. Homosexuals could accept or reject and disclose or conceal their sexual identity. Only acceptance and disclosure, however, promised the blessings of solid sexual relationships, community ties, and protection against oppression.

There was, however, a paradox in the juxtaposition of the political idea of community with the idea of homosexual monogamy. Subscription to the doctrine of paired relationships, which presumably combined both sexual and emotional gratification in a single unit, was also the major sociological thrust in the normalization of homosexual relationships. Yet the gay and lesbian communities were portrayed by these writers as existing as political cells dedicated to revolutionizing social norms. The paradox of how the tradition of monogamy could lie at the heart of a revolutionary community was not addressed by these authors.

There was still another paradox inherent in the lesbian-feminist ideology as expressed by Wolf and Brooks. Within that doctrine the issue of sex in relationships was subordinated to the issue of sex-role stereotypes. Stereotyped femininity, invented and imposed by a male-dominated society, held women in economic, psychological, and social subjugation. If the stereotype could be shattered the real potentialities of women would be liberated. What were these potentialities? The descriptions of feminine values, as reflected by Wolf and Brooks, consisted largely of attributes traditionally associated with the feminine stereotype: nurturance, cooperation, intuition, tenderness, and bonding. The challenge to the sex-role stereotypes was based on an assumption that there were innate sex differences between females and males. The qualities of femininity were intrinsic to the female sex. Males were unavoidably masculine. In order to challenge the social order, feminine values had to be combined with such qualities as aggression, strength and leadership. In women, however, these were qualities that had to be learned. Brooks praised lesbians for their androgyny, that is, a highly developed femininity and masculinity. In this ideology the amalgam was virtuous only in women because of their core femininity. In men, even those perceived as highly feminine, androgyny was always suspect because it was rooted in a core masculinity.

In this way the lesbian-feminists endorsed that part of the concept of the male-female design which looked for the roots of femininity and masculinity in biological sex as created by nature. Yet it was that very male-female design, as conceived by psychoanalysis that formed the bedrock of the psychological heterosexual identity which prescribed that men be masculine and women be feminine in appearance and mental attitudes.

18

The Collective Homosexual Identity:
II. Homophobia and the Gay and Lesbian Identity

In the 1970s, clinical and social psychologists joined the effort of sociologists and urban anthropologists to collectivize the homosexual identity. The psychologists added an internal, cognitive dimension to the collective identity that heretofore had been described essentially as an external social phenomenon. The psychologists conceived the cognitive dimension in two forms: (1) a socio-clinical mental state called homophobia and (2) behavioral theories describing how individuals mentally acquired a fully-developed gay or lesbian identity.

A number of psychologists wrote about and investigated personal and social prejudice against homosexuality and its practitioners. This prejudice was initially viewed as a clinical phenomenon called homophobia.[1] The first extended treatment of the concept was by George Weinberg,[2] who

---

[1] As Boswell stated (1980: 46, Note 11), the Greek derivation of homophobia is "fear of what is similar" *not* "fear of homosexuality. Boswell, in passing, defined homophobia as "an irrational fear of gay people and their sexuality." He called "homophobia" a "macaronism," adopted because of its superficial similarity to homosexual. Fear of homosexuality, he pointed out, would properly be rendered HOMOSEXOPHOBIA. Boswell made no reference to Churchill's more accurate (in derivation) term HOMOEROTOPHOBIA, the fear of homoeroticism. In the psychological literature, the word homophobia first appeared in 1971 (see Smith, 1971). Smith, a clinical psychologist, defined homophobia as "negative or fearful responding to homosexuality" (1091).

[2] Weinberg, George (1972/1973). *Society and the Healthy Homosexual.* New York: St. Martin's Press. (The Doubleday Anchor edition of 1973 is referenced here.) Weinberg acknowledged the assistance of Clarence Tripp and gay writers or political leaders such as Lige Clarke, Arthur Evans, Franklin Kameny, and Jack Nichols. Weinberg referred to Kenneth Smith as "a colleague of mine … who read a paper of mine on homophobia" (129) and as the person who did the first research on homophobia. Weinberg attributed his own knowledge of homosexuality to patients and personal acquaintances. He identified himself

conceived of homophobia as a clinical condition detectable by an individual's "revulsion against homosexuals and the desire to inflict punishment as retribution" (Weinberg, 1972/1973: 129). It was prejudice that had complex and not easily discernible motives. Weinberg identified five possible motives. The first or **RELIGIOUS MOTIVE** derived from the Judeo-Christian tradition which imposed strictures against "spilling the seed" and severely limited the permissible sources of sexual pleasure. A second motive was the **SECRET FEAR OF BEING HOMOSEXUAL ONESELF.** It was a reaction formation, in psychoanalytic parlance, in which the individual warded off an impulse in the self by opposing its expression in others. The stentorian opponents of homosexuality were perhaps propelled by this motive. **REPRESSED ENVY** was a third motive for homophobia. It was found lurking in those heterosexuals disturbed by homosexual men who were "disdainful of the basic requirements of manhood" (17). It also afflicted those heterosexuals who resented the possibility that homosexual men and women may have easier lives. A fourth motive was the belief that homosexuality constituted a **THREAT TO ONE'S VALUES**: "The mere fact of the homosexual's not striving for marriage, for example, makes it harder to include him or her in appeals made to the populace" (15). A final motive was the fear of **EXISTENCE WITHOUT VICARIOUS IMMORTALITY**. Homosexuals, Weinberg believed, awakened the fear of death which in heterosexuals was assuaged by the vicarious immortality of "having children and grandchildren" (17). Because homosexuals did not start families of their own, heterosexuals viewed them as frightening departures from the standardized pattern of existence. In intellectuals this motive surfaced in their endlessly raising the question of the causes of homosexuality. Weinberg concluded:

> Implicit in all this is the unwarranted assumption that at bottom we all crave the same ends and advantages. In the last analysis, the homophobic reaction I have been describing is a form of acute conventionality. Ultimately, it condemns because of difference. It has every basic attribute of an irrational social prejudice. (Weinberg, 1972/1973: 20)

Weinberg was critical of the homophobia he believed psychoanalysts promulgated in their treatment of homosexual patients. As a body of theory and practice he saw psychoanalytic conclusions about homosexuality as "merely restatements of the Judeo-Christian code" (22). Psycho-

---

as a clinical psychologist and author of a college statistics text for psychologists (66).

analysts considered homosexuality "neurotic" or "perverted" because it led individuals away from heterosexuality, towards nonreproductive forms of sexual intercourse. By focusing on the origins of homosexual urges, psychoanalytic treatment implanted misgivings in patients' minds. By substituting introspection for action psychoanalysis preoccupied patients: "The very decision to arrest a trial-and-error process and to replace it by inquiry is a decision about how life should be lived" (28). Finally, under the impetus to change homosexuals into heterosexuals, psychoanalysts accounted for all their patients' difficulties in terms of homosexuality. Contemporary psychoanalysts, in Weinberg's view, were radically departing from the practices of traditional Freudians:

> The whole art of analysis, in their (the traditional) view, is to elicit the patient's own, true, private predilection for viewing people. What the patient brings is the stuff of the analysis. This is the classical Freudian view, and according to it, the analyst must step back, and not offer opinions. (Weinberg, 1972/1973: 31)

Weinberg believed therapists should help patients discover their own solutions to everyday problems.

Another form of therapy used for converting homosexuality to heterosexuality was criticized by Weinberg. Behavioral therapy, in the form of "systematic desensitization" (43) to homosexual stimuli was merely the imposition of societal norms. The behavioral therapists decided, "on the basis of what they were taught as children, that members of one's own sex are not to be included among stimuli" (49).[3]

---

[3] Weinberg particularly mentioned the work of Joseph Wolpe, Thomas Kraft, and H. J. Eysenck. He was especially critical of Kraft's application of behavioral techniques for the eradication of homosexual urges. Weinberg also described other methods of "therapeutic intervention": (a) "Emetic persuasion" (55) was the method in which the homosexual was shown pictures of nude males after he had been injected with a drug (e.g., apomorphine) which caused him to vomit, hopefully inducing the association between the arousal of homosexual desire and pain; (b) The "masturbation method" (52) required the patient to masturbate in the dark in the presence of pictures of almost nude women. Just before reaching orgasm the patient was to signal the therapist, who would immediately hit a switch which would illuminate one of the pictures. (c) The method of "brain surgery" (53) involved the removal of part of the hypothalamus that had supposedly suffered from inadequate masculinization in prenatal males because of fetal androgen deficiency.

In his criticism of efforts to change homosexuals into heterosexuals Weinberg conveyed his belief that homosexuality was a deeply imbedded psychological identity:

> [T]he texture of one's fantasies and ambitions is so delicately woven that any attempt to rend it with a needle, to rip out some skein running through it, is an act of destruction.... If one is homosexual ... this highest yearning for intimacy will appear in the image of a love relationship with another homosexual. What could be simpler than this? (Weinberg, 1972/1973: 65-66)

Homosexuals could also be afflicted with homophobia. This internalized homophobia took two forms. One was chronic self-denial, in which the homosexual viewed himself through the eyes of rejecting heterosexuals and even sided with them against fellow homosexuals. Each time this form of self-betrayal was practiced it became reinforced as a belief: "once a person acts on any belief—in this case, disdain for homosexuals—among the outcomes is that he makes the belief seem righter than ever" (75-76). The other form of internalized homophobia was a flight into guilt. In this form homosexuals accepted the psychiatric view of homosexuality as illness while perceiving fellow homosexuals as enemy. If these homosexuals tried to masquerade as heterosexuals they felt fraudulent and bored. They could even become enraged at heterosexuals who accepted them in their deceptive role.

Based on his notion of homophobia and the homosexual identity, Weinberg developed a portrait of the "healthy homosexual" and "being gay" (69). Being homosexual, he stated "was to have an erotic preference for members of one's own sex. One may be homosexual for a minute, an hour, a day, or a lifetime" (68). Being gay meant considerably more:

> Being gay means having freed oneself of misgivings over being homosexual.... It means remaining free to invent, to imbue life with fantasy. It means being able to investigate one's preferences and desires in sexual roles where one chooses, without having to construct a personality elsewhere consistent with this, to justify it, to account for it. In essence, it means being convinced that any erotic orientation and preference may be housed in any human being. (71)

The healthy homosexuals—gay persons—did not limit their options to fit conventional prejudice. The attitude of pessimism and self-abnegation was replaced with one of entitlement: "This (replacement) occurs where the attitude is the sense of absolute entitlement to a good life, just as it did with guilt. To produce this sense of entitlement to happiness, one must seize the belief that one deserves full rights and use it as a motivation for decisions whenever possible" (Weinberg, 1972/1973: 85).

There were three decisional areas that were critical for attaining the status of the healthy homosexual. One was an attitude toward self that was to consist of full acceptance of one's homosexuality: "whether to pursue homosexual love with full commitment" (86). A second area was relationships with others. Here the decision was whether or not to let others know about one's sexual identity, activities, and relationships. Weinberg implied that the healthy homosexual would make all the necessary disclosures. Finally, there were the decisions about supporting homosexuals as a group. Here he seemed to press for joining the gay liberation movement. The homosexual's practice and acceptance of the homosexual identity was the way to achieve individuality: "He or she becomes the spiritual ally of everyone—homosexual or heterosexual—who has staked out his own path in life" (88).

During the seventies, several social scientists, for the most part psychologists, investigated homophobia, using quantitative techniques. Some of these researchers designed tests to detect homophobia in individuals.[4] The conceptualizations of homophobia upon which these

---

[4] Smith, Kenneth T. (1971). Homophobia: A Tentative Personality Profile. *Psychological Reports* 29: 1091-1094; Dunbar, J., Brown, M., and Amoroso, D. M. (1973a). Attitudes toward Homosexuality among Brazilian and Canadian College Students. *Journal of Social Psychology 90:* 173-183; Dunbar, J., Brown, M., and Amoroso, D. M. (1973b). Some Correlates of Attitudes toward Homosexuality. *Journal of Social Psychology* 89: 271-279; MacDonald, P. A., Huggins, J., Young, S., and Swanson R. A. (1973). Attitudes Toward Homosexuality: Preservation of Sex Morality or the Double Standard? *Journal of Counseling and Clinical Psychology* 40(1): 161; MacDonald, A. P. and Games, R. G. (1974). Some Characteristics of Those Who Hold Positive and Negative Attitudes Toward Homosexuals. *Journal of Homosexuality* 1(1): 9-27; Levitt, E. E. and Klassen, A. D. (1974). Public Attitudes toward Homosexuality: Part of the 1970 National Survey by the Institute for Sex Research. *Journal of Homosexuality* 1(1): 29-43; Lumby, M. E. (1976). Homophobia: The Quest for a Valid Scale. *Journal of Homosexuality* 2(1): 39-47; Minnigerode, Fred A. (1976). Attitudes toward Homosexuality: Feminist Attitudes and Sexual Conservatism. *Sex Roles* 2(4): 347-352; Millham, J., San Miguel, C. L., and Kellogg, R. (1976). A Factor-Analytic Conceptualization of Attitudes toward Male and Female Homosexuals. *Journal of Homosexuality* 2(11): 3-10; Nyberg, Kenneth L. and Alston, Jon P. (1976/1977). Analysis of Public Attitudes Toward Homosexual Behavior. *Journal of Homosexuality* 2(2): 99-107; Hudson, W. W., and Ricketts, W. A. (1980). A Strategy for the Measurement of Homophobia. *Journal of*

investigations were based emerged over a period of about ten years (1971 to 1980).

The first empirical study was conducted by Kenneth Smith (1971) who conceived of homophobia as the "negative attitude" of individuals, presumably heterosexuals, "toward homosexuals" (1091).[5] Smith's intent was to shift the focus of research away from homosexuals as victims to the examination of the "system." By "system" he meant individuals who were "particularly negative or fearful regarding homosexuality" (1091). Such persons Smith called the "HOMOPHOBIC GROUP," which he contrasted with the "NON-HOMOPHOBICS." Smith developed and used a "homophobic scale" that included items dealing with attitudes about patriotism, mental illness, material success, sexual fidelity, male passivity, the divine basis for morality, and occupational attainment. The results of his endeavor, he believed, yielded the following profile of the "homophobic personality:

> It appears that the homophobic individual is status conscious ... authoritarian ... and sexually rigid.... He does not seem to be rigid about appropriate non-sexual behavior for men and women.... He probably does not see homosexuals as a minority group, per se, since he is accepting of rights for blacks but not homosexuals.... Instead, he may view homosexuals as sick, in which case his anxiety about mental illness ... may be projected onto the homosexual. His attitudes toward security and the pleasure motive appear comparable to those of non-homophobics. His stance on pacifism ... and censorship ... and his religious affiliation require additional study. He may be attracted to the nursing profession. (Smith, 1971: 1093)

Another empirical effort to assess homophobia was led by A. P. MacDonald (MacDonald et al., 1973 and MacDonald et al., 1974). As in the case of Smith, MacDonald focused on the "nonhomosexual's" attitude toward homosexuality. He and his associates conceived of homosexuals as constituting a minority group such as poor blacks: "Increasingly, we are recognizing that difficulties experienced by minority groups can be better attributed to characteristics within the

---

Homosexuality 5(4): 357-372. For a general discussion of theory and reports of research on homophobia see DeCecco, John P. (Ed.) 1984. *Homophobia: An Overview.* New York: Haworth Press. (Simultaneously published as Vol. 10(1/2) of the *Journal of Homosexuality*.)

[5] Smith's sample consisted of 130 undergraduate students enrolled in psychology classes at the New York State University College at Fredonia.

majority that discriminates against them than to the minorities themselves.... The **ORGANISM DEFICIENCY** model is slowly giving way to a **SOCIAL DEFICIENCY** model" (1974: 10).

MacDonald assumed that there were two possible sources of homophobia: conservative attitudes about premarital sex and about the social sex-roles of men and women.[6] He concluded that homophobia was more powerfully associated with conservatism about social sex-roles than with premarital sexual permissiveness.

In 1974, MacDonald and Games undertook a more extensive study of the "characteristics of heterosexuals that are associated with their positive or negative attitudes toward homosexuals" (11).[7] The authors concluded, as Smith before them, that "the authoritarian personality is associated with negative attitudes toward homosexuals" (24). They added that such negative attitudes were correlated with "intolerance of ambiguity and cognitive rigidity" (25). Their most interesting finding, they averred, was that respondents generally believed that "girls are made of 'sugar and spice and everything nice' and boys are made of 'snips and snails and puppy dog tails'" (24). They thought their conclusions had two implications for the gay liberation movement: "They (the results) suggest that increased visibility of 'masculine' male homosexuals may do much to further the success of that movement" (1974: 26). At a more speculative level, they suggested that the choice of the word "gay" for male homosexuals may have been an unfortunate one. The authors' advice implied, but did not state, that lesbians should try to appear more feminine.

The study of homophobia continued under the leadership of James Millham. His group attempted to identify a broad spectrum of attitudes of heterosexuals associated with homophobia.[8] They developed a

---

[6] For respondents he used 104 students and some faculty members from West Virginia University (MacDonald et al., 1973). His measure of homophobia was called the Attitude Toward Homosexuality Scale.

[7] For this study, 197 undergraduate students in sociology classes at West Virginia University were utilized. A battery of tests was administered, including the Premarital Sexual Permissiveness Scale, Sex Role Survey (by MacDonald), Attitude Toward Homosexuality Scale, Semantic Differentials for Man, Woman, Male Homosexual, and Lesbian, value factors derived from Rokeach's 36 Instrumental and Terminal Values, a version of the F scale, the Gough-Sanford Rigidity scale, and the Ambiguity Tolerance Scale (by MacDonald).

[8] The first study of the Millham group (Millham, San Miguel, and Kellogg, 1976) involved 795 undergraduate students in introductory psychology classes

seventy-six-item Homosexuality Attitude Scale, containing statements that reflected both positive and negative attitudes toward female and male homosexuals. Using a statistical technique known as factor-analysis, the Millham group believed that they had identified the following component attitudes of homophobia as a complex concept: (1) the belief that homosexuals were dangerous and therefore required legal and social restraint; (2) the emergence of feelings of anxiety and disgust in the presence of homosexuals; (3) opinions that female homosexuals were preferable to male homosexuals or the converse of this; and (4) the belief that homosexuality is sinful and morally wrong.

The most striking finding, according to the authors, was that re-spondents believed that institutionalized restriction of male homosexuality was more important than restriction of female homosexuality. They also concluded that respondents were more anxious in the presence of same-sex than opposite-sex homosexuals and that heterosexual females more than heterosexual males attributed cross-sex mannerisms to male homosexuals.[9]

As part of a national survey of sexual attitudes sponsored by the Alfred C. Kinsey Institute, Eugene Levitt and Albert Klassen included research on attitudes toward homosexuality (MacDonald, et al., 1974).[10] A scale was developed to measure what the authors called HOMOSEXOPHOBIA (41). It consisted of five items dealing with such issues as associating with homosexuals, the quality of their citizenship, never

---

at the University of Houston. Students who believed they were homosexuals were requested to "eliminate themselves" (4) from the survey.

[9] Hudson and Ricketts (1980) challenged the notion of homophobia as a unidimensional concept. They proposed that "the entire domain or catalogue of anti-gay responses be regarded as homonegativism" (358). Homonegativism included negative reactions to such issues as the legality, morality, and social desirability of homosexuality. Responses of fear, disgust, anger, discomfort, and aversion to "gay people" were considered by Hudson and Ricketts as the core ingredients of homophobia which, in turn, was only one dimension of homonegativism.

[10] The survey, conducted in 1970, was based on a national probability sample of 3,018 men and women. There were several series of questions dealing with beliefs about homosexuality: moral attitudes about its practice; attitudes about which occupations homosexuals should be allowed to enter; perceptions of homosexuals as dangerous, threatening, or offensive; opinions distinguishing homosexuals from heterosexuals; opinions on what rights should be accorded to homosexuals; opinions concerning the causation and cure of homosexuality; and homosexophobia. Only the last category of items is discussed here.

liking them, their right to equal treatment as a group, and feeling no particular love or hate for homosexuals as a group. The authors concluded that respondents expressed apparently conflicting attitudes. While many, for example, indicated that they had no particular love or hate for homosexuals, they also expressed the feeling that they did not wish to associate with homosexuals and did not believe that they should receive treatment equal to that of other groups.

Based on data obtained in other parts of the survey, Levitt and Klassen concluded that premarital heterosexual intercourse was judged less harshly than homosexuality and that only extramarital sexual relationships were judged as harshly as homosexuality. Sex under affectional circumstances was greatly preferred to sex under nonaffectional circumstances: "The data leave little doubt that Americans still cherish the concept of love as a basis for sexual behavior (30).[11]

Contemporaneous with assessment of homophobia through questionnaires, psychologists, using experimental situations, attempted to ascertain the impact of homophobia on interpersonal relations.[12] One of the earliest social experiments was designed by Christopher San Miguel and Millham (1976).[13] The subjects were placed in situations where they could display "aggression" toward the experimenters. Aggression consisted of the subjects making critical evaluations of experimenters' competence which, if negative, they were led to believe resulted in the experimenters receiving smaller payments for their services.

---

[11] A subsequent survey of opinions regarding homosexuality was reported in Nyberg and Alston (1976/1977). The sample consisted of 1,197 adult females and males selected from all parts of the United States. They reported that 75% disapproved of homosexual relations. The most tolerant group were those younger than 30, living in large cities, and with some college education.

[12] San Miguel, C. L. and Millham, J. (1976). The Role of Cognitive and Situational Variables in Aggression Toward Homosexuals. *Journal of Homosexuality* 2(1): 11-27; Millham, J., and Weinberger, L. E. (1977). Sexual Preferences, Sex Role Appropriateness, and Restriction of Social Access. *Journal of Homosexuality* 2(4): 343-357; Morin, S. F., and Garfinkle, E. M. (1978). Male Homophobia. *Journal of Social Issues* 34(1): 29-47; Storms, M. D. (1978). Attitudes Toward Homosexuality and Femininity in Men. *Journal of Homosexuality* 3(3): 257-263; and Karr, R. G. (1978). Homosexual Labeling and the Male Role. *Journal of Social Issues* 34(3), 73-83.

[13] The Homosexuality Attitude Scale was administered to male students in introductory psychology classes at the University of Houston. From the pool of students who scored at the extreme ends of the attitude scale, 156 were randomly selected for the experimental study.

The experiment had three phases. In the first phase subjects had the opportunity for an initial interaction with an experimenter which was either "cooperative" (in which the subjects earned extra course credit) or "uncooperative" (did not earn extra credit). In the second phase the experimenters identified themselves as homosexuals to some subjects but not to others. In the final phase some subjects were led to believe that they had personalities that were very similar or dissimilar to those of the experimenters.[14]

The authors arrived at the following conclusions. Homosexuals were exposed to more aggression than heterosexuals simply because of their sexual orientation. Those homosexuals who were perceived by heterosexuals as similar to themselves in personality traits were likely to experience heightened rather than diminished aggression. Experimenters identified as homosexuals were aggressed against whether the prior interaction had been cooperative or uncooperative. However, in the various experimental situations, the group that had been identified as nonhomophobic tended to aggress against the "homosexual" experimenters much less than the homophobic group.

In a second experimental study, Millham and Weinberger (1977) attempted to discover the reactions of men and women toward hypothetical individuals (i.e., targets) who were described as heterosexual or homosexual and as "gender congruent" (i.e., feminine females, masculine males) or "gender incongruent" (i.e., feminine males and masculine females).[15]

The authors arrived at these general conclusions. Both female and male subjects were less willing to work with a homosexual than a heterosexual, the males even less so than the females. Homosexuality overrode gender incongruence as a basis for unwillingness of heterosex-

---

[14] Four male students were used as experimenters. The authors described them as follows: "The experimenters were chosen to be of average college age, were dressed in typical style for the university, presented typical male mannerisms, and in no way were characteristic of the stereotype of effeminate homosexuals" (15). The purposes of the experiment and the fact that the experimenters were acting as "confederates" were revealed in a debriefing of subjects that followed the conclusion of the experiment.

[15] The study involved 117 male and 150 female subjects recruited from classes in introductory and child psychology at the University of Houston. The "targets" in this experiment were not actual individuals but written descriptions of individuals depicted as stereotypic or non-stereotypic in sexual orientation and social sex-roles. Subjects rated their own willingness to participate in three hypothetical experimental situations with the "targets" involving self-disclosure, cooperation, and competition.

uals to interact with homosexuals. Even when the behavior of the homosexuals was presented as gender congruent, male homosexuals were more rejected than female homosexuals.

The subjects' own social sex-roles were assessed for congruity. Incongruity did not alter negative attitudes of subjects toward targets depicted as homosexual and gender incongruent. This conclusion, the authors felt, cast doubt on the assumption that "negative reactions to homosexuals and to persons displaying out-of-sex-role characteristics has its roots in personal threat to the subject's own sexual identity" (356). They attributed the homophobia to learned values about social sex-roles and sexual styles. These values, the authors held, existed apart from the individual's perception of self.

In an article reviewing research on male homophobia, Stephen Morin and Ellen Garfinkle (1978) referred to an experimental study of the behavioral reactions of presumably heterosexual females and males to putative homosexuals.[16] The measure of homophobia was the relative spatial distance that subjects established between themselves and experimenters who were either identified as homosexuals or, in the absence of any mention of sexual identity, were tacitly presented as heterosexuals. To indicate a homosexual identity, female or male experimenters wore "gay and proud" buttons and were introduced as working for the Association of Gay Psychologists. The "heterosexual" experimenters were introduced simply as graduate students. All subjects were interviewed about their attitudes toward homosexuality among other issues. The authors reported that subjects placed their chairs further away from the experimenters who were presented as homosexuals than as heterosexuals. The male subjects kept a greater distance than the females from the male homosexual interviewers. Such distances from the homosexual interviewers were maintained even when subjects reported positive attitudes toward homosexuals. Morin and Garfinkle concluded: "As we conceptualize it, body language speaks more loudly than words" (37).

Homophobia, in the view of Morin and Garfinkle (1978), was both a cultural and personal phenomenon. At the cultural level it was "any belief system which supports negative myths and stereotypes about homosexual people" (30). Cultural homophobia endorsed the heterosexual lifestyle

---

[16] This is a secondary account of the study. The original report was identified as follows: Morin, S. F., Taylor, K., and Kielman, S. (1975, August). Gay is Beautiful at a Distance. Paper presented at the annual meeting of the American Psychological Association, Chicago.

over the homosexual. It also led to the "use of the language or slang, e.g., 'queer,' which is offensive to gay people" (30).

At the personal level, homophobia led to fearful reactions on the part of heterosexuals to homosexuals. Some of these reactions took the form of classically conditioned fears, as revealed in the laboratory responses of heterosexual males to the photographs of nude males.[17] At the personal level, homophobia also appeared to stem from the heterosexuals' fear of their own homosexual impulses:

> [A] man who is basically afraid of his own latent homosexual feelings attempts to reassure himself and convince others that he is really a 'healthy, normal heterosexual,' by actively and vigorously suppressing all homosexual impulses. (Morin & Garfinkle, 1978: 35)

Finally, personal homophobia could be the result of anxiety or fear surrounding the expression of any sexual impulses.

The issue of whether homophobia was directed more toward sexual identity or departures in social sex-roles was addressed in an experimental study by Michael Storms (1978).[18] The target in this experiment was a fictitious character called "John," who was presented in various forms: feminine and homosexual, feminine and heterosexual, masculine and homosexual, or masculine and heterosexual. In the feminine form "John" was described as majoring in fashion design, interested in dancing and dressing in tight-fitting trousers and stacked-heel shoes, In the masculine form "John" was described as majoring in business, playing intermural sports, and wearing hiking boots. Students rated one of these descriptions for how much they liked or disliked "John."

Storms drew this conclusion:

---

[17] They were referring to experiments that showed there was a decrease in "penile volume" of heterosexual men in response to nude photographs of males, *viz.*, the experimental studies of N. McConaghy and particularly of Kurt Freund and his collaborators.

[18] Subjects (130 males, 128 females) were recruited from introductory psychology classes at the University of Kansas. They rated their own sexual orientations and social sex-roles. The correlations between these ratings, according to Storms, indicated that there was (259) "a small 'grain of truth' behind the common stereotype that homosexual men are more feminine and homosexual women more masculine." The correlations between self-ratings and ratings of the experimental "target" were not reported.

Femininity appears to be a strongly disapproved trait in heterosexual men. But in homosexual men, masculine characteristics
elicited greater disapproval.... When a feminine man turns out to
be heterosexual and when a homosexual man turns out to be
masculine, both are disliked even more for violating the stereotype. (Storms, 1978: 261)

The author suggested three possible explanations for his conclusion.
First, masculinity in male homosexuals was resented because it
contradicted people's belief that male homosexuals really wanted to be
women. Second, heterosexual women would be upset because masculinity
was used as a screening criterion for eligible males. Heterosexual men
used masculinity as the basis for surrounding themselves with "safe"
males. Finally, sex-role conformity was the way heterosexuals could
contrast themselves with homosexuals and feel secure in the heterosexual
identity.

Fear and rejection of the individual labeled "homosexual" was the
issue addressed in an experimental study reported by Rodney Karr.[19] In
designing his experiment Karr entertained the following possibilities:
heterosexual males would sit further away from men labeled as
homosexual than those assumed to be heterosexual; they would also talk
less and work less effectively with the putative homosexuals; they would
rate the personality traits of the homosexuals less favorably than those of
heterosexuals; and they would like homosexuals less. Karr also
conjectured that men who were assessed as highly homophobic would
display more alienation from homosexuals than those who were less
homophobic.

Each research team consisted of five subjects and three experimenters.[20]
The three experimenters were confederates presented as ordinary subjects.
In the experimental condition one of these experimenters was labeled as
homosexual and thereby assigned the role of LABELEE. The homosexual
label was affixed to him during a conversation that occurred while he was

---

[19] Karr, R. G. (1978). Homosexual Labeling and the Male Role. *Journal of Social
Issues* 34(3): 73-83. Karr employed attributional theory which purported that
the individuals' perceptions of others reflected both the personality of the
perceivers and the social situation in which the perceptions occurred. The
subjects were ninety male students recruited form introductory psychology
courses at the University of Washington.

[20] The subjects were organized into eighteen teams, half of which constituted
the experimental condition and half the control condition. There were twelve
experimenters.

absent from the room. One confederate, the SECONDARY LABELER, asked the other, the PRIMARY LABELER, what the labelee had talked about in a presentation the labelee had made to a sociology class. The primary labeler responded: "He came and talked about being a homosexual" (77). The secondary labeler replied, "Do you mean that guy is a homosexual?" a fact the primary labeler confirmed. The naive subjects sometimes unwittingly joined in this conversation. In the control condition this exchange did not occur. The homophobia scale designed by Smith (1971) was given to all subjects at the end of the experiment.

Karr concluded that subjects who received high scores on the homophobic scale sat further away from the homosexual labelees and worked less efficiently with them on a group problem-solving task. The homosexual labelees were rated as less masculine than unlabeled targets and the primary labelers as more masculine. The direction of these ratings was most pronounced in the "high homophobic group."

These results, in Karr's view, supported the contention that "perceptions of others may not represent a consensual reality but rather are a function of already existing dispositions on the part of the observer to attribute certain characteristics to another based on the label homosexual being applied" (81). He believed that his most intriguing finding was that men who labeled other men as homosexuals were perceived as being more masculine:

> Thus, it would appear that men are reinforced for publicly identifying homosexual men. Presumably the primary labeler is viewed more positively both because he is assertive enough to publicly label a societal deviant and because he helps group members conform to societal expectations by that act. (82)

The search for homophobia was later extended to include psychological research itself. In 1977, Morin wrote about "heterosexual bias" in psychological investigations of homosexuality.[21] Heterosexual bias

---

[21] Morin, Stephen F. (1977). Heterosexual Bias in Psychological Research on Lesbianism and Male Homosexuality. *American Psychologist* 32(8): 629-637. The article was based on 139 empirical studies published in English between 1967 and 1974 and listed in *Psychological Abstracts*. The articles reviewed appeared in Morin's 1976 Annotated Bibliography of Research on Lesbianism and Male Homosexuality (1967-1974) (*J.S.A.S. Catalog of Selected Documents in Psychology* 6(1): 15. (Ms. No. 1191). Morin chose 1974 as the cutoff point because, in January 1975, the American Psychological Association had passed a resolution which declared that homosexuality per se did not imply mental disorder or

was defined as a "belief system that values heterosexuality as superior to and/or more 'natural' than homosexuality" (629). In research, Morin believed heterosexual bias was most obvious in studies that viewed homosexuality as pathological. Morin also believed that heterosexual bias undergirded discrimination against homosexuals.

The roots of heterosexual bias were to be found in the value systems of individual investigators or in the climate of opinion within which the research was conducted. It was most clearly revealed in the types of questions pursued in this research. Questions about how homosexuality could be diagnosed assumed an impaired mental stability or social maladjustment. The search for the "causes" of homosexuality, particularly within the framework of psychoanalytic, learning, or biochemical theories led "either to suggestions for treatment to change the homosexual orientation or to early family interventions to preclude its development" (634). The investigation of possible pathology in homosexuals was used, in Morin's view, "to study adjustment and to make inferences about the inferiority or superiority of homosexuals" (634).[22] Usually, however, these investigations pointed to deficiencies in homosexual adjustment.

Two areas of research won Morin's endorsement. One comprised the ethnological studies which dealt with "unique aspects in the lives of lesbians and gay men" (1977: 635). The other consisted of studies of homophobia, which Morin called "heterosexual attitudes toward homosexuality" and "anti-homosexuality" (635). The studies of homophobia, he believed, were the clearest examples of research "that is on the offense rather than the defense with regard to the advancement of gay civil liberties" (635).

The samples used in research on homosexuality also came under Morin's purview. Because lesbians and gay men were "essentially a hidden or invisible population" (636), there could be "no such thing as a representative sample." In past research, he observed, samples were

---

social and vocational maladjustment and which urged mental health professionals to work to remove the stigma from homosexuality. See Conger, J. J. (1975). Proceedings of the American Psychological Association Incorporated for the Year 1974: Minutes of the Annual Meeting of the Council of Representatives. *American Psychologist 30*: 633. Morin apparently assumed that the "heterosexual bias" in research on homosexuality would gradually diminish with the passage of this resolution.

[22] Morin acknowledged that a few instances of "homosexual bias," in studies claiming superiority of homosexuals, were beginning to crop up in the research literature(634).

selected on the basis of overt behavior, assessed sexual preference, or self-identity. His recommendation was that samples be based on self-identity only:

> Future research will be even more complex as samples are selected that identify themselves as "gay" and not as "homosexual." The emerging definition of "gay" or "lesbian" is different from that of "homosexual." The term *gay*, like the terms *black*, *Chicano*, and *woman*, connotes a value system as well as designates group membership. *Gay* is proud, angry, open, visible, political, healthy, and all the positive things that *homosexual* is not. (Morin, 1977: 633; emphasis added)

The label of homosexuality, he contended, referred only to "same-sex object choice"; it did not reveal "what [homosexuality] represents to the individual so categorized" (634).

Among Morin's research priorities was the inclusion in the study of homophobia of "methods by which pejorative attitudes could be changed" (636). He also strongly urged research on the various aspects of the "positive gay identity" (636), including its development, disclosure, and solidity and its manifestations in gay relationships, adolescence, and aging.[23]

The research on homophobia conducted in the seventies reified the homosexual and heterosexual sociocultural identities. The homosexual identity was self-evident to those who possessed it and one which could be quickly revealed to others. Homosexual subjects, for example, in the studies of the Millham group knew who they were and were expected to take steps to eliminate their questionnaires from the data analysis. It was also generally assumed that subjects who were not homosexuals could only be heterosexuals. In the experimental research, the procedures used implied that the authors believed that unless confederates were identified

---

[23] There was little doubt that Morin was fostering the idea of a gay and lesbian "minority" with its own "gay community." This intention was clearer in his preface to a 1978 volume he and Dorothy Riddle edited under the title, *Psychology and the Gay Community*, a theme issue of the *Journal of Social Issues* 34(3). Despite the title of the volume, none of the articles was a description or analysis of the entity designated as the "gay community," although Morin averred that the articles dealt with issues which were "of importance within the community of lesbians and gay men" (4). The issues discussed were the love relationships of lesbians, sexual fantasies of gay men, gays as role models for children, coming out, psychotherapy, and aging. He also identified the gay cause with that of the Third World and women's movements.

as homosexuals, subjects would assume they were heterosexuals. Throughout the research on homophobia, therefore, a sociocultural homosexual or heterosexual identity was assumed but never delineated.

Instead, this research delineated a new identity, the **HOMOPHOBE**. He, or possibly she, was the adversary of the **HOMOPHILE**, as created in the ethnographic literature of the sixties. The homophobes were heterosexuals who believed in traditional sexual morality, marital fidelity, and law and order. They feared physical closeness among people of the same sex, departures from stereotypic feminine and masculine roles, possibly their own latent homosexuality, and the expression of a non-reproductive sexuality as pleasure. Homophobes viewed both homosexual and extramarital sexual liaisons as equally insidious threats to the family.

Homophobes suffered from **HOMOPHOBIA** which was described in the language of mental illness as a clinical entity. It was characterized by fear, dread, disgust, or rage associated with homosexuality. The intensity of these feelings and their apparent irrationality suggested that homophobia was a product of disordered minds and personalities. Weinberg went so far as to aver that homophobia should be treated in all patients: "I would never consider a patient healthy unless he had overcome his prejudice against homosexuality" (1972: 1).

The psychologists of homophobia were engaging in what Foucault (1976/1978) called a "reverse discourse." Using the homosexual identity and portraying it as pathological, these psychologists created a new clinical identity, that of the homophobe, which they could now pin on the oppressors of homosexuals. They were implying that it was not the homosexuals who were sick but those who were disturbed by the homosexual identity. The psychologists of homophobia made it possible for individuals to retain their homosexual identity while labeling detractors as mentally ill.

Although originally conceived as a clinical concept, homophobia had obvious relevance for the collective homosexual identity. As a way of labeling social intolerance it bolstered the ideas of the homosexual identity as a minority status, equivalent to the racial or female identity. Homophobia corresponded to racism and sexism as a form of prejudice against minorities. It suggested the existence of and the need to maintain a community of men and women huddled together against the enveloping intolerance of the majoritarian heterosexual culture. Homophobia presumably identified the adversary who had to be confronted if the homosexual identity were to endure. The best defense, Morin implied, was an offense against the heterosexual identity.

In the late seventies several clinical psychologists of homosexuality tried to adumbrate the process through which the "homosexual identity" was developed. This effort was led by Joel Hencken and William O'Dowd, who proposed a three-stage model for the development of a "gay identity."[24] The first stage involved the child's dawning EMOTIONAL AWARENESS, at the ages of four or five, of feeling or being "different" in some undefined way. In childhood this awareness was accompanied by feelings of alienation from the peer group. In adolescence it took the form of sexual or romantic attraction to individuals of the same sex. This attraction, according to Hencken, "is generally felt as significantly uncomfortable, threatening, shameful, dangerous, or wrong and something to be kept secret" (1982: 19). Eventually the adolescent retrospectively applied the homosexual label to those feelings.

The second stage, called BEHAVIORAL AWARENESS, was the one in which the individual engaged in actual sexual or romantic relationships. In retrospect the individual in this stage labeled the self as homosexual in action as well as feeling. The final stage was PUBLIC DISCLOSURE. Here the individual's homosexuality was self-disclosed first to friends, then to family and colleagues, and finally, publicly to the community and the world.[25]

---

[24] Hencken, J. D. and O'Dowd, W. T. (1979). Coming Out as an Aspect of Identity Formation. *Gay Academic Union Journal: Gai Saber* 1: 18-22; and Hencken, Joel D. (1982). *Homosexual Identities: An Exploration of Issues.* A prelim paper presented to the faculty of the University of Michigan, Department of Psychology, Clinical Area.

[25] The sequence of awareness of feelings, self-labeling, and behavior, postulated by Hencken and O'Dowd, was not confirmed in a study by a sociologist, Weinberg, Thomas S. (1978). On "Doing and "Being" Gay: Sexual Behavior and Homosexual Male Self-Identity. *Journal of Homosexuality* 4: 143-156. Weinberg interviewed thirty male homosexuals to find out the sequence of events that led to the development of a homosexual identity. The most common pattern was for individuals to engage in same-sex activity *before* they actually labeled themselves as homosexuals. Men who followed this pattern perceived their sexual behavior with other men to be "just having sex," "fooling around," or "nothing worth thinking about." Even those men who did perceive their behavior as homosexual rarely labeled themselves homosexual. The men applied the homosexual label to their behavior (and later themselves) when they came in contact with self-defined homosexuals, when they changed their definitions of what constituted homosexual behavior, or when they began to perceive changes in their behavior.

In subsequent reflections, Hencken identified some deficiencies in the three-stage model: (1) it emphasized the individual at the price of social and interactive factors; (2) its covert-overt dimension started with the individual and proceeded directly through the surrounding community, while ignoring many possible detours; (3) it implied that those homosexuals who were maximally disclosed were also the most psychologically mature; and (4) it assumed that there was only one "gay identity" rather than a variety of "homosexual identities" (1982: 22).

In an effort to tie the process of homosexual identity formation to societal reactions and to account for individual fluctuations, Carmen de Monteflores and Stephen Schultz proposed a somewhat different conceptualization.[26] They called the process "coming out," which they defined as "a developmental phenomenon in which the individual experiences, at different points in the process, all the aforementioned elements defining homosexuality, i.e., same-sex attraction, homosexual behavior, homosexual identity, and gay identity" (61). The process was punctuated by four milestones: awareness of same-sex attractions, first same-sex experience, coming out to friends, and coming out publicly. Coming out was viewed as a "feedback loop." As the individual reached each of the milestones, societal reactions were elicited that affected that person's future actions. A "continual existential crisis" (63) hung over the coming out process:

> In forming a new relationship with another, one must always decide how much intimacy is desired. Each of us has hidden facts about ourselves, debating the revealing of which leads to inner tension. However, few of these hidden facts carry with them social penalties as extreme as those imposed for being gay, and few affect as many dimensions of one's personal life. (63)

The goal of the coming out process, in the view of de Monteflores and Schultz, was "the integration of homosexual feelings and behavior in the individual's personal and social life" (63). Three areas of psychological and social experience were affected by coming out: identity formation, self-disclosure, and socialization. In the area of identity formation three changes occurred: the individual surrendered the negative homosexual identity for the positive gay identity; feelings of attraction to members of the same sex, which had been disowned in the past, were now explored; and the self-labeling as "gay ... integrates experience by synthesizing

---

[26] De Monteflores, Carmen and Schultz, Stephen J. (1978). Coming Out: Similarities and Differences for Lesbians and Gay Men. *Journal of Social Issues* 34(3): 59-71.

events and aspects of self which seemed disparate" (65). Through self-disclosure, the individual won both self and social validation. The real self was made congruent with the public self. Social banishment was defied: "To be openly gay in such a society says a clear 'no more' to oppression and both confirms the individual gay person and challenges society's norms" (66). Finally, the usual socialization was reversed. Whereas it usually molded the individual to fit society, coming out was a process "through which individual identity asserts itself to create social change" (66).[27]

A theoretical model of homosexual identity formation was constructed by Vivienne Cass to show how the individual could fully integrate this identity within an overall concept of self.[28] The model consisted of six stages: identity confusion, identity comparison, identity tolerance, identity acceptance, identity pride, and identity synthesis. The individual's progress through these stages depended on self perceptions of sexual behavior and on the actions that arose as a result of those perceptions.

The motivation for moving through the stages stemmed from the "incongruency" that resulted when the individual held (1) a private identity of being homosexual and a public identity of being heterosexual or (2) a public identity of being homosexual in a heterosexual milieu. Cass believed that the individual with a homosexual identity could never be completely congruent with Western society. It was possible, however, for "incongruency to be reduced to a level both tolerable and manageable" (Cass, 1979: 222). **IDENTITY FORECLOSURE** could result during any stage when the individual chose not to move on to the next stage.[29]

---

[27] In formulating their position on socialization and the coming out process, the authors acknowledged their debt to Eric Erikson's notion of the interaction of social stability with social change and George Herbert Mead's view of the complementarity of social reconstruction and personality reconstruction.

[28] Cass, Vivienne C. (1979). Homosexual Identity Formation: A Theoretical Model. *Journal of Homosexuality* 4(3): 219-235. Cass reported that her model was based on "several years of clinical work with homosexuals" (219). It was also based on interpersonal congruency theory. See Secord, P. F. and Blackman, C. W. (1961). Personality Theory and the Problem of Stability and Change in Individual Behavior: An Interpersonal Approach. *Psychological Review 68*: 21-32. In a subsequent publication, Cass critiqued the various models of gay identity formation: Cass, Vivienne C. (1984). Homosexual Identity: A Concept in Need of Definition. *Journal of Homosexuality* 9(2/3): 105-126.

[29] The description of the stages in Cass's model is limited to those strategies that avoided identity foreclosure.

The first stage, **IDENTITY CONFUSION,** occurred when the individual began to entertain the thought that "my behavior may be called homosexual" (222). Such a perception was incongruent with the perception of self as heterosexual. The individual became confused over the erosion of the heterosexual identity. As the person acquired more information on homosexuality through books, friends, and therapists, the incongruence became acute and was relieved by moving on to the next stage.

In stage two, **IDENTITY COMPARISON,** the individual accepted the possibility of a homosexual identity and made the "first tentative commitment to a homosexual self" (225). To reduce the pain of feeling estranged, the individual welcomed the notion of being different for various reasons. Some attributed the feeling to their homosexuality. Some felt different because of their nonconformity to the heterosexual role and sought in the homosexual identity the legitimation of their nonconformity. Others found being different an exciting prospect. While thinking that the opinions of others were less important than they once were, the individual continued to present a public image of heterosexuality, what Cass called "passing." The passing strategy was successfully utilized by maintaining social contact with the opposite sex, avoiding behavior that could be labeled homosexual, by deliberately cultivating the image of heterosexuality or nonsexuality, or by adopting a stance that suggested indifference to homosexuality. If identity foreclosure had not taken place, by the end of stage two the individual's self-image was more homosexual than heterosexual. The person's greater commitment to the homosexual identity led to great acknowledgment of social, emotional, and sexual needs. This growing awareness, however, increased the incongruity between the self-image of being homosexual and the public perception of being heterosexual, propelling the individual into the next stage.

Cass called the third stage **IDENTITY TOLERANCE**. The individual "tolerates rather than accepts a homosexual identity" (229). The sense of estrangement from a heterosexual identity was counterbalanced by increasing contacts with other homosexuals. If the contacts proved to be rewarding to the person, other homosexuals began to appear as important and acceptable. This in turn led "to a greater commitment to a homosexual identity and a desire for further contacts with the homosexual culture" (230). The individual discovered the values of involvement:

> Mixing with the gay subculture offers P [the person] the chance
> to observe that it offers several positive features such as opportunity to meet a partner, provision for role models who

present homosexuality as acceptable, the chance to learn techniques for better management of a homosexual identity, practice in feeling more at ease by socialization to subculture behavior, and a ready-made support group. Therefore, even where contact with other homosexuals is minimal, it still allows P to observe the potentially rewarding aspects of mixing with homosexuals. (Cass, 1979: 230)

By the end of Stage 3 the individual could acknowledge that he or she was probably a homosexual. The person's extended participation in the gay subculture, however, spawned a growing incongruity. The demand for commitment to the homosexual identity progressively undermined commitment to the heterosexual identity. The gay subculture came to play a central part in the person's life. Less weight than ever was given to the "nonlegitimizing policy" (232) of the heterosexual world. The incongruence between the individual's positive view of the homosexual identity and its social rejection, however, was accentuated and led the individual to the next developmental stage.

IDENTITY PRIDE was the fifth stage. Here the individual minimized the heterosexual view of homosexuality. The world was dichotomized into homosexuals and heterosexuals and the commitment to homosexuals became univocal and superordinate: "There is a strong sense of pride in being gay, typified in slogans such as 'Gay is good' and 'Gay and proud'" (Cass, 1979: 233). In the individual's life outside the gay subculture, however, the sense of incongruity was heightened and led to "feelings of anger born of frustration and alienation" (233). This led the individual to take on the role of the gay "activist," which, in turn, resulted in the abandonment of a public heterosexual identity. Disclosure, according to Cass, reified the homosexual identity for the individual and resolved the dissonance between the private homosexual and public heterosexual identities. The incongruity in this stage arose when the individual met with acceptance by heterosexuals as a person with a public homosexual identity. Heterosexual approval moved the individual into the next stage.

IDENTITY SYNTHESIS marked the last stage in the development of the homosexual identity. No longer did the person view all heterosexuals as negative and all homosexuals as positive. With growing contact with supportive heterosexuals, the possibility of greater similarity between heterosexuals and homosexuals was accepted. Again referring to the individual P, Cass stated:

P's personal and public sexual identities become synthesized into one image of self receiving considerable support from P's interpersonal environment. With this development process completed, P is now able to integrate P's homosexual identity with all other aspects of self. Instead of being seen as the identity, it is now given the status of being merely one aspect of self. This awareness completes the homosexual identity formation process. (Cass, 1979: 234-235)

A fourth psychological model of homosexual identity development was proposed by Eli Coleman as a set of guidelines psychotherapists could use in treating homosexual patients.[30] It consisted of five stages: pre-coming out, coming out, exploration, first relationships, and integration. In the PRE-COMING OUT stage the person had a "pre-conscious awareness of a same-sex identity" (Coleman, 1982: 15). This was insulated from conscious awareness by such ego-defenses as denial and repression. Even this glimmering of homosexuality had a negative impact on the individual's self-concept because of social intolerance. The "healthy resolution" of the developmental task of this stage was for individuals to acknowledge their homosexual feelings.

With this self-admission the individual was prepared for the second and most important stage, COMING OUT. Coleman suggested: "Once these homosexual feelings are identified and acknowledged, the next developmental task is to tell others" (151). If the individual's disclosure met with acceptance a positive self-concept could replace the negative self-concept present in the first stage. Calculated risks, Coleman averred, were important in coming out because "each positive reaction can help the person take greater risks of disclosure and yet negative reactions can inhibit the process" (158). With the renewed self-esteem and self-confidence resulting from the first successful disclosures the individual was then prepared to withstand negative reactions in any future disclosures.

In the third stage, EXPLORATION, the individual made contact with the gay and lesbian community. It was a sexual as well as a social exploration. The "surge of interest and intrigue" (153)surrounding the individual's erotic development, Coleman suggested, could appear as "making up for a lost adolescence" (153). It was a stage of "awkwardness, intensity, and confusion" (153). Coleman's advice to therapists was not to foreshorten

---

[30] Coleman, Eli (1982). Developmental Stages in the Coming-Out Process. In W. Paul, J. D. Weinrich, J. C. Gonsiorek, and M. E. Hotvedt, Eds., *Homosexuality: Social, Psychological, and Biological Issues*. Beverly Hills, CA: Sage Publications, 149-158. (Another version of this article appeared in *Behavioral Scientist* 25(4): 397-405, in 1982.)

this stage in the treatment of homosexual clients. The individual needed the time to "develop a sense of personal attractiveness and social and sexual skills needed for a more integrated adult lifestyle."

FIRST RELATIONSHIPS was what Coleman called his fourth stage:

> When gay men and lesbians conceive of themselves as capable of loving and being loved, they are ready to enter this next stage of first relationships. The period of exploration has lost its intrigue, and there is a yearning for more stable and committed relationships.... Intimacy becomes the primary need to be fulfilled in this stage. (Coleman, 1982: 155)

Coleman postulated an intense need for intimacy in gay men and lesbians as the reason they desperately wanted workable sexual relationships. The first relationship was, therefore, turbulent because of extravagant expectations for success. In later phases of the relationship one of the partners may attempt to assert independence as a reaction to feeling trapped. The failure of the first relationship can lead the individual into believing that no homosexual relationship could work and to regression to a concept of themselves as a "sexually deviant adolescent, and ineligible for long-term committed relationships" (155). Lasting relationships became possible when partners realized that romantic expectations, mistrust, and jealousy undermined commitment.

Coleman called the final stage INTEGRATION. Here relationships were stabilized because individuals could act in an "open, warm, friendly, and caring way" (156). Coleman was referring to psychological integration, what he called an "integrated identity." If achieved, he believed that it could support the individual through middle and old age.

The models of the homosexual identity formation shared many assumptions.[31] There was the common assumption that the homosexual identity was immanent and predetermined. Unless the process of development was disturbed, the homosexual identity would naturally unfold. In this way it resembled the fertilized ovum which could be expected to develop into a mature organism. The assumption that the homosexual identity as an essence lodged in the individual psyche was implicit in the

---

[31] An additional model of homosexual identity formation, partially couched in psychoanalytic terminology, but based on the notion of a socially constructed homosexual identity, was advanced by Henry Minton and Gary McDonald in 1984 in Homosexual Identity Formation as a Developmental Process, *Journal of Homosexuality* 9(2/3): 91-104.

idea of "coming out." Coming out was analogous to the birth of the organism.

The models also assumed that the homosexual identity was realized through sequential stages. Like Freud's model of psychosexual development, these models implied that (1) the later stages embodied higher levels of achievement than the earlier and (2) the last stage embodied the quintessential homosexual identity beyond which further change was neither expected nor necessary for satisfactory homosexual relationships.

Because of the belief in the mechanism of development, the models provided impoverished motivational explanations of why individuals would abandon the security of the heterosexual identity for the uncertainty of the homosexual identity. Individual action, it appeared, was guided by conscious assessment of desire and behavior and objective appraisal of societal reactions. There was the implicit assumption that self-awareness triggered action either as resistance to the unfolding of the homosexual identity or as the steady march toward its full realization. Unconscious motivational states were not considered, such as a desire to experiment with unconventional structures for sexual relationships.

All the models discussed the process of identity formation in the psychological terms of development, awareness, self-acceptance, and disclosure. Yet the individual's successful negotiation of the stages depended largely on social circumstances. The crucial developmental steps involved displaying the homosexual identity to heterosexuals and handling their reactions. The personal elements of the homosexual identity were less clearly delineated than the public impact of its disclosure. The act of coming out was ultimately an effort to define the boundaries of acceptance by others, what de Monteflores and Schultz called "social validation." The success or failure of coming out was finally measured by the access it granted the individual to the gay community and the re-entry into heterosexual society.

The models precluded the formation of the bisexual identity and required the full abandonment of the heterosexual identity.[32] Even in the last stage of Cass's model, in which homosexuals re-entered heterosexual society and exercised more discretion in dealing with other homosexuals, they still stood forth as fully-formed homosexuals purged of all heterosexual longings and facades. The possibility that a full integration of

---

[32] This point was first suggested by Hencken (1982) who observed that the Cass model implied "the idea that bisexuality is only a homophobically defensive concept" (168).

the individual with self and society would embrace both homosexual and heterosexual relationships was precluded.

The models differed in scope and flexibility. Those of Cass and Coleman appeared to be less associated with particular ages. For them the process of homosexual identity formation could begin or end at any age. The models of Hencken and O'Dowd and de Monteflores and Schultz appeared to tie the process to childhood, adolescence, and adulthood. Some models allowed for more individual control over the course of development. Cass's model surrounded individuals at each stage with an array of options that allowed them to forestall or continue the developmental process. The other models appeared to depend more on social feedback. The course of development in the models of Coleman and de Monteflores and Schultz leaned heavily on the rejection or approval which individuals experienced in the process of coming out and stabilizing a homosexual identity.

These models contributed to the detoxication of the homosexual identity by distinguishing between "positive" and "negative" sociocultural identities. Individuals who took on the positive identity were free of pathology. Pathology continued to reside, however, in those homosexuals who retained the negative identity or resisted the gravitational pull of the positive identity.

The clinical psychologists who constructed these models were presumably inspired by the need to chart a course of psychological development and adjustment within the boundaries of a detoxicated homosexual identity. The cognitive and behavioral manifestations that correlated with each developmental stage were the evidence for locating the particular individual on the identity map. The fact that clinical psychologists took the lead in detoxicating a homosexual identity that had originally been pathologized by their therapeutic predecessors, the European and American psychiatrists, implied two things about their motivation. First, their chief concern was to reverse the work of those psychiatrists by replacing a sick with a healthy homosexual identity. Second, their models were not dispassionate inquiries into sexual relationships but efforts to bolster the belief in the homosexual identity particularly in those men and women in whom it faltered and who came to them for reparative treatment.

The models contributed to the normalization of homosexual relationships by making awareness of the homosexual identity precede behavior in either purely sexual or romantic relationships. This sequence of knowing before acting resembled the conventional expectation that partners "know" each other before they enter into sexual relationships. The individual, it appeared, was ideally expected to court a homosexual identity before seriously engaging in its practice. The models implied that sex or love that preceded awareness were at best relationships of questionable authenticity and at worst shoddy and illicit.

The models also contributed to the normalization of homosexual relationships through the emphasis on their enduring qualities. This emphasis was clearest in the Coleman model which made looking for, experimenting with, and finally attaining a "long-term committed relationship" the central theme in the process of homosexual identity formation. Such relationships were to save the individual from the miasma of lust that characterized the exploration stage. Sexual adventure could be fun, Coleman implied, but the serious business of the homosexual identity resided in lasting relationships.

Coming out, which was pivotal in all the models, was an expression of solidarity with the gay community. Pride and political activism replaced the secrecy, self-rejection, and submissiveness of pre-coming out years. By coming out, homosexuals could build their own communities and thereby be on an equal political footing with other minorities. The achievement of the homosexual identity became the criterion for judging eligibility for membership in the gay community just as the historic criteria of race, ethnic background, and religious belief were used by other minorities.

To the normalization of sexual relationships the models contributed in two ways: (1) by detoxicating the homosexual identity and (2) by purging it of all heterosexuality. Thus the homosexual and heterosexual identities were made analogous. By strictly separating the two identities the boundaries of permissible sexual relationships were pulled back. The straying of heterosexuals or homosexuals into each other's erotic territory could now be viewed as betrayal to self and community. With the creation of the pure homosexual, heterosexuals could feel secure behind the borders of their own sexual relationships.

Although essentially sociocultural in perspective, the collective homosexual identity retained elements of the biological and psychological. Minority status implied common biological roots as it did in the case of women and the racial and ethnic minorities. The psychological identity was retained in several forms. There was the oft-repeated assertion that the die for sexual orientation was cast before the age of four or five, an obvious revival of psychoanalytic theory of psychosexual development. Moreover, the formation of the collective homosexual identity was conceived as a developmental process organized into stages which individuals temporarily occupied in their forward march to the achievement of the fully realized and manifest gay or lesbian identity. Finally, the concept of homophobia, besides reifying a minority identity, also became a clinical diagnosis for heterosexuals and recalcitrant homosexuals who attacked or denied the social validity of the gay identity.

As a collective status the homosexual identity embodied the three cosmological views of sexual relationships. The polytheistic forms of sexual relationships were implicit of the descriptions of those homosexuals who failed to join the political efforts to resist oppression and refused to acknowledge their sexual identity in the public ritual of "coming out." They were depicted as marauders of the gay community, who raided it for sexual partners only to desert it after their lustful appetites had been sated. Those homosexuals who failed to acknowledge their sexual identity were consigned by the sociologists to anonymity and isolation and by the clinical psychologists to states of mental confusion and internalized homophobia.

In keeping with the major thrust of the scientific discourse, it was the view of sexual relationships embodied in the monotheistic cosmology that the collective homosexual identity reflected. The ethnic, racial, and religious minorities had been historically depicted as extensions of the family. The perpetuation of the family was believed to be the vital ingredient for ultimate success in their struggle with the majority. In western history, the family was conceived within the framework of Judeo-Christian tradition and doctrine. It was the product of the monogamous union of husband and wife and the nucleus of social organization. It extended outwards to relatives and community.

Sexual relationships that were based on the homosexual identity presumably precluded the formation of families as conceived within the monotheistic cosmology. Although leaders of the Gay Liberation movement were eager to claim minority status, ethnic and racial groups who established a prior claim to that status did not welcome them to their ranks. This cool reception by the established minorities can be at least partly attributed to their allegiance to the idea of the family and their belief that homosexual relationships constituted a threat to that institution.

As part of the normalization of homosexual relationships within the monotheistic cosmology, the homosexual "community" served as an extended, surrogate family. Community as family was the organizing principle of lesbians, who were collectively viewed as a network of couples. Coupledom granted women access to the lesbian community and the means for maintaining membership in it. Sexual partners from past relationships were retained as friends who could then be matched with other friends to form new sexual relationships. In the discourse on sexual identity, from the time of Krafft-Ebing, the female as wife and mother was considered the bedrock of the family. Deutsch considered the lesbian relationship to be a symbolic mother-child dyad with the partners alternating roles. The lesbian community, as an extension of the lesbian sexual relationship, therefore embodied the notion of family.

The idea of community as family served to bring the heterosexual and homosexual identities into greater harmony. The normalization of homosexual partnerships within the structure of monogamy aligned them with heterosexual relationships. By adding the idea of the homosexual community, homosexual partnerships were further normalized as family relationships. With both heterosexuals and homosexuals properly domiciled, there was less reason than ever for either group to wander into each other's territory or for homosexuals to feel isolated and rejected by heterosexuals.

Cast as minority, community, and lifestyle, homosexual relationships restricted the elements of choice as embodied in the scientific cosmological view of sexual relationships. Choice consisted essentially of acknowledging or not acknowledging membership in the female or male homosexual community. Open acknowledgment of minority membership required the individual to join in the resistance to heterosexual oppression. Community and lifestyle membership required the choice of sexual partners from within the community. Such requirements were tests of piety and allegiance, the results of which distinguished between individuals who accepted or rejected their sociocultural homosexual identity.

Scientism reigned supreme in the conception of the collective homosexual identity. It was conceived more and more as a force in the lives of homosexuals rather than a respite from heterosexual intolerance. It could exercise a determinative effect on psychosocial development, marking the difference between a full and attenuated personal and social development. The existence of the minority status was reified in homophobia scales and social psychological experiments that measured, presumably with increasing reliability and validity, antipathy to homosexuals as a group. The collective homosexual identity also conferred a historical past and future on homosexuals, as if there were social processes at work that would eventually liberate them from social intolerance.

Part Four:

THE RECRUDESCENCE OF THE BIOLOGICAL SEXUAL IDENTITY

19

The Hormonal and Genetic Sexual Identity:
Psychomedical and Sociobiological Approaches

Each successive reconceptualization of the sociocultural sexual identity, from the anthropological, behavioral, and ethnographic to the socially constructed and collective versions, tended to minimize the biological basis of the idea of sexual identity. The erosion of the idea of a sociocultural identity, divorced from its biological determinants and conceived essentially as a product of human invention, as we have seen, first occurred within the ranks of sociologists who had been unable to find empirical support for the idea of the socially constructed sexual identity. Moreover, they claimed that their social science data supported the notion of an innate, biological identity. This erosion was unwittingly intensified by those advocates of the collective homosexual identity who presented it as a minority status, on a par with those minorities apparently rooted in biology, such as women and ethnic and racial groups.

The recrudescence of the idea of the biological sexual identity was inevitable because the crucial distinction between the heterosexual and homosexual identities, even in their psychological and sociocultural avatars, was always tied to the biological sex of partners in sexual relationships. Those writers who were to revive the idea of the biological sexual identity, however, could not ignore the psychological and sociocultural conceptualizations that had dominated the discourse on sexual identity for most of the twentieth century. In reviving the idea of the biological sexual identity they were forced to reconceptualize it so that it could include psychological and sociocultural ingredients.

The recrudescence of the biological sexual identity took two forms: the psychomedical and sociobiological. The psychomedical approach included the study of the relationship of hormones to femininity in boys, masculinity in girls, and the homosexual identity. The sociobiological approach addressed the question of how homosexuality as a genetic trait could be transmitted to future generations.

The luminary figures in the formulation of the psychomedical view of sexual identity were John Money, Richard Green, and their collaborators, whose publications extended over a period of more than thirty years.[1] Money's view of sexual identity rested on his conceptualization of the differences between the sexes. These differences were polarized as female and male and were expressed through the individual's gender identity and role. **GENDER IDENTITY** referred to the person's perception of self as female, male, or ambivalent. **GENDER ROLE** was "everything a person said and did to indicate to others or to self the degree that one was either male, or female, or ambivalent" (1972: 4), including sexual arousal and response. Gender role was unique to the individual: "[Y]our role is not a script that was handed out to you, as a role given to an actor by a playwright. It is your own personal compilation, put together during the course of your development, from various social and cultural inputs" (1980: 12). Identity and role included "anything and everything that has to do with behavioral and psychologic differences, no matter whether the differences are intrinsically related to the genitalia" (1980: 12). In an oft-repeated statement, Money and Ehrhardt declared: "Gender identity is the private experience of gender role, and gender role is the public expression of gender identity" (1972: 4).

Money stressed the close relationship of mind and body in his use of the terms sex and gender:

> It is erroneous to follow the example of some writers who juxtapose sex and gender, allocating sex to the body and what they call biology (as if there is no biology of the mind!) and gender to the mind and social learning, apparently unmindful of the biology of learning. In correct usage, gender is a more inclusive term than sex—a kind of umbrella that shelters sex as

---

[1] Money's first study appeared in 1952: Money, John. *Hermaphroditism: An Inquiry into the Nature of a Human Paradox*. Doctoral Dissertation, Harvard University, Harvard University Library. Although Money was trained as a psychologist, most of his research has been published in medical or sexological journals. We have generally confined our treatment of his work and that of his associates to three primary works: (1) Money, John, and Ehrhardt, Anke, A. (1972). *Man and Woman, Boy and Girl*. Baltimore: The John Hopkins University Press; (2) Money, John, and Tucker, Patricia (1975). *Sexual Signatures: On Being a Man or a Woman*. Boston: Little Brown; and (3) Money, John (1980). *Love and Love Sickness: The Science of Sex, Gender Differences, and Pair-Bonding*. Baltimore: The Johns Hopkins University Press. Extensive bibliographies of his publications appear in the 1972 and 1980 books.

a manifestation of anatomy and of civil status as well. Sex is a term that needs to be reserved to signify that which pertains to the genitals and their functions. (Money, 1980: 12)

In 1980, Money presented the two concepts as gender identity/role (G-I/R) in an effort to emphasize "the unity of mind and body" (8). Gender identity and role had several components including the "erotic, procreational, vocational, recreational, ornamental, legal, and so on" (1980: 12). If erotic sexuality were used as the basis for classification, Money held, "one could speak of a heterosexual, bisexual, or homosexual G-I/R, each with its own variety of manifestations." Or one could have complex combinations such as "sadomasochistic heterosexual G-I/R" (1980: 12).

To link sexual identity and behavior to biological development, Money utilized the concept of "gender dimorphism," which designated distinct female and male forms as evidenced in body shape and appearance and, by extension, to behavior and language. He conceived of human development as beginning with "genetic dimorphism at conception and reaching completion with behavioral dimorphism in adulthood" (1980: 15).

Money's focal interest was in the prenatal and post-natal origins of sex differences. As for prenatal factors, he emphasized the effects of hormones on the development of the central nervous system. It was his belief that female and male forms of behavior resulted from the influence of prenatal hormones on the developing brain. Following contemporary research on embryonic and fetal development, Money believed that the male genital structure was produced when hormonal substances were added to the basic female form, a process he designated as the "Adam principle": "Nature's rule is, it would appear, that to masculinize, something must be added" (1972: 7).[2]

Money and Tucker stated: "Unless there is a sufficient push in the male direction, the fetus will take the female turn at any subsequent fork, whether there is a female push or not" (1975: 47). It was the Adam principle that accounted for the fact that "[m]ales were generally more vulnerable to sex differentiation errors than females" (1975: 4).

Besides influencing the structure of the genital anatomy the sex hormones developed different pathways in the brains of females and males. Money and Ehrhardt acknowledged that these pathways had not been anatomically identified but they believed that they were linked to such behaviors as "tomboyism" in females. Tomboyism was evidenced by such behaviors as interest in athletics, self-assertiveness in competition,

---

[2] The designation "Adam principle" appeared in Money and Tucker, 1975: 46-47.

functionalism and utility in clothing, postponement of the prospect of motherhood, valuing career above romance and marriage, and responsiveness to visual erotic stimuli. Money and Tucker did not believe that the hormones created new brain pathways or eliminated old ones. Both sexes had pathways for all human behaviors. Rather, the hormones formed a prenatal mixture that lowered or raised thresholds for the amount of stimulation necessary to push the individual toward various forms of behavior: "More androgen prenatally means that it takes *less* stimulus to evoke your response as far as strenuous physical activity or challenging your peers is concerned and *more* stimulus to evoke your response to the helpless young" (Money & Tucker, 1975: 78).

The final product of prenatal development was the irreducible differentiation of females and males. Money and Tucker called these differences the "biological imperatives" (1975: 38): "When it comes down to the biological imperatives that are laid down for all men and women, there are just four: only a man can impregnate; only a woman can menstruate, gestate, and lactate." Those differences in reproductive functions did not in themselves guarantee the necessary cooperation between men and women for the rearing of their young. The "gender stereotypes … provided the framework for cooperation" (1975: 38-39) based on "some kind of division of labor between the sexes, a sorting of behavior in sex, love, work, and play" (39). Society could redesign gender role and stereotypes as long as it did not interfere with the basic reproductive functions. The gender stereotypes, however, were not requirements of nature: "Beyond the four basic reproductive functions, nothing—*nothing*—of the differences between the sexes is immutably ordained along sex lines" (1975: 40).

Gender destiny was the wiring needed for the development of gender identity and role: "You were born with something that was ready to become your gender identity. You were wired but not programmed for gender in the same sense that you were wired but not programmed for language" (Money & Tucker, 1975: 89). Without formal instruction and with little awareness, parents throughout the world and history shouldered the responsibility of programming their children from the moment of birth:

> [A]s soon as the shape of the external genitalia is perceived, it sets in motion a chain of sexually dimorphic responses, beginning with pink and blue, pronominal use, and name choice, that will be transmitted from person to person to encompass all persons the

baby ever encounters, day by day, year in and year out, from birth to death. (Money & Ehrhardt, 1972: 12)

Parental shaping of children's behavior involved the processes of identification and complementation. As described in psychoanalytic theory of psychosexual development, the preheterosexual boy ultimately identifies as a male with his father, the girl as a female with her mother. According to Money and Ehrhardt, psychoanalytic theory left out the process of complementation wherein the behaviors the child acquired through identification with the same sex were practiced by the child with the parent of the opposite sex: "just as a small daughter dances with her father, and her brother with his mother" (Money, 1980: 32).[3]

Parents who switched roles, Money and Ehrhardt believed, made it very difficult for children to acquire the proper gender identity and role. For example, they criticized the confusion the openly transvestite father could produce in his son who, when his father was convincingly dressed as a female, may not realize that the father retained a penis under the clothing and that the penis was the "final arbiter" of being male. Parents who appropriately reared their children would be certain that the children know "the reproductive roles of the sex organs and to be able to look forward with approval to the proper use of their own, when the time is right" (Money & Ehrhardt, 1972: 14).

Money held that female and male behaviors were encoded in the brain as two separate schemas, one acquired through identification and labeled "for personal use," the other acquired through complementation and labeled "for predicting the responses of the other sex" (Money, 1980: 32-33). In 1972 the use of schemas had been described more restrictively: "For the ordinary little boy growing up, everything pertaining to the female gender is brain-coded as negative and unfit for use. The opposite holds true for little girls" (Money & Ehrhardt, 1972: 19). Everyone was bisexual in the sense that both schemas were encoded in the brain. Some individuals were better than others at transposing female and male gender roles. The proper development of the females and male schemas occurred when "parents together give a unified message as to what constitutes masculinity and femininity, instead of a garbled and contradictory one" (Money, 1980: 33).

The basic aspects of the child's gender identity, according to Money and Ehrhardt (1972: 16), were consolidated between eighteen months of age, when the child begins to use language, and the age of three or four. During this period, the failure of parents to maintain clear distinctions

---

[3] In his 1980 book, Money renamed complementation "reciprocation" (32).

between female and male gender roles was as confusing for the child as teaching it two languages at once: "[H]e is then likely to be slower than unilingual children in mastering either language" (1972: 18).[4]

The metaphor of the locked gate was employed by Money and Tucker to dramatize what they believed to be the irreversible course of gender development: "When the gender identity gate closed behind you it locked tight. You knew in the very core of your consciousness that you were male or female" (1975: 119). For some children who would become transsexuals or obligative homosexuals, "the gates may stay open a little longer" (119). The authors also speculated on the possibility that some types of homosexuality originated when the child, confused by parental signals, did not properly sort behavior for its own and the opposite sex.

Money continued to emphasize the psychobiological aspect of sexual identity, when he and his associates defined homosexuality as "erotic response to individuals with the same kind of external sexual anatomy as oneself" (1975: 19) and "erotic pairing with a person of the same genital morphology" (Money, 1980: 7). He and Ehrhardt differentiated between "homosexuality defined as a behavioral act, versus homosexuality defined, by inference, as a permanent erotic disposition and preference" (Money & Ehrhardt, 1972: 228). The first type they called FACULTATIVE HOMOSEXUALITY, consisting of "optional" (1972: 228) homosexual behavior which could be found in the sexual play of prepubescent children, in sex-segregated situations such as schools, prisons, and the military, and wherever there were injunctions against heterosexual relations. In prisons, men known as "gorillas," whose "sexual activity on the outside is, by strong preference, heterosexual ... are not so moralistically and inhibitedly heterosexual, however, as to be incapable of achieving erection and orgasm by means of oral or anal insertion" (1972: 228-229).

The second type was labeled OBLIGATIVE HOMOSEXUALITY. It consisted of involuntary homosexual behavior which reflected a core homosexual erotic propensity. Although obligative male homosexuals did not have uniform personalities, there was one trait they shared:

> They were not fighters. They avoided challenges to compete for dominance in the dominance hierarchy childhood groups. The obligative homosexual female, by contrast, is likely to have

---

[4] This contention is not supported by research on bilingualism nor is it consistent with Piaget's theory of cognitive development from which the authors borrowed the idea of mental schemata.

competed for dominance as a child, and to have been weak in maternalistic play interest. (Money & Ehrhardt, 1972: 234)[5]

The homosexual was one of three "psychosexual types" (Money & Ehrhardt, 1972: 229), the other two types being bisexual and heterosexual. It was not clear in what ways bisexuality was a distinct type because it seemed to consist of a basic heterosexuality to which a homosexual capacity was added. In 1980 Money asserted: "To be more precise, this changeable form of facultative homosexuality should have been defined not as homosexuality but bisexuality" (7).

Heterosexuality seemed to be the core identity of bisexuals: "The change from a homosexual to a heterosexual partnership in bisexuals is easily attributable to free will or voluntary choice, whereas it is actually no more than an acceptable alternative, usually more acceptable than the prior homosexual pairing" (1980: 7). Money seemed to assume that there were basically two sexual identities, homosexual and heterosexual, and that both were the involuntary products of prenatal and postnatal development. The heterosexual identity was treated as a unitary phenomenon without subdivisions into types. The bisexual, usually discussed as a male, was essentially the heterosexual who was able to substitute men for women in sexual intercourse when there were no women around, reserving the role of inserter for himself with either sex: "[T]he insertor thus demonstrates to himself that, despite his former heterosexual self-definition, he does in fact have some degree of bisexual gender identity, at least with respect to copulation and ejaculation, though falling short of falling in love" (1980: 85-86).

In addition to viewing bisexuals, heterosexuals, and homosexuals as distinct psychosexual types, Money and his coauthors conceptualized sexual identity as distributed along a continuum of gender identity and role. At one end of the continuum stood those individuals who took on the gender role of the opposite sex. At the other there were those who projected the gender role of their own sex. Presumably gender identity followed gender role so that transsexuals and transvestites who took on the role of the opposite sex also perceived themselves as members of that sex. Those who "chronically" took on the gender of the opposite sex were further toward the "reversal" end of the continuum than those who did so "episodically." Thus

---

[5] In Money and Tucker, facultative homosexuality was called "transient or episodic" (1975: 23), while obligative homosexuality was called "chronic or obligative." All these distinctions of homosexuality were absent from Money's 1980 book.

the transsexual was a more extreme case of role reversal than the transvestite; the "effeminate" homosexual male or "butch" homosexual female showed more gender reversal than "masculine" homosexual males or "feminine" homosexual females; the chronically homosexual female and male showed more gender reversal than the episodic bisexual; and so on. It was, of course, harder to determine the degree of reversal in gender identity than gender role because the former had to be inferred from observations of the latter. In most discussions, however, it appeared as if Money and his coauthors assumed that gender identity approximated gender role at least for the individual's erotic experience.

The position of Money and his coauthors on the gender identity of homosexuals changed in the course of almost a decade of speculation. In 1972, they presented homosexual men as not seeing themselves as fighters and homosexuals women as not seeing themselves as mothers. In 1975, some homosexual men were described as wholly masculine in role but still homosexual in erotic aim. In 1980, the homosexual male could be predominantly masculine in gender identity except for his choice of male partners: "[I]n an erotic partnership he does what one normally expects of a woman, namely, performs with a person with a penis, even though he may perform only the stereotypic masculine role of being an insertor" (Money, 1980: 87).

The continuing theme throughout these discussions was that homosexuals were "unfinished" in sexual identity because they were neither completely feminine nor completely masculine. For example, in describing the homosexual male who appeared masculine, Money and Ehrhardt had this to say:

> Actually, such a person has an identity/role that is partially masculine, partially feminine. The issue is one of proportion: more masculine than feminine. Masculinity of identity manifests itself in his vocational and domestic roles. Femininity of identity appears in his role as erotic partner; it may be great or slight in degree, and it is present regardless of whether, like a woman, he receives a man's penis or, also like a woman, he has a man giving him an orgasm. (1972: 146)

In 1972, homosexuality, transvestism, and transsexualism were considered "incongruities of gender identity" (1972: 147). Each of these sexual identities was classified as a paraphilia because it consisted of "distortions of gender identity" (1972: 148). In 1980, however, Money removed "bisexualism" and "homosexualism" from his list of paraphilias because "like heterosexualism, they do not, of and by themselves alone, interfere with or intrude restrictions or limitations on falling in love" (83).[6]

The major thrust of all these speculations by Money and his coauthors was to sponsor the belief that there was only the appearance of choice in sexual behavior. According to Money what appeared as erotic choice, particularly in adolescence, was really subjective illusion:

> Pubertal adolescents do not choose their erotic sexualism. They encounter it as performed in the mind. That does not preclude the possibility of one's having the personal subjective experience ... of choosing or selecting among options, for there are different weightings to the different preprogrammed components of each newly pubertal individual's sexualism. The protruding shape of girl's nipples, for example, may be heavily weighted as an erotic turn-on in a particular boy, so that it enters imperatively into his erotic fantasies, whereas the shape of the buttocks is relatively insignificant and lightly weighted by comparison. This boy will classify himself as a "tit man," rather than an "ass man." He will probably say that he prefers breast imagery as an erotic turn-on, and even persuade himself that his preference is a voluntary choice, whereas in point of fact it is an option that was preprogrammed into him without his informed consent, perhaps as early as the age of three, when he was still unweaned and suckling at his mother's nipples. (Money, 1980: 37)

A major contribution to the psychomedical discourse on sexual identity was made by Richard Green through his studies of feminine boys and masculine girls.[7]

---

[6] For Money, the major criterion for classifying paraphilias remained distortions in gender identity. However, "falling in love" apparently counteracted "distortions of gender identity." Transvestism and transsexualism also did not appear in the list of paraphilias but were given a separate classification as "transpositions of gender identity-role" (Money, 1980: 84-85). Money was silent on whether the removal of these forms from the list of paraphilias was also based on the belief that transvestites and transsexuals could and did "fall in love."

[7] Green's most extended treatment of this work is in his 1974 *Sexual Identity Conflict in Children and Adults* (New York: Basic Books). His interest in feminine boys grew out of his collaboration with John Money, which started in 1958 when Green was (xvii) a "fledgling medical student" at Johns Hopkins University. It was during that period that he conducted a pilot study of eleven boys who were classified as "behaviorally feminine"; see Green, 1974: 243; and Green (1979a). Childhood Cross-Gender Behavior and Subsequent Sexual

The original focus of Green's research was to identify the specific characteristics of femininity in boys.[8] He believed there was a possible link between adult homosexuality and boyhood history of feminine behavior. A general overview of the feminine boys' behavior, he reported, showed considerable similarity to the childhood behavior associated with male-to-female transsexuals: "The typically feminine boys, from the early years of life, cross-dresses, prefers girls as playmates, is rejected by boys', prefers girls' toys, avoids the rough-and-tumble games of boyhood, and takes a female role in fantasy games" (Green, 1974: 149).[9]

The behavior of these boys was so essentially feminine that Green suggested that they could be seen as females: "[F]eminine boys did not emerge as 'a third sex.' Instead, they exhibited preferences for roles and activities similar to those of typical girls and distinct from the average males of the same age" (1974: 204).

Preference. *American Journal of Psychiatry* 136(1): 106-108, 107. His first major study (Green, 1974) of feminine boys was conducted in Los Angeles while he was a psychiatric resident and researcher at the University of California, Los Angeles, and an associate of Robert Stoller.

[8] The sample in his first major study consisted of thirty-eight feminine boys who ranged in age from approximately three to eleven years (Green, 1974: 142). A comparison group of twenty-five masculine boys was also used. Data on the feminine boys were obtained through clinical interviews, parental description, observations, and most importantly, the administration of psychological tests for determining "gender preference." Most of the feminine boys chosen for this study were described as cross-dressing before the age of four. This meant using a variety of female adornment, including jewelry and cosmetics. The feminine boys were administered two standard psychological tests of social sex roles, the *It Scale for Children* and the *Draw-a-Person Test*, as well as several others devised by Green. Their scores were compared with those of the masculine boys. On the *It Scale* the feminine boys appeared significantly more feminine than the masculine boys in the choice of toys, activities, and playmates stereotypically associated with girls and depicted themselves as females or feminine. On the *Draw-a-Person Test* the feminine boys were reported as initially drawing more female than male figures.

[9] Green's interest in feminine boys appeared to stem from his early exposure to Money's and Stoller's work on transsexualism. He co-edited a volume with Money (Green, Richard and Money, John (Eds.) (1969). *Transsexualism and Sex Reassignment*. Baltimore: The Johns Hopkins University Press) and collaborated on at least one article with Stoller: Green, Richard, Newman, L., and Stoller, Robert (1972). Treatment of Boyhood "Transsexualism": An Interim Report of Four Year's Duration. *Archives of General Psychiatry 26*: 213-217.

In his later work, which included both male and female samples, Green arrived at similar conclusions about cross-gender behavior.[10] Feminine boys preferred the dress, toys, activities, and companionship of girls, played feminine roles, displayed feminine gestures, and sometimes said they wanted to be girls. Their favorite toy was the Barbie Doll. With the single exception of swimming, rough-and-tumble play and sports were avoided. When the boys played "house" or "parent," they usually took the role of mother or sister. The study of masculine girls, showed a corresponding pattern. The tomboys preferred to play with toys traditionally associated with boys, preferred boys as playmates, participated in rough-and-tumble sports, took male roles in playing "house," and sometimes stated that they wished to be boys.

One purpose Green had in studying the "cross-gender" behavior of children was to determine if it could be used reliably to predict adolescent or adult homosexuality.[11] In examining his samples of feminine boys, he found several who had reached mid-adolescence.[12]

His intention was to find out whether or not these boys were homosexual. His conceptualization of sexual orientation included four ingredients: "masturbation fantasies, reported erectile response to heterosexual stimuli, reported erectile response to homosexual stimuli, and interpersonal genital expression" (Green, 1979b: 107). The stimuli were simply nude photographs of females or males. Interpersonal genital ex-

---

[10] Green, Richard (1976). One hundred Ten Feminine and Masculine Boys: Behavioral Contrasts and Demographic Similarities. *Archives of Sexual Behavior* 5: 425-446; and Green, Richard, Williams, K., and Goodman, M. (1982). Ninety-Nine "Tomboys" and "Non-Tomboys": Behavioral Contrasts and Demographic Similarities. *Archives of Sexual Behavior* 11(3): 247-276. The study of tomboys was also preceded by a pilot study involving four girls, alluded to in Green, 1974, Chapter 7, and mentioned more specifically in Green, 1979a: 107.

[11] Green, Richard (1979a). Green was following the tradition in psychiatric research which assumed that adolescents and adults but not children had sexual preferences. His first assessment of the sexual identity of adult males, originally studied as feminine boys, was reported in Green, 1974: 243-244. Of the five males examined, three were described as "clearly homosexual" (243) and one as heterosexual in behavior but bisexual in fantasies. One respondent proved to be intractable. He refused "to return for an interview [and] is reported by his family to collect photographs of nude males" (243). Green distinguished his research approach as "prospective" while acknowledging that most of the available data were "retrospective."

[12] The precise number of boys was not stated in the report (Green, 1979a) although nineteen was the largest number reported for any major category of response.

pression referred to sexual intercourse or "heavy genital petting." Green reported that few boys were exclusively heterosexual or homosexual in fantasy, response to the photographs, or in sexual experience; several were "bisexual" in most of these aspects of sexual identity. He concluded:

> It is clear that feminine boyhood behavior, as defined by clothing, toys, peer group, activity, and role-playing preferences, does not consistently predict later homosexual orientation. However, from preliminary data, it does appear to load in favor of such an outcome in some persons. (1979b: 107)

The outcomes for the follow-up study of the sexual identity of four tomboys who had reached adolescence were equally inconclusive. Two of the girls were described as being heterosexual while one was in the process of becoming a female-to-male transsexual and the other was described as "asexual."

Although the results of his preliminary studies hardly confirmed the theory that feminine boys and masculine girls invariably became homosexual, Green believed that a closer look at the behavioral and test data, parental traits, and unique developmental events would make it possible to distinguish among pretranssexual, pretransvestite, preheterosexual, prehomosexual, and prebisexual children.

Green's beliefs about sexual identity were implied in his views on the origins of "cross-gender" sexual identity. In 1979, after a decade of research he concluded: "There is a growing body of research information linking childhood cross-gender nonerotic behavior with adolescent and adult sexuality (1979b: 1).[13] In effect, he believed that feminine boys and masculine girls were more likely to become homosexual than heterosexual.

In 1974, Green listed a constellation of factors he thought contributed to the development of feminine behavior in boys:

1. Parental indifference to feminine behavior in a boy during his first years.
2. Parental encouragement of feminine behavior in a boy during his first years.
3. Repeated cross-dressing of a young boy by a female.
4. Maternal overprotection of a son and inhibition of boyish or rough-and-tumble play during his first years.

---

[13] Green, Richard (1979b). "Sissies" and "Tomboys." *SIECUS Report* 7(3): 1-2, 15.

5. Excessive maternal attention and physical contact resulting in lack of separation and individuation of a boy from his mother.
6. Absence of an older male as an identity model during a boy's first years or paternal rejection as a young boy.
7. Physical beauty of a boy that influences adult to treat him in a feminine manner.
8. Lack of male playmates during a boy's first years of socialization.
9. Maternal dominance of a family in which the father is relatively powerless.
10. Castration fear. (1974: 212-213)

Among these factors he stressed "atypical" areas of intrafamily relationships: "father-son separation, marital-role division or the relative power within a family of mother and father, parent-child emotional closeness, and the biological sex and the birth order of siblings" (1974: 231).[14]

According to Green, however, the *necessary* factor in the development of femininity in boys was adult reinforcement:

[A]s any feminine behavior begins to emerge, there is no discouragement of that behavior by the child's principal caretaker.... For some extended period of time … parents do not consider the behavior distasteful, unusual, or in any way significant in terms of the boy's future. (238)

Green acknowledged that his list of etiological factors resembled Stoller's theory for explaining extreme femininity in boys except that it veered away from psychoanalytic conceptions pertaining to the mother's bisexuality and child's symbolic processes. Instead, Green believed his theory embraced peer-socialization factors as they related to a prenatal "neuroendocrinal factor":

As the [feminine male] child begins peer relationships, girls are primarily available. The few boys available, if any, are more aggressive than he, intimidate him, and meet with parental disapproval. The boy asserts that he likes to play with girls

---

[14] The empirical results of the study of the 1974 sample of feminine boys, for the most part, did not show that these intrafamilial factors were consistently present. Green appeared to believe that there was greater egalitarianism in the marital relationships of parents of the masculine as compared with those of the feminine boys.

because boys are "too rough." Possibly here too an innate
feature is operating to influence early socialization. A lower
level of aggressivity, influenced perhaps by an intrauterine
endocrine factor such as lowered androgen levels, may
facilitate his companionship with girls because he is more
comfortable in their play activities. Hence, his earliest learned
social skills are those more typical to girls. (239-240)[15]

Accustomed to playing with girls, the boys failed to make friends
with other boys. Their obvious preference for feminine activities and
styles led to the feminine boys being teased by masculine boys. This
rejection resulted in further alienation of the feminine boys. Finally, their
increasingly manifest femininity resulted in their being labeled sissies.
Concern over the influence of parents on the sexual identity of children
led Green to study children of homosexual or transsexual parents.[16]

The homosexual, in this research report, was distinguished from the
transsexual in "manifesting an erotic preference for same-sex partners"
but having a gender identity consistent with anatomy and behaving "in a
gender-role fashion typical for his or her own sex" (692). Some of the
transsexual parents were undergoing the modification of their biological
sex while rearing their children. Green reported that "psychosexual
development appears to be typical in at least 36 of the 37 children" (696).
The children who were teenagers or young adults were described as
being heterosexual in erotic fantasies. In explaining these results, Green
proposed that peer group members and relatives outweighed the
influence of the "unconventional" home.

---

[15] Green later referred to intrauterine hormonal secretions as contributing to
the development of the brain in modifying sexual identity: "Possibly a
nonspecific input such as cuddliness or aggressivity is hormone-influenced so
that parent-child relations are affected" (303). An innately cuddly child,
therefore, could stimulate the mother to cuddle him more. Green entertained
the possibility that some of the child's toy and activity preferences were not
entirely learned: "Consider doll play and infant care, more commonly shown
by girls and feminine boys.... Are these entirely cultural accidents, could there
be here any heritage from subhuman species?" (304).

[16] Green, Richard (1978). Sexual Identity of 37 Children Raised by Homosexual
or Transsexual Parents. *American Journal of Psychiatry* 135(6): 692-697. Eighteen
were boys, nineteen were girls. Twenty-one of the children were raised by
female homosexuals, seven by male-to-female transsexuals, and nine by
female-to-male transsexuals. The children ranged in age from six to twenty.
They lived in the "atypical households" for an average of five years.

Green's interest in exploring the relationship between cross-gender behavior in children and a future homosexual identity was not entirely academic. As physician and psychiatrist he was concerned with early and accurate diagnosis and preventive treatment.[17]

Diagnosis was intended to distinguish those feminine boys and masculine girls who still claimed membership in their respective biological sexes from those who believed they belonged to the opposite sexes: "We distinguish those boys whose behavior does not fit the cultural stereotype, yet who are nevertheless comfortable in being boys, from those who want to be girls" (Green, 1979b: 2). The prognosis for eliminating cross-gender behavior and a future homosexual identity was better for children under eight years of age.

Treatment for the feminine boys consisted of halting reinforcement of feminine behavior, especially by unwitting parents, and approval of masculine behavior. Fathers were advised to encourage sons to engage in "noncompetitive activities" (1974: 278) such as hiking and outdoor cooking, handicrafts, and board games but to avoid emphasizing rough-and-tumble play. The feminine boys were to be encouraged to play with masculine boys "who are themselves not wholly sports or roughhouse minded" (1974: 278). The parents were also to monitor closely the child's behavior: "The child should be sensitized to his actions of walking, sitting, or using his hands 'like a girl'" (279).[18]

Five years later, Green, in considering treatment, seemed to require less modification of femininity in boys:

> [Children] … should know that disinterest in sports or rough-house play does not leave becoming a girl as the only remaining option. They need to know that many boys and men have es-thetic interests, do not enjoy roughhouse play, and that in a world they perceive as black or white, grays exist. (1979b: 15)

---

[17] Two chapters were devoted to treatment (Chapters 6 and 16) in his major work (Green, 1974); diagnosis and "management" make up the bulk of the material presented in two other pieces: (1) Green, Richard (1975). Adults Who Want to Change Sex, Adolescents Who Cross-Dress, and Children Called "Sissy" and "Tomboy." In R. Green, Ed., *Human Sexuality: A Health Practitioner's Text*. Baltimore: Williams and Wilkins, 83-96; and (2) Green, Richard (1979b). "Sissies" and "Tomboys." *SIECUS Report* 7(3): 1-2, 15.

[18] Green did not address the treatment of masculine girls. He stated that some tomboys would eventually abandon their masculine ways when they reached adolescence which provided "heightened social rewards for being female *and feminine*" (1974, 298).

He disavowed the perception that his views on treatment looked like a program for preventing homosexuality:

> Not only does the writer not know how to prevent it [homosexuality], but it is also debatable as to whether one can or should do it. The article is specifically directed at providing some guidelines for members of the helping professions to follow in reducing concerns of parents who fear their child (usually male) is not developing "normally," and, in rare instances in which a child is significantly distressed over his or her gender, at reducing the conflict. (1979b: 1-2)

If treatment could prevent homosexuality, however, Green felt there were good reasons to invoke it. Adult male homosexuals faced the hardship of legal harassment and social intolerance. Others wanted to enjoy the privileges of heterosexuality:

> Many homosexual adults contend they are proud to be "gay." Their pride is not challenged here. However, some homosexuals do suffer because of their sexual orientation. Some long for a family. Those who undergo expensive psychoanalysis or painful aversion treatment do so not only out of feelings of guilt or fear of discovery; some genuinely seek the features of a lifestyle currently available only in a heterosexual union. (1974: 244-245)

Even as youngsters feminine boys faced intolerance; they were "teased, ostracized, and bullied" (Green, 1974: 245) and they could expect little reduction in social hardship in the years ahead

> unless the whole society changes dramatically during the next few years, the distress already experienced by these children will augment and their alienation will increase as society continues to stigmatize them. While one might prefer that society immediately change its often irrational values of what constitutes desirable gender-role behavior, realistically, there is more basis for optimism in helping a single person to change. (245)

Treatment also held a benefit for the behavioral scientist: "The opportunity is presented for testing hypotheses about the development of atypical behavior by directing intervention toward its suspect developmental causes" (245-246).

It would at first appear that Money and Green contributed to the detoxication of the homosexual identity. Treating this identity as an involuntary condition removed it from the realm of moral judgment. The individual who engaged in homosexual behavior and maintained homosexual relationships was obeying dictates handed down by "nature" and "nurture" as engraved on her or his brain. Indeed Money viewed the psychiatric classification of homosexuality as mental illness a disguised form of religious judgment:

> To define noncomplaining nonsufferers as sick, simply because they constituted a statistical minority, is to confuse the statistical minority with the ideological minority, and the statistical norm with the ideological norm. The sickness classification was really the old sin classification in disguise. (1980: 870)[19]

He still advocated treatment for bisexuals (who he believed were really heterosexuals) who suffered from the incompatibility of their heterosexual and homosexual proclivities.

It was more likely, however, that Money, Green, and their collaborators did considerably more to toxicate than detoxicate the homosexual identity by portraying homosexual men and women as "unfinished" males or females. As "intersexuals" neither homosexual females nor males fulfilled the basic requirements for membership in their own sexes. Homosexual women did menstruate but, *qua homosexuals*, they did not gestate and lactate. Homosexual men, *qua homosexuals*, did not impregnate.

This "incompleteness" they believed, was a product of "errors" (i.e., abnormalities) in prenatal and postnatal development. Homosexuals were conceived as victims of prenatal deficiencies, excesses, or temporal errors in the secretion of the male sex hormone. A hormonal excess "masculinized" the fetal brain of the to-be homosexual female. Homosexuals were the postnatal victims of fathers and mothers who provided imperfect identifying models or sent confusing and ambiguous signals about femininity and masculinity to their prehomosexual children. Because there was as little evidence to support the prenatal as the postnatal theory, Money and Green inevitably took the position that the homosexual identity was the product of the malfunctioning of both nature and nurture.

----

[19] Green agreed with Money's basic position that the psychiatric classification of homosexuality as a mental illness was a moral judgment. A full discussion of Green's views on this issue was provided in our analysis of the debate on homosexuality within the American Psychiatric Association. (See Chapter 11.)

Although Money eventually acknowledged that homosexuals could "fall in love," the homosexual relationship was never conceived by him as a relationship between two complete men or two complete women. Even when the male acted only as insertor in intercourse with another male, he was doing with a man what a complete male did only with a woman. Similarly, even if the woman acted only as receiver in intercourse with another woman, she was doing with a woman what a complete female would experience only with a man.

Because of their toxication of the homosexual identity, Money, his coauthors, and Green could contribute little to the normalization of homosexual relationships, except to argue for their acceptance as a minority status. Yet the tolerance Money urged for homosexuals was little more than the medical compassion of the nineteenth-century physicians and psychiatrists who, like them, viewed the homosexual identity as unfortunate and irreversible.

The contribution of Money and Green to the normalization of sexual relationships was considerable. That contribution was to shrink the limits of permissible sexual relationships so that they coincided with the male-female design. A "true" sexual relationship was that which transpired between the female and the male, in whom there was a harmonious confluence of genital anatomy, gender identity, and gender role. Biological sex of partners was not a matter of choice for either the heterosexual or the homosexual. Heterosexuals, however, were more fortunate because sexuality as gratification was tied to sexuality as a reproductive act, what Money and his coauthors called the "biological imperatives" of the two sexes. This concern that men be fully masculine and women be fully feminine was a resounding endorsement of the biological and psychological heterosexual identity as constructed in the scientific discourse.

The medical search for possible links between homosexuality and abnormalities in hormonal secretions began in the 1940s after the techniques for synthesizing and assaying sex hormones were developed.[20] The intention of at least some of that research was to treat

---

[20] The hormones, in general, consist of fats or solid states of alcohol. They are secreted directly into the bloodstream by the endocrine glands (e.g., the pituitary, the thyroid, and the adrenal cortex). The sex hormones are secreted chiefly through the endocrine glands located in the testes of the male and the ovaries of the female. The testis produces the male sex hormones, collectively called androgens. The most potent androgen is testosterone, The ovary produces the female sex hormones, collectively called estrogens. The most

homosexuality by "corrective" doses of hormone injections. Lynda Birke, in her review of the hormonal studies on homosexuality, categorized them on the basis of two implied assumptions: (1) those studies based on the belief that abnormal amounts of sex hormones were secreted by the endocrine glands of adult homosexuals and (2) those which assumed that sex hormones had produced abnormal sex differentiation in the brains of homosexuals during the prenatal period.[21]

Those studies based on the premise that there were abnormal amounts of sex hormones secreted by the glands of homosexual men typically compared testosterone level of men who were identified as homosexual with men who were identified as heterosexual. The expectation was that the level would be lowest in homosexual men, higher in bisexual men, and highest in heterosexual men. There was also the implicit assumption that men with higher testosterone levels would appear more masculine than those with lower levels. The number of homosexual subjects used in the various studies was typically very small, ranging from three to less than fifty (West, 1977).

---

potent estrogen is progesterone, which is produced at the time of ovulation and pregnancy. The adrenal cortex in both females and males produces small amounts of both androgens and estrogens, as does the male testis. The male testis also produces small amounts of estrogens and the female ovary small amounts of androgens. The hormones are called steroids because they contain sterols, which are solid alcohols. Cholesterol is one of the more widely known sterols. The function of hormones is to excite and regulate bodily functions.

[21] Birke, L. I. (1981). Is Homosexuality Hormonally Determined? *Journal of Homosexuality* 6(4): 35-49. Beside Birke we have used the following summaries of research on the hormonal basis of homosexuality: Baker, Susan W. (1980). Biological Influences on Human Sex and Gender. *Signs: Journal of Women in Culture and Society* 6(1): 80-96; Ehrhardt, Anke A. and Meyer-Bahlburg, H. F. (1981). Effects of Prenatal Sex Hormones on Gender Related Behavior. *Science* 211: 1312-1318; Gartrell, N. (1982). Hormones and Homosexuality. In W. Paul, J. D. Weinrich, J. C. Gonsiorek, and M. E. Hotvedt, Eds., *Homosexuality: Social, Psychological and Biological Issues*. Beverly Hills, CA: Sage Publications, 169-183; Hoult, T. K. (1984). Human Sexuality in Biological Perspective: Theoretical and Methodological Considerations. *Journal of Homosexuality* 9(2/3): 137-155; Meyer-Bahlburg, H. F. (1977). Sex Hormones and Male Homosexuality in Comparative Perspective. *Archives of Sexual Behavior* 6: 297-325; Meyer-Bahlburg, H. F. (1979). Sex Hormones and Female Homosexuality: A Critical Examination. *Archives of Sexual Behavior* 8(21): 101-119; Rubin, R. T., Reinisch, J. M., and Haskett, R. F. (1981). Postnatal Gonadal Steroid Effects on Human Behavior. *Science* 211: 1318-1324; and West, D. J. (1977). *Homosexuality Re-Examined*. Minneapolis: University of Minnesota Press, 67-74.

A similar approach was used for females who were identified as homosexual. The expectation, as phrased by Heino F. Meyer-Bahlburg, was that lesbians would show "elevated male sex hormone levels [of testosterone] and lowered female sex hormone levels [of estrogen]" (1979: 103) than heterosexual females. Of the eight studies he listed, four were based on data collected on presumably homosexual females; the other four contained data on subjects he called "female transsexuals."[22] In the four studies on female homosexuals the number of subjects ranged from four to twenty-one.

The results of investigations comparing hormonal levels in heterosexual and homosexual females and males were inconclusive, some showing the expected result (favoring the hormonal theory), others no differences at all, and even a few showing higher testosterone levels in homosexual males. In her summary review of the hormonal studies since 1971, Nanette Gartrell (1982) reached three conclusions: (1) most homosexual males and all homosexual females had testosterone levels that were normal for healthy individuals of their respective biological sexes; (2) the negative correlation between degree of homosexuality, as measured by the Kinsey heterosexual-homosexual rating scale, and testosterone level was not substantiated; (3) heterosexual and homosexual males had comparable amounts of chemically active or inactive testosterone.[23]

The typical conclusion reached by those who sponsored such studies was:

> We can conclude that the majority of female homosexuals appear to have testosterone and estrogen levels within the normal female range, whereas there seems to be a significant subgroup of about one-third of all subjects screened with an elevation of male sex hormone levels.... The reported findings

---

[22] The title of Meyer-Bahlburg's 1979 article referred only to female homosexuality. The studies discussed, however, were a mixture of data on "female homosexuals," "female transsexuals," and female infrahuman mammals.

[23] Of the thirteen studies that compared testosterone levels in heterosexual and homosexual males reported in the literature between 1971 and 1977, three reported higher levels in heterosexual males, eight reported no differences, and two reported higher levels in homosexual males. In most of the studies, sexual orientation was determined by using the heterosexual-homosexual rating scale; in some it was not assessed or the means of assessment was not clearly stated (Gartrell, 1982: 171-173).

themselves do not establish a causative role for androgens in the development of homosexual behavior in women" (Meyer-Bahlburg, 1979: 109)

Later in the same review, Meyer-Bahlburg stated "but the interpretation of these findings as to a causative role of androgens in female homosexuality is open" (1979: 117).

The second group of studies dealt with the prenatal effects of the sex hormones on the development of feminine and masculine behavior (Baker, 1980; Ehrhardt & Meyer-Bahlburg, 1981; and Rubin, Reinisch & Haskett, 1981). Femininity and masculinity were referred to as "gender-dimorphic" behavior. Ehrhardt and Meyer-Bahlburg identified six bases for determining "gender-dimorphic" behavior in children (1981: 1313): (1) ENERGY EXPENDITURE as revealed by active outdoor play, rough-and-tumble body contact, athletic skills—all characteristics of masculinity and therefore of males; (2) SOCIAL AGGRESSION, including pursuing, threatening, and fighting—also masculine characteristics one expected in males; (3) PARENTING REHEARSAL, such as playing with dolls, playing "house" or "mother," and "caring for babies,"—ingredients of femininity and therefore of females; (4) PEER CONTACT, which in masculine boys should be with other boys and in feminine girls with other girls; (5) GENDER ROLE LABELING, which for the masculine boy should not be "sissy" and for the feminine girl should not be "tomboy"; and (6) GROOMING BEHAVIOR, which presumably for boys should follow masculine styles and for the girls feminine styles.

Data for prenatal studies were collected on children who were born as "intersexuals," whose genitalia bore both female and male characteristics such as penises that were the size of the clitoris, clitorises that were enlarged and elongated, testicles that had not descended, and underdeveloped labia. As hermaphrodites these children were referred by physicians to psychologists and psychiatrists who advised parents on whether to raise the child as female or male. The decision was often based on whether the female or male genitalia were more prominent and the likelihood of their future development. Corrective surgery was employed to remove the undesired characteristic and hormonal treatment introduced to suppress the unwanted sex and enhance the development of the sex of choice. Parents were then instructed on the care to be taken in keeping the behavior of the child exclusively feminine or masculine.

The clinical follow-up studies suggested that the child raised as a boy thought of himself as a boy and behaved in masculine ways. The child reared as a girl thought of herself as a girl and behaved in feminine ways. Even for those children who were raised as girls but were genetic males, this pattern prevailed. The suppressed sex, however, appeared to survive in the child's behavior. Those genetic males raised as girls showed more tomboyism than the average girl. Those raised as boys showed femininity not found in the average boy.

These clinical studies were based on the scientific observation that the lack of sexual differentiation in these children was produced by excesses or deficiencies in hormonal secretions during the course of fetal development. In the case of the male fetus, the abnormalities were often attributed to inadequate amounts of androgens, the male sex hormones. For the female fetus, abnormalities were attributed to excessive amounts of androgens.[24]

This observation was based on a number of assumptions about the prenatal effects of hormones. One assumption was that the hormonal imbalances affected the differentiation of the brain as female or male. The deficiency of androgens in theory "feminized" the brain of the male, preventing it from properly differentiating as male. An excess in females masculinized the brain, preventing it from properly differentiating as female.[25]

A second assumption of the clinical, hormonal studies was that the effects of faulty brain differentiation would show up in children and adults as inappropriate gender-dimorphic behavior. Male children who were affected, when compared with those unaffected, would display less energy in play, less social aggression, possibly more interest in playing house, more peer contact with girls than with boys, would be more likely

---

[24] The theory has become more complicated with the inclusion of hormones other than androgen, such as progesterone. Androgens are now known to convert into estrogens and to produce masculinizing effects. See Ehrhardt and Meyer-Bahlburg (1981: 1312).

[25] Apparently the part of the brain that was believed to be affected was the subcortical region known as the hypothalamus (Ehrhardt and Meyer-Bahlburg, 1981: 1312). This is the relatively primitive region that regulates involuntary responses of the human organism, including those associated with the reproductive system. For example, the hypothalamus sets the pace for the female menstrual cycle. It also has been viewed as the "regulatory center" for emotions and aggression (West, 1977: 70). There is currently no reliable evidence that structural differences exist in the brains of the human female or male. The present evidence is based entirely on infrahuman mammals, usually the rat (See Baker, 1980: 92-93). It is extremely dubious that the theory or technology for systematically isolating specific "gender-dimorphic" behaviors will be developed in the foreseeable future.

be labeled "sissies," and would want to put on make-up and dresses. Correspondingly, female children who were affected would display more interest in vigorous activity and aggressive behavior than in playing house, prefer the companionship of boys to that of girls, be labeled "tomboys," and prefer male over female clothes and grooming. After reviewing the clinical studies, Ehrhardt and Meyer-Bahlburg stated:

> Any conclusion drawn on the basis of human research studies have to remain tentative, but it is already obvious that prenatal hormones have to be considered along with other factors [i.e., parental rearing] that interact in exerting their influence on the expression of sex-dimorphic behavior" (1981: 1317).[26]

The search for the link between abnormal prenatal hormonal secretions and feminine and masculine behavior inevitably led to the speculation about the possible connection of prenatal hormonal influences to adult sexual orientation. In this context Ehrhardt and Meyer-Bahlburg described sexual orientation as "sexual responsiveness to the same or other sex, as indicated by erotic attractions, sexual fantasies and dreams, and sociosexual experiences" (1981: 1316). As applied to sexual orientation the prenatal hormonal theory, according to Ehrhardt and Meyer-Bahlburg,

> predicts that the effective presence of androgens in prenatal life contributes to the development of a sexual orientation towards females, and that a deficiency of prenatal androgens or tissue insensitivity to androgens leads to a sexual orientation towards males, regardless of the genetic sex of the individual. (1981: 1316)

Since 1968, the effort to establish the connection between prenatal hormonal abnormalities and homosexuality was led by Gunter Dörner

---

[26] Since 1976, there has been a debate over the biological and psychological nature of gender identity. One group believes that gender identity is mostly the product of rearing, with the child taking on the identity of the biological sex to which the parents expect the child to conform. The other group holds that gender identity is mostly a product of hormonal influences that biologically program the development of gender identity throughout childhood and adolescence. In defense of the latter position, see Imperato-McGinley, J. and Peterson, R. E. (1976). Male Pseudohermaphroditism: The Complexities of Male Phenotypic Development. *American Journal of Medicine* 61(2): 251-272; and Imperato-McGinley, J., Peterson, R. E., Gautier, T., and Sturla, E. (1979). Androgens and the Evolution of Male Gender Identity among Male Pseudohermaphrodites with 5α-Reductase Deficiency. *New England Journal of Medicine* 300(22): 1233-1279.

and his coworkers in East Berlin.[27] The basic assumption of their work was that there was inadequate masculinization of the hypothalamus in the homosexual male due to an insufficient supply of androgen during a critical period of prenatal development. Conversely, in the homosexual female, there was an over-masculinization of the hypothalamus during a critical period. The experimental basis for this assumption was the work of the Dörner group in inducing "homosexual mating behavior" in female and male rats. In the case of female rats, androgens were administered shortly after birth to masculinize the hypothalamus, followed by additional doses given at puberty. The androgenized females, which they called the "homosexual" rats, mounted and attempted to copulate with other females. The male rats were castrated the day after birth to prevent masculinization of the mating centers in the hypothalamus. On the third day they were given testosterone to override the induced androgen deficiency. When the male rats reached puberty they displayed "homosexual" behavior by presenting their hindquarters to other sexually aroused male rats in the position known as **LORDOSIS**.[28]

In extrapolating their findings to humans, the Dörner group argued that there were abnormalities in the anterior lobe of the hypothalamus of

---

[27] Dörner, Günter and Hinz, G. (1968). Induction and Prevention of Male Homosexuality by Androgen. *Journal of Endocrinology 40*: 387-388; Dörner, Günter (1968). Hormonal Induction and Prevention of Female Homosexuality. *Journal of Endocrinology 42*, 163-164; Dörner, G., Rhode, W., Stahl, F., Krell, L., and Masius, W. S. (1975). A Neuroendocrine Predisposition for Homosexuality in Men. *Archives of Sexual Behavior 4*: 108; Krell, L.; Dörner G., Massius, W. G., Rhode, W., and Elste, G. (1975). Beziehungen zwischen klinisichen manifester Homosexualität und dem oestrogenfeedback Effekt. Dermatologishe Monansschrift *161*: 567-572; Dörner, Günter (1976). *Hormones and Brain Differentiation*. Amsterdam: Elsevier; Dörner, Günter (1977b). Hormones, Brain Differentiation, and Fundamental Processes of Life. *Journal of Steroid Biochemistry 8*: 531-536; Dörner, Günter (1977a). Hormone Dependent Differentiation, Maturation, and Function of the Brain and Sexual Behavior. *Endokrinologie 69*(3): 306-320; and Dörner, Günter (1979). Hormones and Sexual Differentiation in the Brain. In R. Green, Ed., *Sex, Hormones, and Behavior*. CIBA Foundation Symposium, 81-112.

[28] Lynda Birke noted that the "homosexual" rats were only those who fit the prevailing stereotypes: the female rat who mounted another female and the male rate who was mounted by another male (1981: 42). Birke's point was that both the "mountee" and "mounter" were homosexual in the sense that each relationship consisted of two rats of the same sex. Thus the stereotypes of the masculine homosexual female and the feminine homosexual male were imported into animal studies.

homosexual females and males. These abnormalities could result in peculiarities of sensitivity to "estrogen feedback effect." The estrogen feedback effect was observed in the female mammal when estrogen levels increased prior to ovulation. They theorized that the estrogen feedback effect may occur in homosexual males because of insufficient masculinization of the hypothalamus which would make them inappropriately sensitive to estrogen.[29]

In the case of homosexual females, effect would not occur because the masculinized hypothalamus would be insensitive to a rise in estrogen. The implication of these speculations, as discussed by Dörner (1976), was that corrective psychosurgery on the ventromedial hypothalamus combined with hormonal treatment, could eliminate or induce the proper feedback functions.

In addition to the experimental program of the Dörner group, support for the prenatal hormonal theory of homosexuality was sought in clinical studies of women who were known to have been exposed to high levels of prenatal androgen.[30] Some of these women received corrective postnatal hormonal treatment in early childhood for virilization while others did not start treatment for many years after birth.[31]

Neither the early nor late treatment groups, Ehrhardt and Meyer-Bahlburg observed, showed a predominance of homosexuality, although some showed bisexuality in their erotic dreams and fantasies.[32] Genetic males who were subject to deficiencies in androgens in the prenatal period were also studied. Most were reared as females because of the feminization of their bodies and as adults were sexually attracted to males.

---

[29] The experimental procedure used to test this theory involved injecting males with estrogen and monitoring levels of luteinizing hormone (LH) released from the anterior pituitary. The results of these experiments were inconclusive. The Dörner group was not particular about their choice of experimental subjects. Much of their work was on males who were hospital patients being treated for sexually transmitted and skin diseases, mental patients, and prisoners. (See Dörner et. al., 1975).

[30] These genetic females are diagnosed as having "congenital adrenal hyperplasia" (CAH). They are born with various degrees of virilization, which progresses unless they are treated.

[31] Ehrhardt and Meyer-Bahlburg described women who received delayed treatment as the "human analogue" of Dörner's female rats (1316).

[32] Curiously, none of the CAH women in the Soviet Union study reported homosexual fantasies or dreams. See Lev-Ran, A. (1974). Sexuality and Educational Levels of Women with Late-Treated Androgenital Syndrome. *Archives of Sexual Behavior 3:* 27-32.

The authors concluded "their sexual orientation can be ascribed to the prenatal hormonal deficiency as well as to rearing factors" (1981: 1316). Those raised as males developed a heterosexual orientation. Such evidence, Ehrhardt and Meyer-Bahlburg believed, suggested that "sexual orientation mainly followed the sex of rearing and identity, and therefore, is based on social learning rather than on hormones" (1316), but the possibility of hormonal influences should not be excluded. Their final conclusion:

> [W]e have to assume that prenatal hormonal conditions by themselves do not rigidly determine sexual orientation. It seems possible that prenatal hormonal abnormalities contribute to the development of sexual orientation in a minority of homosexual subjects, but this has not been sufficiently documented so far. (1981: 1316-1317)

The medical search for the causes of homosexuality extended beyond hormones and the central nervous system to include the possibility of identifying an inherited factor.[33] The inheritability of homosexuality had been a matter of speculation and some investigation since the time of Krafft-Ebing, Ellis, Moll, and Hirschfeld.

There were generally two approaches to the search for the genetic origin of homosexuality. In the "family studies" the investigators would begin with a group of identified homosexuals and then search for others among their relatives. West described a 1941 study carried out by Theo Lang, a German researcher, who looked for homosexuals among the relatives of male homosexuals held as prisoners in Munich (1977: 77).[34]

What Lang found more striking than the incidence of homosexuality was the large number of relatives with serious mental illness. West believed this finding suggested "a familial tendency toward homosexuality is linked with a tendency to serious psychiatric disorder" (West, 1977: 77).

---

[33] For summaries of these studies we have relied on West (1977: 77-84) and Pillard, C., Poumadere, Jeannette, and Caretta, Ruth A. (1981). Is Homosexuality Familial? A Review, Some Data, and A Suggestion. *Archives of Sexual Behavior* 10(5): 465-475. An earlier review appeared in Rosenthal, D. (1970). *Genetic Theory and Abnormal Behavior.* New York: McGraw-Hill.

[34] The study is cited as follows: Lang, T. (1941). Untersuchungen an männlichen Homosexuellen und deren Sippschaften mit besonderer Berücksichtung der Frage des Zusammenhangs zwischen Homosexualität und Psychose. 1. Die Probanden und deren engere Familie. *Zentralblatt für die Gesamte Neurologie und Psychiatrie 171*: 651-679.

In the same year G. W. Henry, an American investigator, conducted a study of the family trees of a nonclinical sample of forty female and forty male "sexual variants."[35]

Sometimes subjects were asked about the sexual orientation of their siblings and sometimes the investigator simply guessed. In a reanalysis of these data, Richard Pillard and his associates concluded that the number of homosexual or bisexual siblings identified supported a belief in the "familial factor" (Pillard, Poumadere & Caretta, 1981: 466). In another investigation of familial factors it was concluded that heterosexual subjects reported a much lower incidence of homosexuality among relatives than did homosexual subjects.[36]

In Pillard's own investigation of homosexuality among the siblings of thirty-six men who identified themselves as homosexual, he concluded that the incidence of homosexuality was "substantially higher than the random expectation" (468). After reviewing six family studies Pillard and his associates thought that these added up to a convincing conclusion: "Homosexual subjects report more HS [homosexuals] siblings than HT [heterosexual] subjects and more than would be expected given population frequencies" (468).[37]

The second approach to the question of inheritability of homosexuality consisted of studies of identical (i.e., monozygotic) and fraternal (i.e., dizygotic) twins. Because identical twins are produced by the splitting of a single egg, that is, fertilized by a single sperm cell, they share the same genetic inheritance. Fraternal twins are little more than ordinary brothers and sisters. The governing assumption of the twin studies was that identical twins would show more commonality of traits than fraternal twins. A higher incidence of homosexuality in identical twins would, therefore, support the theory that a genetic factor lay at the base of homosexuality. Perhaps the best known study was published by Franz J. Kallmann in 1952.[38]

---

[35] Henry, G. W. (1941). *Sex Variants: A Study of Homosexual Patterns*. New York: Paul B. Hoeber.

[36] Margolese, M. S. and Janiger, O. (1973). Androsterone/Etiocholanolone Ratios in Male Homosexuals. *British Medical Journal* 3: 207–210.

[37] Pillard and his associates entertained the possibility that heterosexuals provided less trustworthy estimates of homosexual siblings and relatives than homosexuals who "are certainly more attuned to this characteristic and more adept at recognizing it in others" (470).

[38] Kallman, F. J. (1952). Comparative Twin Study of the Genetic Aspects of Male Homosexuality. *Journal of Nervous and Mental Disease 115*: 282-298; and

Although he did not describe his recruitment procedures, it was believed that he relied on the help of psychiatric, penal, and charitable agencies (West, 1977: 79). Kallmann claimed to have found eighty-five pairs of male twins, forty of whom had identical twin brothers and forty-five of whom had non-identical twin brothers. He also claimed to have traced the brothers of thirty-seven of the identical twins and that all of them proved to be homosexual, what in the literature was referred to as a 100% "concordance rate." He found only three homosexual brothers in the twenty-six fraternal twin pairs he traced, for a concordance rate of 11.5%.[39]

Another study of homosexuality in identical and fraternal twins was even less conclusive than Kallmann's.[40] Part of the study by Heston and Shields was based on a registry, which had been maintained by Maudsley Hospital in London since 1948, of twins who had been psychiatric patients. Of the eighty-two identical twins, 6.1% were identified as homosexual in the registry. Of the ninety-seven fraternal twins, 7.2% were identified as homosexual. Another part of the study required research assistants to ascertain through direct contact the sexual orientation of twins selected from the registry. In this way the sexual orientation of five sets of identical twins and seven sets of fraternal twins, all males, was determined. They found concordance for homosexuality in two pairs of identical twins and one pair of fraternal twins. Each of the homosexual identical twins had

---

Kallman, F. J. (1952). Twin Sibships and the Study of Male Homosexuality. *Journal of Human Genetics 4*: 136-146.

[39] The study has been criticized on several bases: (1) it was carried out as part of Kallmann's research on schizophrenia so that, as West stated, "the subjects he started out with were seriously abnormal apart from their homosexuality" (1977: 79); (2) Kallmann did not specify the criteria he used in distinguishing between monozygotic and dizygotic twins; (3) his reported success rate in finding the brothers of thirty-seven of the identical twins was suspect because this was much higher than that reported in most twin studies (Futuyma and Risch, 1983/1984); (4) Kallmann's research on schizophrenia has been regarded as generally inept (see, for example, the calculation error in the twin study found by Pillard, Poumadere, and Caretta, 1981: 469n); (5) it was not clear which twins had been reared together and which apart, a major consideration in twin studies for distinguishing between the effects of heredity and environment(Hoult, 1984). Kallmann himself expressed some skepticism about his results as being a "statistical artifact." See Kallman, F. J. (1960). [Brief notice.] *Psychosomatic Medicine 22*: 258-259. This is a brief discussion of a research report on the sexual orientation of identical twins.

[40] Heston, L. L. and Shields, J. (1968). Homosexuality in Twins: A Family and A Registry Study. *Archives of General Psychiatry 18:* 149-160.

developed his homosexual interest without any knowledge on the part of his brother.

There were several studies of twins in which only one of the pair was identified as homosexual.[41] The homosexual member of the twin pair was explained as a product of maternal over solicitude or favoritism, parental encouragement of cross-sex behavior, brain damage sustained at birth, or being slighter in build.

Although the evidence of the twin studies left the question of the inheritability of homosexuality open, both West and Pillard held to the belief that homosexuality had a genetic basis. The Pillard group appeared to be firmer in this belief:

> Thus, the concordance for sexual orientation in MZ [identical] twins is probably closer to 50%, though higher for MZ than for DZ [fraternal] twins.... To summarize, there is substantial evidence from twin and family studies and from pilot data we have gathered that male and probably female homosexuality is a disposition than runs in families. (470)

West was more tentative:

> The current state of research into homosexual twins scarcely permits firm conclusions to be drawn. However, both the statistical findings and the descriptive studies suggest that hereditary factors may have considerably more importance than is generally acknowledged. (84)

The psychomedical research on sexual identity was not conducted in the interest of developing biological theory. It was medical research that used biology and was carried out under the aegis of psychiatrists and psychologists who viewed the homosexual identity as a condition and diagnosis. Because they were searching for its pathological origins, the research could hardly be described as dispassionate. It was based on the

---

[41] Among the more recent studies cited by Pillard and associates are the following: Friedman, R. C., Wollesen, F., and Tendler, R (1976). Psychological Development and Blood Levels of Sex Steroids in Male Identical Twins of Divergent Sexual Orientation. *Journal of Nervous and Mental Disorders* 163: 282-283; Green, Richard and Stoller, R. J (1971). Two Monozygotic (Identical) Twin Pairs Discordant for Gender Identity. *Archives of Sexual Behavior* 1: 321-327; Perkins, M. W (1973). Homosexuality in Female Monozygotic Twins. *Behavior/Genetics* 3: 387-388; and Zuger, B. (1976). Monozygotic Twins Discordant for Homosexuality: A Report of A Pair and Significance of the Phenomenon. *Comparative Psychiatry* 17: 661-669.

unquestioned assumption that the homosexual identity represented a biological failure of females to achieve full femininity and of males full masculinity.

Psychoanalysis, under Freud's leadership, had carved out the concept of the psychological sexual identity. Freud did not believe that biology entirely prefigured destiny. Much of sexuality, he believed, had to be determined after birth. For Freud, the heterosexual identity was a psychosocial achievement in which the child, as a biological female, attained femininity or, as a biological male, masculinity. Although Freud's approach to sexual identity clearly rested on the biological differentiation of the two sexes, it was essentially a psychological theory that attempted to keep sexual identity harmonious with genital endowment.

The psychomedical speculations revived the pre-Freudian idea of the biological sexual identity. Now, as before, the question was what could have gone wrong to produce human anomalies who lusted after members of their own sex and acted like members of the opposite sex. Now as then, the inquiry was conducted in the dim corridors of human biology, beginning, of course, with the reproductive process and ending in the recesses of the brain stem.

The psychomedical researchers were unwavering in their view of the homosexual identity as a developmental failure. Their search always centered on the reproductive process because that was where biological sex differentiation occurred. It was medically known, however, that this differentiation sometimes failed and the failure was due to hormonal influences on the developing fetus, as in the case of the hermaphrodites. Because the homosexual identity was viewed as improper sex-role differentiation, the extrapolation from the research on hermaphrodites was a rather simple step.

The trouble with this reasoning was that homosexuals like heterosexuals usually had clearly differentiated inner and outer genitalia. Sexual differentiation, however, comprised more than morphologically distinct genitalia. It included the differentiation of the brain which keeps the reproductive system operating properly, for example, to produce menstrual cyclicity in females. With the brain drawn into the explanation, it was argued that even though homosexuals looked normal, as far as their genitalia were concerned, it was quite possible that their brains were abnormal. Homosexual females may have brains that were prenatally masculinized and homosexual males brains that were prenatally feminized. Although such deficiencies could not be scientifically observed, the putative abnormalities were linked to the putative occurrence of feminized behavior in homosexual males and masculinized behavior in homosexual females. Regarding the prenatal hormonal theories of the homosexual identity, Gartrell remarked that a "hormone resistance or deficiency of the fetus in the uterus can only be *inferred* from postnatal observations. Furthermore, testosterone resistance in male external genitalia and breast does not necessarily imply a testosterone resistance or deficiency in the developing brain" (1982: 179).

In the twin studies the homosexual identity was subjected to epidemiological investigation much in the manner that medical research might attempt to determine the incidence of inheritable diseases like diabetes. In fact, the research on homosexual twins grew out of the epidemiological studies on the inheritability of mental illnesses such as schizophrenia. Homosexuality was said to "run in families," something that would be awkward to report about heterosexuality.

For these psychomedical investigators homosexual men and women were seen as living in contradiction to nature's design for the human race in which the sexual differentiation that occurred in utero was to continue to unfold as "gender dimorphic behavior" after birth. Within the framework of the reproductive imperatives, the homosexual identity was a flouting of nature's design, in which the role of impregnator (or insertor) was viewed as masculine and the role of receiver (or insertee) as feminine. Neither human beings nor animals were spared this stereotyping. The homosexual rats were those females who mounted other females or those males who presented to other males, but not their partners. Such serious disobedience of nature's commands earned the homosexual identity the diagnostic labels of chronic, obligatory, and gender dysphoric.

Within the psychomedical approach, partners of the true homosexuals could still retain a heterosexual identity. If two females or two males were to have sex together, then both partners would be included in a homosexual relationship. The discussion of homosexuality within the framework of the biological imperatives always faced the thorny problem of explaining the sexual identity of men and women who conformed to gender dimorphic behavior yet had a propensity for homosexual relationships. If, at least, the female took the role of receiver and the male the role of insertor in their homosexual liaisons, they would appear less egregious in their defiance of the reproductive mandates because male insertion into another male was at least a symbolic impregnation and female reception of stimulation from another female a symbolic fertilization. It was possible to consider them true though tarnished females or males. Their homosexual involvements, if they persisted, could be viewed as a form of bisexuality or flawed heterosexuality. If it was whimsical and opportunistic, it could be seen as functional, episodic, and transient.

The psychomedicalization of sexual identity incorporated ingredients of both the psychological and sociocultural formulations. It made palpable the psychological heterosexual and homosexual identities as adumbrated by Freud by clothing them in hormonal and genetic theories. It gave credibility to post-Freudian theories of sexual identity, which propagated the belief that anatomy was destiny, the male-female design the basis of sexual relationships, and the homosexual identity a miscarriage of nature's intentions. Psychomedicalization incorporated a basic premise of the sociocultural conceptualization by attributing the formation of sexual identity to factors that lay beyond individual responsibility and control. In the psychomedical approach to sexual identity biological "forces" were substituted for and amalgamated with the sociological.

In the nineteen seventies the sociobiologists joined the scientific discourse on sexual identity. The biologist who was most vigorous in propounding the thesis that sociobiology could be used in the study and explanation of human social behavior, including sexual behavior, was Edward Wilson.[42]

He defined sociobiology as "the systematic study of the biological basis of all social behavior" (Wilson, 1974: 4). It was a hybrid discipline comprising three areas of biology: ETHOLOGY, the study of adaptive and evolutionary patterns of animal behavior in natural environments; ECOLOGY, the study of the relationship of organisms to their environment; and GENETICS, the branch of biology dealing with heredity and variation among related organisms.

---

[42] Wilson, Edward O. (1974). *Sociobiology: The New Synthesis.* Cambridge, MA: The Belknap Press of Harvard University Press, and Wilson, Edward O. (1978). *On Human Nature.* Cambridge, MA: Harvard University Press. The first book was a broad, detailed delineation of the field of sociobiology, including social evolution, social mechanisms, and social species, human and sub-human. The second book was a "speculative essay" (x) that attempted to show how sociobiology could be used to bridge the gap between two "cultures," the social sciences and the natural sciences" (x). Although we have relied on Wilson for much of our elucidation of sociobiology, the field originated in the sixties with the theoretical work of Wynne-Edwards, V. C. (1962). *Animal Dispersion in Relation to Social Behavior.* New York: Hafner. Important contributions to sociobiological theory were made by J. H. Crook, W. D. Hamilton, R. D. Alexander, and R. L. Trivers. For references to their books and articles see Wilson (1974), "Bibliography": 599-663.

In the past sociobiology had concentrated on animal societies. It was Wilson's intention to explore its applications to the social behavior of man. This extension of sociobiology was possible, according to Wilson, because some forms of invertebrates and vertebrates were organized into societies. These societies were not separated by an "immense gulf" but shared many "functional similarities" (4).

By expanding the purview of sociobiology to include human society, Wilson was invading the disciplinary territories of the social sciences and humanities. In fact, he was not reticent to claim that this extension of sociobiology would cannibalize the social sciences and humanities by bringing them into what he called the "Modern Synthesis" (1974: 4). Within this synthesis:

> [E]ach phenomenon is weighed for its adaptive significance and then related to the basic principles of population genetics. It may not be too much to say that sociology and the other social sciences, as well as the humanities, are the last branches of biology waiting to be included in the Modern Synthesis. (1974: 4)[43]

In arguing in support of Wilson's vision of the grand synthesis of the biological and social sciences, David Barash remarked:

> It stretches credulity to imagine that *Homo sapiens* is unique among animals in possessing no biological components of social behavior. If nothing else we must possess a genetically mediated *capacity* for culture, learning, language, etc., in the same sense that wolves have the capacity for developing complicated dominance relationships. (1977: 287)[44]

Barash believed that culture was mankind's major biological adaptation.

Basic to sociobiological theory is the Darwinian concept of NATURAL SELECTION. It describes the tendency for some individuals in a given population to produce more successful offspring than others. Success is a

---

[43] Wilson defined population as "a set of organisms belonging to the same species and occupying a limited space at the same time" (1974: 592). Population genetics constituted the study of the gene pools, that is, all the genes (or hereditary material) of various populations.

[44] Barash, David P. (1977). *Sociobiology and Behavior*. New York: Elsevier. Barash was writing as both a psychologist and zoologist. In the preface Barash described his book as a "persuasive primer" (x) for students in the behavioral and social sciences.

matter of survival and reproduction. The more successful are those individuals capable of surviving such conditions as the onslaught of parasites, predators, and change in the physical environment. Survivors have a better chance to be represented in the next generation than their less fit competitors. The process of natural selection produces a gradual change in the genetic make-up of the population, holding together particular ensembles of genes. This change is what is meant by evolution.

Within the process of natural selection the individual organism is viewed as only the vehicle for transmitting the winning genes. Wilson recalled the aphorism of Samuel Butler that the chicken is only an egg's way of making another egg. The gene is the basic unit of heredity. The individual's constitution represents its genotype with regard to a particular set of traits. As a process natural selection assures the transmission of higher proportions of certain genes to future generations by promoting prolonged survival, superior mating performance, and superior care of the young.

The picture of the genetic basis of human society, Wilson believed, emerged most clearly when the social similarities of certain infrahuman mammals and humans were observed: (1) intimate social groupings contain from ten to one hundred individuals; (2) males are larger than females; (3) the young are raised through long periods of socialization first by mothers and then by peers; and (4) social play involves role rehearsal, mock aggression, sexual practice, and exploration (1978: 20-21). Wilson concluded:

> These facts are in accord with the hypothesis that human social behavior rests on a genetic foundation—that human behavior is, to be more precise, organized by some genes that are shared with closely related species and others that are unique to the human species. The same facts are unfavorable for the competing hypothesis which has dominated the social sciences for generations, that mankind has escaped its own genes to the extent of being entirely culture-bound. (1978: 32)

Wilson also believed that it would ultimately be within our scientific capability "to identify many of the genes that influence behavior" (1978: 46). There would not be specific links to behavior such as particular sexual practices:

> The behavioral genes more probably influence the ranges of the form and intensity of emotional responses, the thresholds of arousals, the readiness to learn certain stimuli as opposed to

others, and the pattern of sensitivity to additional environmental factors that point to cultural evolution in one direction as opposed to another. (1978: 47)

Whereas natural selection was portrayed as essentially a competitive process in which only the fittest survived, Wilson believed that cohesiveness, altruism, and cooperation were key properties of social existence (1974: 32). For Wilson, the central theoretical problem in sociobiology was "how can altruism, which reduces personal fitness, possibly evolve by natural selection" (1974: 3). He defined altruism as "self-destructive behavior performed for the benefit of others" (1974: 578).[45]

He distinguished between two forms of altruism. Hard-core altruism was the more selfless form (1978: 155). The bestower neither expected nor did anything that led to an equal return. Soft-core altruism was basically selfish and calculating (155-156). The donor expected reciprocity for self or for close relatives. In human society, Wilson asserted, there were far greater amounts of soft-core than hard-core altruism.

The basis of the concept of altruism was the sociobiological theory known as kin selection.[46] It referred to the selection of genes that occurred when the altruist favored the survival of relatives who were not offspring. In kin selection the production and care of offspring was seen as a special case of concern for others with whom the altruist shared genes. Kinship theory, thereby, expanded the idea of personal fitness by way of offspring to the idea of inclusive fitness by way of relatives. With the theory of kinship selection it was now possible to answer the question posed by Wilson. Altruism could evolve by natural selection in the following manner:

If the genes causing the altruism are shared by two organisms because of common descent, and if the altruistic act of one organism increases the joint contribution of these genes to the next generation, the propensity to altruism will spread through the gene pool. This occurs even though the altruist makes less of a solitary contribution to the gene pool as the price of its altruistic act. (1974: 3-4)

---

[45] In his 1978 book, Wilson added the following amplification to the definition: "Altruism may be entirely rational, automatic and unconscious, or conscious but guided by innate emotional responses" (213).

[46] Barash credits W. D. Hamilton, a population geneticist, with originating the idea of kin selection (1977: 79). See Hamilton, W. D. (1964). The Genetic Theory of Social Behavior: I and II. *Journal of Theoretical Biology* 7: 1-52.

Germane to the analysis of the normalization of sexual relationships are the sociobiological views of human sexual reproduction and bonding. Wilson held that the female and male sexes were designed for neither reproduction nor pleasure. He observed that there were more efficient means for organisms to mate and fertilize. As for pleasure, he noted that the sexual act was performed mechanically in the vast majority of animal species. The presence of two sexes, however, allowed for diversity and, consequently, adaptability in offspring: "[S]ex creates diversity. And diversity is the way a parent hedges its bets against an unpredictably changing environment" (1978: 122).

The presence of the two sexes, in Wilson's view, also led to a conflict of interest stemming from the division of reproductive tasks and effort. The female has a limited number of eggs to be fertilized while the male has an enormous oversupply of fertilizing sperm. With fertilization the female's commitment to reproduction vastly increased while the male's physical commitment ended with fertilization. Wilson observed: "During the full period of time it takes to bring a fetus to term, from the fertilization of the egg to the birth of the infant, one male can fertilize many females but a female can be fertilized by only one male" (1974: 125).

Wilson believed that there were some modest genetic differences between the human female and male that undergirded cultural variations in sex-roles. These differences he conceived as both physical and temperamental. He observed that men on the average were heavier than women. Pound for pound they were stronger and faster in most sports. The few sports in which women surpassed men, such as long-distance swimming and gymnastics, were those "furthest removed from the primitive techniques of hunting and aggression" (1978: 127). These physical differences were mirrored by psychological differences: "Women as a group are less assertive and physically aggressive" (1978: 128).

The contrast in the psychological development of boys and girls, Wilson thought, reflected the genetic differences of the two sexes. Boys were more physically venturesome and more aggressive in both words and actions. They had more hostile fantasies and they threatened and strove more for dominance. From birth girls were more intimate and social. They smiled more than boys and paid closer attention to the sights and sounds used in communicating. They were more reluctant to leave their mothers' side in new situations. Older girls were more companionable and less adventurous than their male peers.[47]

Wilson concluded:

> I am suggesting that the contradictions [between the sexes] are rooted in the surviving relics of our prior genetic history, and that one of the most inconvenient and senseless, but nevertheless unavoidable of these residues is the modest predisposition toward sex-role differences. (1978: 135)

Wilson believed, however, that most variation in female and male sex-roles could be attributed to cultural rather than biological evolution. Any effort to eliminate all sex differences in behavior, Wilson predicted, would "place some personal freedoms in jeopardy" (1978: 133).[48]

The family was also viewed in sociobiology as an entrenched evolutionary development: "The family, defined broadly as a set of closely related adults with their children, remains one of the universals of social organization" (1978: 135). Wilson saw the family as emanating from a compromise reached in the hunting-gathering phase of social development and dictated by the differences in the female and male roles in reproduction. As large primates human beings developed slowly both inside and outside of the womb. It was to the advantage of each female to hold on to a male-hunter who provided material support while she was bearing and nursing their children and who also shared in the children's care. It was to the male's advantage to obtain exclusive sexual rights to his female and monopolize her economic productivity as a gatherer: "Sexual love and emotional satisfaction of family life can be reasonably postulated to be based on enabling mechanisms in the physiology of the brain that have been programmed to some extent through genetic hardening of this compromise" (1978: 139-140).[49]

---

[47] Wilson was following the conclusions in Maccoby, Eleanor and Jacklin, Carol (1974). *The Psychology of Sex Differences.* Stanford, CA: Stanford University Press.

[48] Barash was sensitive to the fact that the position of sociobiology on sex differences opened it to the charge of sexism: "Sociobiology is sexist if sexism is recognition of male-female *differences*; however, it does not imply that either sex is *better*" (1977: 283n).

[49] Presumably the male's investment in this compromise was somewhat smaller than the female's because, in most cultures, the males took several wives, a practice Wilson attributed to the male capacity to breed at shorter intervals than females (Wilson, 1978: 140). Polygamy evolved into monogamy when the advantage of cooperation in the rearing of children outweighed the

The monogamous bonding of men and women Wilson attributed to the continuous sexual responsiveness of human beings who, in this respect, were unlike most mammals. This responsiveness provided extended opportunity for sexual pleasure. But it was pleasure, in Wilson's view, in the service of bonding. In glancing back over human evolution, Wilson saw the elimination of the female estrus as creating the opportunity for frequent sexual intercourse and conferring upon humans "a Darwinian advantage by more tightly joining the members of primitive clans" (1978: 141). Pursuing the theme of pair-bonding, Wilson held:

> Human beings are connoisseurs of sexual pleasure. They indulge themselves by casual inspection of potential partners, by fantasy, poetry, and song, and in every delightful nuance of flirtation leading to foreplay and coition. This has little if anything to do with reproduction. It has everything to do with bonding. If insemination were the sole biological function of sex, it could be achieved far more economically in a few seconds of mounting and insertion. Indeed, the least social mammals mate with scarcely more ceremony. The species that have evolved long-term bonds are also, by and large, the ones that rely on elaborate courtship rituals. It is consistent with this trend that most of the pleasure of human sex constitutes primary reinforcers to facilitate bonding. Love and sex do indeed go together ... all that we can surmise of humankind's generic history argues for a more liberal sexual morality, in which sexual practices are to be regarded first as bonding devices and only second as means for procreation. (1978: 141-142)

Some theorists attempted to apply the principles of sociobiology to the explanation of the origin of the homosexual.[50] Their interest stemmed from

---

disadvantage of either the female or male having additional partners (Wilson, 1974: 330).

[50] See, for example, Hutchinson, G. E. (1959). A Speculative Consideration of Certain Possible Forms of Sexual Selection in Man. *American Naturalist* 93(869): 81-91; Trivers, R. L. (1974). Parent-Offspring Conflict. *American Zoologist* 14: 249-264; and Alexander, R. D. (1975). The Search for a General Theory of Behavior. *Behavioral Science* 20: 77-100. Their work, as well as that of other sociobiologists, is summarized by Michael Ruse as four hypothetical explanations of the genetic origins of homosexuality. See his 1981 Are There Gay Genes?: Sociobiology and Homosexuality. *Journal of Homosexuality* 6(4): 5-34); and Kirsch, John A. and Rodman, James Eric (1982). Selection and Sexuality: The Darwinian View of Homosexuality. In W. Paul, J. Weinrich, J. C.

the reported presence of homosexual behavior in most cultures and most historical periods. The theoretical problem was to explain how homosexuality as a non-reproductive form of sexuality could be transmitted from one generation to the next.

One explanation preferred by evolutionary ecologist George Evelyn Hutchinson could be called superior heterozygous fitness. Heterozygous fitness suggested that an organism carrying both a heterosexual and homosexual gene may be more fit than those homozygotes carrying two heterosexual or two homosexual genes. This superior fitness meant that the organism in the heterozygous state would survive into maturity better, produce more children, or both. The homozygous states, of course, would result in inferior fitness because individuals in those states would be unlikely to reproduce.[51]

A second hypothesis of the genetic origin of homosexuality as developed by Trivers rested on the sociobiological concepts of "kin selection" and "altruism." This hypothesis assumed that by not having children of their own homosexuals could enhance the fitness of close relatives by altruistic acts. Their altruistic presence in the family would enable their relatives to have and rear more children. As Wilson stated: "Thus it is possible for homosexual genes to proliferate through collateral lines of descent, even if homosexuals themselves do not have children" (1978: 145).

A third hypothesis was called "parental manipulation," also first proposed by Trivers. In sociobiology the concepts of parental manipulation and altruism were tied together. Parental manipulation meant that when conflicts of survival arose between parents and children, the parents prevailed. That is, the parents would manipulate their children to enhance their own chances of survival (or fitness) at the cost of the survival (or fitness) of their children. The manipulation involved the parents inducing their children to behave in altruistic ways toward them and possibly toward their siblings. Michael Ruse suggested that parental

---

Gonsiorek, and M. E. Hotvedt, Eds., *Homosexuality: Social, Psychological, and Biological Issues.* Beverly Hills, CA: Sage, 183-195.

[51] There is only one documented case of superior heterozygous fitness. In individuals living some parts of Africa, the heterozygote pairing of the gene for sickle-cell anemia with the gene for "normal" hemoglobin provides protection against both malaria and anemia. There are two homozygous states: those with only the "normal" gene who are subject to malaria; those with only the sickle-cell gene who are subject to anemia. See Futuyma, Douglas and Risch, Stephen (1983/1984). Sexual Orientation, Sociobiology, and Evolution. *Journal of Homosexuality* 9(2/3): 157-168.

manipulation could be the means parents used to get a child to switch from a heterosexual to a homosexual identity. As a homosexual the child would transfer energies that would ordinarily be invested in a reproductive role to the altruistic role of aiding parents and heterosexual siblings. The presence of homosexual genes in both parents and offspring was a necessary presupposition for this hypothesis. Ruse suggested some possible family conditions under which parents may resort to manipulation:

> As the family gets larger and larger and, coincidentally, as the parents grow older, it becomes more in the parents' interest to raise a child to be altruistic towards other children, rather than as yet another competitor. So, unwittingly, the mother smothers her youngest with affection, turning the child to homosexuality. Conversely, the father may start to lose interest, with the same effect occurring. (26)

A final hypothesis on the genetic origin of homosexuality Ruse referred to as "homosexuality as a by-product" (13) of normal heterosexual development.[52] Masturbation, in this formulation, had adaptive significance for heterosexual development because it was a way for the boy to learn about sex. Within the practice of masturbation, however, there lurked the possibility that the boy would become homosexual because he was playing with and visually stimulated by the organ of his own sex. Ruse quoted the following explanation provided by Alexander:

> We all know that males masturbate more than females.... Moreover, male masturbation provides visual as well as tactual stimuli that are very similar to those involved in some homosexual activities. If one is stimulated sexually a great deal by seeing his own erect penis, then to be sexually stimulated by seeing someone else's is not such a great leap. Even if tactual and other stimuli are not greatly different between the sexes (and they may actually be), this great difference in visual feedback seems to be potentially quite significant. (Ruse, 1981: 14)

Ruse believed that Alexander's thesis rested on a number of assumptions: that the homosexual identity was the result of the

---

[52] Ruse based this explanation on the "unpublished speculations" (13) of R. D. Alexander, a sociobiologist at the University of Michigan. Alexander's hypothesis pertained only to the male homosexual identity.

withdrawal from intense heterosexual competition; that homosexual males masturbated more often and more intensely than heterosexual males; and that some physical differences may exist between the two types of males.[53]

The uniqueness of homosexuals as nonreproductive altruists was a theme in the work of James Weinrich.[54] Weinrich contended that homosexuals were unusual as children and adults. Heterosexual males, he claimed, were usually stronger and weighed more than homosexual males, although they were not taller. Homosexual males had less subcutaneous fat, were longer in proportion to bulk, and were smaller in muscle to bone ratio. This meant as children they were weaker boys. Faced with diminished prospects of reproductive success, these boys adopted a homosexual "strategy," which could include feminine mannerisms. In this maneuver the cost of being non-reproductive was balanced against the satisfaction in aiding siblings to raise children. For example, if a feminine boy became a religious figure (e.g., priest or shaman) he could bring status and financial gain to his family. An implied gain was that sexual gratification would be obtained with other males.[55]

Although less fit than heterosexual siblings for a reproductive role, Weinrich believed that homosexuals were superior in some respects. Most notable, in his estimation, was the greater acting ability of homosexuals. Even before they knew they were homosexual or knew about the theatre, the prehomosexual child showed uncommon interest and skill in stage-acting and role-playing. Homosexuals, in Weinrich's view, were also superior to heterosexual in intelligence.[56] He concluded:

---

[53] Futuyma and Risch (1983/1984) pointed out that this final hypothesis was not sociobiological because it neither viewed homosexuality as adaptive nor postulated any genetic basis for homosexual behavior.

[54] Weinrich, James D. (1976). Human Reproductive Strategy. I. Environmental Predictability and Reproductive Strategy: Effect of Social Class and Race. II. Homosexuality and Non- Reproduction: Some Evolutionary Models. Harvard University, PhD dissertation. See also Weinrich (1982). Is Homosexuality Biologically Natural? In W. Paul, et al., Eds., Homosexuality: Social, Psychological, and Biological Issues. Beverly Hills, CA: Sage, 197-208.

[55] As supporting evidence, Weinrich used anthropological reports of transvestism in primitive societies as well as some later psychological data.

[56] Weinrich, James D. (1978). Non-Reproduction, Homosexuality, Transsexualism, and Intelligence: A Systematic Literature Search. *Journal of Homosexuality* 3(3): 275-289. Weinrich's conclusions were based on fourteen studies in which IQ scores were reported for groups of individuals (mostly males) who were assumed to be homosexual or heterosexual. Most of the subjects in the studies

> As one moves from prisoners, to soldiers, to a clinical sample,
> to unmatched nonclinical samples, the results move from
> highly mixed to vaguely positive, to nearly ironclad. That is,
> the "better" the sample and study, the clearer it is that the
> more homosexual group scored higher [in intelligence] than
> the more heterosexual group. (1978: 286)

It appeared that Weinrich was claiming artistic and intellectual
superiority for homosexuals which would more than compensate for
what might be seen as their physical and reproductive inferiority.

The theory of sexual identity as kinship selection and altruism
furnished the basis for the detoxification of the homosexual identity. If
the homosexual identity fitted into the evolutionary process, then it
could not be considered "unnatural" as in the Judeo-Christian moral
tradition:

> There is, I wish to suggest, a strong possibility that homosexual-
> ity is normal in a biological sense, that it is a distinctive benefi-
> cent behavior that evolved as an important element of early
> human social organization. Homosexuals may be the carriers of
> some of mankind's rare altruistic impulses. (Wilson, 1978: 143)

Wilson believed that: "Most completely homosexual men prefer masculine partners, while their female counterparts, are attracted to feminine
ones" (144).[57] Homosexual men and women did not differ in dress and
mannerisms from heterosexuals. A strong "homophile preference" suggested to Wilson the close association between homosexuality and
heterosexuality: "Homosexuality is above all a form of bonding. It is
consistent with the greater part of heterosexual behavior as a device that
cements relationships" (144).

Wilson provided for the normalization of homosexual relationships by
bringing them within the purview of the family and society. Homosexual
bonding produced no offspring but homosexuals as, for example, brother
or sister, aunt or uncle, were in the position "to operate with special
efficiency in assisting relatives" (145). The social contribution was defined
by the special roles and statuses homosexuals occupied:

---

were institutionalized as prisoners or mental patients but there were also samples drawn from student groups, socio-political groups, or friendship
networks.

[57] Wilson assumed that there was a latent bisexuality in the brains of
infrahuman and human primates. This potentiality, he believed, was lost in
"full homosexuality" and "full heterosexuality" (1978: 144).

They select white collar professions disproportionately and regardless of their initial socioeconomic status are prone to enter specialties in which they deal directly with other people. They are more successful on the average within their chosen professions. Finally, apart from the difficulties created by disapproval of their sexual preference, homosexuals are considered by others to be generally well adapted in social relationships. (146)

The postulation of the existence of heterosexual and homosexual genes revealed the belief of the sociobiologists in the biological sexual identity. It was a tenet of sociobiology that genes controlled human social behavior. In the realm of human sexuality, however, the genes bestowed an entire sexual identity on the individuals whose behavior they presumably controlled. Wilson could speak therefore of the "fully heterosexual" or "fully homosexual" person as distinct human types. Weinrich and Alexander could assume that homosexuals were physically distinguishable from heterosexuals. Although Ruse mused over alternative destinies of homosexual genes, in each hypothesized scenario the individual's biological homosexual identity was prefigured.

In their biological speculations on the origins of the homosexual identity the sociobiologists showed little awareness that the biological sexual identity they attributed to genes had been variously ascribed to quirks in the development of the embryo, hormones, and the central nervous system by earlier writers like Ulrichs, Hirschfeld, and Krafft-Ebing. Even the efforts of the sociobiologists to show the positive side of the homosexual identity followed the historic tradition of Ulrichs and Hirschfeld who were among those who claimed that homosexuals were a superior as well as a unique human species. That superiority lay in the realm of the artistic, intellectual, and the humane.

Once created, however, this biological sexual identity was clothed in the trappings of the psychological sexual identity as conceived in psychiatric theories. Freud had proposed that individuals whose sexual development had been arrested were faced with either neurosis or perversion. Those who were neurotic experienced little or no sexual gratification because they were trapped between the failure to achieve a heterosexual identity and the resistance to perversion. The sexual abstinence that the church may have viewed as sanctified chastity was seen by Freud as a frozen, pleasureless state. The spinster daughter or aunt and the bachelor son or uncle who devoted their lives to parents and relatives were familiar figures in the literary and sociological landscape of the nineteenth and twentieth centuries. The homosexual altruists, as portrayed in sociobiology, resembled those individuals who sublimated their sexual desires, expressing them only as charity and service to family and society. The altruists appeared to be homosexual only in the absence of heterosexual behavior.

There were other examples of how the sociobiologists subscribed to the idea of the psychological sexual identity. The "parental manipulation" theory of Trivers was an unadorned revival of the position of the Bieber group in which the parents, particularly the mother, to meet her own needs, engulfed and seduced her son and, in the process, alienated his father. The major difference between the positions of Trivers and the Bieber group lay in the explanation provided for the sacrifice of the child's heterosexual identity. For Trivers it was to gain the child's assistance in helping parents shoulder parenting responsibilities. For the Bieber group, it was to placate a mother who was besieged by unresolved conflicts centering around her own heterosexual identity.

Alexander's theory that masturbation was the process wherein males were ushered into homosexuality was a revival of a notion vigorously propounded by Krafft-Ebing. Although Krafft-Ebing held that most homosexuals were born rather than environmentally created (and that they indeed masturbated), he also believed that it was possible to become homosexual through masturbatory indulgence. His reasoning was identical to that of Alexander: autoeroticism, in which the "self" and the "erotic object" were one and the same sex, was only a step away from a homosexual relationship.

The sociobiologists, as in the case of the psychiatrists, subscribed to the idea of the male-female design. Wilson linked his observations of the differences in the sexual behavior and bonding practices of the two sexes to the limited number of ova available to the human female and the superabundance of sperm to the human male. What made human evolution work was the complementarity of the hypersexuality of males and the hyperbonding of females so that a propitious balance was struck between promiscuous fertilization and steady nurturance of the newborn. In Wilson's depiction of the sexes this complementarity in reproductive functions became the metaphor for delineating sexual relationships. These were described as consisting of polar opposites so that male aggressiveness, fearlessness and hostility were paired with female intimacy, timidity, and friendliness. Although Wilson acknowledged that so rigid an assignment of traits to one sex to the exclusion of the other led to considerable awkwardness in the conduct of human affairs, he blamed nature and genes as the responsible parties.

Within the genetic framework of the male-female design it was easy for sociobiologists to espouse pair-bonding as the penultimate evolutionary purpose of sexual relationships. By placing pair-bonding at the center of sexual relationships Wilson was able to relegate sexuality as reproduction and as pleasure to subordinate positions while retaining them as essential ingredients of his theory. This amalgam of sexual pleasure and the reproductive imperative was reminiscent of the position of the post-Freudians who proclaimed heterosexual monogamy to be the only stable form of human bonding. Clara Thompson and Simon Rado, for example, argued that heterosexuality would always be the preferred sexual orientation because it alone provided the "natural fit" of the sexual organs as agencies of both reproduction and pleasure. Wilson was even able to accommodate homosexual relationships within the framework of the male-female design by claiming that these relationships consisted of either genuine females or genuine males. He could overlook the absence of genital complementarity in homosexual relationships as long as the integrity of the basic units in the male-female design was preserved.

The biological merits of the sociobiological conception of homosexual behavior as an evolved trait were assessed by two evolutionary biologists, Douglas Futuyma and Stephen Risch (1983/1984). They viewed the sociobiological explanation of homosexuality as a plausible story with little scientific basis. To achieve scientific credibility, the sociobiological theory of homosexuality would have to answer at least two questions: (1) Is homosexuality a special trait or, more simply, an expression of a generalized trait such as sexual behavior? They suggested that a comparable question would be to ask if speaking French is due to a special trait or merely the expression of the human capacity for language. If humans have a single set of genes for sexual behavior, then their expression as a homosexual or heterosexual orientation would depend on environmental circumstances, as in the case of different languages. (2) If homosexual genes exist, what is the evidence that they are adaptive? To answer this question it would be necessary to demonstrate that individuals with homosexual genes were more capable of passing them on than individuals who lack this genetic capacity.

The chief source of evidence for the existence of homosexual genes were studies of the sexual identity of identical and fraternal twins. Generally, in twin studies, to assess the relative influence of heredity and environment, only those twins reared apart in two different families qualify for inclusion. The assumption is that the identical twins will show more similarity in a given trait than the fraternal twins because the identical pairs have the same genetic heredity. Futuyma and Risch concluded that the published twin studies did not fully meet this methodological requirement or provide evidence that sexual identity was inherited.

Futuyma and Risch did not belief that sociobiology provided convincing evidence for the adaptability of the so-called homosexual genes. They thought the kin selection theory, upon which the sociobiological argument heavily depended, lacked or even contradicted available evidence. Anthropological data often showed that kin groups were not based on genetic descent and that altruism was often a manifestation of group loyalty. There was no evidence in the early history of the human race, they contended, that individuals who engaged in homosexual behavior had fewer offspring than those who were exclusively heterosexual. There was little evidence that homosexuals in most societies occupied privileged positions from which they could dole out favors and advantages to relatives. Even if they had occupied such positions, the theory failed to explain how privilege would have been translated into superior genetic fitness. The argument that homosexuals were more altruistic, intelligent, and artistic did not consider the possibility that these traits could be acquired by homosexuals trying to survive in a heterosexual milieu. The parental manipulation theory would have to show that parental behavior was adaptive and not merely a product of the parents' own learning and experience.

In contradistinction to the theory of homosexual genes, Futuyma and Risch proposed that the heterosexual and homosexual identities be conceived as varied expressions of emotional and sexual drives generally shared by mankind. They held that flexibility was the most noteworthy characteristic of human sexual behavior, just as individuals were capable of speaking different languages and preparing and enjoying a variety of cuisines. If preferences in sexual identity had to be explained at all, they would trace them to environmental circumstances.

In the nineteenth century the origin of the biological sexual identity was first attributed to feminine or masculine sex drives by Ulrichs and Kertbeny. If the direction of the drives corresponded to genital anatomy the individual would be heterosexual. Those individuals who were born with feminine drives and male genitalia or masculine drives and female genitalia would be homosexual. Building on Ulrichs' concept of the biological sexual identity, Krafft-Ebing developed the idea of a sexual instinct that was regulated by sex centers lodged in the cerebral cortex. When these were normally formed and functioning they directed the sexual instinct to respond to heterosexual rather than homosexual stimuli. Ellis rooted the biological sexual identity in the "germ plasm" of early embryonic development. In uterine development, when the germs of one biological sex completely vanquished the germs of the other, the individual was born heterosexual. The biological homosexual identity resulted from inadequately differentiated germ plasm. Hirschfeld ultimately believed that the biological sexual identity was a product of hormonal secretions. If the secretions of female hormones outweighed those of male hormones in the anatomical female, her sexual identity would be heterosexual. There was a parallel equation for heterosexual males. The homosexual identity was attributed to hormonal imbalances: an excess of female hormonal secretions in males or of male hormonal secretions in females.

The nineteenth-century theorists of the biological sexual identity agreed that it was an inherited identity. The heterosexual identity was the product of evolutionary progress, the homosexual identity of evolutionary digression or retrogression, which took the form of degeneracy or atavism. The twentieth-century theorists also believed sexual identity was inherited, but they turned to the developing science of genetics for a mechanism with which to explain its intergenerational transmissibility. The early genetic explanations followed the formula in which "good" genes accounted for the heterosexual identity and "bad" genes for the homosexual. This penumbra of genetic taint continued to hang over the speculations of the sociobiologists even when they tried to detoxicate the homosexual identity by harnessing its putative genetic advantages to the evolutionary service of the heterosexual identity.

Because it followed on the heels of the psychological and sociocultural formulations, the recrudescence of the biological sexual identity absorbed and transformed many of their attributes. The psychological sexual identity was given a physical palpability that perhaps had been sacrificed in the symbolism of psychoanalytic formulations. The doctrine of the post-Freudians that anatomy was destiny and that a non-pathological sexual identity conformed to the male-female design was infused with new biological authority. The sociocultural sexual identity was given a boost in two ways. First, the reborn biological identity constituted a resounding endorsement of the belief that the normative biological expectation was that females should fit into feminine sex-roles and males into masculine roles. Second, it reinforced a basic premise of the sociocultural identity, namely, that sexual identity was a product of factors external to the individual's control and discretion, indeed, the inexorable product of both sociological *and* biological forces.

All three cosmological views of sexual relationships were preserved within the psychomedical and genetic approaches to the discourse on sexual identity. In the polytheistic view variations in biological sex, such as hermaphroditism, were seen as evidence of the wonders of nature and the ingenuity of the gods. The polytheistic view was preserved within the psychomedical approach, in which the homosexual was one in a stunning array of anomalous sexual identities produced by hormonal imbalances. In the psychomedical approach, however, announcements of new sexual anomalies were breathlessly made as they were revealed by patients in the gender identity clinics of the medical schools. The apparent femininity of boys and masculinity of girls were also viewed as anomalies of "gender roles," in themselves purportedly the product of the hormonally "feminized" or "masculinized" brain.

In the sociobiological approach polytheism survived as the recounting of the anomalous roles the homosexual male played in exotic cultures, as transvestite, priest, or seer. In an effort at detoxication of the homosexual identity these roles, mostly present in polytheistic cultures, were sometimes described for their grandeur and power which presumably more than compensated for the inescapable fact that their occupants failed to make the crucial evolutionary contribution by not bearing offspring.

The permissive view of biological sex embodied in the polytheistic cosmology was transformed into the prescriptive view of sexual identity embodied in the psychomedical approach. In this shift of viewpoints there were corresponding restrictions on the boundaries of sexual relationships.

The monotheistic view of sexual relationships was fully endorsed in the psychomedical discourse on sexual identity. The implicit assumption of that discourse was that a biologically authentic sexual relationship conformed to the male-female design. Although the sexual relationships of partners of anomalous sexual identities were recognized as possible and existing, they were defined in terms of their conformity to or departure from the normative expectation for complementary pairings. Similarly, in the sociobiological approach, by defining the homosexual identity as ancillary to heterosexual parenting relationships, the biological authenticity of homosexual relationships was obscured if not tacitly denied.

The scientific cosmological view of sexual relationships was chiefly characterized by the element of choice of partners and boundaries. In both the psychomedical and genetic discourse on sexual identity individual choice was virtually eliminated because all sexual relationships were reduced to the biological predestination of their partners. Individuals were faced with the dubious option of either rejecting or accepting their biological fate. As an egregious example of scientism, the psychomedical and genetic discourse on sexual identity was phrased in the language of biology and medicine even though the research was conducted mostly by psychologists or psychiatrists or by biologists who attempted to subsume a form of social relationship under an evolutionary theory designed to explain biological phenomena.

20 Identity As Physiology

T he early recrudescence of the biological sexual identity was based on hormonal and genetic speculations. In the formulations of William Masters and Virginia Johnson, which were to follow, it was recast as a physiological sexual identity. This was conceived more as an extension of a sexual relationship than an attribute of sexual partners. Masters and Johnson believed that partners in homosexual relationships approached sexual intercourse differently than partners in heterosexual relationships. Further, female partners in homosexual relationships used different techniques than males. The various approaches, they purported, resulted in qualitatively different levels of physical and psychological gratification.

In 1954 a physiological approach to the study of sexual identity was launched by William Masters, who was joined later by Virginia Johnson.[1]

---

[1] We have chiefly relied on the following sources: (1) Masters, William H. and Johnson, Virginia E. (1966). *Human Sexual Response*. Boston: Little, Brown; (2) Masters, William H. and Johnson, Virginia E. (1970). *Human Sexual Inadequacy*. Boston: Little, Brown; and (3) Masters, William H. and Johnson, Virginia E. (1979/1982). *Homosexuality in Perspective*. New York: Bantam Books. (Originally published in 1979 by Little, Brown. The first book, *Human Sexual Response*, was based on their eleven-year study of the physiological and behavioral sexual responses of 382 females and 312 males. (When the program began in the mid-fifties the sample consisted of 118 female and twenty-seven male prostitutes. Data collected on these subjects were not included in the report.) Pairs of female and male interviewers obtained "detailed, medical, social, and sexual histories" (22) from individual subjects. They were then physically examined to eliminate those whose reproductive organs showed "any gross pathology" (22). The most unique part of the research was the direct observation of the subjects' sexual activity. This included manual and mechanical stimulation and female-male intercourse with the female in the supine, superior, or knee-chest position. Female subjects, in addition, were observed moving an artificial penis in and out of the vagina. This device provided "cold-light illumination"

The major goal of their work was to describe and explain physiological and psychological response to sexual stimulation. They believed that the sociological studies of the Kinsey group had paved the way to a "definitive investigation of human sexual response" (1966: 2). The direct interrogation of individuals about their sexual practices, they held, did not provide answers to a basic question: "What physical reactions develop as the human male and female respond to effective sexual stimulation?" (4). The answer, in their opinion, would enable the "medical and behavioral professions" to treat successfully "human sexual inadequacy" (4).

For the most part their subjects consisted of what Masters and Johnson called "family units" (1966: 311), i.e., husbands and wives. Over an eleven-year period these pairs were interviewed each year of their participation. After separation from the research program they were interviewed at five-year intervals. On the basis of information from these follow-up interviews, Masters and Johnson concluded that participation in the research program neither inhibited sexual performance nor developed an extravagant preoccupation with sex. In anticipation of the criticism that their program would stimulate an inordinate interest in sex or a lack of sexual restraint, they wrote:

> Any assumption that definitive sexual stimulation accrues directly from exposure to research personnel or environment seems contradicted by the fact that overt exhibitionism has not been a factor in the laboratory. In fact, modesty, social control, and even excessive concern for social mores has been the general response pattern. (1966: 314)

Previously, little was known about the physiological responses of men and women engaged in sexual activity. Through their research, Masters and Johnson defined four phases of arousal, which they called the sexual response cycle. The **EXCITEMENT PHASE** consisted of increased muscle tension and vasocongestion caused by physical and psychological stimulation. The **PLATEAU PHASE** represented reaching and maintaining a high level of sexual tension. The shortest phase was **ORGASM**, a total body response involving the sudden discharge of tension. Finally, in the **RESOLUTION PHASE** the body returned to an unaroused state.

---

which in turn "permitted observation and recording without disturbance" (21) The original work was carried out at the Washington University School of Medicine in St. Louis, Missouri. Masters was a member of the Department of Obstetrics and Gynecology. Their work came under the auspices of the Reproductive Biology Foundation in 1964.

A distinction was made between female and male orgasm and male ejaculation:

> Orgasm refers specifically to the sudden rhythmic muscular contractions in the pelvic region and elsewhere in the body that effectively releases accumulated sexual tension. Ejaculation refers to the release of semen, which sometimes can occur without the presence of orgasm. (Masters, Johnson & Kolodny, 1982: 67)[2]

The authors pointed out that it was possible to have orgasms without ejaculation as in the case of boys before puberty. Both men and women had orgasms but only males ejaculated.[3]

The major contribution of their first published study was to observe and describe in detail the genitalia and extragenital reactions of females and males during the four phases of the sexual response cycle. In the excitement phase the extragenital reactions of the females includes nipple erection, increase in breast size, a flush in the region around and above the breast, tensing of voluntary muscles, and an increase in heart rate and blood pressure. In the plateau phase there is further increase in breast size, a well-developed flush, further tensing of muscles in the facial, abdominal, and rib areas, and contraction of the rectal sphincter. In the orgasmic phase there are involuntary contractions and spasms of muscles, including the rectal sphincter. Finally, in the resolution phase there is involution of the nipples, decrease in the breast volume, relaxation of muscles, and the return to a normal heart rate and blood pressure. There is also a film of perspiration over the body.

There is a corresponding set of genital responses in females. During the excitement phase there is tumescence of the clitoris, appearance of vaginal lubrication, partial elevation of the uterus, and elevation of the labia minora which slightly extends the vaginal barrel.[4]

---

[2] Masters, William H., Johnson, Virginia E., and Kolodny, Robert C. (1982). *Human Sexuality*. Little, Brown: Boston.

[3] The authors remained skeptical about the possibility of female ejaculation. There is now speculation that some women ejaculate from a vaginal area known as the Grafenberg spot. See Perry, J. D. and Whipple, B. (1981). Pelvic Muscle Ejaculators: Evidence in Support of a New Theory of Orgasm. *Journal of Sex Research* 17(1): 22-39.

[4] The genital reactions in the labia majora differed in women who were "nullipara" (had not born children) from those who were "multipara" (had born two or more children).

In the plateau phase the tissues in the outer third of the vagina swell as do the vaginal lips. This increased concentration of blood (i.e., vasocongestion) hide the clitoris. The labia minora changes in color, ranging from bright red to maroon. In the orgasmic phase there are contractions of the vagina, uterus, and anal sphincter. In the resolution phase there is detumescence of the clitoris and vagina, a return of the uterus to the resting position, a return of the labia majora to normal thickness, and a return of the labia minor to a pink color. Women, unlike men, are able to have additional orgasms without falling below the plateau level of sexual arousal.

The extragenital reactions of males included the following. During the excitement phase there is nipple erection (in some males), voluntary tensing of the abdominal and rib muscles, and an increase in heart rate and blood pressure. In the plateau phase there is a sex flush that spreads from above the stomach over the chest, neck, face, forehead, and occasionally to forearms and shoulders, voluntary contraction of the facial, abdominal and rib muscles, contraction of the rectal sphincter, and some hyperventilation. In the orgasmic phase there is a well-developed flush and involuntary contraction and spasm of muscles and the rectal sphincter. In the resolution phase there is involution of nipple erection, disappearance of flush, loss of muscle tension, and return to a normal heart rate and blood pressure. In some men there is a sweating reaction, usually confined to the soles of the feet or the palms of the hands.

The genital reactions of males were also phasic. In the excitement phase the penis rapidly becomes erect and the scrotal sac and testes elevate. During the plateau phase there may be an increase in penile circumference at the coronal ridge, change in color of the coronal area, and enlargement and further elevation of the testes. In the orgasmic phase there are several contractions of intervals of less than a second along the entire length of the penile urethra and of the prostate. As these contractions begin the male has the sensation of "ejaculatory inevitability," a point at which the ejaculation cannot be stopped. In the resolution phase there is detumescence of the penis, relaxation of the scrotum, and full descent of the testes. In males, unlike females, there is a refractory period of varying lengths during which further orgasm or ejaculation is physiologically impossible.

Their elucidation of the sexual response cycle of females and males showed that there was great commonality. The primary physiological reaction in both females and males was superficial or deep vasocongestion, an increased concentration of blood in the skin but especially in the genitals. The secondary reaction in both sexes was myotonia, the voluntary and involuntary contractions of muscles. The authors concluded:

> The parallels in reaction to effective sexual stimulation emphasize the physiologic similarities in male and female responses rather than the differences. Aside from obvious anatomic variants, men and women are homogeneous in their physiologic responses to sexual stimuli. (1966: 285)

As for relative sexual capacity, Masters and Johnson believed that females far surpassed males. There was more dramatic variation in female sexual response: "The mercurial tendency to shift rapidly from peak to valley has been exemplified by female study subjects, while levels of sexual expression that remain essentially constant are observed most frequently in male study subjects" (1966: 314-315). They labeled as "myth" the belief that males had greater sexual capacity: "Females have an almost unlimited orgasmic potential, while men, because of the refractory period, are unable to have a rapid series of ejaculations."

Despite the fact that women were multiorgasmic and more undulating and sustained in sexual responsiveness than men, Masters and Johnson believed that there was still only grudging popular acceptance of female eroticism in the post-Victorian era: "To date, a sexual role for the female in which she freely participates has not received total acceptance in Western culture, despite the currently nebulous status of the double standard" (1966: 301). Instead, male eroticism was still perceived as mostly invincible, defeated only by the aging process. The authors' physiological studies, on the contrary, showed that male sexual performance was extraordinarily fragile: "[A]ny fear of performance, displeasing sensation, or sense of rejection affects male eroticism and 'age' does not necessarily deplete the male's physiologic ability or psychologic interest in sexual performance" (1966: 301).

On the basis of their physiological research Masters and Johnson challenged several popular conceptions and attitudes about orgasm in females and males. The notion that "all orgasms are intense, earth shattering, explosive events" (1979/1982: 74) was deemed a misconception. While some orgasms were "block-busters" others were "mild, fluttery, or warm" (71). The intensity of orgasms, they thought, varied with times and circumstances just as the taste of food or drink did. The popular notion of women who had orgasms was that they were aggressive or masculine. Masters and Johnson believed that orgasmic achievement for females was more dependent on social acceptability than overt aggression. In the case of males, popular attention focused on penile erection rather than ejaculation. Little attention was given to male ejaculation because it was generally assumed to be a part of the male's reproductive destiny. Such popular beliefs and attitudes about orgasms burdened the sexual performance of both men and women: "Fears of performance in the female have been directed toward orgasmic attainment, while in the male the fears of performance have related toward the attainment and maintenance of penile erection" (1966: 218).

Based on their subjects' recollections of early sexual feelings and experiences, Masters and Johnson, like the biological identity theorists before them, held that sexuality could be viewed "as an instinctual activity arising from an undifferentiated sexual state" (1966: 139). Although sexual capacity was transmitted genetically, in their view, sexuality was shaped by "both immediate and continued learning processes" (40). Sexual responsiveness, therefore, within the formulation of Masters and Johnson, was a product of the interaction between biological endowment and psychological influences to which individuals were exposed.

After obtaining physiological data on human sexual response, Masters and Johnson devoted their study to formulating an approach for the treatment of inadequate sexual functioning.[5] The uniqueness of human sexual functioning, as compared with other physiological processes such as breathing and digestion, was underscored by the authors: "Sexual responsivity can be delayed indefinitely or functionally denied for a lifetime. No other basic physical process can claim such malleability of physical expression" (10). This adaptability was useful because it enabled individuals to control the times and the stimuli to which they sexually responded. However, those individuals who suffered from sexual inadequacy involuntarily suspended sexual functioning by fearing that

---

[5] Masters, William H. and Johnson, Virginia E. (1970). *Human Sexual Inadequacy*. Boston: Little Brown. The study was based on 567 "units," of which 510 were married couples and fifty-seven unmarried individuals. In 287 of the couples only one partner was diagnosed as sexually dysfunctional while in 223 both partners were dysfunctional. Among the unmarried group, fifty-four were males and three females. Therefore a total of 790 individuals were classified as dysfunctional. Male patients were treated for a variety of sexual disorders: primary impotence, secondary impotence, premature ejaculation, and ejaculatory incompetence. Female patients were treated for vaginismus, primary orgasmic dysfunction and situational orgasmic dysfunction. Data on treatment were collected between 1959 and 1964. Follow-up data were collected over a five-year period.

their sexual performance would fail or by assuming the role of spectator during their own sexual participation.

Two misconceptions of sexual relationships, the authors believed, found in both men and women, gravely dampened or completely blocked sexual gratification. One, in the words of Masters and Johnson, was "that men by divine guidance and infallible instinct are able to discern exactly what a woman wants sexually and when she wants it" (1970: 87). The other was that sexual expertise lay wholly with the male: "In truth, no woman can know what type of sexual approach she will respond to at any given opportunity until faced with the absence of a particularly desired stimulative factor" (87).

The goal of therapy was to restore sexual responsiveness to its original natural, uninhibited state:

> Spontaneous sexual expression which answers the demand to be sexually needed and gives freedom for comparable male and female interaction, is universally the most stimulating of circumstances. Here the signal systems lead each partner toward and into the specifics that are desirable at a particular time.... Of course, individual preferences will rapidly become known and will repetitively produce the desired pleasure and stimulation.... The point is that sex removed from the positive influence of the total personality can become boring, unstimulating and possibly immaterial. (1970: 87)

The fear of failure was the chief source of inadequate sexual functioning "simply because it so completely distracts the fearful individual from his or her natural responsivity by blocking reception of sexual stimuli either created by or reflected from the sexual partner" (1970: 12). This fear was related to self as well as partner. For the self there was fear that one may lack the necessary sexual prowess. For the partner there was fear that one lacked the ability to relieve the partner's sexual tension.

In males the fear of failure centered around erection and ejaculation. Premature ejaculation was the inability to hold back ejaculation long enough after inserting the penis into the vagina to satisfy the partner. Ejaculatory incompetence was the inability to ejaculate while the penis was in the vagina despite a firm erection. Primary impotence described the condition wherein an erection firm enough to allow insertion could never be achieved or maintained. Secondary impotence defined the condition of males who had once been capable of erection but had lost this ability.

Several forms of sexual inadequacy were identified in females. Primary orgasmic dysfunction described the complete inability of the woman to respond to manipulation or intercourse.[6] Situational orgasmic dysfunction described women who were once regularly but later rarely orgasmic: "Usually when they obtain orgasmic relief, the experience is as much a surprise to them as it is to their established sexual partner" (1970: 240). Vaginismus was the involuntary spasms of muscles in the outer third of the vagina and severe constriction of the vaginal orifice in response to any attempt at penetration. Dyspareunia referred to sensations of severe pain during or after sexual intercourse.

In their program of therapy Masters and Johnson concentrated on the "psychosocial factors" that contributed to sexual dysfunction although they recognized that physical factors could also be the cause. The therapy they developed had several unique features. It departed from the traditional practice in psychotherapy of one therapist attending to only one partner. The one-to-one relationship was replaced by "conjoint" therapy in which both husband and wife were engaged in treatment from the start even though only one might be sexually dysfunctional. Masters and Johnson firmly believed in conjoint therapy:

> It should be emphasized that the Foundation's basic premise of therapy insists that, although both husband and wife in a sexually dysfunctional marriage are treated, the marital relationship is considered as the patient. Probably this concept is best expressed in the statement that sexual dysfunction is indeed a marital-unit problem, certainly never only a wife's or only a husband's personal concern. (1970: 3)

Conjoint therapy promised to identify sexual problems more fully because both partners could provide information and elicit the cooperation and understanding of both partners in overcoming sexual dysfunction.

Treatment also involved two therapists, one female, the other male. Masters and Johnson held that there was an inherent bias in how one sex viewed the sexuality of the other. No matter how objective a man may be, he could not be certain in his understanding of female sexuality "because he can never experience orgasm as a woman" (1970: 4). Conversely, no female would "understand the basic mode of male responsivity, because she will never experience ejaculatory demand nor seminal fluid release" (4). The therapist of one sex, therefore, was seen as the advocate of the same-sex partner, making sure that the sexuality of that partner was

---

[6] In common parlance this condition is called *frigidity*. In current sexology it is often called *anorgasmia*.

adequately represented in the discussion of sexual problems. The therapeutic team, besides acting as a catalyst in the communication between husband and wife, also served as a communicative model that could be emulated by the couple in the discussion of sexual problems.

Treatment extended over a two-week period during which the couple was completely involved in the program. The first segment consisted of a four-day basic program. The second segment, lasting ten days, was devoted to the removal of specific sexual dysfunctions. Each day of the basic program involved specific tasks. The first day was devoted to obtaining detailed sexual histories, the husband being interrogated by the male therapist and the wife by the female therapist. Questions pertained to current sexual practice, childhood, adolescent, and premarital background, perception of self, and awareness and responsiveness to stimulation provided through touching, seeing, smelling, and hearing. There were also general inquiries about chance experiences that had particular sexual meaning for the respondent, sexual expectations, dreams, and fantasies, and traumatic events such as incest, illegitimate pregnancies, abortions, rapes and infidelity. The questions were designed to reveal the quality of the relationship as well as the personalities of the two partners.

Questioning of the couple continued into the second day. At this time the female therapist interrogated the male partner, the male therapist the female. The purposes of this further interviewing was to illuminate material obtained in the earlier interviews, to add depth and color, to clarify the sexual problems, and to crystallize the sexual expectations of both husband and wife. The third day was devoted to a physical examination, **ROUNDTABLE DISCUSSIONS**, and **SENSATE FOCUS**. The physical examination was to uncover any anatomical or metabolic bases for the individual's sexual problems. This was followed by the roundtable discussion in which the co-therapists and marital partners participated(1970: 61). The therapists were to recapitulate and interpret the "psycho-sexual-social histories" (61), and the partners were to interrupt whenever they disagreed or needed clarification. The authors viewed this therapeutic procedure as: "the use of the 'mirror' of unprejudiced objectivity held to reflect the sexually dysfunctional marital unit's patterns of personal interactions" (1970: 63). It was the couple's "first confrontation with the realities of their sexual distress." The roundtable experience constituted a dramatic break with the couple's past:

> Before ... marital partners usually are frozen into patterns of
> self-sacrificing endurance, fear of hurting, or inability to

> understand or analyze the circumstances of their dysfunction. Rarely have they faced or shared together their sexual feelings or even mutually discussed the problems of sexual dysfunction objectively beyond agreeing to seek consultation with authority. (1970: 67)

During the discussion, therapists avoided casting either partner in the role of "victim" or "culprit." Rather, they tried to develop a sense of cooperation in which the attitude of "one-for-all" was established.

Part of the third day was devoted to what the authors called sensate focus. Unclothed and in the privacy of their living quarters, partners were to sexually stimulate each other primarily through touching. They were to continue for as long as the activity provided pleasure and discovery, but never to the point of physical fatigue or boredom. The laboratory epigram was that "A rewarding five minutes is worth much more than a stressful half-hour" (1970: 71). At first each partner took turns touching the other's body except for the genitals. This was followed by mutual touching, an exercise which helped couples to overcome the tendency to be only a spectator. The authors referred to sensate focus as "pleasuring" (86). The couples had to overcome their resistance to the enjoyment of touching: "The feeling that sensate pleasure at best represents indolence and at worst, sin, still permeates society sufficiently to influence the affectional, sexual patterns of many marital relationships" (75). Pleasure was permissible only when fortuitous. The discussion of the couple's reactions to pleasuring was included in the third day of activities.

During the fourth (and final) day of the basic treatment program couples learned to extend sensate pleasure to the entire body, including the breast and genital areas, without any specific goals of sexual arousal. Spontaneous verbal communication was encouraged: "When pleasured, the husband or wife may wish to express his or her pleasure in some manner of verbal release" (1970: 90). But it was not to be a forced communication that would lead to self-consciousness and inhibition.

The remaining ten days of the therapy, constituting the second treatment segment, were devoted to specific sexual dysfunctions. For example, to prevent premature ejaculation, the wife was taught the "squeeze technique," which involved her applying pressure to the coronal ridge of her husband's penis for a few seconds to reduce his urge to ejaculate. To induce ejaculation in a husband suffering from ejaculatory incompetence, the wife was taught "teasing" techniques such as "a demanding style of female pelvic thrust against the captured penis" (131).

In the treatment of primary impotence in single men, female partners known as **SURROGATES** were provided by the program, or a partner of choice (known as a **REPLACEMENT PARTNER**) was brought along by the patient himself. These partners were to "approximate insofar as possible the role of a supportive, interested, cooperative wife" (150). The treatment of orgasmic dysfunction in women involved the husband's and wife's heightened awareness of individual responsiveness to desirable erotic stimuli. They were encouraged to savor the sexual experience by giving up the pretense of enjoying practices that were not gratifying and by not focusing exclusively on achieving orgasm. It was important for them to observe the principle that to "get" gratification one should "give" gratification to one's partner. In the treatment of vaginismus dilators graduated in size were inserted by the husband, at first, with the wife's manual control and then only with her verbal direction.

Masters and Johnson observed that their treatment was not always successful:

> Inevitably, there were failed opportunities on both the patient's and the therapist's sides of the fence. There were instances of lack of sufficient patient motivation and/or psychosexual maturity to accept therapeutic direction. Total dissatisfaction with mate, intense anxiety states, deliberate dissimulation, and revenge motifs clashed with therapeutic process. There were instances of therapist error in judgment, clinical objectivity, and occasionally emotional control. (1970: 370)

Their approach avoided a serious pitfall of one-to-one psychotherapy for sexual problems. Based on the reports of men and women in their program who had psychotherapy, treatment had involved "the therapist seducing the essentially defenseless patient into mutual sexual experience" (1970: 388). The authors were firm in their denunciation of sex between patient and therapist:

> It is easy for psychotherapists to seduce or accede to seduction by their patients, particularly when these patients are under treatment for sexual dysfunction. For therapists have every advantage—the extremely vulnerable patient, the forces of transference and countertransference, the subject matter per se, are significant elements influencing these psychosocial tragedies. There is no greater negation of professional responsibility than taking sexual advantage of an essentially defenseless patient; yet this often happens. (389)

The use of co-therapists, Masters and Johnson believed, provided a built-in protection for all parties because the focus of attention was always on the marital partners and not on their relationship to the therapists: "This innate (i.e., intrinsic) form of patient protection may be one of the stronger arguments for the dual-sex team when professionals are dealing consistently with the vulnerability of men and women lost in the maze of human sexual inadequacy" (391).

It was almost a decade later that Masters and Johnson published *Homosexuality in Perspective* (1979/1982), their study of the physiology and psychosexual behavior of homosexual men and women.[7] The major

---

[7] On a nation-wide basis, 176 subjects were recruited between the years of 1964 and 1968. There were ninety-four males and eighty-two females. Eighty-four of the males and seventy-six of the females were partners in "committed" relationships that had lasted at least one year. The remaining ten males and six females were supplied "assigned partners," usually one but, in a few cases, two to three. Subjects "representing the full range of homosexual preference" (1979/1982: 9) in actual experience were selected, with ratings on the Kinsey heterosexual-homosexual scale ranging from one to six. This broad spectrum of sexual orientation was utilized to see if there was a difference in sexual response patterns of those who were or were not exclusively homosexual. Subjects were interviewed for their sex histories and observed in sexual activity on several occasions. Each subject was observed in at least one episode of masturbation, manual stimulation by partner, and fellatio or cunnilingus. Five homosexual pairs were observed in episodes of what the authors called "rectal intercourse" (1979/1982: 83). Three lesbian couples used dildoes. Only individuals who were "highly functional sexually" (1970: 7) were used as subjects. In addition to the homosexual subjects, twelve AMBISEXUAL subjects (six males, six females) were recruited from 1968 to 1970. As defined by the authors "an ambisexual is a man or woman who unreservedly enjoys, solicits, or responds to overt sexual opportunity with equal ease and interest regardless of the sex of the partners and who, as a sexually mature individual, has never evidenced an interest in a continuing relationship" (1970: 145-146). These individuals were rated in the middle range of the Kinsey heterosexual-homosexual scale and had rarely if ever evidenced a preference for one sex over the other. For partners they were assigned females and males who were exclusively heterosexual or exclusively homosexual. 46 assigned partners were used (nineteen males, twenty-seven females). Also included in this study was a new sample of 114 heterosexual subjects who were recruited as a comparison group. There were fifty-seven males and fifty-seven females. Of these, fifty males and females comprised married couples. Assigned partners were used for seven males and seven females. Heterosexual subjects were limited to those who were rated 0 or 1 on the Kinsey heterosexual-homosexual scale. The authors noted that "heterosexual volunteers leading heterosexual lives with

purpose of the study was to compare the sexual responses of homosexual men and women with those of heterosexual men and women performing the same sexual behavior: masturbation, general approach to partners, partner stimulation, and fellatio or cunnilingus.

As for masturbation, Masters and Johnson observed unique response patterns for the different biological sexes but for different sexual identities. Both heterosexual and homosexual men, for example, during masturbation lay in the supine position, immediately focused on the penis, used the dominant hand for stroking, increased stroking after achieving a full erection, and slowed down the stroking as they ejaculated. Both heterosexual and homosexual women masturbated in the supine position, were indirect in their approach to the clitoris, stroked their breasts, abdomens and thighs, varied the rate and pressure of stroking far more than men, and continued clitoral manipulation through orgasm.

There were differences in the ways homosexuals and heterosexuals approached the sexual act:

> [U]sually, the committed homosexual couples *took their time* in sexual interaction in the laboratory. Generally there was a deliberately slowed approach to the entire stimulative process.... The interacting homosexual couples appeared to be more relaxed and gave the impression of more complete subjective involvement in the sexual activity than did their heterosexual counterparts. (1970: 64)

While the homosexual couples concentrated on the exchange of pleasurable stimulation, the heterosexual couples concentrated on goals: "An apparent pressure to 'get the job done' was usually evident during partner manipulation and fellatio/cunnilingus and was consistently present during coition" (1970: 65). Homosexual partners spent more time at each phase of the sexual response cycle. Heterosexual women appeared

---

sexual preference ratings of 2 through 5 were not recruited for the program" (1970: 9) because it had not occurred to the research team, when their work started in the fifties, that there were heterosexuals with considerable homosexual experience. Heterosexual pairs were observed in the act of coitus as well as those sexual acts performed by the homosexual subjects. Seven heterosexual pairs engaged in anal intercourse. Three heterosexual women used dildoes. The husband of one woman inserted a dildo into her anus. One reason for recruiting this new heterosexual sample was that fellatio and cunnilingus had not been investigated in the original study. A selection of subjects from the original heterosexual pool (1966) was also used as a comparison group.

to be as goal-oriented and hurried as heterosexual men, behavior that Masters and Johnson attributed to cultural pressures on coital performance.

There were striking contrasts in how the woman approached her female partner as compared with the husband's approach to his wife. The female began with full body contact. Breasts were then stimulated manually and orally with particular concentration on the nipples and with equal amounts of time allotted to each breast. The stimulating partner concentrated on the momentary responsiveness of her partner rather than aiming for higher levels of excitation. The labia, thighs, and vaginal opening were explored before the clitoris. Females used two different approaches in bringing female's partners to orgasm. One the authors called the "teasing cycle" (1979/1982: 69) in which the partner was brought several times to high pitches of excitement and allowed to regress before finally coming to orgasm. The other was the "elevator style" in which the partner was stimulated with more continuity and increasing intensity and, in this way, brought to more than one orgasmic experience. Although most female couples preferred one technique to the other, the combination of the two was frequently observed.

In their sexual approach to wives, husbands typically spent little time in close contact, caressing, and stimulating the breasts. They appeared to be more concerned with the release of their own sexual tensions than in arousing their wives. Consequently, breast stimulation produced relatively limited amounts of vaginal lubrication, much less than that produced by the female couples. In fact, several wives did not consider their breasts erogenous zones. Wives received only vicarious pleasure from observing their husbands' gratification with their breasts. Husbands were unaware that their wives' breasts and nipples may become tender during the menstrual cycle. The husbands also directly approached the clitoral glans and maintained contact until the clitoris retracted. Whereas female partners limited vaginal stimulation to the vaginal outlet, husbands frequently inserted their fingers deeply into the vagina even though their wives did not evince any pleasure and were even distracted by the penetration. Because there was little communication between husband and wife, the awkwardness of the husband's approach was not remarked by the wife.

The homosexual male approached his partner in a manner resembling that of the homosexual female to her partner. Sexual activity was initiated with general body contact, including close holding, kissing, and caressing. The nipples were stimulated before genital contact was made, in itself often producing an erection in the stimulated partner and sometimes in the stimulator. Genital play was low-key and non-demanding, involving the anus, thighs, perineal area, scrotum, and abdomen. More attention was focused on the head than the shaft of the penis. Close attention was paid by the stimulator to his partner's responses and he altered the rate of stimulation to prolong gratification. Homosexual males employed almost unfailingly the "teasing technique." As in the case of the female partners, Masters and Johnson believed there was high intragender rapport between male partners: "the committed male homosexual study subjects usually stated in essence that they stimulated their partners the way they (the stimulators) would like to be stimulated" (1979/1982: 73).

The approach of male partners to each other contrasted with that of wives to their husbands. Wives rarely stimulated their husband's nipples, tended to concentrate on the penis to the exclusion of other genital areas, loosely held and stroked only the shaft of the penis, rarely recognized the preorgasmic reactions of their husbands and, therefore, did not vary the rate of stimulation. Husbands rarely made suggestions to improve their wives' techniques.

The contrasts in homosexual and heterosexual patterns of erotic stimulation extended to acts of fellatio and cunnilingus: "The homosexual males did follow the general pattern of proceeding without any sense of haste, slowing and speeding up the fellative activity in a teasing technique" (1979/1982: 75). Apart from the difference in tempo the wives were as proficient at stimulating their husbands' penises as the males were in stimulating the penises of their male partners. Most of the males, however, swallowed the ejaculate while most wives did not.

The female homosexual partners far surpassed the husbands' skill in cunnilingus:

> The lesbian approach to cunnilingus started with the breasts, moved to the lower abdomen and thighs and, in turn, the labia and frequently the vaginal outlet before concentrating on the clitoris. Once focused on the clitoris, the approach varied greatly from forceful stroking to a slow, gentle stimulative technique. And the stimulators varied their approaches significantly from episode to episode with the committed partner. The more variation on the theme exhibited by the stimulators, the higher the levels of subjective involvement evidenced by the stimulatees. (1979/1982: 76)

The husbands were far less inventive. Their major attention was directed to the clitoris, which they forcibly stimulated to orgasm. They appeared to engage in cunnilingus as a means to an end and therefore devoted little attention and imagination to it as a sexual act that could provide unique gratification. Their wives, accordingly, showed little subjective involvement in the husbands' oral stimulation.

The "eye-on-the-goal" tactic also dominated the process of coitus between husband and wife. Intercourse was almost always under the control of the husband. He initiated the mounting process when he felt sufficiently aroused, chose the coital position (usually the top), and controlled the thrusting pattern. The wife could only follow: "This continuing requirement for accommodation distracted many women, at least temporarily, from whatever levels of sexual excitation they previously had attained during the period of precoital stimulation" (1979/1982: 80).

There were a few interesting contrasts between female and male insertees in rectal intercourse. Most of the heterosexual females assumed the knee-chest position while most homosexual males laid face down in a fully prone position. Female insertees met the thrusts of their male insertors with counterthrusting. Most of the females reached orgasm through rectal intercourse but few of the males did.

There was little difference in the use of the dildo by homosexual and heterosexual females. All the homosexual female insertors assumed some manner of "pseudo-coital" position in preparing to place the dildo in the vagina of their partners. The heterosexual or homosexual insertee might respond to the thrusting pattern of the dildo with counterthrusts of her own. Several of the female insertees proved to be multiorgasmic with the use of the dildo.

Whereas most of the laboratory observations were of the sexual activity of "committed" partners, there were also observations of the sexual activity of "assigned" partners. Masters and Johnson defined an "assigned couple" as "composed of sexually responsive men and women formed into a transitory homosexual, heterosexual, or ambisexual partnership by a process of research-team selection" (1979/1982: 211-212). The men and women who formed these couples met for the first time in the laboratory setting. Committed couples were defined as units of two individuals, heterosexuals or homosexuals, who "are reasonably familiar with each other's individual personalities and who, for reasons that they usually cannot define, have chosen to share a life together" (211).

Masters and Johnson were interested in comparing the sexual practices of these two types of couples: "The basic question is, of course, do men and women in a committed relationship tend to function sexually as well as, better than, or less effectively than men and women who have no emotional bond?" (1979/1982: 119). In observing their respective sexual response patterns, the authors concluded that assigned pairs, whether heterosexual or homosexual, were more focused on achieving orgasm than in savoring the sexual experience. In the assigned homosexual couples, as compared with the committed, there was much less use of total-body stimulation:

Orgasm was the end-point goal, and the presumed quickest path toward orgasmic release of the partner was taken with alacrity by the stimulator so that it would soon be 'my turn'" (1979/1982: 78). All assigned heterosexual pairs were fiercely goal-oriented. There was only the most perfunctory precoital stimulation and almost the complete absence of the use of the teasing technique. The authors' apparent conclusion was that the sexual activity of the committed couples qualitatively surpassed that of the assigned couples.

Despite the qualitative differences they reported for the sexual patterns of heterosexual and homosexual committed and assigned pairs, Masters and Johnson found no corresponding differences among these groups in the ability to achieve orgasm:

> The clinical position can safely be taken that when men or women respond to the sexually stimulative techniques of masturbation, partner manipulation, and fellatio/cunnilingus in the laboratory, the gender of the study subjects, their sexual preference, or whether they are committed or assigned couples makes not the slightest bit of difference in their overall sexual functional facility as measured by orgasmic attainment. Gender, sexual preference, or relationship commitment did not influence the sexual functional efficiency. (1979/1982: 120)[8]

In a similar vein, they found no trace of physiological differences in the sexual response cycles of homosexuals as compared with heterosexuals. The total lack of differences led them to express considerable pessimism about the genetic basis for homosexuality or heterosexuality:

> The Institute's current position is simply that the results of these controlled laboratory experiments suggest that it is unlikely that the identification of a genetic determinant for

---

[8] The authors go on to state (121) that committed heterosexual couples had a lower failure rate than assigned couples for coitus. Earlier, however, they reported that there was no failure to reach orgasm by assigned partners in other sexual activities (masturbation, partner manipulation and fellatio or cunnilingus) (120).

homosexuality or heterosexuality will be accomplished in the near future. (207)

The apparently limitless sexual prowess of the ambisexual men and women both captivated and perplexed Masters and Johnson. Ambisexuals were individuals who found sex with either females or males highly satisfying. They also did not form monogamous sexual relationships. They were flawlessly functional in sexual response, capable of achieving orgasm as easily and swiftly with female as with male partners. The ambisexual male and his assigned male partner were more "performance-orientated" than the committed homosexual male pair. He was even more goal-oriented in coitus with a female, taking control as did the exclusively heterosexual male.

The ambisexual female was similar in behavior to her homosexual counterpart in her sexual encounters with females. Although she spent less time touching and sucking her partner's breasts, she quickly took up the pattern of "my turn-your turn" (1979/1982: 168) and used teasing techniques, sharing the initiative. In her sexual encounters with heterosexual males, the ambisexual female let them set the pace in both precoital and coital activity.

Masters and Johnson believed that ambisexual men and women thoroughly enjoyed the novelty and challenge of their encounters with a variety of laboratory sexual partners. How ambisexuals viewed potential sexual partners was explained by the authors:

> From the ambisexual's point of view, heterosexuality and homosexuality are neither right nor wrong, good nor bad, better nor worse. In fact, the true ambisexual really has no frame of reference for evaluating either orientation. Human sexual function is seen as a reality, a birthright, an integral and important part of every man and woman's life, to be directed and controlled as he or she chooses. Sexual opportunity is accepted or rejected on the basis of physical need, and the attractant is the personality and physical attributes of the potential partner, certainly not the gender of that partner. In fact, the most important attractant is the sexual opportunity, and a distant second would be the personality or physical attractiveness of the potential partner. There simply is no thought given to the gender of the potential partner as a qualifying factor in sexual attraction. (1979/1982: 172)

What was troubling about ambisexuals to Masters and Johnson was their lack of interest in starting families and maintaining a committed relationship. The authors were not certain whether this indifference was due to a "diminished capacity for love and affection" (172) or was indeed a free choice. It was possible that their lack of emotional involvement could be traced to their families for whom they had more nostalgia than affection. They ran the danger of loneliness, in the authors' eyes, and this might be their Achilles' heel: "whether the ambisexual can find sufficient resources within himself or herself to counteract the negative aspects of the inevitable social isolation that is concomitant with his or her chosen lifestyle will be the ultimate test of the ambisexual's permanence and prevalence in society" (172).

After describing the sexual behavior of the homosexual, heterosexual, and ambisexual men and women in their study, Masters and Johnson speculated on the reasons for the differences in their sexual response patterns. The central question was why the homosexual couples appeared to enjoy their sexual encounters more than the heterosexuals enjoyed theirs. One basic explanation was INTRAGENDER EMPATHY:

> Men know quite specifically, merely by subjective anticipation, what usually pleases men, and women are indeed the only experts on the subjective appreciation of women's sexual feelings. Subjective involvement in the committed homosexual couple's sexual interaction is usually maintained at highly effective levels by the intragender empathy and by freedom to identify individual sexual needs, distractions, pleasures, or antipathies. (213)

Another reason for heightened sexual enjoyment was that the homosexual relationship lacked a "built-in functional dependency upon a partner" (213), the natural fit provided by the penis and the vagina. Their functional autonomy, the authors assumed, forced homosexuals to use the my turn-your turn approach. With attention focused on only one partner at a time, fears of performance by the stimulated partner were greatly reduced.

A grave disadvantage, however, hung over homosexual intercourse. Homosexuals had to make the most of the stimulative techniques they were biologically limited to: masturbation of one partner by the other and fellatio and cunnilingus:

> The inherent disadvantage of these stimulative approaches is that they are fundamentally my turn-your turn interactions, as opposed to the "our turn" potential of coitus. While the my

turn-your turn approach is obviously a satisfactory means of accomplishing sexual release, the partners' preorgasmic levels of sexual tension and their orgasmic episodes are usually experienced separately, not as an immediate return from mutual stimulation as supplied during coition. (214)[9]

In effect, the explanation given for the sexual inventiveness shown by homosexuals was that they had to make the most of the biologically restricted repertory at their disposal. These biological limitations, the authors believed, also explained the behavior of assigned homosexual partners, men and women who lived without committed relationships: "[T]hey consistently moved to neutralize the long-range disadvantage of the restrictive number of basic stimulative techniques by adding to their subjective appreciation of the sexual interaction the zestful 'seasoning' of regularly recruited new partners" (216). Masters and Johnson feared for the future of the uncommitted homosexuals because new partners would be less available as they grew older and lost their physical and social attractiveness. This often forced them into a committed relationship: "Then the casual homosexual devoted to a 'cruising' lifestyle is in difficulty. He or she usually reacts to reduction in physical attractiveness in a self-protective manner by attempting to establish a committed relationship" (216).

The great advantage that the heterosexual relationship had over the homosexual was that all the sexual techniques were available to be used in any combination:

Variation in stimulative approaches is potentially greater than that available to homosexual couples, and in theory, at least, the heterosexually oriented man or woman has greater opportunity for subjective pleasure derived from the free, inventive interchange of sexual techniques. (217)

The great advantage of the heterosexual relationship was the simultaneous enjoyment of stimulation by both partners. The serious obstacle confronting heterosexual intercourse was "intergender misunderstanding": "Men simply have no frame of reference from which to appreciate the subjective aspects of women's orgasmic experience, any

---

[9] The authors recalled the "pseudo-coital" techniques of rectal intercourse and dildo usage, as well as mutual masturbation, but observed that "these were regularly employed only by a minority of committed homosexuals who volunteered as study subjects" (214).

more than women have the slightest concept of what it feels like to ejaculate" (218). The gender gap could be bridged by the intellectual curiosity of one sex about what the other sex experienced and by "stimulative communicative interchange" (218). Without these adjustments, heterosexual intercourse became a "means of sexual service, or even just a sexual contest" (220)—the attitude that pervaded the sexual pattern of the assigned heterosexual pairs.

Finally there were the ambisexuals, who enjoyed at least two advantages. Because they had access to both biological sexes they had at their beckoning "an almost infinite variety of sexually stimulative activity" (222).[10] Even more that the attached heterosexuals and homosexuals they could rely "on the constantly revolving door of new partner rotation as a continuing source of sexual pleasure" (1979/1982: 222). But they faced a somber future of sexual encounters with little appreciation of their partners' gratification and a life of social isolation: "Whether they continue in the same vein of personal isolation or forsake their ambisexual orientation for a continuing relationship (following the frequently recurrent behavior pattern of the unattached, aging homosexual males or females) remains to be seen" (223).

In the period from 1968 through 1977, Masters and Johnson treated homosexual men and women for various forms of sexual inadequacy.[11]

---

[10] Curiously enough, Masters and Johnson referred to the interest of the ambisexuals in both females and males as "preferential nihilism" (1979/1982: 222), which implied either an absence of the ambisexuals' belief in any moral principles or their desire to destroy social institutions.

[11] Masters and Johnson (1979/1982: 235-411). During a ten-year period they treated 151 homosexuals. Eighty-one couples were treated for sexual dysfunction (fifty-six male couples, twenty-five female couples). Fifty-seven of the male partners suffered from various forms of impotence and twenty-seven of the female partners suffered from various forms of anorgasmia. Another sixty-seven individuals (with their opposite-sex partners) were treated for "homosexual dissatisfaction." Of this group, fifty-four were males, thirteen females. Thirty-one of the males were married, two were living in long-term heterosexual relationships, and twenty-one were without a committed relationship (the latter were treated with their female partners of choice). Seven of the females were married and six were seen with their male partners of choice. The dissatisfied patients were seen for *reversion* or *conversion therapy*. Reversion therapy was provided for those with ratings on the Kinsey heterosexual-homosexual scale of 2 through 4; conversion therapy was given to those with ratings of 5 or 6, indicating little or no prior heterosexual experience. Of the males in the dysfunctional and dissatisfied groups, sixty-

Therapy was provided for those who suffered from sexual dysfunction or who wished to change their orientation from homosexual to heterosexual. The treatment program was based on the premise that both the heterosexual and homosexual identities were "learned preferences" (271).[12]

Treatment was provided only at the request of the client and only after a staff appraisal had been made of the client's strength of motivation to participate. Once the client was accepted into the program, therapy followed the same course laid out in the two-week, rapid treatment program for heterosexuals: "Treat such dysfunctions or dissatisfactions with the same psychotherapeutic techniques, with the same professional personnel, and with the same psychosexual objectivity with which heterosexual dysfunctions are treated" (272-273).[13]

The authors heralded the treatment of the sexually dysfunctional homosexual as an innovation in health-care. Many of their homosexual male clients had borne up under sexual inadequacies for years because of the fears they had about seeking treatment. There was the apparently valid fear that they would be denied treatment once their homosexual identity was disclosed. Then there was the fear that there would be as little success in treating their sexual dysfunctions as they believed there was for changing the homosexual identity to heterosexual. Finally, there was the overriding terror that their sexual identity and sexual problems would become public knowledge.

The major problem of sexual dysfunction faced by the homosexual male clients was impotence, in its various forms. Primary impotence was devastating for homosexual males, in the eyes of the authors, because they were engulfed and constantly aroused by a parade of potent men. Secondary impotence the authors attributed to satiation that could overtake homosexual men in their thirties after having pursued for years a "constant stream of new faces and bodies" (300). The burden of forcing sexual interest and erections made for wear and tear on sexual functioning:

---

two had sought and forty-four had been refused treatment elsewhere. Of the females, nineteen had sought and thirteen had been refused treatment.

[12] The authors implied that, because there was no supporting evidence for the contention that sexual identity had a genetic basis, it was warranted and even humanitarian to proceed on the assumption that it was acquired.

[13] Homosexuals who wanted to function as both homosexuals and heterosexuals were accepted for treatment if their therapeutic partners knew of what the authors called "the applicant's admitted sexual ambivalence" (353).

Since men cannot force erections, these are times when the erective process is slowed, anxiety creeps in, full penile engorgement falters, performance fears swell, and the erective process is progressively impaired. (300)

The homosexual females who were admitted as clients faced the problem of attaining orgasm. This inadequacy, in the eyes of Masters and Johnson, was a double threat to their identity as women. The culture implied not only that "an anorgasmic woman is less than a woman" (314), but also that a lesbian was some anomalous form of male. The authors believed, however, that, as clients in treatment, the homosexual women had an advantage over the heterosexual because their sexual responsiveness did not fall under the sway of the cultural imperative to produce orgasms.[14]

Those homosexual men and women who applied for treatment in order to change their orientation to heterosexual were classified as "dissatisfied" rather than dysfunctional. Those who had little or no heterosexual experience were given CONVERSION therapy; those with considerable heterosexual experience received REVERSION therapy.[15] In accepting clients for treatment, their underlying motivations were appraised. Clients who were accepted included those who feared the consequences of public exposure of their homosexual identity in social and professional situations, those who hoped to establish a sexual relationship with a partner of the opposite sex whom they liked, those who hoped to preserve marriages they valued, those with opposite-sex partners who were interested in the client becoming heterosexual, and those who openly expressed curiosity about heterosexual experience which they had never had.

Both forms of therapy began with an assessment of the client's "social and sexual value system" (1979/1982: 334) and its positive or negative contribution to the client's lifestyle. Studious efforts were made by the therapists to avoid any explicit or implied rejection of the homosexual identity:

---

[14] The treatment failure rate for homosexual as compared with heterosexual female clients was lower (1979/1982: 331, 387-391) .

[15] In the discussion of treatment, the procedural distinctions between the two types of therapy were never specified. Apparently males who had had extremely limited sexual contact with females (and conversely, females with males) in conversion therapy were given a much fuller introduction to the sexual anatomy and physiology of their opposite-sex partners than those receiving reversion therapy.

If the therapist suggests that homosexuality is a psychosocially unacceptable way of life to a man who is in the midst of attempting to alter his sexual value system, the client tends to move to heterosexual expression with a sense that all bridges have been burned. He has the impression that he must succeed in therapy in the immediacy of the present or that his life will have little or nothing to offer in the future. (357)

In the case of the male client, the obstacle to be surmounted in therapy was his fear that he lacked the capacity to perform sexually with a woman.[16] Once the client was able to have sex with his female partner, he was allowed to make his decision about which road to follow:

By the simple expedient of realizing that he has two ways to go, he can decide for himself which road offers the greater reward.... A change in role preference has a far better chance of permanence if it comes as the result of the client's decision rather than as the result of a therapist's imposition. (358)

The homosexual male, Masters and Johnson held, had to leave behind the homosexual for the heterosexual approach. In the homosexual approach one partner had no responsibility for the other's performance except to provide stimulation. In the heterosexual approach the male had the primary responsibility for the female reaching orgasm. Most male clients decided on a full heterosexual commitment.

The fact that so few females applied for treatment suggested to Masters and Johnson that the transition from a homosexual to a heterosexual identity was less perilous for women than for men and could be accomplished without professional support. The woman was not faced with the same fear of performance:

She may be anxious, she may be fearful, she may even be aversive, but if she has been sexually responsive as a lesbian she rarely brings crippling fears of performance into the most important motive for women to change orientations, the social pressure to enter marriage, bear children, and rear a family. (1979/1982: 363).

---

[16] Masters and Johnson acknowledged that the same fear kept heterosexuals from experimenting sexually with members of their own sex: "Fears of performance and of social opprobrium keep many men fully restricted to a heterosexual lifestyle who might otherwise have experimented with homosexual opportunity" (330).

Other motives were protecting good jobs, the desire to experiment with heterosexuality, and a strong attachment to a particular man. For the female client, therapy consisted of preserving the self-expression she had come to value in her homosexual relationships but transferring it to her relationship with a man:

> Most homosexual women who applied for support in attempts to convert or revert to heterosexuality opted for an ongoing heterosexual relationship if within the relationship their status could be established as that of a partner, not merely a provider of sexual service. If the women who requested support in attempted reversion or conversion were satisfied psychosocially as well as psychosexually, they usually remained committed to a heterosexual lifestyle. (378)

According to the authors, one in three clients who underwent treatment failed to achieve or maintain a heterosexual identity. They attributed what they believed to be a high failure rate to the disbelief of the homosexual community that sexual identity can be changed and, within the present climate of opinion, the difficulties in establishing rapport between client and therapist. They did not expect that these attitudes would prevail in the future.

In their concluding remarks Masters and Johnson lamented the doctrinaire belief of exclusive heterosexuals and exclusive homosexuals that they were physically and psychologically different. Laboratory investigations, they held, proved that there were no physical differences in the sexual responses of heterosexual as compared with homosexual men and women:

> We are genetically determined to be male or female and, in addition, are given the ability to function sexually as men or women by the physical capacities of erection and lubrication and the inherent facility for orgasmic attainment. These capacities function in identical ways, whether we are interacting heterosexually or homosexually. When a man or a woman is orgasmic, he or she is responding to sexual stimuli with the same basic physiologic response patterns. (404-405)

The lack of basic physical differences in heterosexuals and homosexuals extended to personality and lifestyle. The exclusive heterosexuals who chose members of the opposite sex as sex objects did so on an individual basis. They were not attracted to all females or all males. Similarly, the exclusive homosexuals who pursued members of the same sex as sex partners also did so on an individual basis. The emotional involvement of heterosexuals with members of the same-sex or of homosexuals with the opposite-sex may be greater than that with their sex partners:

> [T]he Kinsey 0 man or woman is occasionally committed far more closely psychosexually with a same-sex individual than he or she ever is with many opposite-sex acquaintances. The same behavior pattern is followed by Kinsey 6 men and women, who often identify far more closely with an opposite-sex individual than with same-sex acquaintances. (405)

What was ignored by the believers in the "they-are-different" doctrine was the barely audible voice of the "non-exclusives":

> These individuals may indicate a personal bias for either homosexual or heterosexual differences in sexual interaction has been replaced by the more pragmatic process of enjoying sensual aspects of the sexual encounter, regardless of the gender of the partner. (404)

The approach of Masters and Johnson to sexual relationships was a powerful endorsement of the theme of sexuality as gratification. This theme was formulated by Freud almost sixty years earlier and elucidated in the studies of the Kinsey group. In these three formulations, human sexual expression was viewed as an instinctual source of pleasure, available to females and males as a self-contained, renewable resource.

In all three approaches human sexual capacity was viewed, *par excellence*, as natural. For Freud it was an instinctual, libidinous stream that connected innate biological capacity to the intricacies of psychosexual development. The Kinsey group viewed human sexuality as an extension of mammalian sexual capacity but embellished by the cerebrum which could make choice out of necessity. Masters and Johnson traced human sexuality to the sexual response cycles in females and males and the dramatic changes that occurred when the individual was aroused.

In these theories, sexual capacity was viewed as the most malleable and tractable of human biological capacities and therefore most subject to the vicissitudes of experience. Although this amorphous quality contained the promise of unending pleasure, it also made sexual relationships exquisitely vulnerable. Sexual relationships were portrayed as entangled in systems of moral belief and stricture. What was to be perhaps the major source of human pleasure often turned into suffering and tragedy. Freud believed that moral precepts against the enjoyment of sexual expression were internalized as guilt and fear by individuals in their early psychosexual development and, in the form of neuroses, denied them access to sexuality as pleasure. The Kinsey group held that moral and legal dicta intruded on the human desire for sexual gratification and stymied opportunities for satisfying that desire. Masters and Johnson traced human sexual inadequacy to internalized attitudes of social control which made sexual contact more performance and obligation than sensual enjoyment and choice.

The idea that sexual relationships served as a primary source of gratification was intimidating even to these fearless theoreticians. Although they railed against society and culture for stifling sexual pleasure, they worried about removing restraints from a possibly ungovernable human appetite. To dampen sexual ardor each proposed a means for stabilizing sexual relationships. Freud accomplished this containment in the creation of complementary psychological heterosexual identities for females and males as the basis for marriage and the family. Kinsey endorsed marriage as the ideal form of human companionship that allowed for sexual gratification, reproduction, and rearing of children and a regular sexual outlet that curbed promiscuity. Masters and Johnson promoted the idea of the committed relationship. They wrote: "pleasure is an infinitely deeper and more complex matter than simply sensual gratification" (1970: 253).[17]

To be fully enjoyed sexuality was to be expressed in a marriage in which the partners "live according to the commitment of mutual concern, and pleasure is the bond between them" (1970: 254). In all three formulations emotional commitment was seen as a basic requirement rather than a sacrifice necessary for attaining full sexual gratification.

The endorsement in all three stances of a stable, primary relationship between the female and male was based on the assumption that there were irreducible differences in female and male sexuality. In psychoanalytic theory this took the form of the male-female design which conjoined the femaleness and femininity of women to the maleness and masculinity of men. For the Kinsey group the immutable differences between female and male sexuality was more inward and less malleable. In the view of Masters and Johnson, each biological sex was locked into its own understanding of sexuality. Any effort of men to understand the sexuality of women or women that of men, would produce confusion and trauma.

---

[17] Masters, William H., Johnson, Virginia E., and Levine, Robert J. (1970). *The Pleasure Bond: A New Look at Sexuality and Commitment*. Boston: Little, Brown.

Men could never understand the vaginal orgasm and women would never know the experience of male ejaculation.

Masters and Johnson were equivocal in their endorsement of the idea of a biological sexual identity. Their laboratory observations of the sexual response cycles in homosexual men and women showed that they were identical to those of heterosexual men and women. In commenting on the hormonal research on the homosexual identity, their position was clear:

> It is apparent that homosexuality is no more a unitary phenome-
> non than is heterosexuality. Until it is possible to separate sub-
> groups of homosexuals and heterosexuals by precise classifi-
> cation criteria, the heterogeneity that cuts across the basic lines
> of homosexual versus heterosexual—supported by the hetero-
> geneity found in the physiologic and clinical studies reported in
> this text—complicates the identification of hormonal differences
> even if they exist. (1979/1982: 411)

Although they disclaimed a belief in the idea of an exclusive sexual identity, the tacit assumption of a biological sexual identity informed much of their work. Sexual identity was tied to roles in sexual inter-course and emerged from the couple as a unit. These roles were designated as homosexual female, homosexual male, and heterosexual approaches to sexual intercourse. It may be more precise to state that Masters and Johnson probably had in mind two biological sexual identi-ties—one for females, another for males. The identity was heterosexual or homosexual depending on the various combinations of the sexes. The implicit lodging of sexual identity in the approaches to sexual inter-course was clear in the discussion of the ambisexuals. Here the ambisexual female, for example, was described as taking the homosexual female approach when having sex with another female and the heterosexual approach in intercourse with a male.

The tacit belief in a biological sexual identity was further implied in their discussion of intragender empathy. Their position was that the ho-mosexual approach was superior in empathy but that the heterosexual approach was superior in sexual gratification. The potential for empathy resided in the sameness of biological sex in the case of homosexual part-ners. The potential for greater gratification resided in simultaneous, mutual stimulation in the case of heterosexual partners. The biological homosexual identity, therefore, was essentially a mental communion of partners whereas the biological heterosexual identity was an anatomical complementarity.

The idea of the psychological and sociocultural sexual identities implicitly undergirded Masters and Johnson's references to the heterosexual and homosexual lifestyles. For example, a major motivation for some of their homosexual clients to enter conversion or reversion therapy was the clients' desire to change from a homosexual to a heterosexual lifestyle. Although Masters and Johnson never elucidated the differences in lifestyles, there were hints of what they believed they were. The homosexual lifestyle centered on sexual activity for its own sake. This perception was revealed in their allusion to the ceaseless "cruising" of bodies and faces that consumed the lives of uncommitted homosexuals. The heterosexual lifestyle, they implied, was more focused on social events constructed around marriage and occupation. Some of their homosexual clients wanted to switch to a heterosexual lifestyle not only to reap new sexual benefits but also to safeguard and advance corporate or professional careers. It appears, therefore, that although Masters and Johnson subscribed to the idea of the biological sexual identity, they retained a belief in the psychological and sociocultural identities.

The single contribution of Masters and Johnson to the detoxication of the homosexual identity was to show that the sexual response cycles of homosexual men and women were identical to those of their heterosexual counterparts. The psycho-medicalization of the homosexual identity in hormonal and genetic research was based on the tacit assumption that homosexuals suffered from some neurophysiological malfunction even though they appeared to be anatomically normal. Masters and Johnson struck a grave blow against this research. An additional contribution to detoxication was in treating the sexual dysfunctions of homosexual men and women. If fact, their position strongly implied that the past failure of the medical, psychiatric, and psychological professions to provide proper treatment for homosexual dysfunction was a serious flaw in the healthcare system. By providing treatment for making pleasurable the sexual relationships of dysfunctional homosexual men and women, Masters and Johnson repudiated the belief that the homosexual identity was pathological.

It could be argued, however, that their conversion and reversion therapy for homosexuals conveyed the strong implication that the homosexual identity had elements of pathology. Masters and Johnson believed that the motivations for changing the homosexual identity to heterosexual should clearly be those of the client and that entering therapy was a joint decision of client, spouse or friend, and their institute. It appeared that they were providing a therapeutic service which was in very short supply. Unfortunately, they did not make a corresponding effort to provide therapy for heterosexuals who wanted to acquire a homosexual identity.[18]

This one-sided approach exposed them to the charges that they believed that the homosexual identity was a diagnosable and treatable ailment and that the heterosexual was the more desirable identity.

Remnants of the polytheistic view of sexual relationships were present in the theoretical perspective of Masters and Johnson. Reviving the idea of the ancient *ars erotica*, they viewed the body as a rich vein of potential stimulation that could be mined through the proper use of physical techniques and timing. The technique of "sensate focus" brought the touching of the entire body surface within the permissible boundaries of sexual contact. The lips and mouth were no longer limited to mutual kissing but could now be properly applied by one sexual partner to the body surface and the genital organs of the other. The use of at least one sexual device, the dildo, was employed for the stimulation of either a partner or oneself.

Within this polytheistic view Masters and Johnson were able to appreciate the sexual gratification potentially afforded by homosexual relationships. They reported that partners in these relationships gave attention to the entire body, prolonged sexual stimulation, verbalized their desires, vocalized their reactions, and were generally inventive. They held that the artful, mutual stimulation of homosexual partners constituted sexual practice "superior" to that of heterosexuals.

Masters and Johnson's polytheism, however, was a cautious endorsement of pagan sexuality. The stimulation of the anus, either externally or by insertion, was given only passing consideration. The dildo was presumably to be used for vaginal insertion and not for anal stimulation of either females or males. It was the only device, in the historic treasure chest of erotic implements, sexual partners were permitted to use. The positioning of the body for sexual intercourse lacked the imagination of the painters of the ancient Greek vases and Oriental folk art.

The polytheistic remnants that survived in the approach of Masters and Johnson were well circumscribed by their endorsement of the mono-

---

[18] Unfortunately, too, some of the case histories of the conversion and reversion patients suggested that they had turned to homosexual relationships as a result of having had their heterosexual relationships derailed by family, friends, and sociopolitical influences. There were no parallel cases reported in which the development of the individual's homosexual relationships was derailed by a similar array of factors.

theistic view of sexual relationships. They believed that heterosexual relationships inherently possessed the greater erotic potential because partners could experience simultaneous, mutual stimulation.

This position revealed a lack of sophistication with the number of ways in which partners of the same sex can achieve simultaneous orgasms if that is their intention.[19] It also implied a narrow conception of "mutuality," because gratification can be obtained by one partner in stimulating the other. By referring to the vaginal use of the dildo and anal intercourse as "pseudo-coital" activities, Masters and Johnson demonstrated that the post-Freudian notion of homosexual relationships as reparative survived in their thinking.

Monotheistic views were clearest in their conceptualization of the "committed relationship." Like Bell and Weinberg's "close coupleds," for example, the committed relationship required partners to restrict their sexual expression to one partner. Such a requirement could appear to the individual interested in multiple sexual partners as a restriction of opportunities for novel gratification. Masters and Johnson, however, as the Kinsey sociologists before them, held steadfastly to the position that the greatest sexual pleasure was experienced in committed relationships in which each partner felt secure in entrusting her or his body to the other. Committed partners they believed, knew the regions of greatest potential arousal and could be endlessly inventive in providing the desired stimulation. By comparison, sex between uncommitted partners was mechanical rather than spontaneous, driven rather than relaxed, narrowly genital rather than broadly sensual—more the performance of a service than an enveloping erotic experience. The recrudescence of reparative notions of the psychological homosexual identity was visible in their belief that the busy sexuality of uncommitted individuals would ultimately lead to impaired sexual performance and loneliness in advanced years. Although both committed and uncommitted partners had orgasms, those of the committed partners were better because they conjoined sex and love.

The contributions of Masters and Johnson both expanded and contracted the boundaries of permissible sexual relationships. By promoting the idea that sexual partners could capitalize on the sexual response cycle to sustain and intensify the erotic episode, they clearly brought pleasure within the ambit of sexual relationships. The idea that

---

[19] See, for example, Califia (1980); and Morin, Jack (1981). *Anal Pleasure and Health.* Burlingame, CA: Down There Press.

males should be more attentive and responsive to their female partners and that females could and should aggressively pursue stimulation and orgasm challenged psychoanalytic theories that assigned sexual "activity" to males and "passivity" to females. Men could be sensitive and women aggressive without jeopardizing membership in their respective biological sexes or their femininity or masculinity. By describing male ineptness and ignorance of female sexual response and a superior orgasmic capacity of women, the balance of sexual capacity in heterosexual relationships seemed to tip toward females. Their conceptualization of human sexual inadequacy as unnecessary suffering that could be diagnosed and often successfully treated, flew in the face of the conventional belief that marital sex was something that had to be endured rather than enjoyed.

Yet all this potential for pleasure was to be contained, for both heterosexuals and homosexuals, within one primary relationship. This monotheistic constriction of sexual relationships was most clearly revealed in their view of ambisexuals whose sexual adroitness, as described by Masters and Johnson, escaped conventional reticence. Because ambisexuals enjoyed equally the sexual pleasures of both men and women and showed no signs of wanting a committed relationship, Masters and Johnson entertained the possibility that they were incapable of forming close relationships. To do so the ambisexuals would have to select one individual over all others and that person would have to be either female or male. This selection of one biological sex would, in turn, require them to give up ambisexuality for a heterosexual or homosexual identity. Ambisexuality, therefore, no matter how curiously attractive Masters and Johnson found it, could not be included within the boundaries of normalized sexual relationships.

The scientific cosmological view of sexual relationships also prevailed in Masters and Johnson's conceptualization of the physiological sexual identity. Their studies were a unique amalgam of biological and social science. Their study of the physiological reactions of females and males utilized the laboratory setting and included instrumental measures of anatomical and physiological changes associated with sexual arousal.[20]

In pursuing this biological research Masters and Johnson appropriately maintained the scientific posture of removed observation. The authors, however, pursued the study of social phenomena in the same way they investigated the biological. At several points their research passed over the

---

[20] Their reports, however, have been criticized by other investigators as lacking precision and sufficient detail for replication.

boundary dividing the biological from the psychological and sociological. That boundary was traversed, for example, when these investigators described the "subjective involvement" of partners engaged in sexual stimulation or their "sexual value systems." Here too, they maintained the stance of "scientific objectivity," as if each observer would perceive the same involvement and the same sexual value system. Also, in recounting to clients their sexual histories, Masters and Johnson believed they held up a "mirror of unprejudiced objectivity."

The conceptualization of sexual relationships by Masters and Johnson was, therefore, both scientific in cosmology and scientistic. By endorsing the idea of choice in areas of corporeal stimulation and in approaches to and techniques of sexual intercourse, their notions incorporated elements of the scientific cosmology. However, by using the authority of science to endorse an essentially monotheistic view of the structure of sexual relationships, their approach was patently scientistic.

21

Conclusion:
From Sexual Identity to Sexual Relationships—
A Long Look Back and a Short Look Ahead

Our elucidation and analysis of the scientific discourse on sexual identity has shown that it consisted of a mélange of terminology and conceptualizations. In this chapter we will review the variations in terminology and conceptualizations in order to highlight their labyrinthine interrelationships. We shall also review how the specter of biological determinism loomed over the entire discourse and inevitably led to the normalization of both heterosexual and homosexual relationships. Finally, we shall explore how normalization has unwittingly presented the opportunity to abandon the concept of sexual identity and turn to systematic inquiry into sexual relationships.

The terminology for sexual identity referred to the type of identity or to the individuals who were labeled. Ulrichs, as the creator of the idea of sexual identity, called the homosexual identity "the love between men." In his taxonomic edifice the heterosexual female was the "Dioninge," the homosexual female the "Urninge," the heterosexual male the "Dioning," and the homosexual male the "Urning." Heterosexuals constituted the "true females" and "true males," while homosexuals were the "third sex." Kertbeny, following in Ulrichs' theoretical footsteps, coined the word "homosexuality" and the label "homosexuals" to refer to Urnings. Their counterparts he awkwardly called "normalsexuals."

The degeneracy theorists invented a terminology that was derived from two traditions, classical Greek history and medicine and psychiatry. Casper called the homosexual identity "paederastia," particularly in males, although he knew that it was a misnomer for sexual relations between adults. In females, the homosexual identity was "tribadism." Westphal called it "contrary sexual feeling," which for Krafft-Ebing came to be translated "antipathetic sexual instinct." Krafft-Ebing called the homosexual identity a "perversion" which he distinguished from a moral perversity. The French and Italian psychiatrists preferred "inversion"; Chevalier, for example, called it the "inversion of the sexual instinct."

The environmental and evolutionary theorists, writing in the last two decades of the nineteenth century used, for the most part, the terminology of their medical predecessors. Tarnowsky reverted to "pederasty" but Schrenck-Notzing and Moll stuck with "antipathetic sexual instinct." Moll called homosexual males "Uranists." He referred to "Lesbian love," but usually called its practitioners "tribades." Ellis preferred "sexual inversion." Hirschfeld revived and popularized Kertbeny's "homosexuality" but preserved Ulrichs' notion of the third sex in his theory of "intermediate sexuals."

The theorists of the psychological sexual identity largely adhered to the nineteenth-century nomenclature. Freud began by calling homosexuals "contrarysexuals" and "inverts" and their condition "inversion." The "absolute" invert was separated from the "half-inverted" and the "contingently inverted." By 1910 he began using "homosexual" and still later "heterosexual." There was also "latent" homosexuality in which behavior was heterosexual but the underlying psychological identity was homosexual.

The post-Freudians introduced only minor variations in the terminological tradition of their mentor. In their writings the terms "bisexual," "heterosexual," and "homosexual" came into general currency. "Homosexuals" could be either female or male, but female homosexuals were sometimes designated as "lesbians." Ferenczi distinguished between the "subject" and "object homoerotic," considering individuals in the former category to be the true "inverts." In a parallel terminology, Ovesey distinguished between the "obligatory" and "preferential" homosexuals as well as between true homosexuality and "pseudohomosexuality." Three "non-obligatory" forms of the homosexual identity were labeled by Socarides "situational," "variational," and "latent." He also drew a clinical distinction between "preoedipal" and "oedipal" homosexuality. In the psychiatric discourse of the seventies sexual identity was frequently addressed as "sexual orientation." "Sexual orientation disturbance" served as a euphemism for homosexuality in a partial revision of the *Diagnostic and Statistical Manual*, to be replaced later by "ego-dystonic homosexuality."

The early theorists of the sociocultural identity largely preserved the medical terminology. Under the influence of the Kinsey group, Ford and Beach and Churchill, however, sexual identity was cast in behavioral terms. The Kinsey group spoke of "sexual outlet" as either heterosexual or homosexual and of the heterosexual-homosexual "balance."

The early ethnologists of sexual identity utilized medical terminology but applied it to the social milieu. Individuals who bore the homosexual identity were described as occupying a "deviant status," inhabiting the "homosexual subculture" or "homosexual world," or enacting a homosexual "role" or "script." The later theorists of the sociocultural sexual identity spoke of "homophile" organizations or the "gay" and "lesbian" identity, minority, and community. Homosexuals were referred to collectively as "gays" or, on the basis of biological sex, as "lesbians" or "gay men." The term "sexual identity" itself came into general usage in the discourse, first in the form of the "gay identity" and the "lesbian identity," soon to be followed by the "heterosexual" or "straight" identity and, more recently, the "bisexual identity."

Our review of the terminology for sexual identity reveals that there was a confusing admixture of continuity and variation in the labels applied to the idea and to individuals. The same terminology was used for quite different conceptions of sexual identity and new terminologies did not signal fresh conceptions. The psychological theorists used the language of the biological theorists; the sociocultural theorists that of the psychologists. The terminological shift from "homosexual" to "gay" and "lesbian" was made within the framework of the sociocultural conception of sexual identity.

The choice of terms for the homosexual identity implied different opinions about its acceptability. "Urnings" was Ulrichs' effort to show that the homosexual identity was as natural as the heterosexual and perhaps in some ways superior. Kertbeny, masquerading as a physician, replaced Ulrichs' terminology with the scientific term "homosexual." Hirschfeld, as part of his effort to detoxicate the homosexual identity, adopted Kertbeny's term. Ironically, fifty years later, "homosexual" was rejected in the further effort at detoxication and replaced by non-clinical terms.

The early psychiatric terminology pathologized the homosexual identity. Casper's and Tarnowsky's use of pederasty implied an atavism or regression to earlier stages of evolution and history. "Contrary" or "antipathetic" sexual feeling or instinct implied, for Westphal and Krafft-Ebing, an opposition to nature. Chevalier and Ellis in their use of "inversion" suggested that nature had been turned upside down. By adopting "homosexual," Freud made the term clinical and scientistic.

We have distinguished the biological, psychological, and sociocultural conceptions of sexual identity primarily on the basis of what each considered to be the major determinant factors. The biological conception emphasized internal factors that resided in the individual's physical make-up and functioning. The psychological conception also pointed to internal factors but located them in mental apparatus and functioning. We have shown that the break with internal etiological theories came with the sociocultural conception that pointed to formative influences external to the individual, broadly conceived as culture, society, laws, institutions, statuses, or roles.

The three conceptions of sexual identity essentially focused on the homosexual identity. They therefore were more explicit in accounting for it than for the heterosexual identity. It was the homosexual identity that was viewed as problematic even in those theories devoted to its detoxication or celebration.

We have shown that the theorists of the biological conception of sexual identity attributed it to a variety of physical factors. Ulrichs believed sexual identity arose from the embryonic union of female or male sex organs with feminine or masculine sex drives. When the direction of the drives was consonant with the biological sex of the organs, the identity was heterosexual; when the reverse pairings occurred it was homosexual. The psychological dimension of Ulrichs' theory lay in his claim that the sex drives were spiritual rather than physical. The sociocultural dimension rested on the assertion that homosexuals constituted a minority that existed as early as Plato and classical Greece and that was oppressed under Prussian law.

The degeneracy theorists took a different biological tact. They posited the existence of a sexual instinct or drive that developed normally in heterosexuals but that went awry in homosexuals. Krafft-Ebing held that the sexual instinct was under the command of psychosexual centers located in the cerebrum. A biologically normal sexual instinct propelled one biological sex toward the other and ultimately into monogamous unions for rearing children and maintaining the family unit. The homosexual identity was the result of abnormal psychosexual centers and constituted a "functional sign of degeneracy."

Although rooted in biology, degeneracy theory had its psychological and sociocultural dimensions. Krafft-Ebing believed that psychological observation could reveal the presence of physical degeneracy in homosexuals, such as their unrestrained masturbation, exaggerated love, hysteria, neurasthenia, brilliance, or imbecility. The sociocultural dimension was implied in two ways. First, it was through the criminal justice system and his role as forensic psychiatrist that Krafft-Ebing found individuals whom he classified as homosexual. Second, his classifications consisted of psychosocial groups, such as psycho-hermaphrodites, true Urnings, and androgynes.

As conceived by the environmental and evolutionary theorists, the biological sexual identity was moored to physical factors. The homosexual identity, as one form of perversion in a growing roster of aberrant sexual tastes and behaviors, was still linked to degeneracy theory. Binet, for example, alluded to the inherited neuropathic predisposition of fetishists even though he believed chance associations shaped a particular fetish, among which he included the homosexual identity. Schrenck-Notzing held that no sexual perversion was "solely" a congenital disorder. Although Prince considered the homosexual identity, among other so-called perversions, a form of moral perversity, he held on to the belief that inherent neurophysiological weakness in perverts made it more difficult for them than for the unperverted to resist sexual temptation. Even Moll, who more than the others questioned degeneracy theory, held on to the notion that an innate physical predisposition formed the basis of the homosexual identity.

However much their contributions were tied to biology, it was the environmental and evolutionary theorists who paved the way to the psychological and sociocultural conceptions of sexual identity. In a psychological vein, Tarnowsky wrote of the "vicious propensity" and "willful depravity" of boys who, although not congenitally tainted, spread pederastic practices throughout their boarding schools. Binet's theory of association presented the homosexual identity as acquired and fortuitous, the psychological product of learning. The concept of the homosexual identity as a mental disease that lacked a specific biological basis, in Schrenck-Notzing's formulation, was essentially psychological. In Prince's assertion that everybody had homosexual impulses but that only the homosexual lacked the volitional control to suppress them, the psychological speculations of Freud were foreshadowed.

By blurring the distinction between the physical and mental, Moll, more than the other environmental and evolutionary theorists, heralded the psychological conception of sexual identity. He described sexual development as occurring in three parallel and interconnected dimensions: the biological, historical, and psychological. Freud's conception of the heterosexual was prefigured in Moll's description of a psychological and historical process for its development.

The sociocultural ingredients assumed major importance in the environmental and evolutionary theories. Several external factors fostering the development of the homosexual identity were contemplated. Tarnowsky painted a horrifying picture in which pederasty was passed down by students as school tradition. Moreover, he believed that civilization and intellectual development spread such perversions as homosexuality from one culture to another. In the same vein, Schrenck-Notzing believed mental disease spread through environmental contagion. Hypnosis could stern the tide by substituting a healthy contagion. Moll viewed the homosexual identity as a form of historical regression to less civilized stages of sexual development.

The two detoxicators of the biological homosexual identity, Ellis and Hirschfeld, were generally more physical in their conception of sexual identity than the environmental and evolutionary theorists. The heterosexual identity, according to Ellis, was the product of either female or male germ plasm taking the upper hand in embryonic and fetal development. When remnants of the "conquered sex" survived this germinal struggle, the product was the homosexual or bisexual identity. The die of sexual identity was cast during prenatal development and, in Ellis' opinion; the results could not be altered after birth. Hirschfeld also believed that internal factors far outweighed the external in determining sexual identity. The essential factor was "inner secretions," female or male hormones. The heterosexual identity resulted from the proper match of hormonal type with biological sex. When the embryo and fetus were subjected to unusually high amounts of the hormone of the opposite sex, the neonate would possess a homosexual identity. Both Ellis and Hirschfeld believed that the heterosexual and homosexual identities arose out of an initial bisexual stage of development.

There were psychological and sociocultural correlates of their conception of sexual identity. In their psychological portraits of homosexuals, females were depicted as possessing traces of masculinity, the male, traces of femininity. Sexual intercourse between females was described as more sensuous and less genital than that between males. There were artistic strains in the male inverts and an uncommon pragmatism in the females. Hirschfeld believed that homosexuals had irritable nervous systems, the result of not being fully feminine or masculine. Neither Ellis nor Hirschfeld believed, however, that the inverts' emotional lability was caused by degeneracy.

There were distinct sociocultural aspects of Ellis' and Hirschfeld's conception of sexual identity. Ellis believed that acquired sexual inversion could be prevented by protecting school children from homosexual experiences. But his special plea was for tolerance and civil acceptance of homosexuals whose "abnormality," in some cases, he believed could be put to fine uses. Tolerance, however, had its limits. It could not be extended to homosexuals who flouted their identity, particularly those who pursued heterosexuals of their own biological sex. Hirschfeld presented the homosexual identity as an anthropological, social, and political phenomenon, which had collective as well as individual aspects.

The essential determinants of the psychological sexual identity, as conceived by Freud, were the vicissitudes of early child-parent relationships and the child's mental representations of those relationships. In the development of sexual identity there were two central factors: (1) a psychosexual process in which the diffuse zones of potential erotic arousal were genitally organized and focused and (2) the dissolution of the Oedipus complex in which the child identified with either the parent of the opposite or same sex. As products of psychological processes, the heterosexual and homosexual identities stood as mirror images. Each identity was enduringly stamped on the individual and was central to personality and psychological functioning.

There were also physical and sociocultural aspects of Freud's conception of sexual identity. He viewed sexual instinct and bisexuality as basically physical. The sexual instinct was a flow of energy that the individual possessed as a polymorphous biological endowment. Both identities developed from an innate bisexuality, the original physical capacity of the organism to become either female or male, and psychologically feminine or masculine.

The sociocultural elements were supplied by Freud's use of the authoritative support of tradition and civilization for his view of sexual identity. He believed that the historical development of culture had placed the sexual instinct under progressively tighter restraint. Its gratification was limited to monogamy, an institution designed primarily for procreation. The psychological development of the sexual instinct in the child from the polymorphous perverse to genital primacy recapitulated the historical development of institutional restraints.

The post-Freudians emphasized psychological factors almost to the exclusion of the biological in accounting for the heterosexual and homosexual identities. The homosexual identity was seen as an adaptive failure that reflected the individual's lack of self-esteem and self-confidence. The idea of an innate polymorphous or bisexual capacity was jettisoned. The homosexual identity was viewed as a desperate, reparative effort by psychologically damaged individuals to substitute through others of the same sex what they believed was lacking in themselves.

Although the biological aspect of the post-Freudian conception of sexual identity was greatly restricted, it was not absent. The heterosexual identity was conceived as prerequisite for females or males to assume their naturally ordained roles in the male-female design. This design, according to Rado and Socarides, was anatomically determined, the result of an evolutionary process that created two classes of individuals who together formed the perfect human pair. In the heterosexual identity biological endowment combined with the psychical interior and resulted in harmony and completeness for the two sexes. Apart from this abstract notion of biological sex, the post-Freudian conception of sexual identity lacked a specific physical anchorage.

The sociocultural elements in the post-Freudian conception of sexual identity were implicit in the overriding concern with social adjustment. We have shown how the shift in later Freudian formulations of the mental apparatus as well as in those of the post-Freudians focused on the cognitive restraint of the libido. Sexual energy was to be harnessed in the interest of social adaptation, often phrased as the normative expectations for females to fulfill the feminine role, males the masculine role, and both the parental nurturing roles. The homosexual identity was traceable to the confusion in children caused by parents who failed to meet and exemplify these requirements.

The psychological homosexual identity, in the writing of the psychiatric detoxicators, was a slightly modified version of the post-Freudian conception. Szasz referred to it as an expression of "psychosocial immaturity," the twisted product of child development. Marmor viewed it as a psychological state which he called an erotic "preference" usually expressed as sexual behavior. Saghir and Robbins wrote of homosexual "psychologic response," in the tradition of the Kinsey group. In his later writing on the homosexual identity, Marmor moved to a more biological and sociocultural position. He revived Freud's notion of innate bisexuality and lamented how a culturally ingrained "homophobia" could undermine homosexuals' self-acceptance of their sexual identity.

The conceptualization of the sociocultural sexual identity represented a major shift away from a focus on internal biological and psychological determinants toward a concern with external factors. These external determinants were loosely conceived as history or culture, behavioral conditioning or learning, deviant sub-cultures, socially constructed roles or norms, and social collectivities. Each conception reflected the disciplinary context within which it was applied.

The early historical and anthropological study of sexual identity, as reflected in the work of Block, Westermarck, Malinowski, Mead, and Ford, and Beach, assumed that human sexual capacity was malleable, a biological potentiality that could be culturally shaped. In support of this assumption Bloch and Westermarck marshalled historical evidence that demonstrated how sexual expression in the past varied from that of contemporary European culture. Malinowski and Mead studied tribal societies that varied in sexual practices and institutions not only from western culture but also from each other.

None of these historical and anthropological conceptualizations of sexual identity, however, lacked biological or psychological underpinnings. The heterosexual identity represented the full flowering of natural sexuality. Culture either facilitated or impeded its development. Bloch, for example, never abandoned degeneracy theory in accounting for sexual perversions nor the idea that perversions, like contagious diseases, could be transmitted from one culture to another. Mead steadfastly held to the notion that the different roles females and males played in reproduction and child-rearing were biological realities that no culture could afford to ignore. The homosexual identity, according to Mead, required females and males to abandon their reproductive roles as a desperate accommodation to rigidly enforced feminine and masculine stereotypes.

There were psychological ingredients in the anthropological approach to the discourse on sexual identity. Bloch considered freely chosen heterosexual relationships as the healthy manifestation of human sexual identity. Mead believed there were psychological correlates of the female and male roles that pervaded heterosexual relationships.

The behavioral approach to the sociocultural sexual identity of the Kinsey group, Churchill and Tripp, as in the case of the historians and cultural anthropologists, was based on the belief that human sexuality constituted a malleable biological capacity, which was conceived as a reservoir of sexual responsivity to erotic stimuli. The individual's sexual identity consisted of a behavioral repertory of those responses that had been gratified over a lifetime. The ability to respond erotically only to partners of the opposite sex was the result of cultural restriction and moral injunction. It was learned incapacity.

The physical dimension of the behavioral conception of sexual identity was the belief that all human sexual responsivity was grounded in an undifferentiated mammalian capacity. It was not, however, a capacity that could be ignored. The Kinsey group never abandoned the idea of a sexual drive that required periodic "outlets." Beach's research on infrahuman mammals implied that human sexual behavior was basically biological, albeit enormously elaborated by cortical development.

The psychological dimension was contained in the idea of "psychologic response," which, in the conception of the Kinsey group, was essentially mental. We have pointed out that the Kinsey heterosexual-homosexual rating scale was used to assess both sexual practice and psychologic response. The latter clearly included the realm of sexual desire and fantasy.

It was the ethnographers of the sociocultural sexual identity, following in the footsteps of the anthropologists and behavioral surveyors, who treated the homosexual identity as an urban, male subculture. The homosexual subculture was conceived as the product of external forces. Cory, for example, attributed it to hidden sources of hostility. Leznoff and Westley described it as a community in which homosexuals could find social acceptance. Hooker called the subculture the "homosexual world," which she believed consisted of sexually flamboyant public groups and more discrete and sexually restrained private groups. Sonenschein viewed the sub-culture as a network of stable and transitory sexual and social relationships. For Hoffman the homosexual sub-culture was the defensive response of homosexuals to social intolerance. Both Reiss and Humphreys focused their research efforts on public aspects of the subculture, male prostitution and sex in restrooms.

There was little that was explicitly biological in the ethnographic conception of sexual identity except that the heterosexual and homosexual identities were distinguished by the biological sex of the partners in sexual relationships. For the most part sexual identity was treated as a natural phenomenon rather than an idea. When the ethnologists such as Hooker, Schofield, and Hoffman engaged in psychological speculations about the basis of the homosexual identity, they appeared to subscribe to Freudian notions of psychosexual development. Hooker and Hoffman, for example, alluded to narcissism and Schofield wrote about "disturbed homes."

The socially constructed sexual identity constituted a major effort by sociologists to provide an explicit theoretical framework for the idea of a sociocultural identity. In launching this endeavor Mcintosh conceived of the homosexual identity as a "role" individuals took on by behaving in ways that society expected of homosexuals. Gagnon and Simon added the idea of sexual identity as a script or conceptual map that served as guidelines for individuals improvising their sexual conduct. There were heterosexual and homosexual scripts which individuals rarely exchanged.

Building on the concepts of sexual role and script, Plummer explored the contribution of social stigma to the homosexual identity. He believed that this identity originated in people's sense of being different and the social responses made to their behavior. The homosexual identity, therefore, was socially constructed because society erected the categories that defined homosexual behavior as deviant. Under the shadow of social rejection homosexuals went on to develop homosexual "careers" and a homosexual subculture.

The post-Kinsey sociologists launched their empirical investigations on the basis of the socially constructed homosexual identity, which they addressed as the labeling "perspective." They assumed that the deviant status occupied by homosexuals was primarily the product of stigmatization but that it was the behavior of the particular individual that occasioned her or his stigmatization. In their later work the homosexual identity was cast as a typology based on the sexual relationships homosexuals had with other homosexuals.

Although the post-Kinsey sociologists concluded their empirical studies of homosexuality by subscribing to the biological conception of sexual identity, we argued that their conception remained basically sociocultural. Their typology of homosexual relationships and their belief in "gender nonconformity" as a central aspect of the homosexual identity were sociological assertions which they occasionally clothed in psychological or biological metaphor.

Biological ingredients, however, were implicit in the notion of the socially constructed sexual identity. Like all formulations of sexual identity, it was based on the principle that the biological sex of partners in sexual relationships distinguished one identity from another. There was also the implication that the biological constraints that existed prior to the individual's assumption of the socially constructed identity were a necessary, predisposing factor. Plummer, for example, spoke of the individual's original feeling of "primary deviation" as the start of the homosexual career.

It was the psychological sexual identity that the social constructionists aimed to repudiate. However, as we have demonstrated, their theory of sexual identity included psychological elements. A central aspect of both the psychological and social constructionist view of sexual identity was the "meaning" individuals assigned to their sexual thoughts and behavior. "Meaning," of course, was differently construed in the two approaches. In the Freudian conception of the psychological sexual identity meanings were fabrications by the individual, symbolic representations of experience. In the socially constructed sexual identity meanings were largely imports from tradition and the social environment. However, in either view, meaning imposed major constraints on sexual behavior and relationships and, indeed, congealed sexual identity.

The collective sexual identity represented the most recent sociocultural conceptualization. In each of its manifestations the collective identity was formed by forces outside the individual. As a minority identity, it was the product of heterosexual oppression, wittingly or unwittingly abetted by homosexuals. Intolerance was described as embodied in institutions such as the church, law, and psychiatry.

In a more positive vein the collective homosexual identity was described as a distinctive lifestyle. Martin and Lyon, for example, depicted the lesbian lifestyle as quiet and unassuming coupledom, in which emotional attachment was the key element. The "social organization" of gay male "marriages," as described by Harry and DeVal, required emotional more than sexual fidelity. The ways in which gay people overcame their inferiorization by the dominant group, in Adam's speculations, constituted a lifestyle of skillful coping strategies. The homosexual "subculture" or "world" of the ethnographers was transformed into "community." Wolf, for example, described the lesbian community as "continuing social networks" of women "committed to the lesbian-feminist lifestyle."

The notions of "homophobia" and the "development of the homosexual identity" served as external supports and determinants of the collective homosexual identity. "Homophobia" implied not only the existence of community but also that it was the object of hostility. Its members needed to make their presence known and felt and to band together for protection and liberation. The models for developing a homosexual identity could serve as prescriptions for entering the community, contributing to its programs and goals, constructing and maintaining social relationships, and generally enjoying its lifestyle.

There were clear biological and psychological implications of the idea of the collective homosexual identity. With the articulation of the lesbian identity, as distinct from the gay male identity, the biological sex of partners in sexual relationships as the criterion distinguishing sexual identities became more explicit than ever. In effect, four identities were treated as conceptually distinct, the heterosexual and homosexual identities for females and for males. The collective homosexual identity as a minority status was implicitly biological. By aligning it with racial and ethnic groups and with women, it became a biological object of social intolerance.

The psychological elements were supplied by the clinical and social psychologists. The clinicians, some of whom publicly identified themselves as participants in the Gay Liberation movement, invented a new diagnostic category which they called homophobia. The social psychologists, in their attitudinal scales, tried to show how homophobia was linked to other psychological attitudes, which together formed clusters of authoritarian and traditional beliefs regarding the two biological sexes and sexual relationships. Because homophobia was usually described as an affliction of heterosexuals, the appearance of the term in the seventies seemed almost a retribution for the many decades during which homosexuality was diagnosed as a pathology. In the meantime the clinicians proceeded to develop stage-wise models for the acquisition of the homosexual identity which served both as a set of requirements for gaining and maintaining membership in the gay community and also as benchmarks for gauging the psychological health of each inhabitant.

Our review shows that the overlap and confusion that existed in the terminology also prevailed in the theoretical conceptualizations of the determinants of sexual identity. Although a particular conceptualization was explicitly biological, psychological, or sociocultural, at least implicitly it contained all three sets of ingredients.

This conceptual mélange resulted from the fact that each conceptualization tended to subsume the entire individual and all of that person's social relationships under a particular sexual identity. The heterosexual or homosexual identity was formulated as a biographical core to which all aspects of the individual's life had to be accommodated. As such, each conceptualization had to account for biological, psychological, and sociocultural aspects of the individual's life even though it gave primacy to one set of factors over others.

The conceptual mélange was also a historical product. Each conceptualization was a derivative of those that had preceded it. The biological sexual identity gave birth to the psychological, which, in turn, led to the sociocultural formulation. Although each new conceptualization was often trumpeted as the replacement for the old, it was more accurately an incorporation of the old in an expanded context of personal and social relationships.

The idea of sexual identity itself derived from the general concept of personal identity. In his semantic history of the term identity, Philip Gleason (1983) traced its emergence and diffusion. IDENTITY, he noted, derived from the Latin *idem*, which means "the same." The word has been used in English since the sixteenth century. In the seventeenth and eighteenth centuries it was used by John Locke and David Hume in their conception of PERSONAL IDENTITY, by which they meant continuity of personality throughout the individual's various phases of existence. Locke and Hume questioned the unity of personality or self, which was based on the monotheistic belief in the soul as the core or essence of the individual. According to Gleason, since their time identity has been loosely used to refer to personality or individuality.

It was in the 195, Gleason asserted, that the term IDENTITY was incorporated into the social sciences chiefly through the work of Erik Erikson and sociologists. Referring to Erikson's use of the term as elusive, subtle, and Delphic, Gleason suggests that it had two meanings: (1) a process located in the individual's core and (2) a process located in the core of the individual's communal culture. In Gleason's words (914) Erikson's concept of "identity involves an interaction between the interior development of the individual personality, understood in the Freudian id-superego model, and the growth of a sense of selfhood that arises from participating in society, internalizing its cultural norms, acquiring different statuses, and playing different roles." By IDENTITY CRISIS, Erikson referred to a climactic turning point in the individual's life, the first of which occurred during adolescence.

The concept of identity was considerably broadened, in Gleason's belief, when it was linked to the idea of IDENTIFICATION. In the Freudian sense, identification referred to the child's assimilation to parents and the family. The social psychologists and sociologists used identification to describe the process wherein the individual came to realize "what groups are significant for him, what attitudes concerning them he should form, and what kind of behavior is appropriate" (916).

The idea of identification, according to Gleason, furnished the link between the concept of identity and role and reference-group theory of sociologists such as Ralph Linton, Nelson Foote, Robert Merton, and Alice S. Kitt. Identification proceeded through individuals naming the groups with which they identified and later using the attributes of those groups as the ingredients for constructing a sense of selfhood. Through the sixties, the symbolic interactionists preferred to use the term THE SELF rather than the term IDENTITY. Some sociologists of the sixties, however, notably Erving Goffman and Peter Berger, shifted the terminology from THE SELF to IDENTITY.

By the mid-sixties, Gleason argued, "the word identity was so widely and loosely used that to determine its provenance in every context would be impossible" (918). Although the idea had a common historical origin, it eventually bifurcated into two meanings, one psychological and the other sociological. In the psychological meaning the essential elements of identity was conceived as "an artifact of interaction between the individual and society—it is essentially a matter of being designated by a certain name, accepting the designation, internalizing the role requirements accompanying it, and behaving according to prescriptions" (1000).

As applied to ethnic history, Gleason called the psychological formulation of identity the PRIMORDIALIST position and the sociological the OPTIONALIST. He concluded: "[F]or Eriksonians/primordialists, identity is deep, internal, and permanent; for interactionists/optionalists, identity is shallow, external, and evanescent" (920).

Current uses of the term IDENTITY in the discourse on sexual identity, as we have demonstrated, have both psychological and sociological dimensions that Gleason described for the general concept of identity. In the discourse the individual's sexual identity subsumed personal identity whether described as essentially biological, psychological, or sociocultural.

All conceptualizations of sexual identity were heavily influenced by scientism, treating the individual as the object of unremitting forces, either internal and bio-psychological or external and sociocultural. Individuals did not choose their sexual identity. It was forged for them within implacable biological, psychological, or social processes in which they were the main characters but over which they could exercise minimal control.

The specter of biological determinism loomed over the entire discourse on sexual identity. The biological sex of partners in sexual relationships consistently prevailed as the *sine qua non* by which one identity was distinguished from the other. Both the psychological and sociocultural sexual identities, no matter how arduously their formulators labored for conceptual purity, could not escape the implicit belief in the existence of some biological kernel or essence that predisposed the individual to either a heterosexual or homosexual identity. Finally, the assumption that irreducible biological differences existed in female and male sexual capacity and conduct was never seriously challenged in any conceptualization of sexual identity.

It is therefore not surprising that the idea of the biological sexual identity enjoyed a recrudescence in the formulations of the neuroendocrine theorists, the sociobiologists, and the sex physiologists. They were making explicit those biological assumptions implicit in the psychological and sociocultural conceptions of sexual identity. Without necessarily repudiating the psychological and sociocultural elaborations, they were in effect asserting that sexual identity was still rooted in biology.

Despite the biographical sweep of the idea of sexual identity, it is surprising how little it revealed about different types of individual attitudes, conduct, and relationships. The discourse on sexual identity proceeded more by MORAL INJUNCTION than by DESCRIPTION and EXPLICATION. The "heterosexualists" and "homosexualists" operated as opposing ideological camps. Although they were participants in a presumably scientific discourse, they assumed a defensive posture by criticizing one identity in the interest of shoring up credibility in the other.

We have shown how successive conceptualizations of sexual identity contributed to the normalization of sexual relationships. We have argued that normalization, operating under the aegis of a scientific discourse, constituted an endorsement of the boundaries of sexual relationships prescribed within the Judeo-Christian monotheistic cosmology. The process was accomplished by incorporating only those ingredients of the polytheistic and scientific cosmological views that did not undermine the permissible structure of sexual relationships.

The normalization process was exemplified in the detoxication of the homosexual identity. In our discussion of the historical antecedents of the idea of sexual identity, we explained how the homosexual identity symbolized the sexually impermissible. Through degeneracy theory it was linked to sodomy; through medical diagnosis it was linked to masturbation. For its pathologizers, the homosexual identity was conceived as a voracious, ungovernable, and destructive sexual appetite. As such, it was the heir of the polytheistic view of sexual conduct and relationships, the hedonism and paganism that the Judeo-Christian moral tradition had supplanted. Its recrudescence in modern history was viewed as evolutionary atavism and moral regression.

The detoxication of the homosexual identity, within the scientific discourse, constituted an effort to divorce it from its polytheistic and scientific cosmological antecedents and to incorporate it within the monotheistic view of sexual relationships. This was accomplished by distinguishing between pathological and nonpathological forms of homosexual relationships. Those based on raw sexual appetite, the prototypically polytheistic, remained pathological. Partners in pathological relationships were described as caught up in the grip of sexual instinct and psychological forces over which they had little control. Even sexual gratification eluded them in their endless search for new partners and novel sources of stimulation. The sexual gratification that was central to the polytheistic cosmology was permissible only within a properly structured relationship. Choice, the central ingredient in the scientific cosmology, could be exercised in selecting a partner but not in the form the relationship took.

Within the monotheistic cosmology a permissible sexual relationship contained four basic structural ingredients: a belief in the uniqueness of the biological sexes, a belief in their complementarity, a belief in the reproductive imperative, and a belief in the need for stability and permanence.

The fundamental belief was in the biological uniqueness of females and males. The contrasting female and male primary and secondary sex characteristics were viewed as only the most tangible and observable differences. There were corresponding hormonal, neural, and cerebral differences in both anatomy and physiology. Although the hormonal contrasts were measurable, especially in their reproductive functions, the neuro-cerebral differences were speculative extrapolations. In the discourse on sexual identity, physical differences between females and males were viewed as a set of biological constraints that molded sexual relationships.

The belief in complementarity of the two biological sexes grew out of viewing females and males as more different than alike. We have noted that within the polytheistic cosmology the differences between the two sexes were not viewed as immutable and fateful, as they were within the monotheistic cosmology. The gods could have both female and male forms or both female and male genitalia. Each sex could share the biological capabilities of the other. One biological sex could be transmuted into the other and the process magically reversed.

The belief in the complementarity of females and males, therefore, derived from viewing them as essentially unique biological specimens. The two sexes were complementary only to the extent that they were biologically different. The differences were viewed as a form of incompleteness. The two sexes stood before each other as mirror images, each possessing what the other lacked. It was assumed that only through their union was it possible to achieve biological wholeness.

The physical uniqueness of the two sexes was also thought to have its psychological and sociological correlates. The diffuseness of sexual desire and expression, which presumably typified the female, corresponded to the relative dispersion of her sex organs and functions. The restricted focus of sexual desire and expression in the male was believed to reflect the structure and centralized location of his genitalia. Females lingered over holding and kissing while males were preoccupied with genital contact and release. Females, according to Mead, were receptors, while males were the performers. The female temperament was even and rhythmic while males tended to crave adventure and conquest.

There was a core psychological femininity and masculinity that reflected physical femaleness and maleness. The femininity that men could never achieve through themselves or other males, according to Socarides, was what bonded their masculinity to women. From the sociological perspective complementarity was achieved in the relationships of men and women through an assignment of roles and tasks that was prefigured by the biological sexes to which they belonged.

The belief in the reproductive imperative neatly intermeshed with the belief in the biological uniqueness of the sexes and their complementarity. In requiring sexual relationships to be procreative, the reproductive imperative gave them a transcendent purpose. It was not morally acceptable that they exist only for the personal enjoyment of the partners. Relationships had to fit within the general fabric of the social order. Although lamenting the sacrifice of sexual gratification that appeared necessary to meet the requirements of procreative monogamy, Freud believed this was the inescapable fate of civilized men and women.

The belief in the need for stability and permanence in sexual relationships was a corollary of the belief in the reproductive imperative. If reproduction was the overarching purpose, then the rearing of offspring was the central responsibility. The ultimate form of the sexual relationship was, therefore, the family. The family, however, was foremost a social institution rather than a personal relationship. It was ideally devoted to the nurturance of children and their schooling for future parenthood. Although psychoanalytic theory depicted the family as a hotbed of incestuous rivalry, it assumed that responsible parents would take steps to dampen the sexual passions of their children.

The type of relationship that resulted from these beliefs we have called the male-female design. It has been our contention that the idea of sexual identity was rooted in the male-female design. It served as the fundamental premise upon which the discourse on sexual identity was based. The male-female design was what inextricably tied the idea of the heterosexual identity to the idea of the homosexual identity.

Throughout the discourse on sexual identity the male-female design served as a point of departure for the various conceptualizations of the homosexual identity. For example, the biological homosexual identity, as conceived by Ulrichs, consisted of individuals of a "third sex," who occupied an intermediate point between pure femaleness and pure maleness. In the Freudian conception of the psychological homosexual identity, anatomy had failed to prefigure the individual's psychological destiny. The happy confluence of biological sex, mental attitude, and sex object choice that characterized the heterosexual identity had failed to materialize in the case of the homosexual identity. In the sociocultural sexual identity, particularly in the form of the gay male and lesbian identity, the belief in the biological uniqueness of the two sexes remained a central ingredient of sexual relationships.

The pathologizers of the homosexual identity considered homosexual relationships to be an inversion of the male-female design. Because they consisted of two individuals of the same biological sex, they were viewed as precluding any complementarity and incapable of obeying the reproductive imperative. Lacking these basic structural ingredients, homosexual relationships could not reasonably be expected to meet the partners' need for stability and permanence.

We have shown, however, how the attitudinal ingredients of the male-female design were symbolically incorporated in the normalization of homosexual relationships. Ulrichs, for example, believed that a spiritual complementarity replaced the physical in the homosexual's choice of partners. Those with strong feminine or masculine drives were attracted to their spiritual counterparts. Freud believed that male homosexuals who were masculine in mental attitude sought male prostitutes who were feminine. Tripp asserted that the lack of complementarity in homosexual relationships threatened their stability.

Theorists of the sociocultural conceptualization of the homosexual identity bridled at the suggestion that homosexuals formed relationships by fitting together the feminine role of one partner and the masculine role of the other. Their irritation, however, stemmed from the opinion that such complementarity weakened the claim of homosexual females and males to be pure representatives of their respective biological sexes. Yet complementarity was an inescapable ingredient of relationships cast in terms of biological sex. The sociocultural theorists, especially those who created the collective homosexual identity, retained the idea of complementarity in their notion that the "complete" homosexual was one who was coupled. The social constructionists agreed that the lives of "uncoupled" homosexuals were less healthy and fulfilling.

The normalization of homosexual relationships also included symbolic obedience to the reproductive imperative and the need for stability and permanence. The best example of symbolic reproduction was provided by the sociobiologists, who wrote of the altruism of homosexuals who, lacking offspring of their own, were genetically programmed to devote their lives to brothers and sisters or nieces and nephews. The need for stability and permanence in homosexual relationships was fulfilled by viewing them as the basic units of the gay and lesbian communities. Relationships bound individuals together as "lovers," but community bound them together as "brothers" and "sisters." The responsibility of individuals to nurture each other in enduring sexual relationships and to serve as community leaders constituted a symbolic parenthood.

We have shown how the scientific discourse on sexual identity had the unforeseen consequence of normalizing both heterosexual and homosexual relationships. The normalization of homosexual relationships, as we have explained, was the unwitting result of the detoxication of the homosexual identity. Detoxication involved equating the homosexual identity to the heterosexual. The equation of the two, however, implied that homosexual relationships could embody the essential ingredients of heterosexual relationships. Normalized homosexual relationships, therefore, were incorporated into the male-female design.

Heterosexual relationships were also normalized as a fortuitous consequence of the discourse on sexual identity. Bringing homosexual relationships within the ambit of the male-female design constituted a bolstering of the design. As the discourse on sexual identity evolved in the nineteen-sixties and seventies, the fact that the male-female design was a central concern became remarkably explicit, as for example, in the speculations of the post-Freudians. As a set of prescribed components for sexual relationships, the male-design was as binding for heterosexual relationships as for the normalized homosexual. Rado and Stoller, for example, lyrically claimed that the height of orgastic pleasure and affection could be achieved only in those sexual relationships that were perfectly modeled after the design. Sexual pleasure provided by other forms of relationships they considered qualitatively inferior.

The normalization of heterosexual and homosexual relationships, in turn has had unanticipated consequences of its own. By undermining the belief in the biological uniqueness of the two sexes as the basic premise of sexual relationships, it has brought into question the entire male-female design. The premise was that the two sexes were biologically unique and that this uniqueness determined the structure of their sexual relationships. That partners either of the same biological sex or of opposite sexes could have sexual relationships that were identical in structure, however, implies that one sex can be substituted for the other. This has brought the male-female design under fresh scrutiny.

The belief that one sex can be substituted for the other without modifying the structure of sexual relationships inevitability focuses attention on the structure itself. Homosexual relationships, only because they consisted of partners of the same biological sex, had always posed a contradiction. If the sexes could be variously arrayed to form the same type of sexual relationships, is it not possible that relationships themselves could be variously structured? This question was foreshadowed, for example, in Freud's reluctant critique of monogamy, Churchill's bitter ruminations on the family, and Master's and Johnson's uneasy musings over ambisexuals.

If the discourse on sexual identity were to remain within its present theoretical boundaries two results could be anticipated: (1) prolonged debates among advocates of competing conceptualizations and (2) the proliferation of specific forms of sexual identity. First, debates will rage over the relative validity of the biological, psychological and sociocultural conceptualizations, with each successively occupying the position of prominence and popularity. We have shown how the biological conceptualization, particularly in the form of hormonal and genetic theories and research, is now being revived.

If the discourse were to continue to follow the path established for the homosexual identity, it will probably conceptualize new sexual identities and proceed to detoxicate them. The effort to construct and detoxicate the transsexual and bisexual identities is well underway, soon to be joined by the construction of identities for man/boy lovers, transvestites, sadomasochists, and prostitutes. As these identities come to the attention of the public, the sexual relationships they implicitly embody will then be normalized to fit the prescribed structure.

The scientific discourse on sexual identity, however, through the normalization of sexual relationships, has unwittingly presented the opportunity for systematic inquiry into the possible structures of sexual relationships. We identified the constituent elements of these structures as the knowledge, intentions, beliefs, attitudes, and expectations of partners that inform their treatment of each other. These structures are not those that partners necessarily conceive for their own relationships. They are the theoretical invention of the social scientist who notes the implications of partners holding similar or dissimilar beliefs.

We have listed the conceptual, methodological, and moral advantages that could be gained if the focus of inquiry were to shift from sexual identity to sexual relationships: (1) attention would shift from isolated individuals to their mutual associations; (2) the virtues of the psychoanalytic and symbolic interactionist approaches could be combined, while avoiding the pitfalls of utilizing one to the exclusion of the other; and (3) the conception of sexual relationships would be broadened to include the full scope of the polytheistic and scientific cosmological ingredients, particularly the elements of artful, fortuitous pleasure and choice.

The treatment of individuals as encapsulated units, divorced from historical and social contexts, is probably an unfortunate import by the social sciences from the biological and physical sciences. In biology, including medicine, a phenomenon is understood through a detailed analysis of its parts. The social sciences, according to Hayek, should proceed in the opposite direction. As a composite endeavor, attention should be given to the parts only for the purpose of building up a picture of the whole. Whereas the biological and physical sciences proceed through analysis, the social sciences depend on synthesis.

The idea of sexual identity unavoidably rivets attention on the isolated individual. The biological conceptualization treated the individual as an isolated physical unit, the psychological as an isolated mental unit. Even in the sociocultural conceptualization it was the individual who bore the mark of a particular sexual identity even though it was a product of the social milieu. The sexual relationships of individuals were seen through the lens of their sexual identities. A sexual relationship between a heterosexual and homosexual man, for example, was conceived as more circumstantial and transitory than one between two male homosexuals.

Although individuals were viewed as isolated units in the discourse on sexual identity, they were not conceived as persons who, on the basis of knowledge and belief, consciously or unconsciously exercised choices of their own. The penumbra of determinism surrounded each conceptualization of sexual identity. Even in its psychological avatar, sexual identity engulfed individuals and their sexual relationships; they were seen as the product of psychological forces that often lay beyond their ken and their control.

By shifting the focus of inquiry from the sexual identities of individuals to their mutual associations the uniqueness of individual mentality is recognized while treatment of the individual as an encapsulated unit is avoided. Within the framework of methodological individualism, relationships consist of the partners' treatment of each other, for example, politically, economically, or sexually. The treatment accorded is the reflection of their mentalities, which we have loosely referred to as their beliefs and attitudes. Each sexual relationship is unique because each is composed of the unique mentalities of the partners. Yet there are recurring patterns of attitudes and beliefs that imply structural commonalities. To construct a theory of sexual relationships it would be necessary to conceptualize the possible structural variations.

The switch in focus from identity to relationships could capitalize on the advantages of psychoanalytic and symbolic interactionist theory while avoiding their shortcomings. Psychoanalytic theory, on one hand, is exquisitely sensitive to the fact that individuals create personal meanings that are based on the symbolic representations of their experience. It tends, however, to lose the individual in a sea of private meanings that are only vaguely tied to historical and sociocultural contexts. Symbolic interactionism, on the other hand, is acutely aware that the personal and social categories to which individuals subscribe are meanings largely imported from history and their social milieu. It tends, however, to abandon the individual to a world of social meanings that are minimally subject to personal interpretation and modification. The mentality of the individual, as conceived here, consists of meanings that have both personal and social origins. The structure of sexual relationships lies at the junction of both the uniquely personal meanings of the individual partners and a temporal locus in history and society.

The shift in emphasis from identity to relationships would allow consideration of a broader scope of attitudes and beliefs, particularly those associated with personal pleasure and choice. We have presented the discourse on sexual identity as a moral pronouncement that narrowly circumscribed the exercise of choice in the pursuit of sexual gratification. According to Judeo-Christian doctrine, when individuals made the lustful choices that lay outside the boundaries prescribed for sexual relationships, they seriously jeopardized their souls and salvation. Under the banner of science, medicine warned people that errant sexual behavior constituted a grave threat to their physical and mental health. For both religion and medicine, sexual relationships were to have a purpose that transcended personal gratification and choice; if not procreation and the rearing of the family, then some transporting re-embodiment of the partners in, for example, romantic love, poetry, altruism, or common venture or adventure.

The permissible forms of sexual gratification were limited in the discourse on sexual identity because it was anchored in the biological sexes of partners in sexual relationships. Sexual gratification was viewed as essentially genital and orgasmic even in the comparatively polytheistic approach of Masters and Johnson. For them, sexual stimulation was to be diffuse, but sexual gratification was to center in the clitoris or the penis. Individuals who bore evidence of genital "dysfunctions" were excluded from their samples of "non-clinical" subjects. Even their efforts to make sexual stimulation more diffuse, as for example, in the practice of "sensate focus," had the air of prescription. The fortuitous inventiveness and pleasures of the polytheistic ars erotica were transformed into clinical prescriptions and practices for experiencing the joy of sex.

We have shown how the various conceptualizations of sexual identity constrained the exercise of individual choice in sexual relationships. The awesome inevitability of biological, psychological, or sociocultural forces, working singly or in concert, placed the control of and responsibility for relationships well beyond the grasp of the partners involved in them. If any "choice" has been left to the individual, it is the dubious one of conforming to the stern requirements of an inner or outer "reality," or what is by now commonly referred to as "sexual identity." To ignore or flout this reality was to risk "punishment," visited in the form of biological incapacity, mental suffering, or social rejection.

The social sciences have scarcely explored possibilities for understanding sexual relationships from the perspective of moral choice rather than moral obligation. There are several possible changes in perspective that could transpire if this shift were to occur. First, the structure of relationships would be determined from the mentality and practices of the individuals engaged in them, no matter how accurately or inaccurately this reflected the prevailing morality. Second, decision-making within relationships would be viewed as the prerogative of the partners themselves. Power would be conceived as if it resided within relationships rather than in external forces and authority. Third, rules governing relationships and establishing their boundaries would be seen as products of the relationships themselves rather than of pre-established moral parameters.

The uncharted territory in sexual relationships is the mentality and practices of the partners themselves. The structural similarities of heterosexual and homosexual relationships go unrecognized when it is assumed that different sexual identities require dissimilar structures. Approaching relationships as if they are governed by lawful forces, in the manner in which physical and biological phenomena are organized, the social scientist is blinded to the boundless ingenuity individuals exercise in forming, maintaining, and ending sexual relationships and blinded to the unforeseen consequences that the reformulation of past relationships has for future ones. Projected against these possible discoveries, the concern with sexual identity appears to be a narrow preoccupation.

Works Cited & Bibliography

Abbot, Sidney and Love, Barbara (1972). *Sappho Was a Right-On Woman*. New York: Stein and Day.

Achilles, Nancy (1967). The Development of the Homosexual Bar As An Institution. In J. H. Gagnon and W. Simon, Eds. *Sexual Deviance*. New York: Harper and Row, 228-244.

Ackerknecht, Erwin H. (1968). *A Short History of Psychiatry*. New York: Hafner.

Adam, Barry D. (1978). *The Survival of Domination: Inferiorization of Everyday Life*. New York: Elsevier.

Alexander, R. D. (1975). The Search for a General Theory of Behavior. *Behavioral Science* 20: 77-100.

Allport, Gordon W. (1954). *The Nature of Prejudice*. Cambridge, MA: Addison-Wesley.

Altman, Dennis (1982). *The Homosexualization of America and The Americanization of the Homosexual*. New York: St. Martin's Press.

American Psychiatric Association, Board of Trustees (1974). Anti-Discrimination Resolution. *American Journal of Psychiatry 130*(11): 497.

Arlow, Jacob A. and Brenner, Charles (1964). *Psychoanalytic Concepts and the Structural Theory*. New York: International University Press.

Attwater, Donald (Ed.). (1941). *A Catholic Dictionary*. New York: Macmillan.

Bailey, Derrick Sherwin (1955/1975). *Homosexuality and the Western Christian Tradition*. Hamden, CT: Archon Books. First published in 1955 in London by Longmans, Green.

Baker, Susan W. (1980). Biological Influences on Human Sex and Gender. *Signs: Journal of Women in Culture and Society 6*(1): 80-96.

Barash, David P. (1977). *Sociobiology and Behavior*. New York: Elsevier.

Bayer, Ronald (1981). *Homosexuality and American Psychiatry: The Politics of Diagnosis*. New York: Basic Books.

Bayer, Ronald and Spitzer, Robert L. (1982). Edited Correspondence on the Status of Homosexuality in *DSM-III*. *Journal of the History of the Behavioral Sciences 18*(1): 32-52.

Beach, F. A. (1948). *Hormones and Behavior*. New York: Paul Hoeber.

Becker, Howard S. (1963). *Outsiders: Studies in the Sociology of Deviancy*. New York: MacMillan.

Bell, Alan P. (1972). Human Sexuality: A Response. *International Journal of Psychiatry 10*(1): 99-102.

Bell, Alan P. (1973). Homosexualities: Their Range and Character. In James K. Cole and Richard Dienstbier, Eds., *Current Theory and Research on Motivation: Nebraska Symposium on Motivation 21*. Lincoln: University of Nebraska Press, 1-26.

Bell, Alan P. (1975a). Research on Homosexuality: Back to the Drawing Board. *Archives of Sexual Behavior 4*(4): 421-426.

Bell, Alan P. (1975b). The Homosexual Patient. In Richard Green, Ed., *Human Sexuality: A Health Practitioner's Text*. Baltimore: Williams and Wilkins, 52-72. Reprinted and abridged in Weinberg, Martin S. Ed. (1976). *Sex Research: Studies of the Kinsey Institute.* New York: Oxford University Press, 202-212.

Bell, Alan P. and Weinberg, Martin S. (1972). *Homosexuality: An Annotated Bibliography.* New York: Harper and Row.

Bell, Alan P. and Weinberg, Martin S. (1978). *Homosexualities: A Study of Diversity Among Men and Women.* New York: Simon and Schuster.

Bell, Alan P., Weinberg, Martin S., and Hammersmith, Sue Kiefer (1981). *Sexual Preference: Its Development in Men and Women.* Bloomington, IN: Indiana University Press.

Benedict, Ruth (1934). *Patterns of Culture.* New York: Penguin Books.

Benkert, Karl M. (1864). *Erinnerungen aus Charles Sealsfield.* Leipzig: Ahn.

Bentham, Jeremy (1785/1978). Offenses Against One's Self: Paederasty. Louie Crompton, Ed. *Journal of Homosexuality* 3(4): 383-405 and 4(1): 91-107.

Bieber, Irving (1966). Sadism and Masochism. *American Handbook of Psychiatry* 3: 257-258.

Bieber, Irving (1973). Homosexuality: An Adaptive Consequence of Disorder in Psychosexual Development. *American Journal of Psychiatry* 130: 1209-1211.

Bieber, Irving (1980). On Arriving at the APA Decision. Unpublished working paper, Hasting Center Closure Project.

Bieber, Irving, Dain, Harvey J., Dince, Paul R., Drellich, Marvin G. Grand, Henry G., Gundlach, Ralph H., Kremer, Malvina W., Rifkin Alfred H., Wilbur, Cornelia B., and Bieber, Toby B. (1962). *Homosexuality: A Psychoanalytic Study.* New York: Basic Books.

Binet, Alfred (1887). Le Fetichisme dans L'Amour. *Revue Philosophique* 24: 143-167.

Birke, L. I. (1981). Is Homosexuality Hormonally Determined? *Journal of Homosexuality* 6(4): 35-49.

Bloch, Iwan (1902). *Beiträge zur Aetiologie der Psychopathia Sexualis [Contributions to the Etiology of Sexual Perversion],* 2 Vols. Dresden: H. R. Dohrn.

Bloch, Iwan (1910). *The Sexual Life of Our Times in Its Relation to Modern Civilization.* M. Eden Paul, Trans. New York: Allied Book Company. First published in German in 1907 as *Das Sexualleben unserer Zeit in seinen Beziehungen zur modernen Kultur.*

Bloch, Iwan (1934). *Marquis de Sade's Anthropologia Sexualis of 600 Perversions: 120 Days of Sodom or the School for Libertinage and the Sex Life of the French Age of Debauchery.* Raymond Sabatier, Trans. and Ed. New York: Falstaff Press.

Boswell, John (1980). *Christianity, Social Tolerance, and Homosexuality.* Chicago: University of Chicago Press.

Bray, Alan (1982). *Homosexuality in Renaissance England.* London: Gay Men's Press.

Brenner, Charles (1955). *An Elementary Textbook of Psychoanalysis.* New York: International University Press.

Brooks, Virginia R. (1981). *Minority Stress and Lesbian Women.* Lexington, MA: D.C. Health.

Brunett, J. H. (1972). *The French Enlightenment.* London: Macmillan Press.

Bullough, Vern L. (1976). *Sexual Variance in Society and History.* Chicago: University of Chicago Press.

Bullough, Vern L. (1982). The Sin Against Nature and Homosexuality. In Vern L. Bullough and James Brundage, Eds., *Sexual Practices in the Medieval Church*. Buffalo, NY: Prometheus Books.

Burg, B. R. (1980/1981). Ho Hum, Another Work of the Devil: Buggery and Sodomy in Early Stuart England. *Journal of Homosexuality* 6(1/2), 69-78.

Burgess, Ernest W. (1949). The Sociological Theory of Psychosexual Behavior. In Paul H. Hoch and Joseph Zubin, Eds., *Psychosexual Development in Health and Disease*. New York: Grune and Stratton, 227-243.

Burke, Kenneth (1966). *Language as Symbolic Action*. Berkeley: University of California Press.

Burke, Kenneth (1969). *A Rhetoric of Motives*. Berkeley: University of California Press.

Butts, William (1946-1947). Boy Prostitutes of the Metropolis. *Journal of Clinical Psychopathology* 8: 673-681.

Calderone, Martha (1981). Orgasmic Expulsion of Fluid in the Sexually Stimulated Female. *SIECUS Report (10)*2: 23.

Califia, Pat (1980). *The Book of Lesbian Sexuality*. Tallahassee, FL: Naiad Press.

Caprio, Frank S. (1954). *Female Homosexuality: A Psychodynamic Study of Lesbianism*. New York: The Citadel Press.

Carpenter, Edward (1895). *Homogenic Love and Its Place in a Free Society*. London: Redundancy Press.

Carrier, J. M. (1980). *Homosexual Behavior in Cross-Cultural Perspective*. In Judd Marmor, Ed., *Homosexual Behavior: A Modern Reappraisal*. New York: Basic Books, 101-121.

Casper, Johann Ludwig (1857-1858/1864). *A Handbook of the Practice of Forensic Medicine Based Upon Personal Experience*. G. W. Balfour, Trans. London: New Sydenham Society. Translation of Casper, Johann Ludwig. First published in 1857-1858 as *Practisches Handbuchen der gerichtlichen Medicin*. Berlin: A. Hirschwald.

Casper, Johann Ludwig (1863). *Klinische Sovellen sur gerichtlichen Medicin: Nach eignen Erfahrunger*. Berlin: A Hirschwald.

Cass, Vivienne C. (1979). Homosexual Identity Formation: A Theoretical Model. *Journal of Homosexuality* 4(3): 219-235.

Cass, Vivienne C. (1984). Homosexual Identity: A Concept in Need of Definition. *Journal of Homosexuality* 9(2/3): 105-126.

Charcot, Jean-Martin and Magnan, Valentin (1882). Inversion du Sens Genital. *Archives de Neurologie 3:* 53-60; and *4:* 296-322.

Chevalier, Julien (1885). *De l'Inversion de l'Instinct Sexuel au Point de Vue Medico-Legal*. Paris: Octave Doin.

Chevalier, Julien (1893). *Une Maladie de la Personnalité: L'Inversion Sexuelle; Psycho-Physiologie, Sociologie, Tératologie, Aliénation Mentale, Psychologie Morbide, Anthropologie, Médecine Judiciaire*. Lyon and Paris: A. Storck.

Christenson, Cornelia V. (1971). *Kinsey: A Biography*. Bloomington: Indiana University Press.

Churchill, Wainright (1967/1971). *Homosexual Behavior Among Males: A Cross-Cultural and Cross-Species Investigation.* New York: Prentice Hall. First published in 1967.

Coleman, Eli (1982). Developmental Stages in the Coming-Out Process. In W. Paul, J. D. Weinrich, J. C. Gonsiorek, and M. E. Hotvedt, Eds., *Homosexuality: Social, Psychological, and Biological Issues.* Beverly Hills, CA: Sage Publications, 149-158. (Another version of this article appeared in *Behavioral Scientist,* 25(4): 397-405, in 1982.)

Conger, J. J. (1975). Proceedings of the American Psychological Association Incorporated for the Year 1974: Minutes of the Annual Meeting of the Council of Representatives. *American Psychologist 30:* 633.

Cory, Daniel Webster (1951). *The Homosexual in America: A Subjective Approach.* New York: Greenberg.

Cory, Daniel Webster (1964). *The Lesbian in America.* New York: Citadel Press.

Crompton, Louis (1980/1981). The Myth of Lesbian Impunity: Capital Laws from 1270 to 1791. *Journal of Homosexuality 6(1/2):*11-25.

Dank, Barry M. (1971). Coming out in the Gay World. *Psychiatry 34:* 180-197.

Dannecker, Martin (1981). *Theories of Homosexuality.* London: Gay Men's Press.

De Monteflores, Carmen and Schultz, Stephen J. (1978). Coming Out: Similarities and Differences for Lesbians and Gay Men. *Journal of Social Issues 34(3):* 59-71.

DeCecco, John P. (Ed.) 1984). *Homophobia: An Overview.* New York: Haworth Press. (Simultaneously published as Vol. 10(1/2) of the *Journal of Homosexuality.*)

DeCecco, John P. and Shively, Michael G. (1983). From Sexual Identity to Sexual Relationships: A Contextual Shift. *Journal of Homosexuality 9(2/3):* 1-26.

DeCecco, John (1981). Definition and Meaning of Sexual Orientation. *Journal of Homosexuality 6(4):* 51-67

Dessoir, Max (1894). Zur Psychologie der Vita sexualis. *Allgemeine Zeitschrift für Psychiatrie 50:* 941-975

Deutsch, Helene (1933). Homosexuality in Women. *International Journal of Psychoanalysis 14:* 34-69.

Diamond, M. and Karlin, A. (1980). *Sexual Decisions.* Boston: Little, Brown.

Diderot, Denis (1751-1772). *Encyclopédie, ou, Dictionnaire Raisonné des Sciences, des Arts et des Métiers.* Paris: Chez Briasson.

Diderot, Denis (1772). *Supplément au Voyage de M. de Bougainville.* Paris, Saillant & Nyon, 1772.

Dörner, G., Rhode, W., Stahl, F., Krell, L., and Masius, W. S. (1975). A Neuroendocrine Predisposition for Homosexuality in Men. *Archives of Sexual Behavior 4:* 108.

Dörner, Günter (1968). Hormonal Induction and Prevention of Female Homosexuality. *Journal of Endocrinology 42,* 163-164.

Dörner, Günter (1976). *Hormones and Brain Differentiation.* Amsterdam: Elsevier.

Dörner, Günter (1977a). Hormone Dependent Differentiation, Maturation, and Function of the Brain and Sexual Behavior. *Endokrinologie 69(3):* 306-320.

Dörner, Günter (1977b). Hormones, Brain Differentiation, and Fundamental Processes of Life. *Journal of Steroid Biochemistry 8:* 531-536.

Dörner, Günter (1979). Hormones and Sexual Differentiation in the Brain. In R. Green, Ed., *Sex, Hormones, and Behavior*. CIBA Foundation Symposium: 81-112.

Dörner, Günter and Hinz, G. (1968). Induction and Prevention of Male Homosexuality by Androgen. *Journal of Endocrinology 40*: 387-388.

Dover, K. J. (1978/1980). *Greek Homosexuality*. New York: Vintage Books. First published by Harvard University Press, 1978.

Dunbar, J., Brown, M., and Amoroso, D. M. (1973a). Attitudes toward Homosexuality among Brazilian and Canadian College Students. *Journal of Social Psychology 90:* 173-183.

Dunbar, J., Brown, M., and Amoroso, D. M. (1973b). Some Correlates of Attitudes toward Homosexuality. *Journal of Social Psychology 89*: 271-279.

Ehrhardt, Anke A. and Meyer-Bahlburg, H. F. (1981). Effects of Prenatal Sex Hormones on Gender Related Behavior. *Science 211*: 1312-1318.

Ellis, Havelock (1928/1936). *Studies in the Psychology of Sex*, 3rd ed, revised and enlarged, 7 Vols. Philadelphia: F. A. Davis Co. (Reprinted in two volumes in 1936 by Random House.)

Ellis, Havelock and Symonds, John Addington (1897/1936). *Sexual Inversion. Studies in the Psychology of Sex*, Vol. 1, Part 4. New York: Random House, 1-391. (Reprinted by Arno Press, 1975.)

Erikson, Brigitte (Trans.) (1980/1981). A Lesbian Execution in Germany, 1721: The Trial Records. *Journal of Homosexuality 6*(1/2): 27-40.

Faderman, Lillian (1981). *Surpassing the Love of Men: Romantic Friendships and Love Between Women from the Renaissance to the Present*. New York: William Morrow.

Fenichel, Otto (1930/1953). The Pregenital Antecedents of the Oedipus Complex. In *Collected Papers 1*: 181-204. New York: Norton, 1953. First published 1930.

Fenichel, Otto (1945). *The Psychoanalytic Theory of Neurosis*. New York: Norton.

Ferenczi, Sandor (1914/1963). The Nosology of Male Homosexuality. (Homoeroticism). In Hendrick M. Ruitenbeck, Trans. and Ed. (1963). *The Problem of Homosexuality in Modern Society*. New York: E. P. Dutton, 3-16. First published in *Internationale Zeitschrift für ärztliche Psychoanalyse*, 1914.

Ferenczi, Sandor (1924). *Versuch einer Genitaltheorie*. Leipzig: Internationaler Psychoanalytischer Verlag.

Fisher, Peter (1972). *The Gay Mystique: The Myth and Reality of Male Homosexuality*. New York: Stein and Day.

Ford, Clellan S. and Beach, Frank A. (1951). *Patterns of Sexual Behavior*. New York: Harper and Row.

Foucault, Michel (1965). *Madness and Civilization: A History of Insanity in the Age of Reason*. Richard Howard, Trans. New York: Pantheon.

Foucault, Michel (1976/1978). *The History of Sexuality—Vol. 1: An Introduction*. Trans. Robert Hurley. New York: Vintage Books. First published as *La Volente de Savoir*. Paris: Editions Gallimard, 1976.

Freedman, Mark F. (1971). *Homosexuality and Psychological Functioning*. Belmont, CA: Wadsworth.

Freud, Sigmund. (1960). In E. L. Freud, Ed., *The Letters of Sigmund Freud*. New York: Basic Books.

Freud, Sigmund (1905/1966). Three Essays on a Theory of Sexuality. *Standard Edition 7*: 125-243.

Freud, Sigmund (1908/1963). "Civilized" Sexual Morality and Modern Nervous Illness. *Standard Edition 9*: 177-204.

Freud, Sigmund (1910/1957). The Psycho-Analytic View of Psychogenic Disturbance of Vision. *Standard Edition 11*: 210-218.

Freud, Sigmund (1910/1964) Leonardo da Vinci and a Memory of His Childhood. *Standard Edition 11*: 59-137. First published as *Eine Kinderheitserinnerung des Leonardo da Vinci*. Vienna: Deuticke, 1910.

Freud, Sigmund (1911/1966). Formulations of the Two Principles of Mental Functioning. *Standard Edition 12*: 213-226.

Freud, Sigmund (1912-13/1966). Totem and Taboo. *Standard Edition 13*: 1-161.

Freud, Sigmund (1914/1966). On Narcissism: An Introduction. *Standard Edition 14*: 69-102.

Freud, Sigmund (1915/1966). The Unconscious. *Standard Edition 14*, 161-204.

Freud, Sigmund (1920/1966a). Beyond the Pleasure Principle. *Standard Edition 19*: 3-64.

Freud, Sigmund (1920/1966b). Psychogenesis of a Case of Homosexuality in a Woman. *Standard Edition 18*: 146-172.

Freud, Sigmund (1923/1966). The Ego and the Id. *Standard Edition 14*: 3-66. First published in 1923 as *Das Ich und Das Es*. Vienna: Internationaler Psychoanalytischer, 3-59.

Freud, Sigmund (1924/1966). The Dissolution of the Oedipus Complex. *Standard Edition 19*: 172-179.

Freud, Sigmund (1925/1966). Some Psychical Consequences of the Anatomical Distinction between the Sexes. *Standard Edition 19*: 243-258.

Freud, Sigmund (1927/1966). The Future of an Illusion. *Standard Edition 21*: 3-56.

Freud, Sigmund (1932/1961). Female Sexuality. *Standard Edition 21*: 223-243. (The article first appeared in the *International Journal of Psycho-Analysis 13*: 281-297.)

Freud, Sigmund (1937/1966). Analysis Terminal and Interminable. *Standard Edition 23*: 211-253.

Freud, Sigmund (1937-39/1966). Moses and Monotheism. *Standard Edition 23*: 3-137.

Friedman, R. C., Wollesen, F., and Tendler, R. (1976). Psychological Development and Blood Levels of Sex Steroids in Male Identical Twins of Divergent Sexual Orientation. *Journal of Nervous and Mental Disorders 163*: 282-283.

Futuyma, Douglas and Risch, Stephen (1983/1984). Sexual Orientation, Sociobiology, and Evolution. *Journal of Homosexuality 9*(2/3): 157-168.

Gagnon, J. and Simon, W. (Eds.) (1967). *Sexual Deviance*. New York: Harper and Row.

Gagnon, J. H. (1973). Scripts and the Coordination of Sexual Conduct. In J. K. Cole and R. Dienstbier, Eds., *Current Theory and Research and Research on Motivation: Nebraska Symposium on Motivation* 21: 27-59. Lincoln: University of Nebraska Press.

Gagnon, J. H. (1977). *Human Sexualities*. Glenview, Illinois: Scott, Foresman.

Gagnon, J. H. and Simon, W. (1973). *Sexual Conduct: The Social Sources of Human Sexuality*. Chicago: Aldine.

Gagnon, J. H., and Simon, W. (1970). *The Sexual Scene*. Chicago: Aldine.

Gartrell, N. (1982). Hormones and Homosexuality. In W. Paul, J. D. Weinrich, J. C. Gonsiorek, and M. E. Hotvedt, Eds., *Homosexuality: Social, Psychological and Biological Issues*. Beverly Hills, CA: Sage Publications, 169-183.

Gay, Peter (1964). *The Party of Humanity: Essays in the French Enlightenment*. New York: Alfred A. Knopf.

Gebhard, Paul H., Gagnon, John H., Pomeroy, Wardell B., and Christenson, Cornelia V. (1965). *Sex Offenders: An Analysis of Types*. New York: Harper-Hoeber.

Giallombardo, Rose (1966). *Society of Women: A Study of Women's Prisons*. New York: Wiley.

Gilbert, Arthur N. (1980/1981). Conceptions of Homosexuality and Sodomy in Western History. *Journal of Homosexuality* 6(1/2): 57-68.

Gleason, Philip (1983). Identifying Identity: A Semantic History. *Journal of American History* 69(4): 910–931.

Gley, E. (1884). Les Aberrations de l'Instinct Sexual d'apres des Travaux Recents. *Revue Philosophique* 17: 66-92.

Goffman, Erving (1961). *Encounters*. Indianapolis: Bobbs-Merrill.

Goffman, Erving (1963). *Stigmas: Notes on the Management of Spoiled Identity*. Englewood Cliffs, NJ: Prentice-Hall.

Goffman, Erving (1967). *Interactional Ritual*. Chicago: Aldine.

Gold, Ronald (1973). Stop it, You're Making Me Sick! *American Journal of Psychiatry* 130(11): 1211-1212.

Goode, Erich (1981a). Comments on the Homosexual Role. *Journal of Sex Research* 17(1): 54-65

Goode, Erich (1981b). The Homosexual Role: Rejoinder to Omark and Whitam. *Journal of Sex Research* 17(1): 76-83.

Goodich, Michael (1976). Sodomy in Ecclesiastical Law and Theory. *Journal of Homosexuality* 1(4): 427-434.

Goodich, Michael (1979). *The Unmentionable Vice: Homosexuality in the Later Mediaeval Period*. Santa Barbara, CA: Ross-Erikson.

Gould, Stephen Jay (1983). Genes on the Brain. *New York Review of Books* 30(11): 5-10.

Green, Richard (1972). Homosexuality as a Mental Illness. *International Journal of Psychiatry* 10(1): 77-98.

Green, Richard (1973). Should Heterosexuality Be in the APA Nomenclature? *American Journal of Psychiatry* 130(11): 1213-1214.

Green, Richard (1974). *Sexual Identity Conflict in Children and Adults.* New York: Basic Books.

Green, Richard (1975). Adults Who Want to Change Sex, Adolescents Who Cross-Dress, and Children Called "Sissy" and "Tomboy." In R. Green, Ed., *Human Sexuality: A Health Practitioner's Text.* Baltimore: Williams and Wilkins, 83-96.

Green, Richard (1976). One Hundred Ten Feminine and Masculine Boys: Behavioral Contrasts and Demographic Similarities. *Archives of Sexual Behavior 5:* 425-446.

Green, Richard (1978). Sexual Identity of 37 Children Raised by Homosexual or Transsexual Parents. *American Journal of Psychiatry 135*(6): 692-697.

Green, Richard (1979a). Childhood Cross-Gender Behavior and Subsequent Sexual Preference. *American Journal of Psychiatry 136*(1): 106-108.

Green, Richard (1979b). "Sissies" and "Tomboys." *SIECUS Report 7*(3): 1-2, 15.

Green, Richard and Money, John (Eds.) (1969). *Transsexualism and Sex Reassignment.* Baltimore: The Johns Hopkins University Press.

Green, Richard and Stoller, R. J. (1971). Two Monozygotic. (Identical) Twin Pairs Discordant for Gender Identity. *Archives of Sexual Behavior 1:* 321-327.

Green, Richard, Newman, L., and Stoller, Robert (1972). Treatment of Boyhood "Transsexualism": An Interim Report of Four Year's Duration. *Archives of General Psychiatry 26:* 213-217.

Green, Richard, Williams, K., and Goodman, M. (1982). Ninety-Nine "Tomboys" and "Non-Tomboys": Behavioral Contrasts and Demographic Similarities. *Archives of Sexual Behavior 11*(3): 247-276.

Grosskurth, Phillis (1980). *Havelock Ellis: A Biography.* New York: Alfred Knopf.

Haeberle, Erwin J. (1981). Pink Triangle and Yellow Star: The Destruction of Sexology and the Persecution of Homosexuals in Nazi Germany. *Journal of Sex Research 17*(3): 270-287.

Hamilton, W. D. (1964). The Genetic Theory of Social Behavior: I and II. *Journal of Theoretical Biology 7:* 1-52.

Hamilton, W. D. (1964). The Genetic Theory of Social Behavior: I and II. *Journal of Theoretical Biology 7:* 1-52.

Harry, Joseph, and DeVall, William B. (1978). *The Social Organization of Gay Males.* New York: Praeger.

Hartmann, Heinz (1958). *Ego Psychology and the Problem of Adaptation.* David Rapaport, Trans. New York: International Universities Press. First published in German in 1939.

Hartmann, Heinz, Kris, Ernst, and Lowenstein, Rudolph (1964). *Papers on Psychoanalytic Psychology. Psychological Issues 4.* (Monograph 14).

Hatterer, Lawrence J. (1972). A Critique. *International Journal of Psychiatry 10*(1): 103-104.

Hauser, Richard (1962). *The Homosexual Society.* London: The Bodley Head.

Hayek, F. A. (1979). *The Counter-Revolution of Science: Studies on the Abuse of Reason.* Indianapolis, IN: Liberty Press. First published in 1952.

Hencken, J. D. and O'Dowd, W. T. (1979). Coming Out as an Aspect of Identity Formation. *Gay Academic Union Journal: Gai Saber 1*: 18-22.

Hencken, Joel D. (1982). *Homosexual Identities: An Exploration of Issues*. A prelim paper presented to the faculty of the University of Michigan, Department of Psychology, Clinical Area.

Henry, G. W. (1941). *Sex Variants: A Study of Homosexual Patterns*. New York: Paul B. Hoeber.

Herdt, Gilbert (1981). *Guardians of the Flutes: Idioms of Masculinity*. New York: McGraw-Hill.

Hertz, J. H. (Ed.). (1972). *Genesis. XIX, 3, The Pentateuch and Haftoras: Hebrew Text and English Translation and Commentary*, 2nd Ed. London: Soncino Press.

Heston, L. L. and Shields, J. (1968). Homosexuality in Twins: A Family and A Registry Study. *Archives of General Psychiatry 18*: 149-160.

Hirschfeld, Magnus (1910). *Die Transvestiten*. Berlin: Pulvermacher.

Hirschfeld, Magnus (1913). *Die Homosexualität des Mannes und des Weibes* in Iwan Bloch, Ed., *Handbuch der gesamten Sexualwissenschaft in Einzeldarstellungen*, III. Berlin: Louis Marcus.

Hirschfeld, Magnus (1947), *Sexual Pathology: A Study of Derangements of the Sexual Instinct*. Jerome Gibbs, Trans. New York: Emerson Books

Hirschfeld, Magnus (1948). *Sexual Anomalies: The Origins, Nature and Treatment of Sexual Disorders*. New York: Emerson Books, Inc.

Hoenig, J. (1977). Dramatis Personae: Selected Biographical Sketches of 19th Century Pioneers in Sexology. In John Money and Herman Musaph, Eds., *Handbook of Sexology I: History and Ideology*. New York: Elsevier, 21-43.

Hoffman, Martin (1968). *The Gay World: Male Homosexuality and the Social Creation of Evil*. New York: Basic Books.

Hoffman, Martin (1972). Philosophical, Empirical, and Ecologic Remarks. *International Journal of Psychiatry 10*(1): 105-107.

Hoffman, Richard J. (1980a). Some Cultural Aspects of Greek Male Homosexuality. *Journal of Homosexuality 5*(3): 217-226.

Hoffman, Richard J. (1980b). Review of *Greek Homosexuality* by K. J. Dover. *Journal of Homosexuality 5*(4): 418-421.

Hoffman, Richard J. (1984). Vices, Gods, and Virtues: Cosmology as a Mediating Factor in Attitudes Towards Male Homosexuality. *Journal of Homosexuality 9*(2/3): 27-44.

Hooker, E. (1968). Homosexuality. *The International Encyclopedia of the Social Sciences*. New York: MacMillan and Free Press, 222-233.

Hooker, Evelyn (1956). A Preliminary Analysis of Group Behavior of Homosexuals. *The Journal of Psychology 42*: 217-225.

Hooker, Evelyn (1957). The Adjustment of the Male Overt Homosexual. *Journal of Projective Techniques 27*: 18-31.

Hooker, Evelyn (1958). Male Homosexuality in the Rorschach. *Journal of Projective Techniques* 22: 33-54.

Hooker, Evelyn (1959). What is a Criterion? *Journal of Projective Techniques* 23: 273-281.

Hooker, Evelyn (1962). The Homosexual Community. *Proceedings of the 14th International Congress of Applied Psychology, Personality Research.* Copenhagen: Munksgaard, 40-49. (A revised version of this paper was reprinted in *Perspectives in Psychopathology.* New York: Oxford University Press, 1965, and, later, in Gagnon, J. and Simon, W., Eds, *Sexual Deviance.* New York: Harper and Row, 1967, 167-184.)

Hooker, Evelyn (1965). An Empirical Study of Some Relationships between Sexual Patterns and Gender Identity in Male Homosexuals. In John Money, Ed., *Sex Research: New Developments.* New York: Holt, Rinehart, and Winston, 24-52.

Hooker, Evelyn (1965). Male Homosexuals and Their Worlds. In J. Marmor, Ed., *Sexual Inversion: The Multiple Roots of Homosexuality.* New York: Basic Books, 83-107.

Horney, Karen (1924). On the Genesis of the Castration Complex in Women. *International Journal of Psychoanalysis* 5: 50-65.

Horney, Karen (1926). The Flight from Womanhood. *International Journal of Psychoanalysis* 7: 324-339.

Horney, Karen (1933). The Denial of the Vagina: A Contribution to the Problem of Genital Anxieties Specific to Women. *International Journal of Psychoanalysis* 14: 57-70.

Hössli, Heinrich (1836-1838). *Eros: Die Männerliebe der Griechen, ihre Beziehungen zur Geschichte, Literatur und Gesetzgebung aller Zeiten. Oder, Forschungen über platonische Liebe ihre Würdigung und Entwürdigung für Sitten-, Natur- und Volkerkund.* Two Volumes. Vol. I: Switzerland: Glarus; Vol. II: Switzerland, Sankt Gallen.

Hoult, T. K. (1984). Human Sexuality in Biological Perspective: Theoretical and Methodological Considerations. *Journal of Homosexuality* 9(2/3): 137-155.

Hudson, W. W., and Ricketts, W. A. (1980). A Strategy for the Measurement of Homophobia. *Journal of Homosexuality* 5(4): 357-372.

Humphreys, Laud (1970). *Tearoom Trade: Impersonal Sex in Public Places.* Chicago: Aldine.

Humphreys, Laud (1972). *Out of the Closet: The Sociology of Homosexual Liberation.* Englewood Cliffs, N J: Prentice- Hall.

Hunter, John (1786). *A Treatise on Venereal Disease.* London: Privately printed.

Hunter, Richard and Macalpine, Ida (1963). *Three Hundred Years of Psychiatry, 1535-1800: A History Presented in Selected English Texts.* London: Oxford University Press.

Hutchinson, George Evelyn (1959). A Speculative Consideration of Certain Possible Forms of Sexual Selection in Man. *American Naturalist* 93(869): 81-91.

Imperato-McGinley, J. and Peterson, R. E. (1976). Male Pseudohermaphroditism: The Complexities of Male Phenotypic Development. *American Journal of Medicine* 61(2): 251-272.

Imperato-McGinley, J., Peterson, R. E., Gautier, T., and Sturla, E. (1979). Androgens and the Evolution of Male Gender Identity among Male Pseudohermaphrodites with 5α-Reductase Deficiency. *New England Journal of Medicine* 300(22): 1233-1279.

Jersild, Jens (1956). Boy Prostitution. Copenhagen: C. E. Grad.

Johnston, Jill (1973). *Lesbian Nation: Feminist Solution*. New York: Simon and Schuster.

Jowett, Benjamin (Trans.) (1937). *Dialogues of Plato*. Two vols. New York: Random House.

Kallman, F. J. (1952). Comparative Twin Study of the Genetic Aspects of Male Homosexuality. *Journal of Nervous and Mental Disease 115*: 282-298.

Kallman, F. J. (1952). Twin Sibships and the Study of Male Homosexuality. *Journal of Human Genetics 4*: 136-146.

Kallman, F. J. (1960). [Brief notice.] *Psychosomatic Medicine 22*: 258-259.

Kardiner, Abram (1954/1963). *Sex and Morality*. Indianapolis, IN: Bobbs Merrill. Reprinted in Ruitenbeek, H. R. (Ed.). (1963). *The Problem of Homosexuality in Modern Society*. New York: E. P. Dutton, 17-39.

Kardiner, Abram, Karush, A., and Ovesey, Lionel. (1959). Methodological Study of Freudian Theory. *Journal of Nervous and Mental Disease 4*: 11-19.

Karlen, Arno (1971). *Sexuality and Homosexuality: A New View*. New York: W. W. Norton.

Karlen, Arno (1972). A Discussion of Homosexuality as a Mental Illness. *International Journal of Psychiatry 10*(1): 108-113.

Karr, R. G. (1978). Homosexual Labeling and the Male Role. *Journal of Social Issues 34*(3), 73-83.

Karsch, H. F. (1903/1975). Der Putzmacher von Glarus Heinrich Hössli, ein Vorkämpfer der Männerliebe. Ein Lebensbild. *Jahrbuch für sexuelle Zwischenstufen 5*: 449–556. Max Spohr, Leipzig 1903. Reprinted in 1975 under the title *Documents of the Homosexual Rights Movement in Germany, 1836-1927*. New York: Arno Press.

Katz, Jonathan. (Ed.). (1976). *Gay American History: Lesbians and Gay Men in the U.S.A.* New York: Thomas Y. Crowell.

Kellogg, J. H. (1882). *Plain Facts for Old and Young*. Burlington, IA: I. F. Senger.

Kennedy, Hubert C. (1980/1981). "The 'Third Sex Theory" of Karl Heinrich Ulrichs. *Journal of Homosexuality 6*(1/2): 103-111.

Kertbeny, Károly Mária [aka Karl Benkert] (1869/1905). § 143 des Preussischen Strafgesetzbuches vom 14. April 1851 und seine Aufrechterhaltung als § 152 im Entwurfe eines Strafgesetzbuches für den Norddeutschen Bund. *Jahrbuch für sexuelle Zwischenstufen*. Jahrgang I. Band. Leipzig: Verlog von Max Spohr.

Kiernan, James G. (1891). Psychological Aspects of the Sexual Appetite. *The Alienist and Neurologist 12*: 188-219.

Kinsey, Alfred C., Pomeroy, Wardell B., and Martin, Clyde E. (1948). *Sexual Behavior in the Human Male*. Philadelphia: W. B. Saunders.

Kinsey, Alfred C., Pomeroy, Wardell B., Martin, Clyde E., and Gebhard, Paul H. (1953). *Sexual Behavior in the Human Female*. Philadelphia: W. B. Saunders.

Kirsch, John A. and Rodman, James Eric (1982). Selection and Sexuality: The Darwinian View of Homosexuality. In W. Paul, J. Weinrich, J. C. Gonsiorek, and M. E. Hotvedt, Eds., *Homosexuality: Social, Psychological, and Biological Issues*. Beverly Hills, CA: Sage, 183-195.

Kitsuse, John I. (1962). Societal Reactions to Deviant Behavior: Problems of Theory and Method. *Social Problems 9*: 247-256.

Klein, Melanie (1928/1950). Early Stages of the Oedipus Conflict. *Contributions to Psychoanalysis: 1921-1945*. London: The Hogarth Press.

Klein, Melanie (1932/1975). *The Psychoanalysis of Children*. A. Strachey, Trans. London: The Hogarth Press. (Revised edition published in 1975.)

Kohn, Melvin L. (1969). *Class and Conformity: A Study in Values*. Homewood Illinois: Dorsey Press.

Krafft-Ebing, Richard von (1901). Neue Studien auf dem Gebiete der Homosexualität. *Jahrbuch fur sexuelle Zwischenstufen 3*: 1-36.

Krafft-Ebing, Richard von. (1886/1935). *Psychopathia Sexualis*, 12th edition. F. J. Rebman, Trans. Brooklyn: Physicians and Surgeons Book Company. First published in 1886 as *Psychopathia Sexualis: Eine Klinisch-Forensische Studie*. Stuttgart: Ferdinand Enke.

Krell, L.; Dörner G., Massius, W. G., Rhode, W., and Elste, G. (1975). Beziehungen zwischen klinisichen manifester Homosexualität und dem oestrogenfeedback Effekt. *Dermatologishe Monansschrift 161*: 567-572.

Lacey, W. K. (1968). *The Family Life in Classical Greece*. London: Thames and Hudson.

Lallemand, Claude-Francois (1836/1839). *On Involuntary Seminal Discharge*. William Wood, Trans. Philadelphia: A. Waldier. First published in French in three volumes between 1836-1842 as *Des Pertes Séminales Involontaires* [Involuntary Seminal Losses].

Lang, T. (1941). Untersuchungen an männlichen Homosexuellen und deren Sippschaften mit besonderer Berück-sichtung der Frage des Zusammenhangs zwischen Homosexualität und Psychose. 1. Die Probanden und deren engere Familie. *Zentralblatt für die Gesamte Neurologie und Psychiatrie 171*: 651-679.

Lauritsen, John and Thorstad, David (1974). *The Early Homosexual Rights Movement: 1864-1935*. New York: Times Change Press.

Lemert, E. M. (1967). *Human Deviance, Social Problems and Social Control*. Englewood Cliffs, NJ: Prentice-Hall.

Levine, Martin P. (1979). Gay Ghetto. *Journal of Homosexuality* 4(4): 363-375

Levitt, E. E. and Klassen, A. D. (1974). Public Attitudes toward Homosexuality: Part of the 1970 National Survey by the Institute for Sex Research. *Journal of Homosexuality* 1(1): 29-43.

Lev-Ran, A. (1974). Sexuality and Educational Levels of Women with Late-Treated Androgenital Syndrome. *Archives of Sexual Behavior 3*: 27-32.

Lewis, Sasha Gregory (1979). *Sunday's Women: A Report on Lesbian Life Today*. Boston: Beacon Press.

Leznoff, Maurice and Westley, William (1956). The Homosexual Community. *Social Problems 3*: 257-263.

Lombroso, Cesare (1881). L'Amore nei Pazzi. *Archivio di Psichiatria, Scienze Penali ed Antropologia Criminale* II: 1-33.

Lumby, M. E. (1976). Homophobia: The Quest for a Valid Scale. *Journal of Homosexuality* 2(1): 39-47.

Lydston, Frank G. (1889). Sexual Perversion, Satyriasis, and Nymphomania. *Medical and Surgical Reporter 61*: 253-258, 281-285.

Maccoby, Eleanor and Jacklin, Carol. (1974). *The Psychology of Sex Differences*. Stanford, CA: Stanford University Press.

MacDonald, A. P. and Games, R. G. (1974). Some Characteristics of Those Who Hold Positive and Negative Attitudes Toward Homosexuals. *Journal of Homosexuality 1*(1): 9-27.

MacDonald, P. A., Huggins, J., Young, S., and Swanson R. A. (1973). Attitudes Toward Homosexuality: Preservation of Sex Morality or the Double Standard? *Journal of Counseling and Clinical Psychology 40*(1): 161.

Malinowski, Bronislaw (1929). *The Sexual Life of Savages in North-Western Melanesia: An Ethnographic Account of Courtship, Marriage and Family Life Among The Natives of the Trobriand Islands, British New Guinea*. New York: Eugenics Publishing Co.

Marcuse, Herbert (1955). *Eros and Civilization: A Philosophical Inquiry into Freud*. Boston: Beacon Press.

Margolese, M. S. and Janiger, O. (1973). Androsterone/Etiocholanolone Ratios in Male Homosexuals. *British Medical Journal 3*(5873): 207-210.

Marmor, Judd (1972). Homosexuality: Mental Illness or Moral Dilemma? *International Journal of Psychiatry 10*(1): 114-117.

Marmor, Judd (1973). Homosexuality and Cultural Value Systems. *American Journal of Psychiatry 130*: 1208-1209.

Marmor, Judd (Ed.) (1965). *Sexual Inversion: The Multiple Roots of Homosexuality*. New York: Basic Books.

Marmor, Judd (Ed.). (1980). *Homosexual Behavior: A Modern Reappraisal*. New York: Basic Books.

Martin, Del and Lyon, Phyllis. (1972). *Lesbian/Woman*. San Francisco: Glide Publications.

Martin, John R. (1980, April). Sexual Perversion or Vice? A Late 19th Century Debate. Paper presented at the annual convention of the Organization of American Historians, San Francisco.

Masters, William H. and Johnson, Virginia E. (1966). *Human Sexual Response*. Boston: Little, Brown.

Masters, William H. and Johnson, Virginia E. (1970). *Human Sexual Inadequacy*. Boston: Little, Brown.

Masters, William H. and Johnson, Virginia E. (1979/1982). *Homosexuality in Perspective*. New York: Bantam Books. (Originally published in 1979 by Little, Brown.)

Masters, William H., Johnson, Virginia E., and Kolodny, Robert C. (1982). *Human Sexuality*. Little, Brown: Boston.

Masters, William H., Johnson, Virginia E., and Levine, Robert J. (1970). *The Pleasure Bond: A New Look at Sexuality and Commitment*. Boston: Little, Brown.

Mcintosh, Mary (1968/1981). The Homosexual Role. *Social Problems* 15(2): 182-192. Reprinted in Plummer, Kenneth (Ed.) (1981). *The Making of the Modern Homosexual*. Totowa, NJ: Barnes and Noble, 30-44.

Mead, Margaret (1935). *Sex and Temperament in Three Primitive Societies*. London: Routledge and Kegan Paul.

Mead, Margaret (1949/1955). *Male and Female: A Study of the Sexes in a Changing World*. New York: New American Library. First published 1949.

Meyer-Bahlburg, H. F. (1977). Sex Hormones and Male Homosexuality in Comparative Perspective. *Archives of Sexual Behavior* 6: 297-325.

Meyer-Bahlburg, H. F. (1979). Sex Hormones and Female Homosexuality: A Critical Examination. *Archives of Sexual Behavior* 8(21): 101-119.

Millet, Kate (1977). *Sita*. New York: Farrar, Strauss, and Giroux.

Millham, J. and Weinberger, L. E. (1977). Sexual Preferences, Sex Role Appropriateness, and Restriction of Social Access. *Journal of Homosexuality* 2(4): 343-357.

Millham, J., San Miguel, C. L., and Kellogg, R. (1976). A Factor-Analytic Conceptualization of Attitudes toward Male and Female Homosexuals. *Journal of Homosexuality* 2(11): 3-10.

Minnigerode, Fred A. (1976). Attitudes toward Homosexuality: Feminist Attitudes and Sexual Conservatism. *Sex Roles* 2(4): 347-352.

Minton, Henry and McDonald, Gary (1984). Homosexual Identity Formation as a Developmental Process. *Journal of Homosexuality* 9(2/3): 91-104.

Moll, Albert (1889). *Der Hypnotismus*. Berlin: Fischer's Medizinische Buchhandlung, H. Kornfeld.

Moll, Albert (1891/1931). *Die Konträre Sexualempfindung*. Berlin: Fischer's Medicinische Buchhandlung, H. Kornfeld. (Translated by Maurice Popkin, the volume appeared in English as *Perversion of the Sexual Instinct: A Study of Sexual Inversion Based on Clinical Data and Official Documents*. Newark, NJ: Julian Press, 1931.)

Moll, Albert (1897/1933). *Libido Sexualis: Studies in the Psychosexual Laws of Love Verified by Clinical Sexual Case Histories*. David Berger, Trans. New York: American Ethnological Press. (Translation of *Untersuchungen über die Libido Sexualis*. Berlin: Fischer's Medizinische Buchhandlung, H. Kornfeld, 1897.)

Money, John (1952). *Hermaphroditism: An Inquiry into the Nature of a Human Paradox*. Doctoral Dissertation, Harvard University, Harvard University Library.

Money, John (1980). *Love and Love Sickness: The Science of Sex, Gender Differences, and Pair-Bonding*. Baltimore: The Johns Hopkins University Press.

Money, John and Ehrhardt, Anke A. (1972). *Man and Woman, Boy and Girl*. Baltimore: The John Hopkins University Press.

Money, John and Tucker, Patricia (1975). *Sexual Signatures: On Being a Man or a Woman*. Boston: Little, Brown.

Monter, E. William (1980/1981). Sodomy and Heresy in Early Modern Switzerland. *Journal of Homosexuality* 6(1/2): 41-53.

Morel, Benedict Augustin (1857). *Traite des Degenerescences Physiques, Intellectualles et Morales de l'Espece Humaine et ses Causes qui Prodisent ces Varietes Maladives*. Paris: J. B. Bailliere.

Morin, Jack (1981). *Anal Pleasure and Health*. Burlingame, CA: Down There Press.

Morin, Stephen F. (1976). Annotated Bibliography of Research on Lesbianism and Male Homosexuality: 1967-1974. *J.S.A.S. Catalog of Selected Documents in Psychology* 6(1): 15. (Ms. No. 1191).

Morin, Stephen F. (1977). Heterosexual Bias in Psychological Research on Lesbianism and Male Homosexuality. *American Psychologist* 32(8): 629-637.

Morin, Stephen F. and Garfinkle, Ellen M. (1978). Male Homophobia. *Journal of Social Issues* 34(1): 29-47.

Morin, Stephen F. and Riddle, Dorothy (Eds.). (1978). *Psychology and the Gay Community*. Special issue of *Journal of Social Issues* 34(3).

Murphy, Timothy (1984) Freud Reconsidered. *Journal of Homosexuality* 9(2/3): 65-77.

Noonan, John T. (1966). *Contraception: A History of its Treatment by Catholic Theologians and Canonists*. Cambridge: Belknap Press of Harvard University.

Nyberg, Kenneth L. and Alston, Jon P. (1976/1977). Analysis of Public Attitudes Toward Homosexual Behavior. *Journal of Homosexuality* 2(2): 99-107.

Omark, Richard C. (1981). Further Comment on the Homosexual Role: A Reply to Goode. *Journal of Sex Research* 17(1): 73-75.

Opler, Marvin K. (1965). Anthropological and Cross-Cultural Aspects of Homosexuality. In Judd Marmor, Ed., *Sexual Inversion: The Multiple Roots of Homosexuality*, 108-123.

Ovesey, Lionel (1954). The Homosexual Conflict: An Adaptational Analysis. *Psychiatry* 17: 243-250. Reprinted in Ruitenbeek, H. R. (Ed.). (1963). *The Problem of Homosexuality in Modern Society*. New York: E. P. Dutton, 127-140.

Ovesey, Lionel (1969). *Homosexuality and Pseudohomosexuality*. New York: Jason Aronson.

Ovesey, Lionel and Woods, Sherwyn M. (1980). Pseudohomosexuality and Homosexuality in Men: Pseudodynamics as a Guide to Treatment. In Judd Marmor, Ed. *Homosexual Behavior: A Modern Reappraisal*. New York: Basic Books, 325-341.

Padgug, Robert A. (1979). Sexual Matters: On Conceptualizing Sexuality in History. *Radical Historical Review* 20: 3-23.

Parkes, A. S. and Bruce, H. M. (1961). Olfactory Stimuli in Mammalian Reproduction Odor Excites Neurohumoral Responses Affecting Oestrus, Pseudopregnancy, and Pregnancy in the Mouse. *Science* 134: 1049-1054.

Paul, William, Weinrich, James, Gonsiorek, John C., and Hotvedt, Mary E. (Eds.). (1982). *Homosexuality: Social, Psychological, and Biological Issues*. Beverly Hills, CA: Sage.

Perkins, M. W. (1973). Homosexuality in Female Monozygotic Twins. *Behavior/Genetics* 3: 387-388.

Perry, J. D. and Whipple, B. (1981). Pelvic Muscle Ejaculators: Evidence in Support of a New Theory of Orgasm. *Journal of Sex Research* 17(1): 22-39.

Pillard, C., Poumadere, Jeannette, and Caretta, Ruth A. (1981). Is Homosexuality Familial? A Review, Some Data, and A Suggestion. *Archives of Sexual Behavior* 10(5): 465-475.

Plummer, Kenneth (1975). *Sexual Stigma: An Interactionist Account.* London: Routledge and Kegan Paul.

Plummer, Kenneth (1981). Building a Sociology of Homosexuality. In K. Plummer, Ed., *The Making of the Modern Homosexual.* Totowa, NJ: Barnes and Noble, 19-20

Prince, Morton (1898). Sexual Perversions or Vice? A Pathological and Therapeutic Inquiry. *The Journal of Nervous and Mental Disease* 25: 237-256.

Rado, Sandor (1940/1965). A Critical Examination of the Concept of Bisexuality. *Psychosomatic Medicine 2:* 459-467. Reprinted in Judd Marmor, Ed., *Sexual Inversion: The Multiple Roots of Homosexuality.* New York: Basic Books, 175-189.

Rado, Sandor (1949/1963). An Adaptational View of Sexual Behavior. In H. R. Ruitenbeek (Ed.) (1963). *The Problem of Homosexuality in Modern Society.* New York: E. P. Dutton, 94-126. Originally published in P. Hoch and J. Zubin (Eds.) (1949). *Psychosexual Development in Health and Disease.* New York: Grune and Stratton.

Read, Kenneth E. (1980). *Other Voices: The Style of a Male Homosexual Tavern.* Novato, CA: Chandler and Sharp.

Reiss, Jr., Albert J. (1961). The Social Integration of Queers and Peers. *Social Problems* 9(2): 102-120. Reprinted in H. R. Ruitenbeek, Ed. (1963). *The Problem of Homosexuality in Modern Society.* New York: E. P. Dutton, 249-278.

Rieff, Phillip (Ed.) (1963). *Sexuality and the Psychology of Love.* New York: Collier Books.

Robinson, Paul (1976). *The Modernization of Sex: Havelock Ellis, Alfred Kinsey, William Masters and Virginia Johnson.* New York: Harper & Row.

Rosenthal, D. (1970). *Genetic Theory and Abnormal Behavior.* New York: McGraw-Hill.

Ross, H. L. (1971). Models of Adjustment of Married Homosexuals. *Social Problems* 18: 385-393.

Ross, H. Laurence (1959). The Hustler in Chicago. *The Journal of Student Research* 1: 13-19.

Rubin, R. T., Reinisch, J. M., and Haskett, R. F. (1981). Postnatal Gonadal Steroid Effects on Human Behavior. *Science 211*: 1318-1324.

Ruitenbeek, H. R. (Ed. and Trans.) (1963). *The Problem of Homosexuality in Modern Society.* New York: E. P. Dutton.

Ruse, Michael (1981). Are There Gay Genes?: Sociobiology and Homosexuality. *Journal of Homosexuality* 6(4): 5-34.

Sachs, Hans (1923/1978). On the Genesis of Perversions. *Internationale Zeitschrift fur Psychoanalyse 19*: 172-182. Reprinted in 1978 in C. W. Socarides, Ed., *Homosexuality.* Hella Freud Bernays, Trans. New York: Jason Aronson, 531-546.

Saghir, Marcel T. and Robins, Eli (1973). *Male and Female Homosexuality: A Comprehensive Investigation.* Baltimore: Williams and Wilkins.

Saghir, Marcel T. and Robins, Eli (1980). Clinical Aspects of Female Homosexuality. In J. Marmor, Ed., *Homosexual Behavior: A Modern Reappraisal*. New York: Basic Books, 280-295.

San Miguel, C. L. and Millham, J. (1976). The Role of Cognitive and Situational Variables in Aggression toward Homosexuals. *Journal of Homosexuality* 2(1): 11-27.

Schafer, Roy (1968). *Aspects of Internalization*. New York: International Universities Press.

Schenck, Jerome M. (1960). *A History of Psychiatry*. Springfield, IL: Charles C. Thomas.

Schofield, Michael (1965). Sociological Aspects of Homosexuality: A Comparative Study of Three Types of Homosexuals. Boston: Little, Brown.

Schrenck-Notzing, Albert von. (1892/1956). *The Use of Hypnosis in Psychopathia Sexualis with Special Reference to Contrary Sexual Instinct*. Charles G. Chaddock, Trans. New York: The Julian Press, 1956. (Translation of *Die Suggestions-Therapie bei krankhaften Erscheinungen des Geschlechtssinnes, mit besonderer Berücksichtigung der konträren Sexualempfindung*. Stuttgart: Ferdinand Enke, 1892.)

Secord, P. F. and Blackman, C. W. (1961). Personality Theory and the Problem of Stability and Change in Individual Behavior: An Interpersonal Approach. *Psychological Review 68*: 21-32.

Shively, Michael G. and DeCecco, John P. (1977). Components of Sexual Identity. *Journal of Homosexuality* 3(1): 41-48.

Shively, Michael G., Rudolph, J. R., and DeCecco, John P. (1978). Identification of the Social Sex-Role Stereotypes. *Journal of Homosexuality* 3(3): 225-234.

Simon, W. (1973). The Social, the Erotic, the Sensual: The Complexities of Sexual Scripts. In J. K. Cole and R. Dienstbier, Eds., *Current Theory and Research and Research on Motivation: Nebraska Symposium on Motivation* 21: 61-83. Lincoln: University of Nebraska Press.

Simon, W. and Gagnon, J. H. (1967). Homosexuality: The Formulation of a Sociological Perspective. *Journal of Health and Social Behavior 8*: 177-185.

Simon, W. and Gagnon, J. H. (1969). On Psychological Development. In D. A. Goslin, Ed., *Handbook of Socialization Theory and Research*. Chicago: Rand McNally, 733-752.

Smith, Kenneth T. (1971). Homophobia: A Tentative Personality Profile. *Psychological Reports 29*: 1091-1094.

Socarides, Charles (1973). Homosexuality: Findings Derived from 15 years of Clinical Research. *American Journal of Psychiatry 130*: 1212-1213.

Socarides, Charles (1978). *Homosexuality*. New York: Jason Aronson.

Socarides, Charles W. (1972). Homosexuality: Basic Concepts And Psychodynamics. *International Journal of Psychiatry 10*(1): 118-125.

Socarides, Charles. (1960). Theoretical and Clinical Aspects of Overt Male Homosexuality. *Journal of the American Psychoanalytic Association 8*: 552-556.

Socarides, Charles. (1962). Theoretical and Clinical Aspects of Overt Female Homosexuality. *Journal of American Psychoanalytic Association 10*: 579-592.

Sonenschein, David (1966). Homosexuality as a Subject of Anthropological Inquiry. *Anthropological Quarterly 68*: 188-193. Reprinted in Weinberg, Martin S. (Ed.) (1976). *Sex Research: Studies from the Kinsey Institute.* New York: Oxford University Press, 140-155.

Sonenschein, David (1968). The Ethnography of Male Homosexual Relationships. *The Journal of Sex Research 4*(2): 69-83.

Spitzer, R. L. and Endicott J. (1978). Medical and Mental Disorder: Proposed Definition and Criteria. In R. L. Spitzer and D. F. Klein, Eds., *Critical Issues in Psychiatric Diagnosis.* New York: Raven Press, 15-39.

Spitzer, Robert J. (1981). The Diagnostic Status of Homosexuality in DSM-III: A Reformation of Issues. *American Journal of Psychiatry 138*(2): 210-215.

Spitzer, Robert L. (1973). A Proposal About Homosexuality and the APA Nomenclature: Homosexuality as an Irregular Form of Sexual Behavior and Sexual Orientation Disturbance as a Psychiatric Disorder. *American Journal of Psychiatry 130*, 1207-1216.

Steakley, James (1975). *The Homosexual Emancipation Movement in Germany.* New York: Arno Press.

Stekel, Wilhelm (1922). *The Homosexual Neurosis.* James S. van Teslar, Trans. New York: Emerson Books. (Vol. 2 of *Onanie und Homosexualität.*)

Stekel, Wilhelm (1927). *Impotence in the Male: The Psychic Disorders of Sexual Function in the Male,* Vol. 2. Oswald H. Boltz, Trans. New York: Boni and Liveright.

Steward, Samuel (1981). *Chapters from an Autobiography.* San Francisco: Grey Fox Press.

Stoller, Robert (1973). Criteria for Psychiatric Diagnosis. *American Journal of Psychiatry 130*(11): 1207-1208.

Stoller, Robert (1975). *Perversion: The Erotic Form of Hatred.* New York: Pantheon.

Stoller, Robert (1975/1976). *Sex and Gender,* 2 Vols. New York: Jason Aronson. First published in 1975 in England by Hogarth Press.

Stoller, Robert (1979). *Sexual Excitement: Dynamics of Erotic Life.* New York: Pantheon.

Stone, Lawrence (1982, 16 December). Madness. *New York Review of Books 29*(20): 28-36.

Stone, Lawrence (1983, 31 March). Rejoinder to Foucault's Reply. *New York Review of Books 30*(5): 42-44.

Storms, M. D. (1978). Attitudes Toward Homosexuality and Femininity in Men. *Journal of Homosexuality 3*(3): 257-263.

Sullivan, Harry Stack (1965). *Personal Psychopathology.* Washington, DC: William Alanson White Psychiatric Foundation.

Sulloway, Frank J. (1979). *Freud: Biologist of the Mind.* New York: Basic Books.

Suppe, Frederick (1981). The Bell and Weinberg Study: Future Priorities for Research on Homosexuality. *Journal of Homosexuality 6*(4): 69-97.

Suppe, Frederick (1984). Classifying Sexual Disorders: The Diagnostic and Statistical Manual of the American Psychiatric Association. *Journal of Homosexuality 9*(4): 9-28.

Symonds, J. A. (1896/1936). *A Problem in Modern Ethics, Being an Enquiry into the Phenomenon of Sexual Inversion.* London: Privately published. (In 1897, published as an Appendix to Ellis and Symonds' *Sexual Inversion.*)

Symonds, J. A. (1897/1936). Ulrichs' Views. In Havelock Ellis and John Addington Symonds, *Sexual Inversion*, Appendix C. London: Wilson and MacMillan, 258-272.

Szasz, Thomas (1961). *The Myth of Mental Illness*. New York: Hoeber-Harper.

Szasz, Thomas (1965). Legal and Moral Aspects of Homosexuality. In Judd Marmor, Ed., *Sexual Inversion: The Multiple Roots of Homosexuality*. New York: Basic Books, 124-139.

Szasz, Thomas (1970). *The Manufacture of Madness*. New York: Delta Books.

Tardieu, Ambroise (1857). *Étude Médico-Légale sur les Attentats aux Moeurs*. Paris: J. B. Failliere.

Tarnowsky, Benjamin Mikhailovitch [Вениамин Михайлович Тарновский] (1886/1898). *The Sexual Instinct and its Morbid Manifestations from the Double Standpoint of Jurisprudence and Psychiatry*. W. C. Costello and A. Allison, Trans. Paris: Charles Carrington. First published in 1886.

Thompson, Clara (1947/1963). Changing Concepts of Homosexuality in Psychoanalysis. *Psychiatry 10*: 183-189. Reprinted in Hendrick M. Ruitenbeck, Ed. (1963). *The Problem of Homosexuality in Modern Society*. New York: E. P. Dutton, 40-51.

Tripp, C. E. (1975). *The Homosexual Matrix*. New York: McGraw-Hill.

Trivers, R. L. (1974). Parent-Offspring Conflict. *American Zoologist 14*: 249-264.

Troiden, Richard (1974). Homosexual Encounters in a Highway Rest Stop. In E. Goode and R. Troiden, Eds., *Sexual Deviance and Sexual Deviants*. New York: William Morrow, 211-228.

Trumbach, Randolph (1977). London's Sodomites: Homosexual Behavior and Western Culture in the Eighteenth Century. *Journal of Social History 11*(1): 1-33.

Ulrichs, Karl Heinrich (1864/1879). *Forschungen über das Ratsel der Mannmännlichen Liebe*. Reprinted as part of the Arno Press series, "Homosexuality: Lesbian and Gay Men in Society, History, and Literature," Jonathan Katz, General Ed. Twelve volumes. New York: Arno Press, 1975.

Ungaretti, John (1978). Pederasty, Heroism, and the Family in Classical Greece. *Journal of Homosexuality 3*(3): 291-300.

Ungaretti, John (1983). De-Moralizing Morality: Where Dover's *Greek Homosexuality* Leaves Us. *Journal of Homosexuality 8*(1): 1-18.

Vida, Ginny (1978). *Our Right to Love: A Lesbian Resource Book*. Englewood Cliffs, NJ: Prentice-Hall.

Voltaire. (1764/1962). *Philosophical Dictionary*. Peter Gay, Trans. and Introd. New York: Basic Books.

Warren, Carol B. (1974). *Identity and Community in the Gay World*. New York: John Wiley.

Weeks, Jeffrey (1977). *Coming Out: Homosexual Politics in Britain from the Nineteenth Century to the Present*. London: Quartet Books.

Weeks, Jeffrey (1979). Movement and Affirmation: Sexual Meanings and Homosexual Identities. *Radical Historical Review 20*: 164-179.

Weinberg, George (1972/1973). *Society and the Healthy Homosexual.* New York: St. Martin's Press. (Reprinted by Doubleday Anchor in 1973.)

Weinberg, Martin S. (Ed.) (1976) *Sex Research: Studies from the Kinsey Institute.* New York: Oxford University Press.

Weinberg, Martin S. and Williams, Colin J. (1974). *Male Homosexuals: Their Problems and Adaptations.* New York: Oxford University Press.

Weinberg, Thomas S. (1978). On "Doing and "Being" Gay: Sexual Behavior and Homosexual Male Self-Identity. *Journal of Homosexuality* 4: 143-156.

Weinrich, James D. (1976). *Human Reproductive Strategy. I. Environmental Predictability and Reproductive Strategy: Effect of Social Class and Race. II. Homosexuality and Non-Reproduction: Some Evolutionary Models.* Harvard University, PhD dissertation.

Weinrich, James D. (1978). Non-Reproduction, Homosexuality, Transsexualism, and Intelligence: A Systematic Literature Search. *Journal of Homosexuality* 3(3): 275-289.

Weinrich, James D. (1982). Is Homosexuality Biologically Natural? In W. Paul, et al., Eds., *Homosexuality: Social, Psychological, and Biological Issues.* Beverly Hills, CA: Sage, 197-208.

West, D. J. (1977). *Homosexuality Re-Examined.* Minneapolis: University of Minnesota Press.

Westermarck, Edward (1908). *The Origin and Development of the Moral Ideas.* 2 Vols. London: Macmillan.

Westphal, Carl (1869). Die Konträre Sexualempfindung: Symptom eines Neuropathologischen. (Psychopathischen) Zustandes. *Archiv fur Psychiatrie und Nervenkrankheiten* 2: 73-108.

Whitam, Frederick L. (1981). A Reply to Goode on the Homosexual Role. *Journal of Sex Research* 17(1): 66-72.

Williams, Colin J. and Weinberg, Martin S. (1971). *Homosexuals and the Military: A Study of Less than Honorable Discharge.* New York: Harper and Row

Wilson, Edward O. (1974). *Sociobiology: The New Synthesis.* Cambridge, MA: The Belknap Press of Harvard University Press.

Wilson, Edward O. (1978). *On Human Nature.* Cambridge, MA: Harvard University Press.

Wolf, Charlotte (1971). *Love Between Women.* New York: Harper, Colophon.

Wolf, Deborah Goleman. (1979/1980). *The Lesbian Community.* Berkeley: University of California Press. (Reprinted in 1980.)

Wynne-Edwards, V. C. (1962). *Animal Dispersion in Relation to Social Behavior.* New York: Hafner.

Zuger, B. (1976). Monozygotic Twins Discordant for Homosexuality: A Report of A Pair and Significance of the Phenomenon. *Comparative Psychiatry* 17: 661-669.

www.ingramcontent.com/pod-product-compliance
Lightning Source LLC
Chambersburg PA
CBHW020559270326
41927CB00005B/99